Tax Director's Guide to International Transfer Pricing:
2010 Edition

Copyright © 2010 by Global Business Information Strategies, Inc.

All rights reserved. No portion of this book may be reproduced in any form or by any electronic or mechanical means including information storage and retrieval systems — except in the case of brief quotations for use in critical articles or reviews — without written permission from the publisher.

Cover photo of cargo ship taken in San Francisco, California from the Golden Gate Bridge copyright © 2010 GBIS, Inc.

Editor: Kenneth R. L. Parker

Authors: Brian Andreoli, Svein Andresen, Robert Baldassarre, Anthony Barbera, Marius Basteviken, Anjali Bhasin, Patrick Breslin, George Carlson, Philip Carmichael, Tanmoy Chakrabarti, Jose Casas Chavelas, Patrick Cauwenbergh, Pamela Church, Jeffrey Cole, Xavier Daluzeau, Christopher Desmond, Hareesh Dhawale, Horacio Dinice, Pierre-Jean Douvier, Sean Foley, David Fox, Sheila Geraghty, Tamara Gracon, Michael Granfield, Thijs Heijenrath, Tobin Hopkins, Lyndon James, Erik Jan van Sten, Satoko Kawamura, Yukiko Komori, Ted Keen, Elizabeth King, Andreas Köster-Böckenförde, Joanna Lam, Ryan Lange, Ben Lannan, Marc Levey, Fernando Matos, Niels Melius, Robert Miall, D. Clarke Norton, Alexander Odle, Ken Okawara, Danny Oosterhoff, Kari Pahlman, Michael Plodek, Silvia Rodriguez, Nathan Richards, Linwood Smith, Geoff Soh, Monique van Herksen, Kimberley Webb, and Jens Wittendorff.

For updates, supplemental materials, and other information about this title, please visit:

www.InternationalTransferPricing.com

For questions about quantity discounts, distribution agreements, and other sales-related matters, please contact the publisher directly:

Global Business Information Strategies, Inc.
P.O. Box 610135 • Newton, MA • 02461 • USA
+1 (617) 795-0519 • info@gbisi.com

Publisher's Cataloging In-Publication Data:

Tax Director's Guide to International Transfer Pricing: 2010 Edition / edited by Kenneth R.L. Parker — 2nd edition

p. cm.

ISBN: 978-1-60231-004-9

[1. Transfer pricing — taxation. 2. International business enterprises — taxation. 3. International business enterprises — valuation. 4. Transfer pricing — accounting. 5. Intangible property — valuation.]

Library of Congress Control Number: 2010927582

Printed in the United States of America

Tax Director's Guide to International Transfer Pricing:

2010 Edition

Edited by Kenneth R. L. Parker

Global Business Information Strategies, Inc. • Newton, Massachusetts USA

Table of Contents

I. Introduction

From the Editor. 12

Overview of the Transfer Pricing Analysis Process 14

Executive Summaries 22

II. Advance Pricing Agreements

Using Advance Pricing Agreements to Mitigate Transfer Pricing Risk 36

Documentation Requirements, FIN 48, and APAs: Have New
Disclosure Requirements Introduced Risk Factors that Make
Advance Pricing Agreements More Advantageous?. 41

III. Cost Sharing Arrangements

A Discussion of the Latest IRS Views on the Investor Model and
Intangible Valuation Under Cost Sharing Arrangements. 50

IV. Intangibles

Issues Arising in the Application of the Comparable Uncontrolled
Transaction Method 60

Marketing Intangibles and Transfer Pricing: Economic Issues and Tax Enigmas . . 78

Marketing Intangibles Require Close Legal and Tax Scrutiny 96

Table of Contents

V. Organizational Structure

Business Restructuring— "Conversion" Issues and a Framework for Analysis . . 120

Applying the Arm's Length Principle to Valuing "Exit Charges" 127

Business Restructuring Expenses — Tax Challenges and Opportunities 134

VI. Services

Key Considerations when Applying the New Service Regulations –
Treas. Reg. § 1.482-9T. 142

A Practical Process and Approach to Implementing the New
Transfer Pricing Service Regulations 148

VII. Supply Chain Management

Issues in Supply Chain Management 160

VIII. Trade Finance

Commodities Trading and Global Dealing: Transfer Pricing Challenges
and Proposed Methods 170

IX. Treaties

Mandatory Arbitration Procedures: A New Tack for Resolving Double
Taxation Disputes between Competent Authorities 188

X. Country Overviews

Overview of the Transfer Pricing Environment in Argentina 200

Australian Transfer Pricing Rules in Practice 210

Transfer Pricing in Belgium 220

Transfer Pricing in Brazil. 224

Table of Contents

Overview of Canadian Transfer Pricing 232

China's Transfer Pricing Regime. 241

Denmark – Transfer pricing overview 254

Overview of Transfer Pricing in France 258

German Transfer Pricing Rules in Practice 271

Hong Kong Introduces Transfer Pricing Guidelines 280

Transfer Pricing in India 287

Transfer Pricing Developments in Japan: Law and Practice. 295

Transfer Pricing in Mexico 302

Transfer Pricing: The Dutch Approach (the Netherlands) 310

Transfer Pricing in Norway. 313

Singapore Transfer Pricing Requirements. 317

UK Tax Authorities Plan Stricter Enforcement of Transfer Pricing Rules:
What will these Changes Mean for International Companies? 321

XI. Supplemental Materials

United States Advance Pricing Agreement Revenue Procedure
(IRS Revenue Procedure 2006-9) 328

European Union Transfer Pricing Documentation Guidelines (EU TPD) 366

China Special Tax Adjustment Implemenation Measures 385

China Implementation Measures List of Attached Forms 423

Japan Directive on the Operation of Transfer Pricing 424

Norway Transfer Pricing Regulations 456

Table of Contents

XII. Glossary

A Note About Transfer Pricing Terminology	464
Advance Pricing Agreements	465
Arm's-Length Principle	466
Best Method Rule	468
Comparable Profits Method	469
Comparable Uncontrolled Price Method	481
Cost Plus Method	485
Cost of Services Plus Method	489
Cost-Sharing Arrangements	491
Gross Services Margin	492
Indirect Costs	494
Intangible Property	495
Profit Split Method	496
Related-Party Transaction	498
Resale Price Method	501
Services Cost Method	503

XIII. Directory of Contributors

Brian Andreoli	506
Svein G. Andresen	507
Robert D. Baldassarre	508
Anthony J. Barbera	509
Marius Basteviken	510

Table of Contents

Anjali Bhasin 511

Patrick Breslin 512

George Carlson 513

Philip W. Carmichael 514

Jose Casas Chavelas 515

Patrick Cauwenbergh 516

Tanmoy Chakrabarti 517

Pamela T. Church 518

Jeffrey Cole 519

Xavier Daluzeau 520

Christopher Desmond 521

Hareesh Dhawale 522

Horacio Dinice 523

Pierre-Jean Douvier 524

Sean F. Foley. 525

L. David Fox 526

Sheila Geraghty 527

Tamara Berner Gracon 528

Michael Granfield. 529

Thijs Heijenrath. 530

Tobin Hopkins 531

Lyndon James 532

Erik Jan van Sten 533

Satoko Kawamura 534

Table of Contents

Yukiko Komori 535

Ted Keen 536

Elizabeth King 537

Andreas Köster-Böckenförde 538

Joanna Lam Luk Yu 539

Ryan Lange 540

Ben Lannan 541

Marc M. Levey 542

Fernando Pereira de Matos 543

Niels Melius 544

Robert Miall 545

D. Clarke Norton 546

Alexander R. T. Odle 547

Ken Okawara. 548

Danny Oosterhoff 549

Kari Pahlman 550

Michael Plodek 551

Nathan Richards 552

Silvia B. Rodriguez 553

J. Linwood Smith 554

Geoffrey K. Soh 555

Monique van Herksen 556

Kimberley Webb 557

Jens Wittendorff 558

I. Introduction

Introduction

From the Editor

Kenneth R. L. Parker
Global Business Information Strategies, Inc.

We were gratified by the success of the first edition of the *Tax Director's Guide to International Transfer Pricing*, but did not want to rest on our laurels, instead setting out to make the second edition even better. We started by asking readers what they found to be lacking or in need of improvement in the original and then went back to our authors, asking them to update their articles, incorporating reader feedback. We also sought out new articles to fill gaps in the first edition. The majority of the articles in this new edition contain significant substantive updates and we are pleased to report that we have expanded our Country Overviews section to include five new articles discussing transfer pricing rules and practices in Australia, Hong Kong, India, Japan, and Singapore. This edition also includes an entirely new China section, reflecting the major transfer pricing legislation that recently went into effect. The other important addition is a discussion of supply chain management.

Overviews and Insights from More Than Fifty Leading Transfer Pricing Practitioners

In putting together the first edition of the Tax Director's Guide to International Transfer Pricing, we set out to produce a book that offers overviews of important transfer pricing concepts and insights from experienced transfer pricing practitioners into strategies that can help to keep your company in compliance with the transfer pricing regimes of the countries in which you do business, while protecting your company from double taxation and other hazards of operating in a complex tax environment. Toward this end, we reached out to some of the world's leading transfer pricing professionals and asked them to write articles that highlighted important transfer pricing concepts and offered their insights into the subject matter. Forty-two of them rose to the challenge, providing clear explanations of complex transfer pricing concepts and offering their advice on how best to address those issues. This second edition builds on that team of experts, with a dozen new authors contributing their observations, insights, and analysis.

Significant Changes in the Global Transfer Pricing Environment

The updated articles in this second edition reflect the intense competition for tax dollars among various countries in a time of global recession, during which many tightened their transfer pricing rules and increased enforcement. These changes include new rules for Advance Pricing Agreements, intangibles, Cost Sharing Arrangements, reorganizations, and services. In addition to the five new Country Overview sections listed above, this edition also includes significant revisions to many of our other Country Overviews.

Another new feature of this second edition is a greatly expanded Supplemental Documents section.

Introduction

While space constraints prevent us from including every document that might be of use to transfer pricing practitioners, we have more than doubled the size of the section, adding China, Japan, and Norway materials that we believe will not only be of use to readers preparing transfer pricing documentation in these countries, but will also be of broader interest, as they contain discussion and examples that may be helpful in structuring transfer pricing documentation in other jurisdictions.

Readers who are interested in additional Supplemental Documents omitted from this volume due to space constraints are invited to register their copies of the book by emailing us at info@gbisi.com. Additional documents will be provided via email to purchasers of registered copies.

Organizational Structure of this Guide

The *Tax Director's Guide to International Transfer Pricing* is organized into twelve sections. In addition to this editor's note, the introductory section offers an overview of how to conduct a transfer pricing analysis as well as executive summaries of the articles that appear in the rest of the book. Sections II through IX offer subject-area specific articles on major international transfer pricing issues: Advance Pricing Agreements, Cost Sharing Arrangements, Intangibles, Organizational Structure, Services, Trade Finance, Supply Chain Management, and Treaties, respectively. Section X provides country-by-country overviews of the transfer pricing rules in a sixteen major economies. Section XI includes supplemental materials: the U.S. Advance Pricing Agreement Revenue Procedures, the European Union Transfer Pricing Documentation Requirements, China's new Implementation Measures, Japan's Transfer Pricing guidelines, and Norway's Transfer Pricing regulations. Additional supplemental documents of interest are posted on the publication's web site: www.InternationalTransferPricing.com.

Section XII is a glossary of some of the transfer pricing terminology used in this book and Section XIII provides biographical information and contact data for the book's authors.

While the articles in Sections II through IX are focused in specific subject areas, they also make country-specific references to transfer pricing rules and regulations. By a similar token, the articles in Section X review many of the concepts of the earlier sections in the context of a given country's transfer pricing regime.

Designed to Meet Your Needs

Our hope is that you will find this volume useful in identifying important transfer pricing issues that can affect your company's bottom line and that it will help to point you in the right direction as you set out to address those issues. This book, however, does not attempt to do what it cannot do: it does not constitute legal advice, nor does it attempt to provide an exhaustive list of transfer pricing concepts, issues, rules, or laws. In putting the book together, we have rendered judgments about what is likely to be of interest to our readers. Please let us know what topics you find most useful and what areas require further discussion— as well as the areas of coverage that are less relevant to your company. You may reach us by phone at (617) 795-0519 or by email at info@gbisi.com. As we did in this second edition, we will endeavor to respond to your suggestions and other input by making appropriate changes to the next edition.

Overview of the Transfer Pricing Analysis Process

J. Linwood Smith, Senior Manager
Deloitte Touche Tohmatsu

The arm's length standard is satisfied when the results of a controlled transaction are consistent with the results realized by uncontrolled taxpayers engaged in comparable transactions under comparable circumstances. Making this determination can be an enormously complicated task, as it involves both economic and legal principles, as well as overlapping rules from multiple taxing jurisdictions. However, like many complex problems, the process of conducting a transfer pricing analysis can be simplified by breaking it down into its component steps.

This article provides a brief overview of the steps of a transfer pricing analysis that apply in most circumstances, from the perspective of the U.S. practitioner. These steps are as follows: 1) identify and characterize the intercompany transaction; 2) conduct a functional analysis; 3) select a transfer pricing method under the "Best Method Rule;" 4) search for comparables; and 5) calculate an arm's length range.

I. Identifying and Characterizing Intercompany Transactions

The first step in conducting a transfer pricing analysis is to identify and characterize the transaction to be analyzed. The transfer pricing rules of most countries categorize transactions into four groups: tangible goods, intangibles, provision of services, and loans/financial transactions. In the U.S. and other jurisdictions with well developed transfer pricing rules, regulations organize transfer pricing methods according to these categories.[1]

In some cases, identifying and characterizing a controlled transaction may not be straightforward. Multinationals may have operations that are integrated to an extent that controlled transactions may be difficult to identify and characterize. It is straightforward when a manufacturing subsidiary transfers finished goods to a distribution subsidiary. However, some transactions may be less visible, such as when an employee with knowledge of proprietary manufacturing processes is seconded from one manufacturing affiliate to another, or when a central office provides administrative functions on behalf of several affiliates. Other transactions may be easy to identify but difficult to characterize, such as factoring arrangements that may combine services and loans.

In addition, transactions are often aggregated for purposes of the transfer pricing analysis, particularly when using profit-based methods (such as the comparable profits method). A typical example of when aggregation would apply is when a distributor sells several products, and the best method is the comparable profits

---

1 The U.S. regulations address tangible goods in Sections 1.482-3 and 1.482-5; intangibles in Sections 1.482-4, 1.482-5, and 1.482-6; services in section 1.482-9T; and loans/financial transactions in Section 1.482-2.

method. Transactional methods like the comparable uncontrolled price method (for tangible goods) or the comparable uncontrolled transaction method (for licenses) usually treat each product or transaction separately.

II. Functional Analysis of the Controlled Entities

Once a controlled transaction has been identified and characterized, a "functional analysis" of the controlled entities whose transactions are being tested should be performed. The ultimate purpose of a functional analysis is to establish a basis for comparisons between controlled and uncontrolled transactions. However, it is usually performed early in the analysis for the controlled entities to facilitate the selection of a transfer pricing method. It is also important as a measure of diligence. The inquiries made during a functional analysis often uncover additional intercompany transactions or data that may be useful as internal comparables.

The objective of a functional analysis is to identify and analyze the economically significant activities of the participants in a controlled transaction.[2] Such activities may include:
(A) Research and development;
(B) Product design and engineering;
(C) Manufacturing, production and process engineering;
(D) Product fabrication, extraction, and assembly;
(E) Purchasing and materials management;
(F) Marketing and distribution functions, including inventory management, warranty administration, and advertising activities;
(G) Transportation and warehousing; and
(H) Managerial, legal, accounting and finance, credit and collection, training, and personnel management services.

In addition, a functional analysis looks at the resources employed by a controlled taxpayer. Many of these resources may be easy to identify from a balance sheet, such as property, plant, and equipment; or current assets such as receivables and inventory. Other resources may not be as obvious, such as valuable intangibles that have been developed in-house.

III. Selection of the Best Method

Establishing the arm's length character of an intercompany transaction is accomplished using a transfer pricing method. Several of these methods are described in regulations, and taxpayers may also apply methods of their own invention. Which method is appropriate is determined under the "best method rule." This rule states that "The arm's length result of a controlled transaction must be determined under the method that, under the facts and circumstances, provides the most reliable measure of an arm's length result."[3]

Under the best method rule, there is no priority or hierarchy of methods, and no method is regarded as inherently superior to another. This approach diverges from approaches taken by other countries that express preferences for certain methods over others. Because different jurisdictions have different legal principles for selecting a transfer pricing methodology, it is possible that a multi-jurisdictional transfer pricing study will need to apply more than one methodology to the same fact pattern.

In selecting the best method, the two primary factors to take into account are the degree of comparability between the con-

---
2 Treas. Reg. § 1.481-1(d)(3)(i).

3 United States Treasury Regulations, § 1.482-1(c)(1).

trolled transaction (or taxpayer) and any uncontrolled comparables, and the quality of the data and assumptions used in the analysis.[4] In addition, it may be useful to analyze a transaction under multiple methods to see if the results of the best method can be corroborated by alternate methods. A transfer pricing method that confers implausible results (such as extremely high operating profits or losses) likely suffers from a defect that has not been identified. In such cases, alternate methods may be useful as a "sanity check."

The sections below summarize the transfer pricing methods described in the regulations for transfers of tangible goods and intangibles, and describe the classic applications of each of these methods. Recently released regulations have added several new methods applicable to intercompany services, most of which correspond to existing methods. These methods are discussed in detail in Section VI (beginning on page 131).

A. Comparable Uncontrolled Price Method

The comparable uncontrolled price ("CUP") method "evaluates whether the amount charged in a controlled transaction is arm's length by reference to the amount charged in a comparable uncontrolled transaction."[5] The CUP method is the classic transactional method for tangible goods and is most often applied when internal comparables exist. The most common example for the CUP method is when a company sells identical products to a related entity and to an unrelated entity. If the circumstances of both transactions are the same (i.e., quantity, shipping terms, economic conditions, territory, date, etc.), the price charged to the unrelated entity may be used to establish an arm's length price for the transaction with the related entity.

With the proper data, the CUP will usually prevail as the best method for tangible goods. However, the CUP method requires a very high degree of comparability, and it is rare that the requisite data are available. Because the CUP method is based on price, it is sensitive to differences in any factor that may affect price. If differences exist that are minor, and their effects on price are definite and reasonably ascertainable, adjustments must be made to eliminate the effect of such differences. However, the regulations warn that "if there are material product differences for which reliable adjustments cannot be made, [the CUP] method ordinarily will not provide a reliable measure of an arm's length result."[6] The CUP method is not likely to be the best method if any of the following items affect pricing and reliable adjustments for them cannot be made:

- Quality of the product
- Contractual terms (e.g., scope and terms of warranties, sales or purchase volume, credit terms, transport terms)
- Level of the market (i.e. wholesale, retail)
- Geographic market in which the transaction takes place
- Date of the transaction
- Intangible property associated with the sale
- Foreign currency risks

A special situation in which the CUP method may be appropriate is when a controlled transaction involves a product that is listed on public exchanges or in quotation media. In this context, a CUP may be established if:

---

[4] United States Treasury Regulations, § 1.482-1(c)(2).

[5] United States Treasury Regulations, § 1.482-3(b).

[6] United States Treasury Regulations, § 1.482-3(b)(2)(ii).

- The data are widely and routinely used in the ordinary course in the industry to negotiate prices for uncontrolled sales;
- The data derived from public exchanges or quotation media is used to set prices in the controlled transaction in the same way it is used by uncontrolled taxpayers in the industry;
- The amount charged in the controlled transaction is adjusted to reflect differences in product quality and quantity, contractual terms, transportation costs, market conditions, risks borne, and other factors that affect the price that would be agreed to by uncontrolled taxpayers; and
- The transaction does not take place during a period of "extraordinary market conditions."[7]

B. Comparable Uncontrolled Transaction Method

The comparable uncontrolled transaction ("CUT") method applies to transfers of intangible property. It is similar to the CUP in that it determines an arm's length price by reference to the amount charged in a comparable transaction, and most applications of the CUT method involve internal comparables. The classic application of the CUT method occurs when a company licenses the same intangible to related and unrelated entities under similar circumstances. In such cases, the arm's length consideration may be determined by reference to the royalty charged to the unrelated entity.

While the CUT method is similar to the CUP method, it has two additional comparability requirements. The intangible used in establishing a CUT must (i) be used in connection with similar products or processes within the same general industry or market; and (ii) have similar profit potential.[8] The "similar profit potential" requirement generally involves a computation of the net present value of the controlled intangible and the uncontrolled comparable(s). Thus, even when internal comparables are used, the data needed to compute net present value are rarely available. Except in limited circumstances, establishing a reliable CUT is difficult.

C. Resale Price Method

The resale price method ("RPM") applies to transfers of tangible goods. It evaluates whether the amount charged in a controlled transaction is arm's length by reference to the gross profit margin realized in comparable uncontrolled transactions."[9] The gross profit margin (gross profit divided by sales) is often expressed as a discount from list price.

The RPM is ordinarily used in cases involving distribution, in which tangible property is purchased and resold, and in which the reseller has not added substantial value to the tangible goods by physically altering the goods before resale. The requisite degree of comparability for the RPM is less than the CUP and is particularly dependent on similarity of functions performed, risks borne, and contractual terms. In addition, because the RPM relies on measures of gross profit, it requires consistency among the controlled and uncontrolled transactions in classifying items as cost of goods or operating expenses.

The classic application of the RPM occurs when an entity sells products to both a related and unrelated distributor, and the

---

[7] United States Treasury Regulations, § 1.482-3(b)(5)(i)-(ii).

[8] United States Treasury Regulations, § 1.482-4(c)(2)(iii)(B).

[9] United States Treasury Regulations, § 1.482-3(c)(1).

price for the products is expressed as the resale price minus a gross margin. In such cases, the discount provided to the unrelated distributor is used to establish the transfer price to the related distributor.

The importance of the RPM in the U.S. has diminished since the comparable profits method was added to the regulations. Because the CPM is based on measures of operating profit rather than gross profit, it requires a less stringent standard of comparability, and lends itself to the use of external companies as comparables. However, outside the U.S., particularly in jurisdictions that disfavor methods based on operating profit, the RPM remains widely used.

D. Cost Plus Method

The cost plus method "evaluates whether the amount charged in a controlled transaction is arm's length by reference to the gross profit markup realized in comparable uncontrolled transactions."[10] Gross markup in this context means gross profit divided by cost of goods.

The cost plus method is ordinarily used in cases involving the routine manufacture of goods that are sold to related parties. Because the cost plus method is based on a measure of gross profit, it is similar in its comparability requirements as the RPM. It also requires consistency among the controlled and uncontrolled transactions in classifying items as cost of goods sold or operating expenses.

E. Comparable Profits Method

The comparable profits method ("CPM") "evaluates whether the amount charged in a controlled transaction is arm's length based on objective measures of profitability derived from uncontrolled taxpayers that engage in similar business activities under similar circumstances."[11] The CPM does not compute transfer prices directly; rather, it tests whether transfer prices satisfy the arm's length standard by comparing the operating profit of a tested party to the operating profit of uncontrolled comparables.

In applying the CPM, the participant in a controlled transaction whose operating profit is measured is referred to as the "tested party." Ordinarily, the tested party will be the participant in the controlled transaction that performs fewer and less complex functions and whose operating profit can be reliably measured.[12] The reason for this is that comparables are difficult to find for complex entities that perform multiple functions with valuable intangibles.

Once a tested party is selected, its profitability must be measured and compared with uncontrolled comparables. Measures of profitability under the CPM are financial ratios called profit level indicators ("PLIs"). Although a variety of PLIs may be used, the regulations discuss the following three:

- Operating profit margin (operating profit / net sales). This PLI is the most used PLI.
- Rate of return on capital employed (operating profit / operating assets). Also referred to as return on operating assets, this PLI may be appropriate for tested parties who engage in asset-intensive operations, such as manufacturers. However, its usefulness as a PLI is reduced if there are difficulties in valuing operating assets, or if there are differences in the composition of assets among the

---

10 United States Treasury Regulations, § 1.482-3(d)(1)

11 United States Treasury Regulations, § 1.482-5(a)

12 United States Treasury Regulations, § 1.482-5(b)(2)(i).

tested party and the comparables.
- Berry ratio (gross profit / operating expenses). The Berry ratio, named after economist Charles Berry, is typically applied in situations where the tested party is a distributor that purchases and resells goods without modifying them. The Berry ratio is vulnerable to differences in the composition of operating expenses among the tested party and the comparables, and should not be used in cases involving manufacturing.

The selected PLI must be derived "from a sufficient number of years of data to reasonably measure returns that accrue to uncontrolled comparable."[13] Ordinarily, such a period must include at least three taxable years.

In the U.S., the CPM is by far the most widely used transfer pricing method. It requires a lesser degree of comparability than the CUP method, CUT method, RPM, or cost plus method. As a result, it tends to be the default method in situations where internal transactional comparables are not available. In addition, the Securities and Exchange Commission and several commercial vendors offer databases of financial information for public companies, from which profitability information for comparables may be obtained. In other parts of the world, the CPM is emerging as a permitted method, but it remains disfavored or prohibited by many tax authorities.[14]

F. Profit Split Method

The profit split method ("PSM") evaluates whether the allocation of the combined operating profit for one or more controlled transactions is arm's length by reference to the relative value of each controlled taxpayer's contribution to that combined operating profit. The profit split method comes in two flavors – the comparable PSM, and the residual PSM. In both cases, the PSM will usually be applied as a method of last resort in cases where more than one controlled entity owns valuable intangibles.

Under the comparable PSM, a profit split percentage is derived from the combined operating profit of uncontrolled taxpayers whose transactions and activities are similar to those of the controlled taxpayers in the relevant business activity.[15] Applying this method requires finding a situation in which unrelated entities are comparable to the controlled entities, particularly with respect to valuable intangibles, and in which sufficient information is disclosed from which a profit split can be computed. Because such data is difficult to obtain, the comparable PSM has rarely (if ever) been applied.

The residual PSM involves the allocation of the combined operating profit from a business, which is allocated in a two-step process.[16] In the first step, each party to the controlled transaction receives an allocation of operating profit to provide a market return for its routine contributions to the relevant business activity. These allocations are usually determined using the CPM. In the second step, the residual operating profit is divided among the controlled taxpayers based upon the relative value of their contributions of intangible

---

13 United States Treasury Regulations, § 1.482-5(b)(4).
14 The OECD Transfer Pricing Guidelines do not list the CPM as a specified method, but instead list the similar Transactional Net Margin Method ("TMNM"), which is described as a method that should be applied only if "traditional" methods (such as the CUP method, RPM, or cost plus method) cannot be reliably applied. See OECD Transfer Pricing Guidelines, Section III-A.
15 United States Treasury Regulations, § 1.482-6(c)(2)(i).
16 United States Treasury Regulations, § 1.482-6(c)(3)(i).

property to the relevant business activity.

The classic application of the residual PSM involves multiple entities that own valuable intangibles. For example, assume that the parent company of a multinational owns the patent to its products and performs manufacturing functions. The parent sells the finished products to a distribution subsidiary that owns valuable trademarks used in its selling function. Under the residual PSM, the combined operating profit of the parent and subsidiary would first be allocated to the parent's routine manufacturing function and the subsidiary's routine distribution function. The residual operating profit would then be allocated to the parent and the subsidiary based upon the relative value of their contributions of intangible property. Thus, if the fair market value of the patents are three times the fair market value of the trademarks, the parent would receive 75% of the residual operating profit, and the subsidiary would receive 25%.

G. Unspecified Methods

The U.S. Regulations permit the use of "unspecified" methods in cases where a method devised by the taxpayer can be shown to be the best method. When an unspecified method is used, it should "take into account the general principle that uncontrolled taxpayers evaluate the terms of a transaction by considering the realistic alternatives to that transaction, and only enter into a particular transaction if none of the alternatives is preferable to it."[17]

IV. Search for Comparables

Once a transfer pricing method has been selected, comparable transactions or companies must be identified. The first source utilized for potential comparables should always be internal data. However, if sufficient internal data cannot be obtained, the next step is to search for external comparables in commercial databases. Commercial database vendors include:[18]
- EdgarStat (for company financial information)
- Standard & Poor's (Compustat Database)
- Thomson (One Banker Database)
- Bureau van Dijk (Amadeus Database); and
- RoyaltyStat (for royalty rates and license agreements).

Once potential comparables have been obtained, comparability be established. To this end, the regulations provide that the following factors must be analyzed, regardless of which transfer pricing method is used:
- Functions performed
- Contractual terms
- Risks
- Economic conditions
- Property or services[19]

Oftentimes, close comparables cannot be obtained from either internal comparables or commercial databases. This difficulty is experienced not only by taxpayers, but also by tax authorities. However, the objective is not to obtain perfect comparables, but rather, the best comparables given the limitations in the data. In this regard, the regulations state that "an uncon-

---

17 United States Treasury Regulations, § 1.482-3(e)(1).

18 Many commercial database vendors obtain company financial information from the U.S. Securities and Exchange Commission ("SEC"). The SEC offers substantially the same information without charge through its EDGAR database. However, EDGAR is not easily searchable, which has led to the widespread use of commercial databases with efficient search engines.

19 United States Treasury Regulations, § 1.482-1(d)(3)

trolled transaction need not be identical to the controlled transaction, but must be sufficiently similar that it provides a reliable measure of an arm's length result."[20]

V. Determining the Arm's Length Range

The regulations state that the application of a transfer pricing method may produce a single result that is the most reliable measure of an arm's length result. In other cases, application of a method may produce a number of results from which a range of reliable results may be derived. In limited cases, an arm's length range may be based on all of the available comparables, if the following conditions have been satisfied:
- All material differences have been identified between the controlled and uncontrolled transactions;
- Such differences have a definite and reasonable ascertainable effect on price or profit; and
- Adjustments have been made to eliminate the effect of such differences.

If the above conditions cannot be satisfied, the reliability of the analysis must be increased using a "valid statistical method."[21] One such method is the interquartile range, which is determined by using the middle 50% of observations. Other methods that take a similar approach (such as the 50% confidence interval) may also be used.

A taxpayer will not be subject to a transfer pricing adjustment if its results fall within this "arm's length range." If outside of the arm's length range, the IRS will usually adjust to the median.[22]

VI. Conclusion

While the steps outlined above are representative of what occurs in a typical transfer pricing analysis, they do not address the entire transfer pricing function required of a taxpayer. After the analysis is performed, the results must be integrated into the taxpayer's business operations and accounting systems. In addition, the analysis must be properly documented in order to protect the taxpayer from penalties (in the U.S.) or to comply with the various requirements of taxing authorities. Companies with complex intercompany financial transactions, multiple research and development centers, and cost sharing arrangements face additional burdens. As transfer pricing rules continue to mature across tax jurisdictions and enforcement becomes a priority for tax authorities, transfer pricing promises to remain a significant challenge for multinational taxpayers.

---

[20] United States Treasury Regulations, § 1.482-1(d)(2)
[21] United States Treasury Regulations, § 1.482-1(e)(2)(iii)(B).
[22] United States Treasury Regulations, § 1.482-1(e)(3)

J. Linwood Smith, is a senior manager in the tax and transfer pricing division of Deloitte Touche Tomatsu's Hong Kong office. Linwood has more than a decade of experience as a transfer pricing consultant. He can be reached at **+852 2852 1953** or by email at **linwsmith@deloitte.com.hk**. For more information on the author, please see Section XIII.

Executive Summaries

Using Advance Pricing Agreements to Mitigate Transfer Pricing Risk

by Anthony J. Barbera, Ph.D. and Anjali D. Bhasin, Ph.D., *The Ballentine Barbera Group, a CRA International Company*

Advance Pricing Agreements offer companies engaged in related party transactions a useful tool to mitigate transfer pricing risk, as well as some ancillary benefits, but the decision whether to seek an APA should be based on a number of factors. Careful consideration of these factors is necessary to determine whether a given company would be well-advised to seek an APA. Once the decision is made to pursue an APA, there are some additional steps that can be taken to expedite the APA process. *Page 36*

Documentation Requirements, FIN 48, and APAs: Have New Disclosure Requirements Introduced Risk Factors that Make Advance Pricing Agreements More Advantageous?

by Brian Andreoli, Partner, and Sheila Geraghty, Of Counsel, *DLA Piper LLP*

While the U.S. APA program offers companies involved in related-party transactions an opportunity to mitigate transfer pricing risk, the burdens of participation in the program have discouraged some companies from participating. This article examines whether recent changes in documentation requirements and mandatory disclosures, including those of FIN 48, will cause greater transfer pricing uncertainty, leading some previously reluctant firms to seek APAs. The article offers some background on U.S. documentation requirements before delving into the details of the APA program, including a discussion of the various types of APAs and the possibility of using a retroactive APA to resolve an ongoing transfer pricing dispute. *Page 41*

A Discussion of the Latest IRS Views on the Investor Model and Intangible Valuation Under Cost Sharing Arrangements

by Patrick Breslin (Principal), *PTB Consulting*, LLC and Jeffrey Cole (Partner) *Transfer Pricing Associates, LLC*

The recently issued final and temporary cost sharing regulations and the IRS Coordinated Issues Paper (CIP) on cost-sharing buy-ins have laid the groundwork for a new emphasis on acceptable methods in applying the best method rule to cost sharing arrangements. The CIP guidance emphasized an income approach to initial buy-in valuation and an acquisition price-based approach to subsequent buy-ins. The temporary rules reinforce many of the CIP's views. Such guidance challenges some of the traditional valuation methods for cost sharing buy-ins, forcing taxpayers to re-examine the way they define and quantify intangible contributions. This article examines this new landscape and offers some recommendations for how best to examine initial buy-in transactions in a world where the IRS does not always believe that valuation based on the sum of the parts (of individual contributed intangibles) adds up to the whole of intangible value contribution. *Page 50*

Issues Arising in the Application of the Comparable Uncontrolled Transaction Method

By Hareesh Dhawale *(KPMG)*, George Carlson *(Deloitte Tax LLP)*, and Niels Melius *(Deloitte Tax LLP)*

This article offers practical guidance regarding the application of the comparable uncontrolled transactions method (CUTM) of valuing intangible property transfers between related parties. The article discusses the comparability requirements under U.S. law and the OECD guidelines, including an examination of the methods available for evaluating the profit potential of intangibles under the basic arm's length return method (BALRM). This examination includes an illustrative calculation of the BALRM's application. The article goes on to look at the comparability of circumstances of intangible transfers and the selection of comparables relevant to the CUTM. The article concludes with a review of the available databases for identifying comparable licensing agreements and some strategic recommendations regarding use of multiple sources to anticipate the identification of comparables by tax authorities. *Page 60*

Marketing Intangibles and Transfer Pricing: Economic Issues and Tax Enigmas

by Dr. Michael E. Granfield, *Senior Managing Director, Ceteris*

This article examines the role marketing intangibles play in transfer pricing valuations, raising and answering a number of key questions, including whether the existence of marketing intangibles justify increases in royalty rates and other related-party charges, how marketing intangibles can be valued, and when other factors trump these calculations. The author employs a fictional case study to engage the reader in an analysis and discussion of this important topic. *Page 78*

Marketing Intangibles Require Close Legal and Tax Scrutiny

Marc M. Levey *(Baker & McKenzie, LLP)*, Pamela T. Church *(Baker & McKenzie, LLP)*, Monique van Herksen *(Ernst & Young/Holland Van Gijzen)*, Alexander Odle *(A.R.T. Intellectual Property BV)*, and Philip Carmichael *(Baker & McKenzie Consulting)*

Tax authorities in many countries are beginning to recognize the concept of "marketing intangibles" with respect to the calculation of taxable income realized from related-party transactions. While a uniform international definition of marketing intangibles has yet to be formed, several countries are taking their lead from the U.S. recognition of this type of intangibles, such that companies with international related-party transactions should take notice of the policies and practices with respect to marketing intangibles of the tax authorities in the countries where they have operations. Also, the influence of civil law rules relating to intellectual property on the concept of marketing intangible should be taken into consideration as early as possible. This article examines the evolving definition of marketing intangibles as applied in the United States, Europe, Japan, Australia, and China, and recommends some strategies and actions for mitigating transfer pricing risk associated with marketing intangibles. *Page 96*

Business Restructuring— "Conversion" Issues and a Framework for Analysis

by Tobin Hopkins, *Ernst & Young*

Business restructurings can lead to changes in taxable profit in a given country, as compared with the situation before the restructuring. A natural consequence of this development is the increased scrutiny of business restructuring by tax authorities negatively impacted by the business change. This scrutiny has come on a number of fronts. One area of obvious focus is the new transfer pricing paradigm that results from the business restructuring. This article discusses so-called "conversation gains" — asserted occasions of charge when a business activity changes. The article suggests that the typical approaches used by tax administrators are often inappropriate and proposes a different approach based on robust and detailed legal analysis and alternative valuation techniques. *Page 120*

Applying the Arm's Length Principle to Valuing "Exit Charges"

by Robert Miall, *Ernst & Young*

This article examines the loss of profit approach taken by some tax authorities in evaluating business restructurings. The OECD has recently supported this view and set out some principles to be followed in considering whether a compensation payment would be made at arm's length on transfer pricing principles. This article builds on these principles and develops a framework in which restructuring decisions are viewed in the context of the options available to the parties and their interests. Toward this end, two case studies are presented that apply "bargaining theory" to restructuring transactions. The article concludes that without examining the profits that would be available under other scenarios, the loss of profits approach is not consistent with the arm's length principle. *Page 127*

Business Restructuring Expenses — Tax Challenges and Opportunities

by Danny Oosterhoff, *Ernst & Young*

This article examines the tax treatment of business restructuring expenses in light of the risk of non-deductibility in the country where costs are initially incurred and the associated exposure to double taxation. The article discusses the application of the arm's length principle to business restructuring expenses, proposes an analytical framework for evaluating associated costs, and offers an illustrative case study to demonstrate some of the concepts. The article concludes with some suggestions to mitigate the risks of double taxation. *Page 134*

Key Considerations when Applying the New Service Regulations – Treas. Reg. § 1.482-9

by Sean F. Foley, Robert D. Baldassarre, and Tamara Berner Gracon, *KPMG LLP*

The Final Services Regulations issued by the IRS raise significant issues for companies involved in related-party services transactions, including the cost safe harbor, the Services Cost Method (SCM). However, to take advantage of this provision, companies must prepare appropriate documentation and meet required deadlines. While the SCM allows documentation to be filed after the tax return, non-contemporaneous documentation does not provide penalty protection. Also of note is the inclusion of stock-based compensation in the Final Regulations and the treatment of some services which may have been considered non-beneficial in the past as beneficial. The article also discusses the contingent payment agreement documentation requirements under the Final Regulations and offers taxpayers some advice on working with the various provisions discussed. *Page 142*

A Practical Process and Approach to Implementing the New Transfer Pricing Service Regulations

by Christopher Desmond and Ryan Lange, *Ceteris, Inc.*

The new transfer pricing services regulations recently issued by the IRS pose significant challenges for many companies with international operations. This report walks the reader through the necessary steps to determine which provisions of the regulations are applicable to a given transaction and how to achieve compliance. The practical review and implementation process described by the authors offers guidance on key issues, including how to identify fully-loaded cost pools for each cost services center, how to conduct a functional analysis, and how to determine the arm's length charge. The report also examines the transfer pricing methods allowed for services transactions, including the new Services Cost Method, and offers guidance regarding which method is appropriate to a given transaction. Also included is a checklist of necessary implementation actions. *Page 148*

Issues in Supply Chain Management

by D. Clarke Norton, *DLA Piper LLP*

Companies seeking to optimize their supply chain management should be aware of the tax implications of their organizational structure and supply chain planning choices. This article offers some background on supply chain planning in a global tax context, then uses a hypothetical example to illustrate the principles at work and the transfer pricing considerations of which companies should be aware. The article also offers some observations about the enforcement environment and discussion of practical choices facing companies considering changes to their global supply chains. *Page 160*

Commodities Trading and Global Dealing: Transfer Pricing Challenges and Proposed Methods

by Elizabeth King, *Beecher Consulting Group*

The global trading of commodities and financial instruments can present challenges vis-a-vis transfer pricing because of the highly integrated nature of this activity and the fungibility of financial capital. This article offers some background on the mechanics of commodities trading, then identifies the shortcomings with both the three-factor formulary methodologies used in APAs and the more flexible formulary approaches incorporated into the proposed global dealing regulations. The article goes on to put forward a simpler alternative transfer pricing method, which is consistent with the separate entity concept. The author argues that, in lieu of value, risk, and activity factors, one should utilize assets alone to allocate global trading firms' free cash flows. In lieu of subjective weights, one should use the fair market values of such assets. With these modifications, the formulary apportionment method becomes a residual profit split method, and many of the shortcomings of the former approach are ameliorated. *Page 170*

Mandatory Arbitration Procedures: A New Tack for Resolving Double Taxation Disputes between Competent Authorities

by Michael Plodek, *Lockheed Martin*

Current mutual agreement procedures leave taxpayers vulnerable to double taxation when tax authorities from different countries disagree about the arm's length value of a transaction. Under current procedures, the taxpayer has no guarantee that differences of tax treatment resulting in double taxation will be resolved between the tax authorities in a timely manner and even when a decision is reached that relieves the taxpayer of the burden of paying taxes twice on the same income, there is no relief from accrued interest penalties available. Recent income tax agreements, including the Proposed U.S.-Belgium Convention, which is currently being considered for ratification, would offer additional protections to taxpayers, including a definite timeline for the resolution of these disputes, but further improvements are needed if problems such as accrued interest penalties and the possibility of failure by both competent authorities in a dispute to file proposed resolutions are to be addressed. *Page 188*

Overview of the Transfer Pricing Environment in Argentina

by Horacio Dinice and Silvia Rodriguez, *Deloitte Argentina*

Over the course of a decade, Argentina has made strides toward the adoption of such internationally-accepted transfer pricing concepts as arm's length valuation, comparability, and the best method rule. However, Argentine regulations differ significantly from U.S. and OECD rules in a number of important areas, including such basic matters as how related parties are defined. Argentina currently does not allow the full range of transfer pricing methodologies widely accepted elsewhere and lacks procedures for corresponding adjustments and Advance Pricing Agreements. Penalties for late submission of documentation are also inflexible and transfer pricing studies are required to be signed by an independent CPA before filing. Also, there can be difficulty finding documentary support of the segregation of operating results for companies doing business in Argentina that have more than one operating unit, as Argentine companies are not required to disclose the same level of detail as publicly-trade companies doing business in the U.S. The article also discusses the recent audit practices of the Argentine tax authorities. The significant penalties for late or incomplete submission of transfer pricing documentation, combined with recent aggressive enforcement efforts by the Argentine tax authorities in which data are gathered from the Central Bank and Customs Department, make compliance with filing requirements more important than ever. *Page 200*

Introduction

Australian Transfer Pricing Rules in Practice

by Lyndon James and Ben Lannan
Partner PricewaterhouseCoopers, Australia

Australia has a fully-developed transfer pricing regime that shares many traits with other OECD-compliant countries, including reliance on the arm's length standard, a variety of available methodologies, and an active APA program. However, Australian transfer pricing rules also feature some unusual characteristics, including broad applicability not simply to companies with related-party transactions, but also to companies with non-ownership connections. Also, Australia's transfer pricing rules do not mandate that taxpayers prepare contemporaneous transfer pricing documentation, although such documentation is strongly encouraged by Australian tax authorities and disclosures regarding the extent of contemporaneous documentation are required as part the annual income tax return. In addition to reviewing the existing laws and regulations governing transfer pricing in Australia, this article also examines a number of recent developments including two significant transfer pricing court cases and a number of administrative guidelines, practice statements and enforcement actions, which taken together have significant implications for the future of transfer pricing in Australia. *Page 210*

Transfer Pricing in Belgium

by Patrick Cauwenbergh, *Deloitte Touche Tohmatsu*

While Belgium's tax authorities did not begin the process of developing a transfer pricing regime until after many other European countries had taken steps to establish transfer pricing standards, Belgium has acted swiftly to catch up by issuing a series of administrative circulars and updating key provisions of its tax code. Belgian tax authorities prefer traditional transaction methods of transfer pricing valuation to the profit-based methods, but are open to the profits-based methodologies when the taxpayer demonstrates that the facts of the case do not allow application of a transaction-based method. Given the difficulty in finding local comparables in a small country, Belgium welcomes pan-European comparables. Contemporaneous or advance documentation is not required, but lack of such documentation can be seen as a red-flag, triggering an audit. Belgium has a long tradition of issuing Advance Pricing Agreements and its APA program is widely viewed as being business-friendly. Non-compliance penalties range from ten percent to 200 percent, depending on whether bad faith is involved. *Page 220*

Transfer Pricing in Brazil

By Fernando Matos, *Deloitte Touche Tohmatsu*

This article examines the complexities of applying the Cost Plus Method (CPL) under Brazilian law, beginning with a review of the legal requirements and then examining a hypothetical case study of a U.S. company that imports products into Brazil. The case study discusses the effects on transfer pricing analysis of changes in production quantity, cost-per-unit, and competitive factors, as well as the calculations that need to be performed to arrive at appropriate pricing and the documentation requirements for justifying those prices. The article also reviews the tax authorities' role in examining costs associated with the transaction. In cases where costs are disallowed, taxable income increases, which can result in substantial fines and interest penalties. The judicial appeals process and alternative methodologies are also addressed. *Page 224*

Overview of Canadian Transfer Pricing

by L. David Fox, *Fasken Martineau DuMoulin LLP*

In recent years, owing to the scale of business activities conducted by Canadian companies with non-arm's length non-resident entities, the Canada Revenue Agency has been taking a pro-active approach to ensuring that taxpayers are not using transfer pricing to inappropriately allocate income to other jurisdictions. This article provides an overview of Canada's transfer pricing regime, including its adherence to the arm's length standard and reliance on OECD transfer pricing guidelines, the relevance of Canada's withholding tax system in the transfer pricing context, downward transfer pricing adjustments, the imposition of transfer pricing penalties, Canada's contemporaneous documentation requirements, and the periods during which transfer pricing adjustments may be assessed. Canada's broad tax information disclosure and sharing rules, in the domestic and treaty contexts respectively, are also discussed. The article concludes with a discussion of the dispute resolution processes available to taxpayers who have been assessed with respect to transfer pricing adjustments, including the Canada Revenue Agency's internal administrative appeals system, appealing transfer pricing assessments to the courts and competent authority relief under Canada's tax treaties. General guidance on the use of Advance Pricing Arrangements is also provided. *Page 232*

China's Transfer Pricing Regime

by Joanna Lam, *Deloitte Touche Tohmatsu*

Over the course of the past two years, China has passed and begun implementation of a series of laws and regulations designed to overhaul its transfer pricing regime. These new transfer pricing rules include many provisions that will directly impact MNCs with related-party transactions in China. The new provisions include strict new contemporaneous documentation requirements, the creation of an APA program, allowance of CSAs, adoption of a best method rule, and the broadening of the definition of what constitutes a related party. The rules include a number of provisions that will create significant burdens on taxpayers in China, including requirements that documentation be prepared by each taxpayer separately and that all documents, regardless of their original language, be provided to the tax authorities in Chinese.

The new rules do contain some good news for taxpayers, however. In additional to allowing CSAs and APAs, the new regime incorporates other features found in the OECD transfer pricing guidelines, including acceptance of the Cost Plus Method with the same mark-up requirements as are common in OECD-compliant countries. Taxpayers will also benefit from the clarification of reporting requirements and other obligations that are part of the new regime.

The article also includes advice on common audit triggers and what the practical implications of the new regulations are likely to be for MNCs operating in China. *Page 241*

Denmark – Transfer pricing overview

by Jens Wittendorff, *Tax Partner, Deloitte Copenhagen*

Denmark has enacted legislation in recent years to bring its transfer pricing practices into conformity with OECD guidelines, but some country-specific practices remain, including the frequent use of secondary adjustmens by Danish tax courts to account for the economic benefit realized by one of the related parties involved in a given transaction. These secondary adjustments may be avoided if the party benefiting from the transaction makes a corresponding payment to the other party. While Danish law does not have an APA provision, bilateral and multilateral APAs are available through tax treaty provisions and it is possible to obtain a unilateral APA by requesting a binding ruling from the Danish tax authorities. The article also discusses documentation requirements, disclosure requirements, penalties, and other important aspects of Danish transfer pricing practice. *Page 254*

Overview of Transfer Pricing in France

by Pierre-Jean Douvier and Xavier Daluzeau, *CMS Bureau Francis Lefebvre*

France has made great strides in recent years to make its transfer pricing laws and regulations consistent with the latest OECD and EU guidelines. The most recent change is the new requirement, effective January 1, 2010, that large companies established in France prepare contemporaneous documentation of related-party transactions. French tax authorities will automatically assume there is an unlawful transfer of profits when they can show a link of dependence between a company in France and a company that is engaging in transactions that are not at arm's-length pricing. In cases where the other party is in a low-tax country, the link of dependence does not need to be demonstrated. In both cases, the company can rebut the presumption of unlawful transfer of profits by demonstrating that there is an advantage to them in terms of indirect profits associated with the transaction. The French tax authorities are empowered to ask taxpayers to justify their related-party pricing. Failure to do so results in the tax authorities setting the pricing based on comparable transactions. All transfer pricing methodologies described in the OECD guidelines are accepted by the French tax authorities. For practical purposes, the TNMM is the most frequently employed method. In addition, France has a fully-developed APA program and makes use of Mutual Agreement and Arbitration Procedures to resolve transfer pricing disputes. The article also discusses the burden of proof in transfer pricing cases under French Supreme Court decisions and the French definition of related party, which is based on a link of dependence, as well as some thoughts on the future direction of transfer pricing in France. *Page 258*

German Transfer Pricing Rules in Practice

by Andreas Köster-Böckenförde, *Jones Day*

Germany has implemented a new tax law that tightens and updates transfer pricing rules, including specifying which transfer pricing methodologies are acceptable, clarifying documentation requirements, and establishing rules for selection of comparables. Under the law, the comparable profits method is prohibited. German law also does not allow agreements between taxpayers and the tax authorities, but a creative solution has been developed to allow for Advance Pricing Agreements despite this prohibition. The article also discusses noncompliance penalties, appeal procedures, the transfer of intangibles, cost sharing arrangements, and employee compensation for relocation of functions, as well as other relevant issues for companies engaged in related party transactions in Germany. *Page 271*

Hong Kong Introduces Transfer Pricing Guidelines

By Kari Pahlman, Nathan Richards and Kimberley Webb, *KPMG China*

After years of being one of the world's few major economies without a substantive framework for regulating transfer pricing, Hong Kong adopted major new rules in 2009. With the issuance by the Internal Revenue Department of two Departmental Interpretation and Practice Notes in 2009 Hong Kong has begun implementation of a transfer pricing regime that adheres to the arm's length standard, largely following the OECD Guidelines. Hong Kong now specifically accepts the five transfer pricing methodologies specified in the Guidelines, as well as "unspecified methods," and offers greater guidance with respect to documentation, intra-group services and permanent establishments. There remain areas that may need further clarification, such as the definition of "associated enterprises," for which a common ownership percentage is not specified. Also, Hong Kong has yet to offer Advance Pricing Agreement (APA) or Cost Sharing Arrangement (CSA) rules. This article reviews the newly-adopted transfer pricing rules and discusses their potential implications going forward. *Page 280*

Transfer Pricing in India

by Tanmoy Chakrabarti, *Ernst & Young*

While India is a very attractive business location for international companies with an ample supply of English-speaking skilled labor and generous tax incentives, it is burdened by a complicated and inconsistent transfer pricing regime. Not only does India share some of the transfer pricing difficulties common in other countries, such as poor availability of comparable data, India also suffers from a lack of clear regulation to inform taxpayers of their obligations and options. Other significant aspects of India's transfer pricing regime include strict contemporaneous documentation requirements, the lack of an APA program, and the unusual requirement that single-year data generally be used in comparability analyses, rather than the three years of data usually required in OECD-compliant countries. Also, despite the primitive nature of the available transfer pricing databases in India, the use of foreign comparables is not favored. Despite these challenges, there are signs that needed reforms, including the introduction of an APA procedure and other measures to improve clarity of requirements, will be enacted in India soon. The Indian government has increased its focus on cleansing up its taxation system including transfer pricing procedures in order to invite more foreign participation in India's growth story. The article offers three strategies for minimizing transfer pricing risk in India. *Page 287*

Introduction

Transfer Pricing Developments in Japan: Law and Practice

by Ken Okawara, Satoko Kawamura, and Yukiko Komori, *Baker & McKenzie*

Japan has long had a reputation for aggressive transfer pricing enforcement and unclear transfer pricing rules, but new administrative guidelines that clarify taxpayer responsibilities go a long way toward improving the transfer pricing environment in Japan. Another positive development for taxpayers has been the first ever successful court appeal overturning a transfer pricing assessment in Japan. In addition, the recently published transfer pricing case studies can be very helpful to taxpayers. Japan also has a robust APA program that Japan's tax authorities have given great emphasis recently. This article discusses these developments and also examines some of the major features of Japan's transfer pricing regime and some potential pitfalls. For example, while Japan has no official contemporaneous documentation requirement, other rules combine to create a de facto need for documentation. However, an amendment to the relevant rules which took effect from April, 2010 may make it easier for the tax authorities to conduct "deemed assessments" more easily than previously where taxpayers fail to provide the required documents timely at the audit. Taxpayers who disagree with transfer pricing rulings have three domestic appeal options. In addition, Japan has an extensive network of tax treaties with other countries, providing taxpayers access to Mutual Agreement Procedures (MAP) to resolve disputes involving double taxation. Japan does not have a best method rule, but instead gives priority to what it calls the "three basic methods," Comparable Uncontrolled Price, Resale Price, and Cost Plus. *Page 295*

Transfer Pricing in Mexico

by Jose Casas, *KPMG*

As a member of the OECD, Mexico has enacted transfer pricing laws that are generally consistent with OECD guidelines. Mexico's best method rule favors traditional methodologies, starting with the CUP method, over profit-based methods. Given the aggressive enforcement by Mexico's tax authorities in recent years, careful compliance with filing requirements for transfer pricing studies and documentation is advisable. Although there are no statutory penalties for failure to file required documentation and the penalty for failure to file a transfer pricing return is less than ten thousand U.S. dollars, failure to file either item can result in rejection of deductions associated with related-party transactions. Mexican courts have supported the tax authorities' approach, ruling that otherwise permissible deductions may be disallowed solely on the basis of failure to have transfer pricing documentation in time for the annual tax filing deadline.

Further complicating transfer pricing compliance in Mexico are strict requirements that do not permit the use of documentation prepared for another taxpayer, and tend not to allow parent-company transfer pricing analysis. Also, data must be provided from the current fiscal year, which in Mexico is the same as the calendar year, so companies that do not operate on a calendar year basis must make appropriate adjustments. There is also great difficulty in finding comparable data in Mexico, although companies filing annual reports with the U.S. Securities and Exchange Commission are generally accepted as comparables. Mexico also has a well-developed, active APA program that may be attractive to taxpayers wishing to avoid the uncertainty associated with transfer pricing. Contract manufacturers operating in Mexico under the Maquiladora program have a special set of transfer pricing rules, which is also discussed. *Page 302*

Transfer Pricing: The Dutch Approach

by Erik Jan van Sten and Thijs Heijenrath, *Deloitte*

The Dutch Tax Authorities (DTA) are taking a proactive approach to transfer pricing. Even prior to the first Transfer Pricing Decree of March 30, 2001, the DTA offered taxpayers the opportunity to seek advance rulings on transfer pricing matters. The ruling practice was replaced in 2001 with an APA program. In addition to discussing the Dutch APA program, this article examines the Dutch approach towards transfer pricing audits, documentation requirements, and the use of mutual agreement procedures for dispute resolution. *Page 310*

Transfer Pricing in Norway

by Svein G. Andresen and Marius Basteviken, *KPMG*

In June, 2007, Norway adopted new transfer pricing rules that seek to clarify and supplement the framework established under the General Tax Act of 1999 and the Tax Assessment Act. While the new Norwegian transfer pricing filing and documentation rules are generally consistent with those of other European counties and the OECD guidelines, they contain some provisions that may prove onerous, including a requirement that intangible property transactions be described in greater detail than is required in many other countries. The Norwegian rules also have such strict requirements for identifying comparables that some taxpayers may find it difficult to identify any comparables at all for use in their transfer pricing documentation. Norwegian law has no provision for Advance Pricing Agreements, although the authors expect that an APA program will be available in Norway at some point in the future. There are also no specified penalties for non-compliance with transfer pricing rules, which are enforced under the general tax provisions that allow Norwegian authorities to estimate tax liability and charge surtaxes in cases where filings are incomplete or delinquent. *Page 313*

Singapore Transfer Pricing Requirements

by Geoffrey Soh, *KPMG*

Since the introduction of the transfer pricing guidance in 2006, Singapore has been increasing its focus on transfer pricing. Additional circulars have been released by with the aim of fostering taxpayers' transfer pricing awareness and compliance. Several steps have been taken to monitor the level of transfer pricing compliance, including sending questionnaires to, and conducting in-depth reviews and field visits with selected taxpayers with sizeable related-party transactions or with recurring losses for no apparent reasons.

The developments in transfer pricing over the last two years reiterate Singapore's strong adoption of the arm's-length principle and its need for taxpayers to perform rigorous transfer pricing analysis for their significant or complex related-party transactions. However, considering the large number of multinationals that have their regional headquarters and support centers based in Singapore, Singapore is likely to take a pragmatic approach and may be willing to concede to certain flexibilities to facilitate compliance. *Page 317*

Introduction

UK Tax Authorities Plan Stricter Enforcement of Transfer Pricing Rules: What will these Changes Mean for International Companies?

by Ted Keen, *The Ballentine Barbera Group, A CRA International Company*

While the UK has had a fully-developed set of transfer pricing laws and regulations for the better part of a decade, there has been criticism of the UK tax authorities for alleged lax enforcement of transfer pricing rules. Consequently, there has been a recent push by Her Majesty's Revenue and Customs (HMRC) to challenge more aggressively transfer pricing practices apparently designed to shift income to other jurisdictions. This article discusses some of those enforcement initiatives, including a new focus on issues with the most significant tax consequences and the development of a new litigation and settlement strategy for transfer pricing disputes. The article also discusses some of the changes to documentation requirements that are under consideration, including the possibility of requiring contemporaneous documentation filings. Under the new approach, larger companies can expect additional scrutiny of their related-party transactions from specialized teams of investigators. There may also be some good news for taxpayers in the new initiatives, as they seek to speed up the dispute resolution process and to avoid imposing additional compliance costs, where possible. *Page 321*

II. Advance Pricing Agreements

Using Advance Pricing Agreements to Mitigate Transfer Pricing Risk

Anthony J. Barbera, Ph.D. and Anjali D. Bhasin, Ph.D.
The Ballentine Barbera Group, a CRA International Company

Tax authorities in many jurisdictions have intensified scrutiny of transfer pricing in recent years, resulting in significant adjustments and penalties. This heightened scrutiny could have a significant impact on the tax obligations of companies engaged in related-party transactions. Many jurisdictions allow companies to mitigate this risk by entering into an Advance Pricing Agreement ("APA") with tax authorities that establishes agreed-upon arm's-length prices for related-party transactions.

But is it worth the time and expense to negotiate an APA? The answer depends upon the particular situation of a given company. Essentially, the decision whether to enter into an APA is similar to the decision whether to purchase insurance: it is a cost-benefit analysis that weighs an initial expenditure against a quantifiable risk. To analyze this cost-benefit equation, it is necessary to factor in some of the other advantages offered by APAs, the situation and characteristics of the company in question, the APA rules of the relevant countries, and whether the company is currently involved in a transfer pricing dispute. Once a decision is made to seek an APA, there are also some steps that can be taken to expedite the APA process.

Other Advantages of APAs

In addition to mitigating future risk, an APA can offer the opportunity to resolve transfer pricing issues over the past five years or more. The APA approach often offers creativity and flexibility where regulations may not provide clear guidance. Also, as U.S. treaty partners are not bound by U.S. regulations, for example, the IRS may consider a hybrid transfer pricing methodology or a hybrid profit level indicator, which may not necessarily be available outside of the APA program. In addition to the above, an APA virtually eliminates the risk of documentation related penalties and double taxation. No transfer pricing penalties may apply for past years once the years have been accepted for rollback treatment.

Company Characteristics and Practices

Based on our broad experience, companies with the following characteristics should consider the APA approach:

- Companies involved in exotic transactions (e.g., using swaps to transfer risk and cash flows from one related party to another related party for an arm's length compensation)
- Companies utilizing unspecified methods for valuing arm's length transactions, as permitted under Section 1.482-3T of the U.S. regulations.
- Companies utilizing hybrid profit level indicators.
- Companies utilizing creative working

Advance Pricing Agreements

capital or risk adjustments.
- Companies currently under transfer pricing audit.
- Companies with significant tax reserves related to intercompany transactions.
- Companies that are now more likely to be challenged based on recent tax court decisions.
- Companies involved in intellectual property ("IP") migration.
- Companies that are risk averse.

Companies that are involved in exotic transactions or non-routine type of transactions should consider going into the APA process. The economic analysis related to such transactions, while reasonable is likely to be non-traditional. In such situations, especially if the transaction is significant, the APA process could potentially offer certainty in a cooperative environment. An audit would be a difficult venue to resolve such an issue and could be extremely time consuming and expensive. The same arguments apply to companies utilizing unspecified methods.

When using hybrid profit level indicators to more accurately reflect the arm's length operating profits of a subsidiary, for example, a Company may use gross margins from transactional comparables and adjust them for specific operating expenses to establish an operating margin target for the subsidiary. In another example, to reflect the limited risk operations of a large subsidiary, where it may only bear the financing costs of the business as opposed to all market and economic risks associated with the business, certain adjustments can be made to allow this subsidiary to earn a return consistent with its operations. To avoid expensive audits, APA would be a good choice in such scenarios.

If a company is currently under audit, an APA may offer a cooperative environment to resolve the audit. While an APA focuses on future tax years, the tax authorities will usually agree to accept a request to roll back the terms and conditions of an APA to open tax years where substantial audit work has not taken place. Audits are often very expensive and time consuming and can drag on for years.

The Financial Accounting Board's Interpretation No. 48 ("FIN 48") which covers accounting for uncertain tax positions makes an APA a more attractive option. Companies may not need to reserve big dollars for large intercompany transactions with significant uncertainty. For example, Google announced on February 1, 2007 that it concluded an APA with the IRS in December 2006 allowing it to reduce contingency reserves and recognize tax benefit of $90 million. Similarly, Campbell announced on April 29, 2007 that it recorded a $22 million tax benefit from a bilateral APA between the United States and Canada covering royalties.

Many companies with routine intercompany transactions may find themselves in unique situations where their chances of getting audited may increase significantly as a result of a recent court case decision. For example, the GlaxoSmithkline court case has put many U.S. subsidiaries of foreign multinationals with a marketing role at risk. In such circumstances, it is advised to be proactive and approach the tax authorities to reach an agreement as opposed to dealing with a lot of uncertainty and possibly an expensive audit with an unfavorable outcome.

IP migration and related buy-in transactions face a high likelihood of being challenged by tax authorities as these transactions are viewed as high value transactions. For large U.S. companies with valuable marketing IP that may be considering expanding their operations in non-U.S. jurisdictions, could consider migrating their non-U.S. IP in the early stages of the expansion when their trademarks or trade names are not highly recognized and may not have much value outside of the U.S. A relatively small buy-in may be the correct technical answer in this situation as the value of the non-U.S. IP could be relatively small. Under these circumstances, an APA would be highly recommended to avoid controversy.

Each company has a different level of risk appetite. If a company is fairly risk averse, and would like to avoid playing the audit lottery and the uncertainty that comes along with it, an APA offers a good solution. A company like Wal-Mart has made a strategic decision to pursue APAs where appropriate to achieve certainty, timeliness and cost savings in administering its global tax obligations. Wal-Mart completed its first bilateral APA in 2005 and has filed requests for eight more APAs. It has also concluded its bilateral APA between U.S. and China, which also happens to be the first bilateral APA between the United States and China.

When APA is not the Optimal Solution

While an APA offers fine solutions to many companies, it may not always be the best option. For example, if a Company has utilized an overly aggressive transfer pricing approach, the APA process exposes its methodology to the tax authorities, who may decline the request for an APA and begin a transfer pricing audit. In another example, an APA may sometimes provide an optimal solution based on the Company's expected long-term projections. However, if the Company experiences significant changes to its business during the APA period, the taxpayer could be locked into what is now considered to be a bad deal. For example, a Company enters into an agreement where it compensates its foreign subsidiaries with a target operating margin leaving the residual with the entrepreneurial parent company. However, with unexpected changes in the business, the parent Company ends up with residual losses while stuck with a huge tax liability with respect to its subsidiaries earning target operating margins.

Taxpayers need to go into the APA process with their eyes open, as it can take longer than expected and one may need to settle for a result that is less than perfect. An APA will require investment of taxpayer's time and resources and may require a taxpayer to disclose information that may be sensitive in nature. Although the tax authorities endeavor to resolve all APAs accepted into the program, there is a possibility that the APA request may not be resolved or may be resolved in a manner different from what was originally proposed in the APA request. However, a taxpayer still may have a better chance to resolve thorny issues in an APA as opposed to an audit as APA teams tend to be technically savvy and the environment is more cooperative.

Unilateral vs. Bilateral APAs

From a U.S. perspective, a unilateral APA eliminates the risk of a transfer pricing adjustment initiated by the IRS. In many cases, the elimination of the transfer pricing adjustment by the IRS is sufficient to substantially reduce the risk of double taxation. In most cases, however, the elimination of a transfer pricing adjustment and double taxation requires involvement of other tax authorities that have jurisdiction over the taxpayer. Tax treaties and the mutual agreement procedure ("MAP" or Competent Authority procedure) provide a mechanism to eliminate double taxation.

Advance Pricing Agreements

Under MAP, if Country X makes a transfer pricing adjustment, the taxpayer can request the tax authorities of Country X and Country Y to consult to avoid double taxation. MAP has generally worked well. Country X will typically reduce its adjustment and Country Y will provide a corresponding adjustment for the reduced amount. Unfortunately, many MAP cases have not been progressing very well, leaving double taxation unresolved. In addition, MAP generally does not deal with inconsistent laws with respect to refund and deficiency interest or with imposition of penalties for failing to satisfy inconsistent tax rules. An APA would generally eliminate the taxpayer's risk of incurring these costs in the country or countries issuing the APA.

Bilateral/Multilateral APAs avoid many of the above problems. The IRS and the foreign tax authority or authorities, provide specific guidance to the multinational group to satisfy the transfer pricing requirements of all of the jurisdictions that can examine the transactions at issue, thereby eliminating the risk of double taxation, penalties, and interest. Companies that operate in more than one tax jurisdictions, which have transfer pricing legislation in place with the local tax authorities auditing transfer pricing issues aggressively, should consider a bilateral or a multilateral APA.

Cost and Time Frame for APA Negotiation

Companies can expect to pay user fees in the range of $22,500 to $50,000 to file an APA. The user fee for an APA request is $50,000; the user fee for an APA renewal request is $35,000; and the user fee for a small business APA request is $22,500.[1]

Additional time/costs are incurred by Companies in preparation of the APA submission and negotiations/meetings with the IRS. The time/cost associated with preparation of the APA submission is slightly higher than the preparation of the annual contemporaneous documentation report. The time/cost associated with meetings/negotiations with the IRS will depend on facts and circumstances.

The completion of an APA can take two to three years or longer.[2] The APA Team tries to arrange an initial meeting with the taxpayer to take place within 45 days from the assignment of an APA Team Leader and following receipt of the substantially complete APA request. The function of the initial meeting is to review the taxpayer's facts, to discuss and clarify issues, and to reach an agreement on the scope and nature of the APA Team's due diligence. The APA Team and the taxpayer generally agree on a Case Plan to which both the IRS and the taxpayer personnel are expected to adhere. The Case Plan is signed by both an APA manager and an authorized official of the taxpayer. Case milestones include: (a) submission of any necessary additional information by the taxpayer; (b) any planned site visits or interviews; (c) evaluation of the information by the IRS; (d) meeting dates; and (e) presentation of the competent authority negotiating position or recommended agreement to the APA Director.

Expediting the APA Process

Once a decision has been made to seek an APA, there are several steps that can be taken to expedite the APA process. These steps include: participating in pre-filing

---

1 A small APA covers companies with gross income of $200 million or less or the aggregate value of the covered transactions does not exceed (i) $50 million annually, and (ii) $10 million annually with respect to covered transactions involving intangible property.

2 A small APA could be completed in a shorter period of time.

Advance Pricing Agreements

conferences, preparing submissions that anticipate questions from the APA team, and timely and thoroughly responding to questions from the tax authorities. The pre-filing conference can potentially reduce the processing time by several months as it allows the taxpayers to better respond to concerns and questions from the IRS. If the pre-file conference is on a named basis, the APA team may effectively be in place by the time the taxpayer makes its submission.

During the post-filing period, companies need to be very responsive to additional information request for information from the tax authorities on financial data, information on comparables utilized in the analysis, the transfer pricing methodology, and any other related items. If a specific request for information from the tax authorities appears to be unreasonable, it is okay to push back. All parties need to recognize the time and effort required to collect some of this additional information and the relative importance of such information.

Conclusion

APAs can be very helpful in mitigating transfer pricing risk and offer several ancillary benefits, as well, including the possibility of resolving past disputes, eliminating double taxation, and allowing creativity and flexibility in areas where applicable regulations do not provide clear guidance. Determining whether it would be advisable for a given company to seek an APA depends upon a number of factors, including the characteristics of the company and its related party transactions, as well as the jurisdictions in which it is operating. Ultimately, the decision whether to seek an APA should be based on a cost-benefit analysis of the risk mitigation and other benefits offered by an APA against the cost in time and effort of negotiating an APA.

Companies that anticipate major changes in their international operating model should also be cognizant that it may not be to their advantage to lock in a pricing structure if their expected revenues and costs are likely to be significantly different from actuals during the effective dates of the APA.

In cases where an APA is the best choice, it is worthwhile to take available steps to expedite and facilitate the APA process.

CRA International Vice President **Anthony Barbera** has nearly two decades of transfer pricing experience and is a former principal of the Ballentine Barbera Group. He can be reached at **(202) 662-7830** or by email at **tbarbera@crai.com**.

Anjali Bhasin, Vice President, is a member of CRA's Competition practice. Dr. Bhasin has over thirteen years of experience in conducting economic analyses of intercompany pricing of services and tangible and intangible property. She can be reached at **(703) 201-8869** or by email at **abhasin@crai.com**. For more information on the authors, please see Section XIII.

Documentation Requirements, FIN 48, and APAs: Have New Disclosure Requirements Introduced Risk Factors that Make Advance Pricing Agreements More Advantageous?

by Brian Andreoli, Partner, and Sheila Geraghty, Of Counsel
DLA Piper LLP

The U.S. Advance Pricing Agreement (APA) program has long offered companies transacting with related-parties the opportunity to mitigate transfer pricing risk, but the intensive and time-consuming APA application process has discouraged many taxpayers from seeking APAs. Recent developments, however, have introduced new risk factors, potentially increasing the appeal of the relative certainty of the APA program. In particular, the disclosure requirements of FIN 48 could increase the likelihood of a transfer pricing audit. Given the potential tax consequences of an unfavorable ruling, the predictability of an APA may be attractive despite the time, effort, and expense associated with the APA application process.

To examine and weigh these factors, it is necessary to have an understanding of U.S. transfer pricing documentation requirements and the impact of FIN 48 on transfer pricing. This article offers some background in those areas before delving into the requirements and procedures of the APA program.

U.S. Transfer Pricing Documentation Requirements

Transfer Pricing has been identified by the IRS as its top priority in regard to corporations with international operations. In January 2003, then IRS Commissioner Larry Langdon issued a directive that instructed audit teams to issue a request for the taxpayer's documentation, if any, as prepared to document the taxpayer's intercompany transfer pricing pursuant to Internal Revenue Code Section 6662(e) and the regulations thereunder within a thirty (30) day period. If the taxpayer failed to provide the requested documentation within the 30 day time period (pursuant to the regulation), the taxpayer would receive a notification from the IRS that the penalties of IRC Section 6662 may apply if there are proposed transfer pricing adjustments. Prior to issuing the directive, the IRS was on notice by taxpayers that agents were not requesting the Section 6662(e) studies, and this determination was confirmed by an IRS study released in 2002.

Neither IRC Section 6662 nor IRC Section 482 requires transfer pricing documentation. Instead IRC Section 6662 is a procedure to avoid penalty if there is an adjustment.

Advance Pricing Agreements

A 2004 internal IRS study of the compliance of IRS auditors requesting such documentation indicated a moderate level of compliance by IRS audit teams. In May 2005, the IRS Audit Manual updated the audit procedures to state that it was IRS policy to request the IRC Section 6662 documentation. Thus, an IRS Agent who fails to request the taxpayer's documentation may be held to have not complied with the IRS Manual.

By 2004, Congress had enacted Sarbanes-Oxley ("SOX"). Section 404 of SOX required corporations subject to the act to document their internal controls to support the level of reliability in the financial presentation of publicly traded corporations. One aspect of complying with Section 404 concerned the internal controls for the computation of income taxes. A subsidiary concern focused on the controls concerning transfer pricing. Even though the Internal Revenue Code does not require transfer pricing documentation, the lack of such documentation would be cited as an internal control deficiency since the failure to have such "contemporaneous" documentation increased the likelihood that if the IRS were successful in pursuing a transfer pricing adjustment, then the taxpayer would have a greater likelihood that transfer pricing penalties of IRC Section 6662 would apply. As such, the lack of contemporaneous documentation raised the issue of the application of the penalty. This would be noted in the management letter as a material weakness.

Even where documentation exists in the proper contemporaneous format, a corporation subject to SOX would find itself subject to a greater likelihood of a transfer pricing reserve analysis. In July 2006, the FASB issued Financial Interpretation Number 48 (hereinafter "FIN 48") for Accounting for Uncertain Tax Positions ("UTP"). FIN 48 was generally effective as of January 1, 2007 for calendar year corporations. While a complete discussion is beyond the scope of this article, FIN 48 sets forth a framework for the determination of an uncertain tax position and the recognition and measurement of the tax position to be reflected on the financial statements. FIN 48 is applicable to financial statements subject to GAAP. The Standard for recognition was determined as to whether a UTP met or exceeded a more likely than not ("MLTN") standard.

FIN 48 and Transfer Pricing

When applied to transfer pricing, a FIN 48 review would focus on the intercompany transactions and the quality of the support that the corporation had for its position or positions. The lack of contemporaneous documentation would increase at least the likelihood of additional audit fees.[1] Even where the corporation had contemporaneous documentation, the typical review by the auditors would have to reach the conclusion that all intercompany transactions had been covered by its documentation and that such documentation resulted on a UTP that met or exceeded the MLTN standard.

Throughout 2007, there were discussions as to whether the IRS would request a corporation's FIN 48 workpapers. In the 1980s, the IRS successfully won the right to request and review the taxpayer's tax accrual workpapers in the Arthur Young Case. Thereafter, the IRS announced a policy of restraint. That policy stated in general, that IRS auditors would not routinely request such workpapers. As tax shelters became the focus of IRS scrutiny, this policy of restraint was modified and exceptions were allowed for the

---

1   Many found that they needed to develop the documentation before the auditor would agree that the UTP had met or exceeded the more likely than not (MLTN) standard.

Advance Pricing Agreements

nondisclosure of tax shelters and certain other matters.

Public statements by IRS officials however in regard to FIN 48 left an uncertain impression as to its application. Moreover FIN 48 requires footnote disclosure of the difference between tax return positions versus the benefit recognized on the financial statements.

While there has not been a report or study of the use of the FIN 48 for audit selection or more specifically as it applies to transfer pricing, the disclosure footnoting the amounts indicated as the reserves could lead an IRS auditor to conclude that there is a need for an audit. As a result, more corporations looked toward the alternatives available to reduce uncertainty. The APA Program offers an opportunity to try to minimize or eliminate that uncertainty in advance.

The Purpose and Principles of the APA Program

The principle source document in regard to the purpose, principles and the requirements of the APA program is embodied in Revenue Procedure 2006-9, 2006-2 I.R.B. ___, Released December 19, 2005 and published January 9, 2006. Basically the APA program is a voluntary program that "increases the efficiency of tax administration by encouraging taxpayers to come forward and present to the Service all the facts relevant to a proper transfer pricing analysis and to work toward a mutual agreement in the spirit of openness and cooperation".

In light of the above, the basic reason for a corporation to seek an APA is consistently stated "the prospective nature of APAs lessens the burden of compliance by giving taxpayers greater certainty regarding their transfer pricing methods, and promotes the principled resolution of their issues by allowing for their discussion and resolution in advance before the consequences of such resolution are fully known to taxpayers and the Service."

From a financial statement point of view, the resolution in advance of UTP, minimizes or eliminates the uncertainty that a stated reserve leaves in the mind of the reader and the investment community. In general, the risk that an APA will not be respected is predicated on the taxpayer's lack of compliance with the terms of the agreement, rather than a future IRS auditor's alternative transfer pricing theories based on the same facts.

An APA is an agreement, contractual in nature, between the taxpayer and the Service, in advance of the execution of controlled transactions (that is, the related party transactions) that agreement specifies the "best transfer pricing method ("TPM") under IRC Section 482 and the regulations thereunder in regard to the intercompany transactions. This agreement specifies the controlled transactions or transfers (covered transactions), the best TPM, the terms of the APA, operational and compliance provisions, appropriate adjustments, critical assumptions regarding future events, required APA records and annual reporting requirements.

The APA Process

The APA process is voluntary and represents an agreement between a taxpayer and the IRS on an appropriate TPM for the transactions at issue. An APA may be "unilateral", "bilateral" or "multilateral". A "unilateral" APA involves an agreement between the Service and the taxpayer; whereas, bilateral and multilateral APAs involve an agreement between the Service, the taxpayer, as well as a negotiated agreement with one or more foreign competent authorities under

Advance Pricing Agreements

Table 1: APA Applications, Executed APAs. And Pending APAs

	Status	Unilateral	Bilateral	Multilateral	Total	Cumulative
2006	Filed	42	67		109	1037
2006	Executed	42	39	1	82	692
91-05	Executed	282	320	8	610	180
2006	Renewals	21	14		35	33
2006	Amended	2	1		3	
APAS	Pending	92	406		498	
APAS	Canceled	0	0		0	5
APAS	Withdrawn	3	13		16	121

Table 2: Months to Complete APAs

All New		All Renewals		All Combined	
Average	33.9	Average	27.5	Average	31.2
Median	35.3	Median	25.9	Median	28.1
Unilateral		**Unilateral**		**Combined**	
Average	22.0	Average	18.5	Average	20.3
Median	22.9	Median	17.4	Median	18.7
Bilateral/Multilateral		**Bilateral/Multilateral**		**Combined**	
Average	43.6	Average	40.9	Average	42.7
Median	45.4	Median	38.5	Median	42.7

applicable income tax treaties.[2] A unilateral APA establishes an approved TPM for US purposes and binds the taxpayer and the IRS, but it does not protect a taxpayer from an adjustment by a foreign taxing adjustment. If the APA involves a taxpayer operating in a country which is a treaty partner, information relevant to the APA (including a copy of the APA and APA annual reports) may be provided to the treaty partner. It is the policy of the United States to encourage taxpayers that enter into the APA Program to seek bilateral and unilateral APAs when competent authority

---

[2] Part 32. Published Guidance and Other Guidance to Taxpayers, Chapter 4. Special Pre-filing Agreement Programs Section 1. Advance Pricing Agreements (32.4.1.1.1) (08-11-2004)

Advance Pricing Agreements

procedures are available with respect to the foreign country or countries involved.[3]

The APA process has five phases: (1) application; (2) due diligence; (3) analysis; (4) discussion and agreement; and (5) drafting, review and execution.[4]

The application is generally preceded by a pre-file conference, which may occur on an anonymous basis and no payment or user fee is required. Upon filing the application, however, the taxpayer must make full disclosure of the taxpayer's identity and pay the appropriate user fee on or before the due date, including extensions, of the tax return for the first taxable year that the taxpayer proposes to be covered by the APA. The application is assigned to an APA team leader who is responsible for organizing the team and assigning the appropriate international expertise to the team. An opening conference is generally scheduled within 45 days of the assignment of the case to a team leader.[5] At the opening conference the team leader proposes a case design with a goal of negotiation an agreement within 12 months from the date the full application is filed. The actual median and average times for completing unilateral APAs and recommended negotiating positions[6] are set forth in Table 2.

The due diligence process is fact intensive and collecting relevant facts and data is critical to the IRS's ability to reach an agreement with the taxpayer. The APA team must be satisfied that the facts submitted by the taxpayer are complete and accurate. Generally, the APA team leader will submit a list of questions to the taxpayer in advance of the opening meeting and are focused on the transfer pricing issues that are the subject of the APA application.

The IRS economist assigned to the case performs a significant portion of the analytical work associated with an APA. Generally this analysis requires additional information to be provided by the taxpayer.

Once the due diligence and analysis is completed, the team begins its discussion and negotiations with the taxpayer. The discussions include reviewing the various aspects of the covered transactions, the TPM, the selection of comparable transactions, asset intensity and other adjustments, the critical assumptions, the APA term, and other relevant issues. In a unilateral APA case, the discussions proceed solely between the APA Program and the taxpayer. In a bilateral or multilateral APA case, the discussions proceed in two parts and involve two IRS offices - the APA Program and the U.S. Competent Authority. In a bilateral or multilateral APA, the APA generally office works together with the taxpayer to prepare a recommended U.S. negotiating position. Upon completion, the process shifts to the U.S. Competent Authority analyst assigned to the case and prepares the final U.S. negotiating position.

The final step is the drafting and review an drafting of the final APA. The language of the APA is based on standard language that is incorporated into every APA.[7] An APA is deemed executed when signed by the Director of APA and the taxpayer.

The current U.S. APA Director Matthew Frank has advised taxpayers that they can speed the resolution of APAs by participating in pre-filing conferences, preparing submissions that anticipate

---

[3] Rev. Proc. 2006-09 §§ 2.08 and 7, __C.B._

[4] See attached APA Case Management Summary

[5] Announcement 2007-31, Announcement and Report Concerning Advance Pricing Agreements, February 26, 2007

[6] Announcement 2007-31

[7] The current version is found in Attachment A of Announcement 2007-31.

issues, and fully responding to questions from the APA team.

Term and Rollbacks

In general, APAs are issued for a three year advance period. In rare cases, that term may be modified. It should be noted that in the case where similar facts existed in prior audit cycles, it may be advantageous to request that the APA methodology be rolled back to resolve the prior periods.

A rollback request must be made with the APA request or at any time prior to the execution of the APA. Bilateral or multilateral APAs with a rollback request are deemed to constitute an application for accelerated competent authority (See Rev. Proc. 2002-52). As such, an APA rollback request may be a valuable tool in lessening the uncertainty under FIN 48.

Unexpected Complications

The APA process depends very heavily on the taxpayer's facts. Sometimes, despite the statistics provided, an issue arises concerning a particular industry, the interplay of other regulations and treaty or lack of that tax treaty can significantly change the timeline for the APA.

In a recent APA several concerns arose. First, the IRS Audit Team appeared to have exerted a very high level of influence over the APA process. This type of activity can occur when the Audit Team has issued an adjustment related to the rollback period. The Field Team is part of the process.

Second, the APA Team proposed methods that are variations, rather than the specific methods in the regulations. While it is not uncommon for the APA Team to use unspecified methods, in this particular case they were using an unspecified method and termed it as one of the specified methods. This caused confusion at the Competent Authority ("CA") level. When such one-off methods are proposed, delve into the reasons. Also, even if a method appears to work for the APA period, consider whether the market is changing in the future.

Third, the use of aggregation should be considered where the activities are intertwined and provide an end to end service (for example, if an overnight delivery business is comprised of services such as pick-up, trucks, planes, warehouse and sorting, each is probably interdependent on the other. Aggregation gives a result similar to set-off. Set-off is another option when there are a series of transactions that meet the regulatory requirement.

Fourth, in regard to a bilateral or multilateral APA, Competent Authority ("CA") will be involved. On the U.S. side, the CA representative may or may not actively interact during the taxpayer meetings with the APA Team. CA is free to disagree with the APA Team's Recommended Negotiation Position ("RNP").

Fifth, keep the lines of communication open with the APA Team. When the Team proposes an "Economist Meeting" to resolve the economics there should always be another representative of the taxpayer present. This person should be one who can facilitate the facts if the economists have made incorrect assumptions.

Sixth, be careful of the comparable sets. If your situation does <u>not</u> include the use of non-routine intangibles, then the comparables should reflect that fact.

Seventh, in aggregation or set-off be wary of proposals to use different profit level indicators ("PLI"). The use of "cost plus" <u>and</u> the use of a "return on assets" method may cause an unjustified result. The methods should be consistent.

Advance Pricing Agreements

Other Considerations

As previously stated, an APA is a voluntary act. Under appropriate circumstances, a taxpayer may want to withdraw an application. The decision to do so carries certain aspects. The taxpayer may feel that the audit team or competent authority is the "better course" based on the reaction or concerns from the APA team.

In addition, there is required maintenance associated with an APA. There is a required annual report from the taxpayer that must be filed by the later of 90 days after the tax returns are due (including extensions) or 90 days after the effective date of the APA. The annual report must describe the actual operations over the last year and the taxpayer must demonstrate compliance with the APA's terms.

Conclusions

The APA process is intensive and time consuming with myriad compliance dates. It is essential for the taxpayer seeking an APA, to examine the facts carefully before starting the process in order to determine the extent of the commitment in terms of time and resources.

While no two APAs are precisely alike, the basic requirements must be followed. Failure to reach an agreement opens the uncertainty issue again. Proper pre-planning and analysis is necessary to avoid many of the missteps that have led to the breakdown of the process. In many aspects, it is a more intense economic study than an annual documentation study. The offset is the certainty for a specified time period as to the view by the U.S. government and other governments. In a FIN 48 world, the costs of the APA can be but a fraction of costs associated with the uncertainty of the Transfer Pricing issues for a corporation.

DLA Piper Partner **Brian Andreoli** has been a tax professional for more than 30 years, with experience in public, accounting, corporate (both foreign and domestic) law, and litigation. He can be reached at **(212) 335-4553** or by email at brian.andreoli@dlapiper.com.

Sheila Geraghty, Of Counsel at DLA Piper focuses her practice on transfer pricing and international tax matters. Ms. Geraghty has been a tax professional for more than 20 years, with experience in both public accounting and Fortune 500 corporate tax practices. She can be reached at **(212) 335-4599** or by email at sheila.geraghty@dlapiper.com. For more information, please see Section XIII.

III. Cost Sharing Arrangements

A Discussion of the Latest IRS Views on the Investor Model and Intangible Valuation Under Cost Sharing Arrangements

Patrick Breslin (Principal), *PTB Consulting, LLC* and Jeffrey Cole (Partner) *Transfer Pricing Associates, LLC*

On January 5, 2009 the final and temporary cost sharing regulations ("the temporary rules") under Treasury Regulations Section 482-7T[1] took effect, leaving intact most elements of the 2005 proposed regulations[2] ("the proposed rules") and solidifying the investor model as the central concept in valuing intangible contributions to a cost sharing arrangement ("CSA").

The modifications to the 2005 proposed rules are largely technical in nature. They clarify allowable divisions of rights among CSA participants, for example, and provide clearer, if broader, definitions regarding the scope of intangible development activity under a CSA. Grandfather provisions that allow taxpayers to retain treatment under the old rules[3] were also revised; a 50 percent change in ownership or a material change in the scope of the CSA activity no longer automatically terminate grandfather treatment of a cost sharing arrangement as occurred under the proposed rules. However, the IRS may impose periodic adjustment provisions to revalue intangible contributions that occur after a material change in the scope of a CSA.

Much attention remains on the implications the new CSA rules have with respect to past CSA transactions in an IRS audit context. An IRS audit enforcement perspective was formally introduced on September 27, 2007 in a Coordinated Issues Paper (the CIP) providing guidance to IRS personnel concerning methods that may be applied to evaluate cost sharing buy-ins.[4] The guidance discussed two types of buy-ins: 1) initial buy-ins at the time that a U.S. parent and a non-U.S. related party enter into a cost sharing arrangement (CSA) for the purposes of joint development and exploitation of intangible property and 2) subsequent buy-ins when an intangible is acquired by the U.S.-led group from an uncontrolled party and contributed to the CSA.

The CIP identified an income-based valuation method as generally being the best method for valuing initial buy-in intangibles and an acquisition price-

---

1 US Treasury Regulations Section 482: Methods to Determine Taxable Income in Connection With a Cost Sharing Arrangement, REG-144615-02, T.D. 9441, 74 Fed. Reg. 340, January 5, 2009.
2 REG-144615-02, 70 Fed. Reg. 51116, August 29, 2005 (first issued August 22, 2005)
3 US Treasury Regulations Section 482-7 effective prior to the temporary rules, issued in final form in 1996.
4 Under the temporary rules, a CSA buy-in transaction is referred to as a "platform contribution transaction" ("PCT") , signifying a payment for rights to further develop pre-existing—or platform—intangible assets as opposed to fully developed intangibles.

Cost Sharing Arrangements

based method for valuing subsequent buy-in intangibles. Like the temporary rules, the CIP also reinforced the investor model concept introduced in the proposed rules that rejected some of the previously accepted approaches to valuing intangibles contributed to CSAs.

While many practitioners have been reluctant to accept the merits of the investor model, the CIP provided evidence that cost sharing arrangements will likely have to withstand scrutiny under the investor model in an audit context. The temporary rules reinforce this likelihood. In light of the CIP and the temporary rules, the authors discuss the implications surrounding CSAs and the IRS formal adoption of the investor model.

Primary Reliance on the Income Method for Initial Buy-ins

Both the temporary rules and the CIP place considerable emphasis on the income method—which the CIP considered as "generally the best method" for the valuation of initial buy-ins, citing only limited exceptions. While it is reasonable to conclude that the income method is the best method under the examples provided in the CIP itself, it is not inherently clear that the income method is the only reliable method under such circumstances. The CIP's emphasis on a single method is also inconsistent with traditional valuation literature which requires that the analyst consider multiple methods.

To many practitioners, the CIP guidance seems formulaic—a strict dictum that further narrows reliable method options and broadens the scope of intangibles that may contribute to the value of a buy-in. To be fair, the CIP guidance substantiated its choice among available methods. It also articulated the IRS' intention to target potential contributions to intangible development that buy-in analyses often omitted prior to the proposed cost sharing rules.

The temporary rules largely reinforce many views presented in the CIP. Given its audience (IRS examiners) and its intended purpose, it is likely that the CIP continues to occupy IRS thinking from an enforcement perspective, further supported by the temporary rules. What informs the CIP guidance on application of methods? Two key factors: First is adherence to key principles of the investor model—principles to which some methods are better-suited than others. Second is attention to the relationship between scope of rights granted in buy-in intangibles and selection of valuation methods.

The IRS Base Case: Using an Income Method

The baseline hypothetical case in the CIP guidance is a "typical initial buy-in fact pattern" that involves a US parent participant (the US group) and a foreign participant (the CFC). The former brings substantially all intangible asset contributions and the latter has limited functions and risks prior to the CSA. Given this "one-way" flow of intangible contributions between the parties to the CSA the CIP rules out potential justification for use of other methods, such as the profit split method.[5]

---

5   The baseline facts also indicate that the US-contributed "buy-in intangibles" include technology-based platform intangibles and "make-sell" rights to current generation technology. The CSA focuses on long-term R&D based on the platform technologies intended to develop future generation intangibles. While the US group has other "operating intangibles" (such as marketing and manufacturing intangibles), these are excluded from the buy-in intangibles in the base case.

Cost Sharing Arrangements

In fact, the CIP is unequivocal in its review and elimination of all specified methods for transfers of intangible property in the Section 482 regulations, including methods that were specified in the proposed rules. As a result, an unspecified method, the income method, is determined to "constitute the most reliable method for measuring an initial buy-in..."[6]

This method determination is only revisited slightly under other scenarios, such as cases involving CFC contributions of pre-existing intangibles. Even then, the CIP remains emphatic that the income method is the primary and most reliable method, though it allows for a supplementary carve-out analysis to address the CFC intangible contribution.[7]

Notwithstanding the IRS audit focus on the income method, the question remains: Couldn't other reliable methods also apply? Assuming facts, circumstances and sufficient available data support their use, they may.

At a minimum, the authors believe that corroborative analysis of CSA transactions applying multiple methods is warranted. Traditional valuation methods often call for corroborative analysis to check the consistency of results; CSA buy-in valuation should be treated no differently. Furthermore, the temporary rules require analysis and consideration of any realistically available alternative in order to examine the reliability of a given method. In this sense, the temporary rules will likely also inform IRS audit review of CSA transactions, including those taking place before their effective date.

Measuring Future Returns to Future Intangibles

Literature on valuing intangible assets commonly discusses three main categories of methods, including income-, market- and cost-based approaches. Reilly and Schweihs note, "Analysts attempt to appraise intangible assets using methods from all three of the generally accepted valuation approaches in order to obtain a multidimensional perspective on the subject intangible asset."[8]

The income approach translates well to evaluating the key principles of the investor model. For example, *ex ante* expectations regarding income from the CSA are reflected in the projections of the CFC's business related to the CSA activity. The income method also requires evaluation of an appropriate discount rate. This not only helps determine the present value of the buy-in, it addresses risks assumed by the CFC and generally sets forth *ex ante* the expectations for the required return to the buy-in investment.

Similarly, the market capitalization method captures investor expectations about future returns to all of the company's investments, as reflected in the share price. Cost-based methods generally do not directly address expectations about future returns. Rather, they reflect the replacement cost to the owner. However, the cost of obtaining the same expected income flow by otherwise acquiring a similar asset is a reasonable investment alternative available to the CFC in some cases. Thus, even the replacement cost approach may fit within the parameters of

---

[6] Though the income method was introduced as a "specified" method in the proposed rules and adopted as such in the final and temporary rules, it was previously an "unspecified" method under the Section 482 regulations in effect at the time the CIP was issued.

[7] The method for deriving the relative value of this CFC intangible contribution is not described in the CIP.

[8] Reilly, Robert F. and Schweihs, Robert P., *Valuing Intangible Assets*, McGraw Hill, Copyright 1999, p. 115

the investor model.

Scope of Rights and the Sum of the Parts

Underlying the CIP guidance is a view that the income method overcomes many issues related to defining the scope of rights in buy-in intangibles. An income approach focuses on value (in terms of projected income) resulting from *all* of the combined investment in intangible development, regardless of how such contributions may be defined.

The CIP emphasizes the interaction between scope of rights issues and past applications of buy-in methods. It alleges taxpayer attempts to reduce the buy-in through "express designation" that limits the scope of rights in the buy-in intangibles through terminology (e.g. "license" instead of "sale"). According to the CIP, such designations are often semantic but at odds with economic substance.

Instead, the CIP emphasizes the distinction between rights to current generation intangibles, fully developed and ready for commercial exploitation, and the rights to share in the development and exploitation of future intangibles based upon "platform intangibles." The buy-in must address *both* of these, not just the former.

For example, a CUT based solely upon "make-sell" rights reflects only a limited subset of buy-in intangibles and generally excludes development rights. Furthermore, limited useful life estimates based on a licensed technology are considered "irrelevant" to the right to develop new intangibles based upon platform technology. The CIP addresses other areas related to the scope of buy-in intangibles, including the definition and treatment of goodwill, going concern value and the potential presence of workforce in place intangibles.

Methods other than the income method encounter difficult issues related to the scope of rights in intangibles. CIP discussion of the market capitalization method is mainly limited to scope-related difficulties in its application, such as the potential need to carve out benefit related to US operating intangibles that do not benefit the CFC.

The CIP does not address cost-based methods *per se*. Valuation literature notes that "basic economic principles assert that an investor will pay no more for an investment than the cost to obtain" it—this often translates into a classic "make or buy" decision.[9] But the ability to substitute or replace an asset depends upon the comparative utility of the asset. With respect to intangibles, utility should be considered in economic terms rather than simply functional terms.

Implications

Given the CIP, application of the income method appears to be a given from the IRS audit perspective. This remains likely regardless of whether an initial buy-in is grandfathered under the temporary rules. Taxpayers that may be audited should thus view the income method as at least one approach that must support the calculation of an initial buy-in. To the extent that other methods have been considered or used by taxpayers, the authors recommend undertaking corroborative analysis, taking into account results under an income-based approach to assess whether this and the other methods value the buy-in intangibles in a consistent manner and achieve consistent results.

Valuation professionals usually prefer to employ multiple methods in a corroborative analysis. This provides

---

9   Ibid, p. 97

a test of the relative reliability of the methods, information and data used—consistency generally implies that two or more methods are reliable. To the extent that different methods yield very different results, appropriate questions arise and explanations for such differences can be addressed.

In some cases, corroborative analysis of buy-ins can be analogous to the concept of "value additivity," which is defined as a "Rule that the value of the whole must equal the sum of the values of the parts."[10] In a corporate finance context, this rule means that adding the present values of all of the firm's individual assets is necessarily equal to the total value of the firm.[11]

How is this relevant? Methods for valuing buy-ins vary in terms of their level of aggregation. But regardless, different methods (or combinations of methods) that value the same pool of intangible assets benefiting the CSA should theoretically produce consistent results.

Generally speaking, income-based approaches such as those discussed in the CIP are more apt to capture the aggregate value attributable to any combination of intangible assets that generate such value. Any precise separation and identification of each underlying intangible does not necessarily affect the aggregate value. Of course, this all depends upon the reliability of the projections and other assumptions in the application of the method.

Market-based approaches vary in terms of aggregation. A market capitalization method should capture the market value of all underlying intangible assets (and that of other assets). However, transaction specific market-based analysis, such as a CUT, may analyze only a component part of intangible value, such as licensed rights in commercially developed technology.

Cost-based approaches generally identify and value individual assets or groups of similar assets. Methods that separately value individual assets often depend on a "build up" approach that sums values produced by multiple methods, thereby resulting in a "composite" buy-in value. Thus, cost-based approaches may often have to work in combination with other methods to arrive at a sum total value of intangible contributions, unless by definition there is only one individual intangible that is subject to the buy-in.[12]

The CIP's discussion of methods conveys an IRS view that aggregate valuation methods are likely to be more reliable. As discussed, the CIP emphasizes use of the income method and, to a lesser extent, the market capitalization method. Generally, both of these are aggregate approaches that capture total value and subtract value associated with items unrelated to the intangible development area. For example, the income method subtracts routine returns and, under one CIP variation to the baseline case,

---

[10] Brealy, Richard A. and Myers, Stuart C., *Capital Investment and Valuation*, McGraw Hill 2003, p. 547.

[11] According to Brealy and Myers, in capital markets investors are unwilling to pay a premium for diversification of risk among the assets held *within* a given firm, because their portfolios are already diversified by holding securities of many firms. Thus, a firm that lowers its risk (and expected return) through diversifying its own assets is not more attractive to the diversified investor. Brealy and Myers state that finance managers understand this and implicitly add the many present values associated with the firm's assets daily.

[12] This is also based on the assumption that the cost-based method is most reliable for the component intangible asset valuation. Valuation literature further notes that "the cost approach may be less applicable (but certainly not totally inapplicable) when the analyst is estimating the value of the intangible asset to the marketplace (and not the current owner)." (Reilly and Schweihs, p. 120) Thus, a distinction is drawn between cost and market value.

subtracts income attributable to CFC-contributed operating intangibles. The market cap approach must carve out value attributable to assets not contributed to the CSA activity.[13]

What about other methods? Below is a more detailed hypothetical example derived from the CIP baseline scenario that utilizes a composite of different methods.

Case Study: Revisiting the CIP's Hypothetical Scenario

Consider the baseline scenario under a more specific yet consistent set of facts. For example, assume that the platform intangibles consist of a software platform, including a copyrighted code base as well as some related patents. Staying consistent with the CIP example, the "buy-in intangibles" include the platform technology intangibles and the "make-sell" rights to the current generation software based on the platform, inclusive of all needed use rights for related intellectual property.

Given this more detailed scenario, at arm's length one may not necessarily conclude that the only reliable method is an income-based approach that aggregates the component intangibles. Understandably, the original baseline example is too high level to separate and value multiple hypothetical components that underlie the buy-in intangibles. But under arm's length conditions, methods that deconstruct the aggregate intangibles may be considered.

[13] Whether the market capitalization method is reliable depends in part on the whether the transferred buy-in intangibles should reflect "the whole" in terms of the full scope of intangible value benefiting the overall company. When the buy-in intangibles should reflect only a subset of this value, scoping challenges arise and "warrant careful consideration," as additional components of the total market value unrelated to the CSA must be quantified and subtracted.

For the buyer, this may be necessary in order to fully assess realistic alternatives.

Potential buyer questions might include: What are the replacement costs (and possible performance efficiency gains) associated with re-engineering the entire legacy platform code base? This is especially important with a software code base consisting of obsolescing modules from multiple outdated versions. How defensible are the patents, when do they expire, and what countries do they cover? Based on analysis of the patents, can the software be re-engineered in a non-infringing manner? Are certain modules now available cheaply from third parties? Such alternative cost and IP risk evaluation would likely be considered by any third party deciding whether to make or buy such platform intangibles.

As for the current generation "make-sell" rights, one common market-based approach remains a CUT. Based on this, CFC royalty payments could be projected for the reasonable life of the current generation software and discounted to their present value. Perhaps the model would value royalties differently in the periods before and after patents expire. Comparable third party license agreements may clearly delineate development rights and access to source code—such terms might reflect the division of rights under the buy-in.

The applicability of such alternative method combinations is realistic and reasonable—even under the constraints of the IRS's investor model. However, their reliability would hinge upon the degree to which they properly reflect the full scope of the buy-in intangibles. A large discrepancy between the composite of the individual component values described above and the income method would raise the question: Does the composite approach cover all transferred rights and intangible value?

What else is there? Section III.E of the CIP enumerates several types of intangibles that the IRS feels have been commonly excluded from buy-ins. With this guidance, it is more likely the IRS would assert, for example, "research team intangible contribution" as well as "synergy value of the research team related to the buy-in intangible." Presumably, these two types of intangibles would be covered by the projections in the income method but excluded in the cost- and CUT-based composite example above, warranting separate and additional valuation analyses.

Further Developments

Despite the CIP's emphasis on aggregate valuation methods, recent comments by IRS officials acknowledge the potential that intangibles underlying an initial buy-in, such as workforce in place and licensed "make-sell" rights, could be valued separately. But they also indicated that results when disaggregating individual intangible contributions should corroborate with aggregate intangible valuation methods. A disaggregation approach would also have to uphold the reliability standards for best method selection under the Section 482 regulations.[14]

The CIP devotes little attention to corroborative analysis. It briefly notes that a market capitalization method may be used to corroborate an application of the income method, but otherwise emphasizes a fairly narrow application of an income method as a single reliable method for valuing initial buy-ins under the hypothetical base case.

Practitioners will note, however, that the temporary rules are explicit regarding corroborating results, particularly in a section entitled "Consistency of evaluation with realistic alternatives."[15] Here, the regulations require that the total anticipated present value of a CSA participant's income attributable to its entering into the CSA, as of the date of the buy-in transaction, should not be less than the total anticipated present value of its income through an alternative arrangement realistically available to that participant.[16]

Examples in this section show the preferred alternative prevailing under a "licensing scenario" in which a considerably higher net present value attributes to the owner of the intangibles when they are licensed than would be realized when they are contributed under a CSA. Here, this corroborative licensing approach trumps application of none other than the income method itself, using the same basic underlying assumptions and projections.

Conclusions

While the income method and realistically available alternatives may be new realities of inter-company cost sharing buy-ins, at arm's length, identifying the projected cash flows anticipated from a given venture has always been a critical step in assessing value. However, it is not the only step. The specific risk associated with those projected cash flows, as well as the opportunity costs of similarly obtaining the projected cash flows through alternative investment options, are also

---

14 "IRS Official Says Aggregation Depends on Reliability of Transfer Pricing Methods Used," *Transfer Pricing Report* 10/08/2009, a Bureau of National Affairs publication.

15 Temporary rules paragraph (g)(2)(iii). Similar language was included in the proposed rules issued in 2005.

16 Ibid.

Cost Sharing Arrangements

critical steps in determining value.

Literature on valuing intangible assets discusses these and other approaches, including approaches that combine and synthesize different methods. The degree to which available approaches produce different results warrants careful consideration. Such differences raise questions about the reliability of methods producing inconsistent results.

Another main subject of the CIP is the degree to which taxpayers narrowly define intangible contributions, sometimes by narrowing the scope of rights in the transferred intangibles. The guidance implies that such qualitative judgments overly influence the process of quantifying intangible value. Defining and separately valuing various individual components of intangible value can be reasonable and realistically may occur at arm's length. But implicit in the CIP view is that the sum of the parts does not equal the whole. The IRS will be looking to aggregate methods like the income method (and in some cases the market cap) to define and value the whole.

It is the authors' view that taxpayers should examine buy-in transactions through the same lens as this IRS guidance, even as different interpretations and views on the investor model and the temporary rules remain. Corroborative analysis that includes the income method and other methods will provide further insight on the views expressed in the CIP.

PTB Consulting Founder **Patrick Breslin** has extensive experience conducting economic analysis of intercompany transactions with a focus on intangible property valuation. He can be reached at **(202) 518 0471** or by email at **pbreslin@ptbconsultingllc.com**.

Jeffrey Cole, a Partner at TPA Global, has extensive experience in the valuation of intangible assets in support of IRS audits, documentation studies, and business reorganizations. He can be reached at **(703) 663 8714** or by email at **j.cole@tpa-global.com**. For more information on the authors, please see Section XIII.

IV. Intangibles

Issues Arising in the Application of the Comparable Uncontrolled Transaction Method

By Hareesh Dhawale *(KPMG)*, George Carlson *(Deloitte Tax LLP)*, and Niels Melius *(Deloitte Tax LLP)*

Introduction

The comparable uncontrolled transaction method (CUTM) is one of the methods that may be used to evaluate the arm's-length amount charged for the transfer of intangible property in a controlled transaction under both the U.S. transfer pricing regulations under section 482 of the Internal Revenue Code and under the Transfer Pricing Guidelines for Multinational Enterprises and Tax Administrations (OECD Guidelines).[1] When comparable uncontrolled transactions can be identified, both the U.S. transfer pricing regulations and the OECD Guidelines view an application of the CUTM as yielding the most direct and reliable measure of the arm's length result for the controlled transfer of an intangible.[2] In practice, application of the CUTM is not always straightforward, due in part to differences in the profit potential of the intangible property in the controlled and uncontrolled transactions. For example, even when the profit potential of the intangible in the controlled transaction is "relatively small," and a comparison of the profit potential of the intangible in the controlled and uncontrolled transactions is based on indirect factors such as the terms of transfer or the stage of development of the intangible,[3] an application of the CUTM in practice may yield an arm's-length result that varies materially due to differences in contractual terms or the economic conditions in which transactions take place.[4]

This article analyzes a number of issues that arise in the application of the CUTM method. The article begins with a discussion of the comparability requirements for applying the CUTM under the U.S. regulations and the OECD Guidelines. Next, the article discusses a potential method for evaluating the profit potential of the intangibles under analysis and the similarity of the profit potential of the intangibles in the controlled and uncontrolled transactions, since profit potential is a key consideration in determining if and when the CUTM is applicable. The third section addresses issues that arise in evaluating the comparability of circumstances surrounding the transfer of intangible property. The fourth section examines practical issues relevant to a search for comparable uncontrolled transactions. Finally, the article concludes

---

1   The OECD Guidelines allow for the use of the comparable uncontrolled price (CUP) method in the case of a sale or license of intangible property. OECD Guidelines ¶6.23.

2   Reg. Sec. 1.482-4(c)(2)(ii) and OECD Guidelines ¶2.7.

Copyright © Deloitte Development LLC 2008. All rights reserved.

3   Reg. Sec. 1.482-4(c)(2)(iii)(B)(1)(ii).
4   Reg. Sec. 1.482-4(c)(2)(iii)(A).

with a comparison of the various publicly accessible databases available for a search for comparable uncontrolled transactions.

Comparability Requirements of the CUTM: Evaluating Whether the CUTM is Appropriate to a Given Transaction

The CUTM is one of the methods specified in the U.S. regulations and OECD Guidelines to evaluate the arm's length amount charged for the transfer of intangible property. Depending on the commercial circumstances, the range of intangibles being transferred could be broad, such as legally protected patents, trademarks and copyrights, inventions, formulae, processes, designs, patterns, know-how, etc.[5] Alternatively, the intangible property being transferred could also be "soft" intangibles, such as business processes including methods, programs, systems, and procedures.

A reliable application of the CUTM method requires that the controlled and uncontrolled transactions involve either the same intangible property or comparable intangible property.[6] With respect to comparability, the U.S. transfer pricing regulations specify two fundamental requirements for the intangible involved in the controlled transaction to be considered comparable to the intangible in the uncontrolled transaction: 1) the intangible property must have similar profit potential; and 2) the intangible property must be used in connection with similar products or processes within the same general industry or market.[7] The OECD Guidelines also list the expected benefits from the intangible property as one of the factors relevant to comparability between the controlled and uncontrolled transaction,[8] and require taking into account the perspective of both the transferor of the property and the transferee.[9] For example, from the perspective of the transferee, the price that would be paid by a comparable independent enterprise would depend on the value and usefulness of the intangible property to the transferee in its business.[10] This is generally consistent with the U.S. regulations' emphasis on finding uncontrolled transactions that have a similar profit potential in a market or industry similar to the controlled transaction.

The question then becomes how to measure the profit potential of the intangibles involved in the controlled transaction, given that the intangibles have to be similar in this respect between the controlled and uncontrolled transaction. The U.S. regulations have a clear preference for using the net present value (NPV) approach to valuing the profit potential of the intangibles under analysis. The regulations state that profit potential is most reliably measured by directly calculating the net present value of benefits to be realized from the use of the intangibles.[11] The principal difficulty in performing such a direct profit potential comparison is the lack of data to perform a net present value calculation, because projections of the profit and loss statements relating to the exploitation of the intangible are frequently not available. While such data are more likely to be available for the controlled transaction, it is rare for external license agreements identified from public databases to contain this type of information on the profitability from

---

5 Reg. Sec. 1.482-4(b); OECD Guidelines ¶6.2–¶6.5.
6 Reg. Sec. 1.482-4(c)(2)(iii)(A).
7 Reg. Sec. 1.482-4(c)(2)(iii)(B)(1).
8 OECD Guidelines ¶6.20.
9 OECD Guidelines ¶6.14.
10 Ibid.
11 Reg. Sec. 1.482-4(c)(2)(iii)(B)(1)(ii); see also OECD Guidelines (¶6.20).

exploitation of the intangible.

Practically speaking, the necessary data to perform an NPV calculation is available only with respect to internal comparable license agreements between the taxpayer and third parties. For example, large pharmaceutical companies are actively engaged in licensing compounds (which are in various stages of development) from biotechnology companies. As part of the financial analysis of such a potential licensing opportunity, the business development unit of the pharmaceutical company may develop a projected cash flow statement setting forth the projected net sales and costs of developing and commercializing the licensed compound and the resulting net present value to the company from licensing in the compound after making the projected royalty and milestone payments to the licensor. This type of financial analysis of the projected cash flow statement prepared by the business development unit may be used to seek approval from upper management to enter into a licensing arrangement with the licensor on the terms and conditions being proposed. The net present value of the projected cash flow under these circumstances may provide a reliable measure of the profit potential attributable to the intangible property being licensed by the pharmaceutical company. If similar data is available for the intangible property in the controlled transactions, a direct profit potential comparison could be performed of the intangible property being licensed in the controlled and uncontrolled transactions.

Recognizing this difficulty, the regulations permit comparison of profit potential to be based on other factors if the profit potential from the exploitation of the intangibles is "relatively small in terms of total amount and the rate of return."[12] The regulations provide no specific guidance regarding when profit potential may be considered "relatively small." Data on royalty rates in various industries suggest that in industries in which royalty rates approach or are in excess of the high single digits, the range of royalty rates observed also tends to be very wide. For example, royalty rates as a percentage of net sales for technology in the tools and automotive sectors have been reported to range between 3 percent and 7 percent and 2 percent and 5 percent, respectively.[13] In contrast, royalty rates in the pharmaceutical industry tend to have a broad range. For example, licensors that license compounds that are undergoing Phase I clinical[14] trials receive an average royalty rate as a percentage of net sales that ranges from 5 percent to 10 percent; for compounds licensed in Phase II,[15] the average royalty rate ranges from 8 percent

---

[12] Reg. Sec. 1.482-4(c)(2)(iii)(B)(1)(ii). Examples of those alternative factors that may be used in such an analysis include (i) the terms of the transfer, (ii) the stage of development of the intangible(s), (iii) rights to receive updates or improvements to the intangible(s), (iv) the uniqueness of the property and the period for which it remains unique, (v) the duration of the license, (vi) any economic and product liability risks to be assumed by the licensee, (vii) the existence and extent of any collateral transactions or ongoing business relationships between the licensor and licensee, and (viii) the functions to be performed under the agreement.

[13] Russell Parr, *Royalty Rates for Licensing Intellectual Property*, John Wiley & Sons, Inc., 2007, pg. 54.

[14] Phase I clinical trials are conducted in healthy individuals to establish the basic safety, dose tolerance, and metabolism of the clinical product candidate.

[15] Phase II trials are conducted in patients who have the disorder the compound is designed to treat and are typically designed to identify possible adverse effects and safety risks, to determine the efficacy of the clinical product candidate, and to determine dose tolerance.

to 15 percent; and for compounds licensed in Phase III,[16] the average royalty rate ranges from 10 percent to 20 percent.[17]

Based on the data above, the profit potential of intangibles that would support royalty rates approaching or in excess of the high single digits is likely to yield a very broad range of royalties that presumably stem from wide variations in the profit potential of the intangibles. Under these circumstances, an application of the CUTM is unlikely to provide a reliable measure of the arm's-length result for the controlled transfer of an intangible if the profit potential of the intangible transferred in the uncontrolled transaction cannot be reliably measured and if comparability adjustments are not made when material differences in the profit potential of the intangible exist between the controlled and uncontrolled transaction.

Regulation Section 1.482(c)(2)(iii)(B)(4) (Example 3)(vi) also provides additional guidance regarding the profit potential issue. As that example explains, if the intangible properties licensed under the comparable uncontrolled agreements and under the controlled agreement(s) do not account for a "substantial part of the value of the final products," and if the similarity of the controlled and uncontrolled transactions can be shown to be based on other factors, it may be concluded that the intangible properties licensed under the controlled and uncontrolled agreements have similar profit potential.

In the context of the example above, the "value of the final products" appears to refer to the sale price of the products under consideration. This would be consistent with a traditional economic interpretation of "value of the final products," which is generally equated with the prices at which goods and services trade in markets. Thus, in this example, the licensed intangible properties do not contribute significantly to the "value" (i.e., the price buyers would be willing to pay for the product) as evidenced by the relative insignificance of the component (compared to the total value of the final product) in which the intangible is embedded. If it can be shown that (i) the taxpayer intangibles make a small contribution to taxpayer's products' selling prices, and (ii) this is likely the case for the comparable uncontrolled license agreements used in the CUTM analysis, then these facts may provide evidence that the intangibles covered by the controlled and the uncontrolled license agreements have a similar profit potential.

Once the taxpayer has established that the profit potential of the intangibles being transferred is "relatively small," comparable uncontrolled transactions may be found by focusing on the comparability of circumstances between the controlled and uncontrolled transaction. Factors relevant to the comparability of circumstances of the controlled and uncontrolled transactions include: terms of transfer (exclusive/nonexclusive nature, limitations on geographic area, volume, market level, etc.), the right to receive updates (revisions, modifications of the intangibles), and the duration of the license, contract, or other agreement, and any termination or renegotiation rights.[18] As a first step, however, the taxpayer must assess the profit potential of the intangibles under analysis.

Methods for Evaluating Profit Potential of Intangibles

---

16 Phase III trials involve significantly larger and more diverse populations than Phase I and II trials during which the drug's safety and effectiveness are further examined and evaluated.

17 Russell Parr, *Royalty Rates for Licensing Intellectual Property*, John Wiley & Sons, Inc., 2007, pg. 94.

18 Reg. Sec. 1.482-4(c)(2)(ii)(B)(2).

Intangibles

As discussed, the most direct method for calculating the profit potential of intangibles involves calculating the NPV of the expected future profits realized or costs saved from the use of the intangibles. The preamble to the section 482 regulations recognizes the difficulty of calculating the NPV when it states that "the regulations provide that in certain cases it may be acceptable to refer to evidence other than projections [of the net present value of the intangibles] to compare profit potential. Such *indirect* comparisons of profit potential will be most useful in cases where it is not possible to directly calculate the profit potential of the intangibles."[19] The preamble further states, "given an indirect measure of profit potential, it might be concluded that the profit potential of the intangible property(ies) involved in the uncontrolled transaction might be similar to that of the controlled transaction…when the overall profitability of the intangibles is relatively small."[20]

One indirect method for evaluating the profits attributable to the use of intangibles is the basic arm's length return method (BALRM), which is a variant of the comparable profits method (CPM). The BALRM was initially proposed in the 1988 White Paper Study by the IRS and Treasury Department on the theory and administration of section 482.[21] The BALRM may be used to establish:

- That the intangible property in a controlled transaction does not account for "substantial part of the value of the final products";[22]
- That the profit potential of intangible property in a controlled transaction is "relatively small in terms of rate of return";[23] or
- Similarity of profit attributable to an intangible in controlled transaction with similar intangibles used by competitors operating in the same industry as the taxpayer under certain circumstances.

The steps involved in evaluating the profit potential when using the BALRM method are as follows:

1.) Obtain income statement data for multiple years (for example, three years) for the taxpayer and taxpayer's competitors in the same business line or industry;
2.) Identify the activities or factors of production or functions that can be measured ("measurable activities or factors");
3.) Estimate a market return (return on assets, Berry ratio, or some other profit level indicator) to those activities based on a search for comparable benchmarks;
4.) Subtract the marked-up costs of those functions from net sales of the taxpayer and its competitors to generate a residual (intangible) operating profit;
5.) Subtract R&D expenses to determine residual (intangible) profit; and
6.) Calculate the residual (intangible) profit as a percentage of sales or as a percentage of operating assets to evaluate the profit potential of the intangibles.

Illustrative Calculation of Residual Intangible Profit

The following example illustrates the use of the BALRM method to calculate residual intangible profit in the

---

19 Taken from the preamble to the U.S. transfer pricing regulations referring to Reg. Sec. 1.482-4(c) of the final regulations.
20 Ibid.
21 Notice 88-123; 1988-2 C.B. 458
22 Reg. Sec. 1.482(c)(2)(iii)(B)(4)(Example 3)(vi)
23 Reg. Sec. 1.482(c)(2)(iii)(B)(ii)

Intangibles

Table 1: Summary of Ratio of Intangible Profit to Net Sales: 2004-06

COMPANY NAME	Average Net Sales: 2004-06	Average Intangible Profit: 2004-06	Intangible Profit/ Net Sales: 2004-06
Colgate Palmolive Co	11,406,266.667	1,588,098.667	13.92%
General Mills Inc	11,775,333.333	1,455,160.000	12.36%
Kellogg Co	10,232,600.000	1,269,648.000	12.41%
Kimberly Clark Corp	15,910,900.000	2,191,298.667	13.77%
Nestle Sa -adr	75,346,195.333	3,513,814.240	4.66%
Procter & Gamble Co	58,790,000.000	8,020,320.000	13.64%
Revlon Inc	1,320,300.000	(106,705.333)	NC
Unilever Nv	39,827,666.667	729,400.000	1.83%

Weighted Average Intangible Profit / Net Sales	
Maximum	13.92%
Upper Quartile	13.77%
Median	12.41%
Lower Quartile	4.66%
Minimum	1.83%
# of Companies	7

Units: All data except for Unilever Nv is reported in thousands of U.S. dollars; data on Unilever Nv is reported in thousands of euros.

consumer goods industry. The example uses a publicly available data set of eight companies engaged in the development, manufacture, marketing, and distribution of consumer products such as beauty products, food products, and household care products. The intangibles evaluated in this illustrative calculation include manufacturing and marketing intangibles such as patents, know-how, and trademarks. For purposes of the illustrative calculation, the factors of production or functions for which market returns would need to be estimated were assumed to be manufacturing and distribution. The markup on the manufacturing function was assumed to be 8 percent, and this markup was applied to the cost of goods sold (COGS) of these companies. A Berry ratio of 1.20 on the operating expenses was assumed to provide an appropriate return on the distribution function. Appendix A sets forth data on average net sales, COGS, operating expenses, and operating profit income for the eight companies over the three year period 2004-06.[24] Appendix A

24 The data set was downloaded from

illustrates the calculation of the residual (intangible) operating profit based on an application of the six steps set forth above for the eight companies. Table 1 summarizes the results obtained for the intangible operating profit for these companies over the three-year period 2004-06. The interquartile range of intangible operating profit to net sales for the seven of the eight companies that had a residual intangible operating profit extends from 4.6 percent to 13.8 percent, with a median of 12.4 percent.

To assess the profit potential of the intangibles of a taxpayer operating in the consumer products industry, one could calculate the residual (intangible) operating profit for the taxpayer along similar lines as for the eight companies listed in Table 1, which presumably would represent the taxpayer's primary competitors. A key assumption underlying the BALRM

CompuStat. Any one-time expense that would be classified as restructuring, special, or nonrecurring is generally classified by Compustat as nonoperating and is removed in calculating the company's operating profit.

Tax Director's Guide to International Transfer Pricing: *2010 Edition* Copyright © 2010 GBIS, Inc.

analysis illustrated above is that the intangible in the controlled transaction be the total package of intangibles owned by the taxpayer similar to the total package of intangibles owned by the taxpayer's primary competitors whose value is reflected in the intangible profits calculated in Table 1. If the taxpayer's ratio of intangible operating profit to net sales were close to the lower quartile of the range calculated from companies operating in the same business or industry as the taxpayer, it may be possible to conclude that the intangible operating profit of the taxpayer does not account for a substantial part of the value of the final products. In contrast, if the taxpayer's ratio of intangible operating profit to net sales is close to the upper quartile, the CUTM analysis would tend to be less reliable in the absence of other data supporting the similarity of the profit potential of the intangible in the controlled and uncontrolled transactions.

Alternatively, if the taxpayer's ratio of intangible operating profit to net sales were in the range calculated for similar companies operating in the same industry as the taxpayer, one may conclude that the value of the intangible property owned by the taxpayer is consistent with the value of the intangible property utilized on average throughout the industry in which the taxpayer operates. Under these circumstances, a CUTM analysis based on license agreements entered into by either the taxpayer or its competitors with unrelated parties for the intangibles would arguably yield reliable results, since the taxpayer's intangible profits are consistent with those earned by similar companies operating in the same industry as the taxpayer. This conclusion is not based on the intangible property not accounting for a substantial part of the value of final products but on other data supporting the similarity of the profit potential of the intangible in the controlled and uncontrolled transactions. Specifically, if the intangibles in the controlled transaction are the total package of intangibles owned by the taxpayer, a finding that the taxpayer's ratio of intangible operating profit to net sales is in the range calculated for similar companies operating in the same industry as the taxpayer approximates a direct comparison of the profit potential of the intangibles in the controlled and uncontrolled transactions.

To sum up, the taxpayer could argue that its residual intangible profit as a percentage of sales is either small or is comparable to that of its competitors in the same business line or industry. If the taxpayer had a ratio of intangible profit to net sales close to the lower quartile of the range, the intangible property of the taxpayer may be viewed as having a profit potential that is relatively small and does not account for a substantial part of the value of the final products. Alternatively, if the profit potential of the intangibles owned by the taxpayer is in the range of the profits of the intangible properties of the taxpayer's competitors, then the taxpayer's intangible properties are not exceptionally valuable compared to the intangible properties owned by its competitors. This would also support the use of a CUTM analysis based on uncontrolled license agreements entered into by companies operating in the same industries as taxpayer. That is, if the taxpayer's intangible returns are comparable to the returns generally earned by companies operating in the taxpayer's lines of business, a CUTM analysis based on uncontrolled license agreements in this industry would arguably be based on license agreements covering intangible properties of comparable profit potential to the properties covered in the controlled transaction.

The BALRM approach sketched above

may therefore permit the taxpayer, under appropriate circumstances, to perform a CUTM analysis without performing a direct comparison of the profit potential of the intangible property in the controlled and uncontrolled transactions. When the intangibles transferred by the taxpayer and those of the taxpayer's competitors constitute the key intangibles in the business, the BALRM approach approximates a direct comparison of the profit potential of the intangibles in the controlled and uncontrolled transaction. The next step in the CUTM analysis would then be a careful evaluation of the comparability of the circumstances of the controlled and uncontrolled transactions.

Evaluating Comparability of Circumstances of Intangible Transfers: Identifying Comparable Transactions Needed to Apply the CUTM

Once the taxpayer has established the similarity of its intangibles' profit potential to that of its competitors (or, alternatively, the small size of its intangibles' profit potential), the search for comparable uncontrolled transactions may be performed to determine an arm's length price for the controlled transaction. According to the regulations, a number of factors must be evaluated when determining the comparability of circumstances of the intangible transfer. Some of those factors include:
- Terms of the transfer (exclusive v. nonexclusive right to exploit intangibles, geographic area in which intangible is exploited, and restrictions on use (such as restrictions relating to customer base/sales channel));
- Stage of development of intangible (for example, pharmaceutical intangibles might be licensed at different stages of the development process);
- Rights to receive updates, revisions, or modifications of the intangible; and
- Functions to be performed by the transferor and the transferee, such as marketing support, technical assistance (for instance, implementing manufacturing process, assistance with design of plant/equipment), other ancillary services provided by licensor (for example, training), R&D services to be provided or paid for by the licensee, or the sharing of product liability and other risks (indemnification provisions).

Depending on the industry under review, the taxpayer would select a number of these factors to determine the comparability between the controlled and uncontrolled transactions.

Given the various factors that may influence comparability, it is useful to track the comparability of the uncontrolled agreements to the controlled transaction by making a checklist of the various factors under review and creating a "comparability index." The comparability index is a simple count of the number of contractual terms in the uncontrolled transactions that are similar to those in the controlled transaction. Table 2 illustrates a checklist of some key features that may be used to compare the controlled transaction with a potential uncontrolled transaction involving licensing of intangible property. The key features of the controlled transaction along with a hypothetical uncontrolled transaction are set forth in the table. A '1' indicates the presence of the characteristic/feature, whereas a '0' indicates the absence of the characteristic/feature.

For example, both the controlled and uncontrolled transactions involve

Table 2: Checklist of Key Features of Controlled and Uncontrolled Transactions

Licensor	Licensee	Exclusive	Products	Product Coverage	Marketing Intangibles	Manufacturing Intangibles from Licensor	Technical Assistance by Licensor	Updates to Licensee	Marketing Support
Parent Co	Subsidiary	1	Fragrances and cosmetics	1	1	1	1	1	1
A	B	1	Fragrances and skin care products	1	0	1	0	1	0

exclusive rights to the licensee to use the intangibles to manufacture and sell beauty products. Whereas the controlled transaction involves licensing of both manufacturing and marketing intangibles, the uncontrolled transaction involves licensing of only the manufacturing intangibles. In both the controlled and the uncontrolled transaction, the licensee has the right to receive updates to the intangibles during the period of the license. Unlike the controlled transaction, in which the licensee gets technical assistance from the licensor in exploiting the intangible as well as marketing support, the uncontrolled transaction does not provide this type of assistance to the licensee. Thus, four of the seven features/characteristics are similar for the controlled and uncontrolled transactions.

Comparability indices can be helpful in identifying outliers with contractual terms that are very dissimilar to the controlled transaction. In addition, if a sufficient number of third-party license agreements have been identified, one could estimate the impact of variation in each of the contractual terms on the royalty rate using a dummy variable technique. For example, suppose a regression analysis using dummy variables indicates that exclusivity in exploitation rights increases the royalty rate on average by 30 basis points compared to cases in which exploitation rights are not exclusive. Therefore, if the controlled transaction involves exclusive exploitation rights, then royalty rates in the third-party license agreements in which exploitation rights are not exclusive could be adjusted upward by 30 basis points to make the agreement comparable to the controlled transaction. A final possibility would be the division of the full sample of agreements into two or three subgroups based on the number of contractual terms that are similar to the controlled transaction to test the sensitivity of the interquartile range of royalties to differences in contractual terms. The taxpayer might then evaluate whether the interquartile range differs in material ways among the subgroups.

Potentially comparable agreements can be rejected for a number of reasons, including:

1) Agreements that were entered into to settle prior disputes/litigation relating to the ownership of the intangible. These agreements are typically not good comparables because, presumably, the controlled transaction does not involve a dispute between the contracting parties regarding the ownership of the intangibles;

2) Collateral transactions, such as an asset purchase agreement or a manufacturing agreement may make it

difficult to isolate the return/payment for the intangible being licensed from the provision/receipt of other products/assets;
3) Royalty rate presented in noncomparable terms, e.g., as payment per unit of the product sold or a lump-sum payment; and
4) Agreement is a codevelopment agreement with no licensing of intangible property between the parties.

In some instances a particular license agreement might yield multiple royalty rates that may need to be included in the interquartile range of royalty rates. Two prominent examples would be sales-based royalties and royalties that vary based on the contract year. For example, the royalties specified in a license agreement may either increase or decrease based on the amount of sales the licensee is able to generate from the use of the licensor's intangible property. The taxpayer might then consider using – as a CUTM – the royalty rate that corresponds most closely to the sales volume of the controlled transaction.

As a second example, royalty rates may differ over the course of the term of the license agreement. Consider the following example, whereby the uncontrolled licensing agreement with a five-year term stipulates the following:
- Royalty rates in contract years 1, 2, and 3 are 2 percent, 3 percent, and 4 percent, respectively;
- In contract years 4 and 5, the royalty rate is set at 5 percent.

Suppose the contract year 1 in the uncontrolled transaction corresponds to the year ended December 31, 2003, and that the taxable year that is being tested is the year ending December 31, 2005.

Several options are available with respect to selecting the appropriate royalty rate, including:
- Selecting a royalty rate of 5 percent if in 2005 the intangible in the controlled transaction was used by the licensee to sell a mature product that had been on the market for at least three years;
- Select a royalty rate of 3 percent if in 2005 the intangible is used by the licensee in the controlled transaction to sell a product that was in its second year post-launch; or
- Select a royalty rate of 4 percent, because contract year 3 in the uncontrolled transaction corresponds to the year ending December 31, 2005, for the controlled transaction.

Practical Issues in Constructing Reliable CUTM Searches: Developing a Search Strategy Using LexisNexis or Securities Mosaic

Having discussed some of the theoretical groundwork and some practical issues in applying the CUTM, this section turns to some of the practical issues that arise in designing a search strategy for identifying potentially comparable licensing agreements using the two largest databases that present challenges of constructing search criteria using Boolean logic, LexisNexis™ and Securities Mosaic™. Both of these databases contain license agreements that are publicly available as part of companies' filings with the Securities and Exchange Commission (SEC) in the United States. Companies filing with the SEC are required to file all contracts that are material to their business. Those contracts, included as exhibits to the Forms 10-K or other SEC filings, may include agreements that license the right to use the company's intangible properties, such as patents, trademarks, know-how, inventions, designs, systems, and other similar items.

The LexisNexis™ database can be used to search filings made with the SEC and stored in the EDGARPlus Database. The EDGARPlus Database contains over 2 million EDGAR filings that have been filed with the SEC from 1994 to the present. Each of the corporate exhibits is stored in the EDGARPlus database as a separate document, allowing more focused searching and retrieval.

EDGAR, the Electronic Data Gathering, Analysis and Retrieval System, performs automated collection, validation, indexing, acceptance, and forwarding of submissions by companies and others required by law to file forms with the SEC. As of May 6, 1996, all public domestic companies were required to make their filings on EDGAR, except for filings made in paper because of a hardship exemption. Third-party filings with respect to these companies, such as tender offers and Schedules 13D, are also filed on EDGAR.[25] LexisNexis™ receives EDGAR documents filed electronically and makes them available to users. The two LexisNexis™ files searched contained Exhibits 10 and 4 filed as attachments to 10-Ks, 10-Qs, 8-Ks, Proxy Statements, and Registration Statements. Exhibits 10, which are attached to SEC filings, typically contain agreements between the company and unrelated parties involving the licensing of rights to intangible properties. Occasionally, in SEC filings, those agreements are also listed under Exhibit 4 relating to instruments defining the rights of security holders.

If the taxpayer selects LexisNexis™ as the database to identify comparable uncontrolled transactions, several peculiarities of the LexisNexis™ database should be taken into consideration. It is of primary importance to create an effective "search string," a series of commands written using Boolean language and used to filter the myriad resources LexisNexis™ draws from into a coherent group of potentially comparable license agreements. Boolean language is a search strategy for information retrieval that relies on search operators like "and" and "not" that represent symbolic relationships between the individual keywords being used as search terms.

An effective search string is not only important from an efficiency standpoint, it is also fundamental to performing a LexisNexis™ search, because the database will not produce results if more than 5,000 results are obtained from executing the search strategy.

The following steps may be followed to perform a search for potentially comparable license agreements in the LexisNexis™ database:

1) Select sources. For example, to search for license agreements that license intangible property for use in the food industry, the taxpayer would select Exhibit 10 (Material Contracts) and Exhibit 4 ("Instruments Defining the Rights of Security Holders") as sources. This source searches all Exhibit 10s and Exhibit 4s filed with a company's SEC filings since 1994.
2) Select SIC codes. For the food industry, the taxpayer's SIC code likely falls into one of the following general industry codes: 201, 202, 204, 205, 206, 207, 208, 209, and 514. In LexisNexis™, using Boolean language, this portion of the

---

25 Some documents, however, may be filed on EDGAR voluntarily, and consequently may or may not be available on EDGAR. For example, Forms 3, 4, and 5 (security ownership and transaction reports filed by corporate insiders) and Form 144 (notice of proposed sale of securities) may be filed on EDGAR at the option of the filer.

Intangibles

search string would appear as:

sic(201! or 202! or 203! or 204! or 205! or 206! or 207! or 208! or 209! or 514!)

The exclamation mark is a "wild card" key, which means that LexisNexis™ will search all SICs in that general industry code (for example, 2010, 2011, 2012, etc.).

3) Select types of agreements (for instance, license agreements, trademark agreements, design agreements):

((brand! or know-how! or license! or patent! or trademark! or tradename! or trade name! or technolog! or design! or process! or formul! or develop!) and (fee or royalt!))

4) Add exclusionary language (that is, language that would eliminate agreements you do not wish to review): Select types of agreements that you wish to exclude (for example, asset purchase agreements, loan agreements, indemnification agreements).

(and not (((stock or share! or asset! or lease or employment or credit or financing or brokerage or retention or loan or retirement or settlement or note or deferred payment or deferred compensation or guarantee or investment or convertible) w/2 (purchase or agreement or amendment or plan or note or warrant)) or letter of investment intent or incentive award or share saving scheme or (confidential w/15 filed separately) or promissory note or indemnification agreement or (business financing w/1 agreement) or royalty-free))

Considerable care must be exercised in selecting appropriate exclusionary keywords. For example, using simply the keyword "confidential" to exclude agreements in which the company filing the agreement has requested confidential treatment from the SEC of the payment and other provisions in the license agreement may inadvertently exclude license agreements containing provisions obligating the licensee to treat all information and data provided by the licensor as confidential. Thus, a better search string would exclude agreements containing the keyword "confidential" when followed by the keyword "treatment."

5) The final search string combining each of the above three components:

((sic(201! or 202! or 203! or 204! or 205! or 206! or 207! or 208! or 209! or 514!) and (brand! or know-how! or license! or patent! or trademark! or tradename! or trade name! or technolog! or design! or process! or formul! or develop!) and (fee or royalt!)) and not (((stock or share! or asset! or lease or employment or credit or financing or brokerage or retention or loan or retirement or settlement or note or deferred payment or deferred compensation or guarantee or investment or convertible) w/2 (purchase or agreement or amendment or plan or note or warrant)) or letter of investment intent or incentive award or share saving scheme or (confidential w/15 filed separately) or promissory note or indemnification agreement or (business financing w/1 agreement) or royalty-free))

Although the final search string appears long and somewhat complex, it can be easily understood if broken down into its constituent parts as explained above. A final practical tip is to save the search strings in a word file and to record the number of results or "hits" for later use.

Using the LexisNexis™ Results

Once a search has been performed in LexisNexis™, it is helpful to transform the standard Lexis-Nexis output into a more user-friendly format. The easiest way to do this is to create an Excel macro that selectively collects information from each potential agreement found in LexisNexis™ and reports the data in an easy-to-review format in Excel. An Excel macro is simply an Excel function that represents a sequence of operations. The macro extracts the relevant information from the Excel output and reports it in a more user-friendly format. When downloading the output from Lexis, both the "cite" and "full" versions of the results should be downloaded, since the "cite" version is helpful for the macro and the "full" version will allow the reviewer to read the full text of the potential license agreements.

Securities Mosaic^{SM}

Securities Mosaic^{SM}, a database maintained by Knowledge Mosaic LLC that contains more than 6 million documents filed with the SEC since 1994, has many similarities to LexisNexis™, but also some important differences. Each of the corporate exhibits is stored in the Securities Mosaic^{SM} database as a separate document, allowing more focused searching and retrieval. Like LexisNexis™, the two Securities Mosaic^{SM} files that should be selected for the search are Exhibits 10 and 4, which are typically filed as attachments to 10-Ks, 10-Qs, 8-Ks, Proxy Statements, and Registration Statements. Securities Mosaic^{SM}, however, searches all possible SEC filings that may contain Exhibits 10 and 4. For example, the Securities Mosaic^{SM} database includes filings under Securities Act Rule 425, which consists of Form 425. Exhibits 10, which are attached to SEC filings, typically contain agreements between the company and unrelated parties involving the licensing of rights to intangible properties. Occasionally, in SEC filings, those agreements are also listed under Exhibit 4 relating to instruments defining the rights of security holders.

Like LexisNexis™, Securities Mosaic^{SM} also uses Boolean language to perform a search of all the relevant files in the database. The considerations described earlier for creating an effective "search string" in LexisNexis™ apply with equal force to the Securities Mosaic^{SM} database.

Overview of Databases Used to Search for Comparable Uncontrolled Transactions

In addition to LexisNexis™ and Securities Mosaic^{SM}, several other databases can be used to perform a CUT search. This section examines the advantages and disadvantages of each database. For purposes of comparison, the two discussed in the previous section are also included here.

RoyaltySource Royalty Rates database: an online searchable database of technology and trademark sales and licensing transactions.

– Advantages: includes the following information: a) licensee and licensor, including industry description or codes; b) description of the property licensed or sold; c) royalty rate details; d) other compensation,

such as upfront payments or equity positions; e) transaction terms, such as exclusivity, geographical restrictions, or grant-backs; and f) source of information. The database also covers most major industries: apparel, automotive, biotechnology, chemicals, communications, computer hardware, software, electronics, pharmaceuticals, and semiconductors. The turnaround for using this service is also quick: the user receives detailed reports containing search results within 24 hours of submitting a search request. Therefore, the RoyaltySource database is a good source of initial information on the types of potential agreements and ranges of royalties in the industry being analyzed. The database is also inexpensive: the charge for up to 10 transactions of interest is $250 and only $50 dollars for each additional transaction.
- Disadvantages: lacks the full text of the licensing agreements. The database also does not represent the entire universe of potentially comparable agreements; issues of *Licensing Economic Review* are the main source of information.

RoyaltyStat: a subscription-based database with royalty rates and license agreements.
- Advantages: all license agreements will contain at least one numerical, unredacted royalty rate. The database is updated every month and is searchable by licensor, licensee, intangible property description, territory, date filed with SEC, SIC Code, agreement type, and full text keyword search. The user simply enters the words in natural language (as opposed to Boolean language) to search. One of the value-added functions RoyaltyStat provides is the useful summary of each agreement in a search. The user can view these summaries before downloading the agreement, so they are not deducted from the total allowable number of downloads. Each agreement summary includes a link to the complete license agreement and the SEC filing within which the license agreement was included.
- Disadvantages: there are currently approximately 6,000 license agreements in the RoyaltyStat database, as RoyaltyStat removes agreements it considers unusable, such as agreements in which the information on the royalty rate and other payment terms has been redacted because the filer has requested confidential treatment of those terms. Practitioners, however, may want to perform their own independent review of all the available agreements rather than relying on the screening performed by a third party. Databases such as Lexis-Nexis™ and Securities Mosaic™ allow practitioners to perform a search of all available agreements and perform their own evaluation of the agreements. The RoyaltyStat database is also rather costly; a subscription of $4,000 allows only 100 license agreement downloads (although it does allow unlimited searches with summary results).

Compact D/Thomson Database: lists corporate exhibits from recent 10-Ks.
- Advantages: the user can scroll through a listing of agreements to see if there are any potentially relevant license agreements. The database is also relatively cheap to access.
- Disadvantages: the output is not user-

Intangibles

friendly. Additionally, exhibit source references are often ambiguous, which makes finding exhibit sources and the agreement text rather laborious. Thus, the database is cumbersome and does not offer any practical advantage over Lexis-Nexis.

LexisNexis™ and Securities Mosaic[SM]: enormous databases with applications in the business, legal, and media sectors.

- Advantages: allow individuals to search specifically through corporate exhibits filed with the SEC, such as Exhibit 10 (Material Contracts). The user can search the entire universe of agreements by searching through all SEC filings since the mid-1990s that are stored on the SEC-regulated EDGAR archive. Lexis-Nexis™ can also produce the entire agreement in a user-friendly format.
- Disadvantages: quality of Lexis-Nexis™ search depends on the user's ability to construct a proper search string, as previously discussed. Additionally, the resulting Lexis-Nexis™ agreements are not processed to separate those agreements with explicit royalty rates from those in which the royalty rates are redacted. Also, since companies are often given permission to keep certain information hidden from the public's (but not the SEC's) view, key sections may be confidentially treated and inaccessible. Those sections can include the product lists or the exact intangibles being licensed. Finally, Lexis is a highly trafficked database, which cannot handle large searches and search strings during "peak" times (afternoon EST).

To summarize, the RoyaltySource database remains a good starting point to determine what types of agreements exist in the public domain. Then, as a primary database, LexisNexis™ or Securities Mosaic[SM] can be used to search the entire universe of corporate SEC filings. Despite sounding intimidating, a search in Lexis-Nexis™ or Securities Mosaic[SM] can be managed if proper steps are taken to create a sound search string to filter the results Lexis-Nexis™ or Securities Mosaic[SM] provides. As a final confirming step, it is a good idea to check the RoyaltyStat database for any additional comparable uncontrolled transactions because 1) the IRS and CRA subscribe to RoyaltyStat and use this as a basis for discovering CUTs, and 2) the exclusionary language in Lexis may incorrectly exclude good CUTs.

If the intangibles in the controlled transaction consist of business systems and processes as well as trademark/trade names, the Bond's Franchise Guide[26] is a good research tool for identifying third-party arrangements involving the licensing of these types of intangibles, because those agreements are not always publicly available in SEC filings.[27] To the extent a search of the databases described earlier, such as Lexis-Nexis™, fails to identify any comparable uncontrolled transactions, or identifies an insufficient number of comparable transactions, Bond's may be used as the starting point

---

[26] The Bond's Franchise Guide is an annual publication designed to provide prospective franchisees a detailed profile and description of over 1,000 franchises listed in both the United States and internationally. These profiles include background information about a franchisor's number of operating units, geographic distribution, and specific fees and royalty rates charged to the franchisee. Franchise listings are divided into specific industry segments.

[27] For example, the franchisor/licensor may be a private company with no SEC filing obligations.

Appendix A
8 Companies
For the Average: 12/31/2006, 3 years back (2004 to 2006)
Financial Data

		Colgate Palmolive Co	General Mills Inc	Kellogg Co	Kimberly Clark Corp	Nestle Sa -adr	Procter & Gamble Co	Revlon Inc	Unilever Nv
	Fiscal year end	Dec. 2004-2006	May. 2005-2007	Dec. 2004-2006	Dec. 2004-2006	Dec. 2004-2006	Jun. 2004-2006	Dec. 2004-2006	Dec. 2004-2006
		(USD 000's)	(USD 000's)	(USD 000's)	(USD 000's)	(USD 000's)	(USD 000's)	(USD 000's)	(Euro 000's)
Income Statement									
	Net Sales	11,406,266.67	11,775,333.33	10,232,600.00	15,910,900.00	75,346,195.33	58,790,000.00	1,320,300.00	39,827,666.67
	Cost of Goods Sold	4,745,266.67	6,819,666.67	5,209,900.00	9,782,766.67	31,218,353.67	26,704,333.33	483,233.33	20,166,666.67
	Gross Profit	6,661,000.00	4,955,666.67	5,022,700.00	6,128,133.67	44,127,841.67	32,085,666.67	837,066.67	19,661,000.00
	Operating Expenses (excl. depreciation)	3,950,900.00	2,492,000.00	2,809,133.33	2,678,533.33	31,974,919.33	18,597,333.33	758,400.00	14,588,000.00
	Depreciation	328,600.00	420,000.00	382,200.00	859,200.00	2,808,526.33	2,081,333.33	29,733.33	362,000.00
	Operating Profit	2,381,500.00	2,043,666.67	1,831,366.67	2,590,400.00	9,344,396.00	11,407,000.00	48,933.33	4,711,000.00
a	Manufacturing Costs (COGS)	4,745,266.67	6,819,666.67	5,209,900.00	9,782,766.67	31,218,353.67	26,704,333.33	483,233.33	20,166,666.67
b	Markup on Manufacturing costs	8.00%	8.00%	8.00%	8.00%	8.00%	8.00%	8.00%	8.00%
c=a*b	Total Manufacturing return	379,621.33	545,573.33	416,792.00	782,621.33	2,497,468.29	2,136,346.67	38,658.67	1,613,333.33
d=a+c	Manufacturing costs + return	5,124,888.00	7,365,240.00	5,626,692.00	10,565,388.00	33,715,821.96	28,840,680.00	521,892.00	21,780,000.00
e	Net Sales	11,406,266.67	11,775,333.33	10,232,600.00	15,910,900.00	75,346,195.33	58,790,000.00	1,320,300.00	39,827,666.67
f=e-d	Residual gross profit	6,281,378.67	4,410,093.33	4,605,908.00	5,345,512.00	41,630,373.37	29,949,320.00	798,408.00	18,047,666.67
	Distribution costs: Operating expenses less R&D expenses	3,711,900.00	2,314,666.67	2,635,633.33	2,378,400.00	30,708,199.00	16,658,333.33	733,566.67	13,651,333.33
g	Markup on distribution costs	20.00%	20.00%	20.00%	20.00%	20.00%	20.00%	20.00%	20.00%
h	Total distribution return	742,380.00	462,933.33	527,126.67	475,680.00	6,141,639.80	3,331,666.67	146,713.33	2,730,266.67
i=g*h	Distribution costs + return	4,454,280.00	2,777,600.00	3,162,760.00	2,854,080.00	36,849,838.80	19,990,000.00	880,280.00	16,381,600.00
j=g+1	Residual operating profit	1,827,098.67	1,632,493.33	1,443,148.00	2,491,432.00	4,780,534.57	9,959,320.00	-81,872.00	1,666,066.67
k=f-j	R&D Expense	239,000.00	177,333.33	173,500.00	300,133.33	1,266,720.33	1,939,000.00	24,833.33	936,666.67
m=k-l	Residual profit attributable to intangibles	1,588,098.67	1,455,160.00	1,269,648.00	2,191,298.67	3,513,814.24	8,020,320.00	-106,705.33	729,400.00
	Residual (intangible) profit as a percentage of net sales	13.92%	12.36%	12.41%	13.77%	4.66%	13.64%	-8.08%	1.83%
	Average R&D to sales ratio	2.10%	1.51%	1.70%	1.89%	1.68%	3.30%	1.88%	2.35%

Tax Director's Guide to International Transfer Pricing: *2010 Edition* Copyright © 2010 GBIS, Inc.

Intangibles

for a supplementary search. Depending on the industry in which the taxpayer operates, information on the franchise agreements in the appropriate industries/sectors listed in Bond's should be reviewed with a view to identify a list of potential franchise agreements that would require a detailed review. For these agreements, the standard franchise agreements that is part of the Uniform Franchise Offering Circular (UFOC) must be obtained and reviewed.[28]

The standard franchise agreement is not a signed agreement between a specific franchisee and the franchisor, but a form agreement that provides potential franchisees detailed information on the intangibles that would be licensed, along with payment and other terms. A careful analysis of the standard franchise agreement should be performed to evaluate the comparability of the circumstances of the controlled and uncontrolled transactions along the lines described in the previous section. It is also important to look at these standard franchise agreements because the OECD Guidelines do not limit the application of the CUTM to actual transactions between unrelated parties, but permit the use of offers to unrelated parties as well as genuine bids of competing licensees.[29] While there is a possibility of differences with respect to some of the contractual terms in the executed agreement compared to those in the standard franchise agreement as a result of negotiations between the franchisee and the franchisor, Bond's notes that there is a legal requirement that all of a franchisor's agreements be substantially the same at any point in time.[30]

---

28 Franchisors in the United States are regulated at both the federal and state levels. Federal and state regulations require franchisors to provide a disclosure statement to prospective franchisees containing specific information about their franchise offering. Some states – referred to as registration states - provide additional safeguards to potential franchisees by requiring a disclosure format known as the UFOC to enable the franchisor to provide the required information to a prospective franchisee. The UFOC can be ordered from FranchiseHelp, Inc. which operates a website (franchisehelp.com) or from Source Book Publications which also operates a website (ufocs.com).

29 OECD ¶6.23.
30 Bond's Franchise Guide 2007 (18th Edition), Source Book Publications, 2007, pg. 11.

KPMG Managing Director **Hareesh Dhawale** has conducted numerous transfer pricing studies for clients in industries and sectors as diverse as pharmaceuticals, telecommunications, internet services, computer software, express transportation services, oil & gas exploration and drilling, and automotive parts. He can be reached at **(213) 593-6769** or by email at **hdhawale@kpmg.com**.

George Carlson, a Director with Deloitte Tax, has prepared transfer pricing studies for clients in the apparel, automobile, computer software, distilled spirits, electronics, investment banking, medical products, pharmaceutical, sporting goods, and telecommunications industries. He can be reached at **(202) 378-5241** or by email at **gcarlson@deloitte.com**.

Niels Melius is a senior economic consultant in Deloitte Tax LLP's San Francisco transfer pricing group. He can be reached at **(415) 783-6741** or by email at **nmelius@deloitte.com**. For more information on the authors, please see Section XIII.

Final Thoughts

While the CUTM is the most direct and conceptually intuitive transfer pricing method, an application of the CUTM in practice is less straightforward, given the requirement to evaluate the similarity of the profit potential of the intangible in the controlled and uncontrolled transactions. With a sound understanding of when and how the CUTM can be applied, taxpayers can position themselves to withstand challenges to their transfer pricing policies relating to the transfer of intangibles based on a proper application of the CUTM.

Marketing Intangibles and Transfer Pricing: Economic Issues and Tax Enigmas

Dr. Michael E. Granfield
Ceteris

Introduction

For those familiar with tax transfer pricing issues over the past twenty-five years or so, marketing intangibles and their role in an enterprise's success have periodically taken center stage. Recently, the settlement of the *GlaxoSmithKline Holdings v. Commissioner of Internal Revenue* case (September 2006), apparently on terms favorable to the IRS, has rekindled a concern among MNCs and their advisors that a new wave of similar cases may soon be brought, not only in the U.S., but globally.[1] In response, both the International Fiscal Association and the American Bar Association recently addressed the marketing intangibles issues at their conferences in Kyoto Japan (IFA, Sep. 30th-Oct 5th; ABA and Vancouver, Canada Sept 28th) respectively.[2]

Issues Raised at the IFA Conference

At the IFA conference, one of the major points that was emphasized was that in many jurisdictions, it is only the deemed and/or legal owner of the intangibles that is entitled to compensation. Unfortunately, though, deemed ownership requirements differ by jurisdiction such as: (1) the party that holds legal title is the legal owner (2) the party that bears the costs and risks associated with the intangible is the owner, and (3) the party that exercises practical control is the effective owner.

In addition to the legal owner, the definition of what constitutes an intangible is murky at best. Robert Green, the former head of U.S. Competent Authority, put it most succinctly when he stated: "Nothing is written in stone when it comes to interpreting intangibles. I would observe that while the courts rejected IRS attempts to recast transactions, the courts frequently made transfer pricing adjustments that increased royalty payments of the sub to the parent. I would also add that the tax authority frequently takes inconsistent positions on the same facts depending on whether the taxpayer was inbound or outbound."

With respect to marketing intangibles, specifically, the practitioners at the IFA conference praised the OECD's attempt to differentiate between "marketing" intangibles such as trademarks, tradenames, customer lists and distribution channels from "trade" intangibles such as

---

[1] *Tax Management*, Transfer Pricing, Vol 15, No 4, p. 335

[2] An excellent summary of both conferences can be found in *Tax Management*, Transfer Pricing, Vol 16, No 11, p. 270-281

manufacturing know how and trade secrets. Nonetheless, despite this distinction, all agreed that the most difficult problem was to assign a specific value to these intangibles across multiple transactions and jurisdictions.

Creation of Marketing Intangibles by Affiliated Entities

In a similar vein, one of the IFA industry participants asked what factors should be considered when a new marketing intangible is developed by an affiliated entity. "Is it sufficient to create a new marketing intangible that the affiliate, which does not own the trademarks, incurs marketing and advertising expenses that go unreimbursed?" The response once again came from Robert Green, former head of U.S. Competent Authority when the *Glaxo* case fell out of Competent Authority (CA) negotiations with the UK. Green noted that Glaxo paid the IRS $3.4 Billion in tax and interest to settle a transfer pricing dispute, which settlement has shed light on whether local marketing intangibles can be created separately and distinctly from the legal ownership of patents, trademarks and tradenames: "Even though the patents and legal title to the ownership of the drugs resided in the parent company in the UK and despite the fact that all of the R&D expenses were deducted in the UK, the IRS argued that local marketing intangibles had been created and thus the IRS reduced the effective royalty to be paid to the UK."

More specifically, Green stated that the IRS argued that Glaxo Inc. had developed local marketing intangibles because:

1) The marketing campaign was designed specifically for the U.S. and was customized and tailored to meet its needs. This was because the U.S. was the only developed nation in which prescription drugs could be sold without restrictions on pricing, so Glaxo customized its promotion campaign for the U.S. market.
2) Marketing expenses were deducted in the U.S. to implement the campaign which the IRS defined as creating ownership of a marketing intangible.
3) The U.S. affiliate engaged in activities that transcended those of a mere distributor.

At the ABA conference, participants emphasized that it was critical to uncover the specific facts in each case separately. They emphasized that apparent excess returns did not always indicate that marketing intangibles were present. They also noted that the costs or expenditures employed do not necessarily point to an intangible value that was created – the expensive marketing campaign may have failed or a low budget one succeeded.

Another ABA participant posed the query that if her firm, Shell Oil, entered two new markets and one was growing rapidly (e.g. China or India) and the other was relatively stable (e.g. France), is the growth and higher profitability in the first due at all to local marketing intangibles, and could it be easily characterized as such by the local tax authorities?

Another queried: "If a local distribution affiliate significantly increases marketing expenses and market share also increases significantly but operating profits only rise by a modest amount, does this automatically imply a transfer pricing problem à la *Glaxo*?"

Obviously, the issue of marketing intangibles and their proper assessment is a complex one. However, in the transfer pricing context, there is an additional burden – the assessment, or value of the marketing intangibles must meet the a similar conclusion (i.e. similar range)? (6) Is this "mystery" assignment feasible – or is the answer simply too complex to generate because all of the requisite data is not available?

Your evidence and conclusions will be presented to a "Panel of Experts" employing the "Baseball Arbitration Model" i.e. the panel must choose either the result presented by the relevant Tax Authority (e.g. IRS, CRA, ATO etc.), the "taxpayer," or you. It cannot merge the three or pick a result between the three or some other compromise outcome.[4]

Dyneco and "Coming to America"

Dyneco started out as an "old line" Swiss pharmaceutical company. It began, as have several Swiss pharmaceutical firms, as a producer of dyes made from various plants and sold to apparel manufacturers in the late 19th Century. Employing similar technologies, Dyneco developed the first effective anti-gout medicine (colichene) from the bark of the eucalyptus tree employing techniques learned from Indian tribes in Borneo, the Amazon basin, and Geneva (1915). Their next major breakthrough was a specialized surgical antiseptic widely employed in World War I and World War II and elsewhere.

Being largely family-owned, Dyneco was content to develop niche products for sale in Europe through wholly-owned Affiliates in the UK, France, Italy, Germany and Spain with third party distributors in Scandinavia, Australia and New Zealand. All of this began to change, however, when Dyneco was purchased by a U.S. private equity fund in 1990 that specialized in investing in a variety of pharmaceutical firms. Using the fund's expertise, Dyneco research capabilities were greatly enhanced, including a new state of the art facility in Lausanne built for $800M in 1992, which was then staffed with leading researchers. These new researchers immediately began to attend academic conferences where breakthroughs in biochemistry research were highlighted.

This led the Dyneco scientists to believe that a whole new family of anti-inflammatory drugs could now be developed that avoided the complications of the previous generation of products (e.g. Vioxx, Celebrex). Accordingly, they set to work to develop a unique Dyneco product. Given the overall potential market of $5-6 Billion in global annual sales, even a modestly successful product could transform Dyneco into a major pharmaceutical entrant particularly in the largest two markets for such products, the U.S. and Japan, where Dyneco had no presence.

After only two years of research, Dyneco had its unique product, which was part of a large family of potential products, all based on similar biochemistry. The Dyneco product was dubbed "NOPAIN" which was determined as its global "handle." As fate would have it, though, both Merck (U.S. firm) and Roche (another Swiss firm) had also developed similar products and were already in clinical trials required for FDA approval in the U.S and elsewhere.

In 1995, both the Merck product, "RELIEF," and the Roche product "NUMB" were approved by the FDA for sale in the U.S. Global sales for both products

---

3   Although the case is intended to reflect realistic quantities and outcomes, it is purely fictional and not based on actual companies, cases or outcomes.

4   In transfer pricing cases, the Baseball Arbitration Model was first employed by the Tax Court in the Apple Computer Case. More recently, it was chosen as the arbitration model to be employed to resolve U.S. – Canada competent authority cases when there is a stalemate.

commenced in 1996. Because of their similarities (despite marketing messages to the contrary), the market shares for each product were approximately equal globally at $1B each with $500M for each coming from the U.S.

Nonetheless, despite this substantial lead into the market by Merck and Roche, Dyneco still believed its product could be a major success and prove to be the wedge they needed to enter the lucrative U.S. market. Thus, by 1998, they had approvals to sell in all of Europe. With respect to these European markets, Dyneco decided to continue their prior practices of licensing the production and sale of the active ingredient of NOPAIN to their prior third party firms in Scandinavia in return for a 7.5% patent royalty. Dyneco also allowed each Scandinavian firm to determine whether it wanted to use its name NOPAIN or a name of its choosing.

For its European Affiliates, Dyneco had a two part approach or strategy. First, Dyneco established a new primary manufacturing facility in Ireland to produce the active ingredient for NOPAIN. This Affiliate would be the exclusive seller to all of Dyneco's customers both controlled and uncontrolled. Second, all of the controlled European Affiliates would engage in secondary manufacturing (taking the active ingredient and putting it into proper dosages etc) and market NOPAIN under its tradename.

Because of their larger sales potential, Dyneco charged a 10% royalty to its European Affiliates and directed its Irish Affiliate to charge cost plus 100% for the active ingredient to all customers, both controlled and uncontrolled, which amounted to an effective price of 100 Euros per ounce (i.e. cost equals 50 Euros).

In Europe, despite its later entry, (1998 vs. 1996), NOPAIN achieved an equal market share (33%) by 2000 with the offerings from Roche and Merck. Dyneco attributed this success to three factors: (1) Dyneco only had to be taken once a day vs. twice a day for the competitors (2) there were no known direct or indirect side effects whereas the competitors did negatively impact some patients who were taking any of several cholesterol reducing medications, and (3) Dyneco engaged in direct advertising to consumers via satellite TV whereas the competitors disdained this approach.

Based on this European success, Dyneco confirmed that NOPAIN would be their initial major entrant to the U.S. market. Accordingly, in late 2000, they purchased a small boutique pharmaceutical firm in Princeton, New Jersey that had a state of the art secondary manufacturing facility but not much else in the way of useful assets. Dyneco changed the name to Dyneco US and began to hire both marketing analysts and "detail" professionals.

It soon became apparent to both Dyneco and Dyneco US professionals that, given the headstart of RELIEF and NUMB, an innovative approach to market penetration was needed to achieve its true market potential in the U.S., despite its European success. Accordingly, they decided to do the following:

1) Double the usual number of "detailers" assigned to a new drug entrant by engaging the experienced "detailers" from Bristol Myers Squibb ("BMS") who were very well regarded and were eager to promote this new product.
2) Have BMS also use the same tradename as Dyneco US so that prescribing physicians and hospitals were only looking at one product tradename.
3) Have an entry price 10% below the two major competitors even though the prior convention was no more than a 5% margin or, in some cases, a

higher price to signal higher quality.
4) Placing a large number of ads in both the academic medical journals and the more popular medical magazines touting the technical superiority of NOPAIN over its competitors
5) Initiating a directed TV campaign focusing on those programs (e.g. game shows) most often watched by the elderly.

The overall goal and extensive market forecasts had NOPAIN achieving total sales of $500M (wholesale) by 2005 or three years after initial introduction in 2002. This would be an excellent achievement as Dyneco forecast its major competitors at approximately $1B a piece for a total market of $2.5B. However, much to its astonishment, as well as its rivals, sales in 2005 amounted to $1.8B whereas sales for NUMB and RELIEF had actual fallen from $750M each in 2002 to $500M each in 2005. (see Table 1)

Dyneco's market share, which was 0% in 2001, 14% (250/1750) in 2002, was an astounding 65% (1800/2800) by the end of 2005. Total sales for the first five years which covered the initial co-development contract with BMS were estimated to be $2.4B with both Dyneco US and BMS accounting for $1.2B. In actuality, total sales were $6.4B with Dyneco and BMS both accounting for $3.2B.

The co-promotion contract with BMS which was to pay BMS one fourth of their entire annual costs of $100M (1000 FTE detailers at $100,000 per annum) or $125M over five years if the sales goal of $1.2B was met by BMS's detailers, provided for the continuation of this amount for each increase of $1.2B (or its fraction) above the threshold. Thus, at $3.2B which was $2.0B above the threshold, this was effectively a total multiple of 2.66 which generated commission income of $66.5M per year or $332.5M for BMS on their sales of $3.2B. This was approximately a 10.5% commission. In the fourth year of sales or 2005, Dyneco US and BMS agreed to renew their co-production agreement for five more years but as a straight 8% commission on all sales. This concession by Dyneco US (i.e. no tiered incentive) was reflective of the astounding success of NOPAIN, which Dyneco did not want to jeopardize, in part, because it did not understand exactly why its sales had increased so far above plan.

Having secured the continued participation of BMS, Dyneco then turned its attention to its profit possibilities in 2005 as well. With actual sales now forecast at $1.8B for the year and a new medium (vs. low & high) market analysis showing this to grow more slowly to $1.9B over the next two years and then decline (see Table 2 for the true actuals and their likely profit results), Dyneco US and Dyneco were well aware that this would have Dyneco US earning substantial profits in the U.S. even though its major functions were that of a distributor and secondary manufacturer. That is, Dyneco US had performed no R&D for NOPAIN nor did it engage in any primary manufacturing as did Dyneco EIRE. Consequently, based on a functions, asset and risks approach, some modifications were required to the active ingredient purchases and license from Dyneco.

More specifically, at the outset in 2001/2002, the professionals at Dyneco and Dyneco US had decided that, given the size of the U.S. market and its potential for NOPAIN, a royalty of 12.5% was warranted which was two thirds above the charge to the Scandinavian distributors and 25% above Dyneco's European Affiliates who paid 10%. The license agreement had no terminal date, but did provide for termination by either party. In terms of pricing the active ingredient, this was set at

Intangibles

Table 1: Projected and Actual Sales of NOPAIN (USD millions)

Year	Projected Sales	Actual Sales
2002	150	250
2003	300	650
2004	500	1500
2005	650	1800
2006	800	2200
2007	950	2250
2008	1000	2500
2009	1000	2500
2010	1000	2500
2011	1000	2500
	7,350	18,650

100% above cost from Dyneco EIRE but at a lower U.S. gross margin to undercut the competitors. The pricing agreement was set for five years so Dyneco and Dyneco US could monitor its progress and change the price if desired.

Further, as Dyneco and Dyneco US became increasingly aware that NOPAIN was selling well beyond what either they or BMS thought possible, they also determined that, absent some major changes to their contracts, Dyneco US would be much more profitable than any integrated Pharmaceutical firm and certainly much more profitable than the developer of NOPAIN, Dyneco, which they deemed as inappropriate.

The two most obvious changes, that could alter this outcome would be raising the price of the active ingredient and/or increasing the royalty. In terms of the latter, in 1986, there was a change to the U.S. tax laws (vs. regulations) via an amendment to the 1986 Tax Reform Act A "commensurate with income" standard was adopted when an intangible was transferred across borders that involved U.S. jurisdiction. Although intended to prevent or limit U.S.-based corporations from transferring valuable intangibles outside the U.S. without proper compensation, the law, in theory, would also apply to inbound transfers. Essentially, the law allowed the IRS to increase a royalty due a U.S. parent even if the agreement between the parent and affiliate had no such provision. All other relevant payment terms could also be adjusted to reduce the net return to the foreign licensee.

In terms of adjusting the royalty

Table 2: Actual vs. Projected Operating Profit (OP) for NOPAIN

	Projected Forecast			Actual (no change in Price of AI)		
Year	Sales	OP	%	Sales	OP	%
2002	150	15	10%	250	50	20%
2003	300	30	10%	650	300	45%
2004	500	50	10%	1500	825	55%
2005	650	100	15.5%	1800	1200	67%
2006	800	125	15.5%	2200	1620	74%
2007	950	190	20%	2250	1800	80%
2008	1000	200	20%	2500	2000	80%
2009	1000	200	20%	2500	2000	80%
2010	1000	200	20%	2500	2000	80%
2011	1000	200	20%	2500	2000	80%
	7350	1310	18%	18650	13795	75%

upwards, overall actual sales for 2002-11 were now projected to be 2.8 times their original level via the optimistic or "high" forecast. If the shorter period, 2007-11 were looked at alone, the results were also projected to be 2.8 times their original level. If the initial royalty was multiplied by 2.8, this would result in a royalty of 35.0%. After serious deliberation, Dyneco and Dyneco US decided that this was appropriate, under these unique circumstances, and increased the royalty from 12.5% to 35.0% effective in 2007 citing the "commensurate with income" standard in their internal communications.

In terms of net operating profits for Dyneco US, when total revenues were projected for 2007-2011 based on this optimistic forecast, the total was $12.25 Billion. The 35% royalty would amount to $4287.5B generating post royalty income of $7962.5B (see Table 3). Subtracting the 8% commission owed to BMS on its sales of $6125B amounted to $490M leaving $7472.5B or 61% of sales.

Direct operating expenses for Dyneco US were detailing at $80M, advertising of $470M, secondary manufacturing of $580M, and admin of $720M for a total of $1850M or 15% of sales.

All that is left is to deduct the costs of the active ingredient which effectively become a "plug" figure for Dyneco US. That is, this flexible deduction would allow Dyneco US to meet the profit goals set by Dyneco US and Dyneco executives. By setting a price to the U.S. at the same level as that now charged to both the uncontrolled East European distributors and the new uncontrolled Japanese distributor (i.e. cost plus 200%), the cost of goods sold for the "active ingredient" would amount to $2.00B for the five year period or roughly 16% of sales.

The remaining profit for Dyneco over this five year period would be $3622.5B which was 29.5% of sales. Both the Dyneco US and Dyneco executives believed that this was a very reasonable result.

For the ten year period, the total profits for Dyneco US would be $7617.5B ($3622.5B + $3995.0B) or 40.8% of sales. This was clearly quite high for a distributor/secondary manufacturer but no one could figure out how to alter this result, after the fact.

Having dealt with NOPAIN's issues and based on the enormous success of this product, Dyneco and Dyneco US executives, as well as other pharmaceutical industry experts, believed that they had discovered a new marketing "paradigm" for pharmaceutical products. Namely, with substantial increases in detailers and overall advertising expenditures, a new entrant could overcome incumbents even if labeled a "me too" product or, alternatively, could establish such a leading share as an initial entrant that its dominance could not be overtaken. Accordingly, when Dyneco developed what it thought would be its next "blockbuster" drug for the U.S., based once again on its initial European success, a similar aggressive strategy was followed which was still not being emulated by certain key competitors who were still waiting to see if there actually was a new marketing "paradigm."

The product that Dyneco chose was "XXX", a drug that dealt simultaneously with lowering bad cholesterol and raising good cholesterol. There was only one other such product in the U.S. market as of 2007 which was "CCC" sold by Eli Lilly. For its 2007 U.S. launch, Dyneco U.S. and Dyneco chose Pfizer as their co-promoter which was offered similar terms to what BMS had initially been offered, so it would be properly incentivized.

However, rather than reaching its forecast goal of $500M, $1B and $1.5B of sales in its first three years, "XXX" only

Table 3: Cost and Profit Projections 2007-2011 (USD Millions)

		Residual Profit in U.S. After Deductions
Sales	12250	
35% Royalty	4287.5	
	7962.5	65%
8% Commission to BMS	490.0	
	7472.5	61%
OE Detail	80.0	
Advertising	470.0	
Secondary MFG	580.0	
Admin	720.0	
15% OE Sub-Total	1850.0	46%
16% COGS	2000	29.5%
Dyneco OP		(29.5%)

averaged $300M in sales for its first three years. Rather than earning substantial profits in the U.S., it actually had losses of 10-15% of sales each year. In its fourth year, Dyneco pulled the product from the market awaiting a more significant cholesterol oriented innovation to be generated by its labs.

Undaunted, though, by the failure of "XXX" to repeat the success of NOPAIN, Dyneco US and Dyneco chose to market to women a very exciting new product that dealt more successfully with correcting hormonal imbalance than any of its competitors, "ZZZ". Unfortunately, though, it had a major negative, which was the potential to neutralize certain anti-rheumatoid medications which often were taken in conjunction with "ZZZ" type medications. Nonetheless, choosing Eli Lilly as the co-development partner, led to sales 5-10% above forecast levels and net operating profits of 15-20%.

At this juncture, having had one major success, one failure and one acceptable outcome, Dyneco US and Dyneco decided to proceed along more conventional lines in terms of marketing outlays while they internally tried to determine what worked and what didn't in more detail.

Meanwhile, field agents at the IRS, starting in 2009, began to seriously question the rationale for the change in the royalty and the price of the active ingredient. By 2012, the IRS filed a formal "deficiency of income" assessment with Dyneco US. Dyneco US responded in 2013 with its defense. Both TP analyses were allegedly based on the arm's length standard which will be briefly examined in the next section.

The Arm's Length Standard

As just noted, the results for Dyneco US were assessed by both the IRS and Taxpayer employing the initial agreed upon regulatory standard – the arm's length standard. Briefly, this generically means one must simulate what would have occurred under very similar circumstances if Dyneco and Dyneco U.S. were truly independent from each other. Valuation experts often reference the same standard:

Intangibles

"the price that would be paid by a willing buyer and a willing seller."

In terms of IRS Section 482, the ideal result for Dyneco US would be if Dyneco had licensed NOPAIN to a third party in a market very similar to the U.S. (or the U.S.) under virtually identical terms as that with Dyneco US. Similarly, if Dyneco EIRE had sold the active ingredient for prices virtually identical to that charged to Dyneco US in the U.S. (e.g. to Johnson & Johnson which would market it under its own tradename) or in a market very similar to the U.S.

Since this did not occur, the IRS, the taxpayer and you (the reader), must now develop TP analyses consistent with Section 482 to present to the Expert Panel which the Tax Court has chosen as its dispute resolution mechanism instead of a formal trial.

The findings of each entity as presented to the Panel in 2014 will now be reviewed.

IRS Analysis

The IRS determines that the issues first raised by its field agents and field economists were the correct ones, so it will present these to the Panel starting with the determination of the arm's length royalty.

Royalty Determination

Based on the "Best Method" requirement in the 1993/94 482 Reg's, the IRS asserts that it will employ the "CUT" Method to determine the appropriate royalty. The CUT it chooses is technically an "inexact" CUT which was allowed for in these final regs (but not in the initial proposed version in 1992). The "inexact" CUT chosen by the IRS is the royalty charged to the four uncontrolled Scandinavian firms in Norway, Sweden, Denmark and Finland, respectively.

The royalty charged was 7.5% of sales with the licensee being authorized to engage in primary manufacturing, secondary manufacturing and distribution. To buttress this 7.5% result, the IRS also presented 30 license agreements obtained from SEC filings which they argued involved products broadly similar to NOPAIN and where the licensor was a major international pharmaceutical firm or University and the licensee was a third party in North America, Western Europe, Japan or Australia. The royalties in these agreements ranged from 3% to 12% with an interquartile range of 5% to 8%. The IRS also noted that in the aggregate the Scandinavian countries were sufficiently similar to the population that consumes NOPAIN in the U.S., so that these licenses are reliable CUT's.[5] Furthermore, there was no evidence pointing towards either an increase or decrease in the royalty based on absolute market size so the IRS concluded again that no adjustment to the 7.5% was warranted.

The IRS went on to assert that because it had chosen the CUT method for determining the proper arm's length royalty, as opposed to some other TP method, particularly a profits based method, the "commensurate with income" standard was not relevant, such that the increase in royalty executed by Dyneco and Dyneco US was disallowed.

As for the price of the active ingredient purchased from Dyneco EIRE, the IRS asserted that the Comparable Profits Method ("CPM") was the Best Method and cost plus was the preferred Profit Level Indicator ("PLI"). Based on a set of twenty contract manufacturers of similar chemical compounds in Singapore, Korea, Taiwan, South Africa, U.S. and Canada, the IRS concluded that the appropriate cost mark-up range was cost plus 45% to 50%. The IRS also cited an internal Dyneco US study that indicated it could manufacture the active ingredient in the U.S. at a profit at cost plus 35%, so cost plus 50% was a generous concession to the taxpayer.

Administrative Costs

With respect to administrative costs, the IRS once again chose a CPM approach vs. the Best Method and employed a modified resale margin analysis to fifteen pharmaceutical/vitamin distributors in the U.S., Canada and Mexico which yielded (SG&A) costs of 15% of sales.

The IRS accepted that both the initial 10.5% and subsequent 8% Commissions paid to BMS was arm's length so no further adjustment was required.

Finally, since from the IRS's perspective the sales of "XXX" and "ZZZ" were relatively modest and together they earned a positive profit, the IRS determined that the only income adjustments they would be making to Dyneco US's results would relate to NOPAIN.

In Table 4, the total transfer pricing or income adjustment is displayed. Beginning with the 2007-2011 period after the royalty had been raised to 35.0% and the active ingredient price doubled, the royalty is set at 7.5% by the IRS and subtracted ($920M) from sales of $12250M. Next, the 8% commission to BMS which is deemed arm's length is subtracted as well at $490M. Then the 15% Sales, General, and Administrative Expenses ("SGA") amount is taken out leaving a Gross Profit of $8990M. Finally, the Cost of Goods Sold ("COGS") for the active ingredient is reduced to cost plus 50% based on the IRS CPM analysis. IRS operating profit for Dyneco is now $8255.0M vs. the reported amount of $3622.5M generating a TP or income adjustment of $4632.5M.

For the 2002-06 period, there is only an adjustment to the initial royalty to 7.5% from 12.5% which is the IRS's arm's length estimate. The reduction in the royalty raises income by $320. There is no adjustment to SGA. As for COGS the free samples given to BMS which were not accounted for are, equal to the price adjustment so no further reduction is required.

Overall, the IRS raises Dyneco US's operating profit to $12,570M or 67.5% of sales of $18,650 from Dyneco's reported operating profit of $7617.5M which was 41% of sales.

The total TP adjustment of $4952.5M or 26.5% of sales, the IRS attributes to the return on marketing intangibles created for and paid by Dyneco US with no reimbursement from the Parent Dyneco. That is, the IRS attributes the increment to marketing intangibles despite the paucity of direct evidence because from its perspective there is no other potential "suspect" that could account for these extraordinary returns. In other words, a "me too" drug such as NOPAIN could only succeed as it did because of the marketing resources allocated to it which in turn, created the intangible.

The Taxpayer's Analysis

For the taxpayer, Dyneco US, the IRS proposed adjustment was a great shock because from their perspective they had reported extraordinary profits of 40.8% of sales or $7617.5M on sales of $18,650M. This was certainly well above what any distributor/secondary manufacturer that Dyneco US or Dyneco were familiar with would earn.

In fact, data from Robert Morris & Associates for SIC code 5122, which was

---

5 The IRS also developed a regression model based on the thirty agreements plus the four Scandinavian licenses but decided not to present it to the Panel.

as close one could get for private firms, revealed that for mostly privately held distributors of all pharmaceutical products, including patent medicines, the highest returns were in the 8-12% range.[6] For the fifteen publicly held distributor firms that were much larger with some of them engaging in secondary manufacturing, the interquartile range was 5.0% to 18.8% with the highest three at 21.5, 23.0% and 25.5% respectively. Thus, Dyneco US was more than twice as profitable as the upper quartile and 80% above the highest firm.

Further, because of the reporting requirements under its royalty agreements, Dyneco was able to get the complete Profit and Loss statements for its Scandinavian licensees as well as their profit-by-product analyses. The latter revealed that their operating profits for NOPAIN including licensed primary manufacturing, secondary manufacturing and distribution ranged from 16.5% (Finland) to 26.0% (Sweden). In other words, for the IRS's chosen arm's length CUT benchmarks, profits were well below Dyneco US's.

For Dyneco, this was further — and quite compelling — evidence that the profits earned during 2007-2011 were more than arm's length justifying the increase in royalty to 35% and the cost plus of the active ingredient to, cost plus 200% from cost plus 50%.

Based on all of this consistent evidence, Dyneco US chose as the "Best Method", the Comparable Profits Method (CPM) and operating profit/sales as the PLI.

They further supported the change in the active ingredient price by employing the comparable uncontrolled price (CUP) method. Dyneco cited the identical price charged to uncontrolled East European distributors as well as the uncontrolled Japanese distributor, all of whom paid cost plus 200% set by Dyneco EIRE for the period.

With respect to the increase in the royalty from 12.5% to 35.0%, Dyneco US emphasized that under the "commensurate with income" standard, Dyneco was permitted to raise the royalty to limit Dyneco's US income to an arm's length level as stipulated by its CPM methodology.

Dyneco rejected the IRS argument that the IRS's use of an inexact CUT method trumped the commensurate with income ("CWI") standard.

Dyneco US also stressed that the entire ten year period should be evaluated under a CPM approach as well and that its overall profit of 40.8% was more than twice what was required.

To allocate two-thirds of Dyneco US's sales as taxable income as the IRS had done which was based on dubious adjustments was totally inconsistent with Dyneco US's underlying functions, assets and risks.

Finally, Dyneco US pointed to an extensive marketing study it conducted to better understand the success of NOPAIN. The study went back to the prescribing physicians to determine why they had chosen NOPAIN over its competitors. For those who could specifically recall, the reasons were:

1) No side effects
2) Patients reported they preferred it
3) Quality of the detailer's presentation
4) Clinical research indicating it was somewhat more effective in relieving pain

---

6 Robert Morriss and associates is a data collection firm in Philadelphia. The data they collect is from banks who supply data to RMA based on loan applications and the data supplied by lenders. At one time, it was an aft used data source for the IRS but since the 1993 482 Regulations were adopted, it is rarely employed. The disfavor is because specific firms cannot be identified.

Intangibles

Table 4: IRS Calculation of Dyneco US Profits For NOPAIN 2002-2011 (USD Millions)

<u>IRS Adjustment for 2007-2011</u>

Sales	12250
7.5% Royalty	(920)
8.0% to BMS	(490)
15% SGA	(1850)
Gross Profit	8990
(AI) COGS	(735)
Operating Profit	$8255.0 - $3622.5
	Dyneco US income reported = $4632.5 TP adj

<u>IRS Adjustment for 2002-2006</u>

Sales	6400
7.5% Royalty	480
10.5% to BMS	330
15% SGA	(960)
Gross Profit	4630
COGS	385
Operating Profit	$4245 - $3995
	Dyneco US income reported = $250.0 TP adj
Total	$12,500 - $7617.5 Dyneco income reported = $4882.5 TP adj (2002-2011)

Overall, these physicians accounted for approximately 50% of the sales of NOPAIN. Thus, Dyneco US concluded that marketing intangibles, if they existed at all, played a very small role in "NOPAIN's" success. It was mostly due to its inherent properties. They also concluded that there was a great deal that was still unknown regarding "NOPAIN's" ultimate market impact and success.

Your Independent Analysis

You begin your analysis for the Expert Panel with the following observations and assessments:

(1) If marketing intangibles and their existence or non existence with respect to NOPAIN is a primary differentiator between the IRS and the Taxpayer, why did neither party more directly address the properties and nature of the relevant "marketing intangibles." For example, if

Intangibles

it takes time and continued investment to create an intangible, particularly a marketing intangible, how could Dyneco US possess such an intangible if NOPAIN was effectively the first product sold by Dyneco US?

(2) With regard to economic and related implications:

(i) What would be the direct economic empirical evidence if marketing intangibles were present vs. their absence? Would profits for all marketed products be higher than otherwise would be the case?

(ii) Shouldn't the variance in profitability within a product class and across classes be lower than it otherwise would be, if present?

(iii) Can a marketing intangible exist separate from specific pharmaceutical products i.e. is there a "branding" effect whereby all pharmaceutical products offered by the manufacturer (e.g. Pfizer) are seen as superior to other manufacturers products such as Lexus vs. Cadillac?

(iv) If Dyneco US had created substantial marketing intangibles with NOPAIN, why didn't "XXX" and "ZZZ" fare better? Presumably, they should have performed even better as the marketing intangibles for Dyneco US were constantly improved.

(v) If "detailers" are the most important source of marketing intangibles as some have long asserted, why do many of the more recent academic studies show that detailing: (1) only influences a small fraction of prescription choices (2) although statistically significant in physician drug choice, its overall effect, quantitatively, is modest to very small.[7]

(vi) Was the IRS taken in by the "me too" critics of the pharmaceutical industry such that the success of NOPAIN being chemically and clinically very similar to RELIEF and NUMB, could only be explained by Dyneco US's aggressive marketing campaign and not its unique properties?

(vii) If Dyneco US had substantial marketing intangibles and the accompanying marketing expertise, why were its forecasts for all three of its products so wrong, particularly for NOPAIN, where presumably the most significant intangibles resided?

(viii) In terms of rate of return, the biggest winner by far would appear to be Bristol Myers Squibb whose cost outlay was $250M for the ten years (and economically arguably smaller because the opportunity cost was so low) but who received $826M in commissions which is a return of 330%, even though BMS had fewer risks than Dyneco or Dyneco US?

(ix) Why isn't the return earned by BMS on its marketing intangibles a CUP or CUT for Dyneco US's identical investment in detailing? (or is it?)

Based on the, more or less, transparent answers to these questions, you inform the Expert Panel that you have rejected

---

[7] See "Are Physicians 'Easy Marks'? Quantifying the Effects of Detailing and Sampling on New Prescriptions", N. Mizils and R. Jacobson, ISBM Report 9-2003, Penn State Univ, Oct 2003. "Persistence in Prescriptions of Branded Drugs", O. Richard, I Suponic and L. Van Horn, University of Rochester, Simon School of Business, May 2003. "Heterogeneous Learning and the Targeting of Marketing Communication for New Products", S. Narayanan, Ph.d, Thesis, University of Chicago, Graduate School of Business, Aug, 2004.

the IRS assertion or claim that marketing intangibles played a significant role in the commercial success of NOPAIN so your TP resolution and recommendations will not include any reference to marketing intangibles.

Thus, rather than marketing intangibles being the most significant aspect of this case, from your perspective, it is the fact that NOPAIN's sales and profitability were two to three times what were initially projected by Dyneco, Dyneco US and BMS. This is particularly critical in an arm's length context. Namely, what would have been negotiated by Dyneco and an independent third party in licensing NOPAIN for sale in the U.S.? Whether the pharmaceutical corporation was a major one such as Johnson & Johnson, Pfizer or Eli Lilly or was more of a niche firm, the royalty that they would have been willing to pay, given the presence of two other competing products which were already quite successful, would certainly have been no higher than 7.5% and perhaps as low as 5.0%, the lower quartile of the IRS sample of 30 agreements.

The licensing agreement would also have had to be at least as long as patent expiration if the licensee was to take the risk of developing the product in the U.S., or ten years.

Accordingly, you recommend to the Expert Panel that you believe the arm's length royalty should be in the 5.0% to 7.5% range and the license agreement should have a ten year duration. Pressed further by the Panel, you choose the 7.5% royalty and note that the licensee would have captured most of the profits because of the "surprise" success of NOPAIN. That is, for whatever reasons, including luck, NOPAIN succeeded as it did, therefore the upside result in this case would accrue to the licensee who was taking most of the risks, including the extremes up or down that might occur.

In terms of the price for the active ingredient, normal commercial and economic behavior would posit that the licensee, unless required by the licensor, would not pay cost plus 100% or 200% for the active ingredient if it could produce it for significantly less as demonstrated by the IRS evidence from Dyneco US i.e. cost plus 35%.

However, the arm's length standard is not always consistent with likely commercial reality. More specifically, in this instance, the uncontrolled prices charged by Dyneco EIRE would form the most concrete basis for a defensive transfer price as a CUP i.e. cost plus 200% for the 2007-2012 period.

In other words, even though you firmly reject the IRS's marketing intangibles rationale for a TP adjustment to the royalty in favor of a strict arm's length negotiating outcome of 7.5%, you would still employ their CUT analysis and result to defend this choice under section 482.

Similarly, for the price of the active ingredient, you would again employ the CUP standard even though, from a strictly economic profit maximizing perspective, you have no doubt that the IRS recommendation based on both the internal Dyneco US study and the consistent IRS CPM analysis is the correct outcome, *i.e.* the price is cost plus 100% and then cost plus 200%.

In any other tax jurisdiction, other than the U.S., this would be the end of your analysis and recommendations. However, this is the U.S. and there is the 1986 Tax Reform Act amendment mandating the use of the "CWI" standard when dealing with the transfer of valuable intangibles. The IRS asserted that this legal standard was not relevant in this case because the intent of Congress was to rectify the cases with outbound transfers which were the basis

Intangibles

for the IRS testimony before the House Ways & Means Committee in 1985.

Thus, in order to be as thorough as is reasonable, you review this IRS testimony and congressional intent as revealed by their discussion of the topic. There is no doubt in your mind, after reviewing this material, that the IRS is essentially correct since there is very little mention of, or discussion of, the inbound transfer of intangibles.

However, both in its overall legal structure and implicit in its various tax Treaties, it is fairly obvious that it would be illegal for the U.S. to blatantly discriminate against the inbound licensing of intangibles from a foreign corporation to a U.S. subsidiary corporation (i.e. the subsidiary or affiliate of a foreign corporation) even if it were 100% owned by the foreign Parent.

Therefore, you conclude that the Taxpayer was correct in applying the "CWI" standard and raising the royalty. Because the "CWI" standard not only allows for, but actually requires a results oriented approach, you indicate that the appropriate royalty for the last five years was that set by the taxpayer at 35%.

As for the royalty of 12.5% for the first five years, under the "CWI" standard covering the entire ten year period, this too becomes acceptable. That is, if this is reduced to 7.5% via the IRS's CUT analysis, it would only compel a higher royalty above 35% for the last five years. Since the "CWI" standard covers the entire ten year period, it makes the most sense to preserve what the taxpayer charged in both five year periods.

With regard to the price of the active ingredient, one can accept either the taxpayer argument that it is a CUP for the latter periods or accept that it must be higher than recommended by the IRS due to the "CWI" standard.

Reaction of the Expert Panel

After filing your testimony, the Expert Panel points out the following as best they can understand it:

1) You have firmly rejected the IRS's contention that marketing intangibles played any role in the success of NOPAIN.
2) You agree that certain characteristics of NOPAIN did contribute to its success, particularly the lack of any side effects but at least 50% or more of its sales are probably due to "luck" or other unknowable factors.
3) The IRS correctly employed the CUT method as the "Best Method" for the royalty assessment which yielded an arm's length royalty of 7.5% for the ten-year period.
4) As a U.S. taxpayer, Dyneco US was correct in its citing of the 1986 Tax Reform Act Amendment mandating the application of the "commensurate with income" standard when valuable intangibles are transferred out of the U.S. or into the U.S.
5) When applying the "CWI" standard to Dyneco US, you support the taxpayer or licensee paying the 12.5% royalty for the first five years and 35.0% for the last five years. Furthermore, you agree that the income earned, by the licensee after applying the "CWI" standard can be properly assessed as arm's length under the taxpayer's CPM "Best Method" choice. This was an operating profit of 40.8% for the ten-year period.
6) With respect to the price of the active ingredient, you believe the IRS was correct from a financial economics perspective and the taxpayer would not have paid, in the real world, a transfer price well in excess of what

Intangibles

it would cost to actually manufacture the active ingredient on its own. This cost of manufacturing was estimated to be cost plus 35% to 50% by Dyneco US which was also confirmed by the IRS's CPM method.

7) You support the taxpayer's assertion that there were defensible CUPs for the active ingredient for both time periods of cost plus 100% for the first five years and cost plus 200% for the next five years. You also agree that these CUPs effectively trump the IRS "make or buy" analysis in point (6).

8) By combining the IRS's recommended royalty level and transfer prices for the active ingredient, Dyneco US would earn profits equal to 67.5% of total sales. Because over 63.0% of Dyneco US's sales were a "surprise" to all the experts involved, you believe that the licensee in the real world, acting at arm's length, would have had a similar result. Thus, from a results perspective, you support the IRS's TP/income adjustments, although you firmly reject their causal rationale of marketing intangibles.

9) The taxpayer is correct in asserting that the "CWI" standard equally applies to inbound transfers of intangibles. Therefore, the taxpayer was correct in raising both the royalty and the price of the active ingredient in order to approach their final results, albeit still above the threshold of its own CPM analysis with a return on sales of 40.8% vs. an upper quartile of 20.8%.

In response, you agree with the Expert Panel that these are your conclusions. When the Panel points out that these conclusions appear to be mutually exclusive, you quickly concur but note that these are your opinions based, not on the fact that you are an economist (i.e. on the one hand this, and on the other hand that…), but rather on the nature of U.S. tax transfer pricing regulations and the interpretation and legal application of the arm's length standard.

A major flaw in this arm's length standard and the ensuring regulations is that it does not allow for significant positive surprises and significant negative mistakes particularly on the part of major MNCs. Au Contraire, MNCs are effectively characterized as always in control of their financial fate, be it short or long-term. Thus, actual significant deviations from corporate plans and intentions that often actually occur in the market are not dealt with very effectively under the current regulatory regime. In fact, they are often characterized as part of a complex, strategic plot to keep the tax authorities from discovering what really occurred.

Two suggestions to generate a more tractable outcome in this particular case would be for: (1) employing a contingent arm's length royalty i.e. a royalty that would rise or fall based on sales and/or

---

Dr. Michael E. Granfield, a Managing Director with Ceteris in the areas of Transfer Pricing and Anti-Trust, has more than thirty years experience serving large clients involved in retailing, global sourcing, pharmaceuticals, autos, and high technology. He can be reached at **(214) 946-2298** or by email at **michael.granfield@ceterisgroup.com**.

For more information, please see Section XIII.

Intangibles

profitability[8] and (2) having the issues and ultimate channel profits allocated within the Competent Authority/Treaty framework, although that process is currently not as well equipped to deal with a case of this complexity as it will need to be.

[8] Contingent royalties are not common but do exist when the outcome is dependent on factors outside of the control of the licensor and licensee and is a major determinant of the ultimate profitability and output. For example, a licensor of technology to remove crude oil from torsands has a clause that raises the royalty based on the world price of oil.

Marketing Intangibles Require Close Legal and Tax Scrutiny

Marc M. Levey (*Baker & McKenzie, LLP*), Pamela T. Church (*Baker & McKenzie, LLP*), Monique van Herksen (*Ernst & Young/Holland Van Gijzen*), Alexander Odle (*A.R.T. Intellectual Property BV*), and Philip Carmichael (*Baker & McKenzie Consulting*)

Background

The concept of "marketing intangibles" continues to be a vigorously debated issue within the global transfer pricing community and among various tax authorities. Initially, the concept appeared in the United States in the Internal Revenue Service's ("IRS") transfer pricing regulations and administration announcements, some Tax Court cases, Advance Pricing Agreement proceedings, and has been prevalent in most, if not virtually all, applicable transfer pricing audits. Tax authorities in Germany, France, The Netherlands, Japan, China and Australia, among others, regularly raise the issue - especially for controlled distributors in their own countries. Many of these countries (discussed below) have also issued announcements in various forms on the subject.

While the precise meaning of a "marketing intangible" remains unclear from a tax and legal perspective and may vary in application by company, industry and country, the breadth of its grasp continues to grow as the concept has been variously applied and practitioners consider its legal and tax implications. Generally, the term marketing intangibles can be meant to include tradenames, trademarks and trade dress, logos, the local market position of a company and/or its products, know-how that surrounds a trademark such as the knowledge of distribution channels and customer relationship, and trade secrets. The IRS believes the investment in these intangibles is derived from, among other things, the company's levels of advertising, marketing and promotion ("AMP") expenditures, particularly those that transcend pure routine costs.

The concept initially gained prominence in the late 1980's in a docketed Tax Court case involving the sale of vacation destinations by a U.S. distributor on behalf of a related foreign travel and vacation entity. The transfer price for the destination package was not directly at issue, but the level of AMP incurred by the U.S. distribution entity for these sales was scrutinized. The IRS sought either to (1) disallow a portion of the AMP under the notion that it was incurred on behalf of the foreign trademark owner, or (2) deem a service fee for the marketing efforts performed by the U.S. distributor on behalf of the foreign trademark owner. While the case was settled by the parties prior to litigation, this case foreshadowed issues related to intangibles we see today.

Subsequently in 1994, the IRS issued final transfer pricing regulations under IRC Section 482 wherein it addressed the juxtaposition between the foreign owner of a trademark and the economic costs incurred by its U.S. affiliate to promote and exploit that item of intangible property in its territory.[1] In examples then referred to as the "Cheese Examples," a number of scenarios between the foreign parent trademark owner, Fromages Frères, and its affiliated U.S. distributor were cited: (1) the U.S. distributor was simply given a set transfer price and the development of the U.S. market was at the risk and economic cost of the U.S. distributor; (2) the foreign parent indirectly subsidized the development of the U.S. market through a reduced transfer price; and (3) the foreign parent provided the distributor with a rebate of a portion of the distributor's AMP based on sales volumes. Following the IRS position in the above Tax Court case, the Cheese Examples could require a return for the distributor's investment in the marketing intangibles either in the form of a service fee arrangement with an appropriate profit markup or more robust operating margins to reflect the return for the developed marketing intangible.[2]

The *DHL Incorporated and Subsidiaries v. Commissioner of Internal Revenue* Tax Court case[3] decided in 2002 became the next significant step in the evolution of the marketing intangible concept. This case addressed the IRS' attempt to impute a trademark royalty for the use of the DHL trade name by DHL's foreign affiliates. At issue was the taxpayer's assertion that a royalty should not be imputed from these foreign affiliates because they bore the economic investment for the development of the DHL trademark.

While marketing intangibles surrounding the DHL trade name were not directly discussed, the *DHL* case stood for the proposition that for items of intangible property, the party who bore the economic burden of the investment should reap the economic rewards. The aggregate levels of AMP, as well as certain other expenses that were incurred by the DHL foreign affiliates, were considered for purposes of this economic investment, although there was neither a real analysis of the expenditures that made up the AMP nor what component of the underlying costs were directed to trademark development or surrounding intangibles. While the Tax Court found in favor of the IRS and assessed penalties against the taxpayer, in 2002 the Appellate Court reversed the Decision, holding that under then applicable section 482 regulations, the DHL foreign affiliates made the economic investment for the development of the DHL trademark and were considered the owners of those intangibles for tax purposes. Thus, the foreign affiliates were entitled to the economic return associated with the marketing intangibles. In effect, the Tax Court followed the money in order to match income with expense.

It was the dictum in the underlying Tax Court case, however, that bore real importance for purposes of the marketing intangible concept. Here, the Trial Judge espoused his "bright-line" test which notes that, while every licensee or distributor is expected to incur a certain amount of cost to exploit the items of intangible property to which it is provided, it is when the investment crosses the "bright line" of routine expenditures into the realm of non-routine that, economic ownership, likely in the form of a marketing intangible, is created. Unfortunately, the Trial Judge did not expand on this test to provide practical guidelines to this theory because he essentially held that the taxpayer failed to meet its burden of proof. Stated otherwise, he was concerned that DHL

---

1 Reg. 1.482-4 (f) (3) (iv), Exs. 2, 3, 4. (1994).

2 We observe that the present proposed regulations which update the "Change Examples" maintain the viability of the issue yet arguably bring the issue closer to the OECD Guidelines standard.

3 DHL Corporation, TCM 1998-461, aff'd in part, rev'd in part 285 F.3d 1285, 89 AFTR2d 2002-1978 (CA-9, 2002).

did not expressly identify those costs that were actually incurred in the development of the DHL trade name and whether those costs were truly earmarked for such development.

The marketing intangible issue was most recently considered in the *GlaxoSmithKline Holdings v. Commissioner of Internal Revenue* case in the U.S. Tax Court[4] where the IRS asserted a tax deficiency in amounts approximating almost $20 billion for all open tax years that were impacted by the Court. The underpinning to the IRS claim was that Glaxo's U.S. affiliate was the economic owner of the U.S. marketing intangible through its investment in a marketing strategy conceived and directed by Glaxo U.S. executives. This investment arguably resulted in a fully integrated business and led to the success of its products in the U.S. market. It appeared that the IRS simply reviewed expenditures that were referenced on Glaxo U.S.'s profit and loss statement, namely its detailing and marketing expense, which the IRS believed created the market for the Glaxo product. Critical facts, however, that must have been considered in the parties' resolution of the case included that all items of intellectual property were owned by Glaxo UK and that the marketing platform and strategy were developed by Glaxo UK. As a distributor, Glaxo U.S. earned an approximate 16 percent operating profit margin. The IRS was apparently not satisfied with this profit return, however, especially when compared to the robust return earned by Glaxo UK. Accordingly, the IRS asserted that the U.S. affiliate was entitled to operating income commensurate with its expenditures.

While the *Glaxo* case was settled for approximately $3.4 Billion (a mere 7% at the initial adjustment), it serves as a precursor for the IRS to continue challenging this issue on audit, arguably seeking a better set of facts that would give the potential for meaningful jurisprudence on the issue.[5] Indeed, there are currently other cases in the U.S. Tax Court[6] and IRS audit pipeline that may produce jurisprudence on this issue. Further, the global attention given the *Glaxo* case has alerted many other tax authorities to this evolving issue and as they look for additional ways to raise revenue, a potentially attractive vehicle.[7]

The theories described above continue to be raised in most global tax audits and Advance Pricing Agreement proceedings, and are presently under consideration by the U.S. Tax Court in current pending cases. Numerous unanswered questions remain, however, such as how to define a company's marketing intangibles from a tax and legal perspective, what expenses are truly brand building, how to determine in tax parlance where the level of AMP transcends from routine to non-routine expenditures, what

---

4 GlaxoSmithKline Holdings (Americas) Inc., v. Commissioner, T.C. No. 5750-04. GlaxoSmithKline Holdings (Americas) Inc., v. Comm'r., T.C. No. 6959-05. Note: The Glaxo Docket No. 5750-04 covers years 1989-1996 while the Glaxo Docket No. 6959-05 covers years 1997-2000.

5 Because this case settled for all years at less than 20 percent of the amounts due for all years, one can speculate that the IRS factual position was well compromised. Generally, the government, as a practice, concedes cases where the litigating hazards are 20 percent or less. Notwithstanding, $3.4 billion is a significant amount of money and has drawn much attention.

6 See Mary Kay Holding Corporation and Subsidiaries v. Commissioner, Docket Nos 14352-03 and 18150-02 (March 24, 2006 Stipulation of Settlement) where the IRS questioned market support payments to Petitioner's CFCs that were incurred to build the "Mary Kay" Brand.

7 See e.g., "IRS Answer Charges U.S. Glaxo Subsidiary Developed Marketing Intangibles Under § 482" 13, No. 2 BNA Transfer Pricing Report, p 97, June 9, 2004, "IRS Argues Activities of Glaxo Subsidiary Imported Drugs Sold in U.S." 14 No 4 BNA Transfer Pricing Report, p 157, June 22, 2005.

expenses qualify for these considerations, (e.g. registration costs, legal costs for routine expenses and real broad brand building expenses as such non-routine expenses), whether an analysis of each underlying accounting code requires the segregation of routine from non-routine expenditures, what allocation keys may be employed and what is the "shelf life" of the created marketing intangible, as well as any preexisting marketing intangibles that are included within the considered intangible. One further practical problem, and a significant one, is that not every taxpayer accounts for its AMP within the same accounting classifications.

While there may be merit in the *DHL* "bright line" test from a practical point of view, the definition of non-routine expenditures is so industry and company specific, that it may be impossible to apply in most cases. Similar companies within the same industry may have vastly different approaches to their marketing philosophies, product launches, and/or product dependence or interdependence. This could create very different levels of AMP and different "bright lines." This may even occur within the same companies and for similar product categories. These expenditures can also be influenced by, among other things, the product's position in other countries, the timing of product launches, and the competitors and their products, each of which impacts the "bright line" benchmarking and comparability standards. Also, the legal status of the intangibles concerned may impact the expenditures differently. Even more complexity arises where the company has many product lines and the AMP expenditures are not segregated by those lines.

In the recent Mary Kay Holdings case,[8] [9] docketed in the Tax Court, and the subject of a stipulated settlement, the Petitioner begs the question of whether AMP are deductible under I.R.C. Section 162 when they are incurred for the development of a brand outside the United States. In the facts contained in the Petition, the U.S. parent company seemingly used the AMP spend as a vehicle to make a transfer pricing adjustment to its "limited risk" distribution under the guise that the adjustments (i.e. AMP charge backs) were made by the parent to support the development of the "Mary Kay" brand. The amounts of these expenses were approximately $16.1 million in 1997, $20.6 million in 1998 and $14.2 million in 1999. While the case was settled, and some underlying papers indicate the government was challenging the documentation, it is not clear therefore how the Tax Court would have held on this issue. However, what is clear is that there should be a distinct delineation between how transfer pricing adjustments are made and how AMP support payments and/or chargebacks are addressed so that there is a clean line of demarcation between the two and the AMP payments can truly be tracked to brand development and enhancement expense codes.

Notwithstanding the above, the analysis that has evolved from the prior jurisprudence begs the question of what expenses are truly brand building. For example, some marketing consultants would argue that pure advertising is not a brand building cost. Instead, placements for specific events (e.g., the Super Bowl, the U.S. Open, etc.) may be considered to produce lasting brand equity. The same can be said that celebrity endorsements create more brand building and brand association than pure advertising. Similarly, market campaigns and strategic focus groups geared to market knowledge, spending habits, and market placement can be of equal value. In tax audits, the IRS

8 See Footnote 6
9 See Footnote 6

and other taxing authorities have focused on flagship stores as brand builders, or another form of AMP. The premise is that these flagships are strategically positioned in locations where their presence is of greater value than the revenue, if any, generated from the store (e.g. 5th Avenue in New York City) Michigan Avenue in Chicago, Rodeo Drive in Los Angeles. The taxing authorities have often characterized the "excess rental costs" associated with flagship properties as brand builders to be borne by the brand owner.

The likelihood of attaining a consensus view on these items of brand building is nil. But what is clear is that the brand building/development costs will be company specific and will require a detailed analysis to meet the ever increasing challenges of global tax authorities in this area.

International Developments

The OECD added another twist to the international view of marketing intangibles when it included a discussion of their impact on the allocation of profits to either headquarter or permanent establishment in their "Attribution of Profits to a Permanent Establishment" Report and the previous Discussion Drafts leading up to this Report.[10] The re-drafted part I of the OECD Report on the Attribution of Profits to Permanent Establishment did not help to clarify the concept of marketing intangibles when it established that they include, inter alia, the name and logo of a company and a brand.[11] Intentionally or unintentionally, the draft lends a hand to the inventive fiscal quest for marketing intangibles by sympathizing with the decentralized allocation of "global" marketing intangibles as "significant people functions". In particular, day-to-day risk management efforts are hypothesized to be "dispersed within the enterprise". It must be remembered that the OECD Report is designed to be an analogous application of the OECD Transfer Pricing Guidelines to permanent establishment/headquarters cases. By reverse analogy, therefore, similar principles may be applied to company-to-company transactions. This is explicitly provided in the Final Report on the Attribution of Profits to Permanent Establishments as follows: "This analytical difficulty is not limited to Permanent Establishments, but similarly applies to the analysis of marketing intangibles between associated enterprises under Article 9 (of the OECD Model Convention)"[12] The concept of marketing intangibles should arguably not include tradenames, logos, and brands once they obtain protection under intellectual property laws. The legal owner will generally want to control and preserve the validity of the intellectual property and its enforcement capabilities. The expenditures involved in these efforts are not the same as AMP Expenditure. Also, the legal owner may want to determine that all goodwill associated with the use of its intellectual property is to inure to its own benefit, so to avoid future claims on (part of) the goodwill by its licensees and be able to claim full compensation of lost value in case of infringement, even if the significant people function lies in the distribution country.

European tax authorities have generally observed the marketing intangibles debate in the United States. Not surprisingly, the German Government has seized the opportunity offered to it by the judicial

---

10 OECD, Final Report on the Attribution of Profits to Permanent Establishments (finalized and approved by the committee on Fiscal Affairs on June 24, 2008) and Discussion Draft on the Attribution of Profits to Permanent Establishment – Part I (General Considerations), 2nd August 2004, s. 221, 239 et seq.
11 OECD Final Report, s. 27

12 OECD Final Report, s. 128

development of the concept of business opportunity developed in case law before the turn of the last millennium.[13] Significant clarifications of the concept of business opportunity have been achieved since the early days of the concept. It is currently understood that a business opportunity is an asset, thus, if there is no asset there can be no business opportunity. Accordingly, failed AMP investments cannot lead to an asset nor to a business opportunity. Important questions, however, remain such as when to attribute a business opportunity to a specific group entity among several, or how to value and establish a business opportunity. The spending of resources, such as money, is a widely recognized — though not unambiguous — criterion for the allocation of a business opportunity to an (distributor) entity. This is the link with the rather indiscriminate identification of (alleged) marketing intangibles that is so tempting to tax administrators. Most recently we have also observed situations where initially successful expenditures (such as those related to celebrity endorsements) later could be considered as failed expenditures (when the celebrity fell from grace in the public eye due to personal events) It is not clear at this time whether and how this change in value is to be dealt with.

The look back to an early landmark Federal Tax Court decision of 17-2-1993[14], on excessive startup distribution losses reveals a taxation concept competing with the allocation of marketing intangibles to a distributor. In the 1993 <u>Aquavit</u> decision, the center of the controversy were AMP expenses incurred by the German distributor in the hope of opening up and penetrating the German market for the foreign produced branded spirits. Rather than attributing a deemed marketing intangible and a corresponding return to the distributor, the court disallowed the excessive AMP expenses and instructed the tax office to tax them as disguised dividends. Systematically, and in practical cases, it makes a difference financially whether excessive AMP expenses are taxed as hidden profit distributions or those expenses are capitalized as investment plus an adequate return being allocated on top of it.

Both the deeming and allocation of a marketing intangible and the disallowance of excessive AMP expenses (justified or unjustified) are based on a more general principle of arm's length taxation, namely, that each entity ought to earn a return "commensurate" with the functions exercised, risks taken and the assets actually held by the entity.

The Netherlands and French tax authorities are also enamored with the issue of marketing intangibles. While the concept initially surfaced in corporate restructurings, and remains a major concern of tax authorities in these transactions, it has lately become an issue under audit as to whether the distributors have been sufficiently rewarded for their development of the market. It is now predictable that upon restructurings, tax authorities first raise the issue that the operating profit margin allocated to foreign activities are too high, and to pre-empt that discussion, they add that domestic costs are too high, forcing the taxpayers to allocate local costs to the foreign activities to yield the desired result of retaining revenue domestically. The next determination is that marketing intangibles or goodwill are being transferred to the foreign country.

As marketing intangibles are an

---

13   In 2002 the German Ministry drafted guidance to address potential abuses caused by business restructuring that shifts risk and intangible ownership to affiliates in low-tax jurisdictions. See BNA Transfer Pricing Report, Vol 11 No 10 of September 18, 2002.

14   Federal Tax Gazette II 1993, p. 457

economic, nearly synthetic, concept simply defined by marketing investments and business savvy, which de facto are characteristics that are included in the generic distributor function (if not required to be successful in any case), this development is likely to be countered in litigation by the civil law concept of legal ownership of legally recognized intangibles at some point. Investments made to create, register, maintain and enforce legally recognized intangibles (such as trademarks, tradenames, copyrights, and patents) are not the same as investments made to advertise, market and promote the products or services that may be the result of the intellectual property (e.g., when applying patented technology) or that may distinguish the products or services concerned (such as with trade names and trademarks). Although, the latter category of intellectual property may have a marketing function, investments made to create, register, maintain and enforce intangibles that are legally protected are needed for the very existence of the legally recognized intangibles. When viewed under the "bright lines" test, they should be regarded as routine costs, more than as non-routine costs.

While marketing intangibles are not specifically defined and basically subject to a "you know it when you see it" test, the legal proposition is that a distributor that is particularly good at what it does (e.g., a super-distributor), needs to be rewarded with a margin that is comparable to that of (other) super-distributors who incur similar investments related to their functionality. In any case, the marketing effort and resulting marketing intangibles should not result in base erosion at the expense of the legal owner of the relevant intangibles. Value retention is particularly relevant to the legal owner in case of infringement, to be able to sue for restraint, damages and lost profits.

In audit cases, the French tax authorities have been keen to protect their tax base by pointing at the legal protection granted to trademarks and patents and they often demand a return to the legal ownership for the protected intellectual property, even where all AMP was incurred by the foreign distributors. Taxpayers are, therefore, caught between these tax authorities defending their tax bases. Taxpayers are vulnerable to double taxation over this issue, and the competent authority procedure is one that is ill-equipped to address this issue, as it is factual and reasonable people can agree to disagree on what rises to the level of a marketing intangible, and what value ought to be allocated to the deemed intangible or even if a marketing intangible even exists. Within Europe, arbitration may allow for resolution, but resolution outside this process is not well developed yet.

Although a legal concept, transfer pricing is driven by economics and proportionality between functions performed, risks incurred and earnings. The boundaries of this proportionality are provided by comparables, largely from public databases. As the European countries all largely adhere to a continental system of recording, where costs are classified by type of expenses (i.e., Cost of Goods Sold, Operating Expenses) rather than by stage of production, reliable data of profit margins are lacking and comparables must be reviewed from an operating profit level. Financial ratios must also be consulted, such as the Berry Ratio or ratios of operating expenses to gross receipts or gross profit margins, to derive a realistic sense of comparability. However, because most European tax authorities still prefer the traditional transaction methods (i.e. Comparable Uncontrolled Price, Cost Plus or Resale Price Methods), absent the application of these methods there is little authority or defense against adjustments by tax authorities.

The discussion and issue are likely to peak soon, as the European Court of Justice has been chipping away at the domestic tax bases by breaking down domestic tax rules that discriminate against foreign taxpayers.[15] Because European tax authorities are seeking for a last anchor to base their access to revenue on, transfer pricing, intangibles and marketing intangibles, seem to be ideal for that purpose. One way to attempt to minimize exposure on the marketing intangibles front is to carefully define and allocate ownership of client lists, responsibilities for follow up with clients and potential after sales activities, marketing and merchandizing responsibilities and, in particular, responsibilities for AMP spend in clear contractual arrangements between related parties. Also, carefully defining and allocating legal ownership of legally recognized intangibles (intellectual property) may assist in minimizing exposure. This requires more than mere contract drafting, however, and de facto adherence to contract requirements becomes as important as function and risk allocations. So far, the judiciary generally appears to be quite formalistic, and not in favor of creative economic theories that would merit allocation of income elsewhere than where it legally and contractually belongs, assuming the facts support that allocation and functionality. Therefore, contractual arrangements, documentation, and a conservative economic analysis are important in defending against overindulgent tax authorities creatively construing a marketing intangibles theory to extract (additional) income.

---

15 Most recently in the Bosal case (deductibility of expenses made for foreign participations) and as well as in the Marks and Spencer case (allocation of foreign losses to domestic tax base).

The OECD released a 56-page discussion draft on business restructurings ("Restructuring Draft") on September 19, 2008. Generally, business restructurings involve cross-border redeployment by multinational corporations (MNCs) of functions, assets, and risks. Typically, the OECD provides that MNCs have restructured their global business models from vertically integrated business models with fullfledged manufacturing and distribution activities and associated services through locally incorporated enterprises to a centrally controlled supply chain model. The focus of tax administrations thus far is on these transactions but, as noted in passing, the Restructuring Draft defines "business restructuring" far more broadly in an introductory statement that suggests that a business restructuring may include any cross-border transfer of functions, assets and/or risks. The OECD has been requested to clarify that this broader interpretation is not intended. These centrally controlled models are often located in a tax-benefited jurisdiction, structured with appropriate economic substance, and act as the risk-taking entrepreneur who oversees limited-risk distributors or commissionaires and contract manufacturers typically located in high-tax environments with reduced profitability commensurate with their limited-risk profit.

The Restructuring Draft is composed of four Issue Notes that consider various issues related to restructurings and, among other things, challenge the "pragmatism and appropriateness" commercial rationale for the transactions and appear to revise the tenets of the established arm's-length standard:

- Issue Note No. 1 (Special Considerations for Risk).
- Issue Note No. 2 (Arm's-Length Compensation for the Restructuring).
- Issue Note No. 3 (Transfer

Intangibles

Pricing Aspects of Post-Business Restructurings).
- Issue Note No. 4 (Recognition of the Actual Transaction Undertaken).

Generally, the Issue Notes address (1) general guidance in the allocation of risks by and among the related parties to the restructuring; (2) application of the OECD Transfer Pricing Guidelines for Multinational Enterprises and Tax Administrations ("OECD Transfer Pricing Guidelines") to the restructuring with compensation or indemnifications for any terminations or "buy-ins"; (3) application of the arm's-length principle to "post-restructurings"; and (4) exceptional circumstances where a restructuring may be disregarded by a tax authority.

Focusing largely on risk transfer and the centralizing of functions, the OECD raises the issue of intangibles, by providing that in some cases, the local operation will have developed valuable intangibles which are in effect transferred in the restructuring to other members of the group. The example is provided of "the switch from a full-fledged distributor to a commissionaire, where marketing intangibles, goodwill, clientele, and the like are involved" This allows for the introduction of presumptions that adopt the skepticism and adverse attitudes of many tax authorities and challenge the business judgment of MNCs through a "commercial rationale" standard.

While the OECD Discussion Draft generally annunciates the well known transfer pricing concepts to be applied to a business restructuring, it is apparent that the critical issues involve restructurings where items of intangible property, including marketing intangibles, are transferred as a result of the restructuring. This would be most prominent when a buy-sell or full fledged distributor is converted to a limited risk distributor, but arguably also upon (full) termination of activities. The notion here is that the buy-sell distributor must receive arm's-length consideration for the marketing intangibles that it presumably developed. While the Discussion Draft does not do anything new to the transfer pricing knowledge base, it again highlights the possibility to tax authorities of this significant issue.

Japan

In Japan, there exists no judicial precedent or regulatory authority for the marketing intangibles issue, nor are there yet the same vigorous debates on the issue as in the United States. However, an officer responsible for international taxation at the National Tax Agency ("NTA"), (Director, International Taxation) delivered a lecture on the present situations and problems of international taxation at a meeting held in June, 2004 and referred to intangibles in general, and marketing intangibles specifically.[16] This is presumably the only instance where the tax authorities have formally expressed their views on this issue. Some of the views are set forth below, wherein the Director stated:

> "In Japan, it is generally thought that an intangible, irrespective of whoever has legal rights thereto, belongs not to the registered owner thereof but to the party who has developed or enhanced the value of the intangible. This is an important point."[17]

The Director here quoted paragraph 6.38 of the Organization for Economic Corporation and Development ("OECD") Transfer Pricing Guidelines on Marketing Intangibles, which provides in relevant part:

> "In general, in arm's length dealings

---

16 See, Hiroki Yamakawa Present Situations and Problems of International Taxation, [(Sozei-Kenkyu (Tax Study) (August-October, 2004)].
17 Id.

the ability of a party that is not the legal owner of a marketing intangible to obtain the future benefits of marketing activities that increase the value of that intangible will depend principally on the substance of the rights of that party. For example, a distributor may have the ability to obtain benefits from its investments in developing the value of a trademark from its turnover and market share where it has a long-term contract of sole distribution rights for the trademarked product."

In the Instructions of the Commissioner dated June 1, 2001 (the "Guidelines of Administrative Processes for Transfer Pricing"), the NTA, declares, "The Agency shall exert its efforts to properly administer examinations of transfer pricing or audits for APAs by reference to the OECD Transfer Pricing Guidelines whenever necessary," and clarifies that it will make the OECD Guidelines a base for its administration. The OECD Guidelines may also work as a guideline for the treatment of marketing intangibles. Further, the Director refers to the draft U.S. Treasury Regulations, Section 1.482-4 (f)(4), and comments that "The United States has placed emphasis on the status of legal owners, but we have an impression that the attitudes of Japan and the United States are getting closer." Accordingly, the Director believes that the arm's length consideration for a contribution by one controlled taxpayer that develops or enhances the value — or may be reasonably anticipated to develop or enhance the value — of an intangible owned by another controlled taxpayer shall be determined in accordance with the applicable rules under Section 482 of the U.S. Internal Revenue Code

Lastly, the Director stated that, "On the premise that an intangible belongs to the party who has developed or enhanced the value of the intangible, it must be determined who is the party who has developed or enhanced the value of the intangible." It can be considered that this party is the one who has made a decision to develop or enhance the value of the intangible, managed risks thereof, provided services therefor and bore the costs thereof. "Hence, even if a parent company, for the purpose of unifying the management of all manufacturing patents and trademarks of its group companies unilaterally, holds the entire legal rights thereof, . . . *if the brand value is enhanced through marketing activities by a subsidiary*, we consider that for taxation purposes, the interest in the intangibles in connection with the manufacture and sale thereof shall belong to the subsidiary and the benefits corresponding to the economic value of the intangibles belong to the subsidiary."[18] (Emphasis Added.)

These passages clearly imply that while there is no direct Japanese jurisprudence on this subject, the thinking of the NTA and the IRS regarding marketing intangibles fairly parallels each other and this issue may likely result in similar audit issues in Japan, as in the United States. The good news, however, is that any competent authority proceeding between the United States and Japan will allow for at least agreement on the concept.

Australia

Australia's reaction to the "marketing intangibles" issue is more well-developed. Although the OECD's work in this area has been limited, the Australian Tax Office ("ATO") issued on its website, on January 25, 2006, a new Guideline entitled "International Transfer Pricing – Marketing Intangibles, examples to show how the tax office will determine an appropriate reward for marketing activities performed by an enterprise using trademarks or

---
18 Id.

Intangibles

tradenames it doesn't run."[19] The Guide is a part of a suite of ATO publications about how transfer pricing issues are interpreted by it. The ATO makes reference to a number of its earlier rulings in which it has dealt with this issue.[20] Key matters to the ATO approach are:

- the contractual arrangements between the owner of the trade name and the market with particular reference to:
  - duration of the agreement;
  - nature of the rights obtained by the marketing activities;
  - who bears the costs and risks of the marketing activities;
- whether the level of marketing activities performed by the marketer exceeds that performed by comparable independent enterprises;
- the extent to which the marketing activities would be expected to benefit the owner of the trade name and/or the marketer; and,
- whether the marketer is properly compensated for its marketing activities by a "normal" return on those activities or should share in an additional return on the trade name.

Some scenarios that may possibly be under examination are where:

- A related party distributor acting in Australia is reimbursed as to 100% of all of its marketing spent on behalf of the foreign parent and also receives a marketing service fee based upon a percentage of its marketing expenditure. The distributor is regarded as an agent being reimbursed for its promotional expenditure by the owner of the marketing intangible. Under these circumstances, the distributor is only entitled to compensation appropriate to its sales solicitation activities and would not be entitled to share in any return attributable to the increase in value of the marketing intangible.
- The Australian taxpayer obtains no rights to use the trade name other than in marketing and distributing a branded product. Under these circumstances it is anticipated that the ATO would, in general, not expect the Australian taxpayer to be charged a royalty in addition to the transfer price of the product. Where the marketing expenditure, compared to arm's-length comparables, is "normal," it is likely that the ATO would not propose an adjustment to the distributor because the distributor would be receiving an arm's length return. On that basis, the ATO would presumably accept that any increase in the value of the branded product would remain with the ownership of the parent company. This scenario is comparable to the facts under the DHL case where the marketing expenditure does not exceed the "bright line" test.
- A distributor incurs marketing expenditure above and beyond what independent enterprises are required to do and has no right of recovery or reimbursement from the foreign parent, so that the profits are lower than what unrelated parties would accept and it will therefore be considered to have assumed a significantly greater and higher risk than the arm's-length party. In this case, the expectation of the ATO is likely to be that the distributor would obtain an additional return from the trademark owner, possibly through a reduction in the transfer price or a reduction in any royalty rate. Of course, the marketing

---

19 Australian Taxation Office, Taxpayers and Tax Agents Guide NA 1456-11, 2005. See www.atogov.au

20 See TR 94/14 at para 235 and 334; TR 97/20 at para 1.13 and 2.23; and TR 98/11 at para 5.39 and 5.43

expenditure here would be considered in excess of the "bright line" test.

In the latter circumstance, it is anticipated that the ATO would propose to increase the taxable income of the distributor by applying, in substitute for the taxpayer's transfer pricing methodology, a residual profit split methodology where it would attribute a basic return for the functions, assets and risks of each of the parent and Australian subsidiary and split the residual profit on the basis of the value of the intangible assets relevantly owned by the parent and the subsidiary. Presumably, the subsidiary's intangible assets would constitute the contractual rights it has from the long-term distribution agreement which would need to have been valued at the time of entry into the original Agreement. The ATO is thought unlikely to accept (presumably in retrospect) a reimbursement by the foreign principal of the Australian subsidiary's marketing expenditure because it would not be consistent with the legal arrangements between the parties.

Other Australian Tax Office policies for marketing intangibles include:

- The ATO acknowledges that a distributor would enter into a short-term, non-renewable royalty free distribution agreement, but only where the distributor stands to make a "reward" commensurate with the level of risk it is assuming. On that basis, apparently, the ATO is of the view that independent marketing/distributors who have non-renewable short-term distribution agreements which provide no compensation on termination do not invest large sums on the development of marketing and distribution infrastructure, and that the short-term nature of the distribution agreement will not allow the marketer/distributor to benefit from the marketing distribution expenditure it incurs at its own risk and that the expenditure benefits the foreign parent/principal. Accordingly, it appears the ATO could seek to adjust taxable income of the marketing/distributor, presumably, by decreasing the transfer price to the extent of some form of fee for the marketing services actually undertaken. The ATO would also likely seek to preclude the marketer/distributor from sharing in any increase in the value of the trademark.

- The ATO also accepts that a current long-term distribution arrangement may be renegotiated before expiration without compensation, so that the basis of the new transfer price is automatically indexed for the CPI and a percentage of the previous transfer price provided that the distributor "stood to obtain an adequate net return" and/or there was "adequate compensation" to the distributor. Assuming that the distributor has not passed on to its arm's-length customers the increasing price so that its original profit margin was retained, the ATO is likely to propose an adjustment to the distributor's taxable income by reducing the transfer price.

- The ATO accepts that arm's-length parties could renegotiate long-term contracts before expiration where the future agreement provides for the extension of the range of products subject of the agreement and the payment of a royalty based on selling prices, subject to the distributor receiving an adequate return on an after-royalty basis and that the marketing expenditure is not significantly disproportionate to the amount that a third party would spend. The ATO believes, consistent with paragraph 1.42 of the OECD Transfer Pricing Guidelines, that where separate transactions which are so closely linked or continuous cannot be evaluated on a separate basis, they should be evaluated on an aggregate basis. Accordingly, the ATO might expect the transfer price to be reduced to ensure a comparable return to the distributor or it possibly could deny a deduction for the royalty.

The ATO's scenarios do not securely set out how it would quantify the adjustments it was proposing nor how it would distinguish between routine or non-routine marketing spend. In fact, the examples are quite narrow. In the ordinary course of the self assessment tax system, any amounts of marketing expenditure would not be immediately apparent to the ATO, and would be expected to have been paid to arm's length providers in the first instant. However, there has been the proposition that where the AMP was "excessive" or above a "normal arm's length range" it was likely to have created or developed an "asset" for the local distributor which could be separately identified, valued carved out from the "property" belonging to the legal owner and, either subject to tax in its own right, attributed to a royalty, or reducing the transfer price.

The ATO has not indicated if it would determine, in the limited circumstances, an increase in the value of the intangible property. It is also unclear if the ATO is looking to attack or bifurcate the royalty payments from the transfer prices. The ATO currently recognizes this as an emerging issue.

China

Most recently, China has indicated a growing interest in the marketing intangibles issue as they follow the global trends in transfer pricing[21]. The outgrowth of this announcement is that the State Tax Administration ("SAT") may likely seek more income from the supply chain allocated to Chinese affiliates of foreign companies (called Wholly Owned Foreign Enterprises or "WOFEs") for expanding market share in China through AMP expenditures. Concomitantly, the SAT may challenge royalty rates to foreign affiliates where brand recognition of its products is being developed locally in China by the WOFE. Particularly vulnerable in China are companies who have been unknown to the Chinese market, but are currently launching product into the marketplace.

The SAT is seeking input globally about how to address marketing intangibles, among other things. Most prominently, they may be following the lead of the U.S. IRS and the ATO in this area. Not only is the SAT addressing the technical tax issues surrounding marketing intangibles, but how to properly document the transaction. And, with the elimination of many tax holidays and incentives in a drive for an increased share of the supply chain profit, these issues are at the forefront, particular as multinational companies restructure their Chinese WOFE.

Indirect taxes in China may also be significantly impacted by the role of marketing intangibles. For example, a royalty is subject to a 10 percent withholding tax and a 5 percent business tax. Because the royalty may be part of the cost base of the Chinese affiliate for either tax or customs, there may exist some double counting of the tax base.

---

21 "SAT Studying Marketing, Licensing Intangibles, Practitioners Say," 16 No. 6 BNA Transfer Pricing Report 175 (July 11, 2007)

Economic Benchmarking Challenges

The disparity in approaches to marketing intangibles, as well as the amorphous nature of the issue itself, make the identification and selection of comparable, independent economic benchmarks extraordinarily difficult. Without reliable, independent economic benchmarks (i.e., "comparables"), it is more difficult to establish and defend the arm's length nature of intercompany profit allocations where marketing intangibles are present. Below we discuss some of the problems associated with determining the appropriate allocation of profits to a distributor that engages in AMP activities.

In the context of the "bright line" test cited in the DHL a key component of identifying appropriate economic benchmarks (i.e., "comparables") is to first review the expense categories and subcategories that comprise the company's AMP expenditures. While this exercise may provide a strong basis for establishing routine versus non-routine expenditures, the approach can be difficult to implement. The timing of expenditures, such as for product launches, may distort the relative importance of particular categories of AMP expense compared to others, and underscores the difficulties in assessing investment value and payback periods. Another challenge may be the need to separate routine and non-routine expenditures within a particular expense category, which presents the question of whether particular expenditure thresholds constitute a reliable separation of routine expenditures from non-routine. These factors obviously are fact-specific and must always be evaluated in the context of the company's circumstances, its products and its industry. Nonetheless, even if this important initial step is reliably addressed, the identification of appropriate comparables remains a challenge.

The most significant difficulty in identifying comparables for marketing intangibles is that there are very few (if any) data sources that provide sufficiently detailed information regarding the allocation of profits (i.e., value) of the intangibles. For example, one can consider various rates of return on the cost of the investment, (such as a corporate hurdle rate of return) but that is not entirely reflective of a market value for intangible property. One can also extrapolate certain information by reviewing the relationship of gross receipts to operating expenses to establish ratios to be applied to the taxpayer, but that analysis may be imprecise because operating expenses represent an aggregation of several expenditure classes. Public companies are not required to disclose their AMP expenditures, and even for those that do, there is no way to determine the percentage of these expenses devoted to intangible property enhancement. Other financial statements, such as the balance sheet, do little to address this classification problem. When intangible assets appear on the balance sheet, they generally are the result of an asset allocation exercise that may assign accounting values across various asset classes (e.g., patents, trademarks and goodwill) that are not necessarily consistent with the required economic valuation (i.e., "marketing intangibles").

The idea that there are clear industry standards that establish or provide guidelines for what a distributor should spend on AMP can be problematic. The financial statements of companies within an industry may classify and define AMP expenditures entirely differently. One company may define spending as advertising while another company defines similar spending as media or distribution. Other items, such as market studies, promotional brochures, and media may be classified under completely different accounting codes.

Contributing to the difficulty is the uncertain definition of what exactly constitutes marketing intangibles. In addition to trademarks and trade names, marketing intangibles can be company or product specific, but may also include customer lists and knowledge of distribution channels.[22] Although customers are not considered to be "intangible" property per se, customers (and more broadly, customer relationships) are a key value driver and one of the main indicators of growth potential. Similarly, transfer pricing practitioners often engage in discussions with the tax authorities over the value to be attributed to the "customer list" in the context of business reorganizations and supply chain restructuring processes. It is not precisely clear where in the financial statements expenditures related to the development of these items may be reflected.

The lack of transparency and consistency in reporting practices for AMP expenditures across firms and across jurisdictions makes it difficult to reliably identify comparable levels of routine AMP expenses. There are a number of databases that are commonly used to conduct comparables analysis and benchmarking of financial data within industries, including Compustat, Disclosure, Moody's, Worldscope, Global Vantage, and Amadeus, among others. Although the database providers may attempt to standardize data across companies, they ultimately rely on public filings that present the same challenges regarding the transparency and consistency of financial data. In addition, the database providers may also make certain decisions regarding classification and organization that may not easily align with the needs of the practitioner analyzing AMP expenditures. For example, the Compustat database defines Advertising Expense as follows: "This item represents the cost of advertising media (radio, television, newspapers, periodicals) and promotional expenses. This item excludes selling and marketing expenses." It seems clear that there could be expenditures that relate to the creation of marketing intangibles that are not being captured by this line item. However, the category of Selling, General, and Administrative Expense is defined, as one would expect, far more broadly and includes 27 separate items, such as salaries and related costs, R&D, engineering, legal expenses, marketing, and others in addition to advertising. Using this item as a proxy would surely overstate the investments in marketing intangibles.

Further, most contemporary databases that address trademark royalties (e.g. LiveEdgar, RoyaltySource and RoyaltyStat) contain information on license agreements between unrelated parties, but may not provide sufficient elements to segregate the remuneration paid for the intangible property (e.g. trademark) from the one paid, for instance, for ancillary services. Again, this is generally a factor of the amount of specificity contained in the underlying license agreement. Additional benchmarking and/or economic/financial modeling may provide alternative ways to produce meaningful results. Nonetheless, close comparability in terms of property, market, and profit potential is rare so that the result of the analysis may be a range of values for broadly similar property.

The level and nature of AMP expenditures also can be also impacted by a variety of business factors, including management policies, market share, characteristics of the market, and the

---

[22] See Levey, Shapiro, Cunningham, Lemein and Garofolo, "DHL: Ninth Circuit Sheds Very Little Light on Bright Line Test," 13 J. of International Taxation 10 (Oct. 2002).

timing of product launches. As indicated above, the Annual Reports and SEC documents of public companies, as well as the information organized and distributed by database providers, generally do not provide the necessary level of detail that would be required to reconcile these management considerations and classification differences.

An additional challenge to an analysis of marketing intangibles is that AMP spending generally has spillover effects to or from other products or product lines. Also, the effects of AMP spending are distributed over time and so the accounting practice of expensing these AMP "investments" in the current period can create distortions in determining economic profits. This dynamic is most evident when dealing with issues such as a product launch, where there may be a sharp increase in spending prior to the launch of a product or product line, followed by subsequent decreases to more stable spending levels. It might be appropriate to segregate out the spending related to the product launch, or at least ensure that the data being considered covers a sufficient time period so that the lifecycle dynamics can be properly addressed. This requires estimations of the useful life of AMP spending. Economic modeling of investment cycles and profitability curves may address these types of issues, although the data required for such analyses may be significant and, in many cases, unavailable.

Factors to Consider

In analyzing marketing intangibles for transfer pricing purposes one should consider, among others, the following questions:
- Have the marketing intangibles obtained protection under intellectual property laws and, if so, which entity is the legal owner?
- Will certain costs and expenditures result in an economically valuable asset?
- How should one distinguish developmental (i.e. non-routine) from non-developmental (i.e. routine) expenses?
- Can expenditure on intangibles be compensated by simply reimbursing all expenses above a prescribed amount or identifying specific expense codes with allocation keys where appropriate?
- How are allocation keys established for applicable expense codes?
- What is the "base date" for marketing intangible valuation?
- What is the expected use of the intangible asset by the parties?
- What is the expected useful life of the marketing intangible and how is this economically determined?
- Are there any legal or regulatory restrictions related to use of the intangible?
- What are the effects of obsolescence or other external economic factors?
- What level of expenditures are necessary to maintain the intangible?
- What are the customs and indirect tax ramifications of marketing intangibles expenses and/or royalties?

It also is important to consider the nature of the relationship between the related parties (e.g., manufacturer, licensor/license, etc.). Even assuming that it is possible to estimate a normal level of AMP spending for a particular industry, and that the distributor/license in question spends at a greater rate than this routine level, a critical factor is whether the intercompany arrangements are such that the distributor/license is assuming risks consist with an entrepreneurial role. If the intercompany arrangements are such that the distributor/license is effectively guaranteed a routine profit level regardless of the level of its marketing expenditure, then the question of whether these expenditures are above a normal level is not relevant because any resulting profits would be attributable to the manufacturer that is assuming the entrepreneurial risk.

How Can Marketing Intangibles Be Legally Protected?

"Marketing intangibles" in the tax lawyer's sense is a concept that makes many intellectual property lawyers uncomfortable. The tax community's concept of "marketing intangibles" is far broader than the typical intellectual property lawyer's vision of the discrete package of rights constituting "intellectual property", *e.g.*, trademarks (brands and logos), tradenames, trade dress, copyright interests, (for example, marketing materials, advertising, graphics, photographs and other media and databases such as customer lists), and the unique know-how that surrounds a trademark or otherwise is used by the company for its business operations (such as the knowledge of supply and distribution channels and customer relationships). But marketing intangibles also include a penumbra of other benefits associated with the local market position of a company or its products—benefits and rights that are purely contractual in nature such as franchises and licenses, and other rights and interests not protected under intellectual property laws *per se*. This creates some tension between the objectives of tax lawyers and the civil law implications perceived by intellectual property lawyers.

Marketing intangibles are typically developed by a company through its AMP efforts and expenditures and the value of such marketing intangibles is derived from such efforts. From an intellectual property law perspective, value in intellectual property is created through compliance with the formal legal requirements for intellectual property creation, protection and maintenance, including the filing of applications for registration of trademarks and copyrights with appropriate governmental agencies in the jurisdictions of use, maintaining registrations, policing against infringers and exercise of adequate quality control. Nowhere is the tension between trademark lawyers and tax lawyers more evident than when one asks, "who is the "owner" of the marketing intangibles?"

Trademarks, Service Marks, Trade Names and Trade Dress

First and foremost among marketing intangibles are trademarks and service marks—brands and logos which distinguish the owner's goods or services from the goods and services of others. They designate the source and quality and attendant reputation of the owner's goods and services. Most importantly, trademark law bestows on the legal owner the right to exclude others from using a similar mark on other products in a way that is likely to mislead or confuse the purchasing public. This is a powerful monopoly right premised on the public policy of protecting the public against a danger of confusion—buying something which the consumer believes to be of a certain quality when in fact it is something quite different.

Trademark rights are territorial. Ownership of trademarks generally is acquired on a country-by-country basis by complying with the trademark laws

Intangibles

of each applicable jurisdiction.[23] In the United States, for example, trademark rights arise under common law through use, and, in most cases, the first user of the mark in commerce is the legal owner of the mark.[24] U.S. Federal registration is, however, available to the first user of a mark in interstate commerce and it confers important benefits, including constructive notice throughout the United States that the registrant claims ownership of the mark, incontestability of the mark if the owner of the registration has continuously used the mark in commerce for five years after the registration date and files the appropriate document with the U.S. Patent and Trademark Office and access to the Federal court system for infringement and dilution suits. By contrast, in most non-U.S. jurisdictions the legal owner of trademark rights is the first to register the mark with the appropriate administrative agency, not the first user in the jurisdiction. In those "first to file" jurisdictions, if a mark is not registered, no trademark rights accrue under trademark law. Many jurisdictions, even "first to file" jurisdictions, have use requirements to maintain trademark registrations over time, and these requirements may under certain jurisdictions become problematic when the only demonstrable use is that of a licensee or distributor. This is why license agreements routinely specify that the use of the mark by the licensee "inures to be the benefit of the licensor". The United States and some other jurisdictions require actual exercise of quality control over licensees and distributors and active policing of the market for infringers for trademark rights to continue to subsist. Moreover, certain non-U.S. jurisdictions, *e.g.*, Mexico, require that the relevant licenses or registered user agreements be recorded with the local Trademark Office.

Given the different standards for legal ownership under tax law and IP law, the legal owner under trademark law for protection and enforcement purposes may well be different from the "economic owner" under relevant tax law. Tax law may impute ownership of a mark in some part to the licensee of a mark or distributor of branded products if that licensee or distributor has developed the market for the mark through its own expenditure of AMP. But from a trademark law perspective, there can be only one legal owner in a particular jurisdiction, and neither the licensee nor distributor has the right to register a mark or bring actions against infringers to enjoin infringing use and collect damages, such as for lost profits and/or the infringer's ill-gotten gains.

What this means is that tax and intellectual property lawyers must cooperate on the development of the IP ownership structure to ensure that the structure of trademark ownership meets

---

23   Important exceptions to the general rule that trademark rights are acquired on a county by county basis must be noted. Trademark protection covering all member states of the European Union can be obtained through registration of a "European Community Trademark" with the Office for Harmonization in the Internal Market, located in Alicante, Spain. Moreover international treaties such as the Paris Convention and the Madrid Protocol provide the means for a trademark owner to extend priority rights beyond a jurisdiction's borders.

24   One exception to this use-based rights principle is the concept of constructive use. If a party files an intent-to-use application for a trademark or service mark with the U.S. Patent and Trademark Office and said application matures to registration, a constructive use date as of the filing date is afforded to the owner. Therefore, even if a third party commences use of an identical or confusingly similar mark after the intent-to-use application is filed (and prior to any use by the owner of said application), the owner would still be considered the senior user in an infringement or other type of enforcement action.

both the tax planning objectives and the objective of maximizing protection of the marks, absent which trademark rights may be lost. Tax and IP counsel must both pay close attention in the drafting of relevant intercompany license and distribution agreements to how the parties will allocate responsibility and cost for acquisition, protection and enforcement of marks, through allocation of expenses for trademark portfolio registration and maintenance, quality control and policing the marketplace, as well as allocation of damages collected from enforcement activity. Allocation of ownership and responsibility for protection of related non-registered or non-registrable rights such as in trade names and trade dress (the common law rights associated with product or packaging design and certain design schemes of retail stores, restaurants and the like) must be carefully articulated in the relevant intercompany documents as well to ensure their validity and proper exploitation.

Copyrights

Marketing intangibles taking the form of print media, graphics, video, software, architectural designs, databases (such as customer lists), fabric patterns and jewelry designs may be protected under copyright law. Copyright law arose to protect the writings of authors from unauthorized copying, display, or use in the creation of derivatives for a limited period of time before they must eventually enter the public domain. But copyright law has evolved to cover many other forms of creative work, including works of art, the graphics arts, computer programs, architectural design, sound recordings and audio-visual works. In the US, in addition to protecting jewelry designs and fabric patterns, legislation has been proposed in Congress to extend copyright protection to clothing designs. In many European jurisdictions copyright protection to clothing designs has already existed for years.

The exact criteria may differ from country to country, but in general to qualify for copyright protection, a work must be original and be the result of at least some creative effort on the part of its author. Ownership arises in the individual who authored the work, unless the work is a "work made for hire", *i.e.*, a work created by an employee in the ordinary course of his or her employment or a work specially ordered or commissioned for use by another which is designated in writing to be a work made for hire. For work made for hire, the owner generally is the employer or commissioner of the work.

Countries signatory to the Berne Convention (and most countries are members) do not require registration or the use of a copyright notice for copyright protection to subsist. Thus, unlike trademark rights in "first to file" countries, copyright rights are not acquired through registration; rights arise upon creation of the work in question by the author. Copyright registration is however required in the U.S. of U.S. persons and entities prior to commencing an action for copyright infringement, and is also required in order to be eligible to collect statutory damages and attorneys fees in an infringement action in Federal Court. Accordingly, care must be taken to ensure that title to copyrighted material is properly secured (through proper work for hire agreements and assignments), so that if those rights must be enforced, the proper party is able to take appropriate legal action.

Trade Secrets

Information which derives its value because it is not generally known to the public can also be considered a marketing intangible. This information might include the data in customer and supplier lists, product formulas, manufacturing or production methods, systems, procedures, know-how, studies, marketing surveys, forecasts, estimates or other technical data. These types of intangibles are legally protected in the U.S. under state statutes or common law as trade secrets. In Europe, many countries do not provide specific protection for trade secrets, but protection can be created under contract law. For these rights to subsist, the owner of the trade secret must keep the information secret or at least use reasonable efforts in the circumstances to maintain its secrecy, such as keeping the data in a secure environment and disclosing the information to third parties — such as third party contractors and even employees — only on a need to know basis pursuant to appropriate confidentiality and nondisclosure agreements.

A company that protects its trade secrets properly has the right to obtain an injunction to stop the use of such information by a party who steals, copies or uses the information without the company's permission. Some information that qualifies for trade secret status, such as software programs, may also qualify for protection under patent or copyright laws. As trade secret protection can theoretically last forever, companies sometimes prefer to make use of trade secret protection in order to avoid the public disclosure that ensues from registration of the data. The most famous example of a trade secret is the formula for COCA-COLA®.

In summary, valuable marketing intangibles identified for tax planning purposes are only as valuable as their protection programs. Absent care to ensure the rights are perfected, they become useless. Different types of marketing intangibles require different means of protection. Failure to identify these intangibles early on during business operations, such as through documenting ownership in appropriate entities consistent with how the rights arise under the law, may compromise intellectual property enforcement efforts down the road or even the existence of the intellectual property rights themselves.

Intellectual Property Migration Considerations

Intellectual property rights are negative in nature, that is, they are monopoly rights that allow the owner to prevent third parties from doing specified things, *e.g.*, using the same or similar brand for marketing products not emanating from the brand owner. Accordingly, they have value only if they can be effectively enforced. If an intellectual property migration is not carefully planned and executed, the IP owner's ability to enforce its intellectual property rights could be jeopardized, effectively making those rights worthless. No matter how great the tax savings from a migration, it cannot compensate for intellectual property rights that cannot be enforced and the corresponding lost profits and value of the business in general.

Particular enforcement problems can arise if the establishment or migration of intangibles results in a separation between ownership and exploitation in a group of companies. This is because it can be difficult in some countries for licensees, as opposed to owners, to effectively enforce their rights and to recover certain damages such as lost profits for patent and trademark infringement. A party seeking lost profits is required to establish a factual basis for causation, (*i.e.*, but for the infringer's improper acts, the plaintiff would have made greater sales, charged higher prices or incurred lower expenses).

For instance, in the United States, when a licensing relationship exists whereby the licensee sells a product (using the licensor's IP), it is important to structure that license as an exclusive license to preserve the ability to later recover lost profits. With an exclusive license, the licensee generally has standing to join a suit with the licensor and together the parties can recover lost profits because, but for the infringer's acts, the licensee would have had greater sales. If the license is deemed to be non-exclusive, however, the licensee will not have standing to join the suit, and the licensor will only be entitled to damages measured in terms of a reasonable royalty as it was not the party that lost the actual sales. This scenario typically arises in a distribution relationship in which a manufacturer who owns the intellectual property licenses that intellectual property to a related company operating as a distributor in a defined territory who sells product on behalf of that manufacturer and develops that product through its AMP efforts and expenditures. To ensure the possibility to seek lost sales in an infringement action in the licensed territory, the license agreement between the manufacturer and distributor should be exclusive. Damages may be calculated differently in license relationships involving territories outside of the U.S. Accordingly, a careful review under applicable law of the licensing relationships upon migration is paramount.

Besides preserving the ability to recover lost profits, other intellectual property contractual considerations should be focused on when migrating intangibles, because trademark rights and other intellectual property rights can be lost through improper licensing or assignment. If a license grants rights to U.S. trademarks, the license should include adequate quality control provisions, including rights to inspection and monitoring. Where the use of a trademark is licensed without adequate quality control or supervision by the trademark owner, such uncontrolled licensing may result in a "forfeiture" of trademark rights. This requirement, however, does not exist in many non-U.S. jurisdictions.

Where the rights to a trademark are assigned to another party without the goodwill symbolized by the trademark or the portion of the business pertaining thereto, that "assignment in gross" of a trademark is invalid, and does not pass rights to the purported assignee. In most cases, the most significant impact of an assignment in gross is that the purported assignee does not succeed to the assignor's priority of use of the mark. The rationale for these rules is that, in these situations, the trademark no longer serves its purpose of identifying the goods of a particular provider. Any license granting rights to a trademark must provide that all goodwill (as defined under intellectual property law) associated with that trademark and established by the licensee reverts back to the trademark owner, the licensor, because goodwill associated with a given trademark cannot be separated from that trademark under U.S. trademark law.

Goodwill from an intellectual property perspective refers more to reputation and quality control rather than the financial understanding of the term. Since allocations may be required for tax purposes it is useful to clarify contractually what level of AMP expenditures are to be reimbursed or allocated by and between related parties while also ensuring that appropriate provisions with respect to good will from an IP protection perspective are secured.

Finally, careful consideration must be given to whether the target jurisdiction in which the marketing intangibles are to be legally owned is a member country of, and enjoys treaty protection under, the various international intellectual property treaties that afford intellectual property owners reciprocal rights in other member jurisdictions, such as the Madrid Protocol and the Berne Convention. If not, then this can have a negative impact on the validity of the intellectual property right concerned or the ability to enforce the rights concerned.

What Does Future Hold?

So where does this leave us? If one follows the normal trend that has been experienced in transfer pricing over the past years, this concept will continue to be seriously debated among taxing authorities as they each grapple for a share of a multinational company's global profit such that economic modeling will become in vogue. Indeed, China is the most recent taxing authority to announce that it is following this track. But, generally, it can be assumed that for taxpayers who employ an operating income method as their best or most appropriate method for transfer pricing purposes (i.e., the Comparable Profits Method or Transactional Net Margin Method), all items of cost and expense included in the calculation of operating profit will be subject to detailed reviews. If the item of intangible property (e.g.., the trademark) is owned within the same legal entity, the AMP expenses can be perceived as enhancing the item of intangible property's value and that value should be reflected within its operating profit margin positively or negatively as the case may be. If the intangible is owned by another affiliate, the taxpayer will be perceived as the owner of the local marketing intangible, in whole or in part, based on the contributions of the other affiliate and the taxpayer. Here, the taxpayer's contributions will be considered to the extent its AMP expenditures exceed the "bright line" test, constituting non-routine intangibles.

These facts will signal a real need to engage in planning to assure that any perceived marketing intangible is consistent with the taxpayers' business realities and not inadvertently ignored. This is particularly true where the marketing intangibles are part of a migration exercise. It is here that a more refined and documented definition of the company's marketing intangible is needed for a more reliable economic analysis and financial result. Most important is that the relationship between the parties regarding the expenditures for the development of the marketing intangible must be documented within the parties' distribution and/or license agreement. Failure to do so leaves the parties vulnerable to adjustment by any tax authority.

If an entity is intended to make investments in developing marketing intangibles, the nature and degree of expected spending should be clearly delineated, documented and benchmarked. An attempt should also be made to demonstrate that these activities differ from those undertaken by the distribution comparables, keeping in mind the data and information challenges previously discussed. Not only should the intercompany pricing policies reflect that the entity is making additional investments and assuming additional risks and therefore should reasonably expect to have the potential for non-routine benefits should the intangible-developing activities prove successful, but intercompany contracts should clearly reflect the same. Transfer pricing issues are decided and settled largely based on the burden of proof, and timely prepared and signed intercompany contracts are an important strategic tool in this respect. On the other hand, if an entity is not expected to be permitted to realize the potential benefits from local activities designed to develop, maintain, or expand marketing intangibles, the intercompany pricing policies should be structured such that the entity is not assuming the risk and expense of developing those marketing intangibles.

Conclusion

Accounting for marketing intangibles is complex and becomes more so when the taxpayer fails to properly document as much as possible the nature of these intangibles, their ownership costs and other factors contributing to the value of these intangibles. In the face of inadequate documentation, tax authorities are able to project their own views of the taxpayer's markets, investments, and ultimately marketing intangibles, which at times can be totally at odds with the taxpayer's facts and commercial realities. And, if the matter is resolved adversely to the taxpayer, the company will have to live with those results for subsequent tax years. Accordingly, it is prudent for taxpayers to first take control of this issue by defining for themselves their marketing intangibles in the context of their business, marketplace and investments, and by documenting them in legal agreements between the related parties. These issues can involve substantial tax dollars and create significant tax and financial statement exposure, as evidenced by *Glaxo*. Equally important, these issues can disrupt a taxpayer's transfer policy and planning for future years. Taxpayers therefore must stay on top of the ongoing regulatory and enforcement developments associated with marketing intangibles. Failure to do so could expose companies to significant unnecessary tax risk. Intellectual property law and transfer pricing knowledge go a long way in protecting taxpayers against the resulting unexpected and undesirable tax costs.

Marc M. Levey and **Pamela Church** are International Partners at Baker & McKenzie LLP in New York. **Monique van Herksen** is a Partner with Ernst & Young/Holland Van Gijzen in Amsterdam. **Philip Carmichael** is Director of Economics at Baker & McKenzie Consulting, LLC in New York. **Alexander Odle** is the principal at A.R.T. Intellectual Property BV in Amsterdam. This article is an expansion of "The Quest for Marketing Intangibles," 33 Intertax3 (2005) as prepared by the authors and commentators. The authors wish to thank Stephan Schnorberger and Kazuo Taguchi of Baker & McKenzie's Düsseldorf and Tokyo offices, respectively, for their thoughtful comments and contributions. ® All Rights Reserved

For more information on the authors, please see Section XIII.

V. Organizational Structure

Business Restructuring— "Conversion" Issues and a Framework for Analysis

Tobin Hopkins
Ernst & Young

Introduction

In today's dynamic world, the only thing that seems to stay the same is that change is constant. This is particularly true in the world of business, where companies undergo varying degrees of business change on an almost continuous basis. For multinational enterprises (MNEs) with global supply chains, these business changes often have domestic and international tax implications. An emerging and particularly complex tax issue that can arise from business restructurings with cross-border implications and changes in taxable profits in one or more countries is the so-called "conversion gain" (also known as an "exit charge"). More specifically, many tax authorities assert that cross-border business restructurings can lead, in some cases, to a taxable event on deemed transfers of property.

This article describes the types of business change which may lead a tax authority to assert a conversion gain, evaluates the typical approach undertaken by tax authorities in assessing a potential taxable gain, and concludes with an alternative, arguably more robust, framework for evaluating the conversion issue.

The Issue

In general, there are three business restructuring scenarios that might lead a tax authority to assert that an exit charge or conversion gain is applicable. In the first scenario, a MNE restructures a business or product line in a manner that significantly reduces or completely eliminates the production capacity in one jurisdiction and "shifts" the production capacity to another jurisdiction. A classic example of this scenario is the shut-down of a manufacturing plant in one country and a corresponding ramp-up of production in another country of the same product that was originally produced at the recently closed factory. In addition to the question of whether a taxable asset was transferred as a part of the factory closure, this scenario may also raise questions regarding the deductibility of extraordinary costs related to the restructuring, discussed in the article by Danny Oosterhoff.

In the second scenario, an entrepreneurially oriented, fully functional sales and distribution operation is restructured into a sales focused organization with limited functionality and limited risks. Prior to the restructuring, the sales and distribution entity may have undertaken, for example, functions related to sales, tactical and strategic marketing, inventory management, invoicing, logistics, and strategic pricing. Accordingly, the entity may have incurred risks pertaining to inventory, accounts receivable, forecasting, foreign exchange, and general business and market conditions. After the business restructuring, for example, many of these roles and responsibilities are centralized regionally, and the restructured entity performs functions primarily related to sales activities, with more limited roles in pricing and marketing business processes, and incurs little to no inventory and other key risks. From a transfer pricing perspective, the entity earns a commission or resale margin that provides it an arm's length return for its sales activities.

In the third scenario, a so called "fully-fledged" manufacturer is restructured into a contract or consignment manufacturer that focuses on cost and quality, performs relatively fewer functions, and incurs fewer risks. For instance, the "fully- fledged" manufacturer may have been responsible for activities related to production planning and scheduling, inventory and supply chain management, quality control strategy and policy, long-range capacity planning, and sourcing and procurement. Similarly, prior to the restructuring, the entity may have incurred inventory, product liability, warranty, and plant capacity risks. As a result of the restructuring, for example, the manufacturing entity is now responsible for scheduling day-to- day production, executing quality control procedures, "calling off' raw material and component purchases, and the actual manufacture of the product(s). Additionally, the restructured entity manufactures on a "take or pay" basis for the contracting entity and bears only limited risks relative to its previous role. With respect to transfer pricing, the contract or consignment manufacturer earns a cost-plus type of return.

The Typical Approach of Tax Authorities

In assessing the conversion gain issues, tax authorities are contemplating, in most cases, two fundamental issues: i) did a taxable gain arise from the conversion; and ii) if so, what is the value of the taxable gain?

With respect to the first issue, the differing regulatory frameworks of each tax jurisdiction lead to some variation in how this issue is addressed in each country. The German tax authorities, for example, take perhaps the most expansive view in determining whether a taxable event resulted from the conversion. More specifically, the German regulations focus on the mere loss of "profit potential" as potentially giving rise to a taxable gain from a shift of functions as part of a business restructuring. Thus, to assert a gain there is no apparent need in the German regulatory framework to specifically identify an asset or property that was transferred out of Germany as a part of the business restructuring.

Many other jurisdictions are required, at least from a civil law or regulatory perspective, to identify such an asset that has been transferred in order to assert successfully that a taxable gain has resulted from the business restructuring. The Italian regulations, for example, focus predominantly on the transfer of a commercial or market facing type of intangible asset. However, in practice it seems that many taxing authorities are taking a fairly loose view of what constitutes a specifically identified intangible asset in asserting conversion gains. Furthermore, in some jurisdictions a taxable gain may be asserted due to a perceived "hidden profit distribution" or deemed distribution of goodwill rather than as a result of a transfer of a specifically identified intangible asset.

Regarding the second issue, most tax authorities are employing what can best be described as a "top-down" approach in assessing the value of the conversion gain. More specifically, two discounted cash flow (DCF) analyses are conducted: i) a "current state" DCF incorporating profit levels of the relevant entity prior to the business restructuring; and ii) a "future state" DCF which utilizes expected profit levels of the relevant entity after the business restructuring. Under this approach, the taxable gain is simply the difference between the computed future state value and the current state value. For example, assume that a fully functional buy/sell entity earned a five percent (5%) operating margin on average over the last several years. In the future state, the restructured entity will perform relatively fewer functions and incur relatively fewer risks, and consequently is expected to earn a steady two and a half percent (2.5%) operating margin. After making assumptions for anticipated future revenue growth and determining a discount rate, DCF analyses under the 5% and 2.5% operating margin scenarios can be calculated. The difference between the two DCF values, sometimes referred to as the "gap," is the potential conversion gain asserted by the tax administration.

There are a number of potential limitations associated with the relatively simplistic, "top-down" approach described above. For instance, it implicitly assumes a static business model under which current state profit margin levels are expected to remain constant going forward. This implicit assumption fails to recognize that many businesses restructure because the current state business model is simply no longer sustainable. Put differently, without business change the 5% operating margin described above may be eroded in the future because of location cost disadvantages, competitive threats, changing customer or supplier requirements, etc.

An additional potential limitation of the top-down approach is that the resulting DCF analysis essentially treats the transfer of any functions which may change profit levels as giving rise to taxable gains. The aforementioned German regulations notwithstanding, the relevant tax regulations of most countries generally require the transfer of an identified asset in order to generate a potentially taxable gain. Thus, in order for the top-down, DCF approach to be valid, all transferred, profit generating functions must possess an imbedded intangible asset. It seems unlikely that all routine functions which produce incremental profits must also include an intangible asset.

Another potential limitation of the top-down approach relates to the rather practical issue of historical transfer pricing errors. Despite the increasing attention paid to transfer pricing related issues, it is certainly not uncommon for a MNEs transfer pricing regime to be out of alignment with the underlying business model. This can happen for a variety of reasons (e.g., the original transfer pricing system was incorrectly designed or implemented or has failed to keep pace with change), but the end result is that the current state DCF analysis may incorrectly attribute too much or too little value to the pre-restructured entity. Consequently, the calculated taxable gain under the top-down approach will not be accurate.

A further complicating factor associated with a top-down, DCF approach relates to the choice of discount rate for the DCF analysis. In particular, should the same discount rate be used in the Current State DCF and the Future State DCF? Most "conversion" scenarios result in a lower, but very stable, level of profit for the converted entity relative to potentially higher, but more volatile, profit levels for the entity prior to conversion.

Modern financial theory has long accepted the notion that investors require higher expected returns for incurring risk; consequently, riskier cash flows should be discounted with higher discount rates when calculating net present values. This implies that the Current State DCF analysis should incorporate a higher discount rate than the Future State DCF analysis. A critical issue, however, is determining the appropriate adjustment to the discount rate to account for the differing levels of risk in the Current State and Future State cash flows. Most approaches to this issue relate to either: i) adjusting the Weight Average Cost of Capital (WACC) by adjusting Beta in a Capital Asset Pricing Model (CAPM) type approach; or ii) using a non-WACC based discount rate (e.g., the cost of debt). Regardless of the approach, the analytics are complex and generally not without controversy.

In many cases, the top-down, DCF analysis can be adjusted to address, at least in part, the limitations described above. Indeed, many tax authority audits of conversion gains include detailed discussions between the tax authority and the taxpayer on the type and magnitude of these adjustments. However, this can be a very time- consuming and controversial exercise. Furthermore, at some point, the number and complexity of adjustments to a topdown approach may begin to undermine the reliability of the overall analysis.

Alternative Framework for Evaluating the Conversion Issue

An alternative to the top-down analysis is a more "bottom- up" oriented approach that incorporates a legal analysis of the conversion issue and seeks, where applicable, to value specifically identified intangible property transferred as a result of the business restructuring. The starting point of such an analysis is a detailed legal consideration of the facts and circumstances surrounding the intercompany arrangements of the entity (ies) undergoing the business restructuring as well as the relevant commercial law and jurisprudence. The emphasis of this legal analysis is in determining whether the restructured entity has a legal right to a compensatory payment (e.g., conversion gain) as a result of the restructuring. The potential compensatory payment may be a consequence of an actual transfer of intangible property or because of by the restructuring (e.g., breach of contract).

Including a legal analysis in the evaluation of the conversion is certainly in the spirit of the arm's length standard. According to the OECD Transfer Pricing Guidelines:

> "By seeking to adjust profits by reference to the conditions which would have obtained between independent enterprises in comparable transactions and comparable circumstances, the arm's length principle follows the approach of treating the members of a MNE group as operating as separate entities rather than as inseparable parts of a single unified business."[1]

In a business restructuring or similar scenario (e.g., termination of contracts) involving independent enterprises, "the conditions" relevant to a conversion analysis will often ultimately be determined through or significantly impacted by the legal system of the relevant jurisdiction. There are, for example, several legal cases involving contract termination between third parties where a compensatory payment was ultimately required. There are also a number of fairly similar cases involving third parties where there was no compensatory payment.

---

1   OECD Guidelines, paragraph 1.6

Organizational Structure

Recent OECD discussions on transfer pricing related business restructuring issues indicate a growing awareness of the potential applicability of legal considerations to the conversion issue: "there is significant experience in the legal arena on indemnification due to third-party distributors upon termination of contracts."[2]

Consequently, an important element of the legal approach is the research and analysis of potentially comparable "transactions." Comparable transactions in this case relate specifically to situations in which a contract or arrangement between third parties was terminated or significantly restructured under circumstances similar to the related party restructuring under review. The identification of such comparable transactions can provide useful insight into critical negotiation issues for parties operating at arm's length in similar circumstances, relevant business practices in the specific industry, and historical precedent regarding compensatory payments. Operational and business development personnel of the taxpayer are often a useful source of information regarding potential comparable transactions.

Though each business restructuring is inherently unique, there are a number of legal considerations — in addition to the research and analysis of comparable transactions — that should be evaluated in assessing the conversion issue. At a minimum, the following considerations should be evaluated as a part of a detailed legal analysis:

- duration and termination considerations of existing written intercompany agreements;
- historical conduct of the parties and consistency with the substance of the intercompany agreements;
- past renewal behavior of parties with respect to any intercompany agreements;
- actual or beneficial ownership of intangible assets (e.g., trademarks, trade names, brand names, patents, copyrights, business processes, know-how or other intangible assets);
- existence of long-term sales or supply contracts; and
- statutory and judicial guidance regarding the need to compensate a full risk entity for converting to limited risk entity.

In many cases, a legal analysis of the conversion issue should be supplemented with an evaluation of alternatives realistically available to the parties involved in the business restructuring. The OECD Transfer Pricing Guidelines, as well as the relevant regulations of several countries (e.g., Germany, the United States), indicate the importance of contemplating realistic alternatives in evaluating transfer pricing issues. For example the OECD Transfer Pricing Guidelines state:

> "Independent enterprises, when evaluating the terms of a potential transaction, will compare the transaction to the other options realistically available to them, and they will only enter into the transaction if they see no alternative that is clearly more attractive."[3]

Such an analysis is certainly relevant to understanding how third parties, operating at arm's length, might resolve similar, conversion related issues. Indeed, bargaining theory analysis, which targets an area of price determination difficult to evaluate using standard economic

---

[2] Business Restructuring: Transfer Pricing Issues. Caroline Silberztien, 2nd CPTA Roundtable, Paris 26-27, prepared for the OECD Secretariat.

[3] OECD Guidelines, paragraph 1.15

theory, can be a particularly useful tool in assessing the conversion gain issue. This is discussed in more detail in the following article by Robert Miall. If the legal analysis indicates that an asset is being transferred as a result of the business restructuring and that the converted entity has a legal right to a compensatory payment as a result of the transfer, the final step of a bottom-up approach is valuing the relevant specifically identified intangible asset(s). At this point in the analysis, traditional valuation and transfer pricing techniques can be employed to determine the appropriate value of the transferred asset.

For example, traditional valuation techniques for intangible property generally fall into one of three categories:
i) the income approach, which considers the cash flow generated by the intangible property;
ii) the cost approach, which focuses on the aggregate costs involved in developing the intangible property; and
iii) the market approach, which seeks to identify transactions for comparable intangible property.

To illustrate the potential applicability of the alternative framework discussed above, consider the case of a hypothetical manufacturer and distributor of electrical components. Corp E has manufacturing operations in the United States, Asia, and some countries in Europe, an extensive global distribution network, and a well-regarded product line. Though Corp E has a competitive manufacturing cost structure, its distribution network has considerable operational redundancies, excess inventory levels, above average logistics costs, and a cumbersome decision-making process.

As a result, Corp E is restructuring its distribution network by

i) centralizing duplicative functions (e.g., order processing, customer support) currently performed in each distribution entity;
ii) optimizing its distribution network through the use of a European distribution center and significantly reduced stock levels at the local distribution entities; and
iii) consolidating certain decision-making activities which were previously undertaken at a local level. The intercompany agreements and transfer pricing arrangements are also modified to align the tax and legal structure with the future state operational model. These changes result in a reduction in taxable income in most of the distribution entities and a corresponding increase in taxable income in the entity (CentralCo) in which functions and decision making processes were centralized.

In response to the restructuring, a tax authority in the jurisdiction of one of the distribution entities asserts a taxable gain as a result of the "shift" in profits. In particular, the tax authority argues that the intercompany agreement between the distribution entity and CentralCo was not arm's length because it did not provide the distribution entity with any right to compensation as a result of the restructuring.

Corp E's research indicates that competitors in the industry have restructured relationship with third-party distributors without making compensatory payments. Furthermore, Corp E determines that is has similarly restructured (e.g., walked away from) relationships with independent distributors in certain markets without making compensatory payments. Furthermore, Corp E's legal and economic analysis indicates that CentralCo is not making use of any asset legally owned by the distribution entity.

As a result of its bottom-up oriented legal and economic analysis, Corp E can present comparable "transactions" which involve no compensatory payment and can argue that there was no specifically identifiable asset transferred from the distribution entity to CentralCo. Of course, if the analysis had determined otherwise, it might have been necessary to move to step 2, and value the asset transferred and/or compensation right.

Conclusion

In today's global business arena, operationally driven business restructuring is likely to have unintended, as well as intended, tax implications. The conversion of full risk entities to limited risk entities is creating an increasingly vexing tax issue for tax authorities and taxpayers alike. The top-down, DCF-based approach undertaken by many tax jurisdictions in assessing this issue is limited by its all-encompassing, and often erroneous, view of the potential gain. A more precise determination of the conversion issue is achieved by a bottom-up approach which addresses the appropriate legal considerations and values only those assets, if any, which are transferred and for which the converted entity has a legal right to compensatory payment.

Tobin Hopkins is a Principal in Ernst & Young's National Transfer Pricing Practice in the U.S. and focuses on assisting multinational corporations on transfer pricing and implementation issues within the context of Tax Effective Supply Chain Management (TESCM). He can be reached at **(312) 879-3137** or by email at **tobin.hopkins@ey.com**.

For more information on the author, please see Section XIII.

Applying the Arm's Length Principle to Valuing "Exit Charges"

Robert Miall
Ernst & Young

Introduction

The restructuring of a line of business across a region or the world as a whole, and the associated changes in transfer pricing, inevitably results in the reduction of taxable profits in one or more countries, even though the intended overall result will be to increase profitability for the corporation as a whole.

Tax authorities in the countries in which profitability has fallen will often argue that the restructuring gives rise to a taxable event under capital gains and/or transfer pricing legislation. More particularly, they will generally assert that the reduction in profitability is the starting point for determining the basis for the tax charge, whether that be on a net present value basis or some multiple of the profit reduction. The question arises whether such an approach is consistent with the arm's length principle.

In September 2008, the OECD published a "discussion draft" on Business Restructuring[1] which explores, among other issues, when, at arm's length, a restructuring would result in one party making a compensation payment to the other. Among other points made in the discussion draft are that profit potential is not itself an asset.

This article further develops the framework outlined in the discussion draft and explores when, based on the economic principles underlying the OECD Transfer Pricing Guidelines, a compensation payment would be made in the context of a business restructuring,

Why the Loss of Profits Approach is Partial and Generally Inconsistent With The Arm's Length Principle

As the OECD's discussion draft recognizes, a loss of profit approach is not consistent with the internationally recognized standard for valuing transactions within multinational groups, i.e., the arm's length principle.

In place of the loss of profit approach, a framework is needed which is fully compatible with the arm's length principle. Again, as the OECD recognizes, the starting point must be a recognition of a fundamental requirement for unrelated parties to transact with one another: if the transaction is to take place, both parties must expect that they will be better off, or at least no worse off, as a result. As will be apparent, the application of this, apparently obvious, principle is helpful in narrowing down the range of outcomes from a negotiation which can be regarded as arm's length.

The "loss of profits" approach will

---

[1] Transfer Pricing Aspects of Business Restructuring: discussion draft for public comment, Organisation for Economic Co-operation and Development, September 2008

often not be within this range. Why would the owner of valuable intellectual property make a payment to its existing licensee linked to loss of profit in order to realize the benefits of appointing a new licensee in a lower cost location? Clearly, from the licensor's perspective, the relevant issues are the legal rights of the parties and the potential costs in terms of loss of sales if the transfer of production is not effected smoothly. From the licensee's perspective, the question is whether it has any legal rights and, beyond these, any alternative to agreeing to the restructuring. The loss of profit of the licensee is largely irrelevant to the evaluation of these issues.

As this example makes clear, an arm's length analysis of restructuring transactions must consider the alternatives available to bath parties. In the remainder of this article, two case studies are presented, which are based on our experience of applying "bargaining theory" to restructuring transactions.

Technical Framework

The starting point for a bargaining analysis is a recognition that, in approaching a negotiation, no party will accept an outcome that will leave it worse off than it would be if it adopted one of the other alternatives that are available to it.

In evaluating the alternatives open to them, the parties to a negotiation must recognize that their value may depend on the actions that the other party would take if the negotiation does not succeed. For instance, developing the example earlier in this section, the former licensees would need to take account of the prospect of competition from other producers in evaluating whether to go it alone.

Bargaining analysis therefore goes beyond the familiar insight that opportunity cost (i.e., treating profits foregone as a cost of an alternative strategy) is the appropriate basis for evaluating decisions by taking into account strategic interactions. It builds on the fact that it is an essential feature of a bargain freely entered into by two parties that each party should have no option open to them that yields a better result given the option selected by the other party. For, if this condition is not met, one party will not accept that outcome and the parties must continue to seek an alternative if they are to work together.

The first step in a bargaining analysis is therefore to identify the range of outcomes that meet the condition that neither party should have a better alternative given the strategy of the other party. "Outcomes" are to be seen in this context as combinations of strategic choices (e.g., "close down," "remain in the market," "set up alternative manufacturing capability" and associated payments).

Only outcomes meeting the "neither party has a better alternative" test can be considered "arm's length." This is because other outcomes fail to satisfy the principle that economic agents will choose the best alternative open to them given the constraints that they face. This principle underpins most economic theories, including those relating to the functions of markets which are the starting point for transfer pricing analysis.

A bargaining analysis may lead to the conclusion that there are no outcomes meeting the key requirement that neither party should have a better alternative given the option selected by the other party (when the parties have other, attractive alternatives); many outcomes (when both parties nave a lot to gain from working together); or, at least in principle, a single outcome (this is most likely when one party will gain but the other is largely indifferent to the outcome of negotiations).

Most particularly, in the absence of a

legal right, bargaining analysis suggests that it is unlikely that parties operating at arm's length would agree on payments related to the level of profit to be given up by one party when negotiating a restructuring of the kind analyzed here unless that party had a realistic alternative which would yield a similar level of profitability.

If it is the case that many outcomes meet the fundamental requirements for an arm's length outcome, in a second stage of analysis, it is necessary to predict which of these outcomes would be the result at arm's length. This analysis may be no more than the application of a rule of thumb asserting that the outcome of a negotiation is likely to be a sharing of the surplus arising from working together; or it may involve a detailed contribution analysis or the adoption of gain sharing analysis using other game theoretic techniques.

The two case studies address the two restructuring issues which are encountered most frequently: restructuring of distribution and manufacturing activities. The examples include elements from real cases on which we have advised. However, they are simplified in order to focus on the key message from this article. The simplifications include the fact that it is assumed that only two parties are involved in the negotiation. Including three or more parties considerably complicates the analysis without changing the results that this article seeks to demonstrate.

It should be emphasized that the analysis is not of the "cookie cutter" type. In undertaking a bargaining analysis, it is essential to take account of the facts and circumstances of the industry, the specific taxpayer and the legal environment, as these will determine the alternative opportunities that would (hypothetically) be open to the parties to the transaction and the value of these opportunities.

Case Study One — Conversion From Full Function Manufacturing to Contract or Consignment Manufacturing

Background

Group A established its business in Europe through a series of acquisitions in the mid-1990s. Most of the companies it acquired principally served their own national markets, but some had significant exports or plants elsewhere in Europe.

Group A's products are relatively light. Moreover, there are economies form large scale production. Over the past few years, Group A has therefore been rationalizing production both to reduce the number of plants and to focus each of the remaining production facilities on a smaller number of specific product grades.

At the same time, the Group has been establishing national sales and marketing operations. These work closely with customers to develop packaging solutions which meet their requirements. These are now largely based on research and development undertaken in the U.S.

The national sales companies work with pan-European manufacturing management to determine which plant is best-placed to meet the customer's requirements.

In the interim, as this business model was being developed, the sales and marketing operations were structured as distributors purchasing from the production plants on the basis of a resale minus transfer pricing policy which targeted a 4% operating margin. The overall margin is 12%. The transfer pricing policy therefore resulted in the production entities being highly profitable. However, they have paid a 3% royalty to the U.S.

It was apparent that this policy was not suitable for the new business model, which was essentially driven by the sales and marketing operations. Group A considered adopting a centralized business model under which a principal company would transact with manufacturing and sales entities. However, it concluded that this would not adequately recognize the role of the sales and marketing operations. Under the new policy, the sales companies will therefore continue to purchase from the production plants and will also pay a royalty to the U.S. The production plants will be rewarded on a cost plus basis. As a result their profitability will be significantly reduced.

How should any restructuring payment to the production entities by the sales companies or the U.S. parent be determined?

In order to develop an "arm's length" answer to this question, we need to start by identifying the range of compensation payments which will leave both parties at least as well off as they would have been if they had pursued the next best alternative to conversion to consignment or contract manufacturing status. As a first step, it is necessary to understand the legal rights of the parties. The restructuring will involve the termination of:
- the licenses under which the production entities have used U.S. developed technology;
- the distribution agreements under which the sales companies have purchased from the production entities.

In addition to the provisions of these agreements, it is necessary to understand any rights the parties may have under civil law in relevant jurisdictions.

This is a vital step in the analysis, although it must be recognized that it may not be in the interests of the parties fully to enforce their legal rights.

As a result of the analysis, it is determined that, provided relevant notice periods are observed, the parties will have no right to compensation. However, the production companies have some residual intellectual property as some product grades that they developed are still marketed.

Consideration must now be given to the commercial alternatives available to the parties.

For the sales companies, the issues are:
- on what terms could they themselves manufacture or purchase from another party the packaging products they require?
- can the product IP owned by the production entities be replicated and, if not, what loss of margin would be involved?
- how quickly could an alternative production source be established and what dislocation costs would be incurred in shifting production without the cooperation of the existing production plants?

Unless the production plants have some special cost or other advantage over competitors, the presumption is that alternative supplies could, in time, be obtained on the same terms as would apply if the existing production entity converted to a consignment or contract manufacturer (i.e., the cost plus method can be used to value the sales companies next best alternative).

Taken together, these considerations imply that the maximum compensation the sales companies would be prepared to pay is defined by the dislocation cost of switching to new suppliers including the cost of replicating product IP and any short- or long-term loss of sales. This amount is clearly not related to the loss of profit to the production entities if they convert to contract manufacturing.

In principle, the alternatives for the production entities are:
a) to continue as a full function manufacturer developing a new route to market;
b) to continue manufacturing relying on residual product IP,
c) to act as a contract/consignment manufacturer for other principals realizing any sales value from their IP, or
d) to close down.

The market is a competitive one and the production facilities are flexible. As significant costs would be involved, the last of these options is clearly less attractive than the third and is considered no further.

Moreover, it can reasonably be assumed that the terms available from other principals would be the same as those arising from the application of the cost plus method.

The key question for the production entities is therefore whether they have a more profitable future as full function manufacturers once allowance is made for the costs associated with developing a new route to market and for developing a new product range.

Analysis shows that it would take several years to develop an adequate product range (as compared to a one-year period under the license). In the meantime, the residual product portfolio would not be sufficient to achieve profitability.

In these circumstances, the best available alternative for the production entities would be to act as a contract/consignment manufacturer for other principals.

Conclusion on Arm's Length Compensation Payment

The bargaining position of the production entities is very weak. They do not have the option of continuing in business and generating their historic levels of profitability as they were reliant on the license from the U.S. which will be terminated. Indeed, contract/manufacturing for other principals is their best alternative and the minimum compensation they would accept is the sale value of their residual product IP.

However, the sales companies would be prepared to make a payment to avoid the disruption costs of switching to other suppliers and of replicating the IP owned by the production entities.

The arm's length compensation payment is therefore between the sales value of the product IP of the production entities and the disruption costs of the sales companies.

Case Study Two Restructuring of Distribution Activities

Background

Group B is a long-established consumer products group with products in a number of food categories and sales in all the major markets in Europe. Over time, as a result of pressures form its distribution companies, the Group has developed a profusion of products tailored to the perceived requirements of local markets.

Historically, the group was very profitable with margins of around 10%. The historic transfer pricing policy applied common prices to all countries and these were set at a relatively low level to ensure all distribution affiliates were profitable. Nevertheless, the Group also made significant profits in its domestic market and reasonable margins on exports.

Increased competition has made both the commercial and the transfer pricing model unsustainable. Following a study of the progress of convergence across European markets in its chosen categories, the Group has decided to focus on a core range products within each category. This will reduce manufacturing supply chain costs and permit the centralization of most marketing activity. In addition:
- strategic responsibility for major retail customers will be centralized;
- logistics will be largely outsourced.

As a result, the future role of the distribution companies will be limited to:
- local marketing activities within a framework and budget which is closely controlled from the centre;
- account management for national wholesale and retail customers;
- local implementation of account plans for pan-European customers;
- a limited logistics role focusing on checking orders and dealing with any problems experienced by customers.

In recognition of their reduced responsibilities, the distribution companies will be rewarded in the future on a resale minus basis targeting a 2.5% operating margin. In some countries, this will result in a margin reduction of 5% or more.

How should any restructuring payment to the distribution entities be determined?

Again, in order to provide an "arm's length" answer to this question it is necessary to:
- identify the range of compensation payments which will leave both parties at least as well off as they would have been if they pursued the next best alternative to conversion to the new distribution model;
- set the analysis in the context of the legal rights of the parties.

In particular, in some countries distributors enjoy clearly defined legal rights which are likely to define the minimum level of a compensation payment (e.g., Germany). However, this is not the case in all countries (e.g. generally the UK).

The commercial analysis in this case is somewhat simpler than in the case of Group A. In the event of the impending failure of negotiations with an unrelated distributor, the best option available to Group B would be to terminate with due notice and facilitate the establishment of new distributors.

The cost of doing this, together with any loss of margin resulting from a dip in sales resulting from the transition, would comprise the total cost of implementing the strategy and therefore place a ceiling on the amount Group B would be prepared to pay a distributor to incentivize it to participate in the new business model.

For the distributors, the issue would be whether they would have the opportunity to gain an appointment by another manufacturer and the transitional costs associated with this strategy.

In the product categories in which it operates, and of which its distributors are knowledgeable, Group B has been relatively slow in moving towards a pan-European product strategy and a centralized business model. There is therefore a presumption that it would be difficult for distributors to replace Group B. Their best alternative strategy would therefore be to work with another supplier on a similar basis to the appointment proposed (according to the arm's length principle) by Group B.

Conclusion on Arm's Length Compensation Payment

Like the Group A sales and marketing companies, the central Group B entity was in a strong position in an arm's length negotiation on the restructuring of commercial terms following a change in the business model. This is because, at arm's length, it would have had a credible alternative strategy. Group B's willingness to pay compensation would again be limited by the disruption costs it would avoid if its distribution companies agreed to the restructuring of the relationship.

This amount was very significantly less than the loss of profits earned by the distribution companies.

Conclusion

The clear message from these case studies is that loss of profits is only the relevant basis for compensation payments if the entity which has been converted would, if independent, have the ability to continue to generate a similar level of profits. In practice, within integrated multinational groups this is unlikely to be the case. Instead, the main focus should be on the alternatives available to the principal to the conversion transaction (i.e., the converting entity) and the transition costs it would incur in securing the services of an alternative manufacturer or distributor.

Robert Miall is a Director in Ernst & Young's UK Transfer Pricing Practice with over twenty year's experience of applying economics to business. He can be reached in E&Y's London office at **(44) 2-07-951-1411** or by email at **rmiall@uk.ey.com**.

For more information on the author, please see Section XIII.

Business Restructuring Expenses — Tax Challenges and Opportunities

by Danny Oosterhoff
Ernst & Young

Introduction

Business restructuring represents an area of concern for many developed countries. The trend towards outsourcing, transferring activities to low labor cost countries and associated factory closures, especially in developed countries, has triggered numerous debates. Furthermore, business restructuring that is driven by centralization typically entails a movement of activities, and therefore a potential source of taxable profits, from one country to smother. The focus of today's multinational enterprise on the opportunities that may arise out of business restructuring has attracted the attention of governments and tax authorities. Countries (and/or regions) affected by plant closures, reductions in both back-office and front-end activities, closures of technology centers, etc. are typically confronted with layoffs and the threat of losing valuable know-how embedded with the activities that are moving out. The media, workers' representatives and political parties tend to scrutinize such initiatives in view of the impact this may have on local economies. The opportunities and upsides of globalization are generally embraced but the downsides (such as loss of employment) are highly sensitive.

This article specifically discusses the tax treatment of business restructuring expenses. The risk of non-deductibility in the country where the costs are initially incurred and the associated exposure to double taxation poses a real challenge for multinational enterprise.[1] Nonetheless, the tax treatment of restructuring expenses creates opportunities as well as threats, not least because there is very little case law about this specific topic. This article provides an overview of the key issues and provides suggestions for a framework to mitigate the risks of double taxation.

Applying The Arm's Length Principle to Business Restructuring Expenses

Within many multinational enterprises, the decision to restructure the (global) business, to transfer business activities, to move production and/or close a factory or to transfer service centers are typically not taken at a local country or entity level. On the contrary, this type of decision- making typically takes place at the corporate or regional headquarters while the impact of the underlying decisions can have profound consequences for an affiliated enterprise that may be able to assert little or no control over such decision-making. The impact of centralized decision-making on individual

---

[1] Tax authorities can also bring up the notion of an indemnification payment in order to seek compensation for the costs of business restructuring. Although such scrutiny does not entail the risk of non-deductibility it may effectively result in a similar threat in the sense that business restructuring expenses may not erode the local tax base.

group companies is arguably the starting point for approaching the underlying taxation issues from a transfer pricing perspective. The key question is how the aim's length principle applies to business restructuring, especially in view of the fact that business restructuring cannot always be brought back to specific intercompany transactions for which an arm's length price needs to be determined.

A broad interpretation of the word "conditions," as found in paragraph 1 of Article 9 of the OECCD Model Tax Convention, may provide the most direct link for applying the arm's length principle to business restructuring:

> "[When] conditions are made or imposed between. . . two [associated] enterprises in their commercial or financial relations which differ from those which would have been made between independent enterprises, then any profits which would, but for those conditions, have accrued to one of the enterprises, but by reason of these conditions, have not so accrued, may be included in the profits of that enterprise's and taxed accordingly."

Furthermore, the OECD Transfer Pricing Guidelines state the following:[2]

"Independent enterprises when evaluating the terms of a potential transaction, will compare the transaction to the other options realistically available to them, and they will only enter into the transaction if they see no alternative that is clearly more attractive."

By using a broad interpretation of "condition," one can arguably extend the application of the arm's length principle to business restructuring in general. Bearing the costs of a business reorganization can potentially be viewed as an "imposed condition" for which an "arm's length" analysis should be made to evaluate what conditions should apply, also in light of potential alternative options. The key questions are, however, to what extent can one find third-party comparisons under similar circumstances and to what extent are there real alternatives. Furthermore, the OECD guidance for evaluating alternative options is geared towards establishing comparability for comparing a transaction between affiliated parties with a transaction between independent parties. This guidance cannot necessarily be interpreted as guidance for replacing a transaction between affiliated enterprises for an "entirely different transaction"

The Tax Framework

Restructuring, reorganization and closure costs can be defined as both direct and indirect costs incurred by a company in connection with the restructuring, transfer and/or closure of a certain business activity. Such costs typically include severance costs, accelerated depreciation charged write-offs and costs of external advisers. Local tax authorities tend to scrutinize such expenses, especially if these costs are not perceived to benefit the local company.

The argument used by tax authorities to support the position that costs are not deductible is often based on the notion that the costs should have been allocated to other group companies (in view of the fact that other affiliates either took the decision and/or benefited from the activities). Alternatively, tax authorities simply assert that the extraordinary expenses do not benefit the local activities and cannot therefore be deducted. The latter position is arguably difficult to align with the tax code in many countries, but the underlying arguments of the tax authorities reveal an

---

2   OECD Guidelines, paragraph 1.15.

evolving interpretation of the arm's length principle.

However, whether or not such expenses would be deductible and/or should be borne by other group companies under local tax legislation/practice, depends on a number of different factors, including the following:
- specific local tax provisions pertaining to deductibility, especially since business expenditure should in principle be deductible under most tax regimes;
- the relationship between (extraordinary) expenses and a closure;
- the decision-making model applied (which party made the decision);
- the potential relationship between expenses and services; and
- the benefit test under the OECD Transfer Pricing Guidelines.

As already mentioned, there is little or no case law to narrow the range of potential outcomes, which depends on the specific facts and circumstances under local tax law and practice. If business restructuring expenses in certain cases are deemed non-deductible locally, then an allocation model may be the right method of avoiding/mitigating double taxation.

An Analytical Framework

Under most tax frameworks, one of the first questions that should be investigated is whether the restructuring costs are geared towards improving the business. A distinction can be made between an evaluation of benefits on a company-wide basis (i.e., evaluating the business benefits on an integrated company basis) versus evaluating the benefits on a local country basis (i.e., the starting-point of most tax authorities, although there is room for interpretation whether the "business rationale" of a restructuring should be evaluated from a country versus company perspective). Despite the fact that tax authorities are clearly focused on "local country benefits," there is still very little jurisprudence (internationally) that specifically states that one should focus on local country benefits. Even if local focus is needed, cases can be made to support an indirect local country benefit. For example, local distribution operations can benefit from lower-priced products due to the closure of (expensive) local production and subsequent shift to low-cost production.

The OECD Transfer Pricing Guidelines do not specifically discuss this topic as such. In fact, they recognize that the arm's length principle does not always account for the "economies of scale and interrelation of diverse activities created by integrated businesses. There are, however, no widely accepted objective criteria for allocating the economies of scale benefits or integration between associated enterprises."[3]

Furthermore, it is difficult to align incurred reorganization expenses with specific transactions between associated enterprises. The guidance for applying the arm's length principle under the framework of the OECD Transfer Pricing Guidelines is very much focused on actual transactions. Although they do not discuss specific criteria for either allocating benefits or costs, one can use the rationale of the benefit test under Chapter 7 with regard to intra-group services.

"Under the arm's length principle, the question whether an intra-group service has been rendered when an activity is performed for one or more group members by another group member should depend on whether the activity provides a respective group member with economic or commercial value to enhance its commercial position."[4]

---
[3] OECD Guidelines, paragraph 1.9.
[4] OECD Guidelines, paragraph 7.6.

It can be argued that reorganizing business operations can be qualified as an activity that benefits one or more group companies. Furthermore, it needs to be considered whether "an independent enterprise would have been willing to pay for the activity."[5] Since business restructuring is typically geared towards improving the operations and the profitability of the MNE as a whole and thus its individual subsidiaries, one can expect that an independent party would be willing to pay for an initiative that improves the actual profitability or even the certainty of profitability over time.

The same consideration can analogously be applied to the party who either performed the business restructuring activity or was impacted by this reorganization. Would a company incur reorganization and/or closure costs for transferring/terminating its business operations, under comparable circumstances if it were an independent company?

Approaching the topic from this angle generally strengthens the argument for allocating such costs to the companies that ultimately benefit from the reorganization. Moreover, this type of reasoning does not necessarily provide the local tax authorities with a sufficient position for declaring reorganization costs as non-deductible. A thorough analysis of the specific rules for deductibility under local tax codes will help in determining the likelihood that tax authorities can successfully assert non-deductibility. Furthermore, independent parties are often confronted with the necessity to close sites in view of non-competitive cost-bases and other competitive forces. It may very well be that due to increased competition, it is no longer possible to maintain production in a high-cost jurisdiction and that the options available are very limited.

Finally, the OECD Transfer Pricing Guidelines also provide guidance in their discussion on comparability factors.

They consider "whether there is a plausible expectation that following the business strategy the enterprise will produce a return sufficient to justify its costs within a period of time that would be acceptable in an arm's length situation."[6] Such a consideration is clearly geared towards the perspective of the local company and thus the benefit test from the individual group company perspective. When approaching the topic of business restructuring expenses from this angle, therefore, an additional argument can be found that supports the notion of allocation.

Thus the OECD Transfer Pricing Guidelines offer a number of references that would support the application of economics models that account for the benefits to justify, in some cases, the allocation of the business restructuring costs.

Two different conceptual allocation models are discussed further below — either may be applicable in instances where a case exists for allocation of the relevant costs.

a) Alignment with decision-making model

Alignment with a decision-making model may be consistent with the OECD's continued focus on alignment between functions and risks. If risks can only partially be isolated from the underlying functionality[7] of managing such risks, then an analogue model could be applied to the financial consequences of decision-

---

5 Id.

6 OECD Guidelines, paragraph 1.35.
7 OECD Guidelines, paragraph 1.21 and 1.25.

Organizational Structure

making. Under such a scenario, (the bulk of) closure costs should be allocated to the decision-making entity within a multinational enterprise which typically is a (regional) headquarters.

However, if an MNE's overall transfer pricing system only remunerates the decision-maker/headquarters within the group as a service provider, then this model would conflict with the overall transfer pricing system and/or cannot be easily aligned with the benefit test. Thus, this model would be less appropriate to decentralized organizations with headquarters operating as mere service providers to the operating companies. After all, within such organizations, the headquarters are typically compensated on a cost plus basis, which would not justify absorbing extraordinary closure costs that are incurred locally. Consequently, this model would arguably work best for companies with a principal/centralized business model structure whereby the principal central entrepreneur is the decision-maker as well as the party that is entitled to the excess profits within the MNE.

b) Alignment with the "benefit test"

As previously discussed, the benefit test primarily plays a role in the OECD Transfer Pricing Guidelines Chapter on Intra-Group Services. Nonetheless, there are often distinct anticipated benefits from business restructuring that should be realized within the MNE. A number of options are discussed below that pertain to models for allocating restructuring costs consistently with how (expected) benefits are allocated, specifically in relation to plant closures.

- **Transferred production output allocation key:** It may be possible to apply an allocation based on identifiable transferred production output. If plant closures are combined with increased production capacity (utilization) in other plants, then the other plants could be allocated their fair share of closure costs proportionately to their share in increased production capacity. Such an analysis should account for return on investment considerations. In other words, to what extent does the allocated cost portion translate to a reasonable return on investment over time? The return on investment threshold would function as a cap to limit any extraordinary costs that would prevent the entity from realizing a reasonable return.
- **Lost production output allocation key:** An alternative allocation key could be based on "forgiven" production capacity, especially in cases where no production was transferred to other production sites. If plant closures are driven by less demand or other factors that drive down a MNE's need for production output, then the costs of the lost production output (i.e., the plant closure costs) can be shared amongst the remaining plants relative to their plant capacity (or utilized capacity).
- **Allocation to central entrepreneur:** An allocation to a central entrepreneur is essentially based on a benefit allocation resulting from the overall responsibility model and underlying transfer pricing methodologies. Closure costs can be allocated directly to the ultimate beneficiaries of business restructuring. Under a centralized business model, it will be the principal which manages and bears most business risks and thus is entitled to the anticipated financial benefits, assuming that the other activities are legitimately treated as limited risk-

low return activities.

These options should account for efficiency aspects as well because individual plant closures may be driven by a non-competitive cost-base. This would mean that the parties that benefit from the restructuring would not necessarily absorb all the restructuring expenses.

Application of an Economic Approach

The following short illustrative case study provides an example of how in practice an economic approach to business restructuring provided for a framework for allocating business restructuring costs.

An international organization active in the development, production and sales of small engines for industrial use was confronted with less demand in the marketplace for its products. Its manufacturing facilities had been

Plants	Annual output @75% (units)	Forecast reduction in demand (units)
Plant A	4,000	400
Plant B	3,000	300
Plant C	5,000	500

running (on average) at 75% utilization. The reduced demand meant an expected further reduction in utilization. The organization had three manufacturing facilities in three different locations and was faced with the decision to close one facility and to optimize the utilization in the two remaining facilities.

The forecast annual demand approximated 11,800 units (with no evident risk of subsequent upturn). Plants A and C combined had a production capacity of 12,000 units. Consequently, the organization decided to close plant B and to transfer the production to both plants A and C. The closure of plant B triggered extraordinary restructuring costs of approximately €2 million. In view of the fact that plants A and C benefited from the closure of plant B, it was decided — on the facts — that an allocation of restructuring costs would be reasonable. The starting point of this allocation was based both on the additional output that was transferred to these plants and the simulation of the avoided reduction in capacity utilization (in plants A and C) if plant B would not have been closed.

The resulting allocation of the restructuring cost entailed that Plant A's share approximated €890,000 while plant C's share approximated €1,110,000. However, an additional analysis was done from the perspective of plants A and C.

Based on return on investment calculations, it could be demonstrated that a third party would only have been willing to pay €712,000 and €880,000, respectively. Consequently, approximately €408,000 of the incurred reorganization costs in plant B could not be allocated to plants A and C and was therefore retained locally, and a deduction sought.

The underlying analysis provided the framework for allocating cost aligned with the received benefits. Furthermore, the two-sided approach (i.e., the perspective from the transferor and transferee) provided the framework for substantiating what part of the costs should be kept locally.

It is important to note that the outcome of any such analysis very much depends on specific facts and circumstances. First of all, a detailed analysis should be made that considers all relevant factors, such as those discussed throughout this article. Secondly, the absence of specific case law alongside the twin factors of the risk of double

Organizational Structure

taxation and the opportunity legitimately to enhance the overall tax position are factors in play. They may influence the options to take a position to either deduct costs locally or to allocate costs to other group companies. This article provides a framework for considering different options and developing arguments that can be used for either deducting centrally, or allocating business restructuring expenses (or a combination thereof). This is likely to be a challenge for the foreseeable future, and MNEs are invited to consider this framework in facing that challenge.

Danny Oosterhoff is responsible for Ernst & Young's transfer pricing group in Amsterdam. Danny has specialized in transfer pricing services since 1996 and joined Ernst & Young's economic consulting practice in Chicago for one year in 1998 as a member of the European transfer pricing desk. He can be reached at **(31) 2-0-546-6007** or by email at **danny.oosterhoff@nl.ey.com**.
For more information on the author, please see Section XIII.

VI. Services

Key Considerations when Applying the New Service Regulations – Treas. Reg. § 1.482-9

Sean F. Foley, Robert D. Baldassarre, and Tamara Berner Gracon
KPMG LLP

The IRS released the final service regulations under Code Section 482 in July of 2009 ("the Final Regulations") regarding the treatment of controlled services transactions. While the Final Regulations make relatively few changes to the Temporary Service Regulations released in July of 2006, there are some important items taxpayers and practitioners should be aware of in the Service Regulations. This article highlights certain key provisions in the Final Regulations that, in our experience, raise significant issues for companies engaged in related-party services transactions and discusses how these issues can be addressed for tax years beginning after July 31, 2009. Specifically, the article focuses on 1) documentation requirements when applying the Services Cost Method, 2) the inclusion of stock-based compensation in the cost base that must be charged-out under certain methods in the new regulations, 3) the treatment of U.S. headquarter expenses, and 4) practical applications of contingent-payment service arrangements.

Qualification and Documentation Requirements of the Services Cost Method

Potentially, the most significant methodology specified under the Final Regulations is the services cost method (SCM) which has been carried over from the Temporary Regulations. As described under Treas. Reg. §1.482-9(b)(1), the SCM is essentially a cost safe harbor, allowing certain "covered services" to be charged out or allocated to a related entity without a markup. To qualify for the SCM:

- the service must be a covered service[1];
- the service cannot be an excluded activity;
- the service cannot be precluded from constituting a covered service by reason of the business judgment rule; and
- the taxpayer must maintain adequate books and records with respect to the service.

In addition to the above qualifications, taxpayers are obliged to fulfill certain documentation requirements to support the SCM election. These new documentation requirements initially created a fair amount of taxpayer confusion. In response, the IRS issued Notice 2007-5 (the "Notice"), which set forth several clarifications pertaining to the documentation requirements under Treas. Reg. § 1.482-9T(b)(3)(i).

Consistent with the clarifications provided in the Notice, the Final Regulations confirm that the SCM is an elective method and reiterates that

---

[1] Covered service must be either a low margin services (taxpayer can find a set of comparables with a median of 7.0 percent or less) or be a "specified covered service" as found in a revenue procedure issued by the IRS (currently Rev. Proc. 2007-13).

a statement evidencing the taxpayer's intent to apply the SCM is required as a necessary condition when electing to apply the SCM. The statement must be included in the books and records under Treas. Reg. § 1.482-9(b)(6).

Section 3.06 of the Notice clarified that the documentation and support (books and records) required for services analyzed under the SCM (Treas. Reg. § 1.482-9 (b)(3)(i)) need not be generated contemporaneously with the filing of the income tax return. This clarification means that supporting SCM documentation, which would include a statement that the taxpayer intended to apply the SCM and any comparable set establishing that the transactions are in fact low margin, can be prepared after the tax return is filed, apparently at any time up to and including a subsequent IRS audit of the year in question. This flexibility surrounding the documentation of the SCM can be useful for taxpayers, but also presents a potential trap for the unwary. For a taxpayer that did not prepare documentation supporting the SCM contemporaneously with the filing of its return, it is helpful that the taxpayer can prepare the necessary documentation to support the application of the SCM as needed, e.g., perhaps even as late as the time of an IRS audit. As long as the IRS agrees on audit that the services are SCM eligible, there may not be tax consequences for delaying the preparation of the SCM documentation. However, should the IRS disagree with characterization of the services as SCM eligible, such non-contemporaneous documentation would not provide penalty protection under Treas. Reg. § 1.6662-6. For that reason, a leading practice may be for a taxpayer to prepare the documentation before it files its tax return to mitigate potential penalty risk, no matter how remote.

Stock-Based Compensation[2]

One of the more commented upon aspects in the Temporary Regulations and a lingering issue with the Final Regulations is the inclusion of stock based compensation in the cost base. The preamble to the regulations states that "the Treasury Department and the IRS continue to consider technical issues involving stock-based compensation in the services and other contexts and intend to address those issues in a subsequent guidance project."[3]

Upon closer inspection the issue of how stock-based compensation ought to be treated under the services regulations is much clearer than how it ought to be treated for purposes in other areas of the IRC. The services regulations are concerned with how much a U.S. participant should charge a foreign party for performing services (or vice versa). This generally requires a determination of an arm's-length charge for services. While stock-based compensation expense is a component used in benchmarking such an arm's-length charge under some methods, stock-based compensation is not relevant to the application of other transfer pricing methods. Thus, when stock option expenses distort the analysis because they bear no reasonable relationship to the value of the services rendered, taxpayer may choose (or indeed be required) to apply pricing methods that do not take into account stock-based compensation expenses.

Two pricing methods for services require a measure of stock-based compensation: the SCM and the comparable profits method

---

[2] Thomas Zollo and Charles Cope "The Services Regulations Go Final, But an Issue Lingers" September 14, 2009. Available for external delivery please contact KPMG's What's News in Tax inbox at email address: us-wntwhatsnewsintax@kpmg.com for a copy of this article.

[3] 74 Fed. Reg. at 38835.

applied using the ratio of operating profit to total services costs as the appropriate profit level indicator.[4] In practice, these two methods are the most commonly applied methods. The former is a "cost only" safe harbor for certain specified services that are not core to a controlled group's business.[5] The latter, commonly referred to as the "net cost plus method," benchmarks an arm's-length service charge based upon the net profit markups observed from the public filings of a set of comparable service companies.[6]

The SCM and the net cost plus method both require the determination of the service provider's "total services costs." "Total services costs" is defined as:

> [All] costs of rendering those services for which total services costs are being determined. Total services costs include all costs in cash or in kind (including stock-based compensation) that, based on analysis of the facts and circumstances, are directly identified with, or reasonably allocated…to, the services. In general, costs for this purpose should comprise provision for all resources expensed, used or made available to achieve the specific objective for which the service is rendered. *Reference to generally accepted accounting principles or Federal income tax accounting rules may provide a useful starting point but will not necessarily be conclusive regarding inclusion of costs in total services costs.* Total services costs do not include interest expense, foreign income taxes…or domestic income taxes.[7]

In the context of stock-based compensation, the italicized language from the quotation above raises the question of which accounting rules should be used to compute total services costs. This question is particularly acute in the case of stock options because the measurement of option expense under generally accepted accounting principles ("GAAP") can differ dramatically from the measurement under federal income tax accounting rules.

Under U.S. GAAP, FAS 123R requires that stock option expense be measured based on the fair value of the options at the time of grant. This value is then amortized into expense over the service period to which the options relate, i.e., generally the vesting period of the options. Under federal tax accounting rules, on the other hand, the deduction for stock options generally is allowed in the year of exercise in an amount equal to the difference between the fair market value of the option stock on the exercise date and the option's exercise price.[8]

Now consider how these different measurements of stock option expense might be applied in the context of the services regulations. First, as discussed above, the net cost plus method generally determines an arm's-length return for services rendered in a controlled services transaction by giving the service provider (the "tested party") a return on its total services cost based upon the returns a set of comparables earn on their total services costs. Generally, the acceptable return is limited to the inter-quartile range of the comparables' results.[9] In order to apply the net cost plus method reliably, "[c]onsistency in accounting practices between the relevant activity of the tested party and the uncontrolled service providers is particularly important…"[10] In order to achieve this consistency in

---

4 Stock option expenses may also be relevant to the application of the cost of services plus and the profit split methods.
5 See generally Trea. Reg. §1.482-9(b).
6 See generally Treas. Reg. §1.482-9(f).
7 Treas. Reg. §1.482-9(j) (emphasis added).
8 I.R.C. §83(h)
9 *See* Treas. Reg. §1.482-1(e)
10 Treas. Reg. §1.482-9(f)(2)(iii)

accounting practices, reliably applying the net cost plus method would invariably require using the tested party's GAAP computation of total services costs, including for stock option expenses, as those will be the only figures available for the comparable set. Using the tested party's section 83(h) amounts would create a lack of comparability for which no reasonably determinable adjustments could be made.

Whether stock-based compensation should be measured using GAAP or tax rules is less clear in the case of the SCM. Because that method is a safe harbor that does not depend upon benchmarking an arm's-length charge, no comparability analysis is required. As a consequence there is no requirement to look to publicly available data, i.e., data that would include a GAAP valuation. It appears that either the section 83(h) deduction amount or the GAAP value can be used for purposes of the SCM as referenced above in the definition of total services cost. Whether a taxpayer uses the section 83(h) deduction amount, or the GAAP value, the IRS would expect the taxpayer to take a consistent approach from year to year.

Non-Beneficial Services

For U.S. headquartered companies, the Final Regulations may provide particular challenges. Consistent with the former regulations under Treas. Reg. § 1.482-2(b), shareholder and other services that are not performed for the benefit of non-U.S. subsidiaries should not be charged-out. The issue for U.S. headquartered companies is that certain services, which some taxpayers may have considered non-beneficial in the past, are now to be treated as beneficial as described in the 21 examples in the Final Regulations. See Treas. Reg. § 1.482-9 (l)(5). Non-beneficial services under the Temporary Regulations include the following:
- indirect and remote benefit;
- duplicative activities;
- shareholder activities; and
- passive association.[11]

Collectively, the expenses associated with these non-beneficial services are sometimes informally referred to as stewardship expenses, although they may include expenses unrelated to the stewardship of the shareholder's investment. Under the former services regulations, there was little guidance on what was and was not a non-beneficial service. In our experience, many taxpayers do not charge out a significant share of their headquarters costs, taking the position that these headquarters services do not benefit their non-U.S. subsidiaries. Many taxpayers have found that large charges of headquarters costs can be difficult to sustain in non-U.S. jurisdictions. Non-U.S. tax authorities often challenge large headquarters charges, making it difficult to obtain a tax deduction. The lack of guidance in this area in the past sometimes assisted U.S. taxpayers to argue to the IRS that a relatively large part of their headquarters costs were non-beneficial and need not be charged-out.

The extensive detail on what is beneficial and what is not in the Final Regulations may elicit new scrutiny by the IRS on headquarters charges, and has the potential to create significant tax assessments. Consider the following example. A U.S. parented company has $40 million of U.S. headquarter expenses. This same company earns 50 percent of its revenue from its non-U.S. operations. Historically, this company has charged out $10 million of its U.S. headquarter costs. On audit, the IRS may argue that this company would be expected to charge out

---

11 See Treas. Reg. § 1.482-9 (l)(3)

one-half of it's headquarter expenses, or $20 million. Note that whether the company puts a mark-up on its headquarters charge can be much less significant as compared to the amount of cost base that is subject to the charge. Taxpayers will be well advised to review their headquarters costs in light of the Final Regulations and to better document their position on what costs should not be charged out.

Contingent Payments

Lastly, the Final Regulations provide for contingent payments under Treas. Reg. § 1.482-9(i)(1). Contingent payments arrangements among related parties must follow certain requirements set forth in Treas. Reg. § 1.482-9 (i)(2). The contingent payment arrangement must be documented in a written contract that specifies the contingency and the basis for payment which must be consistent with the economic substance of the controlled transaction in accordance with Treas. Reg. § 1.482-1(d)(3)(ii)(b). Of particular importance here is that this written agreement must be entered into prior to or contemporaneous with *the start* of the controlled services transaction. While contingent payment arrangements are generally well known in third party relationships involving the provision of services with uncertain outcomes, such as research and development or legal representation, such arrangements have been relatively uncommon in controlled service transactions between related parties. The express acknowledgement of the validity of these arrangements for controlled service transactions in the Final Regulations may encourage some taxpayers to structure related party agreements with a contingent payment arrangement. In some circumstance, such contingent arrangements may have significant tax advantages.

Conclusion

Despite the issuance of the Final Regulations in substantively the same form as the Temporary Regulations, taxpayers should remain focused on their intercompany service transactions and keep in mind some key points, such as:

Sean Foley is the U.S. principal in charge of KPMG's Global Transfer Pricing Services (GTPS) practice. **Robert D. Baldassare** and **Tamara Berner Gracon** are tax managing directors with the GTPS practice. Foley (sffoley@kpmg.com) is located in Washington, D.C., Baldassarre (rbaldassarre@kpmg.com) in Boston, and Gracon (tgracon@kpmg.com) in Mountain View, Calif.

KPMG LLP, the audit, tax and advisory firm (www.us.kpmg.com), is the U.S. member firm of KPMG International. KPMG International's member firms have 113,000 professionals, including more than 6,800 partners, in 148 countries.

This article represents the views of the authors only, and does not necessarily represent the views or professional advice of KPMG LLP.

The information contained herein is general in nature and based on authorities that are subject to change. Applicability to specific situations is to be determined through consultation with your tax adviser.

For more information on the authors, please see Section XIII.

- Taxpayers applying the new SCM should determine what level of supporting documentation they should create contemporaneous with their tax return;
- U.S. based taxpayers should review their headquarters charges to determine they have the proper amount charged out and that the reason for not charging out certain non-beneficial services is documented;
- Certain services that are charged with a profit element may be explicitly required to include stock based compensation in the chargeable cost base; and,
- Contingent payment arrangements present potential new opportunities for structuring related party transactions.

These are but a few of the more important elements of the final services regulations. Taxpayers should undertake a careful review of their intercompany services before the conclusion of the 2009 tax year to determine they are in compliance with the new Final Regulations.

A Practical Process and Approach to Implementing the New Transfer Pricing Service Regulations

Christopher Desmond and Ryan Lange
Ceteris, Inc.

With tax years beginning after August 1, 2009 many taxpayers expected to begin fully operating under the new transfer pricing services regulations[1] (hereinafter the "Service Regulations"). Prior to August, the temporary service regulations[2] are effective for tax years beginning after January 1, 2008. With the new regulations, taxpayers are struggling to understand what the impact may be to their companies and, moreover, what they need to do to be compliant.

In the past, services transactions have not appeared on the compliance radar of many, if not most, companies. As such, the new service regulations represent uncharted territory for many taxpayers and have many corporations wondering what they will find once they dig deeper into their services transactions. For many U.S.-Headquartered companies, examining their headquarter services and prospective new charges under the service regulations are getting top priority—not to mention that many believe the IRS also considers this a priority that may bring additional income into a U.S. taxpayers return. For companies operating within the service industry, they now need to document these charges under the new regime.

Taxpayers are asking many questions such as:
- "How do I calculate a fully-loaded cost base?"
- "Do I have to administer the charges with a markup?"
- "How do I interview my service centers for this analysis?" and
- "How do I implement the results?"

These are all valid questions, but afterthoughts to the foremost question of: "Where do I start?"

This article focuses on a practical approach that has been developed to analyze intercompany service transactions, as well as some best practices to complete and implement the results.

Background

Transfer pricing regulations for services have historically been vague and have lacked specific guidance on how to analyze intercompany service transactions when compared to the detailed regulations for both tangible and intangible transactions. Under the 1994 U.S. Treasury Regulations of Section 1.482-2, services transactions were discussed and the guidance for testing and evaluating services existed through such criteria as "peculiarly capable," "substantially in excess of

---

[1] Treatment of Services Under Section 482: Allocation of Income and Deductions from Intangible Property; Apportionment of Stewardship Expense.

[2] Internal Revenue Bulletin: 2007-3, Notice 2007-5, and Revenue Procedure 2007-13.

value," and the "four prong benefits test." This ambiguity and lack of specific transfer pricing methods often led to taxpayers ignoring headquarter and other service charges while the IRS experienced difficulty in enforcing adjustments and penalties on services transactions. Recently, intercompany service transactions have moved to the forefront because of the large impact they can have on one's transfer pricing policy. For example, in the Glaxo SmithKline Holdings (Americas) Case[3], reportedly the largest transfer pricing case ever settled, one of the main points of contention was marketing services and the potential intangibles they created for the U.S. entity. The case resulted in a record $3.4 billion dollar settlement payment from Glaxo to the IRS.

The IRS responded to years of feedback by introducing regulations specific to services transactions that were similar in detail to those for tangible transactions. The IRS' goal was to provide certainty concerning the pricing of certain low margin services and to give comfort with back-office services so taxpayers can invest their time towards transactions involving significant value.[4] The result was the release of the U.S. Department of the Treasury's final regulations for the treatment of services under Section 482[5], which provides taxpayers with the ability to charge routine intercompany services at cost to foreign affiliates under the Services Cost Method (SCM) and to charge non-routine services with an arm's length charge under a myriad of specific service methods.

For many multinational companies, service transactions comprise a significant segment of cross-border intercompany transactions; a growing piece of the corporate pie on which the IRS has been missing out. Now the challenge facing taxpayers is how to comply with the Service Regulations without undue burden.

A Practical Process

To assist many taxpayers who have asked for a practical approach in tackling these new service regulations, Ceteris has developed a systematic approach to analyzing, documenting and implementing intercompany services as illustrated in the Exhibit 1.

---

[3] On September 11, 2006 The Internal Revenue Service and Glaxo SmithKline Holdings (Americas) Inc. & Subsidiaries ("GSK") announced that they had reached a settlement involving their transfer pricing dispute. This case, which was pending in the United States Tax Court, is the largest single payment made to the IRS to resolve a tax dispute. Under the settlement agreement, GSK will pay the Internal Revenue Service approximately $3.4 billion. The Tax Court dispute for the years 1989-2000 involved intercompany transactions between GSK and certain of its foreign affiliates relating to various GSK "heritage" pharmaceutical products. Specifically at issue was the level of U.S. profits reported by GSK after making intercompany payments that took into account product intangibles developed by and trademarks owned by its U.K. parent, other activities outside the U.S., and the value of GSK's marketing and other contributions in the U.S. Under the settlement agreement, GSK conceded over 60% of the total amount put in issue by the two parties for the years pending in Tax Court. (Matthews, Robert Guy and Jeanne Whalen; "Glaxo to Settle Tax Dispute With IRS Over U.S. Unit for $3.4 Billion"; The Wall Street Journal; September 12, 2006; Page A3, and "Glaxo to Pay $3.4 Billion to Settle Largest Tax Dispute in IRS History"; BNA Transfer Pricing Report; Volume 15 Number 9; Wednesday September 13, 2006.).

[4] "Interview: Officials Reveal Thinking Behind IRS Transfer Pricing Projects"; BNA Transfer Pricing Report; Volume 16 Number 9; Thursday September 6, 2007.

[5] Treatment of Services Under Section 482: Allocation of Income and Deductions from Intangible Property; Apportionment of Stewardship Expense.

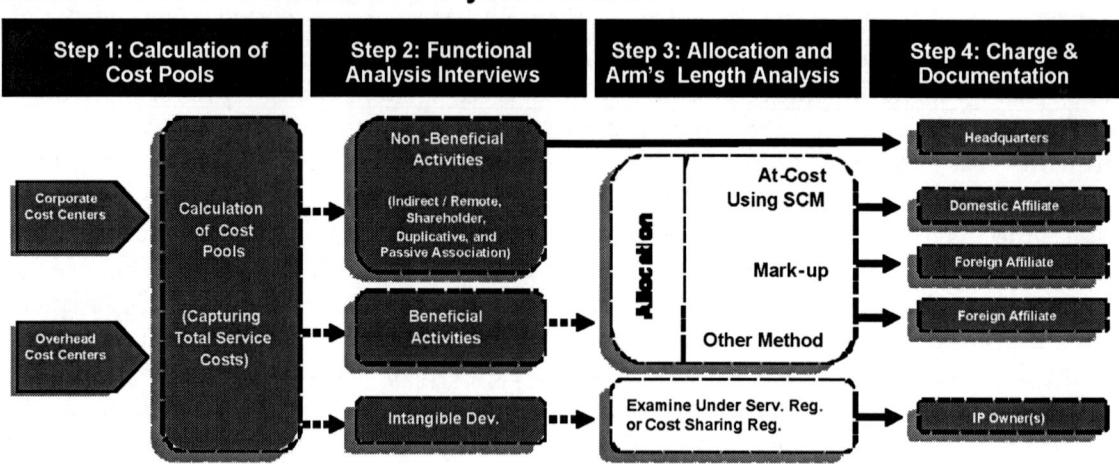

Exhibit 1: Ceteris Services Analysis Process

| Step 1: Calculation of Cost Pools | Step 2: Functional Analysis Interviews | Step 3: Allocation and Arm's Length Analysis | Step 4: Charge & Documentation |

- Corporate Cost Centers → Calculation of Cost Pools (Capturing Total Service Costs) ← Overhead Cost Centers
- Non-Beneficial Activities (Indirect / Remote, Shareholder, Duplicative, and Passive Association) → Headquarters
- Beneficial Activities → Allocation: At-Cost Using SCM / Mark-up / Other Method → Domestic Affiliate, Foreign Affiliate, Foreign Affiliate
- Intangible Dev. → Examine Under Serv. Reg. or Cost Sharing Reg. → IP Owner(s)

© 2009 CETERIS®, All Rights Reserved.

Each of the steps will be discussed in further detail below.

Step 1: Establish Fully-Loaded Cost Pools

Probably the most critical and overlooked step in the process is developing the fully-loaded cost pools. Many taxpayers receive initial cost center reports that only contain salaries and wages, but do not include all the other overhead costs that should be allocated to a cost pool. The purpose of this exercise is to create a cost pool for every Service Cost Center[6] that incorporates all the costs the Cost Center would bear if it were operating as an independent third party performing these services. Many taxpayers either utilize their most recent fiscal year of costs for the analysis or the most recent partial year with an adjustment to annualize the data.

The definition of a fully-loaded cost pool in the Service Regulations is as follows:

"Total services costs include all costs in cash or in kind (including stock-based compensation[7]) that... are directly identified with, or reasonably allocated...to the services. In general, costs for this purpose should comprise provision for all resources expended, used, or made available to achieve the specific objective for which the service is rendered."[8]

This process entails not only identifying all corporate services cost centers, but all overhead cost centers[9] as well, and further verifying that all necessary cost items are included and/or excluded

---

6 The term "Service Cost Center" is used within this article to identify groups of services that may perform functions that directly or indirectly impact foreign affiliates and need to be analyzed under the Service Regulations.

7 Under a fair value method in accordance with U.S. generally accepted accounting principles, companies include in total compensation the value of the stock options attributable to the employees' performance of the relevant business activity for the annual financial reporting period, and treat this amount as an expense in determining operating profit for financial accounting purposes. As such, these expenses should be included in the total services costs of the tested party.

8 § 1.482-9(j).

9 Overhead cost centers represent the operational costs needed to support and maintain core functions of the business. Examples of these costs are utilities expenses associated with a building, office supplies, cafeteria costs, etc.

in each individual cost center. Once all applicable cost centers are identified, it is then necessary to reasonably allocate and apportion the overhead costs to the corporate services cost centers to derive the fully-loaded cost pool for each corporate cost center. This first step is imperative as the new Service Regulations require that "allocation and apportionments of costs must be made on the basis of the full cost, as opposed to the incremental cost."[10] Again, this process is conducted to help calculate all the costs that would be captured by a third party performing the same services on a stand-alone basis.

Table 1 shows typical Service Cost Centers and overhead cost centers.

In Exhibit 1, the typical Service Cost Centers of a headquarter operation are identified on the left. To the right are the common overhead costs that should be reviewed and appropriately allocated to each of the Service Cost Centers. The item "Stock Option Expenses" is highlighted because it is a highly contested issue[11] in the U.S.; the IRS has explicitly addressed stock option expenses in the Service Regulations to ensure it is properly accounted for in fully-loaded cost calculations going forward. In addition, the service regulations do not give guidance on how to value stock options and this is a topic that the Service indicated they need to and will address in the future.[12]

After the fully-loaded corporate cost centers are calculated, the second part of Step 1 is identifying those cost centers that have prospective foreign benefit. This step is important as only those cost centers with prospective foreign benefit will require a functional interview. Taking the time up front to pinpoint those cost centers will streamline the rest of the process and result

Table 1: Service Cost Centers and Overhead Cost Centers

Sample Cost Centers	Sample Overhead Costs
• Finance • Accounting (A/P, A/R, etc.) • Tax • Human Resources • Executive Management • Legal (low margin) • Marketing (low margin) • IT (low margin) • Investor Relations*	• Office rent/lease • Office supplies • Telecommunications • Computers • Stock Option Expenses • Building Security • Cafeteria • Recruiting (HR)

* Typically this function, along with a portion of certain other functions, would be considered a stewardship expense and not be allocated.

in significant efficiencies.

This evaluation should segment each cost center into one of three categories: (i) intangible generating services; (ii) solely U.S. services; and (iii) services with prospective foreign benefit. Each are further described below.

- Solely U.S. Service – these are cost centers with functions that solely benefit the U.S. operations and therefore are not charged out to foreign affiliates (e.g., a cost center that organizes only intra-U.S. logistics). Although a functional and cost allocation analysis is not required, it is a best practice to understand and document the functions performed within these cost centers for the transfer pricing report.
- Cost Centers that Solely Develop Intangible Assets—these are service costs associated with intangible generating activities and they should be borne by the intangible owner even though they may provide benefit to other members within the controlled group. This is important because these services may already be embedded within another intercompany transaction (e.g., a royalty charge

---

10 § 1.482-9(k)(2)(i).
11 See Xilinx Inc. v. Comr., T.C., Nos. 4142-01 and 702-03, opinion filed 8/30/05.
12 "IRS Considering Limited Safe Harbor For Low-Level R&D Operations Cost Sharing;" BNA Transfer Pricing Report; Volume 15 Number 21; Wednesday, March 7, 2007.

for the intercompany license of an intangible). Special consideration should be paid to certain cost centers that may produce intangible assets. Some examples of intangible generating activities are marketing a global brand (marketing), research for a new product (R&D), trademark/patent protection (legal), and creating a proprietary technology platform (IT). The costs associated with these services would be charged to the intangible owner and are typically recouped by the intangible owner through another intercompany charge (e.g. cost share program, a royalty, etc.).

- Cost centers with Prospective Foreign Benefit – these are Service Cost Centers that perform functions with prospective foreign benefit. As such, costs exist that could potentially be allocated to foreign affiliates and therefore will require functional interviews and subsequent cost allocation analysis.

Step 2: Conduct Functional Analysis Interviews

The second step of the process is conducting functional analysis interviews. These interviews are intended to identify the functions performed, the risks assumed and intangible property utilized (if any) by each Service Cost Center. More specifically, the interviews are intended to document the activities performed by each Service Cost Center as well as the benefits received by members of the controlled group with respect to the services performed.

A critical part of the functional analysis for service transactions relates to identifying the benefits received. The services costs should be allocated based on their respective shares of the reasonably anticipated benefits from those services. "An activity is considered to provide a benefit to the recipient if the activity directly results in a reasonably identifiable increment of economic or commercial value that enhances the recipient's commercial position, or that may reasonably be anticipated to do so."[13] Stated differently, a service should be charged out if the recipient would be willing to pay a third party provider to perform the same or similar activity.

It is also critical to discuss and document the benefits being provided for each charge to a foreign affiliate so as to maximize the potential deductibility of that charge in the foreign jurisdiction. This process not only aligns with the U.S. regulations, but also follows the OECD guidelines.[14] Also, documenting the benefits will help assist with other matters such as FIN 48 compliance when evaluating both sides of a transaction accepting the service charge.

As mentioned above, the content from the functional analysis interviews is utilized to determine the respective benefits to members of the controlled party, as well as to classify the costs. When conducting the interviews for each cost center, it is important to remember that one of the major goals of the interview is to walk away with an understanding of how the costs may be segmented into the following two groups: 1) Non-Beneficial Costs and 2) Beneficial Costs, both of which are described below:

Non-Beneficial Services:

The Service Regulations provide guidance for activities performed in a controlled services transaction with the

---

[13] § 1.482-9(l)(3)(i).
[14] Organization for Economic Co-Operation and Development; Transfer Pricing Guidelines for Multinational Enterprises and Tax Administrations.

absence of a benefit.[15] There are four specific guidelines that provide guidance on various services or activities that are "non-beneficial" and should not be allocated. Each of the four guidelines is described below.

- Indirect or Remote Services – Activities are considered non-beneficial if, at the time the services were performed, the "reasonably anticipated benefit from that activity is so indirect or remote that the recipient would not be willing to pay, on either a fixed or contingent-payment basis, an uncontrolled party to perform a similar activity, and would not be willing to perform such activity for itself for this purpose."[16]
- Duplicative Activities – Another category of non-beneficial services are duplicative activities. If, at the time the service is conducted, the activity "performed by a controlled taxpayer duplicates an activity that is performed, or that reasonably may be anticipated to be performed, by another controlled taxpayer on or for its own account, the activity is generally not considered to provide a benefit to the recipient, unless the duplicative activity itself provides an additional benefit to the recipient."[17]
- Shareholder Activities – The third type of non-beneficial services are shareholder activities that are also often referred to as "stewardship activities." Shareholder activities are not considered to provide a benefit if "the sole effect of that activity is either to protect the renderer's capital investment in the recipient or in other members of the controlled group, or to facilitate compliance by the renderer with reporting, legal, or regulatory requirements applicable specifically to the renderer, or both."[18] The Service Regulations further note that "day-to-day management" activities that protect a renderer's "capital investment" do not provide a benefit.
- Passive Association – The final area of non-beneficial services are those that are of passive association. An activity is considered to be of passive association and will not have a benefit if the premise is merely the taxpayer's "status as a member of a controlled group."[19]

If a service meets one or more of the aforementioned guidelines, it is deemed to be non-beneficial and no allocation should be administered.

Beneficial Services:

As mentioned above, under the service regulations, an activity provides a benefit and an allocation can be made if "the activity directly results in a reasonably identifiable increment of economic or commercial value that enhances the recipient's commercial position, or that may reasonably be anticipated to do so."[20] In addition, a service is considered beneficial if "an uncontrolled taxpayer in circumstances comparable to those of the recipient would be willing to pay an uncontrolled party to perform the same or similar activity on either a fixed or contingent payment basis, or if the recipient otherwise would have performed for itself the same activity or a similar activity."[21] Beneficial services generally fall within the following two groups:

1. Direct Costs: These are costs

---
15 Treas. Reg. §1.482-9(l)(3)
16 Treas. Reg. §1.482-9(l)(3)(ii)
17 Treas. Reg. §1.482-9(l)(3)(iii)
18 Treas. Reg. §1.482-9(l)(3)(iv)
19 Treas. Reg. §1.482-9(l)(3)(v)
20 Treas. Reg. §1.482-9(l)(3)(i)
21 Treas. Reg. §1.482-9(l)(3)(i)

associated with activities that provide a benefit directly to one or more related parties and that are not duplicative in nature. These costs generally relate to activities specifically performed for a related party. Examples of direct costs may include litigation costs for an entity-specific lawsuit, costs associated with recruiting personnel for a particular entity and/or costs resulting from a request for specific services by a related entity (e.g., internal audit, financial analysis, etc.). If certain activities are tracked and directly billed/charged to the benefiting member(s), those activities should be defined, the costs associated with those activities should be quantified and directly charged to the benefiting member and the transactions subsequently documented.

2. Indirect Costs: This remaining cost pool (after non-beneficial and all direct expenses are identified), represents the indirect costs. For this category of allocations, the functional interviews should focus on developing a methodology to appropriately allocate these costs among the benefiting members (both domestic and foreign).

These are costs typically associated with activities performed for the general benefit of the group members, including the renderer. These costs are not duplicative in nature and generally involve centralized activities that benefit the entire group as well as individual members. The Service Regulations indicate that the service renderer must charge for activities that provide, or are reasonably anticipated to provide, a direct benefit to a controlled party. For example, costs related to designing and operating a technology system to support global operations would be considered an indirect cost that may directly benefit a foreign affiliate.

It is important to note that any reasonable method may be used to allocate and to apportion indirect costs that produce the most reliable result. Examples of potential allocation metrics include net sales, headcount, and production tonnage.

As explained above, the goal of the functional interviews is to capture three main pieces of information for each cost center: the functions performed, the benefits received, and a classification of costs. Once these items are identified, the qualitative documentation and quantitative metrics to form an allocation for each cost center is available.

Step 3: Determine the Arm's Length Charge

The third step of the process has been the most controversial in the IRS feedback discussion and forums both before and after the final regulations were released. This step involves the determination of the arm's length charge to be applied to the services transaction. Under the Service Regulations, a taxpayer may elect to charge the service out at cost under the "Services Cost Method" or "SCM" method (if they qualify, see discussion below) or apply an arm's length charge under another method.

The Service Regulations provide six methods which must be considered in determining an arm's length amount charge in a controlled services transaction. All methods other than the SCM are similar in form and application to those provided for tangible property analysis. The following chart shows the alignment of the service methods with the tangible property methods.

As illustrated in Table 2, the SCM is the only method that does not have a tangible method counterpart. The SCM is a mechanism that allows taxpayers to administer a charge out at-cost that is unlike any method found for tangible or intangible transactions. This is due to the fact that the tangible and intangible methods do not allow for an at-cost charge. However, similar to the tangible property regulations, when the taxpayer is not administering the charge out at-cost, there are various specified service methods that can be applied: comparable uncontrolled services price method, gross services margin method, cost of services plus method, comparable profits method, profit split method and unspecified methods. All of the services methods are further described in the following sections.

Administering an At-Cost Charge Under the SCM Method

The SCM is an elective method which allows for services to be charged at cost if three conditions are met. First, services that "contribute significantly to key competitive advantages, core capabilities, or fundamental risks of success or failure in one or more trades or businesses of the controlled group"[22] do not qualify for the SCM (referred to as the business judgment rule). In other words, the performed services must be deemed "routine" by the taxpayer. Second, the Service Regulations provide a list of services that are specifically excluded from being charged out at cost under the SCM. These services include manufacturing, production, extraction/exploration/processing of natural resources, construction, reselling/distributing/acting as a sales or purchasing agent, research/development/experimentation, engineering, financial transactions (including guarantees), and insurance or reinsurance.[23] Third, the

Table 2: Services Method/Tangible Method Comparison

Services Method	Tangible Method
Services Cost Method*	None
Comparable Uncontrolled Services Price (CUSP)	Comparable Unconrolled Price (CUP)
Gross Services Margin Method	Resale Price Method
Cost of Services Plus Method	Cost Plus Method
Comparable Profits Method (CPM)	Comparable Profits Method (CPM)
Profit Split Method	Profit Split Method
Unspecified Methods	Unspecified Methods

* The SCM is the only method that does not have a tangible method counterpart.

activity must qualify as either:

a) Specified Covered Service: A taxpayer must match the tested service to a list of 20 service categories and 101 service activities assembled by the IRS[24]; or
b) Low Margin Covered Service: A taxpayer must determine that the service has a median arm's length mark-up on total services costs of less than or equal to seven percent, as determined by independent comparables.[25]

If the service meets all three criteria of the SCM, it is eligible to be charged out at cost.

Administering an Arm's Length Charge with Profit

If transactions are not eligible for cost-based treatment under the SCM or the taxpayer elects not to apply the SCM, a set of methodologies are provided for establishing an arm's length price. The specific methods for testing the arm's length nature of services transactions are described below:

<u>Comparable Uncontrolled Services Price (CUSP) Method:</u>
The CUSP method "evaluates whether

---

22 § 1.482-9(b)(5).
23 §1.482-9(b)(4).
24 Internal Revenue Bulletin: 2007-3, Notice 2007-5 and Revenue Procedure 2007-13.
25 § 1.482-9(b)(3)(ii).

the amount charged in a controlled services transaction is arm's length by reference to the amount charged in a comparable uncontrolled services transaction."[26] When assessing the factors affecting the degree of comparability between controlled and uncontrolled services transactions, similarity of services performed generally will have the greatest relevance.

Gross Services Margin Method:

The Gross Services Margin method relies upon an analysis of the gross profit margins earned in comparable uncontrolled services transactions to test the arm's length nature of charges in a controlled services transaction. The use of this method entails multiplying the applicable uncontrolled price by the gross services profit margin earned in comparable uncontrolled transactions.[27]

Cost of Services Method:

The Cost of Services method evaluates the transfer price by referring to the gross services markup realized in comparable uncontrolled transactions.[28] This method is typically used in circumstances where the same or similar services are performed for both uncontrolled and controlled parties.

The Comparable Profits Method:

The CPM determines an arm's length price by reference to a measure of profitability of unrelated companies that engage in similar activities under similar circumstances.[29] The method compares the profitability of either the related buyer or related seller to the profitability of a comparable company with no related party transactions, by reference to a profit level indicator.

The Profit Split Method:

The Profit Split method determines an arm's length transfer price on the basis of the relative value of each controlled taxpayer's contributions to the combined profit or loss in a particular controlled transaction or set of transactions.[30]

Unspecified Methods:

Other methods may also be used to evaluate the arm's length nature of intercompany transactions, provided they satisfy the best method rule. These methods "should provide information on the prices or profits that the controlled taxpayer could have realized by choosing a realistic alternative to the controlled services transaction."[31]

In order to administer an intercompany service charge (when not using the SCM[32]), the taxpayer must conduct a best method analysis, utilize one of the newly prescribed service methods described above, and conduct an arm's length analysis to establish the appropriate arm's length charge.

The Service Regulations provide taxpayers with the ability to administer a charge out at cost under the SCM or to have an arm's length charge under a specific method similar to those used for a tangible property analysis. It is important to note that the SCM is an elected method and taxpayers have the option to administer charges at-cost for some transactions as well as with a profit component for others. Appropriate attention should be given to this step of the process because, if implemented correctly, it can be beneficial to the taxpayer.

---

26 § 1.482-9(c)(1).
27 § 1.482-9(d)(2)(iv).
28 § 1.482-9(e)(1).
29 § 1.482-9(f)(1).
30 § 1.482-9(g)(1).
31 § 1.482-9(h)(1).
32 If the taxpayer elects to apply the SCM, a best method analysis is not required.

Step 4: Implement the Results

After conducting the analysis the results must be implemented. This is a multi-part process and should involve the following:
- Complete a Transfer Pricing Report: The transfer pricing study will document the analysis conducted and also include other important sections, including an industry overview, functional analysis, methodology selection and economic analysis. These components are required to avoid penalties under U.S. Treasury Regulations Section 6662.
- Implement the Service Allocations: Besides preparing the documentation, the charges must actually be administered. This involves implementing a system to administer the charges and intercompany invoices on a monthly or quarterly basis with an annual true-up at the end of the year. Typically, the audit and tax teams work together to develop this process and system.
- Administer Intercompany Agreements: Formalizing the policy with written agreements (signed by each party) provides support for the charges being administered.
- Perform Foreign Country Reviews: A large concern regarding administration of these services charges is their acceptance by the foreign jurisdictions receiving the charges. Many taxpayers have their transfer pricing reports reviewed by local country experts to increase the potential acceptance of charges by foreign taxing authorities.
- Evaluate the Impact to Other Transfer Pricing Policies: As these are new charges, companies must see how the administration of these charges affects the compliance of other transfer pricing policies. For example, service charges administered to a foreign distributor will decrease their profit margin and if that distributor is already benchmarked under another transfer pricing method (e.g., Transactional Net Margin Method or TNMM), this may result in a dual charge that may disrupt the transfer pricing policy.

Like any new policy, implementing the results is often the most difficult step to complete depending upon how your company captures and accounts for cost center data. In addition to the burden of creating, implementing and maintaining a new transfer pricing policy, the focus on services is a very U.S.-centric initiative. As such, both foreign related parties and

---

Christopher Desmond and **Ryan Lange** are transfer pricing economists with Ceteris, Inc.'s Chicago office. Mr. Desmond advises clients on a variety of transfer pricing matters, including expert witness support, FIN 48, the service regulations as well as global and state documentation strategies. He received a B.S. degree in Management and an M.B.A. degree with a concentration in International Business from Eastern Illinois University. Mr. Lange advises clients' senior management on a variety of transfer pricing matters. He obtained his B.A. degree in Business from the University of Wisconsin. The authors may be reached at **christopher.desmond@ceterisgroup.com** and **ryan.lange@ceterisgroup.com**.
For more information on the authors, please see Section XIII.

foreign tax authorities may initially contest these new charges. Despite this, from a U.S. stand-point, these processes/charges must be made in order to be in compliance with Service Regulations.

Conclusion

The new Service Regulations effective impact tax years beginning after January 1, 2008 and are fully effective with tax years beginning after August 1, 2009. They involve specific methods and processes to document intercompany services for both an at-cost and arm's length charge. The new requirements also focus on key items as calculating the fully-loaded cost base (inclusive of stock options), capturing benefits, determining the appropriate allocation key, and actually implementing and charging the services starting next year.

The new service regulations are a large focus area of the IRS and should not be taken lightly. Taxpayers should take proactive measures to evaluate the impact these regulations will have on their organization—if not, either your auditor or the IRS will.

VII. Supply Chain Management

Issues in Supply Chain Management

D. Clarke Norton
DLA Piper LLP

Perhaps now more than ever, global competition is fierce. Strict credit markets and hesitant consumers are putting enormous pressure on businesses globally across industries. Predicting consumer demand against, in many cases, shareholder value is bringing critical attention to supply chain management. The balance between customer and shareholder brings with it very delicate timing. Guess incorrectly in either direction and one end of the spectrum is going to be dissatisfied. This is especially true in the consumer goods industry where missing one season can determine whether a company will be around for the next.

For companies that rely on their supply chains as a value driver, proactively managing the worldwide effective tax rate can yield dividends—literally and figuratively. In industries that are truly global in scope, and in which tax rates in major centers of activity vary widely, transfer pricing can play an important role in achieving best-in-peer-group tax results.

Background

Most economists agree that we are on the verge of recovery from one of the worst economic downturns in recent memory. As multinational companies plan for economic recovery, optimal supply chain management will be critical. Get it right and the benefits can be substantial; get it wrong and the consequences can be devastating. Supply chain management can:

- Increase growth;
- Enhance margins;
- Leverage resources;
- Lower costs; and/or
- Manage risks.

All of these factors will be vitally important as global economies stabilize.

A well-managed supply chain centralizes value-adding business activities (functions) in locations that provide a favorable environment in terms of general business climate, operating costs and, last but not least, taxation. These functions include, but are not limited to:

- Procurement;
- Production planning;
- Inventory management and warehousing;
- Logistics;
- Manufacturing oversight and quality control; and
- Financing and cash management.

The benefits of supply chain management can include optimization of working capital, improved product availability through better supply chain visibility, efficient asset utilization, rationalization of supplier base, contract compliance, supplier relationship management, increased control and management of spending, and improved financial planning.

Consequences of suboptimal structures include:

- **Increased system-wide costs**
  — Duplication of functions and processes in operating companies or across divisions/business units
- **"Too many cooks"** — Multiple

Supply Chain Management

locations lead to duplication, high transaction costs, divergent policies and service levels
- **Silo mentality** — Lack of standardization leads additional costs, underutilization of resources and operational underperformance
- **Inconsistent Organizational Structure** — Conflicting performance measurement

To reap the benefits of supply chain optimization from a taxation perspective, and make it stand up to the scrutiny of interested tax authorities, optimal supply chain management must establish appropriate business processes and associated transfer pricing policies for the resulting transactions between the entities of a group's structure. The centralization of functions, assets and risks creates clear and long-standing operational benefits to multinational firms and will, if done properly, attract (taxable) income to those supply chain hubs. If possible, allocating those centralized activities to a low tax rate jurisdiction, all other things being equal, may provide additional benefits.

From a financial standpoint, benefits may include:
- Simplified management reporting
- Increased management control
- Tax efficiencies (direct and indirect)
- Stability/predictability of local tax burdens

To further expand on the last point, in the "traditional" conversion, what have historically been entrepreneurial local businesses transition into distributors earning a low but guaranteed margin or manufacturers and service providers earning a markup on their costs. Tax planning arises when value-added functions, assets and risks are migrated to low-tax jurisdictions with high levels of substance.

Business substance is key. Truly optimal supply chain structures can be intrusive to current business operations. Operational changes may require people to completely rethink the way that they undertake jobs that they have been doing for a number of years. However, the greater the business impact (for example, a full principal operating company which owns intellectual property), the greater the return (higher value). Also, transitions to these operating structures can be phased depending on a company's existing business, its organizational model, and its readiness for change. In addition, optimal structures should simultaneously satisfy transfer pricing concepts (as noted above) with particular focus on functions, assets and risks, as well as U.S. tax deferral rules (subpart F).

Hypothetical Example

Hypothetical U.S. company XCo engages in a business restructuring whereby it forms a new company (*"ProcurementCo"*) in a non-U.S. tax-efficient jurisdiciton, which would become XCo's centralized procurement entity for raw materials. Under this restructuring, ProcurementCo would assume the functions and risks of procuring raw materials for the Current Principals and the Current Principals no longer would perform the procurement function or assume the risks associated with that particular function.

In conjunction with this restructuring, the Current Principals would provide ProcurementCo with information related to their current suppliers and other associated information related to their respective procurement activities. ProcurementCo, through its own employees performing services from its offices in its country of residence would identify, negotiate and purchase raw materials on a bulk basis for its own account and risk and then, pursuant to supply contracts with each of the Current Principals, would resell the raw materials that it has purchased to the Current Principals at an arm's length price.

ProcurementCo, depending on the circumstances, could perform some or all of (but is not limited to) the following procurement-type functions:

- **Information gathering**: ProcurementCo would be required to identify suppliers who can satisfy the requirements for the materials sought to be purchased.
- **Supplier contact**: ProcurementCo would be responsible for identifying how may third-party suppliers it may want to contract with.
- **Background review**: It may be necessary for Procurement Co to confirm the quality of raw materials to be purchased or the ability of a third-party supplier to supply certain quantities of raw materials.
- **Negotiation**: ProcurementCo would undertake to negotiate with third-party suppliers as to, among other items, quantity, quality, price and delivery schedules. Once these negotiations are completed, ProcurementCo would enter into written supply contracts with the third-party suppliers.
- **Fulfillment**: Supplier preparation, shipment, delivery, and payment for the raw materials would be effected, based on contract terms. ProcurementCo may also store the raw materials for "just-in-time" delivery to the Current Principals, as part of its centralized procurement services.
- **Renewal**: ProcurementCo would be responsible for renewing supply contracts when they expire or identifying other suppliers to re-order raw materials if the current suppliers.

One of the objectives of this proposed business restructuring would be to enable Xco's group of companies ("the Group") to negotiate lower prices for raw materials through its bulk purchasing program, which benefits ultimately would inure to the Group. ProcurementCo, as a result of performing the Group's bulk procurement activities, would be the entity that retains the profits associated with the the bulk purchasing activity, commensurate with its assets, functions and risks.

We would note that ProcurementCo could obtain an enhanced return if it were to perform additional functions and incurred additional risks; *e.g.*, in addition to performing its centralized procurement functions, it also could function as a centralized manufacturer (through third-party contract manufacturers) of the products and sell the products to unrelated distributors or customers around the world.

Tax and Economic Considerations

A. Transfers of Contracts and Other Intellectual Property

The Current Principals each are likely to have entered into various valuable commercial relationships with third-party suppliers (and contract manufacturers and distributors). To the extent that these relationships or trade information related to these relationships (whether reduced to writing or not) were to be transferred (economically or legally) to ProcurementCo, it may be necessary to value such relationships and to compensate the Current Principals for providing ProcurementCo with trade information that otherwise may not have been available to the newly-formed procurement company. Note, in this regard, compensation would not be for the business opportunity, but for the intangible property ("IP") currently owned by the Current Principals that are associated with this business opportunity. Determination of whether compensation is due and the value of the compensation (*i.e.*, the "buy-in") would depend upon local and international legal and transfer pricing considerations; *i.e.* is the item an asset that is compensable and, if so, what is its value. Other types of IP may also be implicated and, if present, must also be analyzed in a similar fashion.

B. Transfer Pricing on Sales Between ProcurementCo and Current Principals

The proposed transactions between ProcurementCo and the Current Principals must be scrutinized under local and international legal and transfer pricing principles. In this regard, it is essential that ProcurementCo have the requisite substance to perform its designated role: (1) It must be adequately capitalized to perform its functions and bear the risks that it will incur; (2) It must have the tangible and intangible assets necessary to conduct its centralized activities; (3) It must have its own employees that perform services from the company's office in the applicable jurisdiction and the employees must have the experience and authority to conduct the centralized activity and make the requisite business decisions with respect to the overall conduct of the business.

One issue which needs to be considered if ProcurementCo's sole function were limited to that of centralized purchasing is whether any portion of the discount that ProcurementCo realized as a result of its centralized procurement functions would need to be shared with the Current Principals. This issue would depend on how the centralized procurement activity ultimately were structured by analyzing the functions performed, the risks assumed, and the assets employed by ProcurementCo.

C. Structure of ProcurementCo

Assuming that the proposed structure were to result in the retention of significant profits by ProcurementCo, it would be important to structure ProcurementCo in an appropriate jurisdiction that provides a competitive business and tax environment. The jurisdiction should have a broad-based income tax treaty network. Jurisdictions such as Switzerland or Ireland should be considered, among others.

In addition, it would be necessary to establish an appropriate holding company structure in order to repatriate profits in an efficient manner, since a distribution of profits from a treaty-protected jurisdiction to a company in a non-treaty jurisdiction otherwise may be subject to local withholding at source.

D. Taxable Nexus in the United States and Other Jurisdictions

It would be important to determine how ProcurementCo would operate and how its operations would be treated in the various jurisdictions in which the Current Principals and the unrelated customers are located. Specifically, it would be important to determine the extent to which ProcurementCo could become subject to taxation in jurisdictions other than that in which it is resident and the role that bilateral income tax treaties would have in resolving such issues.

With respect to the United States, if ProcurementCo were resident in a jurisdiction that has entered into a bilateral income tax treaty with the United States and otherwise satisfied the limitation on benefits article of the treaty, *e.g.*, the active trade or business requirement, it could potentially minimize its exposure to U.S. Federal income and branch profits taxation, provided, of course, that it were not otherwise engaged in a trade or business through a U.S. permanent establishment as a result of having an office in the United States staffed with employees or a dependent agency relationship. Thus, for example, if ProcurementCo were resident in a treaty jurisdiction and satisfied the limitation on benefits provision of that jurisdiction's bilateral income tax treaty with the United States, it could purchase and sell raw materials within the United States, provided, of course that it did so in a manner that did not result in a U.S. permanent establishment.

In the absence of treaty protection, the threshold for finding that a non-treaty protected is engaged in a U.S. trade or business is much lower, which would necessitate that any non-U.S. company performing services or selling goods related to the United States, carefully structure its activities to avoid having a U.S. nexus that would implicate U.S. direct Federal income taxation.

Clearly, in this latter case, the company, among other activities, (1) should not have a U.S. office or fixed place of business; (2) should not engage an employee or agent, irrespective of whether dependent or independent; to perform services or act as a distributor on its behalf from within the United States; (3) should not pass title in the United States with respect to any goods; (4) should not both purchase raw materials within the United States *and* process such raw materials through a contract manufacturing relationship in the United States, and (5) should not be engaged in the buying and selling of goods that never physically leave the United States, regardless of where title is passed, unless there were compelling, substantive business reasons for the title passage to occur outside of the United States. In effect, the U.S. activities of a non-treaty protected entity would have to be greatly circumscribed compared to the activities of a treaty protected entity and great care would have to be exercised in avoiding a U.S. tax nexus, both from a U.S. Federal and a State taxation point of view.

E. Availability of U.S. Income Tax Treaty Protections

U.S. bilateral income tax treaties require that a treaty beneficiary be a resident of the Contracting State and satisfy a limitation on benefits provisions. While there are various means of satisfying such provisions, the one that appears most likely to be available in the instant case is satisfaction of the so-called "active trade or business test" (which appears in materially identical form in each U.S. bilateral income tax treaty that contains a limitation on benefits provision). Thus, it would be necessary for ProcurementCo (1) to be organized *and* resident in a jurisdiction that has entered into a U.S. bilateral income tax treaty, (2) have the requisite substance in that country to satisfy the active trade or business test of the applicable treaty (see below) and (3) not conduct business from a branch outside of the country in which it is organized or resident.

Generally, under the active trade or business test of a typical limitation on benefits provision of a U.S. bilateral income tax treaty, a resident of a Contracting State that is not otherwise generally entitled to benefits of the treaty may, nonetheless, receive treaty benefits with respect to certain specific items of income that are connected to an active trade or business conducted in its State of residence. As noted above, each of the active trade or business tests appearing in U.S. bilateral income tax treaties are similar. The summary description below generally overviews the requirements that would be required to be satisfied under any of the U.S. bilateral income tax treaties that may be applicable in the proposed restructuring.

In order to satisfy the active trade or

business test, a three-pronged test must be satisfied with respect to a particular item of income:
1) the resident must be engaged in the active conduct or a trade or business in its State of residence;
2) the income derived from the other State must be derived in connection with, or be incidental to, that trade or business; and
3) if the income arises from a transaction with a related party, the trade or business must be substantial in relation to the activity in the other State that generated the income.

1) Trade or Business

Whether the activities of a foreign corporation constitute an active trade or business is determined under all of the facts and circumstances. A trade or business for this purpose comprises activities that constitute (or could constitute) an independent economic enterprise carried on for profit. The active conduct of a trade or business need not involve manufacturing or sales activities but may instead involve services. The activities conducted by the resident ordinarily must include every operation which forms a part of, or a step in, a process by which an enterprise may earn income or profit in order to constitute a trade or business. An enterprise actively conducts a trade or business if it regularly performs active and substantial management and operational functions through its own officers or staff of employees. Although it is possible that one or more of such activities may be carried out by independent contractors under the direct control of the resident, in determining whether the corporation actively conducts a trade or business, the activities of independent contractors are disregarded.

2 Income Derived

An item of income will be considered to be earned in connection with, or to be incidental to, an active trade or business in a Contracting State if the resident claiming the benefits is itself engaged in business, or it is deemed to be so engaged through the activities of related persons that are residents of one of the Contracting States. Thus, for example, a resident of a Contracting State could claim benefits with respect to an item of income earned by an operating subsidiary in the other Contracting State but derived by the resident indirectly through a wholly-owned holding company resident in the other Contracting State and interposed between it and the operating subsidiary.

3) Substantiality Test

Income that is derived from a related party in connection with an active trade or business in a Contracting State must satisfy an additional test to qualify for benefits granted by the other Contracting State. The trade or business in the first-mentioned State (*e.g.*, the jurisdiction in which ProcurementCo is resident) must be substantial in relation to the activity carried on by the related party in the other Contracting State (*e.g.*, the United States) that gave rise to the income in respect of which treaty benefits are being claimed. The substantiality requirement is intended to prevent a narrow case of treaty-shopping abuses in which a company attempts to qualify for benefits by engaging in *de minimis* connected business activities that have little economic cost or effect with respect to the company's business as a whole.

Scrutiny from Tax Authorities

Perhaps not surprisingly, these types of structures and transitions have the

Supply Chain Management

acute attention of tax authorities around the world. Tax authorities will review documentation and interview company personnel in order to understand the operating model in their respective jurisdictions. Tax authorities will want to make sure the tax structure and transfer pricing are appropriate and that the model is operating in practice as it has been documented. It is essential that each company in the structure have the requisite substance to perform its designated role. First, it must be adequately capitalized to perform its functions and bear the risks that it will incur. Second, it must have the tangible and intangible assets necessary to conduct its activities. Third, it must have its own employees that perform services from the company's office in the applicable jurisdiction, and those employees must have the experience and authority to conduct the activity and make the requisite business decisions with respect to the overall conduct of the business. Where this cannot be demonstrated, tax risks may include transfer pricing and permanent establishment adjustments and penalties, and auditors may not permit the enterprise to book the anticipated tax benefits for financial reporting purposes.

Further of the issue of IP. Large multinational enterprises are highly complex organizations with evolving business models. Even in the least complex organizations it is difficult to support a unilateral approach to value creation. Tax authorities around the world see IP as critically important to value creation in the enterprise (and, therefore, see economic ownership of IP as attracting substantial amounts of income to the jurisdiction where it is owned, under arm's-length transfer pricing); they act aggressively to protect their tax bases when IP is transferred out of a jurisdiction without the transferor receiving substantial compensation. Anyone who has transitioned an operating company from full- to limited-risk in Germany, Italy or France (among other jurisdictions) can attest to that.

Conclusions

For companies with global supply chains this is a time of opportunities and challenges.

Consider revisiting your company's intercompany pricing policies and agreements. Don't hesitate to be creative (within the applicable legal and regulatory framework)—the current environment supports adjustments to and optimization of your existing tax and transfer pricing structure.

Even better, evaluate whether this is a good time to make more fundamental changes to your global supply chain. Governments are competing harder than ever to attract foreign investment, the resulting opportunities for their citizens, and of course tax revenue. Tax holidays or even direct subsidies are available in many jurisdictions. Supply chain hubs lend themselves particularly well to taking advantage of such incentives, and may offer opportunities to improve both tax and customs outcomes.

How can you get certainty that it will work? Proper implementation and professional documentation is a

---

D. Clarke Norton is a principal economist in DLA Piper's Tax group and co-head of the Transfer Pricing practice. She can be reached by phone at **212-335-4817** or by email at **clarke.norton@dlapiper.com**.

For more information on the author, please see Section XIII.

Supply Chain Management

prerequisite for success. Depending on your company's appetite for risk, one way is to proactively seek resolution with taxing authorities. Many countries now have Advance Pricing Agreement ("APA") programs. An APA program is designed to resolve actual or potential transfer pricing disputes in a principled, cooperative manner, as an alternative to the traditional adversarial process. An APA is a binding contract between one or more taxing authorities and a taxpayer, under which the taxing authority agrees not to seek a transfer pricing adjustment for a covered transaction if the taxpayer files its tax return for a covered year consistent with the agreed transfer pricing method. An APA can take the uncertainty out of transfer pricing, which can be particularly helpful, especially in these turbulent times.

VIII. Trade Finance

Commodities Trading and Global Dealing: Transfer Pricing Challenges and Proposed Methods

Elizabeth King
Beecher Consulting Group

1. Introduction

Many tax practitioners, both in and outside the government, believe that the global trading of commodities and financial instruments present unique difficulties vis-a-vis the application of transfer pricing regulations. A number of characteristics set trading activities apart from many other types of economic activity: (a) there is often limited division of labor among legal entities constituting a controlled trading group; (b) traders in different jurisdictions often work collectively on a single "book of business" or otherwise collaborate quite closely; (c) debt and equity capital used to finance trades may be fungible across legal entities; (d) traders are not physically tied to a particular geographic location by necessity (that is, they could make the same contributions to the generation of trading profits independent of their geographic base of operations); and, (e) by its nature, trading is a multi-jurisdictional activity.

Given the limited division of labor among controlled trading group members, transfer pricing methods that presuppose a particular division of labor (the resale price and cost plus methods) are not applicable. Because individual members of a trading group can contribute to the generation of joint trading profits in a variety of ways, and, depending on booking conventions, may not purchase (or sell) commodities or financial products from (or to) one another, the comparable uncontrolled price method, likewise, is often not a viable approach. By virtue of the fungibility of financial capital, traders' flexibility regarding their physical location, and the fact that commodities and financial products trading requires a broad geographic reach, the nexus between geographic location and particular profit-generating activities is, in the view of many practitioners, not clearly drawn. This perceived lack of correspondence between activity and location effectively precludes other traditional transfer pricing methods as well.

In lieu of the "separate entity" approach that underlies all of the conventional U.S. and OECD transfer pricing methods,[1] the IRS has endorsed a formulary apportionment methodology for global trading firms, albeit cloaked in profit split clothing. In Notice 94–40,[2] the IRS describes the basic parameters of this formulary approach, incorporated into a number of Advance Pricing Agreements (APAs) that it has concluded with multinational trading groups. In essence, where a trading group is deemed to be "functionally fully

---

1 The "separate entity" approach is part and parcel of the arm's length standard, in that the objective is to determine the amount of taxable income that each member of a controlled group would earn on a separate, standalone basis.

2 See Notice 94–40, Global Trading Advance Pricing Agreements, 1994-1 C.B. 351; 1994 IRB LEXIS 213; 1994-17 I.R.B. 22, April 25, 2004.

integrated," its combined trading profits have been allocated across tax jurisdictions on the basis of three factors: (a) a measure of trading expertise; (b) a measure of the extent to which each legal entity puts the group's worldwide capital at risk; and, (c) a measure of "activity," representing back-office support in various forms. The weights ascribed to each factor and the particular measures of risk used have varied on a case-by-case basis.

Notice 94–40 is "not intended to prescribe a method or factors that will necessarily apply in all APAs with functionally fully integrated global trading operations, . . . limit the use of other methods or factors,"[3] or be used to allocate the trading profits earned by firms that are not functionally fully integrated. However, proposed transfer pricing regulations addressing global dealing operations, issued in 1998, endorse a broadly similar methodology (among others).[4] To date, these regulations have not been finalized, and financial transactions in which members of a global dealing operation engage are expressly exempted from the temporary services regulations issued under IRC Section 1.482-9T in 2006:

Pending finalization of the global dealing regulations, taxpayers may rely on the proposed global dealing regulations, not the temporary services regulations, to govern financial transactions entered into in connection with a global dealing operation as defined in proposed Section 1.482-8. Therefore, proposed regulations under IRC Section 1.482-9(m)(5) issued elsewhere in the Federal Register clarify that a controlled services transaction does not include a financial transaction entered into in connection with a global dealing operation.[5]

Hence, dating back to the mid-1990s, global commodities and financial products trading firms have found themselves in a regulatory limbo of sorts with regard to transfer pricing issues. As such, they have been faced with even greater uncertainty in this sphere than firms engaged in other types of economic activities (and were among the first to avail themselves of the APA option).

The formulary apportionment methodologies described in Notice 94–40 and the proposed global dealing regulations produce arbitrary results and are generally unnecessary, for the following reasons:

1) Trading companies engage in a wide variety of transactions, each of which poses different types of risks. The diversity of risks cannot be distilled down to a single reliable measure.
2) The weights assigned to each factor in individual cases are subjective.
3) Trading is intrinsically fluid and dynamic. As such, it is uniquely ill-suited to tax treatment that, for analytical purposes, "holds constant" both the activities that contribute to the generation of trading profits and their relative importance over a period of years. And,
4) Conventional wisdom substantially understates the degree to which particular trading activities and assets can be identified with specific geographic locales.

---

3   Ibid.

4   IRS Proposed Rules on Allocation and Sourcing of Income and Deductions Among Taxpayers Engaged in Global Dealing Operations, REG-208299-90, 63 Fed. Reg. 11177, 3/6/98.

5   See IRS Final, Temporary Rules on Services Treatment under Section 482, Allocation of Income and Deductions From Intangibles, Stewardship Expenses, 26 CFR Parts 1 and 31, RIN 45-BB31, 1545-AY38, 1545-BC52, "Explanation of Provisions," Item 12, Coordination with Other Transfer Pricing Rules -Temp. Treas. Reg. Section 1.482-9T(m).

Trade Finance

This article provides a more detailed critique of the IRS' formulary apportionment methodology, and suggests an alternative methodology that is consistent with the "separate entity" framework, the 1994 transfer pricing regulations governing intercompany transfers of tangible and intangible property, and the 2006 temporary regulations governing intercompany services. For expository purposes, the article focuses on "physicals trading" (the trading of physical commodities, such as metals, grain, crude, etc., as distinct from the trading of derivative instruments) in certain commodities markets. However, the same principles readily generalize to other commodities and to financial instruments.

The article is organized as follows: Section 2 contains a brief overview of physicals trading in three commodities: Natural gas, aluminum and alumina (treated as a single market), and copper concentrates. Section 3 contains a discussion of the core elements that are prerequisites to trading physicals. (This discussion provides a good deal of contextual information and may be skipped by readers who are familiar with the basics of global trading.) Section 4 contains a discussion of recent developments in the trading environment, and their effects on the relative importance of core trading assets and activities. Section 5 contains a more detailed description of the formulary approach described in the IRS' Notice 94-40 and the proposed global dealing regulations. Section 6 contains the aforementioned critique of this methodology. Section 7 presents an alternative approach to allocating multi-jurisdictional trading firms' combined income for tax purposes, and Section 8 concludes.

2. Overview: Trading in Physical Commodities

This section provides an overview of physicals trading in natural gas, alumina and aluminum, and copper concentrates. These markets are reasonably representative of commodities trading in general, and have many features in common with trading in financial products, as well.

2.1 Natural Gas

Natural gas is consumed by cogeneration plants (to produce energy), industrial companies (to power production equipment), commercial end-users (to heat offices, schools, hotels, etc.) and individual consumers. Gas is extracted from natural reservoirs through a "wellhead," a mechanism that controls the flow of gas to the surface, and is transported along a pipeline system from supplying regions to consuming regions throughout the United States and other countries. The pipeline system consists of small-diameter pipelines, or gathering systems, feeder pipelines, large-diameter pipelines for long-distance transport, storage facilities along the system, and receipt or delivery points. Mineral rights and the wellhead and pipeline systems are generally owned, and natural gas is produced, by separate and independent companies.

Natural gas producers generally contract directly on a long-term basis with large end-users and intermediaries (e.g., utilities). However, an individual utility or other long-term customer may require more or less natural gas than it has directly contracted for, or a producer may have committed to deliver more or less natural gas than it has available at a point in time. Analogously, pipeline operators generally contract directly on a long-term, firm basis with large end-users for most of their capacity. However, the amount of capacity leased out on a long-term basis is somewhat less than total capacity, to allow for peak usage. Long-term users, for their part, want the flexibility to lease out their temporarily excess capacity, or obtain additional capacity on a short-term basis, which their long-term leases with the pipeline owners do not provide.

Natural gas traders take positions and trade in natural gas and pipeline capacity. More fundamentally, they provide an outlet for producers' excess production and assume their market risk, constitute a source of incremental supply to end-users, and take advantage of arbitrage opportunities (or "basis differentials") across markets and over time. Moreover, traders buy and resell the incremental capacity that pipeline companies do not lease out on a long-term, firm basis. They obtain such capacity through leases with the latter, and with end-users, on daily, weekly or monthly bases. Traders typically obtain "interruptible" service, which is less costly than firm service. However, as the term implies, such service is not guaranteed. Rather, one can be displaced by a firm user, and trading strategies must allow for this eventuality through "park and loan" arrangements (permitting traders to draw on pools of natural gas located near their customers).

Traders hedge their physical positions by entering into offsetting positions in the same or a related commodity, thereby mitigating the resulting price exposure and eliminating the open position in whole or in part.[6] Some hedges are done on exchanges (e.g., tradable futures entitling the buyer to claim physical delivery at the contract delivery point and at the specified date, and similarly entitling the seller), and others are done over-the-counter (e.g., swaps negotiated bilaterally and providing for the exchange of the commodity, or a derivative, at some specified future point).

Not all natural gas traders enter into physical transactions, and not all traders entering into such transactions have to make or take delivery. In some instances, traders deal solely in derivative, or financial, instruments, such as futures and swaps. Others buy natural gas into, or sell out of, a hub, involving the transfer of title in a ledger, but no physical movement of product as such. In general, customer-driven business entails the physical movement of product, and the accompanying expertise in pipeline systems. Proprietary business may also involve physical business, but often has a larger financial component.

2.2 Alumina & Aluminum

Alumina and aluminum markets have always been closely linked, because

---

[6] In principle, hedges are entered into as an offset to underlying physical trades. However, the latter may not materialize (due to non-performance of one kind or another), or they may be significantly delayed (due, for example, to production or shipping problems). When the physical trade is delayed, the hedge itself becomes an open position, and carries with it substantial risk. Moreover, futures markets are much more volatile than physicals markets. While one clearly bears a measure of price risk on open positions in physicals, in that the price of a particular commodity is quite likely to fluctuate over time, the potential for backwardation on hedges (where the commodities price in the future is lower than the current price), coupled with the potential for non-performance or delayed performance in the physicals market, poses substantially greater risks. While outright non-performance has historically been relatively uncommon, in part because few contracts are fixed to the day, delays in production and/or shipping, unacceptable variations in quality or volume, and other similarly smaller-scale adverse developments are relatively common.

alumina is the key raw material used in the manufacture of aluminum. It is not unusual for alumina end-users and aluminum smelters to be one and the same firm, or to be part of the same multinational group. A number of metals trading firms traded aluminum exclusively prior to the 1990s. However, with the collapse of the Soviet Union, pre-financing arrangements increasingly became a prerequisite to assured supplies of aluminum from formerly Government-owned Russian producers with limited financial resources. Thus, Glencore, Trafigura, Noble and others began prepaying for aluminum under long-term offtake arrangements circa the second half of the 1990s, and agreed to supply aluminum producers with their alumina requirements.

Aluminum and alumina traders in the physicals market generally have relationships with a number of major suppliers. In addition to Russia, these suppliers are based in Australia, Venezuela, China, India, Mexico and Brazil. Traders source product both in the spot market (i.e., tendered business put out for bid by the large producers) and under long-term contracts.

Counterparties on the buy side of the alumina and aluminum markets consist primarily of major industrial end-users, aluminum producers and, to a lesser extent, independent distributors and small merchants. Large aluminum producers buy alumina in high volumes, which in turn reduces trading firms' administrative and logistical expenses. They also pose substantially less credit risks than smaller customers. On transactions with large aluminum producers, traders' roles entail correcting imbalances in the location of stocks, the availability of raw materials, and the timing of production in these entities' systems. Aluminum can be sold at the prevailing London Metal Exchange ("LME") price at minimum, and sometimes at a higher price, given its particular shape, grade and location.

For much of this decade, China has constituted the main alumina consuming market, and its rapid growth in demand (at the rate of approximately 10% per annum) has fueled the growth of the worldwide alumina market. Alumina is generally sold on a fixed price basis or as a percentage of the LME price. Percent of LME contracts have terms of up to five years, and generally contain specified puts and calls. Under this arrangement, buyers typically have the right to call when prices reach a certain threshold, and sellers have the right to put if prices fall below a specified floor; when prices are within the put/call range, the transactions price is arrived at by mutual negotiation on an annual basis.

2.3 Copper Concentrates

The copper concentrates business is customer-driven, involving the purchase of concentrates from mines for sale to smelters, and is done purely on a principal basis. Traders agree on certain annual tonnages with mines and smelters, and set shipping schedules. Shipments are typically every other month, and traders are responsible for chartering vessels. Collectively, merchants handle only about 30% of transactions between mines and smelters. On the 70% balance, the latter deal directly with one another.

Both mines and copper smelters have very large infrastructure commitments and fixed costs. Therefore, they must be convinced before the fact that traders will perform. Reputation is established over time, and specific merchants are recognized in the field. There are a comparatively small number of merchants in total, some of which are global, and some of which are niche players. Traders must be familiar with each of their customers' smelters, their technology and the concentrates that they can handle and line up acceptable qualities.

Concentrates transactions are long-dated, requiring upwards of six months from beginning to end. After typically lengthy contract negotiations, individual shipments must be transported, delivered, and tested by both producers and refiners. Testing is done by means of a weighing and sampling process to determine the composition of each shipment; copper concentrates contain only about 30% copper, along with silver, gold and other metals. Ocean transport is complicated by the fact that concentrates have a grainy consistency, with an appearance similar to black sand. As such, their movement requires a substantial amount of administration and expertise in vessel chartering, loading rates, discharge rates and port facilities. Moreover, mines are located mainly in Latin America (i.e., Chile), and refiners are located primarily in emerging markets (China, Vietnam, Korea, India, etc.), requiring shipment over considerable distances. All aspects of individual transactions (e.g., payment terms, inspection fees, shipping terms, etc.) are incrementally important in generating trading profits, over and above the spread that traders earn.

Given the lengthy process of concluding individual transactions and the critical importance of reliability, it is not surprising that the supply side of the concentrates business is governed by term contracts, referred to as "frame contracts." These overarching agreements set forth general terms and conditions, which remain fixed throughout. However, pricing and delivery points can be renegotiated at intervals. Most frame contracts provide for indexed pricing.

Absent hedging, traders would be exposed to significant price and basis risk because supply contracts and sales contracts provide for a mix of fixed and indexed pricing. Traders hedge via forward physical sales and futures transactions on the New York Commodities Exchange ("COMEX") and LME. They provide various pricing options to customers and, as noted, generally pay a floating price to suppliers.

3. Core Assets & Skills and Their Relative Importance

As the foregoing discussion suggests, a good deal of trading in physicals is customer-based, although proprietary trading is also fairly common. Traders realize profits, in essence, by creating efficiencies and exploiting short-lived price differentials over time and across markets. For example, on customer-based business, traders engage in time and location swaps, thereby eliminating the need to store and transport product. Through their comprehensive knowledge of infrastructure and their ability to manage risk, they are also able to move product more cost-effectively than producers and consumers when called upon to do so. By maintaining stocks of certain metals in particular shapes and qualities in various locations, they are able to meet specialized demand quickly, and sell metals at higher prices than the prevailing LME price. Proprietary trading generally entails making markets and earning a bid/ask spread, taking positions, and taking advantage of arbitrage opportunities.

There are several key prerequisites to successful physicals commodities trading: (1) access to financing, (2) access to product, (3) a reputation for reliability, (4) a set of administrative controls that prevents enormously costly errors and facilitates the effective management of risk,

(5) a sophisticated IT system that enables traders and risk managers to track activity in "real time," and (6) expertise in market fundamentals, trading strategies, risk management, and market infrastructure and logistics. In some markets (e.g., natural gas and power), traders possess all of these forms of expertise.

In other markets (e.g., copper concentrates, alumina and fuel oils), logistical expertise is "housed" in a separate group.

3.1 Access to Financing

Access to financial capital is a pivotal element of all trading companies' operations. The importance of financing varies to some degree, depending on the type of transaction and commodity at issue. For example, significant financing is essential in structured finance, where producers are capital-constrained, and in alumina markets, where product is traded in very large volumes. In contrast, certain types of precious metals trades require substantially less financial capital by virtue of the way that they are structured. However, with very few exceptions, access to substantial lines of credit is a sine qua non of commodities trading.

Trading firms generally rely almost entirely on European bank lines. European banks have a much greater understanding and appreciation of the complexities of commodities trading than U.S. commercial banks, and have not exited the business, as U.S. lenders have.

Bank loans can be grouped into three categories: (a) structured trade, (b) working capital, and (c) repurchase agreements. Structured finance is provided predominantly to the European (most often Swiss) offices of trading firms. This predilection for lending to European-based borrowers is explained by physical proximity, more effective means of legal recourse and a generally higher comfort level with European entities.

With respect to merchant banking, certain multinational groups or individual group members can only borrow on a transactions-specific basis. Loans are made to particular legal entities in most cases, although banks may also extend "swing lines" on which more than one group member may draw. Individual transactions are almost always financed entirely by one lending institution because this arrangement accords lenders greater legal protections in the event of default. In determining which lender to approach in connection with an individual transaction, a trading firm generally considers the bank's flexibility on transactions financing in general, its proclivity to finance the specific type of transaction at issue, the complexity of the transaction, the potential need to keep unused capacity available for more difficult transactions, and the need to provide each lender with a certain volume of business to preserve the relationship.

Other trading groups or individual group members are able to negotiate more flexible borrowing arrangements and can borrow against inventories. Such loans are generally secured by inventories and receivables. The borrower provides a Letter of Pledge to lenders on each borrowing, which stipulates the specific commodities and receivables that it is pledging as collateral, and provides the requisite supporting documentation.

3.2 Access to Product

In order to trade commodities, one must have access to commodities. As suggested above, such access may take the form of long-term offtake arrangements, and may be dependent on providing financing of various kinds to producers. Traders also source product in the spot market.

In the physicals markets, a knowledge of individual suppliers, their current and projected output, future expansion plans, technologies and alternative distribution channels are key to ensuring reliable supplies of product. Relationships with suppliers (and customers) are often developed and maintained by marketers. Marketers (or "originators") may be part of trading firms' staff or independent agents. The latter are typically compensated by commission or on a fixed fee-per-ton basis.

While pre-financing was often necessary to ensure access to supplies of aluminum in the 1990s, investment in hard assets (ownership interests in mines and smelters) is increasingly viewed as the only truly effective strategy currently. Customers themselves are reluctant to purchase essential raw materials from intermediaries with no direct sources of supply as well. The same trend is evident in copper markets.

3.3 Trading, Risk Management & Logistical Expertise

Traders provide essential expertise in formulating and executing trading strategies, as clearly indicated by their very high compensation levels. An intimate knowledge of the fundamentals that drive individual markets is obviously part of this expertise, but it also often requires an equally extensive knowledge of infrastructural elements of the market, which may create trading opportunities or preclude certain trading strategies at different times. As noted, with respect to certain commodities, traders possess knowledge of both market fundamentals and infrastructural and logistical features.

However, when product is moved via ocean-going vessel, as is true of alumina, aluminum and copper (as well as liquefied natural gas), the chartering function is generally performed by a separate group. The chartering of vessels requires specialized knowledge regarding the optimal means of shipping different metals and bulk raw materials, how quickly one can load, how long the voyage will be, the identities of charter parties and ship owners seeking particular cargo sizes, the availability and locations of ships at specific points in time, which vessels have excess space on particular voyages, discharge rates and depths at individual ports, demurrage charges, etc. In general, local knowledge is extremely important in obtaining the requisite shipping capacity at reasonable cost.[7,8]

While traders typically determine their individual transactions-specific hedging strategies, the trading group also performs a higher-level risk management function, which is often centralized. This activity entails establishing credit and position limits, continuously monitoring the group's exposure, and assessing the potential losses associated with adverse price movements and changes in spread (the differential in value from one month

---

[7] Chartering teams generally work with brokers. Chartering brokers possess important market information that they develop and maintain through daily dialog with other market participants. It is also frequently advantageous to have a middleman in negotiations with vessel owners.

[8] The freight market is a commodity market, with many characteristics in common with other such markets. Freight rates move on a daily basis, and a futures market for freight (the Baltic Exchange) has developed to provide ship owners and firms leasing vessel space a means of hedging their exposure. However, only ships of certain sizes are covered on the Baltic Exchange; smaller vessels, constituting the "Handy Market," are not covered. Some trading firms have "gone long" on ships (i.e., purchased vessels) in recent years, as freight rates have increased dramatically.

to the next).

3.4 Administrative Controls & IT Systems

Because of the large dollar value of individual contracts and the very high cost of potential errors, omissions or missed trades, an effective system of firm-wide controls is essential. Trading firms generally require that every contract for the purchase and/or sale of product be approved in writing from a credit standpoint as part of such internal controls. Every physical trade is also confirmed in writing with the counterparty, clearly specifying the terms that the parties intended. Moreover, all contracts are typically reviewed to ensure that they contain the correct legal clauses and are therefore enforceable, that the terms are correctly stated and accord with those originally agreed on verbally, etc. Such oversight is critically important to trading firms. Similarly, an IT system that permits risk managers to view transactions and hedges in "real time" is essential to the management of risk. While certain trading-specific applications software is available from third parties, it requires extensive customization.

4. Recent Developments & Their Effect on the Relative Importance of Core Trading Elements

While the core trading elements identified at Section 3 above, taken as a whole, do not change overly much from year to year, their relative importance can shift substantially over a comparatively brief period. In the past 3–5 years, the commodities trading landscape has been dominated by four important developments:

Hedge funds have become a very significant factor in these markets.

China has diminished in importance, particularly in the alumina and aluminum markets.

Pre-payment prospects have diminished because few producers require financing. And,

The supply sides of the alumina and aluminum markets are more concentrated than previously, as a result of several large mergers.

4.1 Hedge Funds

Hedge funds take speculative positions and are sufficiently large to influence prices dramatically. As a result of their movement into commodities, commodities prices have increased by as much as 400% over the past several years. Moreover, they are much more volatile than previously, and are no longer driven by market fundamentals. Moreover, while hedge fund money has driven a wedge between market fundamentals and pricing to a significant degree, it has also influenced market fundamentals. High-cost mines that could not operate profitably in more stable markets, generally located in North America and Europe, are now able to produce metals profitably. Moreover, the very high cost of certain metals (notably copper) has motivated end-users to substitute other materials, such as plastics, where feasible (e.g., in plumbing applications).

4.2 China

As previously noted, China was the driving force behind the formerly buoyant alumina market for a number of years and exported significant volumes of aluminum as well. However, it has built up its alumina production capacity from 7–8 million tons several years ago to upwards of 20 million tons currently, and imports commensurately smaller volumes. Moreover, because aluminum production is extremely energy-intensive, and China has been in the throes of a severe energy shortage for some time, it has also shifted from encouraging aluminum exports through tax rebates to imposing a tax on such exports. Hence, traders have been looking elsewhere for aluminum supplies and cultivating relationships with consumers in Asian countries other than China.

4.3 Pre-Payment Opportunities

As previously noted, in the latter part of the 1990s, metals trading firms were able to secure favorable offtake arrangements with Russian aluminum producers in exchange for pre-payment loans, because the latter were cash-strapped and required working capital. However, with metals and other commodities prices at record levels, producers no longer need such cash infusions.

4.4 Consolidation in Alumina and Aluminum Markets

As with many other industries, the alumina and aluminum markets have been consolidating over the past decade, with the rate of consolidation recently accelerating. Alcan previously acquired Alusuisse and Pechiney, and was in turn acquired by Rio Tinto in 2007. Alcoa has acquired Alumax, Inespal, Almix and Renolds. RUSAL and SUAL were formed through the consolidation of Russian smelters and CIS refineries. In late 2006, Glen-core agreed to merge certain of its alumina and aluminum assets with these entities in exchange for a 12% interest in the resulting combined company (United Company RUSAL). Chinese smelters and refiners combined to form Chalco.

4.5 Effects of Developments on Trading Activities

The developments described above have had a profound effect on (a) the risks associated with merchant trading, (b) capital requirements, and (c) the range of viable trading strategies. Each of these points is discussed in turn below.

4.5.1 Enhanced Risk

High and volatile commodities prices magnify price and credit risk, necessitating even greater due diligence and more "bullet-proof" risk management. Moreover, because a customer may enter into a contract to purchase materials at one price on a given day for delivery a month hence, and be able to purchase the materials at a much lower price later in the month, there is a real risk that the customer will not take delivery. Given the increased risk of non-performance, a reputation for reliability is even more important than previously and firms are reluctant to transact with counterparties with which they have limited experience. Moreover, large counterparties that require regular supplies of a given commodity are less apt to renege on a deal than smaller counterparties, and pose a lower credit risk. Hence, smaller counterparties are at a significant competitive disadvantage in these environs.

4.5.2 Increased Need for Financing

Because commodities prices are considerably higher, traders need more money to finance a given transaction, and because prices are more volatile, they must also earn a higher return to compensate them for the increased risk. There is also the potential for very large margin calls on hedging transactions, which banks generally won't finance. Hence, trading firms must have sufficient cash available to meet potential margin calls.

4.5.3 Diminished Range of Viable Trading Strategies

Certain trading strategies are not feasible in the current trading environment. As previously noted, because suppliers generally do not need pre-financing, it is much more difficult to negotiate long-term offtake arrangements. (As a result, trading firms are increasingly acquiring ownership interests in mines and smelters as an alternative means of securing reliable sources of supply.) Traders are also much more reluctant to take positions of any length and to carry inventories (particularly in the copper market, which has been in steep backwardation for some time). Instead, they have focused to a much greater extent than previously on short-term trading.

4.5.4 Greater Transparency, Fewer Counterparties

Both China's diminished presence in the alumina and aluminum markets and consolidation on the supply sides of these markets have substantially reduced the number of potential counterparties, the need for intermediaries in general, and the frequency of arbitrage opportunities.

5. Description of 94–40 Formulary Methodology & Proposed Global Dealing Regulations

In Notice 94-40, the IRS describes the basis on which it has entered into APAs with taxpayers engaged in the global trading of derivative financial instruments and commodities, where such operations are "functionally fully integrated." According to the Notice, fully integrated trading operations manage their business "as one global position for purposes of risk management rather than several discrete businesses." The trading book is not independently maintained for each trading location, but instead, one book (the "global book") is passed from one trading location to another in the adjacent time zone at the close of each trading day.

To assist in the management of risk, a central credit department monitors the Group's credit-related exposure, and establishes credit guidelines and customer credit limits, to be applied by traders throughout the company. In addition, in a functionally fully integrated global trading operation, the book for each product (or group of products) typically has one head trader who allocates trading limits for each trading location and determines guidelines for the book. As the head trader is responsible for the economic performance of that book, he or she is in frequent communication with, and oversees, other traders employed by the company.

Notice 94-40 states that, in the APAs that the IRS has concluded with functionally fully integrated global traders, all parties (the IRS, the taxpayer and the relevant treaty partner) agreed that worldwide income for each global book covered by the APA should be allocated among the taxpayer's trading locations pursuant to a

profit split method that is keyed to three critical factors:
- The relative value of the trading location (the "value factor");
- The risk associated with the trading location (the "risk factor"), and,
- The extent of activity at each trading location (the "activity factor").

The "value factor" is intended to measure the contribution of a trading location to the worldwide profits of the group, and is often equated to the compensation paid to all traders at individual trading locations. The "risk factor" measures the risk to which a particular trading location exposes the worldwide capital of the organization. Risk may be measured in a variety of ways (e.g., the maturity-weighted volume of swap transactions or open commodity positions at year-end by trading location). Finally, the "activity factor" is a measure of each trading location's contribution to key support functions. It is frequently quantified by the compensation paid to such personnel at each trading location.

The Treasury Department issued proposed transfer pricing regulations addressing transactions among participants in a global dealing operation on May 6, 1998 (approximately four years after Notice 94–40 was published). For purposes of these proposed regulations, a global dealing operation "consists of the execution of customer transactions, including marketing, sales, pricing and risk management activities, in a particular financial product or line of financial products, in multiple tax jurisdictions and/or through multiple participants . . . The taking of proprietary positions is not included within the definition of a global dealing operation unless the proprietary positions are entered into by a regular dealer in securities in its capacity as such a dealer ..."[9] The proposed global dealing regulations do not formally encompass commodities, although "the IRS solicit[ed] comments on whether these regulations should be extended to cover dealers in commodities . . . "[10] The arm's length allocation of combined income across tax jurisdictions under these regulations must be determined under one of the following methods, in accordance with the Best Method Rule:
- The comparable uncontrolled financial transaction (CUFT) method;
- The gross margin method;
- The gross markup method; and,
- The profit split method (a total or residual profit split).

Under the CUFT method, one looks to the pricing of uncontrolled financial transactions to establish or evaluate intercompany pricing. Pricing data from public exchanges or quotation media are acceptable under some circumstances, as are applications of internal proprietary pricing models used to establish pricing on arm's length financial dealings. Judging from the examples given in the proposed regulations (as well as simple common sense), the CUFT method would generally apply when (a) a controlled group trades standardized financial instruments, (b) each group member operates as a dealer in its own right vis-a-vis its separate customer base, and (c) intercompany financial transactions take place contemporaneously with third party transactions. While the CUFT approach is reasonable on its face, its applicability is somewhat limited, inasmuch as many trading firms deal in non-standard financial products and commodities, enter into relatively few (albeit large) trades per day, and/or typically conclude contracts

---
9. See Prop. Treas. Reg. 1.482-8(a)(2)
10. Ibid.

in a broad range of geographic markets.

As with the CUFT method, the gross margin and gross markup methods presuppose that each member of a global dealing operation has a substantial book of business that it carries out independently. The gross margin and gross markup methods can be applied when individual group members act as market-makers vis-a-vis third parties and a market-determined bid/ask spread can therefore readily be established in the relevant time frame (that is, when an intercompany transaction takes place).

The proposed global dealing regulations' profit split methods are intended to address more complex situations in which individual group members' activities are more closely integrated. Consistent with Notice 94–40, the proposed regulations advocate apportioning a group's combined operating profits (or losses) by reference to the relative value of each entity's contributions thereto. However, the proposed regulations are more flexible as to the particular factors that should be incorporated into the allocation formula. Depending on the facts and circumstances that characterize individual cases, a multi-factor formula may be indicated, and, in this event, each factor will need to be weighted.

6. Critique of Formulary Methodology

The formulary apportionment methodology put forward by the IRS produces arbitrary results. Moreover, a "separate entity" framework is viable, and would produce more reasonable results. Hence, the use of a formulary methodology—a radical departure from other U.S. and OECD transfer pricing regulations and guidelines—is unnecessary and unhelpful.

6.1 The Formulary Methodology Produces Arbitrary Results

Accepting, for the sake of discussion, that a formulary apportionment methodology is appropriate, it should not produce arbitrary results. However, the formulary method described in Notice 94–40 and the proposed global dealing regulations does not meet this standard for three principal reasons:
1) It does not preserve the nexus between assets (as distinct from "factors") and the generation of income;
2) It distills risk down to a single measure; and,
3) It substitutes subjective weights for fair market values.

6.1.1 "Factors" Should Be Replaced With Assets

While all resources employed in a given activity can be said to generate gross profits, assets alone generate free cash flows. Factors other than assets, such as trader expertise, generic "activity levels," etc., should not be used to allocate free cash flows (or operating profits), because they do not generate free cash flows (or operating profits) in the first instance. Rather, traders, marketers and key support personnel are paid the fair market value of their services,[11] and, for accounting purposes, wages and other forms of compensation are deducted from gross profits. Stated differently, operating profits and free cash flows do not embody the fair market value of services rendered by traders, marketers and key support personnel. The residual

---

11 If they were compensated at less than fair market value, they would presumably seek employment elsewhere.

that remains after paying individuals the fair market value of their services and purchasing or leasing all other resources (including equipment) at their prevailing market-determined prices or rental rates (or imputing such payments if necessary) constitutes the cost of capital to a trading group and the return to investors. Hence, in allocating free cash flows, one should look only to the fair market values of income-generating assets.

6.1.2 Risk is Multi-Faceted

The formulary apportionment method outlined in Notice 94–40 incorporates a single "risk factor," variously measured as the maturity-weighted volume of swap transactions, open commodity positions at year-end, etc. Leaving aside the reasonableness of including this type of risk factor in the allocation formula, risk, in a trading context cannot be reduced to single measure, nor is the nature of risk constant over time.

As discussed at Section 4 herein, the current trading environment, characterized by extremely volatile prices, has greatly exacerbated trading firms' price and credit risk, and effectively precluded open positions of any duration. Non-performance is probably the single most important risk at present and is not addressed at all by the measures of risk described in Notice 94-40. There is also much greater risk that delayed payment (and the attendant interest costs) will eliminate the narrow margins that firms currently earn in traditional merchant trading activities. Moreover, trading firms' investments in hard assets have given rise to other risks not contemplated in Notice 94-40.

6.1.3 Weights are Subjective & Factors Change in Relative Importance

Again, leaving aside the appropriateness of specific non-asset "factors" and their measurement, the weights assigned to individual factors under the formulary apportionment method are purely subjective, and are held fixed for the multi-year term of an APA agreement. In the field, the same tends to be true, although not contractually so. Given the highly fluid nature of global dealing, such constancy is not a viable working assumption.

The subjective nature of weighting is self-evident. However, even if one could objectively establish the relative importance of core trading assets and activities at a given point, these "objective" weights would not remain the same for long. As discussed above, access to financial capital and effective risk management have increased in importance over the past several years. At the same time, the relative importance of trading expertise and established supplier relationships have diminished with the narrowing of potential trading strategies and the "write-off" of established relationships with Chinese alumina buyers and aluminum suppliers.

6.2 The Formulary Apportionment Methodology is Unnecessary

As discussed at Section 3 herein, the core elements of a global trading operation consist of (1) access to financing, (2) access to product, (3) a reputation for reliability, (4) a set of administrative controls that prevents enormously costly errors and facilitates the effective management of risk, (5) a sophisticated IT system that enables traders and risk managers to track activity in "real time," and (6) expertise in market fundamentals and infrastructural and logistical features, trading strategies and risk management.

With the exception of expertise possessed by traders, risk managers and logistical specialists (i.e., "human capital"), these core elements are linked to specific tangible and intangible assets, most of which can be identified with individual group members. Trading firms with established relationships with lending institutions (an intangible asset) have access to funding. Trading firms with long-term offtake arrangements (another intangible asset) and firms that own interests in mines and smelters (tangible assets) have access to product. Customized IT systems are another form of intangible asset. A global dealing operation will necessarily have both administrative controls that facilitate risk management and an established reputation for reliability, elements of going concern value.

As previously discussed, the "worldwide capital" available to a trading group is fungible only if lenders agree to these terms. It is by no means always the case that a single group member has large credit lines and allocates borrowed funds freely among group members, as dictated by trading opportunities. Rather, in some instances, credit is extended directly from third party lenders to individual group members, and the latter have very limited flexibility with regard to the use of borrowed funds. Moreover, even where loans are made to a single entity that performs a centralized treasury function, the relevant metric for profit split purposes (that is, the associated intangible asset) is access to capital in the first instance, not the extent to which individual trading locations put the "worldwide capital" of the group at risk. Such access is generally measurable on an entity-by-entity basis.

Where access to product is formalized in a written contract, generally only one member of a controlled trading group will be the counterparty. While other entities may have assisted in the negotiation of the contract or provided pre-financing, and should be compensated accordingly, the counterparty is the legal "owner" of the established relationship. Where a relationship with a customer or supplier is well-established but not formalized, an individual originator or trader will generally have developed the relationship in the first instance. The entity that compensates this individual should be deemed to "own" the customer or supplier relationship.

Administrative controls, risk management systems and proprietary IT systems are generally developed in one trading location and used by other locations. The developer (or, where applicable, the legal owner) of these controls and systems should be treated as the owner for transfer pricing purposes.

A reputation for reliability may have originated with a single trading location, or it may be a natural outgrowth of the integrated operation. In the first case, the single trading location should be deemed to own the goodwill intangible. In the second case, goodwill should not be used to allocate income across trading locations, inasmuch as it is jointly developed and owned.

---

12. As discussed at length in my forthcoming book, Transfer Pricing in Corporate Taxation (Springer Verlag, 2008), free cash flows should be substituted for operating profits as well.

7. Alternative "Separate Entity" Approach

One can significantly improve on the IRS' formulary apportionment methodology vis-a-vis global dealing operations by substituting assets for factors, and fair market values for weights. With these modifications, the revised profit split methodology has a more solid economic footing, and is consistent with the residual profit split method contained in the 1994 transfer pricing regulations.[12]

Under the residual profit slit method, one (a) imputes a return to each group member's "routine" contributions, and (b) allocates combined residual income (attributable to intangible assets) by reference to the relative fair market values of intangible assets contributed by each group member. As a practical matter, tax practitioners generally value intangible assets for profit split purposes by capitalizing and amortizing the associated "intangibles-creating" expenditures (e.g., advertising, R&D, etc.).

Most of the intangible assets utilized in a global trading context are not the result of investment per se, but a natural outgrowth of conducting a successful global dealing operation over a period of years. Hence, the capitalization–amortization valuation approach cannot be applied. A more standard valuation methodology, such as the discounted cash flow (DCF) method, would be exceedingly difficult and imprecise in a trading context. However, the explicit valuation of intangible assets may be unnecessary. Instead, one might work backwards from realized cash flows in a given reporting period to the intangible assets that generated them, and from intangible assets to their ownership by trading location. Rather than forecasting cash flows over the economically useful life of individual intangible assets, this approach would require only a contemporaneous analysis for individual reporting periods.

Conclusion

This article examines the IRS' formulary apportionment approach, used at times to allocate global trading firms' taxable income across jurisdictions. While certain features of trading operations set them apart from many other forms of economic activity, these distinguishing characteristics do not preclude the use of a "separate entity" framework, consistent with all other U.S. and OECD transfer pricing regulations and guidelines.

In lieu of value, risk and activity "factors," one should utilize assets to allocate global trading firms' free cash flows (or operating profits). In lieu of subjective weights, one should use the fair market values of such assets. With these modifications, the formulary apportionment method becomes a residual profit split method, and many of the shortcomings of the former approach are ameliorated.

Elizabeth King, Ph.D. is the founder of Beecher Consulting LLC, an independent firm specializing in transfer pricing and valuation issues. She has worked in these fields for over 20 years. Dr. King can be reached at **(617) 730-8138** or by email at eking@beecherconsultinggroup.com.

For more information on the author, please see Section XIII.

IX. Treaties

Mandatory Arbitration Procedures: A New Tack for Resolving Double Taxation Disputes between Competent Authorities

Michael Plodek
Lockheed Martin

Negotiating the Byzantine labyrinth of transfer pricing can be a frustrating experience. Perhaps the largest of many traps into which a taxpayer may fall is when two jurisdictions assert inconsistent positions upon an audit of the same transaction, resulting in potential double taxation of the same taxpayer or the same income. Bilateral income tax treaties are supposed to prevent such double taxation, but they are not always effective in doing so. This article highlights some of the deficiencies in the way bilateral tax treaties currently deal with the resolution of inconsistent positions taken by one or another tax authority in connection with transfer pricing and other issues, then analyzes how the new mandatory arbitration procedures included in certain recent protocols and treaties signed by the United States represent an improvement over current methodologies, particularly with respect to establishing a definite timeline for resolution and encouraging Competent Authorities to moderate their positions. The article also discusses potential further improvements that would offer more complete protection against double taxation.

I. Current Mutual Agreement Procedures

Under bilateral income tax treaties currently in force, the United States has the authority to include profits in the income of an enterprise that may otherwise have accrued to a related enterprise.[1] The United States primarily exercises this authority under section 482.[2] However, the other Contracting State is only required to make an "appropriate adjustment" if that Contracting State agrees "profits so included are profits that would have accrued to the enterprise of the first-mentioned State if the conditions made between the two enterprises had been those that would have been made between independent enterprises."[3] Given that such an agreement and the relevant adjustment result in a direct revenue loss to the other Contracting State, disagreements are legion as to the profits that would have accrued between two related enterprises had they

---
[1] See United States Model Income Tax Convention, September 20, 1996 ("1996 Model Treaty"), Article 9(1); United States Model Income Tax Convention, November 16, 2006 ("2006 Model Treaty"), Article 9(1).
[2] All references are to the U.S. Internal Revenue Code of 1986, as amended, unless otherwise noted.
[3] 2006 Model Treaty, Article 9(2).

been independent.

The traditional mechanism for resolving such disagreements is the so-called mutual agreement procedure set out in the applicable bilateral tax treaty.[4] Pursuant to such mutual agreement procedures, a taxpayer which believes that the positions of the Contracting States will result in taxation inconsistent with the terms of the treaty may "present his case to the competent authority of either Contracting State."[5] In response, the competent authority will endeavor to reach a negotiated settlement with the competent authority of the other Contracting State "if the objection appears to it to be justified and if it is not itself able to arrive at a satisfactory solution."[6] The competent authority may endeavor to reach such a settlement notwithstanding any time or other procedural limitations imposed by domestic law.[7] Also of note, the mutual agreement procedures are exempt from the so-called "Savings Clause,"[8] meaning that the mutual agreement procedures of a bilateral treaty may also be used by a citizen of the United States to request appropriate relief from the U.S. Internal Revenue Service ("IRS").[9] The mutual agreement procedures thus represent a flexible method for dealing with potential double taxation caused by, among other things, inconsistent positions taken by both Contracting States regarding the correct transfer pricing to be applied to a taxpayer or related taxpayers.

Consider, for example, the case of Corporation X, a resident of State A that has Branch Z in State B. State A and State B have a bilateral income tax treaty in force that generally incorporates the mutual agreement procedures set forth in the 1996 Model Treaty and both States have a territorial tax system which excludes from the respective tax bases income earned outside that State. Corporation X develops intellectual property used in manufacturing various products, including Product M, while Branch Z has manufacturing facilities which can be used to produce various products, including Product M. Product A costs $20 to make and sells for $50. Pursuant to an intracompany agreement, Branch Z manufactures Product M using Corporation X's intellectual property receiving cost plus 20% ($24 gross revenue and $4 taxable income) while Corporation X receives $50 from the sale of Product M (or $26 taxable income). Upon audit of Corporation X's tax returns, State A asserts that the arm's length agreement between Corporation X and Branch Z should be cost plus 10%, and increases Corporation X's taxable income by $2.

At the same time State B asserts on audit that Branch Z has assumed entrepreneurial risk with respect to the sale of Product M. State B concludes that based on comparable uncontrolled transactions the arm's length arrangement should be only a $10 royalty paid from Branch Z to Corporation X with $40 of revenue attributable to Branch Z. After allowances for costs, this adjustment results in $20 of income attributable to Branch Z and taxable by State B under the Business Profits article of the State A-State B bilateral income tax treaty. Thus, Corporation X as an economic whole would be subject to tax on $48 of "income" ($20 by State B and $28 by State A) on a single economic profit of $30 from the sale of Product M. Under the State A-State B bilateral income tax treaty, Corporation X can request that the competent authority of State A negotiate with the competent authority of State B to resolve the potential double taxation. The competent

---

4   2006 Model Treaty, Article 25; 1996 Model Treaty, Article 25.
    5   Id., Article 25(1).
    6   Id., Article 25(2).
    7   Id.
    8   Id., Article 1(5)(a).
    9   Rev. Proc. 2006-54, 2006-49 I.R.B. 1035.

authorities would then endeavor to reach an agreement on such issues as whether Branch Z has assumed any entrepreneurial risk with respect to the sale of Product M, whether the appropriate method to determine the arm's length price is cost-plus or comparable uncontrolled method, and what is the appropriate royalty or plus factor to be used.

No Enforceable Right to Remedy

There are a few flies in the ointment, however. Most significantly, a taxpayer is not given a judicially enforceable right to remedy double taxation.[10] In Filler v. Commissioner, for example, a taxpayer residing in France received wages for services rendered, including five days of services performed in the United States. France took the position that all of the taxpayer's income was subject to taxation by France while the United States took the position the amounts received by the taxpayer for services performed in the Untied States were U.S. source income, taxable by the United States, and accordingly reduced the foreign tax credits claimed by the taxpayer.[11] The taxpayer subsequently filed a petition in the U.S. Tax Court, claiming that the taxpayer was subject to double taxation in contravention of the then-applicable United States-France income tax convention and, in particular, Article 25 (the mutual agreement procedure thereof).[12] The Tax Court held that Article 25 created an administrative procedure and not a judicial remedy which the taxpayer could assert in Tax Court.[13] The Tax Court further held that any relief to which the taxpayer was entitled should be sought from France, notwithstanding the fact that the taxpayer's request for relief had already been denied by the French authorities.[14]

Filler v. Commissioner illustrates that — notwithstanding the potential resort to mutual agreement procedures — a taxpayer can find itself left twisting in the wind with neither Contracting State willing to negotiate in order to reach a compromise.[15] And according to the statistics released periodically by the IRS, this does arise, even if in only a minority of cases.[16] Of course, it takes two to tango. So even if the competent authority of one Contracting State is willing to negotiate a solution, the process can go nowhere if the competent authority of the other Contracting State is unwilling to compromise. This can then place the taxpayer in the position of having to incur additional expenses in "lobbying" the competent authority of the other Contracting State, where the taxpayer may have few resources in place, no business connections to call upon, and may not even speak the language.

No Relief from Accrued Interest

To add insult to injury, nothing in the mutual agreement procedures requires that the accrual of interest on the amount of any asserted deficiency be suspended or otherwise relieved while the competent authorities negotiate a resolution to the double taxation imposed upon a taxpayer.[17]

---

10   *Filler v. Commissioner*, 74 T.C. 406 (1980).
11   Id. at 406-407.
12   Id. at 407.
13   Id. at 407-408.
14   Id. at 413.
15   It is interesting to note that the amount at issue in the *Filler* case was less than U.S. $400 in tax, hardly a significant revenue loss to either France or the United States.
16   See, e.g., 14 Transfer Pricing Report 688 (Dec. 21, 2005) (referencing the "U.S. Competent Authority statistics for fiscal 2005" showing that an average of approximately 13% of the total dollar adjustments over a five year period resulted in partial or no relief).
17   IRS Non-Docketed Service Advice Review issued April 4, 1996, 1996 IRS NSAR 5874, 1996

In an IRS Non-Docketed Service Advice Review issued April 4, 1996 ("IRS 1996 NSAR"), the IRS concluded that there was "no legal remedy . . . under section 6404, the subject treaty, or Rev. Proc. 96-13 [the then-applicable Revenue Procedure for requesting competent authority relief]" for a taxpayer regarding interest that had accrued while the matter at issue was subject to the mutual agreement procedure by the competent authorities and therefore there should be no reduction in the interest owed by that taxpayer.[18] As a point of reference, issues for one of the taxable years in the IRS 1996 NSAR had been under consideration by the competent authority for 687 days while issues relating to another taxable year had been under consideration for 1,437 days.[19] A taxpayer could, for instance, make a deposit in order to suspend the accrual of interest,[20] but this hardly seems an equitable solution since it requires the taxpayer to bear the economic burden of double taxation without any assurance that it will benefit from an eventual remedy.

II. Proposed Mandatory Arbitration Procedures

On November 27, 2006, the United States and the Kingdom of Belgium signed a new income tax convention (the "Proposed U.S.-Belgium Convention")[21] which contains, in Article 24(7) and (8), provisions establishing mandatory arbitration of unresolved disputes between competent authorities of the two Contracting States. Similar provisions are contained in the protocols amending the U.S.-Germany income tax convention signed June 1, 2006 (the "German Protocol")[22] and the U.S.-Canada income tax convention signed September 21, 2007 (the "Canadian Protocol").[23] These mandatory arbitration provisions were included by the United States in the hopes that they would improve the mutual agreement process,[24] which can result in as many

---

WL 33325635.
18   Id.
19   Id.
20   Section 6603; Rev. Proc. 2005-18, 2005-13 I.R.B. 798.
21   Convention Between the Government of the United States of America and the Government of the Kingdom of Belgium For the Avoidance of Double Taxation and the Prevention of Fiscal Evasion with respect to Taxes on Income, signed November 27, 2006, available at http://www.treas.gov/offices/tax-policy/library/Belgium06.pdf. This convention has not yet been ratified.
22   Protocol Amending the Convention between The United States of America and The Federal Republic of Germany for the Avoidance of Double Taxation and the Prevention of Fiscal Evasion with Respect to Taxes on Income and Capital and to Certain Other Taxes, signed June 1, 2006, available at http://www.treas.gov/press/releases/reports/germanprotocol06.pdf. This protocol has not yet been ratified.
23   Protocol Amending the Convention between The United States of America and Canada with respect to Taxes on Income and on Capital, signed at Washington on 26 September 1980, as Amended on 14 June 1983, 28 March 1984, 17 March 1995, and 29 July 1997, signed September 21, 2007, available at http:www.treas.gov/offices/tax-policy/library/CanadaProtocol07.pdf. This protocol has not yet been ratified.
24   HP-494, Testimony of Treasury International Tax Counsel John Harrington before the Senate Committee on Foreign Relations on Pending Income Tax Agreements, available at http://www.treas.gov/press/releases/hp494.htm ("Based on our review of the U.S. experience with arbitration in other areas of the law, the success of other countries with arbitration in the tax area, and the overwhelming support of the business community, we concluded that mandatory binding arbitration as the final step in the competent authority process can be an effective and appropriate tool to facilitate mutual agreement under U.S. tax treaties."); HP-569, Paulson Remarks on Signing of Update to U.S.-Canada Income Tax Treaty, available at http://www.treas.gov/press/releases/hp569.htm ("There is also a provision for arbitration of unresolved double-taxation cases; this will lead to more expedient and

as 20 percent of cases of double taxation remaining unresolved.[25] This article will use the provisions of the Proposed U.S.-Belgium Convention to illustrate how the mandatory arbitration procedure operates, noting those substantive differences from the procedures established by the German and the Canadian Protocols.

Article 24(7) of the Proposed U.S.-Belgium Convention obligates the competent authorities of the Contracting States to resolve by arbitration, as prescribed in Article 24(8), any matter submitted for mutual agreement on which they cannot reach a complete agreement. There are three prerequisites to the Contracting States' obligation to resolve an outstanding matter by arbitration. The taxpayer must have filed tax returns with at least one Contracting State for the taxable year to which the unresolved matter pertains.[26] All concerned persons[27] and their authorized representatives or agents must agree not to disclose to any other person information received during the course of the arbitration from the Contracting State or the arbitration board.[28] Finally, the competent authorities must not agree that the outstanding matter is not suitable for determination by arbitration.[29] The German Protocol and the Canadian Protocol contain an additional requirement that the unresolved matter involve the application of one or more Articles of the income tax convention.[30] The German Protocol Article XVI(22) states that the relevant matters subject to mandatory arbitration are issues arising under Article 4 (Residence) (but only insofar as it relates to the residence of a natural person), Article 5 (Permanent Establishment), Article 7 (Business Profits), Article 9 (Associated Enterprises), and Article 12 (Royalties).[31] Diplomatic notes between the United States and Canada exchanged in connection with the execution of the Canadian Protocol provide a similar list of subject matter to be covered by mandatory arbitration procedures under the Canadian Protocol.[32]

---

efficient resolutions of these cases. The inclusion of an arbitration provision is a new development for the United States.").

25 Bell, Kevin, "Next Edition of OECD Model Tax Treaty Will Include Arbitration," 114 *Tax Notes* 638 (Feb. 12, 2007) ("Recent statistics from a couple of major OECD countries show that between 9 percent and 20 percent of their mutual agreement cases did not result in a resolution that eliminated double taxation.").

26 Proposed U.S.-Belgium Convention, Article 24(7)(a).

27 Proposed U.S.-Belgium Convention, Article 24(8)(a) defines "concerned person" as "the presenter of a case to a competent authority for consideration under this Article and all other persons, if any, whose tax liability to either Contracting State may be directly affected by a mutual agreement arising from that consideration."

28 Proposed U.S.-Belgium Convention, Article 24(7)(c) & (8)(d). An exception from the non-disclosure requirement may be permitted following a determination by the arbitration board.

29 Id., Article 24(7)(b). The only time restriction specified is that the competent authorities must agree that the matter is not suitable for arbitration "before the date on which arbitration proceedings would otherwise have begun." Id.

30 German Protocol, Article XII, (proposed text of Article 25(5)(b)(aa)(A)); Canadian Protocol, Article 20, (proposed text of Article XXVI(6)(b)(i)(A)).

31 German Protocol, Article XVI(22). This Article also provides for the rules of the arbitration procedure analogous to those set forth in Protocol to Convention Between the Government of the United States of America and the Government of the Kingdom of Belgium For the Avoidance of Double Taxation and the Prevention of Fiscal Evasion with respect to Taxes on Income, signed November 27, 2006 ("Belgian Protocol"), Article 6, available at http://www.treas.gov/offices/tax-policy/library/Belgium06Protocol.pdf., discussed below.

32 Note No. JLAB-0111 dated September 21, 2007, available at http://www.treas.gov/offices/tax-policy/library/CanadaDipNotes07.pdf, provides that the mandatory arbitration procedures apply to issues arising under Article IV (Residence) (but only insofar as it relates to the residence of a natural

Article 24(8) sets forth the operational provisions of the mandatory arbitration procedure. Article 24(8)(c) provides that arbitration of a matter shall begin no earlier than the later of two dates: (1) the date on which all concerned persons and their authorized representatives or agents have submitted their non-disclosure agreement to the competent authorities;[33] or (2) two years after the commencement date,[34] "unless both competent authorities have previously agreed to a different date." This second alternative would seem to indicate that the competent authorities could agree to arbitration before two years have elapsed. On the other hand, allowing the competent authorities to agree to a later date would make the mandatory part of the arbitration superfluous, as the competent authorities could always agree to a date sufficiently far in the future as to make any arbitration effectively useless. Finally, Article 24(8)(e) provides that the taxpayer is not bound to accept the arbitration decision.[35]

The nuts and bolts of the mandatory arbitration procedure are set forth in Article 6 of the Protocol to the Proposed U.S.-Belgium Convention ("Belgian Protocol").[36] However, the rules set forth in Article 6 are not set in stone. Article 6(q) of the Belgian Protocol permits the competent authorities of the Contracting States to "modify or supplement the above rules and procedures as necessary to more effectively implement the intent of paragraph 7 of Article 24 to eliminate double taxation." Thus, the rules of the mandatory arbitration procedure are meant to be flexible, allowing the competent authorities to modify them in order to achieve desired results. On the other hand, as the rules in Article 6 set forth are the default rules (i.e., the rules that apply unless modified), they provide a fairly good indication of how a mandatory arbitration will likely operate in practice.

---

person), Article V (Permanent Establishment), Article VII (Business Profits), Article IX (Related Persons), and Article XII (Royalties) (but only (i) insofar as Article XII might apply in transactions involving related persons to whom Article IX might apply; or (ii) to an allocation of amounts between royalties that are taxable under paragraph 2 thereof and royalties that are exempt under paragraph 3 thereof). This Note also sets forth the rules of the arbitration procedure analogous to those set forth in the Belgian Protocol, Article 6 (discussed below).

33 Proposed U.S.-Belgium Convention, Article 24(8)(c)(ii). Since such an agreement is a prerequisite for the obligation of that Contracting State to arbitrate an issue, this date really appears somewhat redundant.

34 Id., Article 24(8)(c)(i). Article 24(8)(b) of the Proposed U.S.-Belgium Convention defines the commencement date as "the earliest date on which the information necessary to undertake substantive consideration for a mutual agreement has been received by both competent authorities." Article 6(p)(i) of the Belgian Protocol provides that "the information necessary to undertake substantive consideration for a mutual agreement" from the U.S. point of view the United States is the information required to be submitted under Section 4.05 of Revenue Procedure 2002-52, 2006-49 I.R.B. 1035 (or any applicable successor provisions) or, for cases initially submitted as a request for an Advance Pricing Agreement, Section 4 of Revenue Procedure 2006-9, 2006-2 I.R.B. 278, (or any applicable successor provisions). Revenue Procedure 2002-52 is superseded by Revenue Procedure 2006-54, 2006-49 I.R.B. 1035, for requests filed after December 4, 2006.

35 Belgian Protocol, Article 6(c) clarifies that a taxpayer may terminate the arbitration proceeding at any point by withdrawing its request for relief under Article 24.

36 Protocol to Convention Between the Government of the United States of America and the Government of the Kingdom of Belgium For the Avoidance of Double Taxation and the Prevention of Fiscal Evasion with respect to Taxes on Income, signed November 27, 2006, available at http://www.treas.gov/offices/tax-policy/library/Belgium06Protocol.pdf.

Fees and Procedures

First, it is useful to note that Article 6(o) sets forth the fees for the mandatory arbitration procedure and provides that the Contracting States will share such costs.[37] The per diem fee for the members of the arbitration board is US $2,000 (or its euro equivalent), but that can be modified by the competent authorities.[38] The expenses for the members are determined in accordance with the schedule set forth by the International Centre for Settlement of Investment Disputes.[39] The Contracting State that has initiated the mutual agreement proceedings resulting in mandatory arbitration is responsible for providing the facilities and administrative support for the mandatory arbitration at its own costs, with the exception that fees for translation services are to be borne equally by both Contracting States.[40] All other expenses are to be borne by the Contracting State which incurs them.[41]

The arbitration board is to be composed of three members, one appointed by each Contracting State.[42] Those two will then select a third member to serve as the Chair, and the latter may not be a citizen of either Contracting State.[43] From the start of the arbitration procedure, each Contracting State has 60 days to send a written communication to the other Contracting State specifying whom it will appoint to the arbitration board.[44] Once each Contracting State has appointed one member to the arbitration board, the Chair must be selected within 60 days.[45] If either Contracting State fails to appoint a member to the arbitration board, or if the appointed members are unable to agree on a Chair, the chair or other members of the arbitration board will be selected within 60 days of the date of such failure by the highest-ranking member of the Secretariat at the Centre for Tax Policy and Administration of the Organization for Economic Co-operation and Development.[46]

Once the arbitration board has been selected, each Contracting State has 60 days to submit a proposed resolution and a supporting position paper outlining its disposition of the outstanding matters to the arbitration board.[47] Each Contracting State will be notified of the proposed resolution and position paper submitted by the other Contracting State and will have an additional 60 days (i.e., up to 120 days from the date when the Chair is appointed)[48] to submit a reply brief.[49] Any further information may only be submitted to the arbitration board at its request. Once the proposed resolution, supporting position papers, reply briefs, and any additional information requested by the arbitration board have been submitted, the arbitration board has six months to make its decision.[50]

The arbitration board must select one of the proposed resolutions submitted by the Contracting States as its decision.[51] If only one Contracting State has submitted a proposed resolution within the applicable time limit, that proposed resolution shall be accepted as the decision of the arbitration board.[52] In selecting which proposed resolution it will adopt as its decision, the

---
37 Belgian Protocol, Article 6(o).
38 Id.
39 Id. A copy of that schedule dated July 6, 2005 is available at http://www.worldbank.org/icsid/schedule/fees.pdf.
40 Id.
41 Id.
42 Id., Article 6(e).
43 Belgian Protocol,, Article 6(e).
44 Id.
45 Id.
46 Id.
47 Id., Article 6(f).
48 These time periods are 90 days and 180 days, respectively, under the German Protocol, Article XVI(22)(g).
49 Belgian Protocol, Article 6(f).
50 Id., Article 6(h).
51 Id.
52 Id., Article 6(f).

arbitration board will apply, in descending preference, the provisions of the applicable income tax convention, the agreed commentary or technical explanation to the income tax convention, the laws of the Contracting States (to the extent that such laws do not contradict one another), and any OECD Commentary, Guidelines or Reports regarding relevant analogous portions of the OECD Model Tax Convention.[53] The decision of the arbitration board is binding on each Contracting State, but will have no precedential value.[54]

Each concerned person has 30 days from when it is notified of the decision of the arbitration board to decide whether it accepts such decision and advise the competent authority with which it filed the request for mutual agreement procedures of its decision.[55] If the concerned person has previously commenced litigation regarding the matters which were the subject of the arbitration procedure, then such concerned person must also advise the appropriate courts regarding whether it has accepted the decision of the arbitration board.[56] If any concerned person fails to notify the relevant competent authority and, if applicable, the appropriate courts of its acceptance of the decision of the arbitration board within the applicable time period, the concerned person is deemed to have rejected that decision.[57] If the decision of the arbitration board is not accepted, then the matters that were the subject of that decision may not be submitted again for mandatory arbitration.[58] Any applicable interest or penalties will be determined by the local law of the relevant Contracting State.[59]

As an illustration of how the mandatory arbitration provision would operate, consider again the case of Corporation X, discussed supra, with the caveat that the State A-State bilateral income tax treaty has mandatory arbitration provisions similar to those provided in the Proposed U.S.-Belgium Convention. If the competent authorities of State A and State B were unable after two years to reach an agreement regarding how much income should be attributable to Branch Z in respect of its manufacturing activities they would be obligated to submit the matter for arbitration provided that Corporation X signed the requisite non-disclosure agreement. The competent authorities of State A and State B would each select one person to be on the arbitration board within 60 days and those two people would have an additional 60 days to select a third person to be the Chair. The competent authorities of State A and State B would then have 60 days to submit a proposed resolution to the arbitration board which would have 6 months to decide on which proposal to adopt as its decision. Following the decision of the arbitration board, Corporation X would have 30 days to notify the competent authority of State A whether it accepts the decision of the arbitration board. Thus, Corporation X would be assured that once it had signed to requisite non-disclosure agreements, it would have a resolution on its double taxation issue within one year.

III. Analysis and Considerations of the Mandatory Arbitration Procedures

The mandatory arbitration procedures represent a significant improvement over the existing mutual agreement procedures if only because they add a definite time period within which the issue in dispute

---
53 Id., Article 6(i).
54 Id., Article 6(j).
55 Belgian Protocol, Article 6(k).
56 Id.
57 Id.
58 Id.
59 Id., Article 6(m).

must be resolved. In essence, the mandatory arbitration procedures allow a taxpayer to know that after two years from the filing of its mutual agreement request, it can at least expect some meaningful progress. Indeed, assuming that the taxpayer is willing to agree to the non-disclosure provisions, a competent authority must submit its proposed resolution and position paper within 180 days (210 days under the German Protocol) of that two-year mark or risk having the competent authority from the other Contracting State dictate the issue. In any event, the taxpayer can count on a decision within six months from the submission of the proposed resolution, position papers, reply brief, and any further submissions requested by the arbitration board. This affords the taxpayer the certainty that there will at least be some light at the end of the tunnel. In actual fact, however, it is anticipated that the mandatory arbitration procedure's biggest impact will be more prophylactic in nature in that it will encourage competent authorities to pursue more moderate negotiating positions and strategies, thereby avoiding the sort of extreme positions that have often resulted in deadlocked negotiations.[60]

Possible Further Improvements

While a laudable step forward, the mandatory arbitration procedures could nevertheless benefit from a few modifications. It would be a welcome change to allow the taxpayer to submit a proposed resolution and position paper that would be accepted as the decision of the arbitration board if both competent authorities fail to submit a proposed resolution. As currently drafted, there is no provision in the mandatory arbitration rules to provide for this possibility, which could lead to a perverse version of the "prisoner's dilemma" in which both competent authorities can collude to deny mandatory arbitration to a taxpayer by simply failing to present any proposed solution. The mandatory arbitration rules provide a solution for a similar situation in which the two Contracting States fail to appoint someone as the Chair of the arbitration board. In such a situation, the Chair is selected by a neutral third party, the highest-ranking member of the OECD Secretariat at the Centre for Tax Policy and Administration. Allowing the taxpayer to submit a proposed resolution which would be accepted as the arbitration board's decision only if both Contracting States fail to submit proposed resolutions would forestall another similar deadlock. The Contracting States would be motivated to submit proposed resolutions because the taxpayer's proposed resolution would presumably be as favorable to the taxpayer as possible.

It would also be desirable to have a mechanism to deal with interest assessed on a taxpayer which has utilized the mutual agreement and mandatory arbitration provisions to resolve transfer pricing disputes. A taxpayer can end up bearing much of the economic burden of double taxation by reason of interest charges (or by having to make a deposit to prevent the accrual of interest) which are assessed as it attempts to reconcile the differing positions of the competent authorities. In essence, the interest penalty is designed to compensate a government for the loss of the use of taxes not paid to it by the taxpayer based upon an erroneous tax return position and to discourage a

---

60 See HP-494, supra note 25 ("Thus, it is our expectation that these arbitration provisions will be rarely utilized, but that their presence will encourage the competent authorities to take approaches to their negotiations that result in mutually agreeable conclusions.").

taxpayer from avoiding settlement to prolong tax controversies.[61] But in the case of an underpayment asserted on the basis of a transfer pricing error the taxpayer may not have really received such a cash flow benefit because it usually will have paid the taxes assessed by the other Contracting State. While there may be a difference in the tax rates of the two Contracting States, that will not necessarily be the case and,

---

[61] See, e.g., U.S. v. Koppers, 348 U.S. 254 (1955) ("If the instant taxpayer had paid its required tax in 1941, the Government would have received an additional $ 460,408.91 at that time. Accordingly, it would have had the use of that money, without charge, during the crucial war years. Correspondingly, the taxpayer would have been without that money during the same period. Instead, the taxpayer, in fact, retained the funds for its own use and now contends that it need not compensate the Government for such use of a substantial part of it . . . . The detriment to the Government and benefit to the taxpayer was the same -- the use of $ 460,408.91 for eight years."); Manning v. Seeley Tube and Box Co., 338 U.S. 561 (1950) ("The subsequent cancellation of the duty to pay this assessed deficiency does not cancel in like manner the duty to pay the interest on that deficiency. From the date the original return was to be filed until the date the deficiency was actually assessed, the taxpayer had a positive obligation to the United States: a duty to pay its tax. For that period the taxpayer, by its failure to pay the taxes owed, had the use of funds which rightfully should have been in the possession of the United States. The fact that the statute permits the taxpayer subsequently to avoid the payment of that debt in no way indicates that the taxpayer is to derive the benefits of the funds for the intervening period.") (internal citations omitted in both instances).

in any event, some provision ought to be made in the event the Contracting States charge different rates of interest on overpayments and underpayments. In such a case, a taxpayer could end up with a "windfall loss" if, for example, the Contracting State to which there was an allocation of too much taxable income paid only 5% on tax overpayments, but the other Contracting State charges 10% interest on tax underpayments. It would be advantageous and conserve scarce judicial and administrative resources to allow such issues to be decided at the same time as the issues underlying the transfer pricing dispute.

IV. Conclusion

If implemented, the mandatory arbitration procedures set forth in the Proposed U.S.-Belgium Convention and in the German and Canadian Protocols would provide taxpayer with a greater degree of certainty that their potential double taxation will be resolved within a definite time frame. In addition, the possibility of mandatory arbitration will also give competent authorities an incentive to compromise more often with one another as the adoption of extreme positions by one Contracting State could result in a less favorable resolution for that Contracting State in the contexts of mandatory arbitration as it is now conceived to be implemented. This additional incentive to compromise could also result in quicker resolution of taxpayer's requests

---

Michael Plodek is International Tax Counsel at Lockheed Martin. The opinions expressed herein are solely those of the author's and not Lockheed Martin or any law firm with which he was associated. The author wishes to thank Howard Liebman, a Partner of Jones Day's Brussels office, for his invaluable assistance.
For more information on the author, please see Section XIII.

generally. Though not without some room for improvement, the ratification of the Proposed U.S.-Belgium Convention, as well as the German and Canadian Protocols, would represent a significant improvement in the ability of the mutual agreement procedures to resolve potential double taxation disputes.

X. Country Overviews

Overview of the Transfer Pricing Environment in Argentina

by Horacio Dinice and Silvia B. Rodriguez
Deloitte Argentina

Introduction

Following the trend of major world economies, Argentina developed a detailed transfer pricing regime that relies on the arm's length standard for valuing related-party transactions.[1] This process began on December 20, 1998 with the enactment of Law No. 25,063, which added specific transfer pricing regulations to the Argentine income tax code.

Over the course of the first decade of application of the Argentine transfer pricing rules, a significant number of companies failed to comply with mandatory filing requirements leading to recent efforts by Argentine tax authorities to increase their focus on transfer pricing enforcement. These efforts have included the use of a number of new tools designed to identify unreported transactions that may have transfer pricing implications. As part of these enforcement efforts, a six-month transfer pricing amnesty program was implemented during 2009, during which many delinquent filers came forward. These enforcement efforts raise a number of issues for companies with related-party transactions in Argentina.

The first part of this article focuses on summarizing the essence of transfer pricing regulations in Argentina and the current approach taken by Argentine tax authorities in such matters and discusses the interrelationships among the various regulations effective to date, including Law No. 25,063, Law No. 25,239, Law No. 25,784, Decree No. 290/00 (Executive Power -PEN), Decree No. 1,037/00 (PEN) and General Resolution (GR) No. 1,122/01 (Argentine fiscal authorities - AFIP) as amended and supplemented.

The second part of the article discusses the recent enforcement efforts and their implications for companies with related-party transactions in Argentina.

Part I — Transfer Pricing Rules and Requirements

Application of the Arm's Length Principle

Argentine transfer pricing legislation applies the arm's length principle to transactions carried out by local entities with foreign affiliates and with entities located in tax havens. As with other tax authorities, Argentine officials apply the arm's length principle to related-party transactions in an attempt to determine what the values of transacted goods and services would be were the parties independent of one another. However, the definitions of related parties and the best-method rule differ under Argentine law

---

[1] The set of rules responds to the guidelines defined by OECD (Organization for Cooperation and Economical Development) in the document called "Transfer Pricing Guidelines for Multinational Enterprises and Tax Administrations" dated July 13, 1995.

from the standards in place in some other countries. In particular, certain methods are preferred in Argentina and some are not accepted at all.

Definition of Related Parties

According to the Argentinean rules, there does not need to be common ownership or a direct contractual relationship for parties to be considered related for purposes of transfer pricing. Under this broader definition, any economic link between companies can be interpreted as giving the related party status, including:
- Those who carry out transactions with foreign persons that may be directly or indirectly related to be managed or controlled by the same persons; and
- Foreign persons with which an Argentine party operates, who have the decision power to guide or define the activities of any of the Argentine parties, either because of their equity interest, the level of their credit rights, or their influence of any kind — contractual or not.

Some of the criteria defined by Fiscal Authorities do not match the usual concept of economic relationship, usually conceived as a corporate relationship. The "economic link" concept is very broad in current Argentine regulations, including business relationships, which differs from international laws.

Thus, GR No. 1,122/01 lists in a detailed manner the assumptions that will configure an economic relation, among which, for instance, it is understood that there is a relationship upon supplying the technological property, also transactions through exclusive distributors or international franchise systems could be characterized for tax purposes as transactions carried out between related parties.

Transactions with entities (whether or not related) that are located or functioning in a tax haven (as defined by domestic income tax law) are presumed to be related party transactions.

Including such general concepts as those mentioned above is justified by the understanding by tax authorities about the presumed existence of common interest that may covert legal structures designed specifically to conceal relationships.

Consequently, as there are no general guidelines to interpret the standard in the definition of related parties, consideration should be paid to circumstances and facts of each specific case.

Import And Export Transactions of Tangible Goods with Independent Parties

Argentine tax regulations provide for filing information related to import and export transactions of tangible goods with independent parties that do not meet the condition of having a publicly-known international price on transparent markets and whose annual sum exceeds ARS 1,000,000 (about USD 300,000).[2]

Implicit in this standard is a certain degree of suspicion regarding the prices agreed-upon by independent operators about the existence of over- or under-billing, since laws require them to file information with the AFIP to verify whether declared prices "reasonably adjust" to market prices.

Likewise, import and export transactions of commodities with independent operators must be declared.

---

2 By means of General Resolution No. 1918 (O.B. 03/08/05)- amendment of G.R. No. 1122/01.

Application of the Best Method Rule in Argentina

The Argentinean version of the best method rule to verify whether transactions subject to transfer pricing regulations are carried out on an arm's length basis allows consideration of the following methods:
- Comparable Uncontrolled Price Method
- Resale Price Method
- Cost Plus Method
- Profit Split Method
- Transactional Net Margin Method

Similar to the U.S. version of the best method rule, Argentine standards establish that the method that is the most appropriate according to the type of transaction carried out should be used, without assigning a method hierarchy, except for the exceptions mentioned below:
- In the cases of import or export of goods where the international price can be established through transparent markets, such prices should be used to determine the net Argentine-source income.
- In the case of exports of tangible goods with known listed prices on transparent markets, where an international intermediary is involved - that is not the actual beneficiary of the goods - the best method will consist in applying the listed price of the assets on the transparent market on the day the merchandise is shipped, or the price agreed upon with the international intermediary, whichever higher.[3]

Comparability

Comparability is the center of all transfer pricing methodologies. In essence, the transfer pricing analysis consists in determining whether the conditions agree upon in transactions carried out between affiliates correspond to those that may have been agreed upon with independent parties.

Thus, methods are applied to transactions that are comparable, in which case such transactions will be those with which there are no significant differences that may affect the price or the amount of the consideration and when, in turn, such differences are eliminated based on adjustments that allow creating a reliable benchmark.

Additionally, Argentine regulations establish that to apply the methods to determine transfer prices, the comparability analysis should directly be made on the local person's situation.

This implies banning the use of a foreign tested party, unduly limiting, in our opinion, the use of certain methodologies that may be more appropriate to analyze transfer prices (and are accepted under OECD guidelines and U.S. law).

Documentation Requirements

Unlike in the rest of countries with transfer pricing regulations, in Argentina[4] the transfer pricing study is no longer in the taxpayer's hands, available to tax authorities for a possible audit, but such report must be signed by an independent CPA and filed together with the annual sworn statement.

Likewise, these rules describe what type of additional documentation should be produced and kept by the taxpayer upon the filing due date.

Since transfer pricing deals with facts and evidence, the burden of proof falls

---

3   Such method, commonly known as "sixth method" shall not be applicable as long as it is proved that the intermediary jointly meets certain requirements.

4   The same situation takes place in Ecuador.

on the taxpayer to defend its position against tax authorities. Thus, necessary information in support of the valuations arrived at in transfer pricing studies included detailed functional analyses and related documents showing actual costs and prices, such as contracts and bills.

An extremely sensitive matter in this area is what types of documentary support to the financial statements are required in cases of segmentation where the taxpayer analyzes the transactions subject to the regulations based on different functions (for example, manufacturing and distribution).

As Argentine accounting rules do not require a degree of detail similar to that of a 10-K, supporting the fairness of the segmentation of the operating results for various operating units or segments of a company can be difficult, leading to headaches — particularly when being audited by the Argentine tax authorities.

In such cases, it is advisable to try to disclose key accounting information to be used in the transfer pricing studies in the notes to the taxpayer's financial statements that constitute public information and contribute to support the study adequately.

Focused Audit Scrutiny by the Argentine Tax Authorities

Surveys of corporate tax executives at large international companies have shown that transfer pricing is one of the issues that, at a worldwide level, worries them the most. One factor in this concern is that a small adjustment in the profit margin of a company may lead to a huge tax adjustment. For this same reason, national tax authorities have an incentive to examine transfer pricing studies closely. The revenue impacts of a small adjustment in an arm's length price can be considerable. Argentine tax authorities have not been an exception to this principle.

In fact, experience has shown that the Argentine tax authorities developed rapidly from the technical and information access standpoints. For several years, they focused their transfer pricing audit efforts on a few economic sectors, mainly the automotive, pharmaceutical, and commodity industries (especially cereals), but have recently expanded their investigations to include all sectors of the economy. (Please see Part II for discussion of recent enforcement efforts.)

The Argentine tax authority's data justify their recent increase in transfer pricing enforcement from a revenue perspective. Between January and August of 2007, the AFIP made adjustments amounting to ARS 96,446,270 (about USD 30,139,459). This figures stands at 130% above ARS 42,099,443 (around USD 13,156,075) detected over 2006.

"Now, after breaking the paradigm in place for 30 years, we aim at quality rather than quantity of audits and at closing the full audit cycle. This means that even fines and interest are collected apart from the omitted tax," Horacio Castagnola of the AFIP told the Argentine press.[5]

Mr. Castangola stressed that total complete audits went from 20,000 to 4,000. This means collecting more revenue with fewer comprehensive audits by identifying taxpayers with the most conflicting issues and investigating and detecting the highest risk factors.

As regards transfer pricing, the number of audits performed does not follow the same pattern. There are cases in which tax authorities have examined information related to one or more years of activity in a single audit and then used the findings from that audit as a road map for auditing

---

[5] Daily "Infobae", Sept. 14, 2007, "AFIP tightens control over group of companies and remitting funds abroad."

other companies in the same sector. When the AFIP detects the application of comparability criteria or non-accounting adjustments that they consider "debatable" in a given economic sector, they seek to challenge them in other companies in the same sector.

Challenges are mainly based on economic adjustments being made by the tested party to its own financial information based on market factors that appear to affect said taxpayer exclusively without proving in an irrefutable manner that such factors did not affect the situation of other comparable companies.

On the other hand, tax authorities also question those comparable companies that posted recurring losses without evaluating functional comparability. Extreme results can affect the financial indicia which are looked at in the chosen method. However, fiscal authorities often fail to recognize that the difference in the risk profile that would lead to exclude those loss-generating activities would also — for the same reasons lead to the exclusion of those that generate higher profit levels. Extreme results might be rejected in comparability terms, but not solely because they are extreme.

Penalties

Under the last tax reform, failure to comply with transfer pricing regulations subjects taxpayers to a special penalty system.[6]

Unlike in the U.S., Argentine regulations do not allow for the possibility of forgiving fines or even reducing fines because transfer pricing is not an exact science, as is allowed in the U.S. and Mexico.

Taking into account the potential penalties for which taxpayers may be liable to in the event of not filing the documentation required by tax authorities, the cost-benefit equation for taxpayers as regards documentation today is clear cut. The existence of automatic fines for failing to file forms or the transfer pricing study itself makes it important to comply with documentation filing deadlines required by tax authorities.

Corresponding Adjustments and APAs

While Argentina does have some double-taxation treaties with other countries that theoretically require Argentine tax authorities to make corresponding adjustments when the tax authorities of the other country adjust the profit (as a result of a transfer pricing audit) of the related party located abroad due to transactions with Argentina, there are no practical regulations guiding its enforcement, nor are there any cases where Argentine tax authorities have accepted such adjustments.

In addition to being silent on the topic of corresponding adjustments, Argentina's tax rules have no provision for Advance Pricing Agreements (APAs).

Part II — Recent Enforcement Efforts

In response to perceived transfer-pricing related tax evasion, the Argentine tax authorities have engaged in concerted efforts to crack-down on companies that fail to make required filings. Those efforts have included cooperative efforts with the Argentine Central Bank and the Argentine Customs Department in which transactions with low- and no-tax jurisdictions are examined to determine whether they are part of related-party transactions and, if so, whether those transactions were

---

[6] Fines range from ARS 500 to ARS 45,000, with automatic fines of ARS 9,000 and ARS 20,000, based on the type of noncompliance.

adequately documented in filings with the Argentine tax authorities.

Tax Amnesty Program

As part of this enforcement effort, the AFIP implemented a six-month tax amnesty program from March through August of 2009, during which time companies that had previously failed to file required transfer pricing documentation were allowed to come forward without penalties. However, interest was charged for delinquent tax payments made during the amnesty period: up to 30% of the tax claimed if the payment was made during the first two months of the amnesty, up to 40% during the middle two months, and up to 50% during the final two months. Companies that initiated payment plans during these periods were also permitted to take advantage of these reduced interest rates if they prepaid 6% of what they owed and financed the remainder at .75% interest over 120 monthly payments.

As part of this amnesty, the Argentine tax authorities notified companies about transactions with low- and no-tax jurisdictions that had taken place primarily in the 2006 and 2007 tax years, offering these companies the opportunity to come forward.

Focus on "Triangulation Schemes"

Since the conclusion of the tax amnesty program, AFIP has turned its enforcement efforts to "triangulation schemes," in which exports are billed through tax havens. As described by Ricardo Echegaray, head of AFIP, underscored, in an event carried out in April 2009 by an Argentine Tax Journal, "A large number of exports that physically were made to countries with a regular tax situation and had actually been billed through countries known as tax heavens or with irregular tax systems, that is to say, with certain degree of reticence for providing information."[7] AFIP attempts to identify cases in which there was some type of evasion by reviewing customs data to determine whether the prices declared to Argentine customs authorities were the same as those of the destination.

This investigation also made use of information from the Central Bank database: AFIP compared transactions related to bringing currency into the country with the database of companies receiving export rebates or VAT reimbursements. The investigation examined transactions from December, 2008 through May, 2009.

In this context, it should be noted that AFIP continues to make active use of various IT tools and to coordinate its verification activities with the Customs Department. AFIP has also decided to increase its capacity to detect international transactions to verify whether they should be subject to the analysis and documentation provided by the Transfer Pricing System or whether they have duly complied with it. This represents a major expansion in the focus of transfer pricing enforcement from the narrow focus on automotive, pharmaceutical industries and primary production companies of two years ago to all sectors of the economy and cross-border transactions. According to Mr. Echegaray, AFIP is implementing a very tight verification process seeking to guarantee the transparency in foreign trade.

In this sense, the AFIP head reported in October 2009[8] that the agency is signing new information exchange agreements with several no- and low-tax countries. Thus, companies conducting transactions between Argentina and these jurisdictions

---

7 Daily "iProfesional.com," April 3, 2009, "AFIP targets 2.200 large companies for billing via tax havens."

8 Daily "El Cronista.com," Nov. 11, 2009, "Tax havens will provide information on movements by Argentine companies."

should be aware that AFIP may scrutinize these transactions and request information under an investigation into an alleged tax evasion.

Selection of Comparable Companies in a Recessionary Economy

Similar to the tax authorities in many countries, the AFIP prefers that companies that were not profitable in any year of a comparability analysis be excluded. However, since the international crisis that began in 2008 affected strongly affected the level of economic activity in Argentina and throughout the world, often decreasing prices and sales volumes, elimination of companies with a year or two of losses from comparability studies can prove problematic.

Depending on where the market was located, some companies were directly impacted by the crisis, while others were indirectly affected, such as the case of Argentine companies focusing on exports to European and US markets. Many such companies, whether they operate with affiliates or not, carried operating losses for 2008 and will probably carry them again in 2009. It is very probable that many companies that are comparable to the company under study have also carried losses affecting the determination of profit margins. Since comparability is the center of all transfer pricing methodologies, it is important to be aware of whether a given jurisdiction will allow the inclusion of comparables in a transfer pricing study that were unprofitable during one or more of the years in question.

Under the OECD guidelines, it is not expected that an independent company bear recurring losses, except under much justified situation such as startups or under unfavorable economic conditions.[9] This condition of exceptional losses may make the use of comparables with losses to be considered exceptional.

Therefore, comparable transactions generating losses should trigger a deeper investigation to establish the actual comparability. Consequently, those loss making comparables that meet the comparability analysis as regards economic circumstances, business conditions, risk levels, etc. should not be rejected based only on the fact that they have posted losses.

Tax authorities tend to question those comparable companies that posted recurring losses without evaluating functional comparability. Extreme results can affect the financial indicia which are looked at in the chosen method. However, fiscal authorities often fail to recognize that the difference in the risk profile that would lead to exclude those loss-generating activities would also — for the same reasons lead to the exclusion of those that generate higher profit levels. Extreme results might be rejected in comparability terms, but not solely because they are extreme.

Similarly, it is customary that the tax authorities, upon evaluating the comparables selected by the taxpayer, do not add new comparables, but they only challenge one or some of those accepted comparables.

This situation creates uncertainty as follows: if tax authorities in an audit eliminate comparables that have incurred losses, the interquartile range will change, with the possible consequence that the company under analysis is no longer within

---

9 "OECD Transfer pricing Guidelines for Multinational Enterprises and Tax Administrations" 2009 Edition, and "Comparability: Public Invitation To Comment On A Series Of Draft Issues Notes," Working Party No. 6 of the OECD Committee on Fiscal Affairs, May 10, 2006.

the market range, implying adjustment to the taxable income and giving rise to the potential imposition of fines and interest.[10]

In other words, should a company that was not profitable for one or more years during the international economic crisis be allowed to include as comparables other companies that were not profitable during those same years?

Answering this question is not a simple matter, but a strong argument can be made for including such companies with losses during times of international economic crisis as being comparable to the tested party, since a fundamental principle of transfer pricing analysis is to take the general context in which business has been conducted into consideration. The key to determining whether a given non-profitable comparable should be included in the study is to examine the economic sector and market in question, as the crisis may have affected each market differently, depending on the industry. Put another way, demand and supply levels may have changed in different ways in different markets and sectors. Careful documentation of sector-specific factors, including transportation costs and dates of transactions will be of paramount importance in performing the analysis in cases where the inclusion of non-profitable comparables needs to be explained.

It is also important to evaluate whether those circumstances that generated the losses in the potential comparables are similar to those that affected the business of the company under analysis, focusing especially on analyzing economic circumstances in which business was done, taking into account public information available, for instance, by means of evaluating the changes in volumes, prices, loss of customers or markets, inability to decrease production pace in spite of shrinks in sales, changes in exchange rates, inflation effects, among others.

Additionally, as Argentine transfer pricing studies generally use foreign companies as comparables, the probability of finding companies subject to exactly the same conditions as those of the local market is low, further increasing the importance of conducting an individual analysis of each potential comparable to evaluate the actual comparability under a concrete context borne by each company subject to analysis.

Impact on Financial Statements

It is also important to remember that applying transfer pricing regulation goes beyond tax considerations and also affects the preparation of the company financial statements. In this regard, accounting standards effective in Argentina provide that possible payables arising from contingencies should be booked as liabilities when their occurrence probability is high and their economic effect can be quantified. If the possible value of the contingency cannot be fairly determined, the situation should be explained in notes to the financial statements.

As a result, failing to file sworn statements in those cases that it is mandatory for developing activities subject to transfer pricing regulations generates a contingency for fines by tax authorities that should be booked in liabilities under these accounting provisions, since these fines are both highly probable and quantifiable.

Another contingency that should be evaluated is the possible income tax adjustment that tax authorities may impose in cases where transactions with related parties or with no- and low-tax countries

---

10 The fine for failing to pay taxes aggravated for the case of international transactions rates from 1 to 4 times the tax amount not paid.

have taken place, but are not documented and justified as to their arms-length pricing in transfer pricing studies. In these cases, the auditor will require information and the documentation related to those prices agreed upon for operations subject to transfer pricing regulations and should evaluate whether such transactions were agreed upon under market conditions, consistent with the arm's length principle.

If the auditor concludes that transactions have not been agreed upon at market value, an income tax adjustment should be determined. In cases where a reasonable value for the adjustment under discussion can be agreed upon, it should be disclosed as a liability in the financial statement. But if no sufficient information is found to determine market prices, there would be a contingency with a high probability of occurrence, but uncertain as to determining the amount, as defined in the accounting standards. Under these circumstances, the existence of the income tax liability should be disclosed in notes to the financial statements.

In cases where complete transfer pricing documentation has been submitted to the tax authorities in a timely manner, there may still be issues with the financial statements, since preparation and submission of a transfer pricing report does not guarantee that tax authorities will accept the analysis carried out by the company. In other words, transfer pricing studies are subject to review by the tax authorities and can possibly be subject to adjustments that might generate a difference in determined income tax. As such, there is the possibility that the financial statements may not include the correct income tax numbers even in cases where transfer pricing studies have been filed in a timely manner. In this sense, considering the aggressiveness of tax authorities while performing audits, it is evident that a significant dose of uncertainty has been added upon determining whether accounting records reasonably contain the taxpayer's correct income tax charge.

Conclusion

Over the last few years, transfer pricing has attracted the attention of tax authorities, academicians and multinational companies in almost all the world. Everything seems to indicate that it is a matter that has come to stay.

In this environment, multinational companies should painstakingly consider how transactions and organizational agreements should be negotiated and documented. It is important to bear in mind that the documentation not only should be carried out based on international transfer pricing standards, but they also should reflect commercial agreements, related services, use of intangible property and the consistency between such documentation and the circumstances surrounding the agreement between the parties.

While Argentine tax authorities have made recent efforts to bring transfer pricing rules into compliance with internationally-accepted practice, there remain a number of challenges associated with transfer pricing in Argentina. For example, the Argentine tax authorities require strict compliance with documentation deadlines, have no provision for waiving or adjusting penalties, do not have a procedure for making corresponding adjustments when profit levels of a related party are adjusted by another country's tax authorities, and do not have an APA program to offer companies certainty with respect to the valuation of their related-party transactions. The matter is further complicated by the lack of readily-available documentary support of the operating results for functional divisions of companies operating in Argentina.

Recent cooperative efforts between the Argentine tax authorities and the Argentine Central Bank and the Argentine Customs Department have allowed for increased enforcement, including aggressive efforts to detect related party transactions between Argentina and low- and no-tax countries. The possibility of continued efforts of this type make compliance with Argentina's transfer pricing filing requirements more important than ever. Also, the recent expansion of transfer pricing enforcement to all sectors and industries increases the chances that a company's related-party transactions will be scrutinized.

Finally, it is important to note the difficulty of finding comparable companies for inclusion in transfer pricing studies in cases where the tested party had losses during one or more recent years during the global economic crisis.

Horacio Dinice is a tax partner with Deloitte Argentina, where he leads the transfer-pricing practice. He can be reached at **(54-11) 4321 3002** or by email at **hdinice@deloitte.com**.

Silvia B. Rodriguez is Tax Manager with Deloitte in Argentina, with experience in transfer pricing since its creation. She can be reached at **(54 11) 4320 2700 ext. 4714** or by email at **silviarodriguez@deloitte.com**.

For more information on the authors, please see Section XIII.

Australian Transfer Pricing Rules in Practice

by Lyndon James and Ben Lannan
Partner PricewaterhouseCoopers, Australia

Introduction

Transfer pricing continues to be a priority issue for the Australian Taxation Office. While Australia's transfer pricing laws have not been substantively amended since their enactment in 1981, the ATO continues to refine and clarify its approach to international transfer pricing through a series of rulings, tax determinations and practice statements. This is currently reflected by particular focus on specific issues, including financial transactions and business restructures, together with intensified transfer pricing risk review activity. Also, Australia has limited cases to set legal precedent on which to guide transfer pricing considerations, albeit more recently some cases have been heard.

Australia's transfer pricing regime shares many characteristics with other OECD-compliant countries, but also has some less common features. For example, Australia has no legislated requirement for contemporaneous documentation of related-party transactions, albeit it is preferred and disclosures regarding the extent of contemporaneous documentation are required as part of Schedule 25A in the annual income tax return.

Another unusual characteristic is that Australia applies its transfer pricing regime not just to related parties, but also to connected parties, or indeed any international transaction which is not considered to be arm's length. Further, the ATO requires that companies make separate transfer pricing adjustments based on each year's results, rather than aggregating multiple-year averages, as is the practice in the U.S. and most other OECD-compliant countries.

This article reviews the legal and regulatory transfer pricing framework in Australia and discusses some recent developments and their implications.

Scope and Application

Australia's transfer pricing rules are enshrined in Division 13 of the *Income Tax Assessment Act 1936* (SS136AA to 136AF). These provisions form part of Australia's anti-avoidance provisions and are aimed at mitigating international profit shifting. However, the ATO has made it clear that there does not need to be a profit shifting intent for Division 13 to apply.

It is important to note that from the ATO perspective the parties to a transaction do not necessarily need to be related to each other for the transfer pricing rules to apply, merely that there is a connection between them. Section 136 AD provides the Commissioner of Taxation (the Commissioner) the power to adjust an Australian taxpayer's assessable income or allowable deductions in situations where a taxpayer has 'supplied' or 'acquired' 'property', under an 'international agreement' (as broadly defined in Section 136AA and 136AC) and the Commissioner is satisfied that the parties were not operating at arm's length such that:

- the consideration received was less than an arm's length consideration
- no consideration was received in circumstances where it should have been
- the consideration paid exceeded an arm's length amount.

Further, 136AD(4) provides the Commissioner discretion to determine the arm's length consideration for the purposes of applying 136AD where it is not possible or practicable for the Commissioner to ascertain the arm's length consideration.

Section 136AE effectively operates to empower the Commissioner to apply the arm's length principle, by the application of 136AD, in reallocating income and expenditure between a company and its overseas branch, or branches of the same company. In practice, this is achieved through the operation of a notionally separate entity principle in determining the appropriate allocations between the branch and its related party(ies).

Section 136AF provides the Commissioner with discretion to make consequential adjustments in situations where a transfer pricing adjustment gives rise to double taxation within Australia. The more common examples include adjustments to withholding tax where a transfer pricing is made to reduce deductions for royalties or interest. It should be noted however that there is no recognition of secondary adjustments.

The ATO's position is that in applying Division 13, the terms of the relevant double taxation agreement (DTA) should be considered and the Commissioner may apply the provisions of Division 13 and/or the relevant treaty provisions in relation to a transfer pricing matter. This underscores the ATO's traditional view that Australia's DTAs provide the Commissioner with a right to tax, rather than the more limited view that the DTA exists to mitigate the risk of double taxation. This broader ATO view has been questioned in obiter dicta of a recent transfer pricing case, *Roche Products Pty Ltd. v. Commissioner of Taxation,* prompting the ATO to develop administrative guidance clarifying and supporting its traditionally held view. Whilst specific guidance on this issue is yet to be issued, in December 2009 the ATO released a counsel's opinion it sought regarding the interaction of Australia's thin capitalization and transfer pricing rules[1] which supports its views.

Further, to provide guidance in respect of the application of the transfer pricing rules and related issues, the ATO has issued a range of public binding rulings on a range of key issues, including basic concepts, transfer pricing methods, documentation and permanent establishments. In addition, there are a number of specific-issue rulings, covering such topics as intra-group services, loan arrangements and APAs.

Finally, the ATO has supplemented these rulings with publications that seek to provide practical guidance for taxpayers through summaries of key rulings on basic concepts and risk assessments, documentation and APAs, together with guidelines that provide illustrative examples on issues such as marketing intangibles and attribution of profits to deemed permanent establishments.

Alignment with OECD Guidelines

Consistent with OECD guidelines on transfer pricing, Australia's transfer pricing

---

1 The ATO subsequently issued draft Taxation Ruling TR2009/D6 - Income tax: the interaction of Division 820 of the Income Tax Assessment Act 1997 and the transfer pricing provisions in relation to costs that may become debt deductions, for example, interest and guarantee fees.

rules are founded on the application of the arm's length principle. Australia seeks to align its approach to transfer pricing with OECD guidelines generally and references the OECD guidelines in various aspects of its public rulings on transfer pricing.

The ATO has for many years been an active participant in various working parties and discussion forums to shape OECD policy and guidance on key transfer pricing matters, including the attribution of profits to permanent establishments and more recently business restructures.

Penalties

Adjustments made under Division 13 are subject to penalties consistent with Australia's anti-avoidance provisions, with specific guidance found in Taxation Ruling TR 98/16.

Penalties generally range from:
- 10% of the additional tax paid - where the taxpayer had prepared documentation that supported a reasonably arguable position (i.e. as likely as not) and there was no tax avoidance purpose; to
- 50% of the additional tax paid in situations where the commissioner determines there is no reasonably arguable position documented and there was a tax avoidance purpose.

The Commissioner also has the discretion to decrease penalties substantially where voluntary disclosures are made and, in some circumstances reduce penalties to zero. Alternately the penalties may be increased at the Commissioner's discretion in situations where the taxpayer hinders the ATOs progress during an audit or where the taxpayer has previously been penalized under a scheme provision.

In addition to these penalties, in cases where adjustments result in additional tax payable for earlier years the taxpayer will be subject to significant interest charges, including a penalty component, under the General Interest Charge (GIC) provisions.

Transfer Pricing Cases

Australia has until recently had relatively limited legal precedent on which to guide transfer pricing considerations. However, in the last two years, there have been two key cases, the *Roche* case discussed above and the *SNF Australia Pty Ltd v. Commissioner of Taxation*, which have potentially significant implications for the application of Australia's transfer pricing rules.

In 2008 the Administrative Appeals Tribunal (AAT) ruled on the case of *Roche Products Pty Ltd*. This case centered around the transfer price of products purchased by Australian pharmaceutical company Roche Products Pty Ltd from its Swiss parent. Interestingly, the AAT determined that while the ATO's amended assessments were excessive, it did not dismiss the assessment completely, ruling in favor of some adjustment to certain product lines, albeit based on an alternate approach to those proposed by the ATO and the taxpayer.

While an AAT decision does not necessarily carry comparable weight to decisions made by Australia's courts of law, the presiding justice provided a range of comments with implications for a wide range of key transfer pricing issues. Particular insights the AAT's judgment yielded included:
- Strong suggestions that, in contrast to the ATO's long-held view, Australia's double taxation agreements do not provide a mandate to impose tax. Rather Division 13 must form the basis of any amended assessment.
- A clear preference for transactional

over profit-based methods, underlined by the AAT's discarding of the ATO's proposed net margin method in favor of its own simple gross margin approach.
- Challenge to the notion regarding loss making companies that losses are driven by incorrect transfer pricing. This in effect called into the question the reliability of profit based methods and the need to have regard for the commercial basis of operating losses.
- The need to make adjustments based on separate years rather than applying multiple year averages.

While the ATO has publicly claimed the decision in the Roche Case in its favor on the basis that some adjustments were made, the obiter comments from the case have prompted a range of ATO responses. Specifically, the ATO issued a practice statement in 2008 summarizing its views on the AAT's decision in the Roche case and reconciling this to its historic administrative practice. While there is no suggestion that the ATO will change its approach to the selection or application of the TNMM, it does note that taxpayers are advised to closely ascertain the extent and reliability of available uncontrolled data to support the arm's length nature of international related party dealings.

Further, recent experience suggests increased frequency of ATO requests for CUP and gross margin data in transfer pricing risk reviews and audits. Accordingly, in preparing transfer pricing analysis stringent evaluation of available comparable data and method selection by taxpayers would be prudent, particularly where a profit based method is ultimately selected and applied.

More significantly, the ATO has subsequently revisited the issue of the interaction of Division 13 and Australia's DTAs and has publicly disclosed a counsel's opinion that, among other things, indicates a narrow interpretation of Division 13 should be applied, but nevertheless supports the view that Australia's DTA's provide separate and distinct taxing rights, enabling a more broad interpretation of the arm's length principle.

More recently, the case of SNF Australia Pty Ltd was heard before a justice of the Federal court. While a judgment has yet to be delivered, this will be a landmark case in Australia, involving direct challenge by the taxpayer of the ATO's use of profit based methods for valuing SNF's related-party transactions on the basis that Division 13 is a transaction-based provision. This is further underpinned by the presumption that the business profits articles of the DTA do not provide a taxing right for the ATO.

In contrast, the ATO is relying on the onus of the taxpayer to demonstrate that the ATO's assessment is incorrect and the argument that the taxpayer's comparable uncontrolled price data is not reliable. Further, in supporting its position based on a profit based method the ATO appears to have argued to the effect that in applying Division 13 regard should be had for arm's length circumstances and that if SNF Australia had been dealing at arm's length it would not have made continued purchases of goods at prices that generated losses for an extended period of time.

At the heart of this case are key issues relating to the interaction of Division 13 and Australia's DTAs, in addition to the breadth at which the ATO can interpret the application of the arm's length principle under Division 13. The Federal court judgment is expected soon, albeit there has been no indication as yet of when the decision will be delivered.

Other cases have been before the courts since 1999, however these have focused on administrative matters. These have

included:
- San Remo Macaroni Pty Ltd 1999 (challenge to amended assessments on the basis that they were issued in bad faith);
- Daihatsu Australia Pty Ltd 2001 (challenge to amended assessments on the basis the transfer pricing adjustments did not reflect a genuine attempt by the ATO to determine an arm's length amount before exercising the commissioner's discretion);
- Syngenta Crop Protect Pty Ltd 2006 and American Express International 2006 (seeking the Commissioner of Taxation to provide details of the basis of its transfer pricing assessments; and
- WR Carpenter Holdings Pty Ltd and Anor 2007 (similarly seeking the Commissioner to provide details of the matters taken into account in making transfer pricing determinations.

In each case the courts have found in favor of the Commissioner, generally serving to reinforce the burden of proof on the taxpayers by placing the onus on a taxpayer to demonstrate that the ATO's assessments are incorrect, rather than compelling the ATO to demonstrate that its positions are supportable.

Applicable Transfer Pricing Methods and Safe Harbors

Consistent with OECD guidelines, ATO commentary including Taxation Ruling TR 97/20 promulgates the following key transfer pricing methods as the basis for setting and review international related party transactions:
- comparable uncontrolled (CUP) method
- resale price method
- costs plus method
- profit split method(s)
- transactional net margin method (TNMM)

While the ATO acknowledges the suitability of certain methods over others in various circumstances, there is no prescriptive approach in relation to the selection or application of the methods. Rather, the most appropriate method is considered to be the one that provides the most reliable outcome, having regard to the facts and circumstance of the case and the availability of reliable independent comparable data.

In addition to the guidance provided in relation to the selection and application of the methods generally, the ATO has provided certain administrative concessions and safe harbors in relation to transfer pricing.

Most notably Taxation Ruling TR 1999/1 provides a safe harbor method for the transfer pricing of intra-group services in cases where they are non-core to the business or the total value of international related party service transactions is less than AUD500,000 for the year of income (irrespective of whether they are core or non-core activities of the Australian taxpayer). Where either of these criteria is met the taxpayer can rely on applying a 7.5% mark-up to the fully absorbed cost of the services activities. The safe harbor however does not obviate the need to prepare and document supporting analysis.

While not specifically part of Australia transfer pricing rules enshrined in Division 13, a safe harbor debt to equity ratio of effectively 3 to 1 is provided in Division 820 of the *Income Tax Assessment Act 1997*.

The interaction of Division 13 and Division 820 has been a key focus issue in recent times, with the ATO issuing a tax determination in 2007 (TD 2007/D20) outlining its position in relation to transfer pricing thinly capitalized debt. In TD 2007/D20 the ATO indicates that the setting of an arm's length interest rate should be determined having regard to an arm's length level of debt rather than the thinly capitalized debt structure. The implication here is that the ATO may use Division 13 to reduce the taxpayer's interest rate to align with an arm's length level of debt, even when the debt is in line with the debt safe harbor amount. However, the ATO has indicated it will not adjust the level of debt where it falls within the safe harbor debt amount.

These positions have resulted in significant contention and subsequent uncertainty regarding the appropriate basis for approaching intra-group funding. This has been further exacerbated by the introduction of guarantee fees as a specific focus issue following the ATO's release in June 2008 of a discussion paper titled "Intra-group finance guarantees and loans – Application to Australia's transfer pricing and thin capitalisation rules" which contains the ATO's current thinking on intra-group financing arrangements, including parental guarantees.

While the discussion paper is in draft form and cannot be relied upon by taxpayers, consideration is given to how the ATO may approach a parental guarantee. In particular, the ATO paper states that the ATO views credit guarantees as a 'service' and that it is therefore appropriate to examine credit guarantees in light of the benefits they provide to both the recipient of the guarantee and the provider.

Specifically, it would appear to be the ATO view that it may be necessary to adjust the price of a credit guarantee to account for the benefits that the guarantee may provide to the guarantor. This is particularly the case where a parental credit guarantee serves as a substitute for equity. In such instances, the guarantee represents a shareholder service and is therefore not chargeable (or deductible by the recipient). Accordingly, the Australian taxpayer needs to be able to demonstrate that the guarantee arrangement was of commercial benefit and did not replicate benefits that were already available, such as the benefits of association with the parent entities (so-called passive association).

The broader issue of intra-group funding arrangements and the interaction with the thin capitalisation safe harbour continues to be reviewed and debated. As a possible interim measure to provide some certainty to taxpayers, the ATO has recently proposed the so-called "rule of thumb" in Practice Statement Law Administration 3187 (draft), issued in December. It is understood that in essence the rule of thumb would apply to limit the Commissioner making a Division 13 determination on inbound intra-group debt pricing provided the amount of debt is within the safe harbour thin capitalisation limit and the interest rate applied reflects the weighted average cost of debt of the ultimate parent company on a consolidated accounting basis. However, PSLA 3187 (draft) has come under substantial criticism from a wide range of stakeholders since its issuance. For example, in a February 19 2010 comment letter to the ATO, the Institute of Chartered Accountants in Australia wrote that the rule of thumb is a non-arm's length approach, that it increases the risk of double taxation, that it is unfair in cases where Australia's interest rates are higher than those of trading partners, and that it contradicted superceding rules and would therefore not provide meaningful guidance to taxpayers.

Country Overviews

Documentation Requirements

There is no legislative requirement to prepare specific analysis and accompanying documentation to support the arm's length nature of an Australian taxpayer's transfer pricing. However, it is strongly encouraged by the ATO and requests for available transfer pricing documentation are routine as part of compliance review activity.

In this regard, the ATO has issued Taxation Ruling TR 98/11 that provides specific guidance in relation to the compilation of supporting documentation. The ATO advocates its 'four step process' for transfer pricing documentation reflecting the following:

- Step 1 – Understand the transaction. This typically includes relevant industry and business analysis to provide relevant context to the related party transactions, in addition to an analysis of the respective functions, assets and risks of the respective parties to the transaction as the basis for comparability.
- Step 2 – Select an appropriate arm's length transfer pricing method. This step focuses on analysis of available independent comparable data in the context of the related party transaction in order to determine which transfer pricing method can most reliably be applied.
- Step 3 – Apply the most appropriate method. This step seeks to analyse and where appropriate adjust the comparable data and benchmark the pricing outcome by reference to the selected method.
- Step 4 – Review and monitor. This final step reflects the need to review and monitor international related party transactions to ensure that any changes in the transaction and/or available comparable data is considered and the impact on the subsequent selection and application of the appropriate transfer pricing method is considered.

Selection of Comparables

A key challenge in relation to transfer pricing analysis continues to be the availability of comparable data. While Australian public companies and large private companies are required to publicly disclose their audited financial statements, in reality the availability of substantive samples of reliable independent comparable data is limited.

Further, while not formally documented, it is common ATO practice to further limit publicly available data in many circumstances to exclude independent private companies and companies with sustained losses. Accordingly, it is not uncommon to broaden comparability searches to consider analogous industries and overseas jurisdictions to obtain suitable comparables.

The ATO has indicated its preparedness to use controlled data (i.e. comparable data secured through its own investigations of other taxpayers and/or taxpayer data) in situations where it considers there is not sufficient publicly available data to make an appropriate determination on an arm's length price. This has been a particularly contentious issue as privacy legislation prevents the taxpayer from reviewing or assessing the controlled data that the ATO is relying on. For this reason, while the ATO has not precluded the use of controlled data, its use is not prevalent.

Advance Pricing Arrangements (APA)

Australia has established a substantial

APA program which it continues to promote as a key element of its cooperative compliance regime. In this regard, Taxation Ruling TR 95/23 provides specific procedural guidance for bilateral and unilateral APAs.

While the APA program continues to be viewed as a success by the ATO, it is noted that the ATO has demonstrated a tendency to be more selective in accepting APAs into the program, particularly with respect to less complex or material transactions that did not warrant the investment of ATO resources; more contentious issues where agreement on an APA was considered to be unlikely; or where the ATO considered obtaining a tax benefit was a principal element of the dealing.

More recently the ATO has undertaken a substantial independent review, performed by PricewaterhouseCoopers, to review its APA program against the ATO's stated objectives, the needs of taxpayers, and international best practice. The outcome of this review was a wide range of recommendations, including reconsideration of acceptance criteria for the APA program, promulgation of more detailed initial scoping and project planning processes that include consideration of collateral taxation issues, and a stage and gate review process. The ATO has advised that its new Transfer Pricing Management System is expected to address a number of the process issues identified. In addition, the ATO is continuing to work with advisers and taxpayer groups to co-design recommendations and implementation strategies for priority issues such as APA acceptance criteria.

Compliance and Review Activity

Australian taxpayers with international related party dealings, including dealings involving permanent establishments, have specific compliance requirements in relation to those arrangements. Specifically, taxpayers with international related party transactions above a de minimus amount are required to make a range of disclosures in relation to their transfer pricing as part of their annual income tax returns. Included as part of the Schedule 25A, these disclosures provide details of the nature and quantum of the transactions, jurisdictions involved, the level appropriate transfer pricing documentation in place and the arm's length transfer pricing methods applied.

Importantly, as part of the ATO continued vigilance in monitoring related party transactions, the Schedule 25 is in the process of being replaced. For the 2010 tax year it is expected that financial services taxpayers, including foreign banks and branches of foreign banks, together with taxpayers who can be classified as financial services providers with gross revenue exceeding AUD 250 million will be required to complete an International Dealings Schedule. Further, an International Dealings Schedule is also expected to be introduced for other taxpayers in the future. Based on initial drafts, the schedule will require taxpayers to disclose a significantly greater level of detail relating to specific international related party transactions including financial instruments, asset transfers associated with business restructures and dealings with tax havens.

The data included in the Schedule 25A continues to be routinely reviewed by the ATO and forms the basis of its transfer pricing risk profiling. In this regard the ATO has for a number of years routinely undertaken risk review projects across all segments of the Australian corporate tax base. While more recently transfer pricing reviews of larger taxpayers formed part of broader cooperative compliance reviews, the ATO has recently underlined its intention to vigorously pursue transfer pricing compliance through the reintroduction of dedicated transfer pricing reviews in the large business sector. Initial indications are that in the coming months the ATO will launch a major review project of some 150 carefully selected taxpayers and has been actively recruiting personnel to manage the increased case load. This is expected to be the most substantive and focused transfer pricing project for a number of years and will significantly raise the profile of transfer pricing as a tax issue for a number of Australian taxpayers in the near future.

Dispute Resolution and Mutual Agreement Procedures

Should a taxpayer be ultimately selected for a transfer pricing audit it will typically be required to provide a range of information requested by the ATO to enable it to develop its positions and ultimately amend assessments if required. This may include site visits, interviews with key personnel, in addition to review of documentation and financial data. The ATO has wide ranging power to obtain information from taxpayers which it may invoke in relation to a transfer pricing audit, if necessary.

Under typical circumstances, the ATO will apply steps one to three of its preferred four step process to arrive at its position. This will typically culminate in a position paper which the taxpayer has an opportunity to respond to. While this process may involve some further iteration the outcome will be that the ATO will either accept the taxpayer's view or issue determinations and amended assessments based on its original or refined position.

In the event that the taxpayer does not accept the ATO's determinations, there is an extensive objection and appeals process available. However, as previously indicated the sample of legal proceedings is limited, indicating that matters are ultimately settled directly between the taxpayers or referred to the Mutual Agreement Procedures for ultimate resolution by the relevant competent authorities where available.

In this regard, Australia has an extensive tax treaty network which includes in the majority of cases mutual agreements procedures.

Business restructuring

In addition to financial transactions, perhaps the key transfer pricing issue under consideration by the ATO at present is the treatment of business restructurings. In late 2007 the ATO released a draft discussion paper addressing a number of underlying concerns regarding the transfer pricing implications of business restructurings. In particular, while the ATO acknowledges that many restructures are undertaken for commercial business reasons, the ATO's comments raise the notion of broader comparability of some intra-group arrangements following business restructures, including the extent to which particular intra-group arrangements exist in arm's length circumstances.

Further the ATO will seek to understand the commercial rationale for an Australian taxpayer entering into a business restructuring as distinct and separate from the wider group benefits. In this regard, considerations of particular interest will be the pre- and post-restructuring tax outcomes and consideration of whether compensation should be provided to the Australian entity as compensation for lost value resulting from the conversion.

Specific guidance on business restructures is being prepared through a consultation process. In this regard, following its earlier discussion papers a draft tax ruling is expected to be issued by the ATO imminently, albeit there is no fixed date at this stage.

Conclusion

The growing importance and complexity of transfer pricing as an issue for Australian taxpayers should not be underestimated. Uncertainty around treatment of intra-group financial arrangements and focus on business restructuring create heightened transfer pricing risk for some. Further greater reporting requirements and intensified review and audit activity will ensure that transfer pricing compliance will require increased consideration for all taxpayers.

Further, while draft legislation is still pending, expected changes to the Australia Controlled Foreign Companies Regime, including expected relaxation of the rules for outbound public companies, will generate increased reliance on transfer pricing provisions to ensure appropriate taxation outcomes are achieved.

Lyndon James is the leader of PricewaterhouseCoopers' transfer pricing team in Australia. He can be reached at **(61-2) 8266-3278** or by email at **lyndon.james@au.pwc.com**.

Ben Lanham is a Partner in the PricewaterhouseCoopers transfer pricing team based in Brisbane. Ben can be reachced at **(61-7) 3257-8404** or by email at **ben.lannan@au.pwc.com**.

For more information on the authors, please see Section XIII.

Transfer Pricing in Belgium

Patrick Cauwenbergh
Deloitte Touche Tohmatsu

Introduction

In the early nineties, at the time when transfer pricing had already gained its place in an economic environment of emerging global organizations, it was still treated in a 'stepmotherly' way by the Belgian tax administration. Under pressure from the numerous initiatives on the topic at the international level, the developments in the neighboring countries and the experiences gained by the Belgian tax authorities in the scope of mutual agreement procedures, the realization grew that it was necessary to take action in this field.

Starting in 1999, new administrative guidelines were issued that set out directions for both the tax administration and the taxpayer. Recently, there has also been some action at the regulatory level.

Administrative guidelines and legal provisions

The Belgian tax authorities issued their first administrative circular letter on transfer pricing in 1999.[1] This circular letter aimed at providing practical guidance to tax officials on when and how to perform a transfer pricing audit. Although the 1999 circular letter did not introduce a radically new approach to transfer pricing, it created an increased awareness about the topic in both the tax administration and the business community.

After the first circular letter, other administrative guidelines followed, such as:
- the circular letters of 7 July 2000 and 25 March 2003 commenting on the EU Arbitration Convention of 23 July 1990 and its implementation under Belgian tax law[2];
- the circular letter of 4 July 2006 on the installment of a special transfer pricing audit team, specialized in the (assistance on) transfer pricing audits[3]; and
- the circular letter of 14 November 2006 on transfer pricing documentation and audit[4].

On regulatory level, it was only in 2004 that an important new initiative was taken. By Act of 21 June 2004, the internationally accepted arm's length standard for transfer pricing was introduced formally in the Belgian Income Tax Code ('ITC'), by means of a new article 185 § 2.[5]

Prior to that date, the key article with respect to transfer pricing was undoubtedly article 26 ITC. This article deals with the

---

1 Circular letter, 28 June 1999, AFZ/Intern IB/98-0003.
2 Circular letter, 7 July 2000, AFZ/Intern IB/98-0170 and Circular, 25 March 2003, AFZ/Intern IB/98-0170.
3 Circular letter, 4 July 2006, nr. Cp. 221.4/A/601.321 (AOIF 26/2006).
4 Circular letter, 14 November 2006, nr. Ci. RH. 421/580.456 (AOIF 40/2006).
5 Inclusion of article 185, § 2 ITC by the act of 21 June 2004 (B.S. 9 July 2004). See also circular letter, 4 July 2006, nr. Ci.RH.421/569.019 (AOIF 25/2006).

abandonment of Belgian taxable profits in favor of a foreign country. On the basis of this article, the tax authorities can adjust the taxable basis of a Belgian enterprise to the extent it is considered to grant an 'abnormal or benevolent' advantage to a foreign enterprise.

Besides article 26, other important articles in the tax code in the context of transfer pricing are:
- article 49 ITC which mentions the general conditions for tax deductibility of business expenses;
- article 54 and 344 § 2 ITC which are intended to prevent some specific types of tax avoidance through 'tax havens.'

Besides the formal introduction of the arm's length principle, the new article 185 § 2 ITC established the legal domestic basis for making correlative adjustments (as set out by article 9 § 2 of the OECD model tax convention). It also reorganized the existing 'ruling system' in order to guarantee a more efficient treatment of ruling requests related to transfer pricing.

Transfer Pricing Methodologies

Before the publication of the 1999 circular letter, Belgium did not have a legal (hierarchical) system of transfer pricing methods. The assessment of the arm's length character of a specific transaction occurred on a case-by-case basis.

The 1999 circular letter explicitly referred to the 1995 OECD Transfer Pricing Guidelines, of which a semi-official translation was enclosed. The methods described in chapter III of the OECD Transfer Pricing Guidelines can be considered to be acceptable for Belgian tax purposes.

Under the Guidelines, there is no 'best method rule.' As a general rule, one can state that the Belgian tax authorities preferred the traditional transaction methods (comparable uncontrolled price method, cost plus method and resale price method) to assess the arm's length character of intercompany pricing. Nonetheless, experience shows that the application of other (profit-based) methods is acceptable if the taxpayer can demonstrate that the facts and circumstances of the case do not allow the use of one of the traditional methods.

In the case of transfer pricing audits, the tax authorities apply transactional profit methods, and in particular the transactional net margin method, to select the companies for an audit. In this regard, the 1999 circular letter lists specific financial ratios that can be used to test the arm's length character of the intercompany prices of related entities by comparing them with the standard financial ratios for the taxpayer's industry, namely:
- gross profit/net profit;
- net profit/net sales;
- gross profit/operating expenses;
- operating expenses/net sales;
- operating profit/average equity.

It becomes more and more acceptable that taxpayers use the profit-based methods as some kind of 'sanity check' on the basis of which it is demonstrated that the applied intercompany pricing provides a bottom-line 'reasonable' result. Especially in the scope of Advance Pricing Agreement ('APA') requests, the use of the transactional net margin method ('TNMM') and other profit-based methods are becoming more and more the rule than the exception and this tendency seems not to be rejected by the tax administration. In this regard, the Belgian tax authorities are following the trend within the OECD to support the increased use of profit-based methods (such as the transactional net margin method and the profit split method).

The circular letter of 1999 acknowledged the fact that Belgium's limited geographical scope may cause difficulties in obtaining sufficient relevant information when performing a search for comparables. The circular letter of 14 November 2006, which addresses transfer pricing documentation and audits confirms that the use of pan-European databases can be considered as standard practice to which the Belgian tax administration does not object. As an affirmation of Belgium's position vis-à-vis the work on EU level, the November 2006 circular letter also refers directly to the Code of Conduct on transfer pricing documentation issued by the European Joint Transfer Pricing Forum ('EU JTPF').[6]

Documentation Requirements

To date, no statutory requirement exists in Belgium to prepare advance and/or contemporaneous transfer pricing documentation. However, the 1999 circular letter indicated that the non-existence of relevant transfer pricing documentation can be seen as a 'red flag' to trigger a transfer pricing audit and this is repeated in the circular letter of 14 November 2006.

In the November 2006 circular letter on transfer pricing audits, the Belgian tax administration issues guidelines on what kind of documentation might be called for when an audit on transfer pricing is held. As mentioned, the circular letter refers explicitly to the EU JTPF's Code of Conduct on transfer pricing documentation (EU-TPD), meaning that the Belgian tax authorities will adhere to these guidelines.

6   Code of Conduct (Official Journal C176 du 28/07/2006, p.1) on transfer pricing documentation for associated enterprises in the European Union (EUTPD).

Although the November 2006 circular letter provides for a list of all relevant information and documentation that can be expected to exist within an MNE, it also repeatedly states that any request for information should be made with consideration for the facts and circumstances of each individual case and respecting the proportionality between the efforts to obtain such information and the costs to do so. Tax inspectors should refrain from making excessive information requests. In this regard, it is also important to note that the tax administration cannot always demand a translation of the documentation to one of the three official languages. However, specific documentation only relating to Belgium should be in Dutch, French or German.

The best approach for enterprises is to ensure that their transfer pricing policy is documented and that the necessary supporting documents are available. The Belgian tax authorities usually pay attention to the nature and the conditions of the relevant transactions as described in a factual (i.e., function and risk) analysis, an economic analysis explaining why a certain method is chosen and how it supports the arm's length character of the intercompany pricing, the conditions of relevant commercial third party or intercompany agreements and financial information (i.e., budgets and other documents containing information necessary to determine the arm's length prices or potential adjustments).

Advance Pricing Agreements

Belgium has a long tradition of issuing (unilateral) APAs. With the creation in 2005 of a renewed and modernized ruling commission – focusing on providing as much reassurance as possible to foreign investors interested in coming to Belgium

– the ruling practice gained a significant boost.

A Belgian or foreign company that applies for a ruling can obtain upfront certainty about the tax treatment of one or another transaction. One interesting feature is that the ruling decision can cover various (tax) aspects of a transaction, going from transfer pricing and valuation issues to permanent establishment, VAT and customs issues. Over the past three years, the renewed ruling commission has demonstrated a business-friendly attitude and a willingness to be pro-active and flexible. The ruling commission encourages pre-filing meetings (even on a no-name basis) to have an informal discussion before introducing a formal request.

Since the ruling decision can in principle be granted within a 'reasonable' time frame (usually three to four months, depending on the nature and scope of the question), this procedure can be an important benefit to taxpayers. The ruling decision will be legally binding for a period of a maximum of 5 years.

Non-compliance penalties

No specific transfer pricing related penalties exist. The general penalty regime applies to transfer pricing, meaning that in the event of a transfer pricing audit resulting in transfer pricing adjustments, penalties ranging from 10 to 200 percent of additional tax – depending on the level of bad faith and repeated infringement – can be enforced.[7] If the taxpayer can prove that the incorrect reporting resulted from circumstances beyond its control and that no bad faith is involved, the 10% penalty may be waived. Furthermore, administrative fines varying between EUR 50 to EUR 1,250 can be imposed.[8]

If the taxpayer fails to provide the necessary accounting documents or the requested information in due time, the tax administration can carry out an 'ex officio assessment'.[9] Such measure will basically result in a shift of the burden of proof of the arm's length character of the pricing from the tax authorities to the taxpayer.

Conclusion

The days when transfer pricing was considered only as a 'soft target' are long gone. In an attempt not to be 'the last of the class,' Belgium has been working hard to catch up and to create a transfer pricing awareness within the tax administration.

Administrative guidelines on transfer pricing audits and documentation rules provide the tax administration the tools to perform a post factum review of the arm's length character of intercompany pricing. On the other hand, a rather lenient and transparent APA regime allows foreign taxpayers to obtain advance tax certainty about their cross-border transactions.

---

7 Article 444 ITC.
8 Article 445 ITC.
9 Article 351 ITC.

Patrick Cauwenbergh, a tax partner in the Brussels office of Deloitte Touche Tohmatsu's Belgium affiliate, joined Deloitte in 1999 and is now the partner in charge of Deloitte's Brussels transfer-pricing practice. He can be reached at **(32-2) 600-6927** or by email at **pcauwenbergh@deloitte.com**.

For more information on the author, please see Section XIII.

Transfer Pricing in Brazil

By Fernando Pereira de Matos
Deloitte Touche Tohmatsu

While the transfer pricing rules in most countries have significant similarities to those described in the OECD guidelines and the U.S. transfer pricing regime, Brazil has developed its own system of transfer pricing that has many complex characteristics that can make compliance challenging. This article offers an overview of the Brazilian approach to transfer pricing with some observations regarding successful strategies for satisfying the Brazilian tax authorities.

In particular, the article focuses on the rules for applying the Cost Plus Method (CPL) and discusses the application of the CPL in the context of a hypothetical case study in which a fictional Brazilian Company imports goods from a related party.

The article also includes a brief discussion of the other two transfer pricing methods allowed under Brazilian law, the Independent Price Compared Method (PIC) and the Resale Price Minus Gross Profit method (PRL).

Background on the Brazilian Transfer Pricing Environment

Similar to transfer pricing in other countries, Brazilian transfer pricing legislation addresses a number of complex issues. However, Brazil does not apply the arm's length principle or comply with the OECD transfer pricing guidelines, so transfer pricing compliance in Brazil presents some additional challenges. Also, Brazil does not offer an Advance Pricing Agreement (APA) program to allow taxpayers to control risks. Given the complexity of transfer pricing issues, Brazilian corporate taxpayers need to rely upon the interpretations by the Brazilian tax authorities to clarify compliance issues, which can be difficult given the apparent interest of those authorities in increasing the collect tax for the government rather than easing compliance-related burdens. However, some of those interpretations can benefit the taxpayer by allowing price comparisons that might not otherwise be allowed under the formula provided by transfer pricing Law.

Some of the complex subjects of the Brazilian transfer pricing legislation are:

- How to justify for the tax authorities the differences between the acquisition costs and prices of good, and that the prices agreed to in transaction with related company comply with the arm's length principle;
- Explaining the economic foundation and rational basis for determining the statutory gross margin to be applicable invariable and uniform for all the products and all types of business, when it is possible to prove in unequivocal form that different businesses makes different gross margin.

It is widely understood that businesses that at first glance appear to be similar are actually very different when examined more closely and therefore may differ in their gross margins.

This point can be illustrated by comparing two distributors of the same finished good. The first distributor, as revealed by its functional analysis, assumes all the inherent risks of the business, including the risk of bad debt or nor receiving the invoices of sales, the costs of marketing and advertisement of the products, the costs of obsolescence of the inventories, the costs of storage, among others. The second distributor sells products on commission, but does not manage inventories, does not support any advertisement expenses (which is a responsibility of the supplier), does not have bad debt risk of receiving invoices of sales that is assumed by the supplier, does not have financial costs of inventory, and does not have costs with the obsolescence of the product.

From this example, we can see that it is possible for two companies to perform what appears to be the same distribution activity, while each one is performing completely different functions.

The first company demands high profitability to support the costs of its functions and, economically speaking, there is no reason to them make the same gross profit margin. Brazil's tax authorities recognize this possibility of two apparently similar functions being very different in practice and therefore restrict the use of methods that might otherwise force an invalid comparison. As a result, they have a number of requirements that may seem onerous to taxpayers, including:

- No acceptance of any methods based on the comparison of profits to justify the adequacy of prices in cross border transactions between related companies;
- Requirement for comparing prices product by product individually to each product code or part number level;
- Definition of parameter prices through mathematical formulas and statutory gross margin settled in the Law;
- Great volume of information that is required for inclusion in documentation, so as to justify the parameter price and of the transaction prices that cause repercussions for the taxable profit;
- Complexity of obtaining appropriate documentation to prove the parameter price;
- New requirements for document the transfer pricing study in accordance the implementation of the new electronic documentation model known as –"AUDIN";
- Complex completion of income tax returns with detailed information regarding the transfer pricing, including information for each product individually, its parameter prices, its customers or suppliers identification, the paid price, the methodology to calculate price parameter, etc.

Noncompliance Penalties

Brazil has high fines for noncompliance or errors in the information contained in the transfer pricing studies through the AUDIN that can reach 5% of the value of the error, up to 1% of the total gross revenue. Fines on differences of tax, when identified in an audit process, may be 75% of the value of the additional tax due.

Differences of tax identified by the taxpayer after completion of the income tax return and before initiation of a tax audit are subject to penalties of up to 20%.

In addition, differences in the amount of tax due will be subject to interest charges corresponding to public interest rate (SELIC).

This example of noncompliance penalties represents only one example of the many complex issues that all Brazilian taxpayers have to fulfill as part of their fiscal obligations to justify the adequacy of the prices used in cross border transactions with related companies in order to comply with the Brazilian transfer pricing rules.

To further illustrate some of these issues, it is useful to examine a hypothetical case study.

Hypothetical Case Study

Opera Co., a company located in USA, identifies a chance to export the product Algas Superiores to its Brazilian subsidiary called SubBr Ltda.

Two years ago Opera Co. completed its new plant for production of Algas Superiores.

All the Algas Superiores production was transferred to the new plant due to customized processes that reduce costs, new technology, better quality, economies of scale, better performance of the product, and better logistics of supplier chain that involves purchasing raw materials and operating a distribution center.

The new plant is more efficient and produces double of the amount that was produced in the old plant.

The new plant can produce up to 1,050,000 of units per month, but for security reasons and to guarantee outstanding quality of the products the monthly production must be limited to 1,000,000 units.

Currently, due to market limitations, the plant produces 650,000 units per month.

The fixed costs of the plant for the 2007 calendar year were US$2,500,000.00 per month.

During 2007, the variable costs were US$5.00 per produced unit.

The American market of the product Algas Superiores is at its limit. Moreover, new competitors enter the market every year with lower prices each time. The prices per unit of the product in the wholesale market had fallen from US$14.20 in 2005 to US$13.50 in 2006. In 2007, the prices were expected to fall to US$12.30.

The sales, which in 2005 had reached 750,000 units, in 2006 decreased to 650,000 units.

With this very competitive and limited market, the prices defined the amounts sold. For 2007, with the price of US$12.30 per unit studies estimate the sales of 600,000 units.

Studies carried out by professionals at the Opera Co. had concluded that at the sales price of US$ 12.00, the total units sold could reach 700,000 in 2007.

Using its maximum capacity of production, Opera Co. could increase the production of 2007 from 700,000 units to 1,000,000 units, and the excess production would be sold to Brazil through SubBr Ltda, that represent a better opportunity to use to advantage as a chance to develop the Brazilian market as a new market for the products.

The product Algas Superiores was a new item that was expected to perform well with the Brazilian consumers, as its competitors had not yet initiated efforts to develop the Brazilian market that was demonstrated to be promising for this product.

With the increased production for sales to the Brazilian market, the fixed costs would be reduced to US$2.50 per unit, which, added to the variable costs of US$5.00 per unit, would reach the total production cost of US$7.50 per unit. In this scenario, production becomes more efficient, allowing a reduction in sales price, which in turn makes the product more competitive.

Opera Co. is familiar with the Brazilian transfer pricing legislation and begins the process of documenting its transactions in order to comply with those rules.

Opera Co. considers the experience gained with the operation of SubBr, knows the tax legislation and tax impact on the sales prices in Brazil, and calculates the sales price to be used in Brazil for SubBr to achieve a gross profit corresponding to 10% on the cost of the acquisition.

Opera Co. considered in its plan that its operational and administrative expenses would not increase with this new business.

The additional expenses calculated on FOB value of the SubBr importation that impact on acquisition cost for future sales correspond to freight 4%, insurance 2%, import tax 10 %, and other customs expenses 1%. The total expenses on FOB price reach 17 %.

The price of export sales of the product from the U.S. to Brazil was established in US$8.63, which corresponds the production cost of US$7.50 plus gross profit of 15%, that is less than the maximum limit rate on cost of 20%, allowed under the Brazilian transfer pricing legislation.

The sales price in the Brazilian market was defined considering: 1) the incurred costs to make the product available for sales that are of 17 % of FOB value; 2) Gross profit of 10% calculated on total sales cost; 3) 3% commissions on sales; and, 4) Sales Tax of 24%.

Based on above information, the sales price of the SubBr in the Brazilian market was set at US$15.36, including all sales tax and commission.

In light of defined sales prices, Opera Co. and SubBr Ltda know that under the Brazilian transfer pricing legislation they have to compare the prices of imported product that correspond to FOB values of the importations.

However, the tax auditors during the audit process must compare the costs of the acquisitions that include the FOB values of merchandises, added with the values of: Freight, insurance and Import Tax.

Comparing the FOB import price with the parameter price calculate according to Resale Price method minus Profit - PRL, would not result adjustment on taxable income, considering the price of the acquisition of US$8.63 per unit and PRL of US$8.97 per unit.

Considering the comparison that the Tax Auditor must make, in accordance with the interpretation of the Normative Instruction, that considers the acquisition cost to include FOB price plus freight, Import Tax and insurance, totaling US$10.01, the application of Resale Price Method minus 20% gross margin - PRL, would result in differences of prices of US$ 1.04 per unit and that it would represent a monthly adjustment on net profits for calculating income tax of US$ 310.500,00, that represents 12% of corresponding acquisition price FOB.

Opera Co. and SubBr Ltda had consulted tax consultants and lawyers, who are transfer pricing specialists in the application of the Brazilian legislation and those specialists had concluded that the adequate application of the Law would be to compare the PRL with FOB value of the imported merchandise.

To prevent the tax authorities from questioning the anaysis, which could take a long time discuss with signficant costs associated with defense of the application of PRL method, Opera Co. and SubBr Ltda, had decided to apply the Production Cost plus 20% Gross margin method with the expectation that it could be less onerous in regards possible future questioning, as its application would be clearer.

Opera Co. and Sub Br had been informed by their Tax consultant and their tax lawyers of the Tax Auditors requirements to accept the production costs in accordance with the Brazilian tax and commercial legislation to justify the imported prices from related company.

According to the tax and commercial legislation, the production costs must be integrated to the system of accounting of the company to prove that the production costs effectively had been incurred.

Opera Co. and SubBr, know that Opera Co. does not have integrated production cost with its accounting books as required by Brazil's commercial and tax legislation. The production costs of Opera Co. are calculated using the standard cost model.

Applying standard cost model, variations of production costs due to produced amounts, performance of production or any other variation of the industrial process that has impact on the cost of production during the period will be identified and recognized directly in the profit and losses of the period where it occurred.

The Brazilian tax legislation requires the recognition of the cost variation within the inventory each month to each finished good.

Even considering the deficiency in its compliance with the Brazilian transfer pricing legislation, Opera Co. was confident that the standard cost is very clear-cut and did not expect any variation in costs that are negotiated once a year with the suppliers, who are required not to change their prices during the calendar year.

Opera Co. has also locked-in the prices of the raw materials and components in the Algas Superiores production process, by reaching annual contracts with the suppliers of those materials. In light of this, Opera Co.'s variable production costs will not suffer any variation during the calendar year.

While there could be small adjustments in the operating costs of the plant, either because of set up complications or as a result of variations of the produced amounts, fixed costs would not change and would be uniform for each unit, due to the use of the plan to dedicate the plant's entire capacity to this production.

Opera Co. and SubBr know that during the tax audit of the competent Brazilian tax authority, if the production cost plus

Table 1: Algas Superiores Cost Structure

Raw Materials	Supplier	Quantity	Unit	Price per Unit	Total Cost
Element A	Vegetal Co	1,350	kg	1,30	1,755
Element B	Sal Co.	0,400	kg	3,50	1,400
RMComplent	Raiz Co	1	peças	0,30	0,300
Complex 76	Equivel Co	0,309	kg	5,00	1,545
Total Variable Costs					**5,000**

Fixed Costs

Labor including Tax and Benefict	1.280.000,00
Depreciation and Amortization	950.000,00
Mantenance, Repair e Services	220.000,00
Other Indirect Costs	50.000,00
Total Fixed Costs	**2.500.000,00**

method were chosen to justify the import prices used, the Fiscal Auditor, to accept the application of the method, would audit the production costs of Opera Co.

The production costs of Algas Superiores had been determined in accordance with the standard cost concept and presented to SubBr in summary as shown in Table 1.

The Expected Solution with Production Cost Plus Method – CPL

With the assumptions and guarantees above, Opera Co. and SubBr Ltda, had decided to justify the prices used in the Algas Superiores importations with the application of the Production Cost Method plus gross margin of 20% - CPL.

Considering the production cost per unit of US$7.50, the CPL would be US$9.00. With the price used in the exportation of Opera Co to SubBr Ltda of US$8.63, price excess did not occur and it did not cause adjustment in the taxable profit.

Expected Requirements from Tax Auditor

The Tax Auditor will require all of the relevant information to be available to its disposal at the beginning of its tax audit.

With regard to the variable costs, the Tax Auditor will require copies of some supplier invoices, where possible, identifying the raw material, the invoiced amounts, the total values and the corresponding values to the prices for acquired unit. (All documents in original foreign language should be required translated into Portuguese, notarized).

With regard to the fixed costs, the Tax Auditor will require a copy of the list that includes labor force of the plant, its wages, taxes, charitable contributions, benefit and other labor costs, including all personnel working with the production process where it is possible to verify the values.

With regard to depreciation and amortization the Tax Auditor will require a list of equipment, machines, and installations used in the production process, the values of the costs of the acquisitions of these goods, the depreciation and annual amortization rates, as well as invoices that prove the costs of the acquisitions.

With regard to the expenses with maintenance, repair, services and other indirect expenses of production, the Tax Auditor will require documentation of the values, suppliers and the nature of the related expenses.

To justify the use of the fixed costs and the variable costs, the Tax Auditor will require that Opera Co. demonstrate, through production order or equivalent document, that the direct costs and indirect costs were for materials and services that are used in the Algas Superiores production process in their entirety.

The Tax Auditor will search for evidence that the full production resources applied in the production process was not improperly shared with the production of other products.

The Tax Auditor may require the proof of the number of hours by each employee involved with the production of Algas Superiores and compare it to the total hours contracted and available for the work.

The Tax Auditor may require similar evidence regarding the hours during which equipment that benefits the production of Algas Superiores was in use, compared with the number of available hours for the production.

The Tax Auditor may require the methodology and evidence relative to the appropriation and allocation of common expenses of production cost, such as the indirect costs of production.

With all the available information, the Tax Auditor will be able to issue judgments regarding the appropriateness of the cost calculation for Algas Superiores production and exclude production costs that are not allowed under Brazilian law, as well as costs that are not supported by sufficient evidence necessary to justify that the costs are real, effective, incurred and appropriate.

Risk of Rejection of the CPL Method by Tax Auditor

If the tax auditor refuses to accept the CPL method to justify the prices used in the importation of goods from a related company due to lack of evidence that confirms the real production cost among or because it is not possible to audit the cost information, the tax auditor can disqualify the production cost.

If the production cost is disqualified, the tax auditor will recalculate the parameter price and apply the PRL method plus 20% gross margin to calculate the new parameter price and will also recalculate the acquisition costs of importation of goods, including in the sum import tax, insurance and freight, to be compared with parameter price and subject to adjustment in the taxable income.

If this calculation results in a difference of prices that increases taxable income, the new amount of tax due will be subject to a 75% fine, as well as interest calculated based on the Brazilian Central Bank's Sistema Especial de Liquidação e Custodia (SELIC).

Alternatives to the Cost Plus Method

The Brazilian transfer pricing guidelines provide three methods to prove the adequacy of prices on import transaction with a related company. The taxpayer can chose one method from among these three methods at the beginning of the process. Also, if a taxpayer pursues a transfer pricing method initially that is rejected by the tax authorities, the taxpayer may switch to a different method.

Generally, taxpayers will choose the method that results in the minimum adjustment to taxable income, is simplest to document and easiest to prove.

In addition to the CPL, the other two methods available are the Independent Price Compared method (PIC) and the Resale Price Minus Gross Profit method (PRL).

Overview of the PIC Method

If the product being sold to a related party in Brazil is also being sold to unrelated parties, then the PIC, which corresponds to the CUP method in international guidelines, can be applied.

The Brazilian transfer pricing legislation makes application of the PIC method very simple for cases in which the exporter sells the same product to both related and unrelated companies.

The PIC method corresponds to a weighted average of prices from transactions with unrelated companies. In order to apply the PIC method, the average of prices must be documented by providing the tax authorities with a full database of transaction information, including invoice numbers; customer names; transaction dates; quantities of product sold; and total sales price.

Tax auditors also require some copies of the invoices included in the unrelated-party transaction database of transaction with unrelated companies, translated into Portuguese and notarized.

Factors to Consider When the PRL Method is Applied

Another option is to apply the PRL method, which determines values by subtracting gross profit from net resale prices. In cases where a taxpayer uses the CPL, but the tax authorities reject the application of the CPL, the tax authorities usually apply the PRL to determine valuations. They apply the PRL rather than the PIC because they have all the information they need available to conduct a PRL analysis from the information filed with the CPL analysis and accounting book, but they do not have information available to conduct a PIC analysis.

Taxpayers should be careful under these circumstances to make certain that the tax authorities apply the PRL correctly.

Under the PRL, the FOB price should be used, but sometimes the tax auditor adds in other costs, such as transportation, insurance and import taxes. If the tax auditor includes these amounts, it may be grounds to challenge the tax auditor's ruling in the administrative tax court.

This point can be illustrated using the numbers from our earlier example: a product is produced in the U.S. and exported to Brazil for a price of $8.63. The purchaser pays $1.38 in freight, insurance, and import tax, so the total acquisition cost is $10.01. If the auditor uses the $10.01 figure rather than the $8.63 figure in applying the PRL, it may result in higher taxable income and can be appealed on the grounds that the $8.63 figure should have been used, as transportation costs, import taxes, and insurance are deductible costs under Brazilian law.

Conclusion

While the decision to apply CPL method for valuing transactions with related parties in Brazil is often seen as being a simple choice, the actual execution of the method can be quite complicated and may give a false feeling of security. Because of the complexity of calculating and justifying prices using the CPL method, it is rarely accepted by the Brazilian tax authorities.

In many cases, companies applying the CPL have difficulty proving that the documented costs have been incurred. In some cases, a portion of those costs are disallowed by the tax auditor.

The decision to apply the CPL method to justify the prices should be preceded by a deep analysis of the risks is associated with recalculation of taxable income by the Brazilian tax authorities and the resulting fines and interest penalties.

AUTHOR'S NOTE: All the elements of the case study described in this article are fictitious and they do not represent real cases.

Mr. Fernando Pereira de Matos is a tax consulting partner with Deloitte Touche Tohmatsu's Brazilian member firm. He can be reached at **(55) 11 5186 1179** or by email at **fmatos@deloitte.com**.

For more information on the author, please see Section XIII.

Overview of Canadian Transfer Pricing

L. David Fox
Fasken Martineau DuMoulin LLP

The Canada Revenue Agency (the "CRA") believes that it must be vigilant in protecting the Canadian tax base by making sure that taxpayers do not use transfer pricing to allocate income to other jurisdictions inappropriately. When the Department of Finance introduced the current version of the transfer pricing legislation in the *Income Tax Act* (Canada) (the "Act") in 1997, the CRA identified "the reporting of world income, transfer prices, and proper payment of Canadian taxes by non-residents working or carrying on business in Canada" as "key risk areas"[1] and stated that it intended to devote more resources to auditing cross-border transactions by multinational enterprises.[2]

A transfer pricing dispute will occur when the CRA determines that in its view a taxpayer is paying too much for goods, intangibles, or services that it purchases or receives from non-resident affiliates or is receiving too little for goods, intangibles or services that it sells or provides to non-resident affiliates. The Canadian taxpayer will generally either be a subsidiary of a foreign corporation (possibly with affiliated corporations in other jurisdictions) or a Canadian corporation with one or more foreign subsidiaries.

The article addresses only federal income taxes and does not consider customs and excise taxes.

Statutory Provisions and Special Considerations

Statutory Transfer Pricing Provisions

(i) Arm's Length Principle

The transfer pricing provisions in the Act apply where a taxpayer and a non-arm's length non-resident participate in a transaction (or series of transactions)[3] that has non-arm's length terms and conditions or in a transaction which itself is non-arm's length in nature.[4]

Specifically, pursuant to subsection 247(2) of the Act, the Minister of National Revenue (Canada) (the "Minister") may adjust the quantum or nature of amounts in respect of a transaction or series of transactions where:

a) the terms or conditions of the transaction or series differ from those that would have been made between persons dealing at arm's length; or

b) the transaction or series would not

---

1 CRA Backgrounder on International Tax Administration.
2 September 11, 1997 Department of Finance Press Release on Transfer Pricing.
3 Subsection 247(2) also applies to partnerships.
4 Treaties generally also incorporate the arm's length standard. See, for example, Article IX(1) of the *Canada-United States Tax Convention (1980)* (the "Canada-U.S. Tax Treaty").

have been entered into between persons dealing at arm's length and can reasonably be considered not to have been entered into primarily for *bona fide* purposes other than to obtain a tax benefit.

Whether or not a transaction or series is representative of a transaction or series into which arm's length parties would have entered is a question of fact. The Organisation for Economic Co-Operation and Development (the "**OECD**") recommends certain transfer pricing methods which, when applied correctly, result in an arm's length price or allocation. These methods are:

- Traditional Transaction Methods:
- the comparable uncontrolled price (CUP) method;
- the resale price method; and
- the cost plus method;
- Transactional profit methods:
- the profit split method; and
- the transactional net margin method.

A description of each of these transfer pricing methods is beyond the scope of this article, however, while the Act does not impose a hierarchy of the methods, the CRA endorses the OECD's view that:

- the traditional transaction methods are preferable to the transactional profit methods; and
- the transactional profit methods are used as methods of last resort, when the use of the traditional transaction methods cannot be reliably applied or cannot be applied at all.[5]

(ii) Part XIII of the Act and the Obligation to Withhold

Where certain transfer pricing adjustments are made under subsection 247(2), the Act will deem the adjustment to constitute a dividend paid by the Canadian corporation to the related non-resident company. In such circumstances, Part XIII of the Act requires that 25% of the gross amount of the deemed dividend be withheld as tax and remitted by the Canadian "payor" on account of the non-resident's Canadian income tax liability. The 25% withholding rate is reduced in Canada's tax treaties. A Canadian resident taxpayer who fails to withhold and remit tax when required to do so may be assessed for and required to pay the full amount of tax which should have been withheld and remitted, plus interest and penalties (generally speaking, penalties are 10% of the amount that should have been withheld, 20% in situations involving gross negligence).[6] The Canadian resident taxpayer can then deduct or withhold from future amounts paid or credited to the non-resident in order to recover the tax so remitted.

(iii) Downward Transfer Pricing Adjustments

Pursuant to subsection 247(10) of the Act, the Minister has the authority to make downward adjustments if, in the Minister's opinion, the circumstances indicate that the adjustments are appropriate. Downward adjustments are adjustments which result in a decrease in a taxpayer's income, an increase in a taxpayer's loss, or an increase in a taxpayer's capital expenditures, for the year. The Minister may decide not to exercise his discretion under subsection 247(10) where:

- the taxpayer's request has been prompted by the actions of a foreign tax authority and the taxpayer has the right to request relief under the mutual agreement procedure article of the applicable tax tax treaty; or

---

[5] *Information Circular* IC 87-2R- "International Transfer Pricing" (September 27, 1999) at paragraph 52.

[6] See subsections 227(8), (8.1), (8.3) and (8.4) of the Act.

- the taxpayer's request can be considered abusive.

(iv) Penalties

Subsection 247(3) imposes a 10% penalty in certain circumstances for taxpayers who are subject to a transfer pricing adjustment under subsection 247(2) of the Act. The penalty for a particular taxation year is equal to 10% of the amount of the transfer pricing adjustment (to income and capital) for the year except to the extent that the adjustment relates to a "qualifying cost contribution arrangement"[7] or where the taxpayer has made "reasonable efforts" to determine (and use for the purposes of the Act) arm's length transfer prices or allocations in respect of the transaction giving rise to the adjustment.

The penalty does not apply unless the adjustment exceeds the lesser of: (i) 10% of the taxpayer's gross revenue for the year; and (ii) $5,000,000.

The 10% of gross revenue/$5,000,000 limitation is intended to ensure that the penalty only applies where there is a substantial transfer pricing reassessment. Nevertheless, this penalty (particularly when combined with non-deductible interest applicable to any tax that is assessed) is onerous. It will apply to taxpayers that are not in a taxable position due to losses.

The CRA policy is that taxpayers must be made aware of the transactions under review and the potential for application of subsection 247(3) penalties. Normally this will be done through a proposal letter and this letter will provide taxpayers with an opportunity to provide additional information and representations which they wish to be considered. Prior to a penalty being assessed under subsection 247(3) of the Act, it must be reviewed by a central "Transfer Pricing Review Committee," at CRA headquarters in Ottawa.

A taxpayer is deemed under the Act not to have made "reasonable efforts" to determine and use arm's length allocations or transfer prices in a particular taxation year if the taxpayer does not make or obtain "contemporaneous documentation" on or before the relevant taxpayer's "documentation-due date."

(v) Contemporaneous Documentation

Pursuant to paragraph 247(4)(c) of the Act, taxpayers must provide the contemporaneous documentation specified in subsection 247(4) to the CRA within three months of a written request to do so. Failing to provide the records or documents within this time frame will result in the taxpayer being deemed not to have made reasonable efforts to determine and use arm's length transfer prices or allocations for the purposes of the subsection 247(3) penalty.

Under subsection 247(4) of the Act, the contemporaneous documentation prepared by a taxpayer (and provided to the CRA in response to a transfer pricing request) must include, in respect of each transaction, "a description that is complete and accurate in all material respects" of:

- the property or services to which the transaction relates,
- the terms and conditions of the transaction and their relationship, if any, to the terms and conditions of each other transaction entered into between the participants in the transaction (the "Participants");
- the identity of the Participants and their relationship to each other at the time the transaction was entered into;
- the functions performed, the property used or contributed and the risks

---

[7] Defined in subsection 247(1).

assumed, in respect of the transaction, by the Participants;

- the data and methods considered and the analysis performed to determine the transfer prices or the allocations of profits or losses or contributions to costs, as the case may be, in respect of the transaction; and
- the assumptions, strategies and policies, if any, that influenced the determination of the transfer prices or the allocations of profits or losses or contributions to costs, as the case may be, in respect of the transaction.

The CRA has stated that this list of documents is not intended to be an exhaustive list of documents necessary to substantiate that a taxpayer's transfer pricing is in accordance with the arm's length principle or that the taxpayer has made reasonable efforts to determine arm's length transfer prices or allocations.[8] There is no set list of documents which, if made or obtained, will assure that the transfer pricing penalty provisions of subsection 247(3) will not be applied upon the assessment by the CRA of a transfer pricing adjustment.[9]

The required documentation for a particular taxation year must be made or obtained on or before the relevant taxpayer's "documentation-due date," which (in the case of a taxpayer other than a partnership) refers to the taxpayer's filing-due date on which the taxpayer's income tax return under Part I of the Act is required to be filed.[10] Generally speaking, the filing-due date for corporations under the Act is six months after the end of the corporations' taxation years.[11]

Documentation in respect of transactions spanning more than one taxation year must be updated on or before the documentation-due date, to reflect material changes for that year.[12]

Canada, Australia, Japan and the United States (the "U.S."), as members of the Pacific Association of Tax Administrators ("PATA"), have released principles such that taxpayers can create one uniform set of transfer pricing documentation to meet their transfer pricing documentation provisions.[13]

Use of the PATA documentation package guidance is voluntary for taxpayers. While use of the PATA documentation package should, if properly applied and prepared, allow taxpayers to avoid the imposition of transfer pricing penalties, the CRA (and other PATA member taxing authorities) may still make transfer pricing adjustments and assess interest on such adjustments.

Reassessment Period

Generally speaking, the Minister may reassess a taxpayer in respect of a taxation year no later than the period that ends three-years (in the case of Canadian-controlled private corporations)[14] or four-years (in the case of other corporations) after the earlier of the date of mailing of a notice of an original assessment in respect of the taxpayer for the year and the day of mailing of an original notification that no

---

8 *supra* note 5 at paragraph 183.
9 *Ibid.*
10 Paragraph 247(4)(a) and the definition of "documentation-due date" in subsection 247(1) of the Act.
11 Paragraph 150(1)(a) of the Act.
12 Paragraph 247(4)(b)
13 CRA Document: "Pacific Association of Tax Administrators (PATA) Transfer Pricing Documentation Package," http://www.cra-arc.gc.ca/tax/non-residents/common/trans/pata-e.html (Last Modified January 2, 2007).
14 "Canadian-controlled private corporations" are private corporations that are Canadian corporations that are not controlled, directly or indirectly in any manner whatever, by one or more non-resident persons, or by one or more public corporations.

tax is payable by the taxpayer for the year.[15] This "normal reassessment period" does not apply to transfer pricing transactions since the Act extends the reassessment period in respect of transactions between taxpayers and non-arm's length non-residents by three years, to six and seven years, respectively.[16] The extended reassessment period creates uncertainty for taxpayers but the CRA considers the extended period necessary because of the time it takes to obtain and assess foreign-based documentation.

The extended reassessment period may, however, effectively be shortened under an applicable tax treaty. Some treaties prohibit adjustments that give rise to double taxation after a specified period.[17]

Canada Revenue Agency - Audit Division

Subsection 233.1 of the Act requires residents of Canada and non-residents who carry on business in Canada ("reporting persons") to provide prescribed information concerning non-arm's length transactions with non-residents ("reportable transactions"). On this point, Form T106-"Information Return of Non-Arm's Length Transactions with Non-Residents," must be filed annually by "reporting persons," including corporations, trusts, individuals and reporting partnerships (partnerships a member of which is resident in Canada in the period, or a partnership that carries on business in Canada in the period). The CRA uses the information contained in Form T106 to screen non-arm's length transactions for review and audit (i.e. Form T106 may trigger a transfer pricing audit).

During an audit, the CRA may inform the taxpayer that it proposes to reassess the taxpayer on a transfer pricing issue. The proposed reassessment may be part of a specialized audit of a particular industry. The CRA's practice is to inform a taxpayer by letter of any proposed reassessment and to give the taxpayer an opportunity (often thirty days, sixty days or whatever time is appropriate in the circumstances) to respond. When informed of a proposed reassessment the taxpayer will want to take immediate steps to support its transfer pricing.

Canada Revenue Agency Not Required to Disclose Third Party Information at Audit Stage

Often an auditor will be relying on third party comparables or other third party information as the basis for a proposed reassessment. That is, the CRA may assess whether prices at which services, tangible property and intangible property are traded between Canadian resident and non-resident, related parties satisfy the arm's length principle by assessing information in respect of similar transactions undertaken by independent enterprises. The CRA has stated that auditors should only use third party information as a basis for reassessment as a last resort and that every effort should be made to base assessing positions on publicly available information.[18] Auditors wishing to use third party information as the basis for a transfer pricing assessment must first refer the file to the International Tax Operations Division ("ITOD") of the CRA, prior to sending a proposed assessment to the relevant taxpayer.

When gathering third party information, the CRA has instructed its auditors

---

15 Subsection 152(3.1).
16 Subparagraphs 152(4)(b)(iii) and 152(4.01)(b)(iii).
17 See, for example, Article IX(3) of the Canada-U.S. Tax Treaty.

18 *Transfer Pricing Memorandum* TPM-04 "Third Party Information" (October 27, 2003)

to inform third party taxpayers of the true purpose for gathering such information and that the auditors should not enter into agreements with the taxpayers that promise not to disclose any of the taxpayers' information.[19] Section 241 of the Act prohibits the CRA from disclosing such information, subject to certain statutory exceptions, and, generally, such information will remain confidential. Where the third party information obtained by the CRA is used as a basis for reassessing another taxpayer and that taxpayer appeals the reassessment to the Tax Court of Canada, the CRA is permitted to release the third party information obtained to the appealing taxpayer. However, in such circumstances and prior to releasing this information, the CRA will contact the third parties to allow them to pursue their legal rights regarding their confidential information through court issued confidentiality orders.

If, following a request, third party taxpayers do not provide the information requested by the Minister voluntarily, or the Minister is not satisfied with the information provided, the Minister may issue "Requirements for Information," or "Demands for Information," pursuant to section 231.2 of the Act.

Canada Revenue Agency Access to Foreign-Based Documents

(i) Section 231.6

Section 231.6 permits the CRA to obtain access to foreign-based documents during (or following) an audit. Under subsection 231.6(2), the CRA may serve notice on the taxpayer requiring the taxpayer to produce any information or document that is available or located outside Canada and that may be relevant to the administration or enforcement of the Act.[20]

If a taxpayer fails to "comply substantially" with the requirement, the Minister may bring a motion under subsection 231.6(8) before any court having jurisdiction in a civil proceeding relating to the administration or enforcement of the Act to prohibit the introduction by the taxpayer in the court proceeding of any foreign-based information or document requested in the notice.[21]

Subsection 231.6(4) provides that a taxpayer may apply to a judge to have the requirement set aside on the basis that it is unreasonable. However, the Act provides that a requirement is not unreasonable because the information or document is under the control of, or available to, a related non-resident person that is not controlled by the taxpayer. This means that a taxpayer can be required to produce information or documents relating to transfer pricing that are in the possession of a foreign parent or sister corporation.

(ii) "Exchange of Information" Provisions in Tax Treaties

In addition to section 231.6 of the Act, the "Exchange of Information" provisions in Canada's tax treaties, permit the CRA to obtain information through the applicable foreign competent authority.[22]

For example, Article XXVII of the Canada-U.S. Tax Treaty permits the CRA to ask the U.S. competent authority for

---

19 Ibid.
20 The Minister must serve notice of the requirement personally or by registered or certified mail and must provide a reasonable time for production (at least ninety days). The notice must set out a description of the information or document being sought and the consequences under subsection 231.6(8) of a failure to provide the information or document within the required time period. See subsections 231.6(2) and (3).
21 See *Glaxo Smithkline Inc. v. Her Majesty the Queen*, 2003 D.T.C. 918 (T.C.C.).
22 For a case dealing with Article XXVII of the Canada-U.S. Tax Treaty see, for example, *Thomas G. Andison v. Minister of National Revenue*, 95 D.T.C. 5058 (F.C.T.D.).

information relevant to a transfer pricing issue. If the CRA requests information under this article, the U.S. competent authority is to endeavour to provide the information: (i) in the same way as if U.S. taxation was involved; and (ii) in the form specifically requested, such as depositions of witnesses and copies of unedited original documents, to the same extent such depositions and documents can be obtained under the laws and administrative practices of the U.S. with respect to its own taxes.[23]

Pursuant to Article XXVII(1), the CRA is required to treat any information received under this article as secret in the same manner as information obtained under Canadian tax laws and may disclose the information only to persons or authorities involved in the assessment or collection of, the administration and enforcement in respect of, or the determination of appeals in relation to the taxes to which the treaty applies.[24]

Contesting Transfer Pricing Assessments

Appeals to the Canada Revenue Agency and Canadian Courts

A taxpayer wishing to appeal a transfer pricing assessment may do so by filing a Notice of Objection with the CRA Appeals Division within ninety days after the day of mailing of the notice of assessment. Filing such an objection preserves the taxpayer's right to appeal the transfer pricing assessment to the Tax Court of Canada (if necessary) and provides a second opportunity to communicate with the CRA before going to court (or competent authority). Upon receipt of a Notice of Objection, an Appeals Officer in the CRA Appeals Division (as opposed to the Verification and Enforcement Division which raised the assessment) will review the Notice of Objection and will make a recommendation to the Chief of Appeals of the CRA who, in turn, will vacate, vary or confirm the transfer pricing assessment.

Failure to file a notice of objection will preclude a taxpayer from contesting the assessment further in court but will not preclude the taxpayer from seeking competent authority relief. Nevertheless taxpayers should always file a notice of objection even if they intend to proceed to competent authority so that they preserve their appeal rights in the event that the competent authority result is unsatisfactory.[25]

If the CRA confirms the assessment, varies the assessment or reassesses in a manner that the taxpayer finds unsatisfactory, the taxpayer must then either proceed to the Tax Court of Canada and/or competent authority if the taxpayer wishes to continue to dispute the assessment.

Competent Authority

Instead of (or in addition to) contesting a reassessment in the courts, a taxpayer may seek competent authority relief. Competent authority proceedings have had a high success rate to date in the transfer pricing context and the use of these proceedings is expected to increase in the future.

Competent authority relief is often a

---

23 Article XXVII(2)

24 Disclosure can also be made to the provincial tax authorities in respect of provincial income taxes.

25 If the taxpayer for some reason does not file a notice of objection and proceeds to competent authority the taxpayer should ensure that all necessary federal (subject to the applicable treaty provisions) and provincial waivers are filed. The taxpayer may wish to file waivers in any event.

more effective route than litigation in the transfer pricing context because a transfer pricing adjustment in one jurisdiction will generally result in double taxation unless there is a corresponding adjustment in the other jurisdiction. For example, the CRA may reassess a Canadian taxpayer on the basis that the taxpayer is overpaying for goods purchased from a related non-resident. Unless there is a corresponding reduction in the non-resident's income, the same income will be taxed in both jurisdictions.

The objective of competent authority proceedings is to resolve the double taxation issue to the mutual satisfaction of the Canadian taxpayer, the related non-resident, and the competent authorities of both governments.

The CRA takes the position that a taxpayer may request competent authority relief at any time that the CRA adjusts, or formally proposes in writing to adjust, income related to any transaction to which the taxpayer is a party and the adjustment results, or will result, in double taxation or taxation that otherwise is not in accordance with the treaty.[26] Accordingly, the taxpayer may apply for competent authority relief as soon as the CRA formally proposes in writing to reassess and the taxpayer does not have to wait for the reassessment to be issued. However, the taxpayer's request must be made within the time period (if any) specified in the applicable treaty.

A request for relief from the competent authority is initiated by sending a letter to the Canadian competent authority setting out the facts and an analysis of the issues surrounding the matter for which competent authority assistance is being requested. Wherever possible, electronic copies of the materials should be provided.

Once the competent authorities reach a settlement, the taxpayer may accept or reject the settlement. The CRA takes the position that the taxpayer must accept the entire settlement, and not just the settlement on some of the issues or taxation years involved. That is, it is an all or nothing proposition and there is no right or ability to appeal a competent authority settlement. If the taxpayer rejects the competent authority settlement the competent authorities will consider the case closed and advise the taxpayer accordingly.

In the event that the taxpayer proceeds to competent authority before being reassessed, the normal reassessment process is not affected. The CRA will proceed to reassess the taxpayer and the two procedures will proceed concurrently and independently. Following the reassessment, the taxpayer should file a notice of objection and should ask the CRA to hold the notice of objection in abeyance pending the outcome of the competent authority negotiations.[27]

Similarly, if the taxpayer has filed a notice of appeal and then proceeds to competent authority, the taxpayer should request that the notice of appeal be held in abeyance. The CRA takes the position that the taxpayer is not entitled to pursue the court and competent authority avenues simultaneously and that if the taxpayer proceeds with either a notice of objection or an appeal to a court on a double taxation issue while competent authority negotiations are in progress and does not request that the objection or appeal be held in abeyance, the competent authority process will be terminated.[28]

---

26 *Information Circular* IC71-17R5-"Guidance on Competent Authority Assistance Under Canada's Tax Conventions" (January 1, 2005) at paragraph 10.

27 *Ibid.* at paragraph 38.
28 *Ibid.* at paragraph 39.

Advance Pricing Arrangements

A taxpayer that decides to bring a transfer pricing dispute to competent authority may also want to consider entering into an Advance Pricing Arrangement ("APA") for future years. The:

> ...CRA's APA program assists taxpayers in determining transfer pricing methodologies with the objective of avoiding double taxation that may otherwise occur. Under the MAP article of a tax convention, a taxpayer may request a bilateral APA with respect to specified cross-border transactions. Once concluded, bilateral APAs provide an increased level of tax certainty in both tax jurisdictions, thereby lessening the likelihood of double taxation.[29]

No penalty will be levied under the transfer pricing provisions of the Act in respect of transactions covered by APAs. While APAs are intended to provide certainty of tax consequences in the future, taxpayers can request that the CRA "rollback" APAs to cover transactions occurring in prior, non-statute-barred, taxation years.

APAs may be resolved in a manner different from that which is proposed in the APA request. In such circumstances, the taxpayer can accept the resolution arrived at by the Competent Authorities or reject the resolution and withdraw from the APA process.[30]

APAs may be unilateral, bilateral or multi-lateral.

Conclusion

Taxpayers are best able to resolve transfer pricing disputes by ensuring that their transfer prices comply with the arm's length standard. Proactive and early consultation with and involvement of legal and accounting advisors specializing in Canadian transfer pricing matters will provide taxpayers with some comfort that the arm's length standard is being met and that the taxpayer's contemporaneous documentation meets the requirements imposed under the Act. If a transfer pricing disagreement does arise, competent authority proceedings will generally be preferable to litigation.

---

29 Ibid. at paragraph 63.

30 CRA APA Program Report 2006-2007, Competent Authority Services Division, International and Large Business Directorate, Compliance Programs Branch at 7.

L. David Fox practices in the areas of corporate tax, personal tax planning and wealth management in the Toronto office of Fasken Martineau DuMoulin LLP. He can be reached at **(416) 865 4480** or by email at **dfox@fasken.com**. For more information on the author, please see Section XIII.

China's Transfer Pricing Regime

Joanna Lam
Deloitte Touche Tohmatsu

China has recently enacted a series of laws and regulations that completely overhaul its transfer pricing regime. MNCs with related parties operating in China should carefully review the changes and consider how the new legal and regulatory framework affects their operations. Overall, the new laws and regulations bring China closer to the transfer pricing standards of the OECD regulations, but notable differences remain. China now allows Advance Pricing Agreements (APAs) and Cost Sharing Agreements (CSAs) and applies a "Best Method Rule" similar to that of the United States, and accepts six transfer pricing methodologies. The new rules also include strict contemporaneous documentation requirements and incorporate "General Anti-Avoidance Rules" (GAAR) for companies whose business operations appear to be structured to reduce tax exposure without legitimate business purposes.

Even companies that previously were not subject to transfer pricing requirements in China because their China operations were not considered associated enterprises should take notice of the new rules, which expand the definition of related-party to include some entities that do not share common ownership.

Another factor that will challenge some companies operating in China is the requirement that all documentation be provided to the tax authorities in Chinese, even when the original documents are written in another language.

The new rules do provide some opportunities for companies to mitigate risk of special tax adjustments and clarify compliance requirements.

Overview of Recent Changes

Tax administration in the People's Republic of China ("China") entered a new era in 2008 with enactment of the Unified Enterprise Income Tax Law ("EIT Law"). Articles 41-48 of 'Chapter 6 – Special Tax Adjustments' of the EIT Law and Articles 109-123 of its detailed Implementation Rules ("Implementation Rules") establish a new basis for the Chinese tax authorities to make special tax adjustments related to areas such as Transfer Pricing, Thin Capitalization, General Anti-avoidance Rules ("GAAR"), and Controlled Foreign Corporations ("CFC"). In addition, the EIT Law and its Implementation Rules provide the basis for Chinese enterprises to enter into Advanced Pricing Arrangements ("APAs") and Cost Sharing Agreements ("CSAs"). The State Administration of Taxation ("SAT") in Beijing published the Implementation Regulations for Special Tax Adjustments ("STA Rules") as set out in notice, Guo Shui Fa [2009] No. 2, dated 8 January 2009.

The STA Rules, which take effect as of January 1, 2008, provide more detailed guidance on how special tax adjustment will be determined and enforced going forwards, particularly in regards to transfer pricing. The STA Rules consolidate the contents of the previously issued transfer pricing circulars. After the issuance of the STA Rules, the previously issued Guoshuifa [1998] No. 59 ("Circular 59"), Guoshuifa [2004] No. 143 ("Circular 143"), and Guoshuifa [2004] No. 118 ("Circular 118") will be revoked. The issuance of the STA Rules is seen as a landmark in the history of Chinese transfer pricing rules. It demonstrates the SAT's determination to tighten up transfer pricing compliance enforcement and to take China a step further closer to international transfer pricing standards.

In order to evaluate a company's China operations for potential transfer pricing issues and to take necessary measures to mitigate the potential risk of special tax adjustments, it is important to understand the main features of the STA Rules, which include contemporaneous documentation requirements, a broader definition of related parties (i.e. "associated enterprises"), criteria for determining the best transfer pricing method, audit selection factors and procedures, rules for making adjustments, penalty provisions, APA procedures and applicability, CSA requirements and restrictions, a revised definition of "Controlled Foreign Corporation" (CFC), new thin capitalization rules for MNCs operating in China, and the new general anti-avoidance rules (GAAR).

The article also includes a discussion of the practical implications of some of these provisions for companies with related parties operating in China.

I. Contemporaneous Transfer Pricing Documentation Requirements

A) Applicability of Documentation Requirements

In the past, it was not mandatory for Chinese enterprises to prepare transfer pricing documentation in China for compliance purposes. In line with the spirit of the EIT Law and its Implementation Rules, the SAT has introduced contemporaneous transfer pricing documentation requirements in China for the first time.

Based on the STA Rules, enterprises are required to prepare contemporaneous transfer pricing documentation for the fiscal year by May 31 of the following year, unless one of the following exceptions applies:

- the annual value of related party purchases and sales is less than RMB 200 million (for toll manufacturing activities, the amount is calculated based on the import or export customs declaration prices) AND annual amount of other related party transactions is lower than RMB 40 million (for related party financing, the amount is calculated based on the interest received or paid). The determination of the abovementioned related-party purchases and sales or other transactions is exclusive of those amounts already covered by CSAs or APAs that are in effective in the relevant year;
- Related-party transactions are covered by an APA;
- Foreign shareholding in the enterprise is less than 50% and the enterprise only transacted with domestic related parties (not including Hong Kong, Taiwan and Macau).

B) Definition of Associated Enterprises

When defining associated enterprises (or related parties), the STA Rules use a 25% direct or indirect ownership threshold. Where an entity owns more than 25% of an intermediary entity, its indirect ownership of the lower tier entity will be deemed to be the same as the intermediary's direct ownership of the lower tier entity. As a result, two entities could be treated as being related even if their legal shareholding proportion has not reached the 25% related party threshold.

Also, if debts owed by one party to another (except to an independent financial institution) exceed 50% of the party's actual received capital, or 10% or more of the total debts owed by one party is guaranteed by another party (except by an independent financial institution), the two parties are regarded as related.

The STA Rules also put a great emphasis on control when defining associated enterprises. An entity with significant control over the taxpayer's senior management, purchases, sales, production and the intangibles and technologies required for the business is defined as a related party under the STA Rules.

Under certain conditions, two transacting enterprises without a legal ownership relationship could be deemed as associated enterprises and therefore subject to transfer pricing assessment and investigation according to the STA Rules, as follows:

1) If more than half of one party's senior management personnel (including the members of the board of directors and managers), or at least one senior member of the board of directors who is able to exert control over the board of directors, is appointed by another party; or
2) If two parties with more than half of their senior management personnel (including the members of the board of directors and managers), or more than one senior member of the board of directors who is able to exert control over the board of directors, is appointed by the same third party.

C) Required Content of Contemporaneous Documentation

The STA Rules specify that contemporaneous documentation should include:

- **Organizational Structure–** including the organizational structure of the group that the taxpayer is affiliated to, records regarding any development or changes in the relationships between the taxpayer and associated enterprises, information on associated enterprises including applicable tax rates and incentives, and the associated enterprises that exert direct influences on the intercompany pricing;
- **Summary of Business Operations–** including major economic and legal issues affecting the taxpayer and the industry such as a summary of the enterprise's development, summary of the industry's development, business strategy, industrial policy or industrial restrictions; description of the group's supply chain arrangement and the position that the taxpayer is located in the chain;
- **Functional Analysis–** summary showing percentage of enterprise's revenues and profits by business line, market and competition analysis; information regarding the functions, risks, and assets of the enterprise (with a specific requirement to prepare an official 'Functional and Risk Analysis' form) and the group's consolidated financial report that was prepared according to the group's year end;
- **Description of Related Party Transactions–** including the types, participants, timing, amounts, currency and contractual terms of the related party transactions; description of the

transactional model, terms applied and any changes to the model, operational flows including information, product and cash flows and flow comparisons with transactions with unrelated parties; intangible assets utilized and their impact on pricing policies; copies of the inter-company agreements and their execution status; analysis of the main economic and legal factors affecting the pricing of the related party transactions; and segmented financial analysis (with a specific requirement to prepare an official 'Annual Financial Analysis of Related Party Transactions' form);

- **Comparability Analysis** – including factors considered in performing the comparability analysis, information related to the functional profiles of the comparable companies, description of the comparable transactions, source, selection criteria and rationale for selection of comparables, and rationale for use of adjustments on the financial data; and
- **Discussion of Selection and Application of Transfer Pricing Methods** – including rationale and support for selection of transfer pricing method, whether the comparable data can support a reliable application of the selected transfer pricing method, assumptions and judgments when determining comparable prices or profits, determination of the comparable prices or profits and justification of arm's length price or profit of enterprise.

D) Timing of Preparation and Submission of Required Documentation

Contemporaneous documentation must be prepared by May 31 of the following year and maintained for ten years, although the deadline for the preparation of contemporaneous transfer pricing documentation for 2008 was extended to December 31, 2009.

Taxpayers are required to submit their contemporaneous transfer pricing documentation within 20 days of the date of request by the tax bureau. All documents, including those originally in a foreign language, must be submitted to the tax bureau in Chinese.

In addition, enterprises are required to submit nine related-party transaction disclosure forms with their annual income tax filing by May 31st of the following year. These forms, included in Guoshuifa [2008] No. 114 ("Circular 114") released on December 16th, 2008, include a requirement for the enterprise to disclose whether contemporaneous transfer pricing documentation has been prepared, or whether the enterprise is exempt from the preparation of contemporaneous transfer pricing documentation. Companies are also required to disclose whether they have entered into a CSA.

E) Noncompliance Penalties

If a taxpayer refuses to provide documents on its related party transactions, provides false or incomplete materials, or provides untruthful information, the tax bureau may order them to rectify the situation within a certain time limit and impose a fine of up to RMB 50,000 (approximately US$ 7,300). The more critical consequences are that the tax bureau has the right to assess taxable income to the enterprise in accordance with "reasonable" deemed methods.

When a transfer pricing adjustment is assessed – in addition to the additional tax liabilities – normal non-tax deductible interest charges and potential double taxation issues, a non-deductible penalty interest charge of 5% per annum (computed on a daily basis on the amount of underpaid tax) will be levied for related party transactions occurring after January 1st, 2008. However, this penalty interest may be waived if the taxpayer has prepared and submitted contemporaneous transfer pricing documentation according to the STA Rules within the specified time limit.

As the new transfer pricing documentation requirements apply to each individual taxpayer separately and may not be prepared on a consolidated basis, they will create a significant burden on many enterprises in China.

The penalty interest may apply when the adjusted related party transaction amount surpasses the documentation preparation exemption threshold, even if the taxpayer acted in good faith but mistakenly believed that it was exempt from the contemporaneous documentation requirement.

Therefore, one should be cautious when analyzing the relevant transactions in determining if an enterprise constitute as related party transactions and assessing the potential adjustment risks for Chinese transfer pricing purposes.

F) Allowed Transfer Pricing Methods

The EIT Law, its Implementation Rules and the STA Rules have adopted the "Best Method" approach for selecting a transfer pricing method, with no specific ranking among the following reasonable methods:

- Comparable Uncontrolled Price ("CUP") Method;
- Resale Price Method ("RPM");
- Cost Plus Method ("CPM");
- Transactional Net Margin Method ("TNMM");
- Profit Split Method; and
- other appropriate methods that comply with the arm's length principle.

The concept of the CPM is clarified under Article 25 of the STA Rules and is consistent with the concept defined in the OECD Guidelines where the arm's length price is determined based on reasonable costs plus the gross profit of comparable third party transactions. There had previously been some confusion amongst transfer pricing professionals on the Cost Plus concept introduced in Circular 143, in that there was an uncertainty as to whether the basis of the Cost Plus mark up was intended to include both cost of goods sold and operating expenses or just cost of goods sold.

G) Application of the Best Method Rule

In determining the "Best Method" to apply in analyzing a related party transaction, the STA Rules state that a reasonable method should be selected by considering the following factors within a comparability analysis: (i) the characteristics of the assets and services of the transaction; (ii) the functions performed and risks borne by all parties to the transaction; (iii) the contractual terms; (iv) the economic environment; and (v) the enterprise's business strategy. For each method, the STA Rules list several items that should be taken into account when applying the methods, e.g., if significant differences exist, reasonable adjustments should be made to increase comparability. Determining the allocation of functions and risks between related parties is at the heart of any transfer pricing analysis. The STA Rules emphasize the importance of a functional analysis by requiring taxpayers to fill the "Functional and Risk Analysis" form as part of the contemporaneous documents.

This is in line with the intent of Guoshuihan [2007] No. 363 ("Circular

363"), which was issued by the SAT issued in March, 2007 in an effort to strengthen and standardize the functional, risk, and financial analyses performed by the officials of local tax bureaus as part of their transfer pricing investigations.

While China's Best Method Rule bears some resemblance to that of the United States, it should be noted that the new rules also offer indications that transaction-based methods are preferred over the TNMM in a manner similar to the prioritization of methods found in many European jurisdictions. For more discussion of these considerations, please see Paragraph II(D), below, on Set-Offs and Aggregation of Transactions.

H) Conducing the Comparability Analysis

Since the issuance of Guoshuihan [2005] No. 239 ("Circular 239") titled "Notice of the State Administration of Taxation about the Anti-tax Avoidance Work 2005", the Chinese tax authorities have made great progress in using public databases. Specifically, the SAT uses Bureau Van Duk's OSIRIS database for their searches comparable public companies. This database is available for use in preparation of transfer pricing studies on a subscription basis. (For more information, please see *http://www.bvdinfo.com/Products/Company-Information/International/OSIRIS.aspx*.)

However, Article 37 of the STA Rules states that the tax bureaus may use either public or non-public information when conducting transfer pricing analysis and evaluation. Due to the lack of well established and reputable sources of industry data in China and reliability issues related to the financial information of private companies, the use of private data by the tax bureaus may put Chinese taxpayers in an unfavorable position.

In July 2005, the SAT issued Guoshuihan [2005] No. 745 stating that local tax bureaus should not apply capital adjustments in transfer pricing audit investigations, APA negotiations and other transfer pricing comparability analyses, unless certain conditions are met and approvals are obtained from the SAT. The STA Rules extend this position by stating that when the tax bureaus analyze and evaluate an enterprise's related party transactions, differences in operating profit due to variances in operating assets between the tested party and the comparable enterprises should, in principle, not be adjusted.

And if capital adjustments are necessary, the SAT's approval will be required. The restriction and inflexibility of the use of capital intensity adjustments may decrease comparability when searching for comparables for tested parties.

II. Transfer Pricing Audit Targets and Procedures

Compared with Circular 143, the STA Rules provide more detailed guidance regarding the criteria for selecting audit targets and audit procedures. Some salient points under "Chapter 5 – Transfer Pricing Audit and Adjustment" of the STA Rules are summarized below:

A) Transfer Pricing Audit Targets

Potential audit targets include taxpayers that:
- have large amounts of related party transactions or have multiple types of related party transactions; have long-term losses, marginal or fluctuating profits;
- have profit levels lower than that of their the industries;
- have profit levels which obviously do not match with the functions they perform and the risks they assume;

- have transactions with related parties registered in tax havens;
- fail to submit annual related party transaction disclosure forms or fail to prepare contemporaneous transfer pricing documentation; and
- obviously do not comply with the arm's length principle.

Audited enterprises will have a limited period of time to submit the required information to the tax bureaus upon request. Based on the STA Rules, while the submission of the contemporaneous transfer pricing documentation is required within 20 days upon request, other required information must be submitted within the time frame specified by the tax bureau in-charge. Extension of submission deadlines may be granted but will not exceed 30 days. Related parties of the audited enterprise and other unrelated comparable enterprises (hereafter refer to as the "Comparable Enterprises") may also be required to provide information upon request. The tax bureaus have the right to request that related parties and Comparable Enterprises provide relevant information or documentation through the written "Tax Matter Notice" procedure. Generally, documents requested should be provided within an agreed upon time frame, up to a maximum of 60 days.

The contemporaneous preparation of transfer pricing documentation therefore serves two purposes:
1) it allows the enterprise to satisfy the contemporaneous documentation requirement thereby avoiding interest and penalties for failing to meet timely documentation filing requirements, and
2) it relieves, to a large extent, the significant burden to the enterprise in an event of an audit and related requests for information from the tax bureaus.

B) Enterprises Whose Operations are Limited to Process Manufacturing Activities

Article 39 of the STA Rules reiterates the position previously taken by Guoshuihan [2007] No. 236 ("Circular 236") by requiring Chinese tax authorities to conduct economic analysis and determine a profit level for such enterprises should any losses be incurred.

Circular 236 states that a contract manufacturing entity must earn a profit that is reasonable with the functions and risks it undertakes. The STA Rules reiterate this position and emphasize that enterprises with only a processing manufacturing function and which do not bear risks, should not bear losses arising from business issues such as poor management decisions, insufficient capacity, product obsolescence, etc. It is the view of the SAT that these enterprises should maintain a stable level of profit, and that the risks related to volume shortfall should not be borne by the captive contract manufacturer if it solely takes orders from related parties and manufactures products only for related parties.

Further, on July 6, 2009, SAT issued Guo Shui Han [2009] No. 363 (Circular 363) under the title "Circular of the State Administration of Taxation on Strengthening Supervision and investigation of Cross-Border Related Party Transactions" on issues concerning the standardization of the administration of special tax adjustments for Chinese enterprises with cross-border related party dealings. Circular 363 requires loss-making enterprises to prepare contemporaneous documentation and other relevant materials to justify the structuring of related party transactions and arm's length nature of their profits.

C) Transfer Pricing Adjustments

The STA Rules state that the tax authorities can use public as well as non-public information when making transfer pricing assessment. In principle if a taxpayer's profitability is lower than the median of the inter-quartile range established by comparable companies, the tax bureau should adjust the taxpayer's profitability to at least the median of the range. Where an adjustment is made resulting in a reduction in the amount of interest, royalty, rental and other similar payments subject to withholding tax, the STA Rules state that the overpaid withholding taxes will not be refunded.

After a special tax adjustment comes into effect, the tax bureau will implement a follow-up supervision period for 5 years from the last year assessed. During the follow-up supervision period, the enterprise must submit contemporaneous documentation to the local tax bureau in-charge by June 20 of the following year.

In addition, the STA Rules provide a corresponding adjustment regime for the purpose of eliminating double taxation. Enterprises must apply for corresponding adjustments within three years upon receiving an adjustment notice from the tax bureaus. As indicated later, proper preparation and provision of contemporaneous documents is also a pre-condition for APA application based on the APA provisions of the STA Rules.

The rules also suggest that special tax adjustments may not only result in incremental income tax liabilities, but also increases in turnover tax liabilities on Value Added Tax ("VAT"), Business Tax ("BT"), or Consumption Tax ("CT").

D) Set-Offs and Aggregation of Transactions

Under the STA Rules, transactional set-offs will in principle need to be evaluated separately to determine whether they are consistent with the arm's length principle. This could cause additional analytical burden to the taxpayers in terms of separately proving the arm's length nature of the set-off transactions. This requirement could also have further indirect tax and customs duty implications, in addition to income tax implications. For example, if the two transactions in question have different VAT rates or even BT rates, a transfer pricing adjustment could potentially cause additional VAT or BT liabilities.

In practice, the Chinese tax authorities usually require the transfer pricing methodologies be applied on a transactional rather than a 'whole of entity' basis unless the transactions can be aggregated.

Aggregation of transactions is usually allowed if the business activities of the transactions are closely related to each other. Hence, an enterprise with large discrepancies in the profitability of its various segments (either by product line or type of transaction) could still have transfer pricing exposures in China even though the enterprise as a whole earns a decent profit margin in China.

III. APA Program

The Implementation Rules and the STA Rules provide considerable guidance on the APA program in China, implying a genuine desire by the Chinese tax authorities to utilize APAs as a viable tool for taxpayers. The STA Rules describe the six phases of the APA application process including: 1) pre-filing meetings, 2) formal application, 3) tax authority review and evaluation, 4) negotiations, 5) the signing of the agreement, and 6) monitoring and execution. The procedures outlined in the STA Rules are similar to the procedures previously outlined in Circular 118. The STA Rules also clarify certain procedures at various application stages for bilateral or multilateral APAs.

Notwithstanding the positive sign given by the issuance of "Chapter 6 – Administrative Guidance concerning APAs" of the STA rules, APAs may still not be suitable for all MNCs in China. In 2005, the SAT issued Guoshuihan [2005] No. 1172 ("Circular 1172") encouraging local tax bureaus to focus on the quality of the APA applications rather than the number of the applications. In addition, Circular 1172 encourages local tax bureaus first to consider taxpayers that have either been recently audited, or that are in an industry familiar to the tax bureau for entry into the APA program. Under the STA Rules, APA candidates should generally meet the following requirements:

- Annual volume of related party transactions exceeds RMB 40 million (approximately US$ 6 million);
- Fulfilled the obligations to declare their related-party transactions; and
- Prepared, maintained and provided contemporaneous transfer pricing documentation in accordance with the STA Rules.

Under the STA Rules, an APA will have the following features:

- Taxpayers may hold pre-file meetings with the tax bureau in-charge on a no-name basis;
- The term of an APA may range from 3 to 5 years starting from the year after formal application;
- The APA will become automatically invalid after the execution period expires. The taxpayer may apply for a renewal with the governing tax bureau within 90 days before the expiration of the existing APA; and
- If the related-party transactions in the filing year or prior years are the same or similar to those covered in the APA, after the taxpayer's application and the tax bureau's approval, the transfer pricing and calculation method applied in the APA may be applied to evaluate and adjust the related party transactions that occurred during the application year or prior years.

It can be seen that the STA Rules were enacted to make the APA program more effective for enterprises wishing to seek greater certainty through APAs. In practice, local in-charge tax authorities' experience of applying transfer pricing methodologies and attitude towards APAs are also important to the successful conclusion of an APA.

IV. Cost Sharing Agreements

The growing complexity of business operations and commercial dealings has caused MNCs to seek a wider spectrum of support and assistance from both internal and external resources. Cost sharing allows parties to agree to pool risks and resources for the purpose of developing intangibles and to share the benefits of such developed intangibles. As a result, MNCs often put in place CSAs to optimize their available resources, helping them to manage their overall business operations.

The EIT Law and its Implementation Rules introduce the CSA concept to China for the first time and state that CSAs may cover the joint development of intangible assets and the provision of services. For cost sharing related to service activities, Article 67 of the STA Rules restricts acceptable services to group purchasing and group marketing activities.

It should be noted that according to "Chapter 7 – Administrative Guidance concerning CSAs" of the STA Rules, an enterprise must file a CSA with the SAT through the local tax bureau within 30 days of the date when the agreement is signed. Local tax authorities need to report to the SAT for approval before determining whether a CSA is arm's length. The relevant tax treatment of an arm's length CSA is as follows:

- Costs allocated according to the CSA would be deductible for tax purposes;
- Compensating adjustments would be included in taxable income for the year in which the adjustment is made; and
- In cases where a CSA involves intangible property development, a buy-in or buy-out payment, or distribution of outcomes, termination of CSAs should be treated as a purchase or disposal of assets.
- During the enforcement period of a CSA, enterprises must prepare and maintain contemporaneous CSA documents specified in the STA Rules. The CSA related contemporaneous transfer pricing documents must be submitted to the tax authorities by June 20th of the following year regardless whether it is reached via an APA or not.

Costs allocated for a CSA are not deductible where:

- The CSA does not have a bona fide commercial purpose or economic substance;
- The CSA does not comply with the arm's length principle;
- The allocation of costs and benefits among CSA participants does not comply with the 'cost and income matching' principle;
- The enterprise has not filed the CSA with the tax authorities or prepared, maintained, and provided contemporaneous documentation for the CSA in accordance with the STA Rules; or
- The enterprise will not be in operation for at least 20 years since the CSA is signed.

Based on the above, it appears that the qualifying conditions of a CSA are quite stringent. However, CSAs may also be reached in the form of an APA as per the STA rules.

V. Controlled Foreign Corporations

According to "Chapter 8 – Administrative Guidance concerning CFCs" of the STA Rules, CFCs are foreign companies that meet the following criteria:

- They are controlled by Chinese tax residents
- They are established in a country (or region) where the effective tax rate is 50% lower than the PRC income tax rate; and
- They have no distribution or reduced distribution of profits without business needs.

In relation to CFCs, the concept of "control" is defined as "actual control" in share holding, financing, operation, or purchase or sale, etc. Actual control in shareholding refers to any single one of the Chinese tax resident shareholders directly or indirectly owning at least 10% of the foreign company and the Chinese resident shareholders collectively holding directly or indirectly more than 50% of the foreign company on any date of the fiscal year. Where there is an indirect shareholding relationship, the ultimate shareholding percentage will be calculated by multiplying the share-holding percentage of each layer.

If an intermediary shareholder holds over 50% of the shares of lower layer entity, this percentage will be counted as 100% when calculating the ultimate shareholding percentage.

One of the related-party transaction disclosure forms issued in Circular 114 is designed to assist enterprises and the tax authorities in determining whether, for China tax purposes, CFCs exist in an enterprise's outbound investment. If a foreign related party meets the above criteria and is defined as a CFC of an enterprise, that enterprise will have to include its share of any deemed dividend in its taxable income for enterprise income tax purpose. There would be no deemed dividend income if a CFC meets any of the following:

- The CFC is located in a non-low-tax rate country (or region) designated by the SAT;
- The CFC primarily derives income through active business activities; or
- The CFC's annual profits do not exceed RMB 5 million.

VI. New Thin Capitalization Rules

There have historically been no applicable thin capitalization rules for foreign MNCs operating in China. For domestic enterprises, a debt-to-equity ratio threshold of 0.5:1 was applied to determine the allowable level of related party interest expenses deduction. In September 2008, the Ministry of Finance and SAT jointly issued Caishui [2008] No. 121 ("Circular 121") that announced the safe-harbor debt-to-equity ratio of 5:1 for financial enterprises and 2:1 for all other enterprises.

"Chapter 9 – Administrative Guidance concerning Thin Capitalization" of the STA Rules provides further guidance on the new thin capitalization rules that would apply to all enterprises involved in various types of inter-company financing in China. The STA Rules provide detailed guidance on the criteria to apply in determining whether an enterprise is thinly capitalized. According to the STA Rules, the related party debt-to-equity ratio is defined as the sum of the average monthly related party debt divided by the sum of the average monthly equity. According to the Implementation Rules, related party debt also includes back-to-back loans through unrelated parties (e.g., entrusted loans) and debt with third parties that have been guaranteed or supported by a related party. In determining the equity component of the equation, the book value of equity is to be used rather than the fair market value of equity.

The STA Rules further provide that where a taxpayer's related party debt-to-equity ratio as calculated under the prescribed rules has exceeded the allowable ratio, it should prepare, maintain, and submit contemporaneous documentation based on requirements from the tax authorities to demonstrate that its ratio is arm's length, if it is seeking the full deduction for the related-party interest expenses.

Relevant contemporaneous documentation includes analysis of the borrower's repaying ability and crediting ability; analysis of repaying ability of the group and its financing structure; explanation of changes in the equity investment of the enterprise; explanation of the nature, purpose of the related party debt and the market condition when the financing was made; currency, amount, interest rate, term and conditions of debt; information on collaterals and guarantees received; and interest rates of comparable loans.

If an enterprise fails to prepare, maintain and provide contemporaneous documents, or the documents are unable to prove that the enterprise's debt-to-equity ratio conforms with the arm's length principle, the excess interest expense on the debts over the specified ratio will not be deductible for income tax purposes, unless such interest expenses are paid to a domestic related party with higher effective tax rate. In addition, any non-deductible interest amounts paid to overseas related parties will be recharacterized as dividends and subject to dividend withholding tax. If any interest withholding tax has been withheld that is in excess of the applicable dividend withholding tax, there will be no refund.

Therefore, in the event that the dividend withholding tax rate is lower than the tax rate for interest, this re-characterization will represent an additional cost to the taxpayer.

Notwithstanding the above, there is little guidance to taxpayers on how to prepare contemporaneous documents to support the arm's length nature of the inter-company borrowings.

VII. General Anti-Avoidance Rules ("GAAR")

"Chapter 10 – Administrative Guidance concerning GAAR" of the STA Rules also provide guidance on the newly introduced GAAR concept. These rules allow the tax bureaus to initiate investigations towards enterprises believed to be engaged in tax avoidance activities such as: (i) abuse of tax incentives; (ii) tax treaty shopping; (iii) abuse of a company's legal form; (iv) transactions with companies registered in a tax haven to avoid taxation; and (v) other business arrangements without bona fide commercial purposes.

The inclusion of GAAR in the EIT Law provides emphasis on the importance of business substance and commercial purpose in an arrangement involving a Chinese enterprise and this creates a need for companies to substantiate their tax planning structures with commercial substance and business rationale.

According to the STA Rules, when tax bureaus start GAAR investigations, they will send a "Tax Audit Notice" to an enterprise. Within 60 days of receiving the notice, the enterprise should provide documents to prove its arrangement has a bona fide commercial purpose. If the enterprise does not provide documents within the period or if the documents are unable to prove that its arrangement has a bona fide commercial purpose, tax bureaus may send a "Special Tax Audit Adjustment Notice" to the enterprise and make a tax adjustment based on information it already has.

In addition, the STA Rules state that any GAAR investigations or adjustments must be reported to the SAT for its approval, demonstrating the SAT's caution in applying the GAAR in practice. However, this should not be interpreted to indicate that the SAT will itself refrain from applying the GAAR rules where it deems necessary. The uncertainty regarding how the GAAR rules will be implemented is caused by the lack of precedent cases on which the SAT can rely, which may result in the SAT applying its own interpretation and judgment when settling actual cases.

VIII. Practical Implications of the China Transfer Pricing Regulations

The Chinese tax authorities have become more confident in their abilities and are now able to deal with more sophisticated transfer pricing issues. In addition, their mindsets are much closer to the international transfer pricing practice and the OECD Guidelines, although deviations are also obvious, as can be seen from the STA Rules. The STA Rules emphasize substance over form and an investigative approach that assesses the taxpayer's transfer pricing position by taking into consideration a variety of business reasons such as market strategy, industry factors, and supply chain management.

According to the provisions of the STA Rules, the SAT will be responsible for approving cases related to APAs, CSAs, and GAAR and will therefore have more power to manage and control complicated transfer pricing issues. As such, the issuance of the STA Rules demonstrates the continuing standardization of the rules and procedures for transfer pricing enforcement among local tax bureaus in China. In addition, the STA Rules provide clearer guidance to both taxpayers and the Chinese tax authorities on their respective responsibilities.

Under the STA Rules, the definition of related party is broader and the related party information disclosure requirement is more burdensome. Chinese taxpayers are now obligated to provide substantial intercompany information and documentation in a timely manner. Maintaining contemporaneous documentation is a must for taxpayers applying for APAs, entering into CSAs or having thin capitalization issues in China. Enterprises failed to prepare, maintain, and provide contemporaneous documents will not be protected from the 5% interest penalty and other penalties on special tax adjustments, in addition to a greater risk of being audited. Taxpayers should take a proactive approach to reviewing their transfer pricing methodologies and preparing relevant contemporaneous documentation based on the STA Rules for their entities in China. In the meantime, MNCs should take this opportunity to revisit their Chinese entities' transfer pricing positions to ensure that their transfer pricing methodologies and arrangements are appropriately planned and implemented on a going-forward basis.

Joanna Lam is a senior manager in the Transfer Pricing Group in Deloitte Touche Tohmatsu's Hong Kong office. She can be reached by email at **joalam@deloitte.com.hk** or by phone at **+852 2852 6373**.

For more information on the author, please see Section XIII.

Denmark – Transfer pricing overview

Jens Wittendorff
Deloitte Copenhagen

Legislation

Denmark's transfer pricing legislation was reformed in 1998 bringing it in line with the OECD Transfer Pricing Guidelines. The cornerstones of the Danish transfer pricing legislation are section 2 of the Tax Assessment Act, which sets out the arm's length principle; section 3 B of the Tax Control Act, which contains the documentation requirements; and section 17(3) of the Tax Control Act, which contains the penalty provisions. The arm's length principle is also embodied in section 6 A of the Hydrocarbon Tax Act and section 13 of the Tonnage Tax Act. Other tax law provisions of a more general nature which may also form bases for transfer pricing adjustments includes section 4-6 of the State Tax Act. All Danish tax treaties contain a provision similar to article 9(1) of the OECD Model Tax Convention, and most of the tax treaties contain a provision similar to article 9(2). In 2006, the tax authorities issued regulations setting out binding rules regarding the content of a transfer pricing documentation. In 2006, a comprehensive guideline was issued setting out the tax authorities interpretation of the documentation rules and the arm's length principle.

Taxpayers Subject to Transfer Pricing Rules

Section 2 of the Tax Assessment Act requires taxpayers to apply the arm's length principle to transactions with both Danish and foreign affiliates. Taxpayers are affiliated for transfer pricing purposes if they are under common control. The control concept is based on *de jure* control. Accordingly, the term covers taxpayers that directly or indirectly own more than 50 percent of the share capital or control more than 50 percent of the voting power of a legal person. In determining whether decisive influence exists, a shareholder should consider the share capital and voting power of other shareholders, if an agreement regarding the exercise of common control has been made between the shareholders.

Accordingly, if three unrelated taxpayers each own one-third of a company and a shareholder agreement regarding the exercise of common control has been concluded, transactions between the company and the shareholders will qualify as controlled transactions. Companies may be "affiliated" for the third category above based either on de jure control or *de facto* control. The term covers legal persons in which the same group of shareholders has decisive influence, or that share the same management even if the shareholders are not the same. Accordingly, if three unrelated taxpayers each own one-third of two companies, the two companies will be affiliated. Moreover, two companies may be affiliated even if they are not owned by the same group of shareholders, if the two companies have the same management. The term "management" has not been defined, and the exact scope of this rule is uncertain.

All transactions between a head office and PE are deemed to be controlled transactions for the fourth and fifth categories above. However, the arm's length principle is applicable only to internal transactions that have a close connection with the income-generating activities of the company. Other internal transactions should be conducted on a cost-only basis. The transfer pricing legislation does not apply to foreign insurance companies that are conducting insurance business through a PE in Denmark and are calculating the Danish taxable income in accordance with section 12 of the Companies Tax Act. Section 12 requires foreign insurance companies to calculate the taxable income on a formulary apportionment basis. Similarly, the transfer pricing rules do not apply to companies that are calculating the taxable income according to the Tonnage Tax Act for controlled transactions concluded with foreign legal persons or PEs, if the income is covered by the Tonnage Tax Act.

Transactions Covered by the Transfer Pricing Rules

The transfer pricing legislation is applicable to commercial and financial transactions between affiliated taxpayers. These include transfers of goods and services, management fees, intangibles, license agreements, loan agreements, guarantees, leasing, and so on.

Transfer Pricing Methods and PLIs

Controlled transactions may be documented using the comparable uncontrolled price method, the resale price method, the cost-plus method, the profit split method, and the transactional net margin method. The traditional methods have priority over the profit methods. However, since the election of the most reliable transfer pricing method depends on the quality of the available data the result is often a profit method.

Moreover, any other method that makes it possible to test the arm's length nature of controlled transactions may be used. For purpose of the TNMM, the PLI's used by the tax authorities includes the return on operating assets, operating margin, and the Berry ratio.

Transfer Pricing Adjustments

The tax authorities may make an upward transfer pricing adjustment (primary adjustment) if the prices for controlled transactions deviate from arm's length prices. If controlled transactions have been subject to a primary adjustment by the tax authorities in a foreign state, the Danish affiliated company may ask the Danish tax authorities for a downward transfer pricing adjustment (corresponding adjustment). The Danish tax authorities must examine the case, but are required to accept a corresponding adjustment only if that would bring the transfer prices in line with the arm's length principle. Because the actual allocation of the excess profit represented by the adjustment is not at arm's length, the primary and corresponding transfer pricing adjustments do not alter that. To account for the economic benefit realized by one of the parties, Danish courts make use of secondary adjustments.

Secondary adjustments may take the form of a constructive distribution if the economic benefit is received by a parent company, or a constructive contribution if the economic benefit is received by a subsidiary or sister company. A constructive distribution will be tax exempt if the Danish participation exemption regime applies. A constructive contribution will be taxable income at a rate of 25 percent unless it qualify as contribution according to section 31 D of the Corporate Tax Act. A secondary adjustment made at the subsidiary or sister company level may therefore result in economic double taxation even if a corresponding adjustment has been made. For this reason, a company may avoid a secondary adjustment by undertaking an obligation at the time of the corresponding adjustment to repay the economic benefit to the affiliated company (payment adjustment). A further requirement is imposed regarding cross-border transactions, insofar as the foreign tax authority must have made a primary adjustment equal to the corresponding adjustment made in Denmark. However, the Commission of the European Communities has published a procedure for concluding EU APAs which the Danish tax authorities are expected to follow.

Statute of Limitations

A tax return ordinarily may be reopened by the tax authorities or a taxpayer to make a transfer pricing adjustment concerning controlled transactions until May 1 of the sixth year after the end of the financial year. The tax return may be reopened extraordinarily by the tax authorities or a taxpayer for any fiscal year if a foreign tax authority has made a tax assessment that affects the Danish tax assessment of the taxpayer. Accordingly, concerning corresponding adjustments, tax returns are never timebarred in Denmark.

Advance Pricing Agreements

Taxpayers are able to obtain bilateral and multilateral binding advance pricing by way of the mutual agreement procedure in the tax treaties. It is also possible to obtain a unilateral advance pricing agreement by requesting an ordinary binding ruling from the tax authorities, which has been done by several companies. No special procedures have been established for requesting an advance pricing agreement.

OECD Transfer Pricing Guidelines

The OECD Guidelines are central to the interpretation and application of both the Danish domestic and tax treaty transfer pricing rules. Accordingly, the OECD Guidelines form basis of the legislative history of section 2 of the Tax Assessment Act. Moreover, as an integral part of the OECD Commentary to Article 9, the OECD Guidelines are important for purposes of interpreting Article 9 of the Danish tax treaties. The status of the OECD Guidelines is confirmed by the Documentation Guidelines stating that the Danish transfer pricing legislation has been prepared in accordance with the OECD Guidelines.

Documentation Requirements

Taxpayers are required to prepare and retain transfer pricing documentation for national as well as cross-border controlled transactions. The basic requirement to the transfer pricing documentation is that it must show (1) that the transfer prices meet the arm's length principle, and (2) how the prices, terms, and conditions of the controlled transactions were determined. Pursuant to Regulation No. 42 of 24 January 2006, transfer pricing documentation should include the following items:

1) Description of the business including the legal structure, organisational structure, turnover and EBIT for all affiliated companies for the past three years with which controlled transactions have been concluded, historical review, and industry review.
2) Description of the controlled transactions including any cost contribution arrangements.
3) A comparability analysis.
4) A description of the implementation of

the transfer pricing method including any price adjustments made.
5) Copies of written agreements.

Alternatively, the taxpayer may prepare the transfer pricing documentation as an EU Transfer Pricing Documentation (EU TPD).

Taxpayers are required to prepare a database search if specifically required by the Danish tax authorities. While there is no specific regulatory reference to which databases should be used, the Amadeus of Europe datbase appears to be preferred, although other searches of other databases are also accepted. The tax authorities will provide taxpayers with a deadline of 60-90 days to complete and submit a database search.

The transfer pricing documentation must be available upon request from the Danish tax authorities within 60 days. The documentation is covered by the Danish Bookkeeping Act and must be retained for at least five years after the end of the financial year in question.

There is a small taxpayer exception from the documentations requirement. Accordingly, taxpayers, who alone or together with affiliated companies have less than 250 employees, and either have total assets of less than DKK 125 million or net sales of less than DKK 250 million, shall only prepare and retain written documentation regarding how prices and terms are determined for:
1) controlled transactions with natural and legal persons who are tax resident in a foreign state that has not concluded a tax treaty with Denmark and which is not a member of the EEC or EEA,
2) controlled transactions with a permanent establishment situated in a foreign state that has not concluded a tax treaty with Denmark, and which is not a member of the EEC or EEA,
3) controlled transactions with a permanent establishment, situated in Denmark provided that the taxpayer is resident in a foreign state that has not concluded a tax treaty with Denmark, and which is not a member of the EU or EEA.

Tax return disclosure requirement

Taxpayers are required to disclose the nature and volume of controlled transactions. Guidelines dealing with the tax return disclosure requirements were issued on 1 December 2000. The disclosure requirement is satisfied by completing form 05.022 "Controlled transactions".

Penalties

Non-compliance with the transfer pricing documentation requirements is sanctioned with a penalty of up to 200 percent of the operating costs saved by the taxpayer by not preparing the documentation, and a penalty of up to 10 percent of any adjustment. Both penalties may be avoided by preparing the transfer pricing documentation. While documentation should be prepared in advance, unlike the U.S. there is no specific filing deadline.

Jens Wittendorff has seventeen years of professional experience as an international tax adviser. He is a tax partner in the Deloitte Copenhagen office and has previously worked in the London office of Deloitte. He can be reached at **(45-36) 10-34-11** or by email at **jwittendorff@deloitte.dk**. For more information on the author, please see Section XIII.

Overview of Transfer Pricing in France

Pierre-Jean Douvier and Xavier Daluzeau
CMS Bureau Francis Lefebvre

Introduction

The transfer pricing environment in France has undergone several recent changes, including new documentation requirements enacted in December, 2009. The changes build on France's history of transfer pricing enforcement based on the application of the arm's length standard to related-party transactions, consistent with the OECD guidelines.

Since 2002, France has participated in the EU Joint Transfer Pricing Forum ("EU JTPF")[1]. The French legislation and regulations are more and more influenced by the works performed by the EU JTPF.

This article provides an overview of the French rules governing transfer pricing and examines a number of specific transfer pricing provisions and their application. In addition to the new documentation requirements, the article discusses the definition of related party, allowed methods, adjustment procedures, guidelines for small and medium-sized companies, court decisions, international exchange of information, the enforcement environment, Advance Pricing Agreements, and procedures to avoid double-taxation.

Background and Authority

As in many other countries, the aim of the French transfer pricing rules is to insure the cross-border pricing relationships within a group are appropriate and accordingly avoid loss of income for a French entity (and the French Government) belonging to an international group in case of international transactions. For this purpose, the French legislation has at its disposal specific provisions, which have to abide by the French legal system and particularly by the general principle of the hierarchy of rules, such principle implies that an inferior rule is not allowed to add some provisions to a superior one, but can only explain it[2]. As inferior rules, there are two types of administrative publications: the first kind is issued by the highest executive political authority (government) and is called "Décret." The second kind of administrative publications are inferior rules called "Instruction" (statement of

---

[1] Further to a Communication of the EU Commission dated 23 October 2001, the EU JTPF was set up in 2002. The overall objective of the JTPF is a more uniform application of transfer pricing tax rules within the EU. One chairman, representatives of the Member States and experts from business participate in the EU JTPF. Representatives of the OECD also participate as observers. The EU JTPF aims at working on the basis of consensus. The outcome must be pragmatic, non-legislative solutions within the framework of the OECD Guidelines to the practical problems posed by transfer pricing practices in the EU. The outcome of the efforts undertaken by the EU JTPF is transmitted on a regular basis to the Commission (which assesses the need for appropriate action) and then by the Commission to the Council for endorsement.

[2] The scale of the hierarchy of rules coming from the French Constitution is 1) the Constitution, 2) the Treaties, 3) the Law, 4) the Decree (Décret), 5) all administrative Statements of practice or Circulars published.

practice). And the French tax authorities, FTA, are bound by each administrative official position, such as rulings or APA (Advance Pricing Agreements).

The French transfer pricing provisions can be found in the CGI (French Tax Code) and the LPF (French Tax Procedure Code). The interpretation and explanation of the transfer pricing legislation is given by Administrative statements of practice published in the bulletin officiel des impôts (BOI) (official tax journal). Though it is not a statement of practice, the Guide on transfer pricing to the attention of small and medium-sized companies issued in 2006 (Guide sur les prix de transfert à l'usage des PME) serves in practice as a reference for tax auditors in France.

France, like other European countries, has to transpose in its domestic law the European rules, like Directives, decisions or recommendations derived from the European official authorities like Council of Ministers (Conseil des ministres), especially through the Economic and Financial Affairs Council of the European Union (ECOFIN) sessions.

Scope and Application

Article 57 of the French Tax Code[3] ("FTC") allows the FTA to make tax reassessments on the basis of non-arm's length transfer prices between associated enterprises.

In order to reassess transfer prices, the FTA must:
i) prove that the French enterprise and the foreign enterprise are dependent and
ii) demonstrate that profits were transferred by the French enterprise to the foreign enterprise (concomitantly, the FTA must assess the profits that were transferred).

Condition (i) does not need to be fulfilled when the foreign company is established in a low tax territory, as discussed in the second paragraph of Article 57 of the CGI. This provision was introduced because of the great difficulties experienced by French tax authorities in trying to prove the link of dependence in countries that keep information about the shareholders of their resident companies secret. According to Article 238 A, paragraph 2, of the CGI, the threshold for determining whether a given country can be categorized as a low-tax country is if the level of direct taxation in the country where the foreign entity is located is more than half lower than the level of taxation to which this entity would be liable if it were located in France.

The burden of the proof is borne by the FTA even if the taxpayer has not answered (or has given an insufficient answer) to a request for information issued on the basis of article L 13 B of the French Tax Procedure Code[4] ("FTPC")[5]. Article L 13 B of the FTPC provides that, in the course of a tax audit, when the FTA have collected elements allowing them to presume that an enterprise has indirectly transferred profits in the meaning of article 57 of the FTC, they can request certain information and documents relating in particular to the relationship of this enterprise with associated enterprises and the transfer pricing methodologies used. However, in this case, the FTA are allowed to make tax reassessments in relation with transfer prices on the basis of the elements at their disposal.

---

3   *Code Général des Impôts.*
4   *Livre des Procédures Fiscales.*
5   In such a case, the taxpayer can be subject to a penalty of € 10,000 for each fiscal year covered by the request for information.

Definition of Related Party

French and foreign enterprises are dependent in the meaning of article 57 of the FTC (i.e. are associated enterprises) where (i) one owns directly or indirectly more than 50% of the share capital or voting rights of the other (or where a third enterprise owns directly or indirectly more than 50% of the share capital or voting rights of the two enterprises) or where (ii) one enterprise is de facto dependent upon the other, for example in case an enterprise is the sole supplier or client of the other.

Allowed Methods

The French tax authorities officially follow all methodologies described by the OECD Guidelines: the three traditional methods, Comparable Uncontrolled Price (CUP), resale minus and cost plus methods, and the two transactional profit methods, Transactional Net Margin Method (TNMM) and the profit split method.

Where appropriate, for practical purposes, the TNMM is the most frequently applied by practitioners (and accepted by the French tax authorities), because of its lower sensibility to differences within the industry (which allows an increase number of comparables) and in accounting standard (the operational margin is generally more precisely delineated than the gross margin). The concrete application of TNMM is the same as for resale minus and cost plus methods, except for the usage of the operational margin in the place of the gross margin.

Transfer Pricing Adjustments

The FTA can use two approaches to reassess transfer prices:
- Direct assessment of the profits transferred. According to this method, the FTA assess the profits transferred on the basis of the characteristics of the reassessed transaction. This approach consists, for example, of comparing the prices at which a French enterprise sells the same service to a third party and to an affiliated enterprise.[6]
- Indirect assessment of the profits transferred. This method can be used when the FTA cannot make a direct assessment of the profits transferred. This approach consists in comparing the profits of the audited enterprise with the profits realized by uncontrolled enterprises engaged in the same activity.

In practice, this second approach is often used by the FTA. It assumes the selection of appropriate comparable companies. Where appropriate, for practical purposes, the FTA frequently applies the TNMM because of its lower sensibility to differences within the industry (which allows an increase number of comparables) and in accounting standard (the operating margin is generally more precisely delineated than the gross margin).

Guide for Small and Medium-Sized Enterprises

In November, 2006, the FTA issued a guide on transfer pricing designed to draw France's transfer pricing regime to the attention, in particular, of small and medium-sized enterprises ("SMEs").

This guide summarizes the French provisions applicable to transfer prices and explain certain concepts such as the functional analysis, the comparable study and the OECD transfer pricing methodologies.

---

6   Conseil d'Etat 31 July 1992, n°61286, SNAT.

The guide occupies an interesting position in the French hierarchy of rules because formally it is not a statement of practice but only an explanation of the transfer pricing regulations. Nevertheless, the principles included into the guide are fully respected by the administration members.

Though it is addressed to SMEs, the guide proves very helpful to larger companies since (i) it is the first official publication from the FTA that describes the practical steps that must be taken to build an arm's length transfer pricing policy, (ii) it contains a number of useful information as regards the "expectations" of the FTA in terms of definition and justification of a transfer pricing policy and (iii) it gives indications on FTA's general approach of transfer pricing.

Appeals and Court Decisions

Taxpayers can refute the loss of profits with respect to transactions with another company from the same group; to do so, taxpayers must indicate and demonstrate their strict interest to the transaction.

To determine if the personal interest of the French company exists behind the apparent loss of income, the French Supreme Tax Court (Conseil d'Etat[7]) states that this company may have an indirect interest to such an apparently unfair transaction. But the French company has to prove such an indirect personal interest. The most important is that the two mutual advantages (i. e. the price difference between arm's length pricing and the amount charged on the one hand and the indirect interest on the other hand) should have an equivalent value.

For example, The Supreme Tax Court (Conseil d'Etat[8]) has accepted that a French company may argue that the guarantee granted free, i.e. without any compensation, to the foreign related company was compensated by a proportional increase of its own sales.

Significant transfer pricing court decisions include:

- The Supreme Administrative Court[9] has accepted the idea that a trademark royalty rate could vary over time and depending on the market on which it is used. As a result, the FTA did not prove that the absence of royalty paid by foreign affiliates to their French parent was abnormal by referring (i) to the royalties paid by the French affiliates over the audited years and (ii) to the royalties paid by foreign affiliates in subsequent years, whereas the trademark licensed was at the time little known on the foreign markets and sometimes used with the original trademark of the foreign affiliates.

- The Administrative Court of Appeal of Nancy considered that, in order to establish a transfer of profits, the FTA could not compare the selling price of a taxpayer with the selling price of other companies when the companies retained as comparables were not exporting their products in the same conditions as those of the products exported by the taxpayer. In particular, one comparable was not exporting the same products and another comparable was not using the same currency as the reassessed taxpayer. Furthermore, the Court considered that the selling price of the reassessed taxpayer on the French market could be different of its selling prices to a German company.[10]

---

7 *Conseil d'Etat* (CE) Plen., of July 27th, 1988, n°50020, *Boutique 2 M*.

8 CE, of March 3rd, 1989, n°77581, *Société Lainiere de Picardie*.

9 Conseil d'Etat 7 November 2005, n°266436 and n°266438, Cap Gemini; RJF 1/06 n°17.

10 CAA Nancy 26 January 1995, n°92-490, SARL Moulin de la Chée. See also Conseil d'Etat 21 February 1990, n°84483, SARL Solodet.

- The Administrative Court of Paris considered that the FTA did not prove the existence of a transfer of profits (i) by providing comparables the names of which were not specified and (ii) by comparing the transactions of the reassessed taxpayer with transactions that had not the exact same characteristics.[11]

- The Administrative Court of Appeal of Paris considered that the FTA did not prove the existence of a transfer of profits by arguing that enterprises having an activity similar or comparable to the one of the reassessed taxpayer were compensated by a commission of 8% without establishing that this rate was compensating the same services as those provided by the reassessed taxpayer.[12]

- The Administrative Court of Paris recognized that the FTA proved that a royalty rate for the license of a trademark and of pharmaceutical specialties was too high (and, therefore, proved the existence of a transfer of profits) by providing nominative comparables pertaining to the license of the same trademark and of similar pharmaceutical specialties to companies having comparable turnovers.[13]

- More recently, the Administrative Court of Appeal of Versailles considered in particular that, when the FTA provide comparable companies operating on foreign markets, the FTA must prove that such markets have the same characteristics as the French market (on which the taxpayer was operating). It also indicated that the fact that a company incurs losses several years in a row does not, as such, prove that the transfer pricing policy applied was not arm's length.[14]

[11] TA Paris 13 February 1997, n°93-7089 and 93-7090, SARL Les amis de l'histoire.
[12] CAA Paris 20 November 1990, n°1172, Reynolds Tobacco France.
[13] CAA Paris 12 July 1994, n°92-1392, Sté Pharmatique Industrie.
[14] CAA Versailles, 3e ch., 5 mai 2009, n° 08VE02411, Man Camions et Bus.

Therefore, in the context of an indirect assessment of the profits transferred (which is more and more frequently the approach retained by the FTA), it seems that French courts accept comparable transactions used by the FTA if the FTA provide:
- a sufficient number of comparable transactions covering all years reassessed;
- the names of the comparables or, at least, a precise description of their activity and business conditions; and
- the evidence that the comparable transactions have the same characteristics as the transaction reassessed.

International Exchange of Information

Depending on the bilateral income tax treaty applicable, the FTA can exchange information with the tax authorities of other countries. Such exchange of information can allow the FTA to have a maximum additional two-year period to make a reassessment (end of the fifth year following the year for which the tax is due instead of three years; article L 188 A of the FTPC). Within the EU, tax authorities of several Member States can agree to perform simultaneous tax audits in their respective States and to exchange the information collected during such audits (article L 45 of the FTPC).

New Documentation Requirements

In December, 2009, France enacted major changes to its transfer pricing regime through the passage of the Amended Finance Bill for 2009, which included two new provisions, article L 13 AA and L 13 AB of the FTPC. These articles introduce mandatory contemporaneous documentation requirements for transfer pricing in France. The provisions apply only to large companies established in France that meet certain ownership requirements.

Prior to the new transfer pricing legislation codified under article L 13 AA and L 13 AB of the FTPC, France did not require contemporaneous documentation of transfer pricing policies. The penalties applicable in cases of non-compliance with the documentation requirements are codified under article 1735 ter of the FTC.

Scope and Applicability

The new documentation requirements apply to legal entities established in France that meet the following criteria:
1) which have annual turnover (taxes excluded), or gross amount of assets shown on the balance sheet, greater than or equal to € 400,000,000; or
2) which hold at the closing of the tax year, directly or indirectly, more than half of the financial or voting rights of a legal entity - legal entity, body, trust or comparable institution established or constituted in France or outside of France - satisfying one of the conditions mentioned in (1); or
3) more than half of the financial or voting rights of which is held, at the end of the tax year, directly or indirectly, by a legal entity satisfying one of the conditions mentioned in (1); or
4) which benefit from a ruling granting a worldwide tax consolidation regime (provided by article 209 quinquies of the FTC), and, in this case, all enterprises taxable in France which belong within the perimeter of the consolidation; or
5) which belong to a French tax group under article 223 A of the FTC when the latter includes at least one legal entity meeting the requirements of (1), (2), (3) or (4).

Enterprises that do not meet the above-mentioned criteria would remain subject to the standard obligations as regards the justification of their transfer pricing policy (and, in particular, the obligations set forth by article L 13 B of the FTPC).

Documentation to be Filed

Legal entities subject to the documentation requirements would have to document all transactions carried out with associated enterprises[15]. In line with the Code of Conduct drawn up by the EU JTPF[16], the documentation should include two levels: general information concerning the group of associated enterprises (the concept of a masterfile under the Code of Conduct) and specific information concerning the associated enterprise subject to a tax audit (the concept of country-specific documentation under the Code of Conduct). The list of information to be provided for each level is close to that defined by the Code of Conduct.

The general information should enable the FTA to understand the economic, legal, financial and tax background of the group. The enterprise subject to a tax audit should

---
15 For the purposes of the transfer pricing documentation, associated enterprises are foreign entities with which dependency ties exist. Such dependency ties are deemed to exist between two enterprises where:
a) one enterprise owns directly or indirectly the majority of the share capital of the other or effectively exercises within the other enterprise decision-making powers ;
b) both enterprises are under the control of the same third enterprise (control being defined as under a above).
16 Code of Conduct proposed by the Commission in November 2005 and adopted by the Council in June 2006.

provide the following documents to the FTA:
- a general description of the activity carried out, including any changes which occurred during the period subject to the tax audit in comparison with prior tax years;
- a general description of the legal and operational structures of the group, including an identification of the associated enterprises engaged in controlled transactions;
- a general description of the functions carried out and risks assumed by the associated enterprises, to the extent that they affect the audited enterprise;
- a list of the main intangible assets owned (e.g. patents, trademarks, trade names, know-how), in relation with the audited enterprise; and
- a general description of the transfer pricing policy of the group.

The specific information should include elements allowing the FTA to appreciate the extent that the transfer pricing policy implemented by the audited enterprise complies with the arm's length principle. The enterprise should notably provide the following documents:
- a description of the activity carried out, including any changes which occurred during the period subject to the tax audit in comparison with prior tax years;
- a description of the transactions carried out with other associated enterprises, including the nature of the flows and the amounts thereof, including any royalties;
- a list of any cost-sharing agreements, a copy of any advance pricing agreements and rulings concerning the determination of transfer prices, affecting the results of the audited enterprise;
- a presentation of the method(s) applied to determine transfer prices in compliance with the arm's length principle, including an analysis of the functions carried out, assets used and risks assumed, and an explanation concerning the selection and application of the chosen method(s); and
- when the chosen method so requires, an analysis of the comparison elements (benchmarks) regarded as pertinent by the enterprise.

In addition, article L 13 AB of the FTPC provides that, where transactions are realized with one or more associated enterprise(s) established in a non cooperative State or territory (in the meaning of article 238-0A of the FTC[17]), the documentation should also include for each associated enterprise all documents required from companies subject to corporate income tax, including the balance sheet and profit and loss account established in the conditions set forth by the French CFC rules (article 209 B of the FTC).

For 2010, the list of non cooperative States or territories can be found in Table 1 (this list is updated on a yearly basis).

Effective Date and Timing of Filing Requirements

The new requirements apply for the first time to tax years beginning on or after 1 January 2010. They provide that the documentation described above must be made available to the FTA on the date of the beginning of the tax audit, i.e. on the date of the first on-site arrival as mentioned

---

[17] The definition of a non cooperative State or territory has also been introduced into French tax law by the amending finance bill for 2009.

Table 1: 2010 List of Non-Cooperative States and Territories

Anguilla	Guatemala	Niue
Belize	Cook Islands	Panama
Brunei	Marshall Islands	Philippines
Costa Rica	Liberia	Saint Kitts and Nevis
Dominica	Montserrat	Saint Lucia
Grenada	Nauru	Saint Vincent and the Grenadines

in the notification of tax audit. Although there is usually some delay between the end of a tax year and the beginning of a tax audit, in practice the requirements oblige enterprises to prepare contemporaneous documentation.

Non-Compliance Penalties

If the audited enterprise does not provide the required documentation, or if it provides incomplete documentation, the enterprise is liable to a penalty equal to € 10,000 or, if the corresponding amount is higher and depending on the seriousness of the default, to a penalty of a maximum of 5% of the transfer pricing reassessment made by the tax authorities (under article 57 of the FTC) for each tax year covered by the tax audit. This penalty - which is specific to this documentation requirement - can therefore be very high, as it is not assessed on the tax ultimately due by the taxpayer and can be 5% of the transfer pricing reassessments made by the FTA.

Though it is uncertain for the moment, this penalty should not constitute a serious penalty within the meaning of article 8-1 of the European Arbitration Convention of 23 July 1990. Therefore, this penalty should not deprive the enterprise of the possibility to have recourse to the procedures set forth under this Convention or the mutual agreement procedures set forth under tax treaties (the French practice being generally to refuse also the benefit of the mutual agreement procedures set forth under tax treaties where a serious penalty is applied). One can hope that the issue will be clarified by the FTA in the official guidelines that should be published in the coming months.

Guidelines Expected

In addition to the specific provisions included in the law, guidelines that further clarify the obligations of taxpayers and the procedures for compliance are expected to be issued by the FTA in 2010.

Enforcement Environment

Depending on their size, enterprises depend on a tax audit directorate having a national or regional competence. Within the tax audit directorate having a national competence (and sometimes also at regional level), tax auditors are specialized according to industry sectors. In addition, the FTA have implemented teams of so-called "international consultants". These tax inspectors are specialized in international tax issues and, in particular, in transfer pricing issues. They can assist the audit teams in charge of tax audits. The FTA have also teams specialized in the audit of computerized accounting (brigade de vérification des comptabilités informatisées). These teams can have access to the "raw data" that allow a company to establish its accounting and tax result. They are often involved in transfer pricing audits since their access to accounting "raw data" allow them to establish analytical results of the company, e.g. operating result of a given activity of a company.

Currently, the timing from the introduction of a case before a lower French Administrative Court and a decision by the French Supreme Administrative Court (Conseil d'Etat) is approximately ten years. Besides, the French tax procedure provides that, after the issuance of a tax reassessment notice, taxpayers can further discuss their case with the FTA (in a first step, with the chief of the tax inspectors (chef de brigade) who made the reassessments and, in a second step, with the superior of the chef de brigade). These discussions can allow taxpayers to find acceptable solutions to their cases within a few months (depending on the complexity of the case). Consequently, in practice, transfer pricing cases are mainly resolved administratively.

Advance Pricing Agreements ("APAs")

The French APA procedure was introduced in 1999 by administrative guidelines[18]. This procedure was enacted by the amending finance bill for 2004 and is now codified under article L 80 B-7 of the FTPC. At end 2008, France had concluded approximately 50 APAs. It is possible to conclude unilateral (subject to certain conditions[19]), bilateral or multilateral

---

18 Instruction 4 A-8-99 of 7 September 1999.
19 A unilateral APA can be envisaged if

APAs. In line with the OECD Guidelines, the FTA consider that an APA should in principle be a bilateral (or multilateral) agreement.

An APA allows a group to confirm with the FTA that the prices used for intragroup transactions comply with the arm's length principle: to the extent that the terms of the APA are complied with by the taxpayer, the FTA cannot reassess the prices used for the intragroup transactions covered by the APA.

The main steps of the procedure are as follows:
- Preliminary meeting with the FTA.
- Official filing of the APA request (the filing of an APA request is not subject to a fee in France).
- Review of the case by the FTA. At the end of this phase, the FTA informs the taxpayer of their position on the request and discuss the case / the APA with the taxpayer.
- For a bilateral APA, there is a subsequent phase where the competent authorities of the States involved negotiate the APA.
- Drafting and signature of the APA. A unilateral APA is signed only by the FTA and is accepted by the taxpayer. A bilateral APA is signed by the competent authorities involved (in general, exchange of letters) and is accepted by the taxpayer. In both cases, the taxpayer can refuse the APA proposed.

(instruction 4 A-11-05 of 24 June 2005):
– no APA procedure exists in the other State involved; or
– the transactions covered by the APA request involve a high number of States; or
– the transactions involve specific matters or matters of a limited complexity (e.g., management fees); or
– the French enterprise requesting the APA is a SME.

In practice, (i) for a unilateral APA, the average duration to negotiate and conclude an APA is 6 to 18 months and (ii) for a bilateral APA, the average duration is 18 to 24 months. Indicative lists of the documents to produce upon filing of the APA request can be found in the administrative guidelines of 7 September 1999 (4 A-8-99). In practice, upon filing an APA request, the FTA usually request the following information/documentation:
- Corporate structure of the group.
- Presentation of the group: activity, organisation, main transactions of the companies covered by the APA request.
- List of the group's competitors.
- For the French entities covered by the APA request and for the last three tax years: tax returns, auditors' report (commissaires aux comptes) and management report (rapports de gestion).
- Functional analysis of the entities covered by the request.
- Economic study supporting the proposed transfer pricing methodology.

In addition to these items, the FTA may request additional information during the application process.

The team in charge of the APA program (Bureau CF3) belongs to the central department of the Direction Générale des Finances Publiques. In case of APA negotiation with another State, this team acts as French competent authority.

In principle, the APA request must be officially filed with Bureau CF3 at least six months before the beginning of the first financial year during which the agreement should apply for the first time. However, the administrative guidelines state that, as an exception and if expressly requested by the taxpayer when filing the APA request, the APA could apply as from the financial year during which the APA request was filed.

An APA can be valid for three to five years. In theory, an APA cannot have retroactive effect. Once the APA is signed, the taxpayer must provide an annual report demonstrating that (i) the transfer pricing methodologies used comply with the agreement and that (ii) the critical assumptions described in the APA are fulfilled. The exact content of the annual report is defined in the APA.

In addition to the standard APA, France has introduced in its domestic regulation the possibility of a simplified APA for small and medium-sized companies. According to article 44 septies IV of the CGI, the test of little or medium-sized company is passed if:
- the company has less than 250 employees, and its annual turnover (net of tax) is under 50 million euros or the total of its balance sheet is fewer than 43 million euros; and
- the capital equity or the rights of vote are not held more than 25 percent by one or more companies which do not meet the above size criteria.

The APA can be renewed upon expiration. In principle, assuming the case initially presented to the FTA is not substantially modified, the renewal of the APA should be significantly easier than the initial APA procedure.

Procedures to Avoid Double-Taxation: MAP and the European Arbitration Convention

Further to a transfer pricing reassessment, and to the extent no serious penalty was applied[20], taxpayers can

---
20 Within the meaning of article 8-1 of the European Arbitration Convention of 23 July 1990. The French practice is generally to refuse also the benefit of the mutual agreement procedures set forth

request the elimination of the resulting double taxation (i) either under the mutual agreement procedure ("MAP") set forth by the applicable bilateral income tax treaty (article 25 OECD Model Convention), (ii) or under the procedure set forth by the European Arbitration Convention of 23 July 1990 ("EU Arbitration Convention").[21]

The deadline to file a MAP is generally three years as from receipt of the tax reassessment notice (certain tax treaties provide for a shorter delay or do not provide any time limit). The delay to engage the procedure set forth by the EU Arbitration Convention is three years as from receipt of the tax reassessment notice.

The main differences between the two procedures are the following:
- A MAP deals with any situation in which a taxpayer is subject to taxation that is contrary to the provisions of the relevant tax treaty. This may relate to a variety of situations, one of which being the double taxation resulting from a transfer pricing reassessment. The procedure set forth by the EU Arbitration Convention only deals with transfer pricing.
- A MAP can be conducted with all the States that have concluded a tax treaty with France containing such a provision. This is the case in approximately 110 of the tax treaties concluded by France. The EU Arbitration Convention only applies with EU Member States.
- In the context of a MAP, (except where the applicable tax treaty contains a provision for arbitration) States are bound by an obligation of due diligence, i.e. as regards a transfer pricing reassessment, they are not obliged to effectively cancel the resulting double taxation. However, among States belonging to the OECD, this procedure works well. The EU Arbitration Convention guarantees that the double taxation resulting from a transfer pricing reassessment will be cancelled.

Applying the Directive of 1990 mentioned above is conditioned by the absence of "serious penalty" incurred by the taxpayer. In France, the term "serious penalties" includes criminal penalties and tax penalties such as penalties for:
- failure to make a tax return after receiving a summons,
- lack of good faith,
- fraudulent practices,
- opposition to tax inspection,
- hidden payments or distributions, or
- abuse of law.

It should also be noted that, assuming such procedures are engaged prior to the collection of the corporate income tax (and, as the case may be, withholding tax) resulting from a transfer pricing reassessment, the taxpayer can benefit from the so-called "suspension of tax collection" (article L 189 A of FTPC). In principle, following a tax audit and a tax reassessment, French corporate income tax must be collected at the latest on 31 December of the third year following the year during which the tax reassessment was notified. For example: if a notice of reassessment is issued on 5 November 2009 by the FTA, the tax must be collected by 31 December 2012. Since 1 January 2005, in case a MAP or procedure set forth by the EU Arbitration Convention is introduced, this delay is suspended as from the date the procedure is introduced until the end of the third month during which the

---
under bilateral income tax treaties where a serious penalty is applied.

21 Convention on the elimination of double taxation in connection with the adjustment of profits of associated enterprises of 23 July 1990, 90/436/EEC.

outcome of the procedure is notified to the taxpayer. Before the introduction of this provision, French taxpayers introducing such procedures had in practice to pay the corporate income tax resulting from the reassessments made (or had to constitute guarantees in order to have the possibility to delay the payment of the tax) before the end of the procedure. Now, since the deadline to collect tax is suspended during the procedure, French taxpayers will have to pay tax at the end of the procedure (based on the agreement that will be found between the competent authorities involved), thus limiting the financial cost of such procedure. The Code of Conduct approved by ECOFIN on 7 December 2004 as regards the EU Arbitration Convention recommended the introduction of such provision to Member States.

After their engagement with competent authorities, the steps of the procedures are also different:

- A MAP provides for a procedure that is first conducted in the State of residence of the taxpayer and, if the competent authority involved cannot solve the double taxation, it is then conducted between the contracting States and consists of resolving the dispute on an amicable basis, i.e. by agreement between the competent authorities.
- The procedure set forth by the EU Arbitration Convention provides for the following steps and timelines:
  - there is first a mutual agreement procedure that is similar to the MAP set forth by tax treaties; however, in principle, this mutual agreement procedure cannot last longer than two years;
  - in the absence of agreement, the case is submitted to an advisory committee. The committee must issue an advice within 6 months;
  - this advice is not binding on the competent authorities; however, if they do not find an agreement within an additional 6-month delay, the competent authorities are bound by the advice.

In France, Bureau E1 of the Directorate for Tax Policy (Direction de la Législation Fiscale) is the competent authority for both procedures. The formalities to engage both procedures are in substance the same. Such formalities, as well as other practical issues, are described in detail in the guidelines issued in 2006 by the FTA on these procedures.[22] As regards the procedure set forth by the EU Arbitration Convention, the guidelines expressly take into account the Code of Conduct approved by ECOFIN on 7 December 2004 as regards the EU Arbitration Convention.

---

22 Administrative guidelines of 23 February 2006 (14 F 1-06)

Pierre-Jean Douvier, a partner at CMS Bureau Francis Lefebvre, is in charge of the international department. He can be reached at **(33-1) 47 38 56 76** or by email at **pierre-jean.douvier@cms-bfl.com**.

Xavier Daluzeau is a senior associate in the tax department of CMS Bureau Francis Lefebvre. He can be reached by phone at **(33-1) 47 38 42 25** or by email at **xavier.daluzeau@cms-bfl.com**.

For more information on the authors, please see Section XIII.

Time Frame for Resolution

Except for the cases submitted to the procedure set forth by the EU Arbitration Convention which are disclosed in the context of the works of the EU JTPF, the FTA does not regularly publish regularly statistics as regards cross border tax disputes and their resolution. However, the following statistics on the program are available:
- As at end 2004, France was engaged in 250 MAP (with EU and non-EU States). It can be estimated that one third (90) of these procedures involved transfer pricing disputes. The average duration of a transfer pricing MAP could be estimated at 3.5 years.
- As at end 2008, France was engaged in around 100 procedures under the EU Arbitration Convention (these procedures involve only EU Member States and relate only to transfer pricing).

Conclusion

France has long had a robust transfer pricing regime based on the OECD and EU guidelines. However, unlike many OECD-compliant countries, France had not required contemporaneous documentation of related-party transactions prior to 2010. With new requirements in place and new guidelines expected, companies conducting related-party transactions with entities in France should pay careful attention to the changes in rules and enforcement practices as they develop in the coming months.

German Transfer Pricing Rules in Practice

Andreas Köster-Böckenförde
Jones Day

In recent years, the German government and its Finance Ministry have tightened the legislation relating to transfer pricing, seeking not only to finance a recent cut of the tax rate but also to close loopholes said to be eroding the German tax base. Historically, transfer pricing was an important issue, primarily with respect to domestic transactions, since German tax authorities had focused on the relationships of companies to their German resident shareholders rather than on cross-border issues.

Legislation and Administrative Guidelines

Germany applies the "at arm's length" principle to transactions of related parties. For corporations, this principle is stipulated in Section 8, Paragraph 3, of the Corporation Income Tax Act (*Körperschaftsteuergesetz*) and states that a hidden distribution of profits cannot reduce the taxable income. The term "hidden distribution" is defined by extensive case law and the administrative regulations (*Körperschaftssteuer-Richtlinien*) as a decrease of assets or a prevented increase of assets of a corporation that is caused by the relation of the company to its shareholder and affects the corporation's income. A decrease or prevented increase of profits is based on the relationship of the shareholder to the corporation if a prudent and diligent managing director, under the same facts and circumstances, would not have accepted the decrease or prevented the increase of assets vis-à-vis a person who is not a shareholder.

In 1972, the Foreign Tax Act (*Außensteuergesetz*) was enacted. Section 1 of the Act grants the tax authorities the right to adjust a German taxpayer's taxable income from cross-border transactions with related parties if the transactions were not at arm's length. Section 8, Paragraph 3 of the Corporation Income Tax Act relates to domestic and cross-border transactions, whereas Section 1 of the Foreign Tax Act relates only to cross-border transactions.

In 1983, the Finance Ministry published its first administrative guidelines.[1] These guidelines include instructions for the application of Section 1 of the Foreign Tax Act, along with a detailed description of the applicable transfer pricing methods. Although most of these guidelines are still in force, in 1999 the part dealing with cost-sharing agreements was replaced with a new letter from the Finance Ministry.[2]

A separate letter from the Finance Ministry, dealing with cross-border employees' secondments, was published in 2001.[3]

---

1   Schreiben betr. Grundsätze für die Prüfung der Einkunftsabgrenzung bei international verbundenen Unternehmen (Verwaltungsgrundsätze) as of February 23, 1983; BStBl 83 I, p. 218 („1983 Administrative Guidelines").

2   Schreiben betr. Grundsätze für die Prüfung der Einkunftsabgrenzung durch Umlageverträge zwischen international verbundenen Unternehmen as of December 30, 1999; BStBl 1999 I, p. 1122.

3   Schreiben betr. Grundsätze für die Prüfung der Einkunftsabgrenzung zwischen international verbundenen Unternehmen in den Fällen der

In response to the 2001 landmark decision of the Federal Fiscal Court[4] that put the burden of proof for a taxpayer's failure to adhere to the arm's-length principle on the tax authority, in 2003,[5] the legislation was amended accordingly and extensive documentation requirements were introduced in the General Tax Act (*Abgabenordnung*). It should be noted that the Finance Ministry needed more than three years to decide whether or not this decision should be binding in comparable cases. The taxpayer is obliged to prepare and, upon request, to present appropriate documentation with respect to the transactions between related parties. In October 2003 the Finance Ministry enacted the new decree with respect to the details of the documentation obligations.[6]

In 2005, in response to the revised OECD transfer pricing guidelines and the new transfer pricing documentation obligations, the Finance Ministry issued new administrative guidelines.[7] These administrative guidelines partly replace the 1983 Administrative Guidelines. Recently, Section 1 of the Foreign Tax Act was amended by the Enterprise Tax Reform Act 2008. Beginning in 2008, new rules are in place that dictate the procedures for selecting which method should be used to calculate the applicable transfer price. These new rules limit taxpayers to three transfer pricing methodologies, except in exceptional circumstances where none of these methods can be applied. In addition, it is stipulated that the transfer of enterprise functions cross-border must be treated as a cross-border transaction and the arm's-length principle must apply. In August 2008 a decree on the implication of a transfer of enterprise functions[8] was published by the Finance Ministry. In July 2009 the Finance Ministry published a draft of an administrative guideline regarding relocations of functions.[9] Businesses, organizations and interested parties were given the opportunity to comment on the draft.

Applicable Transfer Pricing Methods

The German tax authorities have historically applied three standard transfer pricing methods, briefly described in the 1983 Administrative Guidelines that conform to the OECD Guidelines: the comparable uncontrolled price method, the resale price method, and the cost-plus method. It was left to the taxpayer to determine which transfer pricing method was most appropriate in a particular case.

Arbeitnehmerentsendung (Verwaltungsgrundsätze – Arbeitnehmerentsendung) as of November 9, 2001; BStBl 2001 I, p. 796.

4 Federal Fiscal Court (BFH), as of October 17, 2001; Der Betrieb 2001, p. 2474.

5 Steuervergünstigungsabbaugesetz as of May 16, 2003; BStBl 2003 I, p. 660.

6 Verordnung zu Art, Inhalt und Umfang von Aufzeichnungen im Sinne des § 90 Abs. 3 Abgabenordnung. (Gewinnabgrenzungsaufzeichnungsverordnung) as of November 13, 2003; BStBl 2003 I, p. 2296.

7 Grundsätze für die Prüfung der Einkunftsabgrenzung zwischen nahestehenden Personen mit grenzüberschreitenden Geschäftsbeziehungen in Bezug auf Ermittlungs- und Mitwirkungspflichten, Berichtigungen sowie auf Verständigungs- und EU-Schiedsverfahren. (Verwaltungsgrundsätze-Verfahren) („2005 Administrative Guidelines") as of April 12, 2005; BStBl 2005 I, p. 570.

8 Verordnung zur Anwendung des Fremdvergleichsgrundsatzes nach § 1 Abs. 1 des Außensteuergesetzes in Fällen grenzüberschreitender Funktionsverlagerungen (Funktionsverlagerungsverordnung – FVerlV) as of August 12, 2008; BStBl 2008 I, p. 1680.

9 Entwurf Grundsätze der Verwaltung für die Prüfung der Einkunftsabgrenzung zwischen nahe stehenden Personen in Fällen von grenzüberschreitenden Funktionsverlagerungen (Verwaltungsgrundsätze – Funktionsverlagerung) as of July 17, 2009.

However, it was assumed that a diligent manager would apply different methods in order to cross-check the result of the chosen method.

The 2005 Administrative Guidelines, released in response to the revision of the 1995 OECD Guidelines, permit use of the profit split method and the transactional net margin method in addition to the three standard pricing methods. However, these two methods are regarded as a last resort, to be used when the other three methods may not give reliable results. The comparable profit method is still not accepted.

The Enterprise Tax Reform Act 2008 now codifies for the first time which transfer pricing methods have to be applied and the manner in which this must be done. Section 1, Paragraph 3, of the Foreign Tax Act stipulates that transfer pricing should be based on the comparable uncontrolled price method, the resale price method, or the cost-plus method. Consequently, other transfer pricing methods, such as the profit split method and the transactional net margin method, should be used only in exceptional cases.

Selection of Comparables

Fully Comparable Data

The law further provides that the taxpayer has to research and present fully comparable third-party data. There is no limitation as to the region where the comparables come from. Such data must be adjusted appropriately in consideration of the functions, the employed assets, and the opportunities and risks. If it is determined that more than one price has been established by this calculation, a couple of potential prices will be considered as a range of prices. If the transfer price used by the taxpayer is outside this range, the median of the range is decisive for the adjustment by the tax authorities. If, on the other hand, the prices used by the taxpayer are within this established range, there is no adjustment by the tax authorities, whether or not the price is equal to the median of the range.

Limited Data

Where the taxpayer is not able to obtain comparable third-party data, he may use limited comparable third-party data that must be adjusted according to the results of the above-described functional and risk analysis. Again, if the actual transfer price of the taxpayer is outside the limited range, the median of the prices is decisive for the tax authority to determine their adjustment. In this respect, the 2005 Administrative Guidelines provide that in cases where no adequate prices could be established, the interquartile method will be used to determine the midpoint for the prices.

No Data

The law further provides that where no third-party data is available, a hypothetical third-party price considering the functional and risk analysis shall apply for the income determination of the taxpayer; the highest price, which is the view of the purchaser, and the lowest price, which is the view of the seller, have to be determined. In such case, the price to be used will be the one most likely to be accepted by unrelated parties. If this likelihood cannot be established by the taxpayer, the midpoint has to be used.

Compensation for Relocation of Functions

The new law further introduces a specific provision relating to the relocation of entrepreneurial functions, including opportunities and risks. It would apply, for example, to the German legislature's recent proposal to tax the relocation of manufacturing functions from Germany to countries that offer lower labor costs. According to the draft of the function relocation guideline[10] a relocation of function will be assumed if a company transfers its assets including opportunities and risks to the related party to enable the related party to perform the function which the transferring company does not conduct anymore or in a restricted way only.

The law requires that the relocation must be adequately compensated by the recipient, taking into account the chances and risks and the transferred assets, including intangibles (like - e.g. know-how), as a single package. The determination of the prices for function relocations follows the standard methods.[11] Otherwise taxpayers are obliged to apply the hypothetical arm´s length price. The value of this "package" has to be calculated by the discounted cash method applying at arm's length interest rates, risk adjustments and estimated terms for the use of the "package."

In cases where no material intangible assets are relocated, the taxpayer is permitted to determine the total transfer price on the basis of each individual asset or service. However, this applies only if the total transfer price compared to the transfer price for the package is still at arm's length.

Transfer of Intangibles

The new law introduces the commensurate transfer pricing calculation in cases where intangibles are part of a cross-border transaction. In such cases, the law assumes — although it can be rebutted by the taxpayer — that the parties to the transaction typically do not have complete knowledge of the future business development associated with the transferred intangibles, and a prudent manager will therefore insist on a price-adjustment clause. It is noteworthy that this legal assumption applies only if the factual business development deviates from the expected development. The law further provides that, if no price-adjustment clause is included in the transfer agreement or license agreement and material deviation occurs within the first 10 years of the term of the agreement, the transfer price adjustment has to be made retroactively for the completed fiscal years.

Special Transfer Pricing Cases

Cost-Sharing Agreements

By the end of 1999, the Finance Ministry had circulated a letter dealing with cost-sharing agreements[12] by which the 1983 Administrative Guideline was partly revised. The letter provided that cost-sharing agreements must be in written form. They must clearly show the benefits and expenses of each party to the agreement. No profit markup is permitted because each party contributes to the pool and receives a right to the results of the work product. The letter further provides details on the required documentation of the expenses and benefits of the pool, the details of other pool members, the right to control and review the expenses of those members and the details of the chosen proportions. The right to terminate the cost-sharing agreement, as well as the right to demand an adjustment, is also required.

---

10 See footnote no. 8, there Section 1, Paragraph 1.
11 See footnote no. 8, there Section 2, Paragraph 1.

12 See footnote no. 3.

Employee Secondments

In 2001, the Finance Ministry published a letter that provides specifics in the case of employee secondments;[13] it states that the company has to bear the expenses that have the main interest in the particular secondment. This could be the "seconding employer" if, for example, it is part of the company's international strategy to second employees to foreign countries, if the employee has reporting and controlling functions in the "receiving employer" for the benefit of the "seconding employer," or if the secondment enables a transfer of know-how from the "receiving" company to the "seconding" company. On the other hand, the "receiving employer" has to bear the cost if it needs specific knowledge of such employee or if it prefers to train the employee for its own benefit. All this must be recorded, as well as the details of the employee's remuneration and associated costs. The letter further provides that the charge-backs of the "seconding employer" to the "receiving employer" have to apply the comparable uncontrolled price method in the first instance. Therefore, it has to be determined what expenses would have been incurred if the employer had hired a person with the same knowledge and capabilities locally. These comparable expenses are the upper limit for which the receiving company can be charged back.

Documentation Requirements

The documentation obligations are qualified in Section 90 of the General Tax Act. The legislation, enacted in 2003,[14] stipulates the obligation of the taxpayer to clarify transactions that occurred outside Germany and to deliver the required supporting evidence. The taxpayer is obliged to use all existing legal and functional options to achieve this, since the burden of proof is on him. He cannot argue that he is unable to clarify the facts or provide evidence if he would have been in a position to do so beforehand.

It is further stipulated that the taxpayer in a cross-border transaction is obliged to record the type and content of the business transaction to related parties. The documentation includes the economic and legal basis of the arm's-length principle with respect to pricing and other business terms. Documentation must be delivered to the tax authorities within 60 days of being requested. For extraordinary business transactions[15] like restructurings or the conclusion of long term agreements, the documentation has to be set up promptly, which is defined to be within a six-month period commencing after the completion of a fiscal year. In cases of extraordinary transactions, the period of document production is reduced to 30 days. The period can be extended upon petition by the taxpayer.

Based on Section 90 of the General Tax Act, the Finance Ministry enacted a decree[16] that provides details on how the evidence has to be provided and what documentation is required. Further details are included in the 2005 Administrative Guidelines. In general, the documentation must be based on the respective transaction, but it is permissible to group comparable transactions if such grouping is determined before the occurrence of the transaction.

To the extent possible, the taxpayer is obliged to collect comparable publicly obtainable data supporting the transfer pricing method applied by him. In particular, the taxpayer has to document comparable data resulting from his own third-party transactions, *e.g.*, pricing,

---

13 See footnote no. 2.
14 See footnote no. 6.
15 The definition of "extraordinary business transaction" was revised and more broadened by the Enterprise Tax Reform Act 2008.
16 See footnote no. 7.

general terms and conditions, cost quota, profit margin, cross margin, net margin, and profit split.

The records have to comprise (i) general information about the group and ownership's structure, business and organization, (ii) business relationships with related parties, (iii) analysis of functions and risks, and (iv) transfer pricing analysis. Some of the information must relate to a general overview, consisting of group structure charts and the type of business (*e.g.*, distribution, manufacturing services, etc.). Other records must show the type and extent of the business conducted with related parties (*e.g.*, purchases, sales services, financing, and other use of assets). In particular, records must include the material intangible assets owned by the taxpayer and that it has licensed to related parties. The functional and risk analysis must record the function and the associated risk of the taxpayer and the related parties within the particular business transaction. It must further record material assets, the business strategy, and relevant market and competition relations and situations. Finally, the chosen transfer pricing method, the explanation of the appropriateness of the chosen transfer pricing method, calculation records, and data about comparable third parties should be documented. The 2005 Administrative Guidelines provide a more detailed list of the information the taxpayer has to record.

Noncompliance Penalties

If the taxpayer does not produce the records or the records are unusable, or if it is recognized that the records have not been filed in due time, it will be assumed that the income of the taxpayer is higher than reported (although the taxpayer is permitted to rebut this legal assumption). The tax authorities are permitted to estimate the income at the upper level if there is a range of possible "correct" incomes.

In addition, the taxpayer has to pay a penalty of at least €5,000 if he does not produce the documentation or if the documentation is unusable. The penalty will be 5 to 10 percent of the additional income that is assessed as a result of the nonproduction of the records, if this amount exceeds €5,000. If the documentation is produced after the 60-day/30-day period, a minimum penalty of €100 per day will be due, up to €1 million.

Advance Pricing Agreements

In 2006, the first letter of the Finance Ministry regarding advance transfer pricing agreements ("APA") was published.[17] Under German law, no agreements between the taxpayer and the tax authorities are permitted. Nevertheless, the German tax authorities are interested in APA's because they believe it is easier to share in the international "tax cake" at the outset rather than try to participate in a controversy after the fact.

In the German context, the international common understanding of an APA is inconsistent with German law, which not permit an agreement between the taxpayer and the tax authorities. Therefore, the German Finance Ministry has assembled the elements of an APA from a German perspective as follows: the APA is an advance competent authority agreement between the German competent authority and the relevant foreign competent

---

17 Merkblatt für bilaterale oder multilaterale Vorabverständigungsverfahren auf der Grundlage der Doppelbesteuerungsabkommen zur Erteilung verbindlicher Vorabzusagen über Verrechnungspreise zwischen international verbundenen Unternehmen (sog. „Advance Pricing Agreements" — APAs), as of October 5, 2006; BStBl 2006 I, p. 594.

authority. As a result, only bilateral and multi-lateral APAs are possible. There are no unilateral APAs with the German tax authorities. In addition, it is a request for a binding ruling by the taxpayer that implements the intergovernmental agreement.

In this context, it is evident that the competent authority procedure is based on a double tax treaty with the relevant foreign country. Consequently, no APA could be obtained in relation to a foreign country with which no double tax treaty is in force. In such cases, the APA, as understood in Germany, simply lacks a legal basis. Nevertheless, since Germany has a broad treaty network, the practical impact should be limited.

The APA procedures are centralized at the Federal Central Tax Office (*Bundeszentralamt für Steuern*), where the application for the APA has to be filed; centralization seems to be more efficient, as each local tax office has to deal with international issues. Please note that the Federal Central Tax Office will not agree with a foreign competent tax authority if the local or state tax authority does not approve such agreement.

While the first part of the APA procedure is an agreement between the German and foreign tax authorities, the taxpayer has to initiate the procedure by filing an application that determines the scope and limits of the intergovernmental negotiations and agreements. This application must include all relevant facts for both tax authorities. In addition, the applicant must consent to the result of the negotiations and has to waive all rights to complain before the intergovernmental agreement becomes valid (although he can withdraw from the process at any time). Before the intergovernmental negotiations start, the taxpayer has to pay an application fee of €20,000. This amount can be reduced to €10,000 in some cases.

It is expected that an intergovernmental agreement will have an effective period of three to five years. Upon application and approval by the foreign tax authority, the term of the APA can be extended. The fee for extending an APA is €15,000, which can be reduced to €7,500 under some circumstances.

The content of an APA is limited to transfer pricing issues. The taxpayer has to outline the scope of the requested APA and to describe in detail the facts and circumstances, the applicable transfer pricing method, and the calculations that verify the results of the applicable transfer pricing method. In addition, the taxpayer must provide supporting documentation.

In cases where the taxpayer has obtained an APA in a foreign country, the German tax authorities are not bound by such unilateral APA. Moreover, the German tax authorities might audit the taxpayer because it is assumed that the taxpayer has concluded an agreement with a foreign country to the disadvantage of Germany.

Taxpayrs who apply for APAs should be aware that any facts and circumstances presented within the APA procedure could be used by a local tax authority in determining taxable income, particularly in cases where no APA is achieved.

Dispute Resolution and Appeals

Administrative Appeal

Transfer pricing adjustments are the typical result of a tax audit. Depending on the size of the company, all fiscal years will be subject to audit. Tax auditing is a standard procedure and takes place every three to four years. The audit ends with a final discussion between the tax authorities and the taxpayer. In most cases, an agreement to the proposed revisions of the tax authorities is achieved. Audit results are summarized in an audit report, which serves as a basis for the revised tax-assessment note.

Irrespective of whether an agreement was achieved during the audit, the taxpayer has the right to appeal the assessment note. The appeal must be filed with the local office that issued the revised tax-assessment note, and the taxpayer should give reasons and provide evidence. The tax office will render a decision on the appeal in writing, stating the reasons for its decision.

At the same time, the taxpayer may apply for a competent authority proceeding. If he does so, the administrative appeal will be on hold until the case is resolved by the competent authorities.

Judicial Appeal

If the taxpayer's administrative appeal is rejected, he has the right to file a claim with the lower tax court (*Finanzgericht*), whereby the taxpayer brings an action against the local tax office that issued the disputed tax-assessment note. It is a tax court's right and duty to review all facts and circumstances as well as the legal consequences of the case. The tax court is not restricted to dealing with the arguments and facts brought forward by the taxpayer or the tax office, but may also take into consideration all facts and circumstances of the case including facts which are new to the taxpayer or the tax office. The lower tax court renders its decision in writing. This decision can be appealed only if (i) the legal issue is of fundamental significance, (ii) the lower fiscal court violated the rules of procedure and the disputed decision is the result of this violation, or (iii) the uniform interpretation of the law requires a decision of the Federal Fiscal Court.

If the Federal Fiscal Court approves the appeal as being correct in form and content, it commences proceedings. In doing so, it will not review the facts and circumstances of the case—only the legal issues, based on the facts established by the lower fiscal court. The decision of the Federal Fiscal Court is not appealable but can be brought up to the Federal Constitutional Court. However, this is the case only if the decision of the Federal Fiscal Court is based on a law that is unconstitutional. In other exceptional cases where the taxpayer believes that the decision of the Federal Fiscal Court violates European law, he may appeal to the European Council Court of Justice.

Competent Authority Procedures

The taxpayer can apply for the competent authority procedure at any time, provided he can claim that the action of the tax authorities will result in a taxation that violates the applicable tax treaty. The double taxation that can result from the adjustment of transfer prices is regarded as such a treaty violation.

It should be noted that the taxpayer can apply for the competent authority procedure, but according to most of the tax treaties to which Germany is a party, the taxpayer has no right to enforce the achievement of an agreement between the relevant tax authorities. However, with respect to the new German-U.S. double tax treaty, the tax payer has the right to enforce an agreement of the tax authorities.

Arbitration

The EU Arbitration Convention[18] entered into force in 1995 for a five-year period. It was extended for a further five-

---

18 Convention on the elimination of double taxation in connection with the adjustment of profits of associated enterprises, 90/436/EEC; Official Journal L 225 as of August 20, 1990, 10

year period in 2000 and again on January 1, 2005. In the meantime, a new convention was proposed, which will become effective after all 25 EU member states have ratified it. The new Convention also contains a provision permitting the member states to apply it on a bilateral basis if it is not unanimously approved.

The convention applies in cases where the profits of a taxpayer who resides in a member state are included in the profits of the resident of another member state, resulting in double taxation because neither of the parties had observed the arm's-length principle. It should be noted that the EU Convention does not apply to a taxpayer resident in the U.S. However, it does apply to European resident subsidiaries of a U.S.-based group among the European group companies.

Resolution of the transfer pricing dispute may require three steps. In the first step, the taxpayer has to inform its foreign related party, which in turn informs its competent authority. If the foreign company and the foreign competent authority agree to the adjustment, the procedure is final. If they fail to reach agreement, formal procedures begin. In the second step, the competent authorities have to agree within two years. Otherwise, they have to set up an advisory commission that has to deliver an opinion within a further six months. In the third step, which applies only if the competent authorities do not agree with the advisory commission, the parties are given another six months to reach an agreement. Otherwise, they have to act according to the advisory commission's opinion.

Andreas Köster-Böckenförde, a partner with Jones Day in Frankfurt, has substantial experience in M&A transactions, both in corporate and tax law. He can be reached at **(49-69) 9726.3968** or by email at **akboeckenfoerde@jonesday.com**. For more information on the author, please see Section XIII.

Hong Kong Introduces Transfer Pricing Guidelines

By Kari Pahlman, Nathan Richards and Kimberley Webb
KPMG China

Historically, Hong Kong's regulatory framework provided limited guidance to taxpayers regarding transfer pricing. Over the course of the last year, Hong Kong has issued significant new transfer pricing guidance in the form of two Department Interpretation and Practice Notes. The net effect of these changes is to establish guidelines for the documentation of related-party transactions, transfer pricing methodologies, treatment of intra-group services, and profit attribution to permanent establishments. As the new guidelines do not address such issues as Advance Pricing Agreements (APAs), Cost Sharing Arrangements (CSAs), or year-end adjustments future developments are still anticipated.

Background

Prior to 2009, Hong Kong had only a very limited regulatory framework for assessing transfer pricing matters, relying primarily on the general provisions of its Inland Revenue Ordinance (IRO) and case law. Notably, the IRO is and was historically built on the principles of source-based taxation and it does not comprehensively address areas such as transfer pricing. Most transfer pricing related cases have historically been interpreted according to the general anti-avoidance provisions of IRO - however there was a notable lack of regulation in relation to determining and reviewing the arm's length nature of normal (i.e., bona-fide), cross-border intra-group transactions.

Of late, there has been substantial pressure for the Hong Kong Inland Revenue Department (IRD) to address transfer pricing more precisely at a regulatory level. In addition, since 2009 there have been important broader developments in Hong Kong's international tax framework as Hong Kong has moved ahead with expanding its Double Tax Agreement (DTA) network and modifying its relevant exchange of information provisions. The expansion of the DTA network is also expected to increase transfer pricing disputes for which the IRD will need to resolve in a DTA context. The fact that almost all other Asian developed or developing jurisdictions already have transfer pricing regulations, coupled with the impact of the economic downturn, were key contributing factors in the IRD's decision to release transfer pricing guidelines.

Thus, 2009 saw the IRD release two Department Interpretation and Practice Notes (DIPN) relating to transfer pricing, namely DIPN 45 Relief from Double Taxation due to Transfer pricing of Profit Reallocation Adjustments and DIPN 46 Transfer Pricing Guidelines – Methodologies and Related Issues. Of these, the latter provides, for the first time, a comprehensive framework of transfer pricing principles for arriving at an arm's length position of a Hong Kong taxpayer. The former provides guidance on relief from double taxation as a result of a transfer pricing adjustment in the context of a DTA.

Exchange of Information

On January 6, 2010, the legislative council of Hong Kong passed an amendment to the 2009 Revenue Bill enabling it to adopt the latest international standard for exchange of information. This amendment will facilitate Hong Kong's ability to enter into many more DTAs. In this regard, since adopting the latest standard for exchange of information Hong Kong has entered into DTAs with the Netherlands, Indonesia and Brunei.

The signing of additional DTAs by Hong Kong will directly benefit taxpayers by providing them with more certainty in relation to the taxation of their operations between Hong Kong and overseas jurisdictions. It will also provide them with an avenue to mitigate double taxation which may arise due to transfer pricing adjustments. This is likely to remove a key disadvantage associated with operating in Hong Kong and will reinforce Hong Kong's position as one of the most favoured locations for Asian operations of multinational enterprises.

DIPN 45

DIPN 45, released on April 30, 2009, relates to transfer pricing strictly in the context of providing relief from double taxation where the related party is located in a jurisdiction which has a signed DTA with Hong Kong. DIPN 45 discusses instances where double taxation can arise and the procedures available to Hong Kong taxpayers for obtaining relief from such double taxation. These avenues relate solely to DTAs. Further, DIPN 45 clarifies the IRD's view that where a transfer pricing or profit reallocation adjustment is made in a non-DTA context, there are no procedures in place for the IRD to provide relief from any resultant double taxation.

However, DIPN 45 does not go so far as to specify the transfer pricing principles or methodologies to be adopted by the IRD, thus creating a need for DIPN 46.

Case Law

The need for the IRD to adopt transfer pricing regulations has been further highlighted by the decisions in *Ngai Lik Electronics Company Limited v CIR*, FACV 29/2008 and *Commissioner of Inland Revenue v Datatronic Limited (Datatronic)* (2009) CACV275/2008.

The *Ngai Lik Electronics* case involved a business reorganization, whereby the manufacturing functions of the group were moved to the PRC and a BVI company became the principal manufacturing entity. The purchases by the Hong Kong taxpayer, Ngai Lik Electronics Company Limited, from the BVI entity were subject to an annual price-fixing arrangement whereby the two parties recorded the quantities of the goods ordered and delivered during the year but only decided on the price on an annual basis.

While the lower courts ruled in favor of the taxpayer and found that no adjustment was required to the taxpayer's annual assessments, the Court of Final Appeal (CFA) agreed with the Commissioner's analysis that there was abusive profit shifting on the basis of section 61A of the IRO. However, the CFA disallowed the quantum of the assessments raised by the Commissioner, namely assessments based on 50% of the profits derived by the taxpayer's subsidiaries from their manufacturing operations, on the grounds that these assessments did not counteract the tax benefit arising from the abusive profit shifting. Rather, the CFA allowed the Commissioner to assess the taxpayer's profits on the basis of an estimate of the assessable profits which would have been earned by the taxpayer if it had transacted with related parties on an arm's length basis. However, given that this decision was reached prior to the release of DIPN 46, the IRD did not have established grounds for determining what constituted an "arm's length basis."

In the *Datatronic* case, the Hong Kong Court of Appeal denied the availability of the 50:50 Concession to Datatronic, a Hong Kong-based seller of products manufactured in China by a related party. In rejecting Datatronic's claim to the 50:50 Concession, the Court of Appeal determined that the profit-producing transaction performed by Datatronic was the sale of the finished products and that its participation in the manufacturing activity in China was only antecedent or incidental to the profit-producing sales transaction. From a transfer pricing perspective, this case highlighted the importance of determining the appropriate functional and risk profile of entities when assessing where profits should be attributed.

Overview of DIPN 46

The IRD released DIPN 46 during December, 2009, establishing the tax authority's views and practices regarding transfer pricing methodologies and related issues. It provided, for the first time, a comprehensive framework for the transfer pricing principles followed by the IRD in arriving at the arm's length position of a Hong Kong taxpayer. Thus, DIPN 46 provides the basis on which the IRD will assess the arm's length nature of taxpayer's intra-group transactions, make transfer pricing/profit reallocation adjustments and interpret a transfer pricing adjustment initiated by a party other than the IRD (i.e., by the taxpayer or another fiscal authority).

DIPN 46 states that the arm's length principle utilizes independent transactions as a benchmark to determine how profits and expenses should be allocated for in transactions between associated enterprises. Importantly, especially for taxpayers already operating in OECD-jurisdictions, DIPN 46 clarifies in paragraph 8 that, "Generally, the Commissioner would seek to apply the principles in the OECD Transfer Pricing Guidelines for Multinational Enterprises and Tax Administrations (OECD Guidelines), except where they are incompatible with the express provisions of the IRO." However, DIPN 46 provides no indication of under what circumstances the IRD would consider the express provisions of the IRO to be inconsistent with those of DIPN 46 – one of several areas of residual uncertainty for Hong Kong taxpayers. Further, the lack of an effective date within DIPN 46 means that, at least in theory, the principles contained in it could be applied retroactively to all open years of assessment, namely six years for Hong Kong taxpayers. DIPN 46 also applies to domestic transactions within Hong Kong, although this is most likely intended to be directed at intra-group transactions where certain entities are in a tax loss position, as there are currently limited opportunities within Hong Kong for taxpayers to be subject to differing tax rates.

Overall, DIPN 46 provides taxpayers operating in Hong Kong with guidance on the transfer pricing principles and practices which will be adopted by the IRD. However, it leaves a number of more complex transfer pricing areas, such as cost sharing arrangements and Advance Pricing Agreements (APAs), to be addressed by the IRD in the future.

The specific areas addressed by DIPN 46 include: 1) Associated Enterprises, 2) Arm's Length Principle, 3) Transfer Pricing Methods, 4) Documentation, 5) Intra-group Services, and 6) Permanent Establishments.

1) Associated Enterprises

The concept of what constitutes "associated enterprises" is central to transfer pricing. In terms of determining when enterprises may be considered associated, DIPN 46, referring heavily to the OECD Model Tax Convention, outlines that "association" may be via direct or indirect participation in management, control or capital. The lack of a common shareholding percentage above which two enterprises will be considered to be associated for transfer pricing purposes within DIPN 46 means the concept of association is a 'grey area' for Hong Kong taxpayers.

2) Arm's Length Principle

Within DIPN 46, the IRD has signalled its intention to adopt the arm's length principle as a framework for the pricing of intra-group transactions, on the basis that it represents "the closest approximation to open market and economic reality and would produce a reasonable allocation of profits and income within a multinational enterprise."

Paragraph 39 of DIPN 46 contains guidance, although not prescriptive, of the implementation of the arm's length principle. These steps refer to the selection of the most appropriate transfer pricing methodology and contain multiple references to documenting the steps.

3) Transfer Pricing Methods

DIPN 46 places reliance on the five transfer pricing methods specified in the OECD Guidelines, but also provides for the use of "unspecified methods" (in particular circumstances). This acceptance of other unspecified methods will enable taxpayers to use the most reliable transfer pricing approach possible, even though it may potentially not fit cleanly into one of the specified methods contained in the OECD Guidelines.

DIPN 46 retains the hierarchy of transfer pricing methods currently contained in the OECD Guidelines, whereby traditional transaction methods are preferred to transactional profit methods. However, the OECD has recently issued proposed revisions to Chapters I - III of the OECD Guidelines, incorporating previously released discussion drafts and the responses received by the OECD in relation to these previous discussion drafts. One of the key changes of the proposed revisions is that the hierarchy of methods would be relaxed. Taxpayers would be required to determine the most appropriate method after having considered the strengths and weaknesses of each method together with the availability of "reasonably reliable information."

The hierarchy of methods has already been disregarded in some tax jurisdictions. Accordingly, it will be interesting to see the path taken by the IRD once the OECD proposed revisions are finalized.

4) Documentation

DIPN 46 contains certain guidance in relation to transfer pricing documentation and provides an explicit recommendation for taxpayers to prepare such documentation. We believe the IRD will treat transfer pricing documentation as a starting point for discussions regarding transfer pricing classifications and methodologies in potential transfer pricing audits. We note in particular, Example 5 of paragraph 60 of DIPN 46, where it would appear that the Commissioner will not recognize deductions related to a market penetration strategy unless the amounts were supported by the taxpayer's "contemporaneous documentation."

DIPN 46 refers to recommendations made by the OECD Guidelines regarding the nature and type of information to be included in transfer pricing documentation. The information listed in DIPN 46 is generally consistent with that which taxpayers are commonly required by tax authorities globally to include in transfer pricing documentation. DIPN 46 also contains some specific recommendations on the steps to be taken when applying and documenting the arm's length principle, including:

- Characterizing the transactions between associated enterprises;
- Selecting the most appropriate transfer pricing methodology;
- Applying the most appropriate transfer pricing methodology to determine the arm's length outcome; and
- Implementing support processes, including a review process for material changes.

5) Intra-group Services

DIPN 46 clarifies that, "basically, the Commissioner accepts the principles defined by the OECD Guidelines surrounding the charging for intra-group services." As such, it is of key importance that Hong Kong taxpayers can substantiate that they have received a benefit from services provided by a related party (the taxpayer can document that they would have been willing to pay for or perform these services itself had they not been performed by a related party), and that the services are not shareholder activities (i.e., activities performed for the benefit of the parent company in its role as a shareholder which do not directly benefit the subsidiaries) or duplicative in nature.

DIPN 46 goes beyond the issues addressed by the OECD as regards intra-group services and discusses instances where recharges for intra-group services should include mark-up and provides several examples of costs associated with shareholder activities. In addition, in relation to permanent establishments, DIPN 46 specifically notes that where the main activity of the permanent establishment is to provide specific services to the enterprise and where these give a real advantage to the enterprise and the costs associated constitute a significant part of the expenses of the permanent establishment, a mark-up should be applied. In contrast, where the provision of such services is merely part of the general management activity of the enterprise taken as a whole, there should be no mark-up.

In terms of determining the quantum of the mark-up, DIPN 46 does not provide any safe harbor thresholds, but rather requires that all mark-ups comply with the arm's length principle.

6) Permanent Establishments

DIPN 46 also indicates that the IRD will adopt the Authorised OECD Approach (AOA) framework provided by the OECD for determining the profits that should be attributed to a Permanent Establishment (PE) in Hong Kong. The AOA has been detailed in the OECD's Report on Attribution of Profit to Permanent Establishments which was finalized in July, 2008. The OECD approach is intended to provide taxpayers and tax administrations with a basis to deal with the potential issues which may arise from the application of Article 7 Business Profits of the OECD Model Tax Convention.

Under the AOA, PEs are treated as if they are functionally separate entities whose profits are determined by the application of transfer pricing methodologies. As such, in accordance with the AOA, DIPN 46 clarifies that the IRD would consider the significant people functions and the key entrepreneurial risk-taking functions when attributing profits to a permanent establishment. DIPN 46 also states clearly that even if profits are not booked to the PE, they can be taxed in Hong Kong if economically significant activities are carried out by the PE in Hong Kong. This is an important revision in relation to IRD's past practices which have typically relied on booked profits

Although the IRD states that they will adopt the "functionally separate entity" approach, DIPN 46 does not specify the IRD's views on specific issues such as the capital attribution mechanism for tax purposes. This implies that the practical application of the AOA by IRD is still somewhat ambiguous. This issue is likely to be very relevant to taxpayers in the financial services industry, which relies heavily on branch structures.

Implications for Taxpayers

DIPN 45 provides the potential for taxpayers to claim relief from double taxation arising from transfer pricing adjustments in the context of a DTA and DIPN 46 provides comprehensive recommendations for addressing the required analysis to be provided in such circumstances. Although Hong Kong has at present signed only a limited number of DTAs, the release of these DIPNs provides greater certainty for taxpayers regarding the treatment of certain intra-group transactions.

Due to the recent transfer pricing developments in Hong Kong, taxpayers should prepare to have their transfer pricing policy questioned in detail in future tax audits. Preparation of appropriate transfer pricing documentation should assist taxpayers with mitigating the risk of potential transfer pricing adjustments and minimize the costs associated with such tax audits.

Although no specific industry/functional profiles have been specifically targeted by the IRD, it is likely that the arm's length nature of intra-group transactions with entities in low-tax jurisdictions will receive significant attention from the IRD. In addition, it is likely that taxpayers with significant intra-group transactions and taxpayers reporting consistent losses are also more likely to be questioned by the IRD.

The modifications to Hong Kong's exchange of information rules and the potential increase in the number of requests received by the IRD from overseas tax administrations should encourage taxpayers to review their transfer pricing documentation and ensure the consistency of their transfer pricing policy at a global level.

In our experience, taxpayers commonly make year-end transfer pricing adjustments so that their intra-group transactions comply with the arm's length principle. However, DIPN 46 does not address the mechanism or timeframe for which taxpayers should finalise any such adjustments. Accordingly, taxpayers should consider this uncertainty when establishing their transfer pricing policies.

In the current economic environment, many financial institutions are transferring assets as part of cleaning up their balance sheets. For example, this may involve moving loss-incurring portfolios to a special purpose vehicle or centralizing the overall management of the portfolio. When undertaking such transfers, taxpayers need to consider the arm's length value of the transferred assets, while bearing in mind the potentially varied tax accounting treatments of the assets across various jurisdictions.

Conclusion

In 2009, the IRD made significant efforts to clarify its position in relation to transfer pricing. DIPN 45 and DIPN 46 provide a significant level of guidance to taxpayers regarding the IRD's view on transfer pricing principles and the allocation of profits.

However, some important aspects of transfer pricing are yet to be addressed by the IRD, including intellectual property, potential cost sharing agreements, intra-group financing and APAs. As the IRD's skills and experience in transfer pricing increases, we would look towards these areas to receive further attention and guidance.

Hong Kong appears committed to participating in the global effort made by tax authorities worldwide to promote transparency and good practices as regards transfer pricing and tax in general. Going forward, the combined actions should help secure that Hong Kong is a favorable jurisdiction.

Kari Pahlman, a partner with KPMG China, can be reached by phone at **+852 2143 8777** or by email at **kari.pahlman@kpmg.com.hk**.

Nathan Richards is a director in KPMG's Global Transfer Pricing Services (GTPS) group in Hong Kong. He can be reached by phone at **+852 2685 7645** or by email at **nathan.richards@kpmg.com.hk**.

Kimberley Webb, a manager with KPMG China, can be reached by phone at **+852 2685 7645** or by email at **kimberley.a.webb@kpmg.com.hk**.

For more information on the authors, please see Section XIII.

Transfer Pricing in India

by Tanmoy Chakrabarti
Ernst & Young

Transfer pricing issues have been cited as the biggest business issue faced by multinationals operating in India. A restrictive law, inadequate guidance and primitive databases have rendered transfer pricing exercises puzzling to most. While the current transfer pricing environment in India is challenging, there as signs that government efforts currently underway will improve the regulatory climate. Some of the problems associated with Indian transfer pricing relate to the difficulty of valuing certain types of transactions that are common in India. For example, global companies that run low-risk information technology captive centers in India must determine what should be the "appropriate" cost-plus mark-up on the services rendered to the associated enterprises. It is not an easy job for transfer pricing advisors to comment on the "appropriateness" of these mark-ups, especially given the recent experience of aggressive transfer pricing audits in India. The dilemma surrounding transfer pricing is not unique just to information technology captive service providers, but the uncertainty has largely purported a feeling of skepticism among the managers and consultants alike across all industries.

A law that came into existence in 2001 is fairly new and in a large country like India, proper implementation is bound to take its time. In this regard, it is of utmost importance for businesses venturing into the Indian market to understand the current transfer pricing regulations and the scenarios surrounding audits to pre-plan and facilitate efficient decision-making.

The *Ernst & Young, Transfer Pricing Global Reference guide (February 2009)*, provides a lucid brief of the Indian regulations but here one can look into some of the important aspects concerning the same. Largely based on the Organisation of Economic Co-operation and Development (OECD) guidelines, the regulations[1] set parameters for determining transfer prices of tangible and intangible property transferred in related party transactions. It delineates specific situations in which two entities are deemed to be related and incorporates anti-evasion provisions to prevent revenue loss arising from shifting profits to low tax incidence jurisdictions.

Broadly, there are three aspects to the regulations; determination of arm's length price, compliance requirements and dispute settlement.

Applying the Arm's-Length Standard: Allowed Methods

Indian regulations require international transactions with related entities to be on an arm's length basis. Regulations prescribe

---
1 Relevant regulations and rules are Sections 92-92F of the Income Tax Act, 1961 and Rule 10-10E of the Income Tax Rules, 1962. Indian Transfer Pricing Regulations are available online at http://law.incometaxindia.gov.in/TaxmannDit/IntTax/tpcont.aspx

five methods to arrive at the arms length price and warrant the usage of the most appropriate one. This entails identifying similar transactions and using prices or profit margins as benchmarks. The proper application of the arm's length principle and the determination of the transfer price hinges on the appropriate choice of transfer pricing method. The prescribed methods are CUP, Resale Price, Cost Plus, Profit Split and TNMM. It is pertinent to note that unlike OECD, Indian transfer pricing regulations do not prescribe any hierarchy of transfer pricing methodologies. The taxpayer is required to identify the most appropriate method based on the facts of the transaction and availability of reliable data.

Documentation Requirements

Indian transfer pricing regulations require maintenance of specified documentation to justify the arm's length nature of international transactions and that taxpayers furnish an Accountant's Certificate to the Department of Revenue detailing the nature and value of international transactions undertaken with related parties.

All taxpayers with related-party transactions are required to compile documentation to support inter-company transfer pricing strategies on an annual basis, prior to filing the Indian income tax returns. This documentation must provide not only the details of each international transaction, but also a logical justification of the prices charged for the transaction.

The details of India's documentation guidelines are provided under Rule 10D of the Income Tax Rules, 1962. The availability of reliable data is critical to facilitating an orderly examination and audit by tax authorities. The information and documents are to be maintained in a prescribed format for a period of nine years from the end of the year subsequent to the financial year. In a given financial year, such information maintained contemporaneously and prepared for submission on or before the due date of filing tax returns.

It is advisable to maintain proper and complete documentation that would assist in substantiating the arm's length nature of the international transaction of the taxpayer in the relevant financial year. Since the initial burden of proving that the international transaction entered into by such taxpayer with its associated enterprise are arm's length lies on the taxpayer, proper documentation will assist the taxpayer as the first line of defense.

In addition to the required documentation, the taxpayer must also obtain an Accountants Certificate in the form 3CEB and furnish it to the tax authorities on or before the due date of filing tax returns. The accountant's certificate is essentially a summary of international transactions carried out in a given financial year. There are heavy penalties imposed as regards to non-compliance, as outline in Table 1.

Making a good faith effort to document transfer pricing should shield companies from penalties in the event of an audit adjustment.

Dispute Settlement Mechanisms

Taxpayers in India have access to two dispute resolution mechanisms for transfer pricing rulings:
- Appeals (under domestic law); and
- Mutual Agreement Procedure ("MAP") – (under Double Taxation Avoidance Agreement between India and the United States)

Country Overviews

Appeals Procedure

The first level of appeal lies with Commissioner of Income Tax (Appeals). An appeal must be filed within 30 days from receipt of the assessment order (which includes the transfer pricing adjustment). If the taxpayer and the Revenue are not in conformity with the order of the Commissioner of Income Tax (Appeals), they may prefer an appeal to a higher court (Income Tax Appeals Tribunal).

Using MAP in India

The Mutual Agreement Procedure ("MAP") is an alternative dispute resolution procedure that may be used to avoid double taxation. Under this scheme, the foreign partner in the international transaction approaches its Competent Authority ("CA"), which in turn will approach the Indian CA for resolution of the dispute. Some transfer pricing cases are currently pending at the MAP stage. The relevant Articles for invoking MAP are typically placed under Article 9 and 25 for most Double Taxation Avoidance Agreements.

No APA Opportunity... Yet

Indian transfer pricing Regulations do not provide for an Advance Pricing Arrangement ("APA") which has globally reduced much of transfer pricing disputes. An APA is an arrangement wherein the taxpayer can determine in advance of the transaction – the transfer pricing methodology or the price in agreement with the revenue. In this sense APA is a pre-emptive mechanism not really a tool for dispute resolution but a tool to reduce uncertainties during transfer pricing audits. Though Revenue is contemplating initiation of APA mechanism in India soon but no timeline can be predicted for its implementation.

Other Rules Affecting Transfer Pricing

While doing business in India along with transfer pricing regulations, some other rules may be worth referring to. These have their direct or indirect bearing on appropriate transfer pricing planning. These are aspects of law governing settling up of establishment in a Special Economic Zone ("SEZ")[2], Manual on Foreign Direct Investment[3], and Indirect tax legislations on customs and service tax[4].

Recent Developments

There have been a number of significant recent developments relating to the transfer pricing enforcement landscape in India. The Union Budget 2009 was a landmark budget to address some of the key issues faced by multinationals operating in India. Some of these issues are summarized below.

Presently, where more than one price is determined by the most appropriate method, the arm's length price is the arithmetic mean of such prices, or at the option of the taxpayer, a price which may vary from the arithmetical mean by an amount not exceeding 5%. Under the new rules, the arm's length price will be the arithmetical mean of such prices determined by the most appropriate method.

Further, it is provided if the variation between the arm's length price and the price at which the international transaction

---

2 Available online at http://sezindia.nic.in/;
3 Available online at http://dipp.nic.in/
4 Available online at http://www.incometaxindia.gov.in/

is undertaken does not exceed 5% of the latter, the price at which the international transaction is undertaken will be deemed to be the arm's length price.

The above amendment took effect as of October 1, 2009.

Additionally, the Union Budget has proposed introduction of safe harbor rules which are sought to reduce disputes. However, the details are yet to be formulated. The Union Budget 2009 has also introduced provisions to set up new dispute resolution panel, which would go a long way to speedy settlement of transfer pricing disputes. Previously, the transfer pricing division of the tax administration has been considerably strengthened as the number of Transfer Pricing Officers (Specialist revenue officers handling transfer pricing cases) has been increased significantly which reduced, the work load of a Transfer Pricing Officer. This ensures speedier resolution of transfer pricing cases.

Audit and Enforcement Experience and Controversies

Recently concluded audits have brought to fore various issues where the Revenue has differed with the taxpayer regarding applicability and interpretation of transfer pricing provisions. While each round of audit has enhanced the Department of Revenue's experience in administration of transfer pricing Regulations, each round has also generated significant controversies. These controversies include:

1) Use of Multiple-Year Data

The use of multiple-year data in determining the range of prices of comparable transactions for computing the arm's length price in a given international transaction has been a debated issue in recent audits. Due to a time lag between the conducting of an economic analysis and commencement of audits for the same, unavailability of financial data at the documentation stage pose a problem. This created an anomaly between the arm's length price computed by the taxpayer vis-à-vis the Revenue authorities.

Recent audit experience suggests that the Revenue authorities are asking for fresh economic analysis of international transactions based on current data of comparable companies that was not available during the documentation stage. Taxpayers have argued that to maintain documentation based on data that was not available at the time of conducting the economic analysis would be impossible.

Almost all taxpayers facing transfer pricing adjustments are in appeals against the stance adopted by the Revenue for the use of single-year data. No relief has been granted at the Commissioner of Income Tax (Appeals) level. The indications provided by the higher court also suggest that the transfer pricing Regulations require use of single-year data only.

Indian Regulations do not specifically deal with the issue. Judicial precedents have said when the taxpayer does not have access to required information at the time of documentation, he cannot be held in default of maintenance of documentation and information at a later date.

However, concrete guidance on this important point remains lacking and is eagerly awaited.

2) Use of Foreign Databases to Identify Comparables

The Department of Revenue generally has inhibitions regarding the use of foreign comparables, arguing that taxpayers should rely on Indian comparables. Taxpayers and the Department of Revenue rely primarily on Prowess and Capitaline Plus databases (which contain Indian companies) to identify comparables. However, in certain cases foreign comparables have been used in transactions where an Indian enterprise had undertaken complex functions and received support services from its overseas group enterprises, e.g. distribution, marketing, administration, etc. Foreign databases have also been resorted to in absence of adequate Indian databases regarding prices paid for receipt of such services. Also, in situations where Indian comparables could not be identified, e.g. distribution of branded watches, accessories, etc, international comparables have been used.

3) Loss-Making Comparables and Entities

The Department of Revenue, in a majority of cases, rejected loss-making companies used as comparables, to arbitrarily deflate the arm's-length price. The underlying principle being that the losses incurred by the comparables were on account of extraordinary or abnormal factors.

In cases where taxpayers attempted to justify losses on account of factors such as start-up costs, market penetration strategies, inefficiencies, economic downturn, etc., the Department of Revenue asked for documentation supporting the taxpayers' claims. In addition, the rationale for losses incurred on account of business strategies in particular was questioned by the Department of Revenue, which required great detail with respect to the strategy adopted, the expected outcome and the risks borne. In most cases, short-term losses were accepted if there was evidence of potential profits in the future.

In cases of royalty payments made by loss-making manufacturing or distribution concerns to their associated enterprise for intangible property, the Revenue questioned the arm's-length nature of such payments. The view adopted was that an uncontrolled loss-making entity would not incur high royalty costs for use of intangible property.

This issue has become especially important in the recent years of recession where like most jurisdictions around the world loss making entities have come under special focus. The Department of Revenue expects that entities that bear limited risks are expected not to incur any losses.

4) Allocation of Head-Office Expenses

With respect to allocation of head office expenses to Indian subsidiaries, the Revenue Department accepted allocations where the allocation keys used were commercially realistic and uniformly applied to other group companies. Another important criterion considered was related to the "benefit test". This requires the taxpayer to demonstrate that the shared services are actually required for the conduct of taxpayer's business and reasonable benefit is derived from such services.

5) Benchmarking Intangibles

One of the challenges faced by the Department of Revenue is determining the arm's-length results for transactions involving intangibles. Since Indian Regulations do not provide any guidelines on benchmarking intangibles, valuing and benchmarking intangibles — including know-how, patents, copyrights, trademarks, franchises or other business or commercial rights of similar nature — is one of the most difficult transfer pricing problems.

In case a CUP is not available and the if there is no comparables for transactions involving intangibles which limits usage of TNMM, an indirect approach is adopted whereby royalty payment is benchmarked by comparing net operating margins of the taxpayer (calculated after considering payment of royalty) with net operating margins earned by comparable independent companies. In cases where the taxpayer has earned a higher net operating margin compared to similar independent companies, the royalty payment can be said to be at arm's-length. The issue with such an approach is that, in cases where the taxpayer has earned a low profit margin due to commercial reasons, there is exposure that the Department of Revenue may hold that the transactions were not priced at arm's length.

6) Benchmarking Interest Payments on External Commercial Borrowings

Interest payments on External Commercial Borrowings are made after approval from the regulator, the Ministry of Finance. Difficulties similar to those faced in the benchmarking of intangibles arise in the benchmarking of loan transactions because the choice of method is restricted to use of CUP and because of the difficult of finding reliable arm's length comparables for transactions of this kind.

In summary, the recent audits have further opened up many such contentious issues regarding Indian transfer pricing regulations, thus greater clarity on the provisions of the law to appropriately reflect the intent of the legislature is urgently required.

Recent Court Rulings

Recent judicial pronouncements have shed light on the tax provisions as interpreted by the Revenue authorities. These pronouncements have largely generated a feeling of optimism since they provide greater clarity and help to improve taxpayer preparedness. Broad observations that can be made based on these recent transfer pricing rulings include:

- The Tribunal has taken a firm stand against any arbitrariness in the determination of arm's length price;
- The Tribunal dealt with comparability issues in detail addressing several nuances. There seem to be reliance on OECD Guidelines, OECD published Draft Comparability Notes and also on IRS Regulations. It has encouraged use of diagnostic ratios such as ratio of fixed to operating assets;
- Generally speaking, there has been a tendency on the part of the taxpayer and Revenue to apply TNMM in a flexible manner without regard to tenets of comparability analysis. The Tribunal has emphasized that even where TNMM is applied, comparability principles should be paid due attention;
- The tribunal has rejected the use of industry averages as part of a CUP analysis. The reasoning underlying this stance is that when considering an average, the factors relevant for examining comparability (such as quality, market conditions etc) tend to get overlooked;
- In line with statutory provisions, the Tribunal has held that transfer pricing adjustments apply despite taxpayer's income being tax exempt (in case of most Indian IT enabled service providers, income is exempt under software technology park scheme as authorized by Section 10A of the Income Tax Act); and
- The Tribunal also noted that while the cost plus revenue pricing model was not disputed, parties should pay due

attention to the computation of cost *per se*.

Transfer pricing rulings in India are often reported by print and online media, but so far they have applied on a case-by-case basis without being conclusive in providing reliable guidance in interpreting the law in other cases. Thus, taxpayers are still waiting for the Indian Ministry of Finance to clarify some of the procedural aspects of transfer pricing law, to introduce an APA procedure, and to take other steps to reduce the cost of compliance with the arm's length transfer pricing standard.

Strategies to Minimize Transfer Pricing Risk in India

Multinationals operating in India face the critical question of how to go about implementing proper solutions to their transfer pricing problems. The question seems to be pertinent considering that the law is open to multiple interpretations and the lack of proper guidance on various aspects of cross-border trade (for example, intangibles). There is no easy answer to such a question but taxpayers can adhere to transfer pricing discipline to minimize risk:

1) Know the Regulations

It is important that taxpayers have knowledge about Indian regulations and how they interrelate with one another. For example, the Manual on Foreign Direct Investment in India describes the procedures for royalty payments, but it is possible to comply with these procedures and to lack a justification for the pricing that is set, thereby failing to demonstrate that the transaction complies with the arm's length's standard;

2) Plan Ahead

Planning eases compliance and audits at a later stage. However, transfer pricing planning in India is complicated by the primitive nature of Indian databases, minimizing the set of available comparables. Consequently, taxpayers should be absolutely certain about the reasons for choosing a particular comparable and should document those reasons clearly. For example, finding potential comparables for a market support service provider in India is not an easy exercise, so taxpayers who provide services should be certain to have a proper assessment of the exact services they provide and examine potential comparables to see how closely the services they provide match; and

3) Document Everything

Robust documentation and adherence to compliance timelines are necessary. Given the unpredictable nature of transfer pricing enforcement in India, having access to clear contemporaneous documentation explaining operations and justifying the selection of comparables and any adjustments will prove extremely valuable in the event of an audit.

Tanmoy Chakrabarti is a Senior Transfer Pricing Consultant with Ernst and Young, New Zealand. He can be reached by phone at **(64 2) 7489-9867** or by email at **tanmoy.chakrabarti@nz.ey.com**. The views expressed in this article are personal and have no bearing on the firm's view.

Conclusion

It is beyond any doubt that lawmakers need to refine Indian transfer pricing regulations to a great extent in order to ensure smooth implementation, but it is also important for taxpayers to understand the intricacies that exist in Indian regulations. Although the recent rulings have not provided much clarity on the existing controversial issues, the Tribunal has not ignored the taxpayers' concerns. Experts and industry representatives have been aggressively lobbying the Government for consistent interpretation of the transfer pricing law and there is tremendous optimism that there will be smoother sailing in the future. India remains an attractive destination for businesses because of availability of quality professionals and English language proficiency. A collaborative effort by businesses, consultants and the Department of Revenue will help to accelerate the evolution of India's transfer pricing framework.

Transfer Pricing Developments in Japan: Law and Practice

by Ken Okawara, Satoko Kawamura, and Yukiko Komori
Baker & McKenzie

Japan has long been one of the most aggressive countries in the world when it comes to transfer pricing audits. However, it seems to have changed its policy in recent years, including the issuance of new administrative guidelines. Prior to the issuance of these guidelines, the Japanese transfer pricing rules were not very informative, but recently, the National Tax Agency (NTA) has endeavored to facilitate taxpayers' understanding of the Transfer Pricing (TP) regulations with the publication of these guidelines and by issuing Case Studies, which was previously uncommon in Japan.

The biggest transfer pricing news in 2009 was a case in which a taxpayer prevailed for the first time in a challenge to a TP assessment. Together with the fact that the NTA has failed to reach agreements through Mutual Agreement Procedures in several cases involving assessments in Japan, this may have led the NTA to put a greater emphasis on APAs. Also, the new "documentation rule" became effective on April 1, 2010.

This article discusses the fundamentals of Japanese transfer pricing as well as the recent developments in transfer pricing issues in Japan.

Allowed Methods

Japan's transfer pricing rules were introduced in 1986 as the "Special Taxation Measure Law (STML) 66-5" (now 66-4). They are broadly consistent with the TP guidelines of the Organization for Economic Cooperation and Development (OECD) and permit the below methods to be used in calculating an arm's length price:

- The comparable uncontrolled price (CUP) method
- The resale price (RP) method
- The cost plus (CP) method
- Similar and "Other" alternative methods, including profit split and the transactional net margin method (TNMM)

The first three methods (CUP, RP and CP) are called the "three basic methods" and are given priority over other methods. However, no priority exists among the three basic methods. "Other" methods (i.e. profit split or TNMM) can be applied only when none of the three basic methods are suitable. Also, TNMM was only formally introduced in 2004.

Documentation Requirements: Previously Implicit Only, But Strengthened in 2010

There has long been discussion on whether strict documentation requirements exist in Japan or not. The Japanese documentation rule has often been called the "implicit documentation rule." Japan's transfer pricing regulation did not explicitly require contemporaneous documentation: taxpayers were not legally required to prepare and retain for production on request a detailed statement or in-depth explanation of their transfer pricing and there were no penalties for failure to provide these, but not providing the documentation when required by the tax authorities could lead to a "deemed assessment" (or presumptive taxation). The amendment of the Special Taxation Measures Law (STML), promulgated on March 31, 2010 with effect from April 1, 2010, has strengthened application of the rule.

The Japanese documentation rule consists of Article 66-4(7) (now 66-4(6) since April 1, 2010) of the STML (the main source of Japan's transfer pricing rules), and Enforcement Ordinance[1] 22-10.

STML Article 66-4(7) authorized the tax authorities to presume an arm's length price and reassess the taxpayer's taxable income (deemed assessment) when the taxpayer failed to provide, without delay, the documentation necessary to calculate the arm's length price. However, what constituted "documentation necessary to calculate the arm's length price" was sometimes unclear as it was not set out in the STML, but was only in the Commissioner's Directive (the so-called "TP Guidelines"). The amended STML 66-4(6) changed this to "documentation listed in the Enforcement Ordinance". In this regard, the documents listed below have been added to Enforcement Ordinance 22-10:

1) The following documents related to intercompany transactions:
   - Assets and services provided in the intercompany transaction
   - Functions and risks of each related party
   - Intangible assets used in the intercompany transaction
   - Intercompany contracts
   - Pricing policies/pricing negotiations
   - Profits and losses of each related party with respect to the intercompany transaction
   - Market analysis
   - Business strategies
   - Other transactions closely related to the intercompany transaction, if any

2) The following documents to compute arm's length price (ALP):
   - The selected transfer pricing method (TPM) and the reason for selection
   - Comparable transaction selection process and details of selected comparables
   - Calculation of profit attributable to each related party where the profit-split method or TNMM is applied
   - Justification and details of each transaction where multiple transactions are aggregated for computation of the ALP
   - Details of adjustments made to the comparable transaction, if any.

Prior to the amendment, Enforcement Ordinance 22-10 also included a requirement for taxpayers to submit a Schedule 17(4) (previously 17(3), until fiscal years ending before April 1, 2009) with their Japanese corporate tax returns, which requires disclosure of information regarding transactions with foreign affiliates. This has not been changed. The information required by 17(4) includes the following:
- Information about the foreign affiliates
- Name, main address, number of employees, sales, operating income
- Information about transactions with the foreign affiliates
- Amounts and Transfer Pricing Methodologies (TPMs) applied to calculate the sales/purchase amounts,

---
[1] Enforcement Ordinance is an order by the Ministry which has the same effectiveness as the STML.

- service fees, royalties, and interest paid and/or received
- APA Status

Although there is no penalty for not submitting Schedule 17(4), failure to submit it may trigger an audit. Also, as Schedule 17(4) requires taxpayers to disclose the TPMs applied, it would be difficult for taxpayers to fill in 17(4) without preparing documentation. Once an audit has begun, a taxpayer would be asked to submit detailed information on its foreign affiliates and the transfer price of transactions listed in amended Enforcement Ordinance 22-10. The amendment moving the list of documentation from the TP Guidelines to tax law (by way of the Enforcement Ordinance) may enable the tax authority to conduct deemed assessments more easily than before when taxpayers cannot provide the information timely.

Transfer Pricing Guidelines and Case Studies

On June 1, 2001, the NTA released the "Commissioner's Directive on the Operation of Transfer Pricing (Administrative Guidelines)"; the so-called TP Guidelines. Although they are administrative guidelines for the use of the tax authorities' TP examiners, they are closely watched by practitioners and taxpayers in Japan. These guidelines have been revised almost every year since their issuance, and have become more detailed to include the following topics:
- Definitions and basic policies
- Examination procedures
- Points to note in calculating arm's length prices
- Treatment of foreign transferred income
- Advance pricing agreements (APAs)

Also, the NTA released "Case Studies for Application of the Transfer Pricing Rules" for the first time in 2007. This includes cases regarding selection of TPMs, intangible property transactions, service transactions, APAs and points to be noted when applying the profit split method.

Audits and Enforcement

Transfer pricing audits are conducted by specialist tax auditors in the Pricing Divisions of the Regional Taxation Bureaus (RTB auditors) and are reported ultimately to the NTA Director (International Examinations).

The audit team usually consists of two or more examiners and typically takes one to two years to complete an audit. Auditors generally request extensive information on foreign affiliates during the audits. As they only have direct authority to demand information on domestic (Japanese) taxpayers and not on foreign affiliates, some discretion exists about whether and to what extent to respond to a request by the auditors for information on foreign affiliates. Japanese auditors were notorious for using secret comparables in their audits and have been criticized not only by other countries but also by Japanese companies in the past. They do not frequently use secret comparables today, except in a case in which a taxpayer is not cooperating with an audit.

Although the points taxpayers should bear in mind during the audit process differ depending on the industry, transaction, function, profitability and other factors, two recent trends in the NTA's focus can be identified:
1) Interest, Service fees, Royalties—Transactional Methods (CUP, RP, CP) are often applied. Although the amount in most cases may not be significant, they are often targeted.

2) Profit Allocation Ratio Among Parties in a Group— Foreign related parties with high Berry Ratios (GP/SGA). Japanese parties that are unprofitable, while their foreign related parties are making profits at the operating profit level.

Regarding the methods applied during an audit, the NTA has tended to prefer RPSM. However, this may change, as in some cases the NTA has failed to reach agreement with the tax authorities of counterparty countries in Mutual Agreement Procedures (MAPs) in cases in which they based their assessments on RPSM.

The NTA announced in November 2009 that the number of assessment cases in fiscal year 2008 (ending June 2009) decreased to 111 cases from the previous year's 133 cases. Also, the total assessed amount decreased to 27 billion yen from the previous year's 169.6 billion yen. This sharp decline in both the number of assessment cases and the total assessed amount may reflect the severity of the economic recession in Japan. However, considering that both the number of cases and the total amount had increased by 131.7% and 161.3% respectively in fiscal year 2007 (ending June 2008), it is likely that the NTA will start conducting tough audits again.

Domestic Appeal Options and Procedures

When an assessment is made in a transfer pricing audit, the taxpayer may either choose a domestic appeal (to the tax authority and to the court) or an MAP in cases in which the transaction was conducted with countries that have double taxation treaties with Japan (to resolve

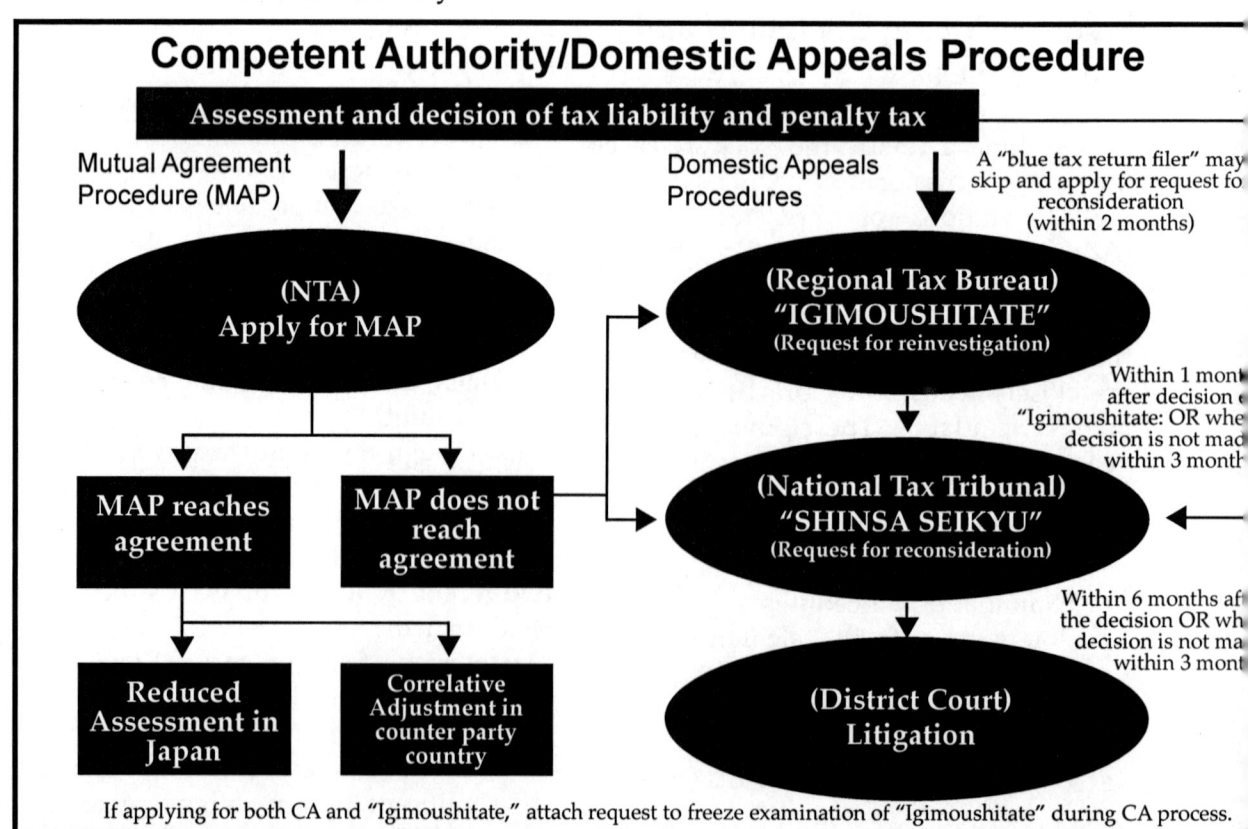

Competent Authority/Domestic Appeals Procedure

Assessment and decision of tax liability and penalty tax

Mutual Agreement Procedure (MAP) → (NTA) Apply for MAP
- MAP reaches agreement → Reduced Assessment in Japan
- MAP does not reach agreement → Correlative Adjustment in counter party country; also → (National Tax Tribunal) "SHINSA SEIKYU" (Request for reconsideration)

Domestic Appeals Procedures → (Regional Tax Bureau) "IGIMOUSHITATE" (Request for reinvestigation) → (National Tax Tribunal) "SHINSA SEIKYU" (Request for reconsideration) → (District Court) Litigation

A "blue tax return filer" may skip and apply for request for reconsideration (within 2 months)

Within 1 month after decision of "Igimoushitate: OR when decision is not made within 3 month"

Within 6 months after the decision OR when decision is not made within 3 month

If applying for both CA and "Igimoushitate," attach request to freeze examination of "Igimoushitate" during CA process.

double taxation). These processes are illustrated in the accompanying diagram, "Competent Authority/Domestic Appeals Procedure."

The three domestic appeals procedures are: 1) Request for Reinvestigation by the Regional Tax Bureau, 2) Request for Reconsideration by the National Tax Tribunal, and 3) Lawsuit in District Court.

1) Request for Reinvestigation (by Regional Tax Bureau)

A taxpayer may file a request for reinvestigation with the Regional Tax Bureau (or District Tax Office in small cases) within two months from the date of the assessment notice. However, the chances are low that the assessment will be changed at this stage. A "blue tax return filer" (a taxpayer who maintains certain books and records) may skip this stage and directly file a request for reconsideration with the National Tax Tribunal as the first step.

2) Request for Reconsideration (by the National Tax Tribunal)

Within three months after receiving a notice of denial from the Regional Tax Bureau, or if the Regional Tax Bureau does not rule on the request for reinvestigation within three months (or within two months from the date of the assessment notice when a blue tax return filer skips this stage), the taxpayer may file a request for reconsideration with the National Tax Tribunal (NTT). The NTT is a quasi-judicial organization within the NTA that is separate from the Regional Tax Bureau. This stage usually takes one to three years depending on the complexity of the case.

3) Lawsuit in District Court

Within six months after receiving the NTT's decision to reject, or if the NTT does not rule on the request within three months of the taxpayer's filing, the taxpayer may file a lawsuit in a district court.

Four transfer pricing court cases have so far been reported in Japan. The first transfer pricing case was an ocean going vessel construction case. The issue was whether the prices of ocean going vessels sold by a Japanese ocean going vessel manufacturer to its Panamanian subsidiary fell short of the arm's length standard or not. The taxpayer lost this case in 2007. The second case involved a loan transaction. The point at issue was the interest paid by a Thai subsidiary. The taxpayer also lost in this case.

The third case was the first ever successful transfer pricing appeal brought by a taxpayer in Japan. The Tokyo High Court upheld an appeal brought by a taxpayer represented by Baker & McKenzie Tokyo, the tax authorities did not appeal, and the High Court's decision become final in October 2008. The taxpayer is a wholly owned Japanese subsidiary of a US-based software company. The taxpayer's foreign related companies sold software products to Japanese third party distributors, and the taxpayer provided certain marketing, training and support services for the benefit of these foreign related companies. The issue was whether the fees for the taxpayer's services fell short of the arm's length standard. In this case, the tax authorities applied a comparable transaction in which similar software products were purchased by a reseller and resold to end users. The court held that the determinative factor in this case was whether the functions performed and risks assumed by the resellers in both the assessed transaction and the comparable transaction were similar enough that the tax authorities could rightfully rely on the selected comparable. The court ruled that it was impossible to ignore the differences in the functions performed by the reseller comparable and the taxpayer, who provided various services to the distributors as required under contractual agreements with the foreign related entities. The court also ruled that the risks assumed are fundamentally different, since the reseller assumed the risk of resale revenues falling below break-even, whereas the taxpayer did not assume such a risk.

The fourth case was an electronic components case in which a Japanese electronic component company sold its products to its Singapore and Hong Kong subsidiaries. This case is still on trial at the High Court.

When a taxpayer considers litigation, careful preparation should be undertaken from the time the audit begins, long before filing a lawsuit, as any discussion or information provided could impact the litigation. Also, it is important to make the points in dispute clear to judges who may not necessarily be very familiar with transfer pricing cases.

Mutual Agreement Procedures (MAPs)

In addition to the avenues for domestic appeal, a taxpayer may opt to seek relief from double taxation with another country with whom Japan has entered into a tax treaty by making use of Mutual Agreement Procedures (MAPS). Japan has entered into 56 tax treaties. The NTA issued the "Commissioner's Directive on Mutual Agreement Procedures" (the so-called MAP guidelines) and has been encouraging taxpayers to utilize the MAP system. The number of MAPs has been growing. The NTA announced in November 2009 that there were 174 cases using MAPs in the

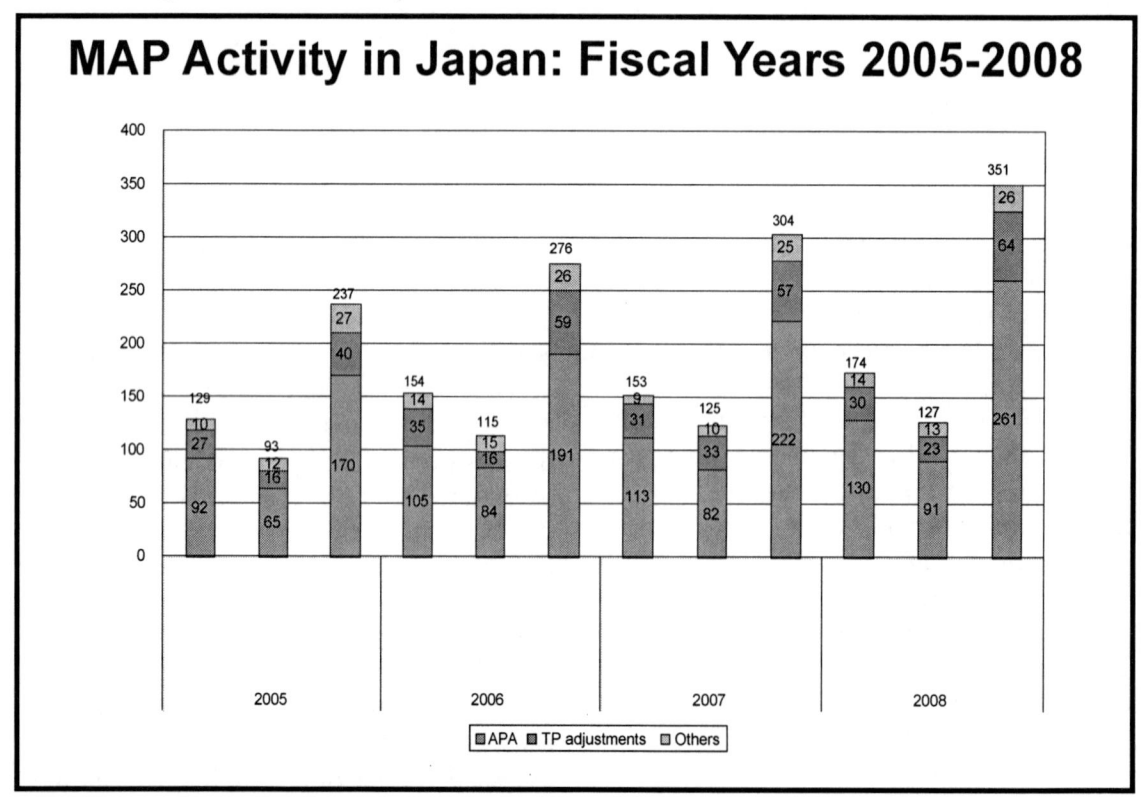

MAP Activity in Japan: Fiscal Years 2005-2008

Year	APA	TP adjustments	Others	Total
2005	92	27	10	129
2005	65	16	12	93
2005	170	40	27	237
2006	105	35	14	154
2006	84	16	15	115
2006	191	59	26	276
2007	113	31	9	153
2007	82	33	10	125
2007	222	57	25	304
2008	130	30	14	174
2008	91	23	13	127
2008	261	64	26	351

fiscal year ending June 2009 (four times the number of 10 years ago) out of which 130 cases dealt with APAs (ten times the number of 10 years ago). However, difficulty remains in conducting MAPs with some countries, such as China.

When a taxpayer intends to apply for an MAP after a transfer pricing assessment in Japan, he or she may request suspension of the payment of taxes until the MAP has been concluded. The accompanying diagram shows the number of the Mutual Agreement Procedures in each of the years 2005 through 2008.[2]

Donation Issue

Transfer pricing issues are sometimes treated as donation issues by the tax authorities. In such a case, a taxpayer may not apply for an MAP as the NTA only accepts MAP applications for international tax issues, and "donation" is treated as a domestic tax issue. However, there have been a few cases in the past in which the NTA has held MAPs to resolve donation issues when the MAP was proposed by the tax authority of the counterparty country. Taxpayers should be aware that resolving donation issues can be much more difficult than resolving transfer pricing issues to relieve double taxation.

APA Program

Japan was the first country in the world to introduce an APA system in 1987. The NTA released the "Guidelines Concerning the Confirmation of the Calculation Method of Arm's Length Prices (the so-called "APA Guidelines") in 1999 and has revised and improved them several times since then. In October 2009, the NTA issued an APA report and announced that 91 APAs were agreed to (64 for manufacturers and 23 for resellers) in the fiscal year ending June 2009. As for the TPM applied, it should be noted that TNMM was applied in 61 cases, CUP in 5 cases, RP in 4 cases, CP in 17 cases and PS in 5 cases the same year. It should be also noted that although there were 18 APAs with the Americas and 5 with Asian Pacific countries in the fiscal year ending June 2002, they increased to 41 and 36 respectively in the fiscal year ending June 2009, showing noticeable improvement in APA negotiations between Japan and other Asian Pacific countries. It is believed that APAs will be an increasingly important tool for resolving controversies in the future.

---

2 The NTA's fiscal year is from July to June (e.g., FY 2008 is the period from July 1, 2008 to June 30, 2009).

Ken Okawara is the Head of Transfer Pricing and Economic Analysis at Baker & McKenzie in Japan. He can be reached by phone at (813) 5157-2965 or by email at **ken.okawara@bakernet.com**. **Satoko Kawamura** and **Yukiko Komori** are economists specializing in transfer pricing and international tax planning with Baker & McKenzie in Japan. Satoko can be reached by phone at **(813) 5157-4304** or by email at **satoko.kawamura@bakernet.com**. Yukiko can be reached by phone at **(813) 5157-2789** or by email at **yukiko.komori@bakernet.com**.

Transfer Pricing in Mexico

Jose Casas Chavelas
KPMG

Background

After joining the Organization for Economic Cooperation and Development (OECD) in 1994, Mexico was required to include transfer pricing rules in its tax legislation. Therefore, a transitory article was included that required companies operating under the "maquila" program to price their related party transactions at arm's length.

The following year, more rules were introduced to provide further guidelines for the maquilas to comply with arm's length transfer pricing requirements, either by obtaining a safe harbor — represented by a taxable profit of at least 5% of the value of total assets used in the maquila program — or by obtaining an APA (Advanced Pricing Agreement), under which the taxpayer and Mexico's tax authorities reached agreement that the transfer pricing of the maquila services were appropriate and complied with the arm's length standard.

Transfer pricing rules for maquiladoras underwent several changes in the following years, of which the main one will be discussed later on.

In 1996, after the impact and growth of tax revenue derived from transfer pricing rules for maquilas, a tax reform act was passed in which Mexico introduced transfer pricing rules for all taxpayers in a general basis. These new rules, which went into effect starting in 1997, are based on the OECD transfer pricing guidelines.

Summary of Transfer Pricing Rules

As of today, the Income Tax Law (ITL) is the law in Mexico that contains the transfer pricing rules. The three transfer pricing obligations of Mexican taxpayers are included in Article 86 of the ITL, with transfer pricing definitions and methodologies appearing in Articles 215 and 216 respectively. Such obligations are the following:

- Section XV requires that all transactions performed with related parties are done in a similar way as if they would have been performed between third parties, applying one of the transfer pricing methodologies contained in Article 216 of the ITL.
- Section XII requires that taxpayers who perform transactions with foreign related parties prepare and maintain documentation supporting that said transactions are valued at arm's length. Such documentation must contain the following:
  - Information about the related parties, including name, domicile for tax purposes, and the relationship between the Mexican taxpayer and its related parties, as defined in Article 215.
  - Information and documentation regarding the related party transactions, including their amounts.
  - For each type of transaction performed with related parties, an analysis of the functions, risks and assets of the taxpayer and its related parties.

- One of the transfer pricing methodologies included in Article 216 of the ITL, including comparables used, applied for each type of transaction performed with related parties.
• Section XIII requires that all taxpayers that perform transactions with foreign related parties present an informative return, along with their tax return.

Taken as a whole, the ITL identifies two particular obligations to fulfill with respect to each related-party transaction with a foreign entity: 1) preparation of supporting documentation and 2) filing an informative return.

When dealing with transactions between Mexican related parties, there is no obligation to prepare supporting documentation, nor to file an informative return. However, there is the obligation to verify that such transactions are priced at arm's length through the application of a transfer pricing methodology.

Starting 2008, a new tax law came into effect in Mexico, the Flat Tax (Ley del Impuesto Empresarial a Tasa Unica, or LIETU). Article 18, section III of the LIETU requires that all transactions performed with related parties, have to be performed at arm's length, and support with one of the transfer pricing methodologies contained in Article 216 of the ITL.

Non-Compliance Penalties

Regarding non-compliance, there is no specific penalty for not preparing supporting documentation. However, failure to provide documentation may result in the tax authorities rejecting the deduction of payments to related parties. The Federal Fiscal Code (FFC) does have specific penalties for failure to file an informative return. In addition to these penalties, which range from $4,000 to $8,500 USD approximately, non-compliance with this filing requirement can also result in the tax authorities may rejecting the deduction of payments to related parties.

It is important to mention that in August 2006, the Courts in Mexico issued a decision, which establishes that if a taxpayer does not have its transfer pricing documentation by the time that the annual tax return is filed, then all transactions incurred with related parties are non-deductible. This ruling was derived from a transfer pricing audit performed by the tax authority several years ago. In said audit, the tax authority established that the taxpayer under review did not prepare transfer pricing documentation as required by the ITL. Therefore, the argument that was used by the tax authority was that the taxpayer did not fulfill with one of the requirements to take a deduction, which is to have, by the time the tax return is filed, all documentation supporting the transaction. The taxpayer decided to take the resolution of the tax authority to court, and the Court found in favor of the tax authorities. This decision and the resolution it upheld give insight as to the date by which the documentation has to be in place, since the ITL is not clear on this aspect.

It is in this manner that — despite the lack of a penalty for not having transfer pricing documentation — failure to prepare said documentation can put at risk the deduction of transactions performed with related parties.

Another issue regarding penalties, is that the FFC grants a reduction of the penalty that may be imposed if the tax authorities establish that a taxpayer underpaid taxes due to transfer pricing. This reduction is granted to taxpayers that prepared transfer pricing documentation. The reduction can be of 50% of the original penalty.

In order to apply the transfer pricing rules established in the ITL, said law establishes that the OECD Transfer Pricing Guidelines can be used for interpretation purposes.

Allowable Methodologies and Best Method Rule

Article 216 of the ITL establishes the transfer pricing methodologies that can be applied in order to test and support the arm's length nature of a transaction between related parties. These methodologies are the following:
- Comparable Uncontrolled Price Method
- Resale Price Method
- Cost Plus Method
- Profit Split Method
- Residual Profit Split Method
- Transactional Operating Profit Margin Method

Until 2005, taxpayers could use any methodology that they considered to be appropriate in order to test and support the arm's length nature of their related party transactions. However, the tax authorities decided that the Transactional Operating Profit Margin was being used indiscriminately. Therefore, as of 2006, Mexico incorporated in its legislation a "best method rule," which establishes that the first methodology to be used when testing and supporting the arm's length nature of a related-party transaction is the Comparable Uncontrolled Price (CUP) Method. Taxpayers who do not use this methodology are required to document why they were not able to apply the CUP Method to a given transaction and their reasons for rejecting it.

Once it is established that the Comparable Uncontrolled Price Method cannot be applied, then taxpayers are allowed to use one of the remaining methodologies, giving preference to the Resale Price Method or the Cost Plus Method.

The description of the methodologies included in the ITL is very similar to the one contained in the OECD Transfer Pricing Guidelines.

Documentation Requirements

As mentioned before, transfer pricing documentation must contain four elements in order to comply with Mexico's requirements: 1) information about the parties, 2) information about the related-party transactions, 3) a functional analysis of the risks, costs, and other economic factors associated with the transactions, and 4) the use of a transfer pricing methodology, including appropriate comparables. In addition to these basic requirements, there are some important considerations to be taken into account when preparing transfer pricing documentation.

First of all, an important aspect to consider is that the ITL is applied on an annual basis, and the fiscal year for Mexican purposes is calendar year. Therefore, documentation has to be prepared for each calendar year. Documentation prepared for the fiscal year of the parent company that does not match the calendar year will very likely be rejected by the tax authorities in an audit. Also, documentation must be prepared each year. It is not possible to use documentation prepared for a prior year to support transactions for the current year, since the former supports only the transactions of the year for which it was prepared.

It is also important to mention that each taxpayer must have its own supporting documentation. It is not permissible to use the documentation prepared for another taxpayer, even though that documentation may contain the transaction which is being tested. The tax authorities have been rejecting this type of documentation under the argument that it corresponds to a different taxpayer from the one that is being audited.

In some cases, taxpayers in Mexico have presented as their transfer pricing documentation the transfer pricing report prepared for their parent company or for head office. Special care should be taken in this situation, as this kind of documentation may be rejected by the Mexican tax authorities for one or more reasons.

In first instance, as mentioned before, said documentation does not correspond to the Mexican entity. Even though it may contain information on the intercompany transactions being performed by the Mexican entity and the use of a transfer pricing methodology to support them, if it corresponds to a foreign entity, it will very likely be rejected by the tax authorities.

Another issue to consider is whether it is prudent to provide the Mexican tax authorities with documentation that contains information on the parent company and its related parties worldwide.

As a result, there are few shortcuts to compliance with Mexico's requirement that taxpayers must prepare documentation every year supporting that the intercompany transactions performed in said year, comply with the arm's length principle.

Maquiladoras

Maquiladoras or "maquilas" are mainly contract manufacturers located in Mexico that belong to a multinational group. Their distinguishing characteristic is that they obtain a registration from the Mexican government to operate under the "maquila program." Under this program, they may import inventory, machinery, and equipment on a temporary basis and are therefore not required to paid duties or value added tax when importing or exporting said items. These were the first type of taxpayers that were required by the ITL to comply with transfer pricing, starting in fiscal year 1995.

In the beginning, maquilas had two options to comply with transfer pricing: obtain a Safe Harbour, representing a taxable profit for an amount of at least 5% of the total assets used in the contract manufacturing services, or obtain an Advanced Pricing Agreement.

Based on the business model of the maquilas, they may be considered to trigger a permanent establishment in Mexico for the foreign entity to which they provide services if the machinery and equipment used to transform the inventories, is owned by a foreign resident. However, the ITL establishes that there will be no permanent establishment if the foreign entity resides in a country with which Mexico has signed a tax treaty and the maquila complies with the transfer pricing requirements established in the ITL.

Maquilas now have three options by which they may comply with transfer pricing requirements. These options, which are described in Article 216-B of the ITL, are the following:

1) Prepare transfer pricing documentation as required by Article 86-XII of the ITL without taking into consideration the assets used by the maquila, which are owned by the foreign resident. Once said transfer pricing is obtained, an amount equivalent to a 1% of the assets used by the maquila but owned by the foreign related party, has to be added to the trans-

fer price in order to come up with the price at which the maquila must charge the foreign related party for its contract manufacturing services.
2) Obtain a Safe Harbor, which is equivalent to the taxable income representing the higher of 1) 6.9% of the assets used by the maquila, regardless if they are owned by the maquila or by a related party, or 2) 6.5% of the costs and expenses incurred by the maquila to provide its contract manufacturing services.
3) Prepare transfer pricing documentation, as required by Article 86-XII of the MITL, but applying only the Transactional Operating Profit Margin Method and take into consideration when applying said method the assets owned by the foreign related party.

In general, this is the way in which maquilas have to comply with transfer pricing in Mexico. Their transfer pricing regime has been modified every year, granting several relieves in some years, changing the safe harbors in others, among some of the changes. The topic of maquilas may well deserve a complete article on them, but for purposes of this article, we will only take a general look at their regime.

Mexico's Advance Pricing Agreement (APA) Program

Since the beginning of transfer pricing in Mexico more than ten years ago, the tax authorities have been very active in issuing APAs.

Mexico's FFC, allows the taxpayers to request and APA from the tax authorities. The APA can be unilateral, in which Mexico's tax authorities and the taxpayer agree on pricing for specific related-party transactions in advance. If the related-party transactions for which the APA is requested involve a country with which Mexico has in place a tax treaty, then the taxpayer may request a bilateral APA. In this case, Mexico's tax authorities are empowered to negotiate the transfer price of the related party transaction with the tax authorities of the country in which the related party resides. Once the two tax authorities have reached agreement on pricing, then Mexico's tax authority will issue the corresponding APA to the Mexican entity.

Under the FFC, an APA can cover up to five years, specifically the year it is requested, the previous year, and the following three years. If an APA derives from a tax treaty, then the period that the APA can cover, may be of more than five years, depending on the tax treaty.

Taxpayers that want to obtain an APA have to pay an application fee of approximately $600 USD and an additional fee of approximately $100 USD must be paid each additional year that the APA is valid.

As mentioned earlier, when Mexico introduced transfer pricing for maquilas, one of the option for this entities to comply with transfer pricing was to obtain an APA. It is estimated that in the first three years of transfer pricing for maquilas more than 400 APAs were issued.

Currently, since APAs are no longer one of two options for transfer pricing compliance by maquilas, APA activity has declined, but Mexico's tax authorities are still active on this function, mainly for bilateral APAs.

Transfer Pricing and the Statutory Tax Report

In Mexico, companies are required to file a Satutory Tax Report preparaed by a CPA, with the tax authorities, if a milestone is reached either in income, number of employees, or value of the assets. This report is generally due in June of the following year. Said report is mainly a review by the CPA of the tax position of a company. Within said report, the CPA has to mention any tax obligations that were not fulfilled by the taxpayer. Since transfer pricing documentation is an obligation stated in the ITL, failure to prepare it has to be disclosed by the CPA in the Statutory Tax Report.

For 2008, three appendix on transfer pricing, as well as a questionnaire on transfer pricing for the CPA, were added to the Statutory Tax Report. The first appendix requested the segmented financial information related to transactions with related parties. However, due to clarity on how it should be completed, its filing was not mandatory for 2008. The second transfer pricing appendix, requested information pertaining to the related party transactions, including the type of transaction, the amount, as well as with which related party it was performed. Also, the transfer pricing methodology and the result of its application, as well as the proposed adjustment, are required. The third appendix consists of a sort of checklist, asking if the taxpayer has an APA, if it filed its informative return, if it prepared transfer pricing documentation, if it faces thin capitalization, permanent establishment, back-to-back loans, cost allocations, among other tax topics, derived from it intercompany transactions. The transfer pricing questionnaire, needs to be filed by the CPA. In said questionnaire, mostly the same questions as in the appendixes are included, but they are aimed directly at the CPA, asking him if he reviewed specific situations of the intercompany transactions. However, for 2008, the questionnaire was not mandatory.

For 2009, it is very likely that the appendixes and the questionnaire will be required in the Statutory Tax Report.

Transfer Pricing Audits

Even though Mexico's tax authorities have been performing transfer pricing audits for several years, they have become more active in the past three years. As of December, 2009, it is estimated that more than fifty transfer pricing audits are currently taking place.

The first step in an audit is that the independent CPA who performed the statutory tax review is asked to present the workpapers used to perform the review and the transfer pricing documentation prepared by the taxpayer. If he did not disclose in his report that the taxpayer did not prepare transfer pricing documentation and it turns out that there was no documentation in place at the time he filed his report, then the CPA may very likely get a sanction. Once the review of the CPA's papers is concluded, then the tax authorities may perform a direct audit of the taxpayer if they consider that the CPA did not have enough evidence in his workpapers to show that the taxpayer complied with its transfer pricing obligations.

When performing an audit, the tax authorities focus mainly on two aspects. The first one is a tax approach, in which they look for possible non-deductible issues and for lack of withholding taxes in cases where they consider that withholding is required. The second one is a transfer pricing approach, in which they try to establish a transfer pricing adjustment by rejecting comparables, challenging adjustments, or raising other technical issues with the transfer pricing study. However, they can also combine these two approaches in an audit.

There are three areas in which the Mexican tax authorities have focused their transfer pricing enforcement efforts recently. These areas are the following:

- Services— The main focus here is to establish if there really was a service provided and that it is not a cost allocation or a stewardship expense being passed on to the subsidiary. In both cases, the service may be considered non-deductible for tax purposes.
- Technical assistance— Besides the issues mentioned for services, the tax authorities are also looking to establish whether there is know-how involved. If they consider that there is, the technical assistance is considered to be a royalty, subject to withholding tax.
- Loans— Mexico has now a 3 to 1 thin capitalization rule for loans with related parties. Therefore, tax authorities have been looking at loan transactions in which they may deem interest to be treated as dividends.

Litigation and Other Dispute Resolution Options

As of December 2009, there are several cases in court that relate to transfer pricing in Mexico. However, none of them has come to a conclusion, based mainly on the fact that Mexican courts are starting to deal with transfer pricing.

There are two mechanisms available to taxpayers who disagree with the transfer pricing assessments of Mexico's tax authorities. The first is the traditional one, going to tax court. The second option is to seek competent authority relief. This option is available only in cases where a tax treaty is in place between Mexico and the country in which the related party resides. As of December 2009, the author is not aware of any taxpayer seeking competent authority relief from a Mexico transfer pricing assessment.

OECD Review

In 2003, the OECD concluded its review of Mexican transfer pricing legislation and practices, for which review Mexico had volunteered. According to the OECD, Mexico was confronted at that time by two major challenges. The first of these challenges was the extensive use of profit based methodologies and the second was the difficulty of finding comparables for the transfer pricing analysis.

Specifically, the first one refers to the fact that since taxpayers were given the opportunity to select any of the transfer pricing methodologies contained in the ITL, they would very frequently choose the profit-based ones. This situation occurred because taxpayers considered that it was easier to support a profit margin than to apply one of the traditional methods. Mexico has since taken action to address this situation by implementing in 2006 a rule that established that traditional methodologies, such as the Comparable Uncontrolled Price Method have to be used before applying any other methodology.

The second challenge identified by the OECD is still considered an issue in Mexico. Due to the fact that, in practice, comparable transactions or companies must be public ones, that is, that their information is available to the public, and there are very few Mexican companies that meet this requirement. Furthermore, the ones that do are mainly holding companies, which do not disclose the information of their subsidiaries. Therefore, practitioners and taxpayers have to refer to other sources to obtain comparable information. Since Mexico is part of NAFTA, the comparable information that has been used is that of companies that file their information with the Securities and Exchange Commission in the United States. Even though there may be differences of economic circumstances, this information has been the one that the tax authorities have been accepting when performing transfer pricing reviews.

In general, the OECD has indicated that Mexico has been performing well on transfer pricing and considers it to be the leader in Latin America. Mexico has made an effort to be in close contact with the OECD, in order to receive training and feedback, and to be able to share insights on the day-to-day issues of transfer pricing.

Conclusion

Mexico has been very active in transfer pricing. It was the first country in Latin America to get into the transfer pricing arena. Over the past ten years, it has gained a great deal of experience in this area, as evidenced by the fact that each year it amends its transfer pricing legislation to be able to increase control and to make other adjustments. Mexico's tax authorities have demonstrated that they are vigilant in enforcing the country's transfer pricing rules and have made significant adjustments to the deductions and taxable income of companies that fail to comply.

Many other Latin American countries have followed in Mexico's footsteps in developing transfer pricing rules and Mexico's tax authorities have provided training to some of their colleagues at tax authorities elsewhere in the region.

There is still a large group of taxpayers in Mexico that are under the impression that the Mexican tax authorities are still in the first stages of transfer pricing regulation and enforcement, and that they do not have the experience or the capacity to perform an audit. However, recent experience has shown that this is not the case, as there is frequent news of new transfer pricing audits being started and assessments being issued.

Even though Mexico has been active in transfer pricing for a long time, it still has a considerable way to go in order to have a solid transfer pricing regime. Recent successes by the tax authorities at collecting increased taxes through transfer pricing enforcement will likely result in more resources being dedicated to transfer pricing.

With a regulatory environment that is largely consistent with OECD guidelines and increasingly sophisticated enforcement, Mexico's transfer pricing regime has made great strides in recent years and continues to be refined with legislative adjustments each year. Companies doing business in Mexico should take notice of this trend toward serious enforcement of transfer pricing rules and take great care in the preparation of transfer pricing studies and documentation.

Jose Casas Chavelas is the partner in charge of KPMG Mexico's Global Transfer Pricing Services Practice. He has more than ten years of experience in the analysis of intercompany transactions for multinational groups and can be reached at **(52-55) 5246 8364** or by email at **jcasas@kpmg.com**.

For more information on the author, please see Section XIII.

Transfer Pricing: The Dutch Approach

Erik Jan van Sten and Thijs Heijenrath
Deloitte

This article provides for a high level overview and some insights into the approach to transfer pricing by the Dutch Tax Authorities (DTA). This overview begins with a discussion of the history of Dutch transfer pricing regulation, including the Decrees issued by the Dutch Ministry of Finance that deal with transfer pricing issues. To help understand the DTA's vision and approach on transfer pricing, the article also addresses the Advance Pricing Arrangements (APA) practice, tax audits situations, and the position of the DTA in international dispute resolution by way of Mutual Agreement Procedures.

Regulatory Framework

As a consequence of the strongly developing internationalization of the Dutch economy, in 2002 the arm's length principle and documentation requirements were incorporated into the Corporate Income Tax Act (CITA). Supporting article 8b CITA, a number of Decrees were issued that deal with a number of key transfer pricing areas. These Decrees aim to explain how the DTA expect that taxpayers should understand and apply the OECD Transfer Pricing Guidelines (OECD Guidelines) in the Netherlands. Since it was recognised by the Dutch tax authorities that in a number of areas the OECD Guidelines leave room for individual interpretation, the Decrees provide insight into the Dutch position regarding these areas and try to deal with potential uncertainties.

The most important published sources of information in relation to the transfer pricing policy of the DTA are as follows:
- The Transfer Pricing Decree of March 30, 2001 nr. IFZ2001/295;
- Decrees DGB2004/1338M & 1339M provide certain organizational aspects of APAs and other requests;
- Decrees IFZ2004/ 126M & 127M both of August 11, 2004 deal with inter group financing activities
- Decree DGB2004/1337M of August 11, 2004 addresses the "good faith versus treaty partners" policy of the DTA
- Decree IFZ2004/680M of August 21, 2004 provides adjustments and additions to the Transfer Pricing Decree of March 30, 2001, and deals, among other things, with the position of the DTA on certain aspects of intra group services and Cost Contribution Arrangements (CCA).

From the number of Decrees and clarifications on the position of the DTA in certain transfer pricing areas, it becomes clear that the DTA has paid close attention to the issue of transfer pricing, both preceding and following the codification of the arm's length principle in the Netherlands as per January 1, 2002.

Advance Pricing Arrangements

To get a good understanding of the development of transfer pricing in the Netherlands, the current APA practice, which has been in place since 2001, has to be viewed in the context of the ruling practice that it replaced.

The DTA has a longstanding ruling practice. Before 2001, the 'old' ruling practice already was characterised by its approachable, transparent and centralized character. The factual and transfer pricing formats were published and taxpayers could discuss a more tailor made approach with the DTA. An international investors desk (dealing with potential new investors in the Netherlands) was already in place.

Partly as a result of comments and pressure of the EU and OECD, the 'old' ruling practice was converted into the current APA practice in 2001. Along with this development, the arm's length principle was formally codified in the Dutch corporate income tax law and transfer pricing documentation requirements were introduced.

As under the old ruling practice, under the current APA practice the DTA provides a Dutch taxpayer (for instance, a part of a foreign-based multinational enterprise) certainty in advance on its Dutch corporate income tax position. The key focus of the newly introduced APA practice was to be compliant with the OECD transfer pricing guidelines and to guarantee a level playing field for all existing taxpayers as well as new investors into the Netherlands. However, the open and approachable character of the DTA and the APA practice remained, with the possibility of arranging pre-filing meetings and to agree on case management plans.

Transfer Pricing Audit Practice

The open, transparent and professional approach of the DTA can also be seen in transfer pricing audits up to and including mutual agreement procedures. The DTA has a group of transfer pricing specialists, which was officially formed in 1998 and is generally involved in all transfer pricing audits.

In the 90's the DTA started an industry audit program that first concentrated on the automotive industry. After that, the DTA targeted pharmaceutical companies and currently is focussing on other areas such as permanent establishments of multinationals.

In addition to its focus on these subject issues, the DTA audit program is based on a risk assessment policy. This implies that based on certain criteria, taxpayers are selected for a field audit. Transfer pricing has become one of the key selection criteria. In order to be able to handle the selected cases on a high professional level and to ensure that the cases are handled OECD compliant the DTA invested and still invests in the education of the professionals of the tax administration in the field of transfer pricing.

The above mentioned documentation requirements, which have been in force from 2002 onwards, can be seen in this perspective. Even though there is no direct penalty for not meeting the transfer pricing documentation requirements, the DTA will give taxpayers only a limited period of time to meet these requirements once, for instance during a tax audit, this is detected. When the taxpayer still cannot meet the requirement within the limited period given, depending on the specifics of the case itself, additional assessments can be imposed. Along with such additional assessments, the lack of documentation can shift the burden of proof on the incorrectness of such assessment in the court to the taxpayer.

Although in general the DTA has a forward looking approach in solving transfer pricing controversies, the DTA is not hesitant to impose severe adjustments and penalties in cases where a transfer pricing policy has lead to an unacceptable erosion and/or underreporting of the taxable base of taxable income in the Netherlands.

International Dispute Resolution

The Netherlands is one of the countries that strongly endeavors to resolve international double taxation resulting from transfer pricing adjustments and to reduce the accompanying (administrative) burden for the business community as much as possible. As a result, the Netherlands built up a strong tax treaty network, comprising of tax treaties that include a provision for mutual agreement procedures (hereafter 'MAP'). Since the outcome of transfer pricing cases in a tax audit or court procedure are very difficult to predict, there is a trend toward solving transfer pricing cases by a MAP, and within the European Union, by the arbitration procedure. While many countries were still discussing the need of arbitration procedures in bilateral tax treaties, most of the treaties the Netherlands has entered into over the last years already allowed for the possibility to enter into an arbitration procedure. Due to its open-minded and pro-active approach, the Netherlands has gained much experience in this area and has solved already many transfer pricing cases through the MAP.

MAP and arbitration cases are handled by a special department of the Ministry of Finance, the competent authority of the Netherlands for MAPs. This department handles these cases in close cooperation with the DTA with specific members of the Dutch transfer pricing coordination group and the APA team.

Conclusion

Transfer pricing is an important issue in the Netherlands. The DTA has professional transfer pricing specialists who are involved in the selection and handling of the cases and in the APA process. It is crucial for taxpayers to be well prepared and have a thorough approach, including up to date transfer pricing documentation, when applying for an APA, or when a tax audit is at hand.

Erik Jan van Sten is a manager in the Transfer Pricing / Tax Aligned Supply Chain team of Deloitte in the Netherlands. He can be reached by phone at **(31-10) 880 1051** or by email at **EvanSten@deloitte.nl**.

Thijs Heijenrath is the service line leader of the Transfer Pricing / Tax Aligned Supply Chain team of Deloitte in the Netherlands. This Dutch team is part of the European and Global Transfer Pricing Group of Deloitte. He can be reached by phone at **(31-10) 880 1059** or by email at **theijenrath@deloitte.nl**.

For more information on the authors, please see Section XIII.

Transfer Pricing in Norway

Svein G. Andresen and Marius Basteviken
KPMG

In June 2007, the Norwegian Parliament adopted transfer pricing documentation rules. Under these rules, taxpayers must submit transfer pricing documentation within 45 days after a request is made from the tax authorities. The documentation requirements were effective as of January 1, 2008. In addition, many taxpayers must file an annual summary statement of all inter-company transactions as an attachment to their tax return with effect from the income year 2007.

The Norwegian Parliament adopted the transfer pricing documentation rules on June 29, 2007. The new rules enable the tax authorities to request more detailed information regarding controlled transactions. Transactions with or between permanent establishments are also covered by the new rules. Furthermore, the rules are meant to be non-discriminatory with reference to Norway's European Economic Area (EEA) obligations. As a result, domestic transactions and cross-border transactions with companies in other EEA countries are treated equally with respect to the burden of proof from a Norwegian perspective.

The transfer pricing documentation rules clarify and update some of the transfer pricing provisions of the General Tax Act 1999 section 13-1 and the Tax Assessment Act, which have formed the basis for transfer pricing requirements in Norway. While the new rules were introduced with the intention merely to formalize and to clarify existing requirements for the preparation and presentation of transfer pricing documentation, several of the provisions of the new rules appear to place increased burdens on companies involved in related-party transactions in Norway.

The new legislation imposed two new disclosure requirements: a filing requirement and a documentation requirement.

Filing Requirements

Taxpayers with a threshold level of related-party transactions in Norway are required to submit an annual filing statement, in accordance with a form prepared by the Directorate of Taxes. The annual summary statement is meant to provide an overview of the type and amount of controlled transactions and outstanding accounts conducted by that entity during the tax year in question. Originally, the filing of the form was not meant to be an extra burden on the taxpayer and detailed estimates were not going to be required at this stage. However, the form that is currently in place is more onerous and detail-oriented than first envisaged. In particular, the fine-grained categories relating to different types of transactions require focus and effort from taxpayers beyond the initial signals from the Ministry of Finance. Furthermore, some industries have experienced challenges in categorising its controlled transactions in accordance with the categories presented in the form.

The threshold to trigger the filing requirement has been set at NOK 10 million for total controlled transactions and NOK 25 million for total intra-group loans. If the

Norwegian taxpayer exceeds one of these limits, the company is bound by the filing requirements.

The open-ended nature of the time frame for possible tax audit under the rules has caused concern among some tax directors at multinational enterprises (MNE) with operations in Norway. In our opinion, a two-year limitation for opening a tax investigation should apply in cases where the taxpayer has filed a correct form and especially if this is done together with an appendix describing the actual facts and circumstances.

Based on information received in the form the Norwegian tax authorities will select subjects for a closer inspection of accounts. It is therefore reasonable to assume that a number of Norwegian companies will be subject to an inspection of accounts as a consequence of the new filing requirements effective as of 2007. In particular, it is reasonable to assume that companies which disclose transactions with companies based in tax havens (category D transactions according to the form RF-1123) will be targeted by the Norwegian tax authorities. The same will probably apply to Norwegian companies with extensive outbound or inbound transactions of intangibles.

Documentation Requirements

The documentation requirements are more onerous than the filing requirements and include companies and branches that are part of a larger group.[1] The scope and category of the documentation required varies according to the type of transaction, complexity and size. Nevertheless, the Government points out that some aspects are common for all transfer pricing inspections and that the Norwegian tax authorities will expect the following elements to be included in the documentation:

- Description of organisation, business and activities
- Description of type and scope of controlled transactions
- Functional analysis
- Comparability analysis
- An account of, and reasons for, choice of transfer pricing method

The Norwegian transfer pricing documentation rules are, to a large degree, based on the Danish transfer pricing rules. In addition, documentation prepared in accordance with European Union Transfer Pricing Documentation approach (EU TPD) will be accepted by the Norwegian tax authorities.

In addition, Directorate of Taxes has prepared transfer pricing guidelines that offer some information regarding the expectations that the Norwegian tax authorities will have with respect to the scope of the documentation. They have also published detailed guidelines in connection with database searches for selecting comparables as part of a transfer pricing analysis.

These guidelines contain certain special provisions of great interest. First, the guidelines require that transactions relating to intangibles be described in more detail than many other national guidelines require. Secondly, financial information for the last three years from all transacting parties must be included – with turnover and EBIT as a minimum requirement. Finally, the guidelines in connection with

---

[1] Small- and medium-sized corporations are exempt from the documentation requirements. Small- and medium sized corporations are defined as companies which, together with closely-held subsidiary companies and affiliates, have fewer than 250 employees and either has turnover under NOK 400 million or a balance of less than NOK 350 million.

database searches contain requirements which, in our opinion, make compliance difficult. In fact, the comparability requirements are so stringent, the result of a comparables company search that follows these guidelines meticulously is most likely to contain no comparable companies at all in the final set.

Favored Methodologies

The Norwegian tax authorities are, in general, sceptical of the transactional net margin method (hereafter TNMM). The strict database search requirements, as mentioned above, are examples of scepticism when facing net margin methods[2]. Nevertheless, the profit split method appears to be attractive to the tax authorities when facing inbound controlled transactions – even in situations where the Norwegian taxpayer is a low-risk commissionaire.

Therefore, although Norway has not introduced a "best method" approach, it is clearly advisable that the taxpayer explain why the applied method is considered the most appropriate. OECD has currently issued a proposed revision of Chapters I-III of the Transfer Pricing Guidelines and we expect the Norwegian tax authorities to apply the final version of said guidelines. It is therefore likely that a "best method" approach will be used in the future.

Timetables and Deadlines

The taxpayer is allowed a period of 45 days from the date the tax authorities has requested disclosure of documents. The documentation has to be in writing and may be in Norwegian, Danish, Swedish or English. In addition, the documentation has to be kept for a minimum of ten years and there will be a lot of documents and financial information relating to the transacting parties to keep it accessible upon request. The documentation requirements came into force as of the fiscal year 2008.

No APA Program at Present

Currently, advance pricing arrangements (APAs) are not available in Norway, except for taxpayers covered by the Petroleum Tax Act. This includes unilateral, bilateral, and multilateral APAs, none of which are possible as the Norwegian tax authorities have yet to establish a system to deal with APAs. However, implementation of more formal documentation requirements will likely lead to the development of an APA program in Norway. While multilateral APAs are not yet available to resolve potential double-taxation issues in advance, some companies in Norway have taken advantage of the Mutual Agreement Procedure (MAP) under Norway's treaty obligations to resolve such issues after the fact.

Sanctions

The Government has decided that the basic penalty for misrepresentation in connection with transfer pricing continues to be estimated tax assessment and surtax. Thus, the general regulations regarding estimated tax assessment and surtax will prevail when there is a breach of the filing and documentation requirements. Moreover, the Ministry of Finance has stated that the threshold for an estimated tax assessment will be lowered at the implementation of the aforementioned set of rules.

If the taxpayer fails to submit the

---

2   Both in respect of tax audits and articles they have argued that TNMM is a form of targeting that is not in accordance with the arm's length principle.

requested documentation, the tax authorities may estimate the taxpayer's tax liability, in practice on a discretionary basis. Similarly, if documentation is not submitted as requested, the tax authorities may reject any appeals. Whether the taxpayer then can bring the case for court is rather uncertain and unlikely in our opinion.

Svein G. Andresen, a tax partner with KPMG, has extensive within the banking, insurance, shipping, oil service and processing industries. He can be reached at **(47-40) 63 90 22** or by email at **svein.andresen@kpmg.no**.

Marius Basteviken assists several multinational companies with their transfer pricing compliance work in Norway. He can be reached at **(47-40) 63 90 32** or by email at **marius.basteviken@kpmg.no**.

For more information on the authors, please see Section XIII.

Singapore Transfer Pricing Requirements

Geoffrey Soh
KPMG

Since the introduction of the transfer pricing guidance in 2006, Singapore has been increasing its focus on transfer pricing. Additional circulars have been released by with the aim of fostering taxpayers' transfer pricing awareness and compliance. Several steps have been taken to monitor the level of transfer pricing compliance, including sending questionnaires to, and conducting in-depth reviews and field visits with selected taxpayers with sizeable related-party transactions or with recurring losses for no apparent reasons.

The developments in transfer pricing over the last two years reiterate Singapore's strong adoption of the arm's-length principle and its need for taxpayers to perform rigorous transfer pricing analysis for their significant or complex related-party transactions. However, considering the large number of multinationals that have their regional headquarters and support centers based in Singapore, Singapore is likely to take a pragmatic approach and may be willing to concede to certain flexibilities to facilitate compliance.

Background

In February 2006, the Inland Revenue Authority of Singapore (IRAS) released the IRAS Circular: Transfer Pricing Guidelines (Main Circular) with detailed guidance on, and documentation requirements for, transfer pricing and Advance Pricing Arrangements (APAs). The guidance in the Main Circular is applicable to all transactions, both local and cross border, between a Singapore taxpayer and its related parties (be it a legal entity or permanent establishment). The guidance on Mutual Agreement Procedures (MAPs) and APAs is only applicable to related-party transactions where the transacting entity is resident in a jurisdiction which has a comprehensive double tax agreement with Singapore.

"Reasonable Efforts" Required

Like its counterparts in most countries, IRAS endorses the arm's-length principle as the standard to guide transfer pricing. This is supported by Section 34(D) of the Singapore Income Tax Act (SITA), effective from the year of assessment 2010, addressing transactions not at arm's length. IRAS is of the opinion that taxpayers should exert reasonable efforts to undertake a sound transfer pricing analysis, to ascertain an arm's-length price, as well as to demonstrate that such analysis has been performed. When reasonable efforts have been exercised, the transfer prices are considered, prima facie, as arm's-length. Accordingly, the burden of proof then resides with IRAS to show that the documented prices are not compliant with the arm's-length standard

Documentation Requirements

Adequate and timely documentation help to demonstrate a reasonable effort. Indeed, IRAS warns that scant documentation of significant transactions may result in transfer pricing reviews and challenges.

Annex G to the Main Circular provides a non-exhaustive list of items that taxpayers should include in their documentation to demonstrate that reasonable efforts have been expended in determining arm's-length transfer prices. Depending on the type and significance of the transaction involved, these items may include:
- details on the product(s) transferred;
- information on the transacting parties and their finances;
- discussion of the functions performed, risks undertaken, and assets used by each related party;
- the rationale for the chosen transfer pricing method and tested party;
- information on transactions between and/or with third parties or comparables chosen; and
- identification of an arm's-length price range.

Enforcement Climate

Since the introduction of the Main Circular, IRAS has been gradually increasing its focus on transfer pricing. A second circular, Transfer Pricing Consultation Circular (Consultation Circular), was released by IRAS in July 2008, with the aim of fostering taxpayers' transfer pricing awareness and compliance. The initiative also seeks to identify areas in which IRAS may further assist and advise taxpayers on good transfer pricing practices.

IRAS has started to monitor the level of transfer pricing compliance by adopting several steps, including:
- sending questionnaires to selected taxpayers with sizeable related-party transactions or with recurring losses for no apparent reasons;
- assessing if a transfer pricing consultation is warranted; and
- providing the taxpayer with its opinions on the adequacy and timeliness of the taxpayer's documentation.

If the taxpayer's transfer pricing deviates significantly from IRAS' opinion of arm's-length pricing, IRAS may make arrangements with the taxpayer to review the issue further. In 2009, a number of questionnaires were sent, and based on the responses received, some companies were selected for in-depth reviews and field visits.

APA Program Formalized

In response to the increasing interest by Singapore taxpayers in APAs IRAS released additional transfer pricing guidance in the form of a circular providing administrative guidance on APAs in October 2008. The guidance provides a formal framework to facilitate the application and consideration of APA requests, and specifically highlights the commitment needed from taxpayers in relation to an APA request.

e-Tax Guide Issued

In February 2009, IRAS finalized transfer pricing guidance for related-party loans and related-party services (e-Tax Guide). In this supplementary e-Tax Guide, IRAS reaffirms its endorsement of the arm's-length principle to determine transfer prices, but recognizes that embarking on a comprehensive transfer pricing analysis to demonstrate compliance may not always be practical or administratively expedient. Accordingly, as stated in the e-Tax Guide, IRAS will allow taxpayers some flexibility to vary from the arm's-length principle under certain circumstances, in order to facilitate compliance.

Intra-Group Loans

Currently, it is common practice for loans made by a domestic entity (that is, a business that is incorporated or registered in Singapore and carrying on a business in Singapore) to another related domestic entity to be interest-free or with an interest charge that is not supported by a transfer pricing analysis. In the past, IRAS has acquiesced to this practice, provided that the domestic lender did not claim a tax deduction for interest costs, should the funds be ultimately sourced from a commercial lender.

Per the e-Tax Guide, IRAS is prepared to allow the current practice to continue for loans between two domestic entities, as long as the domestic lender is not in the business of borrowing and lending (e.g. not a financial institution or a finance and treasury center). IRAS will also extend this concession to existing loans between domestic lenders and related offshore borrowers until January 1, 2011. From that date onwards, all cross-border loan arrangements will need to reflect arm's-length conditions. IRAS is of the opinion that the Comparable Uncontrolled Price ("CUP") Method is the preferred method to establish the arm's-length interest for related-party loans.

Intra-Group Services

The e-Tax Guide also provides specific guidance on intra-group services. Some of this guidance has strong parallels to that of the OECD Guidelines – especially for concepts such as willingness-to-pay, benefits received, direct and indirect charging, allocation keys and rationale thereof. The e-Tax Guide also suggests that the CUP Method and Cost Plus Method are often the most appropriate methods for determining the arm's-length fee for related-party services.

The above notwithstanding, for entities that provide certain routine support services only to related parties, IRAS is prepared to accept an amount equivalent to all service costs plus a safe harbor mark-up of five percent as "a reasonable arm's-length charge for such services". Annex A of the e-Tax Guide provides a list of services considered as routine. These include accounting, computer support, legal, staffing, and training. Although the list will be reviewed and possibly modified from time to time, the e-Tax Guide specifies that only those services currently listed in Annex A will be accepted as routine support services. The e-Tax Guide rounds off the discussion on intra-group services by highlighting that if there is a detailed transfer pricing analysis that supports a mark-up other than the prescribed five percent, this alternative mark-up quantum could be adopted and applied consistently. Furthermore, this mark-up should be regularly reviewed to ensure it continues to reflect arm's-length conditions.

Cost Pooling

Cost pooling refers to the situation where related parties enter into an arrangement to centralize the provision of routine support services and share the associated costs accordingly. Provided certain conditions are met, IRAS may allow taxpayers not to incorporate a mark-up element in the amounts charged from a centralized service provider to a related cost pooling party. The main conditions that must be fulfilled are as follows:

- the services are not also provided to unrelated parties;
- the provision of services does not constitute the principal activity of the service provider;
- the services must be limited to the

routine support services listed in Annex A of the e-Tax Guide (with respect to this, IRAS specifies that this zero mark-up concession will not extend to cost contribution arrangements for the development of intangibles); and
- there must be sufficient documentation supporting the intent to pool resources between the parties involved, prior to the provision of any services.

Penalties

Singapore does not have penalties specifically for transfer pricing. However, IRAS has the legislated power to impose penalties from 100 percent of the tax undercharged (for an incorrect return) to 400 percent of the tax undercharged (for serious fraudulent tax evasion). In the event of insufficient or lack of documentation, IRAS may invoke Section 65, 65A, and 65B of the SITA and thereafter enforce penalties for violation of these provisions.

Outlook: More Focus on Related-Party Transactions

With the release of transfer pricing guidance in Singapore, IRAS has been increasing its focus on related-party arrangements and prices in their tax audits. This is likely due to the fact that many of Singapore's trading partners have toughened their transfer pricing requirements significantly over the past decade. Such developments have caused taxpayers with cross-border transactions to err on the side of caution – by imputing more income into countries with stricter transfer pricing requirements and penalties. Going forward, it is possible that IRAS may focus on cross-border intra-group loans, especially after the expiration of the grace period on January 1, 2011.

Geoffrey Soh is Head of Transfer Pricing in KPMG Singapore. He can be reached by phone at **+65 6213 3035** or by email at **geoffreysoh@kpmg.com.sg**. For more information on the author, please see Section XIII.

UK Tax Authorities Plan Stricter Enforcement of Transfer Pricing Rules: What will these Changes Mean for International Companies?

Ted Keen
The Ballentine Barbera Group, A CRA International Company

The UK's current transfer pricing legislation dates back to the Finance Act of 1998 and coincides with the introduction of Corporate Tax Self Assessment (CTSA) in the UK.[1] Under CTSA, all UK tax-paying companies are expected to self-assess in accordance with the arm's length principle, as set out in the "OECD Guidelines on Transfer Pricing."[2] UK corporate taxpayers must be able to provide evidence to Her Majesty's Revenue and Customs (HMRC, the UK tax authority) that their transactions with related parties adhere to the arm's length principle within 30 days of any request from HMRC's inspectors. In determining the taxpayer's adherence to the arm's length principle, HMRC policy is to follow the OECD's preference for traditional transactional methods over profit based methods. HMRC has an active APA programme and encourages taxpayers with particularly complex and valuable related party transactions to use the APA programme. In these respects the UK's transfer pricing regime is similar to that of many European countries.

While UK's transfer pricing regulations seem as strict as those of most other major European nations, there has been some question as to whether HMRC is enforcing these regulations aggressively enough. Specifically, HMRC has come under fire in recent years for permitting large multinationals doing business in the UK to use tax planning strategies including transfer pricing to shift income out of the UK and thus pay little or no UK corporate income tax.[3] As a consequence, HMRC introduced tough anti-avoidance provisions "which were perceived as creating a climate of heavy compliance costs, uncertainty and to some extent a breakdown in trust."[4] This focus on avoidance has drawn criticism from the UK business community. A survey conducted by the Confederation of British Industry (CBI) published in November 2006 indicated that, despite a steady reduction in the UK corporate tax rate from 33% to 30%, "Seven in ten business leaders believe the UK is a poorer international business location than in 2001, and three-quarters say the corporate tax regime is worse."[5]

---

1 CTSA applies to all accounting periods ending on or after 1 July 1999.
2 "Transfer Pricing Guidelines for Multinational Enterprises and Tax Administrations," issued by the OECD, 1995.
3 See, for example, the opening paragraphs in "Moving Beyond Avoidance? Tax Risk and the Relationship between Large Business and HMRC: Report of a Preliminary Survey," Judith Freedman, Geoffrey Loomer, and John Vella, Oxford University Centre for Business Taxation, June 2007.
4 Ibid.
5 CBI News release,
http://www.cbi.org.uk/ndbs/press.nsf/0363c1f07c6ca12a8025671c00381cc7/5373a784a195669b8025722c00369200?OpenDocument

Mindful of the dissatisfaction with their performance from both camps, HMRC has embarked on an approach to enforcement that tries to strike a balance between reducing the tax gap (i.e. the amount of tax that HMRC would have collected but for tax planning, avoidance and evasion) while maintaining an attractive business environment in the UK for multinationals.

Central to HMRC's strategy is a consultative approach with large business, set out in the Varney report.[6] The report sets out several goals, among them that of establishing "an efficient risk-based approach to dealing with tax matters."[7] The idea is to allow HMRC to use its resources more effectively by focusing on issues of greatest concern and of greatest impact on the tax gap, both in terms of amount of tax at stake and of the value of the precedent these issues represent. The report also recognizes the need to provide taxpayers with greater certainty in complex matters, with "clarity through effective consultation and dialogue," and with a quicker resolution to disputes, particularly in transfer pricing where disputes have been known to last for years.[8]

The Varney report seems to have struck a resonant chord with some corporate taxpayers. One CFO has called the Varney report "a huge step forward for the UK…a major shift in the relationship between HMRC, the treasury and business."[9] But others are not so sure. Hadn't HMRC always taken a risk-based approach to enforcement? It is hard to imagine that HMRC routinely focused their enforcement efforts on taxpayers that could be considered "low risk." Specifically with reference to transfer pricing, it is difficult to imagine that HMRC previously ignored taxpayers with complicated cross-border transactions and with less than transparent compliance practices and focused instead on smaller taxpayers with simpler cross border transactions and with a history of strong compliance practices. Setting aside the question of whether the Varney report represents anything really new, it is hard to condemn the Varney report's vision of an efficient, risk-based approach to enforcement. The question is how would this vision be implemented in practice by a resource-constrained HMRC?

In two March 2007 publications[10] collectively known as the "Varney delivery plan," HMRC attempted to provide the answer. The delivery plan set forth several proposals for implementing the vision articulated in the Varney report, with commitments as to when these proposals would be delivered. The proposals, including the introduction of more advanced rulings, faster resolution of historic issues, an efficient risk-based approach for business taxes, etc., were more statements of intent than specific proposals. Almost all the proposals committed to developing an approach in consultation with business. Transfer pricing was no exception; HMRC committed to:

A comprehensive approach to the settlement of transfer pricing enquiries, based on guidance to be developed with business and published by the end

---

6 HMRC (November 2006) 2006 Review of Links with Large Businesses (hereafter "the Varney Report," so named after HMRC Commissioner David Varney, who commissioned the report).
7 The Varney Report, 1.7, p.5.
8 The Varney Report, 1.7, p.5.
9 John Symonds, CFO AstraZeneca, quoted by Nigel Ash in "Finance Director Europe," 1 January 2007. http://www.the-financedirector.com/features/feature860/
10 "Making a Difference: Delivering the Review of Links with Large Business" and "HMRC Approach to Compliance Risk Management for Large Business." For a more thorough review of these publications, see "Moving Beyond Avoidance?" note 2 supra.

of 2007 so that, subsequently, matters will be settled within 18 months as the norm. This is a significantly shorter timeframe than is currently the case.[11]

As with the other proposals in the delivery plan, any specifics were deferred until after further consultation with business. For transfer pricing these specifics came in HMRC's consultation document on transfer pricing, or the "Condoc" for short.[12] In implementing the vision of the Varney report, the Condoc introduces a new litigation and settlement strategy for transfer pricing, under which HMRC:
- seeks to administer the tax system fairly and efficiently without unnecessary compliance costs for the taxpayer;
- seeks non-confrontational solutions where possible;
- seeks to resolve disputes in a way which best serves the goal of reducing the tax gap;
- takes decisions based on the wider impact of the disputed issue as the amount of tax immediately at stake;
- where there is a strong case, seeks full value from settlement or takes the matter to litigation;
- does not pursue weak arguments;
- uses team-work for cases.[13]

As with the Varney report, it is hard to quarrel with the basic principles outlined in the Condoc. But viewed as a blueprint for implementing change, as HMRC clearly intends it to be, the Condoc contains some striking admissions: did HMRC previously administer the tax system and enforce UK transfer pricing regulations unfairly and inefficiently? Did they impose unnecessary compliance costs upon taxpayers? Did they pursue weak arguments in the past? Was their approach often confrontational? If this was the case, then a break from the past is clearly good news UK taxpayers.

It is important to bear in mind that the Condoc contains no discussion of changing the UK transfer pricing rules, only in how these rules will be enforced. The Condoc reaffirms the primacy of the arm's length principle as the standard to which related party transactions should confirm for UK tax purposes. The Condoc also reiterates the obligation for taxpayers to file a correct self-assessment return; filing a correct return requires that multinational taxpayers have evidence at the time of filing that their transactions with related parties reflect arm's length transfer pricing. This evidence does not need to be presented with the return, nor is there any requirement as to how and in what form that evidence should be documented.[14] Until now the only guidance HMRC has given taxpayers is the cost incurred in assembling evidence of arm's length pricing and recording it in documentation "should be commensurate with the risk involved in arriving at the arm's length result."[15] In other words, a taxpayer should spend more time and money on compiling and documenting evidence of arm's length pricing in a related-party transaction when there is a greater risk of the transfer pricing in that transaction deviating from arm's length pricing. For most taxpayers, that guidance is merely a restatement of the obvious and not really much help. The Condoc recognizes that more guidance from HMRC on how companies should assemble and provide evidence of arm's length transfer pricing is necessary if they are to realize the goal of achieving a more efficient approach to transfer pricing administration.

The Condoc then goes on to consider

---
11 Ibid, Proposal 5, p.9.
12 "HMRC Approach to Transfer Pricing for Large Business," HMRC Consultation Document, 20 June 2007.
13 Ibid 1.6, pp. 5-6.
14 Ibid 1.11, p. 7.
15 Ibid. 1.12 p. 7.

several options for assembling and providing this evidence. Three different approaches are examined: the first one requiring taxpayer submission of all evidence of arm's length pricing at the time of filing; the second recognizing EU transfer pricing documentation as best practice, with submissions required only upon HMRC's request; the third requiring taxpayers to submit with their tax return a standardized form (like form 25-A in Australia, for example) indicating to which transactions the transfer pricing rules apply. HMRC rejected the first option outright, but considered which of the other two approaches would better help it achieve its goal of an efficient risk-based transfer pricing administration and invited interested parties to comment. Several submissions to HMRC expressed disappointment at HMRC's lack of enthusiasm for standardized documentation and cautioned against the UK pursuing a strategy too far out of line with its major trading partners.[16] Moreover, if HMRC elects to require submission of a standardized form on transfer pricing, it is not clear that compliance costs for the taxpayer will be reduced.

The Condoc missed another opportunity to reduce compliance costs in its outright rejection of safe harbours, even though admitting their suitability for low-risk transactions.[17] Dismissing safe harbours for their supposed deviation from arm's length pricing seems overstated, at least for some fairly routine transactions: is there any transfer pricing advisor anywhere who could NOT produce evidence that a cost plus mark-up of 5 percent for administrative services falls within a range established by third party comparables? Once the taxpayer provides evidence of an arm's length cost allocation mechanism, then its scarce budget on transfer pricing compliance, and HMRC's scarce resources, could be better spent focusing on pricing for other transactions than on establishing that a 5 percent mark-up falls within a range of comparables.

Some other elements of the Condoc also have important transfer pricing implications. For example, under the new approach:

> HMRC will devote more specialised resource to transfer pricing, especially for larger businesses. Teams will be set up that will be able to draw on investigators who will tend to specialise in transfer pricing work and who will be able to get to grips with issues quickly and in depth. This will require appropriate training for the investigators involved, including appreciation of general commercial considerations. Where the risks and costs justified it, HMRC will be prepared to buy in expertise from outside.[18]

HMRC has been building expertise on transfer pricing for some time; however, buying in expertise from the outside represents a clear departure from past practice. To the extent that outside experts can help focus HMRC's enquiries and resolve technical issues more quickly, this has to be a positive development for most taxpayers. HMRC's stated willingness to take transfer pricing disputes to litigation[19] also stands out as a clear break from the past: to date not a single transfer pricing matter has been litigated in the UK. It is hard to square this willingness to litigate with a non-confrontational approach, but the

---

16 See for example the "Written Response Submitted on 14 September 2007 by the ICAEW Tax Faculty relating to the Consultation Document issued by HM Revenue & Customs on 20 June 2007.
17 Condoc, 1.58-1.61, pp. 12-13.
18 Ibid., 1.46, p. 11.
19 Ibid., 1.6, p. 6.

current system of negotiated settlement and avoidance of litigation sacrifices potentially valuable legal precedent upon which taxpayers can rely for guidance. A further and perhaps unintended consequence of HMRC's greater willingness to litigate transfer pricing matters may be a shift in the market for transfer pricing advisory services in the UK. HMRC's current preference for negotiated settlements would seem to favour tax advisors from the Big Four accounting firms, many of whom are themselves ex-HMRC and understand HMRC's negotiated settlement process better than anyone. A shift away from negotiated settlements toward litigation would seem to favour law firms with tax litigation specialists, which would bring the UK more in line with the rest of the world. More competition in the market for transfer pricing advisory services can only benefit UK taxpayers.

HMRC already claimed to follow a risk-based approach in deciding where to make enquiries, taxpayers were left wondering what would change? And what were the criteria upon which "risk" would be assessed? Would risk arise from taxpayer's behaviour, or from the nature of the taxpayer's business? Moreover, taxpayers are left wondering what is the benefit of being a low risk taxpayer, and if there is a benefit, how does a taxpayer move from high risk to low risk. It would seem impossible to move from a high risk to a low risk classification if risk assessment were based on structural issues.

Just as with those who resolve to lose weight or to quit smoking, HMRC's resolution to make transfer pricing enquiries faster and more efficient appears to be a genuine effort to make behavioural changes for the better, and in making this resolution, HMRC has garnered a lot of support. But keeping this resolution will require more than just HMRC's collective willpower. How these changes will be measured and made operational will be a huge determinant in how well they are implemented.

CRA International Vice President **Ted Keen** has 16 years of experience consulting on a wide range of economic issues in the United States and in Europe. For the past twelve years he has specialized in developing innovative applications of economic theory to transfer pricing and valuation matters. He an be reached at **44 (0) 20 7664 3671** or by email at **tkeen@crai.com**.

For more information on the author, please see Section XIII.

XI. Supplemental Materials

Supplemental Materials

Rev. Proc. 2006-9

2006-2 I.R.B. ___

Internal Revenue Service (I.R.S.)

Revenue Procedure

Released: December 19, 2005

Published: January 9, 2006

Internal Revenue Code § 482: Allocation of income and deductions among taxpayers

TABLE OF CONTENTS

Section 1: Purpose ....

Section 2: Principles of the APA Program ....

Section 3: Prefiling Conferences ....

Section 4: Content of APA Requests ....

Section 5: Taxpayer Disclosure Obligations..

Section 6: Processing of APA Requests ....

Section 7: Competent Authority Consideration ....

Section 8: Rollback of TPM ....

Section 9: Small Business Taxpayer APAs ....

Section 10: Legal Effect of the APA ....

Supplemental Materials

Section 11: Administering the APA..

Section 12: Renewing the APA ....

Section 13: Disclosure..

Section 14: Effect on Other Documents ....

Section 15: Effective Date ....

Section 16: Paperwork Reduction Act ....

Drafting Information..

Supplemental Materials

SECTION 1:   PURPOSE

.01   This revenue procedure explains the manner in which taxpayers may request an advance pricing agreement ("APA") from the APA Program within the Office of the Associate Chief Counsel (International), the manner in which such a request will be processed by the APA Program, and the effect and administration of APAs. This revenue procedure updates and supersedes Revenue Procedure 2004-40, 2004-2 C.B. 50.

SECTION 2:   PRINCIPLES OF THE APA PROGRAM

.01   The APA Program provides a voluntary process whereby the Internal Revenue Service ("Service") and taxpayers may resolve transfer pricing issues under § 482 of the Internal Revenue Code ("Code"), the Income Tax Regulations ("the regulations") thereunder, and relevant income tax treaties to which the United States is a party in a principled and cooperative manner on a prospective basis. The APA process increases the efficiency of tax administration by encouraging taxpayers to come forward and present to the Service all the facts relevant to a proper transfer pricing analysis and to work towards a mutual agreement in a spirit of openness and cooperation. The prospective nature of APAs lessens the burden of compliance by giving taxpayers greater certainty regarding their transfer pricing methods, and promotes the principled resolution of these issues by allowing for their discussion and resolution in advance before the consequences of such resolution are fully known to taxpayers and the Service.

.02   The APA Program's central goal is the prompt, proper, and fair resolution of APA requests and renewals consistent with the principles of sound tax administration.

.03   The APA Program reserves the right not to accept an APA request or to terminate consideration of an APA request if the request or the continued development of the case is contrary to the principles of sound tax administration.

.04   An APA is an agreement between a taxpayer and the Service in which the parties set forth, in advance of controlled transactions, the best transfer pricing method ("TPM") within the meaning of § 482 of the Code and the regulations. The agreement specifies the controlled transactions or transfers ("covered transactions"), TPM, APA term, operational and compliance provisions, appropriate adjustments, critical assumptions regarding future events, required APA records, and annual reporting responsibilities.

       (1)   APAs are intended to supplement traditional administrative, judicial, and treaty mechanisms for resolving transfer pricing issues.

(2) Taxpayers formally initiate the process for APAs. Thereafter, APAs require discussions among the taxpayer, one or more associated enterprises, and one or more tax administrations, including the Service.

(3) Ordinarily, an APA is reached only on the proposed covered transactions. In some cases, however, the APA Program may require that the scope of the proposed covered transactions be expanded or contracted, or may determine that the TPM proposed by the taxpayer is not appropriate for some subset of the proposed covered transactions.

.05 The taxpayer's participation in the APA process is entirely voluntary. In some cases, the Service may approach a taxpayer to discuss the advantages of an APA.

.06 The APA Program is under the immediate supervision of a Director (the "APA Director") within the Office of the Associate Chief Counsel (International). The APA Director reports to the Associate Chief Counsel (International) who exercises general oversight over the APA Program. The APA Director, directly or by delegation, may take any action – not contrary to statute, regulation, or treaty – necessary to carry out the provisions of this revenue procedure. The APA Director may modify the provisions contained in this revenue procedure (for example, time limits or content of an APA request) if that modification would be consistent with sound tax administration.

.07 Under the APA request procedure, the taxpayer proposes a TPM and provides data intended to show that the TPM constitutes the appropriate application of the best method rule under the § 482 regulations. The Service, through an APA Team, evaluates the APA request by analyzing all relevant data and information submitted with the initial request and at any time thereafter.

.08 Taxpayers may request a bilateral, multilateral, or, if appropriate, a unilateral APA. A bilateral or multilateral APA involves a request for an APA between the taxpayer and the Service, accompanied by a request for a mutual agreement between relevant competent authorities. A unilateral APA involves only an agreement between the taxpayer and the Service. Where possible, in the interest of sound tax administration and to ensure that no potential for double taxation results from an APA, an APA should be concluded on a bilateral or multilateral basis between the competent authorities through the mutual agreement procedure of the relevant income tax treaty or treaties.

.09 The APA Policy Board establishes policy on matters of substantial genuine importance pertaining to the APA Program. It consists of the Associate Chief Counsel (International), the APA Director, the Director, International (Large and Mid-Size Business (LMSB) Operating Division), Treasury's International Tax Counsel, and other senior officials.

.10   In a bilateral or multilateral case, the APA Program prepares a recommended negotiating position for the U.S. Competent Authority. The negotiating position serves as a basis for discussions with the relevant foreign competent authority or authorities under the mutual agreement article of the applicable income tax treaty or treaties. Prior to finalizing its recommendation, the APA Program, through the Team Leader (see section 6.03), conveys the substance of the APA Team's position to the taxpayer to provide an opportunity for the taxpayer to comment. The Team Leader, in coordination with other members of the APA Team, considers the merits of the taxpayer's timely received comments in finalizing the recommended position.

.11   If the U.S. Competent Authority and the relevant foreign competent authority or authorities reach a mutual agreement, the taxpayer and the Service may execute one or more APAs consistent with that mutual agreement.

.12   In appropriate cases, the TPM may be applied to tax years prior to those covered by the APA ("rollback" of the TPM, see section 8). The Service's policy is to use rollbacks whenever feasible based on the consistency of the facts, law, and available records for the prior years. This policy does not apply to unilateral APA requests in which a rollback would decrease taxable income on a return filed for a taxable year not covered by the APA (see § 1.482-1(a)(3)).

.13   Filing an APA request does not suspend any examination or other enforcement proceedings. The APA Program will coordinate its activities with those of other Service proceedings to avoid duplicative information requests to the taxpayer, enhance the efficiency of Service operations, and reduce overall taxpayer compliance burdens.

SECTION 3:   PREFILING CONFERENCES

.01   *General Principles*

A taxpayer may request a prefiling conference ("PFC") with the APA Program to discuss informally the suitability of an APA.

.02   *Discussion Topics*

The taxpayer may use a PFC to clarify what information, documentation, and analyses are likely to be necessary for the Service to consider an APA request. Among the areas of discussion are the covered transactions, the potentially applicable TPMs, the probability of agreement among the competent authorities, and the APA Program's schedule and method for coordinating and evaluating the request. To provide for the efficient use of taxpayer resources, PFCs are recommended in order to ensure that the APA request is appropriate and focuses on relevant issues.

.03   Scheduling

A taxpayer or its representative may contact the APA Program Office in Washington, D.C. or California to schedule a PFC. The taxpayer or its representative should propose three alternative dates, and should generally allow two weeks before the first proposed date. The telephone and facsimile numbers are:

	Washington, DC	**California**
Voice:	(202) 435-5220	(949) 360-3486
Facsimile:	(202) 435-5238	(949) 360-3446

.04   PFC May be Named or Anonymous

The taxpayer may request a PFC either on an identified or anonymous basis.

.05   Participation

If a taxpayer identifies itself, representatives of the Service Operating Division with responsibility for the taxpayer's return normally will participate in the PFC. Representatives from Appeals and the Division Counsel field offices may also attend. In the case of a PFC regarding a bilateral APA request, a Competent Authority analyst may attend. If a taxpayer initially requests a PFC on an anonymous basis but prior to the meeting chooses to identify itself, the meeting may be rescheduled to permit necessary Service personnel to attend. When requesting a PFC on an identified basis, the taxpayer must inform the APA Program whether transactions similar or related to those to be covered by the proposed APA are currently under consideration by a Service Operating Division, an Appeals Office, a Division Counsel, or an Associate Chief Counsel.

.06   Prefiling Submission

A taxpayer must send a brief prefiling submission to the relevant APA Program Office in Washington, D.C. or California that lists the persons attending the PFC for the taxpayer (first names only or job titles are sufficient if the PFC will be on an anonymous basis) and that outlines and describes the issues to be discussed. This brief submission should be provided at least one week in advance of the PFC. If the document is twenty pages or less, it may be sent by facsimile; but if it exceeds twenty pages, eight copies (or if anonymous, only three copies) and one original should be delivered.

SECTION 4:   CONTENT OF APA REQUESTS

Supplemental Materials

.01 Introduction

A complete APA request is essential to a timely and efficient APA process. In the APA Program's experience, a complete APA request may save many months of case processing time and hundreds of hours of labor, as it allows the APA Team to narrow its focus immediately to the core issue or issues and avoids delays caused by the need to supplement the original APA request. The goal of completing a unilateral APA or a recommended negotiating position within 12 months (see section 6.01) is predicated in large part on the assumption that the taxpayer has submitted a complete APA request.

A complete APA request should provide the information specified below and all other information reasonably necessary to permit the APA Program to evaluate fully the taxpayer's proposed TPM. The level of detail required will depend on the particular facts and circumstances of each case and should be governed by relevancy and materiality considerations (keeping in mind that the request should provide enough information to allow the reader to concur that a matter is not relevant or material). The detailed information supporting the APA request should be tailored to the specific facts relating to the taxpayer, the proposed covered transactions, and relevant legal authority. It should also take into account discussions with the APA Program in any PFC.

An APA request will normally be considered not "substantially complete" for purposes of sections 4.08, 4.13, 6.01, and 6.03 unless the request contains the information required below (as may be modified by agreement of the parties).

.02 General Principles

> (1) For purposes of requesting an APA, each taxpayer that is a member of a consolidated group (as defined in Treasury Regulations § 1.1502-1) must comply with the provisions of § 1.1502-77.
>
> (2) All materials submitted with the APA request become part of the APA Program's case file and will not be returned. Therefore, taxpayers should not submit original documents.
>
> (3) The taxpayer must submit copies of any documents relating to the proposed TPM. All materials submitted must be properly labeled, indexed, and referenced in the request. Any previously submitted documents that the taxpayer wishes to associate with the request must be referenced.
>
> (4) If the records or documents to be submitted are too voluminous for transmittal with the request, the taxpayer must describe the contents of

such items in the request and confirm that the items will promptly be made available upon request.

(5) All documents submitted in a foreign language must be accompanied by an accurate English translation.

(6) All documents in the APA request that are available in electronic format should be submitted, on either a CD-ROM or diskette, along with the paper submission. Suitable formats include Microsoft Word, Excel, PowerPoint, and Adobe Portable Document Format. Other formats may be arranged on a case-by-case basis.

.03 *Factual, Legal, and Analytical Items for All Proposed APAs*

Unless otherwise agreed, each APA request must include an appropriate discussion of the items set forth below.

(1) A comprehensive table of contents.

(2) The names, addresses, telephone and facsimile numbers, taxpayer identification numbers (if applicable), and both the Standard Industrial Classification (SIC) and the North American Industry Classification System (NAICS) codes reported on the most recently filed federal tax returns (if applicable) of (a) the organizations, trades, and businesses engaging in the proposed covered transactions, and (b) the controlling taxpayer of the parties, if the controlling taxpayer is not itself engaging in the proposed covered transactions.

(3) The controlling taxpayer's industry (for example, Heavy Manufacturing and Transportation) within LMSB; or if the taxpayer files its tax returns with the Small Business/Self-Employed (SB/SE) Operating Division, a statement to that effect.

(4) A properly completed Form 2848 (Power of Attorney and Declaration of Representative) for any person authorized to represent the taxpayer in connection with the request, disregarding if appropriate the line 3 instruction limiting the authorization to three future tax periods. If the taxpayer or the taxpayer's authorized representative retains any other person (for example, a law firm, accounting firm, or economic consulting firm) to assist the taxpayer in pursuing the APA request, the taxpayer must also provide a separate written authorization for disclosures to the person and such person's employees during the APA Program's consideration of the request, according to the instructions in § 301.6103(c)-1T (see also

T.D. 9011, 31 C.F.R. Part 10 (July 26, 2002)). Such written authorization may be made by completing Form 8821 (Tax Information Authorization), disregarding, if appropriate, the line 3 instruction limiting the authorization to three future tax periods.

(5) A description of the general history of business operations, worldwide organizational structure, ownership, capitalization, financial arrangements, principal businesses, the place or places where such businesses are conducted, and major transaction flows of the parties to the proposed covered transactions. The description must also identify any branches or entities disregarded for tax purposes (see § 301.7701-3) that are involved in the proposed covered transactions.

(6) A description and analysis of the transactions covered by the APA request, as well as the estimated dollar value of each proposed covered transaction for each year of the proposed term of the APA. The discussion must also describe how the proposed covered transactions relate to other controlled transactions that the taxpayer does not propose to cover.

(7) A statement addressing the extent to which the tested party has transactions involving commission sales and ordinary distribution sales (i.e., buying and reselling). If the APA request involves both kinds of transactions, the taxpayer must propose a TPM and analyze the extent to which it is appropriate under the facts and circumstances to (a) test both kinds of transactions on an aggregated basis; (b) test the two kinds of transactions separately; or (c) exclude one of the two kinds of transactions from the APA.

(8) For each party to the proposed covered transactions, a detailed analysis of:

    (a) the functions and economic activities performed;

    (b) the assets employed;

    (c) the economic costs incurred;

    (d) the risks assumed;

    (e) relevant contractual terms;

    (f) relevant economic conditions; and

(g) relevant non-recognition transactions.

(9) Copies of the principal written agreement(s), if any, setting forth the contractual terms for the covered transactions (within the meaning of § 1.482-1(d)(3)(ii), including without limitation the form of consideration charged or paid); and an explanation of any significant discrepancy between the applicable written agreement(s) and the economic substance of the covered transactions (including payment form) to date and as proposed for the APA.

(10) Representative financial and tax data of the parties to the proposed covered transactions for the last three taxable years (or more years if relevant to the proposed TPM), together with other pertinent data and documents in support of the TPM. This item may include (but need not be limited to) data from the following:

(a) Form 5471 (Information Return of U.S. Persons With Respect to Certain Foreign Corporations);

(b) Form 5472 (Information Return of a 25% Foreign-Owned U.S. Corporation or a Foreign Corporation Engaged in a U.S. Trade or Business);

(c) income tax returns;

(d) financial statements;

(e) annual reports to stockholders;

(f) other pertinent U.S. and foreign government filings (for example, customs reports or SEC filings);

(g) existing pricing, distribution, or licensing agreements;

(h) marketing and financial studies;

(i) documentation prepared in consideration of § 6662(e); and

(j) company-wide accounting procedures, budgets, projections, business plans, and worldwide product line or business segment profitability reports.

Supplemental Materials

(11) The functional currency of the parties to the proposed covered transactions and their respective foreign currency exchange risks.

(12) The taxable year of each party to the proposed covered transactions.

(13) A description of significant financial accounting methods employed by the parties that have a bearing on any proposed TPM.

(14) An explanation of any relevant financial and tax accounting differences between the U.S. and the foreign countries.

(15) A discussion of any relevant statutory provisions, tax treaties, court decisions, regulations, revenue rulings, or revenue procedures that relate to the appropriateness of the proposed TPM for the requested APA. For cases in which the taxpayer requests a rollback, the discussion should state whether the period of limitations for the rollback years has expired in the U.S. or in foreign countries, and if not, when the periods of limitations do expire.

(16) (a) A statement describing all previous and current issues at the examination, Appeals, judicial, or competent authority levels that relate to the proposed TPM, including an explanation of the taxpayer's and the government's positions and any resolution of the issues.

(b) If the taxpayer is requesting a rollback that involves any issues relevant to the proposed covered transactions that are unresolved and still under consideration by Appeals, the taxpayer must include with its APA request a waiver of its right to be present during communications between the Appeals Office and the APA Team members (as described in section 6.04). See Rev. Proc. 2000-43, 2000-2 C.B. 404. The following language satisfies this requirement:

Waiver of Ex Parte Communication: [Name of taxpayer(s)] agrees to the participation of the Appeals Office in the consideration of this APA request, and hereby waives its right to be present during, or participate in, communications related to the APA request or the proposed covered transactions between the Appeals Office and the APA Team members.

(17) A statement describing any APAs with, or rulings by, foreign tax authorities relating to the proposed covered transactions (or any pending requests for such APAs or rulings) and, if requested, copies of such APAs

or rulings.

(18) An economic analysis or study of the general industry pricing practices and economic functions performed within the markets and geographical areas covered by the APA request.

(19) A list of the taxpayer's competitors and a discussion of any uncontrolled transactions, lines of business or types of businesses comparable or similar to those addressed in the request.

(20) An explanation of the proposed TPMs, including any method used to convert results from one payment form to another (e.g., to convert from a lump sum to a contingent payment such as a sales-based royalty), and an analysis of why each proposed TPM is the best method within the meaning of § 1.482-1(c).

(21) A detailed presentation of the research efforts and criteria used to identify and select possible independent comparables. This presentation should include a list of potential comparables and an explanation of why each was either accepted or rejected. The taxpayer may request an APA even though no comparable uncontrolled prices, transactions, or companies can be identified. In such cases, a taxpayer must demonstrate that the proposed TPM otherwise satisfies the requirements of § 482 and this revenue procedure.

(22) Detailed financial data (and licenses or other agreements, if applicable) on the selected independent comparables in print and electronic formats. For example, if the proposed TPM uses the comparable uncontrolled price (CUP) method, the comparable pricing information should be included; if the TPM uses the comparable uncontrolled transaction (CUT) method, the comparable license agreements should be included; and if the TPM uses the comparable profits method (CPM), the annual and multiple year period results using the selected profit level indicator should be included. If pertinent, the taxpayer should demonstrate consideration of alternative measurements of profitability and return on investment (for example, gross profit margin or markup, ratio of gross income to total operating expenses, net operating profit margin, or return on assets).

(23) A detailed explanation of any adjustments to the selected comparables, such as: accounting for product line segregations; differences in accounting practices; differences relating to functions, assets employed, risks assumed, and costs incurred; volume or scale differences; and differing economic and market conditions.

(24) An illustration of the application of each proposed TPM by applying the TPM, in a consistent format, to the prior three taxable years' financial and tax data of the parties to the covered transactions. If historical data cannot be used to illustrate a TPM (for example, when the TPM applies to a new product or business), the request should include an illustration based on projected or hypothetical data, as well as a description of the source of the data. If coverage of three taxable years is inappropriate for any reason, the taxpayer should provide data for an appropriate period and explain why the period was chosen.

.04 *Specific Items for a Cost Sharing Arrangement*

In addition to the items in section 4.03, an APA request related to a cost sharing arrangement ("CSA") must include:

(1) A copy of (a) the documents forming or revising the CSA, (b) the documents relevant to the making available of any pre-existing intangible property to the CSA), including the documents relevant to the acquisition or licensing of any pre-existing intangible property that is made available to the CSA, for purposes of research in the intangible development area, and (c) a statement that the CSA conforms to the requirements of § 1.482-7(b).

(2) A specific description of intangible development costs for all participants under the CSA. Such description should include a description of the costs included and excluded (for example, costs of technology acquired from third parties; the treatment of stock-based compensation under the CSA; non-product specific development costs; costs associated with abandoned projects; costs associated with specific stages of product development; relevant labor, material, and overhead costs; and support and administrative costs); a description of any services performed for participants that will be included in intangible development costs (for example, contract research) and how those services would be taken into account; and, for a representative period, a breakdown of total costs incurred, and the costs borne by each participant, according to the CSA.

(3) The basis (as described in § 1.482-7(f)(3)(ii)) used to measure anticipated benefits, the projections used to estimate benefits, and why such basis and projections yield the most reliable estimate of reasonably anticipated benefits.

(4) The method used to calculate each participant's share of intangible development costs; the reason why that method can reasonably be

expected to reflect that participant's share of anticipated benefits; and a statement of the circumstances under which the participants' shares of intangible development costs will be adjusted to account for changes in economic conditions, business operations and practices, and the ongoing development of intangibles under the CSA.

(5) The accounting method used to determine the costs and benefits of the intangible development (including the method used to translate foreign currencies).

(6) Each participant's sales, cost of sales, operating expenses, research and development costs, and operating profit (historical for the five most recently completed taxable years and projected for two taxable years) for the product area covered by the CSA.

(7) A description of any amounts to be received from non-participants for the use of covered intangibles (for example, as a royalty pursuant to a license agreement) and how the participants would take into account such amounts.

(8) Representative internal manuals, directives, guidelines, and similar documents prepared for purposes of implementing or operating the CSA (for example, research and development committee meeting minutes, market studies, economic impact analyses, capital expenditure budgets, engineering studies, reports and studies of trends and profitability in the industry, and financial analyses for financing and cash flow purposes).

(9) A description of any prior research undertaken in the intangible development area; the identification of any pre-existing intangible property made available to the CSA; the amount of any buy-in or buy-out payment (as defined in § 1.482-7(g)(2)); a complete economic analysis to support the payment; the form of the payment, the method used to determine the amount of the payment (that is, the method used to value the pre-existing intangible property and to calculate any royalty, lump sum, or installment payments, including, if applicable, any conversion between different payment forms); and an explanation of any discrepancy between the proposed payment form and the payment form established in the documents listed in paragraph (1) above (see section 4.03(9)); and an analysis demonstrating that the method used constitutes the best method under § 1.482-1(c).

(10) The treatment of cost sharing and buy-in or buy-out payments for U.S. income tax purposes (for example, the source and character of those payments).

(11) Evidence of the participants' compliance with the reporting requirements under § 1.482-7(j) of the cost sharing regulations.

(12) For taxpayers requesting an APA that covers a CSA but does not cover the related buy-in transaction, or an APA that covers a buy-in transaction but does not cover the related CSA, the reasons why an APA limited in this manner is consistent with the principles of the APA process, as set forth in this revenue procedure. The APA Program will evaluate the requests to ensure their consistency with the principles of this revenue procedure and sound tax administration. If an APA request is limited to covering only buy-in payments, the APA must include a representation by the taxpayer, as a term and condition of the APA, that the CSA to which the buy-in payments relate meets the § 482 regulatory requirements for CSAs.

.05 *Critical Assumptions*

The taxpayer should propose and describe any relevant critical assumptions. A critical assumption is any fact the continued existence of which is material to the taxpayer's proposed TPM, whether related to the taxpayer, a third party, an industry, or business and economic conditions. Critical assumptions might include, for example, a particular mode of conducting business operations, a particular corporate or business structure, a range of expected business volume, or the relative value of foreign currencies.

.06 *Contents of Annual Report*

Section 11.01 provides that the taxpayer must file an annual report for each taxable year covered by the APA. The taxpayer should propose in the request a list of items to be included in each report. Consideration should be given to all items listed in Appendix C to the APA Program's current Model APA.

.07 *Term and First Year of APA*

(1) The taxpayer must propose a term for the APA appropriate to the industry, products, and transactions involved. Although the appropriate APA term is determined on a case-by-case basis, a request for an APA should propose an APA term of at least five years unless the taxpayer states a compelling reason for a shorter term. Additionally, the APA Program

strives to have at least three prospective years remaining in the term upon the execution of an APA (in the case of a unilateral APA) or completion of the APA Program's recommended negotiating position for Competent Authority (in the case of a bilateral or multilateral APA), except in unusual circumstances. Accordingly, taxpayers should anticipate that the APA Program may require their agreement to extend the proposed term of an APA if necessary to ensure such prospectivity.

(2) The taxpayer must file its APA request within the time prescribed by statute (including extensions) for filing its Federal income tax return for the first proposed APA year. If the taxpayer receives an extension to file its Federal income tax return, it must file its APA request no later than the actual filing date of the return. An APA request will be considered filed on the date the required user fee is paid (within the meaning of § 7502(a)), provided that a substantially complete APA request is filed with the APA Program within 120 days of the return due date (including extensions) for the first proposed APA year. Because of the need to begin the processing of the APA request in a manner that ensures appropriate prospectivity, the APA Director will consider extending the 120-day period pursuant to section 2.06 only in unusual circumstances. If the APA Program's evaluation of an APA request is delayed due to a lack of responsiveness or timeliness by the taxpayer subsequent to the filing of its request, the APA Director may deem the taxpayer's APA request to have been filed for purposes of this paragraph on a date subsequent to its actual filing.

.08 *Request for Competent Authority Consideration*

(1) The taxpayer must state whether any of the parties to the proposed covered transactions are residents of or conduct activities in a treaty partner country or U.S. possession, and whether the taxpayer proposes an agreement among competent authorities (see section 7 for guidelines). For purposes of this revenue procedure, "competent authority" includes the Director, International (LMSB) and designated foreign competent authorities under income tax treaties to which the U.S. is a party, and also includes the Director, International (LMSB) acting as the U.S. Competent Authority with respect to a possession tax agency described in Rev. Proc. 89-8, 1989-1 C.B. 778, as well as a designated possession tax official within the meaning of that revenue procedure.

(2) If the APA request is unilateral and involves transactions with an entity in a treaty jurisdiction, the taxpayer must provide an explanation of why the request is not bilateral. See sections 2.08 and 7.06.

(3) If the taxpayer requests a bilateral or multilateral APA, the taxpayer's request must include the information described in section 4.05(a) and (b) and, in a separate document, section 4.05(n), of Rev. Proc. 2002-52, 2002-2 C.B. 242 (or its successor), or similar information pursuant to a request for relief under Rev. Proc. 89-8. The following wording satisfies section 4.05(n) of Rev. Proc. 2002-52:

[Name of taxpayer(s)] consents to the disclosure to the competent authority of [name of foreign country] and the competent authority's staff of any or all of the items of information set forth or enclosed in the [bilateral/multilateral] APA request for the taxable year(s) _____ [and accompanying rollback request for relief from economic double taxation of income for the taxable years _____], and any further submissions, within the limits contained in the [name of treaty].

.09 *Perjury Statement*

(1) The taxpayer must include in any APA request and supplemental submission a declaration in the following form:

Under penalties of perjury, I declare that I have examined this [APA request] [supplemental submission relating to this APA request] including accompanying documents, and, to the best of my knowledge and belief, the [APA request] [supplemental submission] contains all the relevant facts relating to the [APA request] [supplemental submission], and such facts are true, correct, and complete.

(2) The declaration must be signed by the person or persons on whose behalf the request is being made and not by the taxpayer's representative. The person signing for a corporate taxpayer must be an authorized officer of the taxpayer who has personal knowledge of the facts, whose duties are not limited to obtaining letter rulings or determination letters from the Service, or negotiating APAs, and who is authorized to sign the taxpayer's income tax return pursuant to § 6062. The person signing for any non-corporate taxpayer must be an individual who has personal knowledge of the facts, and who is authorized to sign in accordance with §§ 6061 or 6063, as applicable.

.10 *Signatures*

The taxpayer or the taxpayer's authorized representative must sign the APA request. If an authorized representative is to sign, the taxpayer and representative must satisfy the relevant instructions on signatures in Rev. Proc. 2005-1, 2005-1 I.R.B. 1 (or its successor).

.11   *Mailing, Deliveries, Copies, and Office Location*

   (1)   User fees (accompanied by an identifying cover letter that includes a justification of the fee amount) must be sent to:

   Internal Revenue Service
   Attn: CC:PA:LPD:DRU
   P.O. Box 7604
   Ben Franklin Station
   Washington, D.C. 20044

   The fee payment may also be hand delivered to the drop box at the 12th Street entrance of 1111 Constitution Avenue, N.W., Washington, DC.

   (2)   All other communications must be mailed or delivered as follows to (unless arranged otherwise, for example, mailing to the California office):

   Office of Associate Chief Counsel (International)
   Advance Pricing Agreement Program
   Attn: CC:INTL:APA; MA2-266
   1111 Constitution Avenue, N.W.
   Washington, D.C. 20224

   (3)   The taxpayer must provide the original and eight copies of its APA request and any supplemental materials submitted while the request is pending.

   (4)   The APA Program is located at:

   799 9th Street, N.W.
   Washington, D.C. 20001

.12   *User Fees*

   (1)   A separate user fee is required for each APA request. For this purpose, an APA request means a substantially complete and timely-filed APA submission, as required by section 4, and includes all such APA submissions filed by the taxpayer within any single sixty-day period. The taxpayer, for purposes of the preceding sentence, includes all members of a controlled group as defined in Treasury Regulations § 1.482-1(i)(6).

   (2)   User fees shall be made payable to the United States Treasury.

(3) Except as provided in paragraphs (4), (5), and (7), the user fee for an APA request is $50,000.

(4) Except as provided in paragraph (5), the user fee for an APA renewal request is $35,000. For this purpose, an APA request will be considered an APA renewal request if its subject matter is substantially the same as in a previous APA request by the taxpayer.

(5) The user fee for a small business APA request is $22,500. For this purpose, an APA request will be considered a small business APA request if the taxpayer has gross income of less than $200 million or the aggregate value of the covered transactions does not exceed (i) $50 million annually, and (ii) $10 million annually with respect to covered transactions involving intangible property.

(6) For purposes of paragraph 5, the gross income of a taxpayer includes the gross income of all organizations, trades, or businesses owned or controlled directly or indirectly by the same interests controlling the taxpayer. Gross income must be computed for the last full (12-month) taxable year ending before the date the taxpayer filed the APA request. If the information on the taxpayer's gross income for the last full taxable year is not available, the taxpayer must use its projected gross income for the first twelve months of the APA term.

(7) The user fee to amend an APA request or to amend a completed APA is $10,000. For this purpose, a request to amend will be deemed to occur if a taxpayer requests changes to an APA request or to a completed APA that requires substantial additional work by the APA Team. Generally, no user fee will be imposed if substantial changes are requested by the Service or by a foreign competent authority.

(8) The APA Director may require a corrected user fee after submission of an APA request if the request does not meet the criteria for the user fee amount initially paid by the taxpayer. The taxpayer may either pay the corrected fee and continue the APA process or withdraw the request.

SECTION 5: TAXPAYER DISCLOSURE OBLIGATIONS

.01 Any information submitted by a taxpayer in connection with its APA request must be true, correct, and accurate (see section 4.09). If the APA Program determines that it needs additional information to analyze the APA request, the APA Program may require the taxpayer to provide such information.

.02   A taxpayer has an obligation to update on a timely basis all material facts and information that it submits in connection with its APA request. In addition, while an APA request is pending and after an APA is executed, a taxpayer is under a continuing duty to timely supplement its disclosures if the taxpayer discovers that information that it provided in connection with an APA request was false, incorrect, or incomplete in some material respect. If a taxpayer discovers such an error or omission after the APA is executed, the taxpayer must disclose the error or omission in its next-filed annual report (see section 11.01(1)).

.03   While the APA request is pending, the taxpayer should be prepared to update the financial data for the selected comparables as new or revised data become available.

.04   If a taxable year is completed while the APA request is pending, the taxpayer should be prepared to update its APA submission following the close of the taxable year by demonstrating the application of the proposed TPM to the taxpayer's actual financial results for that year.

.05   Failure by a taxpayer to provide all materials required by this revenue procedure in its APA request (see section 4), or requested by the APA Program while the request is pending, can cause significant delays in case processing and may result in rejection of the APA under section 6.10.

SECTION 6: PROCESSING OF APA REQUESTS

.01   General

The processing of an APA request follows one of two paths, depending on whether the request is for a bilateral or multilateral APA, or for a unilateral APA. The scheduling of due diligence, analysis, discussion, agreement, and drafting is designed to complete the recommended U.S. negotiating position (bilateral or multilateral APA request), or a unilateral APA, within 12 months from the date the full request was filed. The filing of a full APA request includes not only the payment of a user fee, but also the receipt by the APA Program of the materials specified in sections 4.02 through 4.10. Significant analysis of the APA request will not begin until a substantially complete request has been filed.

.02   Initial Contact

After receiving an APA request, a representative of the APA Program will contact the taxpayer or its representative to discuss any preliminary questions the APA Program may have, or to ask for any additional information or documents necessary in order to initiate processing of the request. The taxpayer must supply the additional information and documents, accompanied by the perjury statement described in section 4.09, by the date specified by the APA Program, as extended for good cause.

.03   Designation of Team Leader

Upon the receipt of a substantially complete APA request, the APA Director will designate a Team Leader to oversee the APA Team's activities in processing the request. If a prefiling conference was held with the taxpayer, the Team Leader generally will be designated from among the APA Program staff attending the prefiling conference.

.04   Formation of APA Team

The Team Leader will organize the APA Team, which normally consists of the following personnel: the Team Leader, an APA Program economist and/or a Service Operating Division economist, an LMSB international examiner, a Division Counsel attorney, and, in bilateral or multilateral cases, a competent authority analyst. In appropriate cases, an LMSB international technical advisor, the international examiner's manager, and other Service Operating Division personnel familiar with the taxpayer may serve on the APA Team. If the APA or a rollback of the APA affects taxable years in Appeals, the appropriate Appeals Officer will be invited to participate. The APA Team Leader will assure that copies of the APA request are distributed to all Team members for review.

.05   Function of APA Team

The function of the APA Team is the following: (1) for a bilateral or multilateral APA, to develop, in consultation with the taxpayer and consistent with sound tax administration, a competent authority negotiating position that it can recommend for approval, and (2) for a unilateral APA, to make best efforts, consistent with sound tax administration, to develop an APA that the APA Program can recommend for approval by the Associate Chief Counsel (International). The Service Operating Division field office responsible for the taxpayer's income tax return will be provided an opportunity to review and comment on the recommended U.S. competent authority negotiating position in the case of a bilateral or multilateral APA, and the proposed APA in the case of a unilateral APA.

.06   Due Diligence and Analysis

The APA Team will evaluate the taxpayer's APA request by discussing it with the taxpayer, verifying the data supplied, and requesting additional supporting data if necessary. The evaluation of the request will not constitute an examination or inspection of the taxpayer's books and records under § 7605(b) or other provisions of the Code.

.07 *Schedule for Discussion and Drafting*

(1) The APA Team will strive to arrange an initial meeting with the taxpayer to take place within 45 days from the assignment of an APA Team Leader (and following receipt of the substantially complete APA request). The function of the initial meeting is to review the taxpayer's facts, to discuss and clarify issues, and to reach agreement on the scope and nature of the APA Team's due diligence.

(2) In connection with the initial meeting, the APA Team and the taxpayer will agree on a Case Plan to which both Service and taxpayer personnel will be expected to adhere. The Case Plan will be signed by both an APA manager and an authorized official of the taxpayer (see section 4.09(2)). The Case Plan may identify issues raised by the APA Team's initial review of the APA request. Firm dates should be agreed upon for resolving all outstanding issues, and case milestones should be cited. Case milestones include: (a) submission of any necessary additional information by the taxpayer; (b) any planned site visits or interviews; (c) evaluation of the information by the Service; (d) meeting dates; and (e) presentation of the competent authority negotiating position or recommended agreement to the APA Director. To minimize delays caused by the need to coordinate different parties' schedules on short notice, the time and place of future meetings required for any steps in the case should be agreed upon at the initial meeting and established in the Case Plan.

(3) The time scheduled for completion of the case milestones will depend to some extent on the scope and complexity of the particular case. In the case of bilateral or multilateral requests, the Service will seek to work with the competent authority of the treaty partner or partners, or the U.S. possession involved to minimize the time needed for competent authority resolution.

(4) Failures by either the taxpayer or the APA Team to meet case milestones will be addressed promptly. The APA Director will assist in remedying any difficulties to ensure a course of action to meet case milestones. Substantial or persistent failure by the taxpayer to comply with the Case Plan may be treated by the APA Program as a withdrawal of the APA request. In this event, if the taxpayer wishes to continue to pursue the APA, the taxpayer must re-file the request and pay a new user fee.

(5) In some circumstances, development of the case will suggest to both the APA Team and the taxpayer that they adjust some milestone dates. To

preserve flexibility, the APA Team and the taxpayer may amend the Case Plan by written mutual agreement, consistent with the need to complete the case expeditiously.

(6) If a case is not completed by the date specified in the operative Case Plan, the APA Team Leader and the taxpayer must submit to the APA Director a joint status report (or separate status reports in the event of disagreement) explaining the substantive or procedural matters causing the delay and specifying how the parties propose to resolve the outstanding issues and complete the case within a reasonable time. If the case is not completed by the new target date, APA Program management will hold a status conference. The purpose of the status conference is to reach agreement on how the case will be resolved. The Associate Chief Counsel (International) may participate in this or subsequent conferences if the case is not resolved satisfactorily in a timely manner.

.08 Execution

Signature of an APA by the APA Director and the taxpayer will constitute agreement to the APA. For purposes of executing the APA, each taxpayer that is a member of a consolidated group (as defined in § 1.1502-1) must comply with the provisions of § 1.1502-77. The person signing the APA request on behalf of the taxpayer must satisfy the requirements of section 4.09(2).

.09 Withdrawing the Request

The taxpayer may withdraw the request at any time before the execution of the APA. The user fee generally will not be refunded if the taxpayer withdraws its APA request after the due diligence process has been initiated.

.10 Rejecting the Request

The APA Program may decline either to accept any APA request or to execute any APA after a request has been accepted. If the APA Program declines to execute an APA after the due diligence process has been initiated, the Service normally will retain the user fee, although the fee may be returned if the APA Program determines that such action would be appropriate under the circumstances. If the APA Program proposes to reject an APA request, the taxpayer will be granted one conference of right with the APA Director. Other conferences may be granted at the APA Director's discretion.

SECTION 7: COMPETENT AUTHORITY CONSIDERATION

.01 When any of the parties to a request are entitled to obtain assistance under the mutual agreement provision of a tax treaty between a foreign country and the United States, or under Rev. Proc. 89-8, the competent authorities may enter into agreements concerning the APA. Requests similar to APA requests that are initiated through treaty partners or possession tax agencies and submitted to the U.S. competent authority will be processed under this revenue procedure and Rev. Proc. 2002-52, as appropriate. In order to provide timely clarification of factual issues, minimize the potential for miscommunication, and assist in development of a multiple party agreement on a timely basis, the Service will generally initiate coordination among the taxpayer, the Service, and the competent authorities of treaty partners at the earliest possible stage of consideration of an APA request, including, where possible, the prefiling stage. In this manner, the U.S. and foreign competent authorities can develop a joint understanding of the case, which should facilitate negotiation and resolution of competent authority issues. The taxpayer should remain available throughout consideration of the request to assist the Service in reaching agreement with the foreign competent authority. Final agreement to the negotiated APA will be sought among the taxpayer, the Service, and the foreign competent authority. As a general matter, the taxpayer should submit APA requests and related correspondence simultaneously to the Service and to foreign competent authorities involved in the requests.

.02 The purpose of a competent authority agreement is to avoid double taxation or taxation not in accordance with the relevant income tax treaty or treaties. If such an agreement is not acceptable to the taxpayer, the taxpayer may withdraw the APA request (see section 6.09). If the competent authorities are unable to reach an agreement, the taxpayer may withdraw its request or, at its discretion, the Service may negotiate and enter into a unilateral APA with the taxpayer (see section 7.06).

.03 The taxpayer must cooperate with the Service and the U.S. competent authority, pursuant to the standards set forth in Rev. Proc. 2002-52 and any other applicable revenue procedures.

.04 Taxpayers have an affirmative obligation to identify relevant concerns that may impact competent authority negotiation of an APA request. For example, it may be necessary for the Service to request sensitive confidential data (including material that may constitute a trade secret), which if disclosed, could harm the taxpayer's competitive position. If the taxpayer identifies such sensitive information, the Service will work with the taxpayer in developing a mechanism to permit consideration or verification by the treaty partner or partners of the information while still preserving its confidentiality.

.05 When the competent authorities enter into an agreement covering an APA, the Service will, to the extent appropriate, agree to a mutual exchange of information with the foreign competent authority concerning any subsequent modifications, cancellation, revocation, requests to renew, evaluation of annual reports, or examination of the taxpayer's compliance with the terms and conditions of the APA.

Bilateral APAs may provide for simultaneous filing of the annual report with the Service and with the foreign tax administration.

.06 To minimize taxpayer and governmental uncertainty and administrative cost, bilateral or multilateral APAs are generally preferable to unilateral APAs when competent authority procedures are available with respect to the foreign country or countries involved. In appropriate circumstances, however, the Service may execute an APA with a taxpayer without reaching a competent authority agreement. The taxpayer must show sufficient justification for a unilateral APA. In some circumstances, procedures agreed upon with particular foreign competent authorities, or the requirements of proper relations with treaty partners, may preclude unilateral APAs.

.07 Section 7.05 of Rev. Proc. 2002-52 provides in part that, if a taxpayer reaches a settlement on an issue pursuant to a written agreement, the U.S. competent authority will endeavor only to obtain a correlative adjustment from a treaty country and will not undertake any actions that would otherwise change such agreement. The restrictions imposed under section 7.05 of Rev. Proc. 2002-52 with respect to the discretion of the U.S. competent authority to negotiate correlative relief will not apply to a unilateral APA. However, a unilateral APA may hinder the ability of the U.S. competent authority to reach a mutual agreement that will provide relief from double taxation, particularly when a contemporaneous bilateral or multilateral APA request would have been both effective and practical (within the meaning of § 1.901-2(e)(5)(i)) to obtain consistent treatment of the APA matters in a treaty country. If there is a settlement with respect to taxable years prior to the first year subject to a unilateral APA based on rollback of the APA's TPM (as discussed in sections 2.12 and 8 of this revenue procedure), section 7.05 of Rev. Proc. 2002-52 will apply to the rollback years in the regular manner.

SECTION 8: ROLLBACK OF TPM

.01 Application of the TPM to tax years prior to those covered by the APA ("rollback" of the TPM) may be an effective means of enhancing voluntary compliance and of using available resources to address unresolved transfer pricing issues. The taxpayer may request that the Service consider a rollback (a "rollback request") in connection with a particular APA request. Under regularly applicable procedures, the Service may determine that the same or a similar TPM as that agreed to in an APA should be applied to prior years even in the absence of a rollback request. When applying the TPM to prior years, adjustments may be made to reflect differences in facts, economic conditions, and applicable legal rules. Those adjustments may be made regardless of whether the taxpayer or the Service initiated the rollback request.

.02 The taxpayer may make a rollback request in its APA request or at any

time prior to the execution of the APA. The principles set forth in section 2.12 generally will govern the Service's consideration of the request. The balance of prospectivity and retroactivity of the total number of years covered by the proposed overall agreement, and the status of any on-going examination, will also be given consideration in the Service's decision to entertain a rollback request. Rollbacks requested after submission of the APA request must be in writing and addressed to the APA Director.

.03　　　　If a rollback request is submitted in connection with a bilateral or multilateral APA, the rollback request will be deemed to constitute an application for accelerated competent authority consideration as described in section 7.06 of Rev. Proc. 2002-52 (or its successor). The Office of Associate Chief Counsel (International), the Service Operating Division field office involved, and the U.S. Competent Authority will coordinate consideration of the request. The taxpayer's request must include all information required for accelerated competent authority consideration under Rev. Proc. 2002-52 (or its successor), subject to the rules set forth therein. The taxpayer's request can pertain to any years prior to the first year to be covered under the requested APA. As necessary to reach a competent authority agreement, the Service may require that the rollback be applied to one or more specified years if accelerated competent authority is to be granted. In exercising its discretion over the conduct of accelerated competent authority consideration, the U.S. Competent Authority will seek to implement the policy concerning APA rollbacks stated in section 2.12.

.04　　　　Rollback requests submitted in connection with a bilateral or multilateral APA and involving a taxable year under the jurisdiction of Appeals will be deemed to constitute an application for simultaneous Appeals and competent authority consideration. That application is described in section 8 of Rev. Proc. 2002-52 and is subject to the rules of that section. The Office of Associate Chief Counsel (International), Appeals, and the U.S. Competent Authority will coordinate consideration of the request. In exercising its discretion in a simultaneous Competent Authority-Appeals proceeding, the U.S. Competent Authority will seek to implement the policy concerning APA rollbacks stated in section 2.12. Taxpayers are encouraged to request accelerated competent authority consideration under section 8.03 above, in conjunction with an application for the simultaneous Appeals and competent authority process.

.05　　　　Subject to the policy stated in section 2.12, the Service official with jurisdiction over the taxable year subject to the rollback has discretion as to whether the rollback is applied. That official may be either the Service Operating Division executive responsible for the taxpayer's income tax return, the National Chief of Appeals, the U.S. Competent Authority (for matters subject to competent authority negotiations), or the Division Counsel (for matters pending litigation). Except to the extent inconsistent with this revenue procedure, APA rollbacks will be implemented using regularly applicable procedures for resolving tax issues. Such procedures include but are not limited to closing agreements and other settlement documents and Forms 870 and 870AD.

Supplemental Materials

SECTION 9:   SMALL BUSINESS TAXPAYER APAs

.01   *Special Provisions Available to Small Business Taxpayers*

At the request of a small business taxpayer ("SBT"), the APA Program may apply any or all of the provisions in this section. A SBT is any U.S. taxpayer with total gross income of $200 million or less, as determined under section 4.12(6). In addition, SBT procedures will be available for APAs that cover small transactions described in section 4.12(5). Although transactions involving valuable intangible property or CSAs would not ordinarily be appropriate for these SBT procedures (because of the complexity of valuing such intangibles), the APA Program will consider employing special procedures for such transactions on a case-by-case basis.

.02   *PFC Procedures*

(1) As set forth in the general rules above, a taxpayer contemplating an APA may request a PFC with the APA Program (see section 3). If a PFC is requested, the APA Program provides informal advice to the taxpayer regarding the taxpayer's proposal, but ordinarily does not begin significant due diligence until the taxpayer formally files an APA request and pays the appropriate user fee (see section 6.01). In the case of an SBT, however, the APA Program will commence its due diligence analysis earlier in the process to accelerate the conclusion of the APA negotiations.

(2) The APA Program and a SBT may hold a PFC to determine as early as possible the best method for the SBT's proposed covered transactions. The APA Program will need a detailed description of the underlying facts and the proposed TPM for the SBT's proposed covered transactions at least 60 days prior to the scheduled conference. The SBT may provide the information it maintains under § 6662(e) to satisfy this requirement. Prior to its prefiling submission, the SBT must consult with the APA Program to determine the information required to evaluate the SBT's covered transactions.

(3) An APA Team will evaluate the APA prefiling information to determine items of concern and the additional documentation needed to evaluate the request. The SBT will be advised of the APA Team's initial conclusions before the PFC so that it can address these items before or at the conference.

(4) At the PFC, the SBT and APA Program will agree on a schedule with the objective of finalizing the recommended negotiating position for a bilateral

APA, or concluding a unilateral APA, within six months of the date the SBT files its APA request. The APA Program expects that performing this analysis earlier in the process should result in a reduced number of post-filing meetings and supplemental information requests.

.03 *Items Required for an SBT APA Request*

Before an SBT submits an APA request, the APA Program and the SBT may agree to reduce or eliminate specific items that would otherwise be required by section 4.

.04 *Locale and Number of Meetings for SBT APA Requests*

The APA Program will endeavor to hold meetings with the SBT at a location convenient to the SBT. To minimize the number of meetings, teleconferences will be employed whenever feasible.

.05 *Assistance in Economic Analysis*

At the SBT's request, the APA Program will assist the SBT in the selection and evaluation of comparables, as well as the computation of any appropriate adjustments to comparables.

.06 *APA*

For unilateral APA requests, a SBT should submit a proposed draft APA in a form substantially similar to the APA Program's current Model APA (see Announcement 2005-27, 2005-16 I.R.B. 918, 950). The electronic component of the APA request should include a "redline" version showing the differences between the Model APA and the SBT's proposed draft APA (see section 4.02(6)).

.07 *APA Program's Consideration of Other Alternative Procedures*

The APA Program may consider other procedures suggested by the SBT to reduce the SBT's administrative and financial burden, consistent with the objectives of the APA Program and the requirements of § 482.

SECTION 10:   LEGAL EFFECT OF THE APA

.01   An APA is a binding agreement between the taxpayer and the Service. See sections 2.01 - 2.04.

.02   If the taxpayer complies with the terms and conditions of the APA, the Service will not contest the application of the TPM to the subject matter of the APA except as provided in this revenue procedure. The taxpayer remains otherwise subject to U.S. income tax laws and applicable income tax conventions.

.03	An APA will have no legal effect except with respect to the taxpayer, taxable years, and transactions to which the APA specifically relates.

.04	Unless provided otherwise by written agreement or regulations, the Service and the taxpayer may not introduce the APA or non-factual oral and written representations made in conjunction with the APA request as evidence in any judicial or administrative proceeding regarding any tax year, transaction, or person not covered by the APA. This paragraph does not preclude the Service and the taxpayer from agreeing to roll back the APA TPM, or the Service's use of any non-factual material otherwise discoverable or obtained other than in the APA process merely because the parties considered the same or similar material in the APA process.

.05	Unless provided otherwise by written agreement or regulations, the Service and the taxpayer may not introduce a proposed, cancelled, or revoked APA, or any non-factual oral or written representations or submissions made during the APA process, as an admission by the other party, in any judicial or administrative proceeding regarding any taxable year of the requested APA term. This paragraph does not preclude the Service's use of any non-factual material otherwise discoverable or obtained other than in the APA process merely because the APA Program and the taxpayer considered the same or similar material in the APA process.

SECTION 11:	ADMINISTERING THE APA

.01	*Annual Reports*

(1) For each taxable year covered by the APA, the taxpayer must file a timely and complete annual report describing its actual operations for the year and demonstrating compliance with the APA's terms and conditions. The report must include all items required by the APA, describe any pending or contemplated requests to renew, modify or cancel the APA, and report any adjustments made pursuant to section 11.02. In addition, the annual report must identify any material information submitted while the APA request was pending that the taxpayer discovers during the taxable year was false, incorrect, or incomplete. See section 5.02.

(2) The taxpayer must file an original and four copies of the annual report by the later of (a) 90 days after the time prescribed by statute (including extensions) for filing its federal income tax return for the year covered by the report, or (b) 90 days after the effective date of the APA. The Service and the taxpayer may agree to alternative filing dates. The taxpayer

should file the original annual report and copies with the APA Director in Washington, D.C., as indicated in section 4.11. For bilateral or multilateral APAs, the Service may require the taxpayer to file simultaneously a copy of the annual report with the treaty partner or partners.

(3) The Service Operating Division or the APA Program Office will contact the taxpayer regarding an annual report if it is necessary to clarify or complete the information submitted in the annual report. The taxpayer must supply the additional information by the date specified.

(4) Any contact between the Service Operating Division, or the APA Program Office, and the taxpayer to clarify or complete the information in an annual report is not an examination or the commencement of an examination of the taxpayer for purposes of § 7605(b) or any other Code provision.

(5) If a filed annual report contains incomplete or incorrect information, or reports an incorrect application of the TPM, the taxpayer must amend it within 45 days after becoming aware of the need to amend the report. The time may be extended for good cause.

(6) An annual report must contain the following declaration:

Under penalties of perjury, I declare that I have examined this annual report including accompanying documents, and, to the best of my knowledge and belief, this annual report contains all the relevant facts relating to the annual reporting requirements pursuant to the APA, and such facts are true, correct, and complete.

[If applicable: An adjustment to conform taxable income and other relevant items to reflect the results reported herein has been reported to the appropriate responsible Service Operating Division personnel.]

[If applicable: An amended income tax return to conform taxable income and other relevant items to reflect the results reported herein [has been] [will be] filed with the appropriate Internal Revenue Service Center.]

(7) The taxpayer must sign the declaration in compliance with sections 4.09 (Perjury Statement) and 4.10 (Signatures).

(8) Failure to file a timely, complete, or accurate annual report may be grounds for canceling or revoking the APA under sections 11.06.

.02 *APA Primary Adjustments, Secondary Adjustments, and Revenue Procedure*

Treatment

(1) APA Primary Adjustments. The APA provides the TPM for determining the proper amount of the taxpayer's gross or net income, deductions, credits, or allowances with respect to the APA's covered transactions. In general, the taxpayer's actual covered transactions during an APA year, as reported in its books and records, should comply with the TPM and be clearly reflected on the taxpayer's timely-filed original return for the year. Under some TPMs, however, the taxpayer may have to wait until the close of the taxable year to determine whether the intercompany prices it actually paid or received complied with the TPM (for example, a comparable profits method providing for a particular operating margin range). If the taxpayer's actual covered transactions do not comply with the TPM, the taxpayer must nonetheless report its taxable income in an amount consistent with the TPM (an "APA primary adjustment") on either a timely-filed original return or an amended return. The generally applicable Code rules, including additions to tax, penalties and interest, apply with respect to an APA primary adjustment. When the taxpayer makes an APA primary adjustment, an appropriate correlative adjustment will also be made with respect to the related foreign entity affected by the APA primary adjustment. See § 1.482-1(g)(2). To the extent the APA covers years for which federal income tax returns were filed prior to, or no later than 60 days after, the effective date of the APA, the taxpayer must file, unless otherwise agreed to in the APA, an amended return or returns that reflect any required primary adjustment and pay any tax due because of such adjustments, within 120 days of entering into the APA. The generally applicable Code rules will apply with respect to the primary adjustment with respect to the APA years for which federal income tax returns were filed before the APA was executed, except: (a) the computation of any required estimated tax installments for the taxable year will not take into account the primary adjustment and related secondary adjustments (see section 11.02(2)); and (b) the taxpayer will not be subject to the failure to pay penalties under §§ 6651 and 6655, or the failure to make timely deposit of taxes penalty under § 6656, by reason of the primary adjustment and related secondary adjustments.

(2) Secondary Adjustments. Absent an election of the APA revenue procedure treatment described in section 11.02(3), an APA primary adjustment requires a secondary adjustment to conform the taxpayer's accounts. The secondary adjustment may result in additional tax consequences. See § 1.482-1(g)(3).

(3) APA Revenue Procedure Treatment. If a taxpayer makes an APA primary

adjustment, the taxpayer and its related foreign entity may elect APA revenue procedure treatment and avoid the possible adverse tax consequences of a secondary adjustment that would otherwise follow the APA primary adjustment. Under APA revenue procedure treatment, consistent with the principles of Rev. Proc. 99-32, 1999-2 C.B. 296, the taxpayer will be permitted to establish an account receivable from, or payable to, its related foreign entity in the amount of the APA primary adjustment as of the last day of the taxable year to which the APA primary adjustment applies. The account will not bear interest and must be paid within 90 days of the later of (a) the date for timely filing (with extensions) of the federal income tax return for the taxable year to which the APA primary adjustment applies, or (b) the APA's effective date. The account must be paid within the 90 day period to receive revenue procedure treatment. Payment must be in the form of money, a written debt obligation payable at a fixed date and bearing interest at an arm's length rate as provided in § 1.482-2(a)(2), or through an accounting entry offsetting such account against an existing bona fide debt between the U.S. taxpayer and the related foreign entity. The taxpayer must document the payment or offset of the account, and disclose it in the APA annual report for the year of the payment.

(4) The Service will give effect to an APA primary adjustment, secondary adjustment, and payment under APA revenue procedure treatment, if applicable, for all U.S. income tax purposes. The tax treatment of any such adjustment or payment depends on the facts and circumstances of the adjustment or payment. For example, if a taxpayer's APA primary adjustment involves the reporting of an additional royalty expense for a transaction with a related foreign entity, the Service will deem a payment in the nature of a royalty in the amount of the APA primary adjustment to have been made by the taxpayer to the related foreign entity. This deemed payment may be subject to U.S. withholding tax, and interest would accrue on the tax required to be withheld from the due date of the taxpayer's federal income tax return without regard to extensions. Similarly, a taxpayer's APA revenue procedure treatment may involve the recharacterization of a dividend paid by its foreign subsidiary as a payment of an account receivable established in connection with an APA primary adjustment. Any foreign tax withheld from the payment may be treated as a noncompulsory payment ineligible for the foreign tax credit, unless the taxpayer exhausts all effective and practical remedies, including invocation of competent authority procedures, to obtain consistent treatment that would eliminate the foreign tax liability. See § 1.901-2(e)(5).

(5) If the Service proposes a tax adjustment or the taxpayer files an amended return that does not require an APA primary adjustment, generally applicable Code rules will apply.

(6) If the taxpayer requests a bilateral or multilateral APA, the U.S. Competent Authority will discuss the principles of this section with the appropriate foreign competent authority to seek substantially identical treatment of the taxpayer's related foreign entity.

.03 *Examination*

(1) With respect to the application of § 482 to the covered transactions, the Service will limit the examination of a taxpayer's income tax return for a tax year covered by an APA to the requirements described in the next paragraph and will not reconsider the TPM.

(2) For the year under examination, the Service may require the taxpayer to establish: (a) compliance with the APA's terms and conditions; (b) validity and accuracy of the annual report's material representations; (c) correctness of the supporting data and computations used to apply the TPM; (d) satisfaction of the critical assumptions; and (e) consistent application of the TPM.

(3) The Service Operating Division must inform the APA Director if the taxpayer has not satisfied any requirement in the prior paragraph. After consulting with the appropriate Service Operating Division personnel, the Associate Chief Counsel (International) may decide to apply the terms of the APA, or revise (see section 11.05), cancel, or revoke (see section 11.06) the APA.

(4) The Service Operating Division may audit and propose adjustments to the taxpayer's operating results as determined under the TPM without affecting the APA's validity or applicability. The taxpayer may agree with the proposed adjustments in the same manner as any other adjustment, and the Service Operating Division will assess any resulting additional tax or refund any resulting overpayment of tax. If the taxpayer does not agree with the proposed adjustment, the taxpayer may contest it through the normal administrative and judicial procedures. The taxpayer must include the audit adjustments as finally determined for the purpose of applying the TPM and, as necessary, make any APA primary, secondary and correlative adjustments under section 11.02. APA revenue procedure treatment under section 11.02(3) is unavailable for audit adjustments.

Supplemental Materials

.04 **Record Retention**

(1) The taxpayer must maintain books and records sufficient to enable the Service Operating Division to examine whether the taxpayer has complied with the APA. The taxpayer's compliance with this paragraph fulfills the record-keeping requirements of §§ 6038A and 6038C as applied to the covered transactions.

(2) Upon examination, the Service Operating Division may submit a written request to the taxpayer requiring the submission of requested information or the translation of specific documents within 30 days, as extended for good cause. The fact that a foreign jurisdiction may impose a penalty upon the taxpayer or other person for disclosing the material will not constitute reasonable cause for noncompliance with the Service Operating Division's request.

.05 **Revising the APA**

(1) An APA may be revised by agreement of the parties, consistent with the principles set forth herein and the interests of sound tax administration. The Associate Chief Counsel (International) may agree to revise an APA in lieu of canceling or revoking it. If the parties agree to revise the APA, the revised APA will indicate its effective date.

(2) If the parties agree to revise a bilateral or multilateral APA, the Team Leader will submit the revised APA to the U.S. Competent Authority to obtain the consent of the foreign competent authority. If the foreign competent authority refuses to accept the revised APA, or if the competent authorities cannot agree on a revised APA acceptable to all parties, the APA Director and the taxpayer may agree to: (a) apply the existing APA, if appropriate; (b) apply the revised APA or agree to further revisions; or (c) request the Associate Chief Counsel (International) to cancel the APA as of an agreed date. If the APA Director and the taxpayer cannot agree on how to proceed, the Associate Chief Counsel (International) will cancel the APA pursuant to section 11.06.

.06 **Revoking or Canceling the APA**

(1) The Associate Chief Counsel (International) may revoke an APA due to fraud or malfeasance (as defined in § 7121), or disregard (as defined in § 6662(b)(1) and (c)) by the taxpayer in connection with the APA, including, but not limited to, fraud, malfeasance, or disregard involving (a) material facts in the request or subsequent submissions (including an

annual report) or (b) lack of good faith compliance with the APA's terms and conditions.

(2) The Associate Chief Counsel (International) may cancel an APA due to the taxpayer's misrepresentation, mistake as to a material fact, failure to state a material fact, failure to file a timely annual report, or lack of good faith compliance with the terms and conditions of the APA.

(3) Unless the parties agree to revise the APA, the Associate Chief Counsel (International) will cancel an APA in the event of a failure of a critical assumption, or a material change in governing case law, statute, regulation, or a treaty (as described in section 11.07).

(4) For purposes of this section 11.06(1) and (2) the Associate Chief Counsel (International) will consider facts as material if, for example, knowledge of the facts could reasonably have resulted in an APA with significantly different terms and conditions. In regard to annual reports, the Associate Chief Counsel (International) will consider facts as material if, for example, knowledge of the facts would have resulted in (a) a materially different allocation of income, deductions, or credits than reported in the annual report, or (b) the failure to meet a critical assumption.

(5) The Associate Chief Counsel (International) may waive cancellation if the taxpayer can satisfactorily show good faith and reasonable cause and agrees to make any adjustment proposed to correct for the misrepresentation, mistake as to a material fact, failure to state a material fact, or noncompliance.

(6) If the Associate Chief Counsel (International) revokes an APA, the revocation relates back to the first day of the APA's first taxable year. The Service may: (a) determine deficiencies in income taxes and additions thereto; (b) deny relief under Rev. Proc. 99-32, 1999-2 C.B. 296; (c) allow the taxpayer relief under Rev. Proc. 99-32, but determine the interest on any account receivable established under Rev. Proc. 99-32, section 4.01, without mutual agreement or correlative relief; (d) revoke the APA as an "egregious case" under Rev. Rul. 80-231, 1980-2 C.B. 219, so as to deny the taxpayer a foreign tax credit; and (e) not make available the unilateral relief provisions of Rev. Proc. 2002-52 (see section 12.07). The Service will seek to coordinate any action concerning revocation of a bilateral or multilateral APA with the foreign competent authority.

(7) If the Associate Chief Counsel (International) cancels an APA, the cancellation normally relates back to the beginning of the year in which the

critical assumption failed, or the beginning of the year to which the misrepresentation, mistake as to a material fact, failure to state a material fact, or noncompliance relates. If, however, the cancellation results from a change in case law, statute, regulation, or treaty, the cancellation normally relates back to the beginning of the year that contains the effective date of the change in case law, statute, regulation, or treaty.

(8) As of the effective date of the cancellation, the APA has no further force and effect with respect to the Service and the taxpayer for U.S. income tax purposes. The Service will seek to coordinate any action concerning the cancellation of a bilateral or multilateral APA with the foreign competent authority.

.07 *Change in Case Law, Statute, Regulation, or Treaty*

If applicable U.S. case law, statutes, regulations, or treaties change the federal income tax treatment of any matter covered by the APA, the new case law, statute, regulation, or treaty provision supersedes inconsistent terms and conditions of the APA.

SECTION 12:   RENEWING THE APA

.01 A taxpayer may request renewal of an APA using the procedures for initial APA requests. To expedite the preparation and evaluation of an APA renewal request, however, taxpayers are encouraged to request a prefiling conference to discuss with the APA Program the suitability of streamlined submission requirements. Taxpayers are encouraged to file the renewal request nine months before the expiration of the APA term.

.02 The APA Program will endeavor to expedite the processing of a renewal APA. Expedited processing will be most likely where the taxpayer demonstrates that the following conditions exist: (a) substantially the same law and policy applied to the existing APA; (b) no substantial differences exist between the taxpayer's proposed TPM and the TPM under the existing APA; (c) no material changes occurred in the taxpayer's facts or circumstances since the parties entered into the existing APA; and (d) for a bilateral APA, a rollback or closed year considerations did not influence the TPM in the existing APA.

.03 If the conditions in the prior paragraph exist, the APA Team begins its evaluation of the renewal APA by considering the continuing applicability of the existing APA, using updated comparables as appropriate. The APA Team will focus on any changed facts and circumstances. While the APA Team will endeavor to streamline the renewal process, certain cases may require additional analysis. That is, experience and insight gained from applying the TPM to actual data (for example, APA annual reports) may provide insight that indicates the need to modify the TPM. The APA Program will use its best efforts to advise the taxpayer at a prefiling conference whether a streamlined APA renewal process will be achievable.

SECTION 13:   DISCLOSURE

.01   An APA, any background information related to the APA, and the taxpayer's APA request for that APA, are return information and are confidential. See §§ 6103, 6105, 894, and 7852(d).

.02   An APA, any background information related to the APA, and the taxpayer's APA request, are not "written determinations," and they are not open to public inspection. See § 6110.

.03   The Secretary must prepare an annual report for public disclosure. See § 521(b) of the Ticket to Work and Work Incentives Improvement Act of 1999, Pub. L. 106-170, 113 Stat. 1860, 1925. That report includes specifically designated information concerning all APAs, but in a form that does not identify taxpayers or their trade secrets or proprietary or confidential business or financial information.

.04   An APA, any annual reports, and any factual information contained in the background files is subject to exchange of information under income tax treaties or tax information exchange agreements in accordance with the terms of such treaties and agreements (including terms regarding relevancy, confidentiality and the protection of trade secrets). In cases where the exchange of information would be discretionary, information may be exchanged to the extent consistent with sound tax administration and the practices of the relevant foreign competent authority, including where relevant the existence and application by the foreign competent authority of rules similar to those described in sections 10.04 and 10.05.

SECTION 14:   EFFECT ON OTHER DOCUMENTS

Rev. Proc. 2004-40, 2004-2 C.B. 50, is superseded.

SECTION 15:   EFFECTIVE DATE

This revenue procedure will apply to all APA requests, including requests for renewal, received on or after February 1, 2006. By agreement, this revenue procedure may apply to any APA resulting from an APA request pending on such date.

SECTION 16:   PAPERWORK REDUCTION ACT

The collections of information contained in this revenue procedure have been reviewed and approved by the Office of Management and Budget in accordance with the Paperwork Reduction Act (44 U.S.C. 3507) under control number 1545 - 1503.

An agency may not conduct or sponsor, and a person is not required to respond to, a collection of information unless the collection of information displays a valid control number.

The collections of information are in sections 3.06, 4, 5, 8.03, 11.01, 11.02(1), 11.04, 11.05 and 12.01. This information is required to provide the Service sufficient information to evaluate and process the APA request or request for renewal of an existing APA, or to determine whether the taxpayer is in compliance with the terms and conditions of an APA. This information will be used to evaluate the proposed TPM, and the taxpayer's compliance with the terms and conditions of any APA to which it is a party. The collections of information are required to obtain an APA. The likely respondents are business or other for-profit institutions.

The estimated total annual reporting and/or recordkeeping burden is 8200 hours.

The estimated average burden for an APA prefiling conference is 10 hours; the estimated average burden for an APA request is 50 hours; and the estimated average burden for preparation of an annual report by a party to an APA is 15 hours. The estimated number of respondents and/or recordkeepers is 230.

The estimated annual frequency of responses is one request or report per year per applicant or party to an APA, except that a taxpayer requesting an APA may also request a prefiling conference.

Books or records relating to a collection of information must be retained as long as their contents may become material in the administration of any internal revenue law. Generally tax returns and tax return information are confidential, as required by § 6103.

DRAFTING INFORMATION

The principal authors of this document are various members of the Advance Pricing Agreement Program of the Office of Associate Chief Counsel (International). For further information regarding this revenue procedure, please contact Mr. Craig A. Sharon or Mr. Craig R. Gilbert at (202) 435-5220 (not a toll free number).

COUNCIL OF THE EUROPEAN UNION

Brussels, 20 June 2006
(OR. en)

9738/06

FISC 74
OC 405

LEGISLATIVE ACTS AND OTHER INSTRUMENTS

Subject: RESOLUTION OF THE COUNCIL AND OF THE REPRESENTATIVES OF THE GOVERNMENTS OF THE MEMBER STATES, MEETING WITHIN THE COUNCIL, on a Code of Conduct on transfer pricing documentation for associated enterprises in the European Union (EU TPD)

COMMON GUIDELINES
Consultation deadline for Bulgaria and Romania: 21.06.2006

RESOLUTION OF THE COUNCIL AND
OF THE REPRESENTATIVES OF THE GOVERNMENTS
OF THE MEMBER STATES,
MEETING WITHIN THE COUNCIL,

of

on a Code of Conduct on transfer pricing
documentation for associated enterprises
in the European Union (EU TPD)

THE COUNCIL OF THE EUROPEAN UNION AND THE REPRESENTATIVES OF THE GOVERNMENTS OF THE MEMBER STATES, MEETING WITHIN THE COUNCIL,

Having regard to the Commission's study entitled "Company Taxation in the Internal Market"[1],

Having regard to the proposal made by the Commission, in its Communication of 23 October 2001 entitled "Towards an internal market without obstacles – A strategy for providing companies with a consolidated corporate tax base for their EU-wide activities[2]", for the establishment of an EU Joint Transfer Pricing Forum,

Having regard to the Council conclusions of 11 March 2002 welcoming this move and the establishment of the Joint Transfer Pricing Forum in June 2002,

---

[1] SEC(2001) 1681, 23.10.2001.
[2] COM(2001) 582 final, 23.10.2001.

Considering that the internal market comprises an area without frontiers in which the free movement of goods, persons, services and capital is guaranteed,

Considering that in an internal market having the characteristics of a domestic market, transactions between associated enterprises from different Member States should not be subject to conditions less favourable than those applicable to the same transactions carried out between associated enterprises from the same Member State,

Considering that in the interest of the proper functioning of the internal market, it is of major importance to reduce the compliance costs as regards transfer pricing documentation for associated enterprises,

Considering that the Code of Conduct contained in this Resolution provides Member States and taxpayers with a valuable instrument for the implementation of standardised and partially centralised transfer pricing documentation in the European Union, with the aim of simplifying transfer pricing requirements for cross-border activities,

Considering that acceptance by Member States of standardised and partially centralised transfer pricing documentation to support transfer pricing on an arm's length basis could help businesses to benefit more from the internal market,

Considering that transfer pricing documentation in the European Union needs to be viewed in the framework of the OECD Transfer Pricing Guidelines,

Considering that standardised and partially centralised documentation should be implemented flexibly and should recognise the particular circumstances of the business concerned,

Considering that a Member State may decide not to have transfer pricing documentation rules at all or to require less transfer pricing documentation than that referred to in the Code of Conduct contained in this Resolution,

Acknowledging that a common approach in the European Union with respect to documentation requirements is beneficial both for taxpayers, in particular in terms of reducing compliance costs and exposure to documentation-related penalties, and for tax administrations owing to enhanced transparency and consistency,

Welcoming the Commission Communication of 7 November 2005[1] on the work of the EU Joint Transfer Pricing Forum in the field of business taxation and on a Code of Conduct on transfer pricing documentation for associated enterprises in the European Union,

Emphasising that the Code of Conduct is a political commitment and does not affect the Member States' rights and obligations or the respective spheres of competence of the Member States and the Community resulting from the Treaty establishing the European Community,

Acknowledging that the implementation of the Code of Conduct contained in this Resolution should not hamper solutions at a more global level,

---

[1] COM(2005) 543 final, 7.11.2005.

HEREBY AGREE TO THE FOLLOWING CODE OF CONDUCT:

Code of conduct on transfer pricing documentation for associated enterprises in the European Union (EU TPD)

Without prejudice to the respective spheres of competence of the Member States and the Community, this Code of Conduct concerns the implementation of standardised and partially centralised transfer pricing documentation for associated enterprises in the European Union. It is addressed to Member States but is also intended to encourage multinational enterprises to apply the EU TPD approach.

1. Member States will accept standardised and partially centralised transfer pricing documentation for associated enterprises in the European Union (EU TPD), as set out in the Annex, and consider it as a basic set of information for the assessment of a multinational enterprise group's transfer prices.

2. The use of the EU TPD will be optional for a multinational enterprise group.

3. Member States will apply similar considerations to documentation requirements for the attribution of profits to a permanent establishment as apply to transfer pricing documentation.

4. Member States will, wherever necessary, take duly into account and be guided by the general principles and requirements referred to in the Annex.

5. Member States undertake not to require smaller and less complex enterprises (including small and medium-sized enterprises) to produce the amount or complexity of documentation that might be expected from larger and more complex enterprises.

6. Member States should:

    (a) not impose unreasonable compliance costs or administrative burden on enterprises in requesting documentation to be created or obtained;

    (b) not request documentation that has no bearing on transactions under review;

    (c) ensure that there is no public disclosure of confidential information contained in documentation.

7. Member States should not impose a documentation-related penalty where taxpayers comply in good faith, in a reasonable manner and within a reasonable time with standardised and consistent documentation as described in the Annex or with a Member State's domestic documentation requirements, and apply their documentation properly to determine their arm's length transfer prices.

8. In order to ensure the even and effective application of this Code, Member States should report annually to the Commission on any measures they have taken further to this Code and its practical functioning.

ANNEX

TO THE CODE OF CONDUCT ON TRANSFER PRICING DOCUMENTATION FOR ASSOCIATED ENTERPRISES IN THE EUROPEAN UNION (EU TPD)

SECTION 1

CONTENT OF THE EU TPD

1. A multinational enterprise (MNE) group's standardised and consistent EU TPD consists of two main parts:

    (i) one set of documentation containing common standardised information relevant for all EU group members (the "masterfile"), and

    (ii) several sets of standardised documentation each containing country-specific information ("country-specific documentation").

The EU TPD should contain enough details to allow the tax administration to make a risk assessment for case selection purposes or at the beginning of a tax audit, ask relevant and precise questions regarding the MNE's transfer pricing and assess the transfer prices of the inter-company transactions. Subject to paragraph 31, the company would produce one single file for each Member State concerned, i.e. one common masterfile to be used in all Member States concerned and a different set of country-specific documentation for each Member State.

2. Each of the items of the EU TPD listed below should be completed, taking into account the complexity of the enterprise and the transactions. As far as possible, information should be used that is already in existence within the group (e.g. for management purposes). However, an MNE might be required to produce documentation for this purpose that otherwise would not have been in existence.

3. The EU TPD covers all group entities resident in the EU including controlled transactions between enterprises resident outside the EU and group entities resident in the EU.

4. The masterfile

4.1. The masterfile should follow the economic reality of the business and provide a "blueprint" of the MNE group and its transfer pricing system that would be relevant and available to all EU Member States concerned.

4.2. The masterfile should contain the following items:

(a) a general description of the business and business strategy, including changes in the business strategy compared to the previous tax year;

(b) a general description of the MNE group's organisational, legal and operational structure (including an organisation chart, a list of group members and a description of the participation of the parent company in the subsidiaries);

(c) the general identification of the associated enterprises engaged in controlled transactions involving enterprises in the EU;

(d) a general description of the controlled transactions involving associated enterprises in the EU, i.e. a general description of:

    (i) flows of transactions (tangible and intangible assets, services, financial),

    (ii) invoice flows, and

    (iii) amounts of transaction flows;

(e) a general description of functions performed, risks assumed and a description of changes in functions and risks compared to the previous tax year, e.g. change from a fully fledged distributor to a commissionaire;

(f) the ownership of intangibles (patents, trademarks, brand names, know-how, etc.) and royalties paid or received;

(g) the MNE group's inter-company transfer pricing policy or a description of the group's transfer pricing system that explains the arm's length nature of the company's transfer prices;

(h) a list of cost contribution agreements, Advance Pricing Agreements and rulings covering transfer pricing aspects as far as group members in the EU are affected; and

(i) an undertaking by each domestic taxpayer to provide supplementary information upon request and within a reasonable time frame in accordance with national rules.

5. Country-specific documentation

5.1. The content of the country-specific documentation supplements the masterfile. Together the two constitute the documentation file for the relevant EU Member State. The country-specific documentation would be available to those tax administrations with a legitimate interest in the appropriate tax treatment of the transactions covered by the documentation.

5.2. Country-specific documentation should contain, in addition to the content of the masterfile, the following items:

(a) a detailed description of the business and business strategy, including changes in the business strategy compared to the previous tax year;

(b) information, i.e. description and explanation, on country-specific controlled transactions, including:

(i) flows of transactions (tangible and intangible assets, services, financial),

(ii) invoice flows, and

(iii) amounts of transaction flows;

(c) a comparability analysis, i.e.:

(i) characteristics of property and services,

(ii) functional analysis (functions performed, assets used, risks assumed),

(iii) contractual terms,

(iv) economic circumstances, and

(v) specific business strategies;

(d) an explanation of the selection and application of the transfer pricing method(s), i.e. why a specific transfer pricing method was selected and how it was applied;

(e) relevant information on internal and/or external comparables if available; and

(f) a description of the implementation and application of the group's inter-company transfer pricing policy.

6. An MNE should have the possibility of including items in the masterfile instead of the country-specific documentation, keeping, however, the same level of detail as in the country-specific documentation. The country-specific documentation should be prepared in a language prescribed by the Member State concerned, even if the MNE has opted to keep the country-specific documentation in the masterfile.

7. Any country-specific information and documents that relate to a controlled transaction involving one or more Member States must be contained either in the country-specific documentation of all the Member States concerned or in the common masterfile.

8. MNEs should be allowed to prepare the country-specific documentation in one set of documentation (containing information about all businesses in that country) or in separate files for each business or group of activities in that country.

9. The country-specific documentation should be prepared in a language prescribed by the Member State concerned.

SECTION 2

GENERAL APPLICATION RULES AND REQUIREMENTS FOR MNEs

10. Use of the EU TPD is optional for MNE groups. However, an MNE group should not arbitrarily opt in and out of the EU Transfer Pricing Documentation approach for its documentation purposes but should apply the EU TPD in a way that is consistent throughout the EU and from year to year.

11. An MNE group that opts for the EU TPD should generally apply this approach collectively to all associated enterprises engaged in controlled transactions involving enterprises in the EU to which transfer pricing rules apply. Subject to paragraph 31, an MNE group opting for the EU TPD would, therefore, need to keep the documentation specified in Section 1 in respect of all its enterprises in the Member State concerned, including permanent establishments.

12. Where an MNE group has opted for the EU TPD for a given fiscal year, each member of the MNE group should inform its tax administration accordingly.

13. MNEs should undertake to prepare the masterfile in time to comply with any legitimate request originating from one of the tax administrations involved.

14. The taxpayer in a given Member State should make its EU TPD available, upon request by a tax administration, within a reasonable time depending on the complexity of the transactions.

15. The taxpayer responsible for making documentation available to the tax administration is the taxpayer that would be required to make the tax return and that would be liable to a penalty if adequate documentation were not made available. This is the case even if the documentation is prepared and stored by one enterprise within a group on behalf of another. The decision of an MNE group to apply the EU TPD implies a commitment towards all associated enterprises in the EU to make the masterfile and the respective country-specific documentation available to its national tax administration.

16. Where in its tax return, a taxpayer makes an adjustment to its accounts profit resulting from the application of the arm's length principle, documentation demonstrating how the adjustment was calculated should be available.

17. The aggregation of transactions must be applied consistently, be transparent to the tax administration and be in accordance with paragraph 1.42 of the OECD Transfer Pricing Guidelines (which allow aggregation of transactions that are so closely linked or continuous that they cannot be evaluated adequately on a separate basis). These rules should be applied in a reasonable manner, taking into account in particular the number and complexity of the transactions.

SECTION 3

GENERAL APPLICATION RULES AND REQUIREMENTS FOR MEMBER STATES

18. Since the EU TPD is a basic set of information for the assessment of the MNE group's transfer prices a Member State would be entitled in its domestic law to require more and different information and documents, by specific request or during a tax audit, than would be contained in the EU TPD.

19. The period for providing additional information and documents upon specific request referred to in paragraph 18 should be determined on a case-by-case basis taking into account the amount and detail of the information and documents requested. Depending on specific local regulations, the timing should give the taxpayer a reasonable time (which can vary depending on the complexity of the transaction) to prepare the additional information.

20. Taxpayers avoid cooperation-related penalties where they have agreed to adopt the EU TPD approach and provide, upon specific request or during a tax audit, in a reasonable manner and within a reasonable time, additional information and documents going beyond the EU TPD referred to in paragraph 18.

21. Taxpayers should be required to submit their EU TPD, i.e. the masterfile and the country-specific documentation, to the tax administration only at the beginning of a tax audit or upon specific request.

22. Where a Member State requires a taxpayer to submit information about transfer pricing with its tax return, that information should be no more than a short questionnaire or an appropriate risk assessment form.

23. It may not always be necessary for documents to be translated into a local language. In order to minimise costs and delays caused by translation, Member States should accept documents in a foreign language as far as possible. As far as the EU Transfer Pricing Documentation is concerned, tax administrations should be prepared to accept the masterfile in a commonly understood language in the Member States concerned. Translations of the masterfile should be made available only if strictly necessary and upon specific request.

24. Member States should not oblige taxpayers to retain documentation beyond a reasonable period consistent with the requirements of the domestic laws where the taxpayer is liable to tax regardless of where the documentation, or any part of it, is situated.

25. Member States should evaluate domestic or non-domestic comparables with respect to the specific facts and circumstances of the case. For example, comparables found in pan-European databases should not be rejected automatically. The use of non-domestic comparables by itself should not subject the taxpayer to penalties for non-compliance.

SECTION 4

GENERAL APPLICATION RULES AND REQUIREMENTS APPLICABLE TO MNEs AND MEMBER STATES

26. Where documentation produced for one period remains relevant for subsequent periods and continues to provide evidence of arm's length pricing, it may be appropriate for the documentation for subsequent periods to refer to earlier documentation rather than to repeat it.

27. Documentation does not need to replicate the documentation that might be found in negotiations between enterprises acting at arm's length (for example, in agreeing to a borrowing facility or a large contract) as long as it includes adequate information to assess whether arm's length pricing has been applied.

28. The sort of documentation that needs to be produced by an enterprise that is a subsidiary enterprise in a group may be different from that needed to be produced by a parent company, i.e. a subsidiary company would not need to produce information about all of the cross-border relationships and transactions between associated enterprises within the MNE group but only about relationships and transactions relevant to the subsidiary in question.

29. It should be irrelevant for tax administrations where a taxpayer prepares and stores its documentation as long as the documentation is sufficient and made available in a timely manner to the tax administrations involved upon request. Taxpayers should, therefore, be free to keep their documentation, including their EU TPD, either in a centralised or in a decentralised manner.

30. The way that documentation is stored – whether on paper, in electronic form or in any other way – should be at the discretion of the taxpayer, provided that it can be made available to the tax administration in a reasonable way.

31. In well justified cases, e.g. where an MNE group has a decentralised organisational, legal or operational structure or consists of several large divisions with completely different product lines and transfer pricing policies or no inter-company transactions, and in the case of a recently acquired enterprise, an MNE group should be allowed to produce more than one masterfile or to exempt specific group members from the EU TPD.

SECTION 5

GLOSSARY

MULTINATIONAL ENTERPRISE (MNE) AND MNE GROUP

According to the OECD Transfer Pricing Guidelines:

– an MNE is a company that is part of an MNE group,

– an MNE group is a group of associated companies with business establishments in two or more countries.

STANDARDISED DOCUMENTATION

A uniform, EU-wide set of rules for documentation requirements according to which all enterprises in Member States prepare separate and unique documentation packages. This more prescriptive approach aims at arriving at a decentralised but standardised set of documentation, i.e. each entity in a multinational group prepares its own documentation, but according to the same rules.

CENTRALISED (INTEGRATED GLOBAL) DOCUMENTATION

A single documentation package (core documentation) on a global or regional basis that is prepared by the parent company or headquarters of a group of companies in a EU-wide standardised and consistent form. This documentation package can serve as the basis for preparing local country documentation from both local and central sources.

EU TRANSFER PRICING DOCUMENTATION (EU TPD)

The EU Transfer Pricing Documentation (EU TPD) approach combines aspects of the standardised and of the centralised (integrated global) documentation approach. A multinational group would prepare one set of standardised and consistent transfer pricing documentation that would consist of two main parts:

(i) one uniform set of documentation containing common standardised information relevant for all EU group members (the "masterfile"), and

(ii) several sets of standardised documentation each containing country-specific information ("country-specific documentation").

The documentation set for a given country would consist of the common masterfile supplemented by the standardised country-specific documentation for that country.

DOCUMENTATION-RELATED PENALTY

An administrative (or civil) penalty imposed for failure to comply with the EU TPD or the domestic documentation requirements of a Member State (depending on which requirements the MNE has chosen to comply with) at the time the EU TPD or the domestic documentation required by a Member State was due to be submitted to the tax administration.

COOPERATION-RELATED PENALTY

An administrative (or civil) penalty imposed for failure to comply in a timely manner with a specific request of a tax administration to submit additional information or documents going beyond the EU TPD or the domestic documentation requirements of a Member State (depending on which requirements the MNE has chosen to comply with).

ADJUSTMENT-RELATED PENALTY

A penalty imposed for failure to comply with the arm's length principle usually levied in the form of a surcharge at a fixed amount or a certain percentage of the transfer pricing adjustment or the tax understatement.

China Regulations

Circular of the State Administration of Taxation on the Issuance of the Implementation Measures of Special Tax Adjustments (Provisional) Circular Guoshuifa [2009] No. 2

State taxation bureaus and local taxation bureaus of all provinces, autonomous regions, municipalities directly under the Central Government and cities specifically designated in the state plan:

In order to implement the PRC Corporate Income Tax Law and its Implementation Rules, and to regulate and strengthen the administration of special tax adjustments, the State Administration of Taxation has formulated the Implementation Measures of Special Tax Adjustments (Provisional). These Measures are hereby issued to you for implementation.

Attachment: Implementation Measures for Special Tax Adjustments (Provisional)

January 8, 2009

Implementation Measures of Special Tax Adjustments (Provisional)

Contents:

Chapter 1 ...... General Provisions
Chapter 2 ...... Related Party Filing
Chapter 3 ...... Contemporaneous Documentation Administration
Chapter 4 ...... Transfer Pricing Methods
Chapter 5 ...... Transfer Pricing Investigation and Adjustment
Chapter 6 ...... Advance Pricing Arrangements
Chapter 7 ...... Cost Sharing Arrangements
Chapter 8 ...... Controlled Foreign Corporation Administration
Chapter 9 ...... Thin Capitalisation Administration
Chapter 10 .... General Anti-Tax Avoidance Rules
Chapter 11 .... Corresponding Adjustments and International Negotiation
Chapter 12 .... Legal Responsibility
Chapter 13 .... Supplementary Provisions

Chapter 1 General Provisions

Article 1 This set of Measures[1] is formulated to administer special tax adjustments in accordance with the PRC Corporate Income Tax Law (the "CIT Law") and its implementation rules (the "Implementation Rules"), the PRC Tax Collection Administration Law (the "Tax Collection Law") and its implementation rules (the "Tax Collection Law Implementation Rules"), and relevant provisions of the avoidance of double taxation treaties (arrangements) between the Chinese government and governments of relevant countries (or regions) (the "tax treaties or arrangements").

Article 2 The Measures shall apply to the special tax adjustment administration by tax authorities, covering business enterprises' transfer pricing, advance pricing arrangements, cost sharing arrangements, controlled foreign corporations, thin capitalisation and general anti-tax avoidance.

Article 3 In respect of transfer pricing administration, tax authorities shall examine business transactions between enterprises and their related parties ("related-party transactions") and evaluate whether they are conducted on an arm's-length basis, in addition to conducting investigations and making adjustments, as required under Chapter 6 of the CIT Law and Article 36 of the Tax Collection Law.

Article 4 In respect of advance pricing arrangement administration, tax authorities shall examine and evaluate enterprises' pricing principles and computation methods of related-party transactions for (a) future year(s), and negotiate with the enterprises to reach an advance pricing arrangement, in accordance with Article 42 of the CIT Law and Article 53 of the Tax Collection Law Implementation Rules.

Article 5 In respect of cost sharing arrangement administration, tax authorities shall examine and evaluate whether cost sharing arrangements among enterprises and their related parties are executed on an arm's-length basis, in addition to conducting investigations and making adjustments, in accordance with Paragraph 2 of Article 41 of the CIT Law.

Article 6 In respect of controlled foreign corporation administration, tax authorities shall examine, evaluate, and investigate the controlled foreign corporations' non-distribution or decreased distribution of profits, and adjust the income tax attributable to Chinese resident enterprises in accordance with Article 45 of the CIT Law.

Article 7 In respect of thin capitalisation administration, tax authorities shall examine, evaluate, and investigate (along with adjustments) whether proportions of related party debt investments to equity investments received in enterprises comply with the prescribed ratio or are set on an arm's-length basis, in accordance with Article

---

[1] The "Implementation Measures of Special Tax Adjustment (Provisional)" are referred to as the "Measures" throughout the text.

46 of the CIT Law.

Article 8 In respect of general anti-tax avoidance administration, tax authorities shall examine enterprises' taxable income and evaluate whether it has been reduced through transactions or actions for non-reasonable business purposes; they shall also conduct investigations and make adjustments, in accordance with Article 47 of the CIT Law.

Chapter 2 Related Party Filing

Article 9 The term "related-party relationships," as referred to in Article 109 of the Implementation Rules of the CIT Law and in Article 51 of the Tax Collection Law Implementation Rules, primarily refers to relationships between an enterprise and other parties, organisations or personnel under one of the following situations:

(i) One party directly or indirectly holds a total of 25 percent or more of the shares in the other party, or 25 percent or more of the shares of both parties are directly or indirectly held by a third party. When either party indirectly holds the shares of another party through an intermediate party, the indirect shareholding will be deemed as the same as the shareholding by that party in the other party if it holds more than 25 percent of the shares.

(ii) Loans between two parties (excluding independent financial institutions) account for 50 percent or more of either party's paid-in capital, or 10 percent or more of either party's total loans are guaranteed by the other party (excluding independent financial institutions).

(iii) More than half of one party's senior management (including board members or managers) or at least one senior board member who has the controlling power over the board is appointed by the other party, or more than half of both parties' senior management (including board members or managers) or at least one senior board member of each of both parties who has the controlling power over the board is appointed by a third party.

(iv) More than half of one party's senior management (including board members and managers) are also senior management of the other party (including board members and managers), or at least one senior board member of either party who has the controlling power over the board is also a senior board member of the other party.

(v) One party's production and business operations can only be carried out normally with rights to industrial property, proprietary technology, etc., provided by the other party.

(vi) One party's purchase and sales activities are largely controlled by the other party.

(vii) The services that either party receives or offers are largely controlled by the other party.

(viii) Other relationships, in addition to relationships of family members and relatives, such as those involving one party's actual control of the other party's production, operations or transactions, or both parties' interests being connected, despite the shareholding percentage not reaching the level specified in the first paragraph of this article.

Article 10 Related-party transactions mainly include the following:

(i) The sale, purchase, transfer and use of tangible property, including selling, purchasing, assigning and leasing tangible property such as buildings, means of transport, machinery, tools, and products;

(ii) The transfer and use of intangible property, including assigning ownership of or providing the right to use licenses, such as land use rights, copyrights, patents, trademarks, client lists, marketing channels, brand names, business secrets, and proprietary technology as well as industrial property rights such as industrial product designs or utility models;

(iii) Financing, including all types of long-term and short-term loans and security, and all kinds of interest-bearing advances and deferred payments;

(iv) The provision of services, including market research, marketing, management, administration, technical services, maintenance, design, consultancy, agency, scientific research, legal services and accounting services.

Article 11 When filing annual tax returns, resident enterprises whose tax is levied according to accounting books as well as non-resident enterprises that have establishments in China and file and pay corporate income tax on an actual basis shall also submit the "Enterprise Annual Reporting Forms for Related Party Transactions of the Peoples' Republic of China" which includes the following forms:

- Related Party Transactions Annual Reporting Forms of the People's Republic of China – Related Parties
- Related Party Transactions Annual Reporting Forms of the People's Republic of China – Summary of Related-Party Transactions
- Related Party Transactions Annual Reporting Forms of the People's Republic of

China – Sales and Purchase
- Related Party Transactions Annual Reporting Forms of the People's Republic of China – Services
- Related Party Transactions Annual Reporting Forms of the People's Republic of China – Intangible Assets
- Related Party Transactions Annual Reporting Forms of the People's Republic of China – Fixed Assets
- Related Party Transactions Annual Reporting Forms of the People's Republic of China – Financing
- Related Party Transactions Annual Reporting Forms of the People's Republic of China – Outbound Investment
- Related Party Transactions Annual Reporting Forms of the People's Republic of China – Outbound Payment.

Article 12 If an enterprise is unable to submit the Reporting Forms in accordance with Article 11 before the relevant deadline and needs to defer the submission, this shall be dealt with in accordance with the Tax Collection Law and its Implementation Rules.

Chapter 3 Contemporaneous Documentation Administration

Article 13 Enterprises shall prepare, maintain, and submit, upon request of tax authorities, contemporaneous documentation regarding their related-party transactions for every tax year, in accordance with Article 114 of the Implementation Rules.

Article 14 The contemporaneous documentation shall chiefly include:

(i) Organisational structure
(a) The related organisation and ownership structure of the group that an enterprise is affiliated with;
(b) Change of relationships between the enterprise and its related parties during the year;
(c) Information on related parties transacting with the enterprise, including related parties' names, legal representatives, senior management, such as board members or managers, registered address as well as actual business address, and related individuals' names, nationality, inhabitancy, and family information. Related parties that directly influence the pricing of related party transactions shall be specified;
(d) Taxes of income tax nature, the rates and tax incentives applicable to the related parties;

(ii) Overview of Business Operations
(a) Business overview of the enterprise, including any changes of business and the enterprise's development; overview of the industry and its development;

business strategy; main economic and legal issues such as industry policies and industry restrictions that will influence enterprises and their industry; group industry chains; and the enterprise's position;

(b) Composition of core businesses, and the proportions of their revenue to the total revenue, as well as the proportions of their profit to the total profit;

(c) Analysis of the enterprises' industry position and related market competition;

(d) The enterprises' internal organisational structure and the respective functions performed, risks assumed, and assets employed by the enterprises and their related parties in the related-party transactions (including completing the "Function and Risk Analysis Form");

(e) Consolidated financial statements of the group, the preparation of which can be extended according to its accounting year, but no later than 31 December of the year after the year the related-party transactions occurred.

(iii) Information on Related-Party Transactions

(a) Types, participants, timing, value amount, currency, and contractual terms of the related-party transactions;

(b) Trade terms of related-party transactions, and any changes during the year, together with explanations;

(c) Comparison of business processes between related-party transactions and third-party transactions, including information flows, logistics flows and cash flows;

(d) Intangible assets involved in related-party transactions, and their influence on the pricing;

(e) Copies of all contracts or agreements in connection with related-party transactions, with explanations of their execution;

(f) Analysis of major economic and legal factors that affect pricing of related-party transactions;

(g) Allocation of revenues, cost, expenses and profits between related-party transactions and unrelated party transactions. When direct allocation is not available, the allocation shall be made by using reasonable ratios, and the determination of the ratios shall be justified (including completion of the "Financial Analysis on Annual Related Party Transactions Form").

(iv) Comparability Analysis

(a) The factors to be considered in a comparability analysis include characteristics of properties or services in the transaction, functions and risks of the parties involved in the transaction, as well as contractual terms, economic environments and operating strategies;

(b) Information on the functions performed, risks assumed and assets employed by comparables;

(c) A description of the comparable transactions, such as physical features, quality, and utility of tangible assets; for financing business, normal interest rates, amounts, currency, duration, and guarantees, borrowers' credit standing, repayment terms, and methods used to calculate interest for financing business; the services' nature and extent; intangible asset types and transaction modes, the right to use intangible assets through the transaction, and benefits from using intangible assets;

(d) Sources of, as well as the conditions and reasons for selecting, the comparable information;

(e) Adjustments made to the comparable data for the differences, together with reasons for making such adjustments;

(v) Transfer Pricing Method Selection and Application

(a) Transfer pricing methods applied and reasons for application. When a profit-based method is chosen, the enterprises' contributions to the overall profit or residual profit level of the group shall be explained;

(b) How the comparable information supports selected transfer pricing methods;

(c) Assumptions and judgments made in the process of determining price or profit in comparable unrelated-party transactions;

(d) Determination of the arm's-length price or profit using an appropriate transfer pricing method and relevant comparable analysis.

(e) Other information that supports the transfer pricing methods selected.

Article 15 Any enterprise that meets one of the following conditions is exempt from preparing contemporaneous documentation:

(i) Per annum related-party purchases and sales totalling less than RMB 200 million (the amount of processing activities is calculated based on declared value of imports and exports during the year) and other related-party transactions totalling less than RMB 40 million (the amount of related-party financing is calculated based on the interest paid or received). These amounts shall not include related-party transactions under cost sharing arrangements or advance pricing arrangements within the year;

(ii) Related-party transactions under advance pricing arrangements;

(iii) Foreign-owned shares account for less than 50 percent and related-party transactions are conducted with domestic related parties only.

Article 16 Subject to Chapter 7 of the Measures, enterprises shall prepare contemporaneous documentation before 31 May of the year after the related-party transactions occur, and the documentation shall be submitted within 20 days of the tax authorities' request. If they cannot provide such documentation on time due to force majeure, they shall do so within 20 days of the elimination of the force majeure.

Article 17 Contemporaneous documentation submitted as required by tax authorities shall be duly stamped with the company chop and signed or sealed by the enterprises' legal representative or someone authorised by the legal representative. If contemporaneous documentation contains quotations, sources should be referenced.

Article 18 Contemporaneous documentation shall be maintained by the successor enterprise after a merger or spin-off if tax registration is changed or tax deregistration is conducted due to mergers or spin-offs.

Article 19 Contemporaneous documentation shall be prepared in Chinese. If the source material is in a foreign language, a Chinese copy shall be submitted as well.

Article 20 Contemporaneous documentation shall be maintained for 10 years from 1 June of the year after the related-party transactions occur.

Chapter 4 Transfer Pricing Methods

Article 21 Enterprises involved in related-party transactions and tax authorities evaluating related-party transactions shall adopt reasonable transfer pricing methods on an arm's-length basis.

In accordance with Article 111 of the Implementation Rules, the transfer pricing methods include the comparable uncontrolled price method (CUP method), the resale price method (RPM), the cost plus method (CPLM), the transactional net margin method (TNMM), the profit split method (PSM), and other methods in compliance with the arm's-length principle.

Article 22 A comparability analysis shall be conducted in order to select reasonable transfer pricing methods. A comparability analysis mainly covers the following five aspects:

(i) Characteristics of assets transacted or services provided, including the physical characteristics, quality, and quantity of tangible assets; characteristics and scope of services provided; as well as types, transactional forms, terms and scopes, and expected returns of intangible assets;

(ii) The functions performed and risks assumed by the parties in transactions. Functions primarily include research and development, design, procurement, processing, assembly, manufacture, inventory management, distribution, after-sale services, advertising, logistics, storage, financing, finance, accounting, legal affairs and human resources management. When performing a functional analysis, the similarity of the assets employed by the parties for performing the functions shall also be examined. Risks to be analysed include research and development risks, procurement risks, manufacturing risks, distribution risks, marketing risks, and management and finance risks;

(iii) Contractual terms, including transaction targets, transaction amounts, prices, modes and conditions of charges and payments, consignment conditions, scopes and conditions of after-sale services, agreements to provide additional services, the right to change and revise contracts, contract durations, and the right to terminate or renew contracts;

(iv) Economic circumstances, including industry profiles, geographic locations, market scales, market segments, market shares, degree of market competition, consumers' purchasing power, substitutability of products and services, prices of production factors, logistics costs, and government control;

(v) Business strategies, including strategies for innovation and research and development, business diversification, risk-avoidance, and market share.

Article 23 Under the CUP method, price setting based on the prices for the same or similar transactions conducted between independent enterprises can be regarded as arm's-length prices of related-party transactions.

Comparability analyses should particularly investigate the differences between related-party transactions and third-party transactions in respect of assets transacted, services provided, contractual terms and the economic environment. The comparability analysis, by the different categories of transactions, should include the following information, according to different categories and substance of business transactions:

(i) Sale, purchase, or transfer of tangible assets:
(a) Processes of sales, purchases, or transfers, including the time and location of transactions, transactional terms, transactional procedures, payment conditions, transaction amounts, time and location of warranty services, etc;
(b) Stages of sales, purchases or transfers of tangible goods, including ex-factory, wholesale, retail, and export stages, etc;
(c) Tangible goods sold, purchased or transferred, including brand names, trademarks, specifications, models, functions, structures, exteriors, and packaging, etc;
(d) Environment of sales, purchases, or transfers of tangible goods, including social customs, consumer preference, political stability, financing policies, taxation, and foreign exchange policies, etc;

(ii) Use of tangible assets, including:
(a) Functions, specifications, models, structures, types, depreciation methods of the property;
(b) The time, period, and the place that the property is provided for use;

(c) The investment expenditure and maintenance fees, etc. of the property owner.

(iii) Transfer and use of intangible assets, including:
(a) Type, purpose, applicable industries, expected return of the intangible properties;
(b) Investment in development, conditions of transfer, degree of exclusiveness in possession, extent and period of protection under relevant State laws, costs and expenses of transfer, functions and risks, and substitutability of the intangible assets.

(iv) Financing, including: amount, currency, term, guarantee, credit worthiness of the borrower, method of repayment, method of calculating interest.

(v) Provision of services, including: nature of the business, technical requirements, level of specialisation, liability borne, terms and method of payment, direct and indirect costs, etc.

If related-party transactions differ significantly from uncontrolled transactions in terms of the afore-mentioned aspects, reasonable adjustments shall be made for the influence of such differences on the prices. If reasonable adjustments cannot be made, other appropriate transfer pricing methods shall be selected pursuant to the provisions specified in this Chapter.

The comparable uncontrolled price method is applicable to all types of related-party transactions.

Article 24 Under the resale price method, the arm's-length price for goods purchased from a related party is determined by deducting the gross profit of a comparable unrelated-party transaction from the resale price to unrelated parties for goods purchased. The formula for calculation is as follows:

Arm's-length price = resale price to unrelated party X (1 – gross margin of comparable unrelated party transaction)

Gross margin of comparable unrelated party transaction = gross profit of the comparable unrelated party transaction / net sales of the comparable unrelated party transaction X 100%

The comparability analysis shall focus on the differences in functions, risks, and contractual terms between the related-party transactions and the unrelated-party transactions, as well as other factors influencing the gross profit, including sales, advertising and service functions, inventory risk, the value and useful life of instruments and equipment, the use and value of intangible properties, stage of wholesale or retail, business experience, accounting treatment and management efficiency.

If related-party transactions differ significantly from unrelated-party transactions in terms of the afore-mentioned aspects, reasonable adjustments shall be made for the influence of such difference on the gross margin. If reasonable adjustments cannot be made, other appropriate transfer pricing methods shall be selected pursuant to the provisions specified in this Chapter.

The resale price method shall apply where the resellers engage in simple processing or buy-sell activities that do not involve substantial value-added processing such as the alteration of appearance, functionality, structure or a change of trademark.

Article 25 The cost plus method determines the arm's-length price of related-party transactions by adding a gross margin derived from the comparable unrelated-party transactions to a reasonable cost base of the related-party transaction. The formula for calculation is as follows:

Arm's-length price = reasonable costs of related party transactions X (1 + cost mark-up rate of comparable unrelated party transactions)

Cost mark-up of comparable related party transactions = gross profit of comparable unrelated party transactions / cost of comparable unrelated party transactions

The comparability analysis shall focus on the differences in functions, risks, and contractual terms between the related-party transactions and the unrelated-party transactions as well as other factors influencing the cost mark-up rate, including such functions as manufacturing, processing, installing and testing, market and foreign exchange risks, the value and useful life of machinery and equipment, the use and value of intangible property, commercial experience, accounting treatments and management efficiency.

If related-party transactions differ significantly from unrelated-party transactions in terms of the afore-mentioned aspects, reasonable adjustments shall be made for the influence of such differences on the cost mark-up. If reasonable adjustments cannot be made, other appropriate transfer pricing methods shall be selected pursuant to the provisions specified in this Chapter.

The cost plus method shall apply to related-party transactions involving purchases and sales, transfer and use of tangible assets, provision of services, and financing.

Article 26 The transactional net margin method determines the net profit of related-party transactions by using profit level indicators of comparable unrelated-party transactions. Profit level indicators include return on assets, operating margin, net cost plus, and berry ratio.

The comparability analysis shall focus on the differences in functions, risks and economic environment between related-party transactions and unrelated-party transactions as well as other factors influencing operating profit, including the functions performed, the risks borne, the assets employed, industry and market conditions, business scale, economic cycle and product life cycle, cost, expense, the allocation of income and assets among respective transactions, accounting treatments and business management efficiency.

If related-party transactions differ significantly from unrelated-party transactions in terms of the afore-mentioned aspects, reasonable adjustments shall be made for the influence of such differences on the operating profits. If reasonable adjustments cannot be made, other appropriate transfer pricing methods shall be selected pursuant to the provisions specified in this Chapter.

The transactional net margin method shall apply to related-party transactions that involve the buy-sell, transfer and use of tangible assets, the transfer and use of intangible assets, and the provision of services.

Article 27 The profit split method determines the profit to be allocated to each party in the related-party transaction based on their contribution to the consolidated profits derived from the related-party transaction. The profit split method can be categorised into the general profit split method and the residual profit split method.

The general profit split method allocates profit to participants in the related-party transaction according to the functions performed, the risk borne and the assets employed by each party.

The residual profit split method first determines residual profit by deducting the routine profit allocated to each participant from the consolidated profits earned by all participants in the related-party transaction. The residual profit is then allocated based on each participant's contribution to the residual profit.

The comparability analysis shall focus on the functions performed, risk borne and assets employed by each participant; the allocation of costs, expenses, income, and assets to each participant; the accounting treatment; and the reliability of the information and assumptions used to determine the contribution of each participant to the residual profit.

The profit split method shall apply to situations where related-party transactions are highly integrated and where it is difficult to separately assess the transaction result of each participant.

Chapter 5 Transfer Pricing Investigation and Adjustment

Article 28 The tax authorities are empowered to select enterprises for investigation, and conduct transfer pricing investigations and adjustments pursuant to the provisions of tax inspection as specified in the Tax Collection Law and its Implementation Rules. The enterprise under investigation shall accurately disclose its related-party transactions and provide relevant information without refusal or concealment.

Article 29 Transfer pricing investigations shall focus on the following types of enterprises:

(i) Enterprises with significant amounts of related-party transactions or several types of related-party transactions;

(ii) Enterprises with continuous losses, low profitability or fluctuating profitability;

(iii) Enterprises with profit levels lower than those of other enterprises in the same industry;

(iv) Enterprises with profit levels which do not correspond with the functions performed and risk assumed;

(v) Enterprises that engage in transactions with related parties incorporated in a tax haven;

(vi) Enterprises that fail to file their related-party transactions reporting forms or to prepare contemporaneous documentation;

(vii) Enterprises that are clearly in breach of the arm's-length principle.

Article 30 A transfer pricing investigation and adjustment will not be made in principle between two domestic enterprises whose tax rate is equal, as long as the transactions do not directly or indirectly decrease the overall tax revenue of the country.

Article 31 Tax authorities shall carry out desktop reviews in connection with the day-to-day tax administration to determine investigation targets. Desktop reviews shall be mainly based on the prior year's annual tax returns for corporate income tax and annual reporting forms for related-party transactions submitted so as to conduct a comprehensive assessment and analysis of the business operations and the related-party transactions.

Enterprises can submit contemporaneous documentation to the tax authorities during the desktop review period.

Article 32 Tax authorities shall conduct on-site investigations of selected enterprises in accordance with Chapter 6 of the CIT Law and its Implementation Rules, as well as Chapter 4 of the Tax Collection Law and Chapter 6 of its Implementation Rules.

(i) On-site investigations shall be carried out by two or more tax officials.

(ii) Tax investigators shall present a "Tax Investigation Certificate" and deliver a "Tax Inspection Notice".

(iii) On-site investigations, by complying with certain legal procedures, could involve inquiry, requests for book records and field check if necessary.

(iv) A specific tax official shall be assigned to prepare the "Inquiry (Investigation) Records". The interviewee shall be informed of the legal liabilities that may arise should he/she not provide true and accurate information. The "Inquiry (Investigation) Records" should be confirmed by the interviewee.

(v) In accordance with Article 86 of the Tax Collection Law, when it is necessary to obtain accounting books and relevant documents, tax authorities shall complete the "Accounting Books Request Notice, and "Accounting Information Request List", follow the relevant legal procedures, safeguard the accounting books and relevant materials and return them to the enterprise within the time period stipulated by law.

(vi) The tax authorities shall keep the "Inquiry (Investigation) Records" in relation to the problems and issues found during the on-site investigations. The records shall be signed by two or more tax investigators and confirmed by the investigated enterprises if necessary. If the investigated enterprises refuse to sign the records, the records can be signed by two or more tax investigators for filing.

(vii) Note-taking, voice-recording, video-recording, photo-recording and photocopying are allowed when necessary to request information related to the investigation, however the sources and holders of the original data must be noted and shall be confirmed by the keeper or provider with a written statement of "checked and confirmed to be the same as the original" and shall be sealed or stamped.

(viii) If witnesses are required, the tax authorities should inform the witnesses of the legal consequences they may bear should they fail to provide truthful information. The information provided by witnesses shall be signed or sealed by the witness themselves.

Article 33 Pursuant to Article 43 Paragraph 2 of the CIT Law and Article 114 of its Implementation Rules, tax authorities are empowered to collect information from the investigated enterprises, their related parties and other relevant enterprises (hereinafter referred to as "comparable companies"), provide relevant documents and issue a written "Notice on Tax-related Matters".

(i) The investigated enterprise shall provide information upon request within the period prescribed by the "Notice on Tax-related Matters". Where timely submission of the required documents is impossible under special circumstances, the enterprise shall file a written application for extension to the tax authorities. An extension of no more than 30 days may be granted upon approval. The tax authorities shall reply in writing to the extension application of the enterprise within five days of receipt. Where such a reply is not delivered within five days, it shall be deemed that the tax authorities have granted the extension.

(ii) The related parties of the investigated enterprise and comparable enterprises shall provide information within the time frame agreed with the tax authorities, generally no more than 60 days.

The enterprise, its related parties, and its comparable companies shall provide the information completely, truthfully and accurately.

Article 34 The tax authorities should verify the enterprise's filing information, and require the enterprise to complete the "Comparability Factors Analysis Form," in accordance with the relevant provisions in Chapter 2 of the Measures.

According to the enterprise's related party filing information and the materials provided, the tax authorities must complete the "Form for Determination of Related Party Relationships," the "Form for Determination of Related Party Transactions," and the "Form for Determination of Comparability Factors," which should be confirmed by the enterprise under investigation.

Article 35 If the tax authorities need to take evidence from related parties and comparable companies during the investigation of related-party transactions, the competent tax authorities must issue and serve a "Tax Inspection Notice" to the enterprise for investigation and evidence collection.

Article 36 The tax authorities should analyse relevant documents provided by the enterprise, its related parties, and comparable companies and confirm their accuracy via a field survey, issuing a written request for investigation assistance by reference to public information. If overseas documents are required, information exchange procedures under the relevant tax treaties can be initiated pursuant to relevant rules. Chinese agencies residing in overseas countries can also be contacted to help collect relevant information and materials. When dealing with relevant documents of related parties overseas, the tax authorities can ask the enterprises for notarised proof.

Article 37 The tax authorities should analyse and evaluate whether the related-party transactions comply with the arm's-length principle by reference to the transfer pricing methods provided in Chapter 4 of the Measures. The tax authorities can use public information as well as non-public information in their analysis and evaluation.

Article 38 When analysing and evaluating related-party transactions, the tax authorities should not make adjustments in principle on differences in operating profits caused by differences between the enterprise and comparable companies in terms of working capital employed. If such adjustments are required, approval from the State Administration of Taxation (SAT) must be obtained.

Article 39 For enterprises that are engaged in processing and manufacturing to the order of related parties and do not undertake functions such as management decision, research and development, and sales, they should not assume any risks or losses caused by wrong decisions, capacity under utilisation and unmarketable products. The profit margin of these enterprises should be kept at a certain level. For enterprises suffering losses, tax authorities should select appropriate comparable prices or comparable companies to determine the profit level based on economic analysis.

Article 40 Where the respective transactions involving payments and receipt between related parties are being offset, tax authorities conducting comparability analysis and making tax adjustments should, in principle, restore the transactions and evaluate related-party transactions separately.

Article 41 When the tax authorities analyse and evaluate an enterprise's profit by using the inter-quartile method, an adjustment should generally be made to no lower than the median if the profit is found to be lower than the median of the comparable companies' inter-quartile range.

Article 42 Based on the investigation, the tax authorities should reach their transfer pricing investigation conclusions and send it via the "Notification of Special Tax Investigation Conclusion" to the enterprise whose related-party transactions do not comply with the arm's-length principle.

Article 43 If investigations show that related-party transactions were not conducted in compliance with the arm's-length principle, resulting in a reduction in enterprises' taxable income and tax payable, the tax authorities should make transfer pricing tax adjustments following the procedures detailed below:

(i) A preliminary special tax adjustment plan should be drafted based on testing, verification and comparable analysis;

(ii) Negotiations should be conducted according to the preliminary adjustment plan. The tax authorities and the enterprise should respectively appoint their chief negotiators and the "Negotiation Records" issued by the tax investigators should be signed and confirmed by both chief negotiators. If the enterprise refuses to sign the record, two or more tax investigators can sign it instead for filing purposes;

(iii) If the enterprise disagrees with the preliminary adjustment plan, further related information should be provided within the time period prescribed by the tax authorities. The tax authorities should review the information and make prompt, appropriate conclusions;

(iv) The tax authorities should issue a "Notice on Preliminary Adjustment Plan of Special Tax Investigation" to the enterprise based on their conclusions. If the enterprise disagrees with the preliminary adjustment plan in the Notice, it should issue an objection in writing within seven days of receiving the Notice. The tax authorities should review and negotiate again after receiving the comments from the enterprise. If the enterprise fails to raise an objection within the seven-day time limit, it is deemed to have agreed to the preliminary adjustment plan;

(v) The tax authorities should confirm the finalised adjustment plan, and send a "Notice on Special Taxation Investigation Adjustment" to the enterprise.

Article 44 After receiving the "Notice on Special Taxation Investigation Adjustment," the enterprise should pay the taxes due and interest within the specified time limit.

Article 45 After the execution of the transfer pricing adjustments, the tax authorities will follow up with the enterprise for five years from the year after the most recent year for which the taxable income was adjusted. The enterprise should provide contemporaneous documentation for each of the follow-up years before 20 June of the year after the relevant follow-up year. The tax authorities should focus on analysing and evaluating the following according to the contemporaneous documentation and tax filing information:

(i) Enterprise's investment, operation and related changes;

(ii) Changes in the value as shown on the tax return submitted by the enterprise;

(iii) Changes in the enterprise's business results;

(iv) Changes in related-party transactions.

If the tax authorities identify abnormal transfer pricing issues during the follow-up period, the tax authorities should contact the enterprise immediately and request a self-adjustment, or start a transfer pricing investigation pursuant to the provisions in this Chapter.

Chapter 6 Advance Pricing Arrangements Administration

Article 46 In accordance with Article 42 of the CIT Law, Article 113 of its Implementation Rules, as well as Article 53 of the Implementation Rules of the Tax Collection Law, an enterprise can reach an advance pricing arrangement (APA) with the tax authorities regarding the pricing policies and calculation methods of its related party transactions in future years. Negotiation and execution of APAs usually involves six stages: pre-filing meetings, formal application, examination and appraisal, negotiation, signing of arrangements, and supervision of implementation. An APA can be one of three types: unilateral, bilateral or multilateral.

Article 47 The application of an APA should be dealt with by tax authorities above the municipal or autonomous prefecture[2] level.

Article 48 Advance Pricing Arrangements generally apply to enterprises that meet all of the following criteria:

(i) Enterprises with annual related-party transactions exceeding RMB 40 million in value;

(ii) Enterprises fulfilling the responsibility of related-party transactions reporting in accordance with the law;

(iii) Enterprises that prepare, preserve, and submit contemporaneous documentation in accordance with the law.

Article 49 APAs are applicable for related-party transactions conducted in a period of three to five continuous years, starting from the year after the year during which formal written application is submitted.

The negotiation and signing of an APA has no influence on the tax authorities' transfer pricing investigation and adjustment of related-party transactions in the year of or before the formal application of an APA.

If the related-party transactions during the year of application or previous years are

---

[2] KPMG Note – These are the levels immediately beneath the province level.

identical or similar to those in the years for which the APA applies, upon approval from the tax authorities, the transfer pricing polices and computation methods determined in the APA can also be applied to the evaluation and adjustment of the related-party transactions conducted in (those) year(s).

Article 50 Before formally applying for an APA, the enterprise should submit a written letter of intent to the tax authorities. The tax authorities will conduct pre-filing meetings on the related content of the APA and the feasibility of an APA with the enterprise on the basis of this written document, and prepare "APA Meeting Minutes." The pre-filing meeting can be conducted anonymously.

(i) Enterprises that apply for unilateral APAs should submit a written letter of intent to the tax authorities. During the pre-filing meeting stage, the tax authorities and the enterprise should discuss:
(a) The applicable years of advance pricing arrangement;
(b) The related parties and related-party transactions involved in the arrangement;
(c) The enterprise's business operations in previous years;
(d) An analysis of the functions and risks of the related parties involved in the arrangement;
(e) Whether the transfer pricing issues of previous years are to be solved using the methods determined in the advance pricing arrangement;
(f) Any other related items requiring explanation.

(ii) Enterprises that apply for bilateral or multilateral APAs should submit a written letter of intent to the SAT and the governing tax authorities at the same time. The SAT will organise the pre-filing meeting with the enterprise. Matters discussed in the pre-filing meeting should include the following topics in addition to those mentioned in the previous paragraph:
(a) Matters relating to the application for pre-filing meetings with competent authorities of the counter-party country of the treaty;
(b) Information about the business operation and the related-party transactions of the related parties in years before the APA application;
(c) The pricing principles and calculation method in the APA to be submitted to the competent tax authorities of the country which is the counter-party of the treaty.

(iii) If a consensus is reached in the pre-filing meeting, the tax authorities should notify the taxpayer in writing within 15 days of reaching such a conclusion to start the formal negotiation of the APA and issue the "Notice on Formal Negotiation of the APA." If no consensus is reached, the tax authorities should notify the taxpayer in writing within 15 days of the end of the last pre-filing meeting, issuing the "Notice on Rejection of APA Application of the Enterprise" to explain the rejection.

Article 51 The enterprise should submit the written APA application report to the tax authorities within three months of receiving the notice of formal meeting from the tax authorities, and submit the "Formal Application for APA." If the enterprise applies for a bilateral or multilateral APA, the "Formal Application for APA" and "Application for Initiating Mutual Agreement Proceeding" should be submitted to the SAT and the competent tax authorities at the same time.

(i) The written application report of the APA should include the following:

(a) Organisational structure of the group, internal organisational structure of the enterprise, a description of the relationship between related parties, and details of the related-party transactions;

(b) The enterprise's financial statements for the last three years, product functions, and information about assets (including intangible and tangible assets);

(c) Types of related-party transactions and tax years to be covered in the APA;

(d) Allocation of functions and risks between the related parties, including the enterprises, human resources, expenses, and assets that the allocations depend on;

(e) The transfer pricing policy and calculation methods applied in the APA, and the supporting functional and risk analysis, benchmarking analysis, and assumptions;

(f) Illustration of the market condition, including industry development trends and the competitive environment;

(g) The enterprise's annual operating scale, forecasted operating performance, and operating plans during the period for which the APA is to apply;

(h) Related-party transactions, operating arrangements and financial performance information including the profit level to be covered by the APA;

(i) Whether the APA is to cover any double taxation issues;

(j) Issues in relation to domestic and international laws or tax treaties.

(ii) If, due to any of the following circumstances, the enterprise cannot submit the written application report on schedule, it can submit a written application to the tax authorities for an extension, together with the "Application for Extension on Submission of APA Formal Application":

(a) Certain information must be specially prepared;

(b) The preparation of the application report involves technical processing such as translation;

(c) Other non-subjective reasons;

The tax authorities should reply in writing to the application for extension within 15 days of receiving the written application from the enterprise, and issue the "Response to the Application for Extension on Submission of APA Formal Application." If no reply is made within the period specified above, the tax authorities are deemed to have accepted the enterprise's application for extension.

> (iii) The enterprise and the tax authorities should properly maintain all the documentation and information specified above, including the supporting documents for the pricing policies and calculation methods and any other documents supporting the fact that the enterprise meets the requirements for an APA.

Article 52 The tax authorities should review and evaluate the formal application for the APA within five months of receiving the written application and all the required materials from the enterprise. Depending on the actual review status, the tax authorities may request the enterprise to provide further information necessary for them to conclude the application.

If the review and examination period needs to be extended under special circumstances, the tax authorities should issue a written "Notice on Extension of APA Review and Evaluation" to the enterprise in a timely manner. The extension period shall not exceed three months.

The tax authorities should review and evaluate the following contents:

> (i) Historical operating status - analyse and evaluate documents in relation to the enterprise's operation plans, development trends, and operation scope. Special attention should be paid to examining the feasibility study report, investment budget (forecasted and finalised), and decisions of the board of directors. The tax authorities should comprehensively analyse documents related to the enterprise's operating performance, for example, financial statements or audit reports;

> (ii) Functional and risk profile - analyse and evaluate the enterprise and the share of functions performed by each enterprise in the related party arrangement of procurement, manufacturing, transportation, sales, research and development of intangible assets, and their risks assumed, including inventory risk, credit risk, foreign exchange risk, and market risk;

> (iii) Comparable information - analyse and evaluate the enterprise's domestic and overseas comparable price information and identify any substantial differences between the comparable enterprises and the applicant (tested party) and make any necessary adjustments. If the enterprise is not able to prove the reasonableness of its comparable transactions and operating activities, the tax authorities should request the enterprise to provide the necessary documentation and information to justify that the transfer pricing policies and calculation methods adopted fairly reflect the nature of the related-party transactions and the operating status of the enterprise, and have been proven by related financial

and operational information;

(iv) Assumptions - analyse and evaluate the factors affecting industry profitability as well as the significance of their influence on the enterprise's particular operation. The tax authorities should justify the reasonableness of the assumptions applied in the APA;

(v) Transfer pricing policies and calculation methods - analyse and evaluate whether and how the transfer pricing policies and calculation methods chosen were applied, are being applied and will be applied to past, present and future related party transactions respectively and relevant financial and operating information, as well as whether they comply with relevant laws and/or regulations;

(vi) Expected arm's-length prices or profit range - further examine and evaluate the comparable prices, profit margins and comparable enterprises' transactions, and estimate the prices or profit range acceptable to both the tax authorities and the enterprise.

Article 53 The tax authorities should negotiate with the enterprise within 30 days of the date they draw a conclusion on the unilateral APA application. If both parties reach an agreement, the draft APA and the assessment report should be submitted to the various higher level tax authorities for the final examination and approval by the SAT.

For bilateral or multilateral APAs, the SAT negotiates with the competent tax authorities of the tax treaty counterparty. In the case that both parties reach an agreement, the draft APA should be prepared according to the negotiation memorandum.

The draft APA should cover the following:

(i) Basic information of related parties, including name, address, etc;

(ii) Related-party transactions and the applicable years covered in the proposed APA;

(iii) Comparable prices or transactions, transfer pricing policies and calculation methods, and forecasted operating results selected in the proposed APA;

(iv) A glossary of the terms in relation to the application of transfer pricing methods and calculation basis;

(v) Critical assumptions;

(vi) The enterprise's obligations on annual filing, records maintenance, and disclosure of changes in assumptions;

(vii) Legal effects, confidentiality of documentation and information in the proposed APA;

(viii) Mutual responsibility clause;

(ix) Revisions to the proposed APA;

(x) Methods and approaches to resolve disputes;

(xi) Effective date of the proposed APA;

(xii) Supplementary provisions.

Article 54 If the tax authorities and the enterprise reach an agreement on the draft unilateral APA, the legal representatives or the representatives delegated by the legal representatives of both sides should sign the unilateral APA. If the SAT and the competent authorities of the tax treaty counterparties have reached an agreement on a bilateral or multilateral APA draft, the representatives delegated by the competent authorities should sign the bilateral or multilateral APA. The competent tax authorities should sign an "Agreement on the Implementation of the Bilateral (Multilateral) APA" with the enterprise according to the bilateral or multilateral APA.

Article 55 Both the tax authorities and the enterprise can suspend or terminate the negotiation anytime before signing the APA. For a bilateral or multilateral APA, the tax authorities can suspend or terminate the negotiation upon consent. In a termination, both sides should return all the information and materials provided in the negotiation.

Article 56 Tax authorities should establish a monitoring and management system to monitor the implementation of the APA.

(i) During the implementation period of the APA, the enterprise should maintain all relevant documents and information (including accounting books, related records, etc.) and should not lose, destroy or transfer any of the documents and information. The enterprise should provide to the tax authorities an annual report on the implementation status of the APA within five months of the end of the tax year.

The enterprise should illustrate in the report its operations during the year, and how it has complied with the relevant provisions of the APA, and any request for modification or de facto termination of the APA. The enterprise should explain any outstanding issues to be resolved or issues that are forthcoming in the annual report for negotiation with the tax authorities on the need to amend or terminate the APA.

(ii) During the implementation period of the APA, the tax authorities should regularly (once every six months in general) check the enterprise's implementation status of the APA. The inspection should cover the following issues: whether the enterprise complies with the provisions and requirements of the APA; whether the information and annual reports provided for the application of the APA reflect the actual operations of the enterprise; whether the information and the calculation methods used as the basis of the transfer pricing method are correct; whether the assumptions stated in the APA remain effective; and whether the enterprise's application of transfer pricing is consistent with those assumptions.

If the tax authorities discover any general violations of the APA by the enterprise, they should take necessary measures, which could include the termination of the arrangement. If the enterprise is found to have hidden any matters in relation to the APA or refused to implement the APA, the tax authorities should deem that the APA is void from its inception.

(iii) During the implementation period of the APA, if the actual operating results of the enterprise fall outside the price or profit range stipulated by the APA, the tax authorities shall, after reporting to the higher level tax authorities for verification, adjust the actual operating results so that they fall within the range of prices or profits stipulated by the APA. In the case of a bilateral or multilateral APA, the deviation should be reported to the higher level of tax authorities in order to obtain final approval from the SAT.

(iv) During the implementation period of the APA, the enterprise should submit a written report to the tax authorities detailing any substantial changes that may influence the APA. The enterprise should submit the report within 30 days of the changes taking place and provide a detailed explanation of the impact of the changes on the APA implementation, together with relevant supporting materials. The submission deadline of the report may be extended for non-subjective reasons. The extension period shall not exceed 30 days.

Within 60 days of receiving the taxpayer's written report, the tax authorities should evaluate and take any steps necessary, including reviewing the changes, negotiating with the taxpayer to revise the APA terms and relevant conditions, or amending or terminating the arrangement based on the extent of impact of such substantial changes on the execution of the APA. After the termination of the original APA, the tax authorities can arrange for the negotiation of a new APA according to the procedures and requirements in this Chapter.

(v) During the implementation period of an APA signed with the enterprise by both the state tax bureaus and the local tax bureaus, the enterprise should submit the annual report of the APA implementation and actual changes to the state tax bureaus and the local tax bureaus respectively. The state tax bureau and the local tax bureau should jointly inspect and examine the implementation of the agreement by the enterprise.

Article 57 The advance pricing arrangement will become invalid immediately after the period is due. If the APA needs to be renewed, the enterprise should submit the renewal application 90 days before the end of the APA implementation period, submitting the "Application for Renewal of APA", as well as providing reliable supporting evidence to prove that the facts and environment as described in the current APA have not undergone any substantial changes, and that it has been complying with the various terms and stipulations of the APA. The tax authorities should prepare a written response on acceptance or not within 15 days of receiving the renewal application and issue the "Response to the Application for Renewal of APA". The tax authorities should examine and evaluate the application materials of the renewal application, draft an advance pricing arrangement with enterprises, and finish the renewal of the arrangement in accordance with the agreed renewal time and place as agreed between the parties.

Article 58 The negotiation and implementation of an APA that involves more than two provinces, municipalities, directly governed city regions, and cities specifically designated in the state plan, or that involves both the state taxation bureau and local taxation bureau should be organised and coordinated by the SAT. The enterprise can submit a written letter of intent to the SAT directly.

Article 59 All state and local tax bureaus shall accept and implement an APA that is concluded between the tax authorities and the taxpayer, provided that the taxpayer abides by all the terms and requirements of the APA.

Article 60 Both the tax authorities and the enterprise are responsible for maintaining the confidentiality of all the information obtained throughout the process, from pre-filing meetings to the official signing, including the examination and analysis. The tax authorities and the enterprise should prepare a written memorandum of the negotiation content every time, and prepare a record of the number of documents and content provided to each other, signed or stamped by the chief negotiators of both parties.

Article 61 If the tax authorities and the enterprise fail to conclude an APA, the non-factual information, such as suggestions, assumptions, concepts and judgments, obtained by the tax authorities during the meeting or negotiation process cannot subsequently be used for a tax investigation related to the transactions covered by the intended APA.

Article 62 During the execution of the APA, if there are disagreements between the tax authorities and the enterprise, the two parties shall solve the disputes through negotiations. If the negotiations fail, the issues should be reported to the higher level tax authorities for coordination; in the case of a bilateral or multilateral APA, the issues should be reported to the SAT through escalated reporting for coordination. The lower level tax authorities should execute the result or decision made by the upper level tax authorities. If the enterprise still does not agree, the execution of the arrangement should be stopped.

Article 63 Within 10 days of the official signing, the tax authorities should submit the official copy of the unilateral APA or the Implementation Agreement of the bilateral or multilateral APA to the SAT for filing. The same should be done within 20 days for any modifications, termination and other matters during the execution of the APA.

Chapter 7 Cost Sharing Arrangements Administration

Article 64 Pursuant to Paragraph 2 of Article 41 of the CIT Law and Article 121 of its Implementation Rules, an enterprise that signs a cost sharing arrangement with its related parties on joint development, transfer of intangible assets, or provision and receipt of services should act in accordance with this Chapter.

Article 65 Participants in cost sharing arrangements can exploit the benefits of developed or transferred intangible property or the participation of services, and assume the corresponding costs. The costs borne by the related parties should comply with the costs paid by unrelated parties for the benefits mentioned above in comparable circumstances.

Participants who use intangible property developed or transferred under a cost sharing arrangement do not need to pay royalties separately.

Article 66 An enterprise should have reasonable and measurable expected benefits of its right to the intangible property and services involved in a cost sharing arrangement based on reasonable commercial assumptions and normal business practices.

Article 67 A cost sharing arrangement on services generally applies to group procurement and group marketing activities.

Article 68 A cost sharing arrangement should mainly include:

(i) Participant's name, country (region), related parties, rights and obligations in the arrangement;

(ii) Content and scope of the intangible assets or services involved in the cost sharing arrangement, the party that performs the research and development or provides the services involved in the cost sharing arrangement as well as its responsibilities and tasks;

(iii) Duration of the arrangement;

(iv) Computation methods and assumptions of the participants' expected benefits;

(v) Amount, form and valuation method for the initial costs as well as subsequent costs paid by the participants, and explanations for the arm's-length nature;

(vi) Specification of the accounting policy application and any changes;

(vii) Procedures and treatments for the entry or exit of the participants;

(viii) Terms and treatment for compensatory payments between participants;

(ix) Terms and treatment for changes to or termination of the arrangement;

(x) Rules for non-participants using the results of the arrangement.

Article 69 The enterprise should report the cost sharing arrangement to the SAT within 30 days of the arrangement being concluded. The tax authorities will report to the SAT to review whether the cost sharing arrangement complies with the arm's-length principle.

Article 70 For a cost sharing arrangement that has already been executed and has led to the creation of certain assets, if there are changes in participations or the arrangement is terminated, the following actions should be taken in accordance with the arm's-length principle:

(i) For the buy-in payment, the new participant should pay a reasonable fee to obtain the benefits in the existing results of the arrangement;

(ii) For the exit compensation, the original participants who exit the arrangement will transfer the benefit to other participants which warrant a reasonable compensation;

(iii) After the changes of participants, the benefits and costs shared by each party should be adjusted accordingly;

(iv) When the arrangement is terminated, the existing results should be allocated among all the participants on a reasonable basis.

If an enterprise does not comply with the arm's-length principle in making the above-mentioned treatments, and thus decreases its taxable income, the tax authorities are empowered to make adjustments.

Article 71 During the execution period of a cost sharing arrangement, the participant's costs should be commensurate with the expected benefits; otherwise a relevant compensating adjustment should be made.

Article 72 The tax treatments for a cost sharing arrangement in compliance with the arm's-length principle are as follows:

(i) The costs allocated to the enterprise under the arrangement should be deducted in each year as stipulated in the arrangement for corporate income tax purposes;

(ii) The compensating adjustment amount should be included in the taxable income in the year it is made;

(iii) For a cost sharing arrangement involving intangible assets, buy-in payments, exit compensation or the allocation of the existing results when the arrangement is terminated, all shall be treated in accordance with the relevant provisions for asset purchase or disposition.

Article 73 Enterprises can reach a cost sharing arrangement in the form of an APA in accordance with Chapter 6 of the Measures.

Article 74 During the execution of the cost sharing arrangement, besides the provisions as stipulated in Chapter 3 of the Measures, the enterprise should also prepare the following contemporaneous documentation for the cost sharing arrangement:

(i) Copy of the cost sharing arrangement;

(ii) Other agreements reached for the implementation of the cost sharing arrangement;

(iii) Non-participants' use of the results and the amount and form of payment;

(iv) Overview of the current year's new participants and exiting participants, including the name, country (region), related parties, amount and form of the payment for the buy-in or exit payments;

(v) Overview of changes to or termination of the cost sharing arrangement, including the reasons, treatment or distribution of the achieved results;

(vi) The current year's total costs and their composition pursuant to the cost sharing arrangement;

(vii) Overview of the current year's cost allocation to each participant, including the amount, form and objectives of the cost payment, and the amount, form, and objectives of any compensatory payments or receipts;

(viii) Comparison of the annual forecasted benefits and actual results as well as the corresponding adjustments made for the current year;

During the execution of the cost sharing agreement, whether or not the cost sharing agreement is in the form of an APA, the enterprise should submit related contemporaneous documentation on the cost sharing agreement to the tax authorities before 20 June of the next year after the applicable tax year.

Article 75 For an enterprise that signs a cost sharing arrangement with related parties, if one of the following scenarios applies, the costs allocated should not be deducted when computing the enterprise's taxable income:

(i) Lack of reasonable commercial purpose and economic substance;

(ii) Failure to comply with the arm's-length principle;

(iii) Failure to comply with the cost-revenue matching principle;

(iv) Failure to file or prepare, preserve and provide contemporaneous documentations for the cost sharing arrangement pursuant to the relevant provisions of the Measures;

(v) The operating period is shorter than 20 years from the signing of the cost sharing arrangement.

Chapter 8 Controlled Foreign Corporation Administration

Article 76 A controlled foreign corporation, as stipulated in Article 45 of the CIT Law, refers to a foreign enterprise established in a country (or region) where the actual tax rate is lower than 50 percent of the tax rate set out in Paragraph 1 of Article 4 of the CIT Law, whose profits are not distributed or are distributed at a reduced rate due to reasons other than viable business needs, and is controlled by a resident enterprise or by a resident enterprise jointly with Chinese individual residents (hereinafter collectively referred to as "Chinese resident shareholders" which includes both Chinese resident enterprise shareholders and Chinese resident individual shareholders).

Article 77 The "control" referred to in Article 76 of the Measures means substantial control in terms of shares, capital, operation, purchase and sales. Of these, control in shares means that a Chinese resident shareholder directly or indirectly holds no less than 10 percent of the voting shares of a foreign enterprise in any single day of a taxable year, and jointly holds no less than 50 percent of the total shares of the foreign enterprise.

Shares indirectly held by Chinese resident shareholders are accumulated by multiplying each proportion of the shares held by each level together. If the proportion exceeds 50 percent, then 100 percent should be used for the calculation.

Article 78 For annual corporate income tax filing purposes, Chinese resident enterprise shareholders shall submit information about overseas investments, submitting the "Outbound Investment Form" together with their annual tax reporting.

Article 79 The tax authorities are responsible for collecting and reviewing the information about overseas investments reported by Chinese resident enterprise shareholders. The tax authorities should deliver the "Confirmation Notice of Chinese Resident Enterprise Shareholders of Controlled Foreign Corporation" to Chinese resident enterprise shareholders who are recognised as shareholders of a controlled foreign corporation, and impose taxes on the Chinese resident enterprise shareholders that satisfy the taxation conditions as specified in Article 45 of the CIT Law.

Article 80 The deemed dividend income from the controlled foreign corporation should be included in the taxable income of the Chinese resident enterprise shareholder. The calculation formula is as follows:

The current period income of the Chinese resident enterprise shareholder = (deemed dividend income×actual number of share holding days)÷(number of days of the controlled foreign corporation's tax year×percentage of shares held)

For multi-level indirect shareholding by Chinese resident shareholders, the proportion will be calculated by multiplying each proportion of the shares held by each level together.

Article 81 If there is a difference in taxable years between the controlled foreign corporation and the Chinese resident enterprise shareholder, the deemed dividend income should be included in the revenue generated in the taxable year of the Chinese resident enterprise shareholder to which the ending date of the taxable year of the CFC can be attributed.

Article 82 If the Chinese resident enterprise shareholder has already paid income tax overseas for the current period income of the deemed dividend, credit or exemptions can be granted pursuant to the relevant provisions in the CIT Law or tax treaties.

Article 83 The actual distribution of profit by the CFC already taxed pursuant to Article 45 of the CIT Law can be excluded from the taxable income of the Chinese resident enterprise shareholder for the current period.

Article 84 If the Chinese resident enterprise shareholder can provide information to prove that the foreign corporation under its control satisfies one of the following conditions, the profits of the foreign corporation that are not distributed or are distributed at a reduced rate can be exempted from being regarded as the deemed dividend and can be excluded from the taxable income of the Chinese resident enterprise for the current period:

    (i) Located in a non-low tax rate country (or region) as recognised by the SAT;
    (ii) The revenue is mainly generated from active business operations;
    (iii) The annual profit does not exceed RMB 5 million.

Chapter 9 Thin Capitalisation Administration

Article 85 As stipulated in Article 46 of the CIT Law, the interest expenses which shall not be deducted from taxable income should be calculated as follows:

Non-deductible interest payments = annual actual interest paid to related parties × (1 - standard ratio / related party debt to equity ratio)

In the formula above, the standard ratio refers to the ratio stipulated in "The MOF and the SAT's Notice on Deducibility of Interest Payment to Related Parties" (Caishui [2008] No. 121).

Pursuant to Article 46 of the CIT Law and Article 119 of its Implementation Rules, the related party debt to equity ratio is the portion of the debt investment received from all its related parties ("related party debt investment") to the equity investment ("equity investment"). The related party debt investment includes all types of debt investment guaranteed by related parties in any form.

Article 86 The related party debt to equity ratio is calculated as follows:

Related party debt to equity ratio = sum of monthly average related party debt investment in a year / sum of monthly average equity investment in a year

Of which:

Monthly average related party debt investment = (book opening balance of related party debt investment at the beginning of the month + book ending balance of related party debt investment at the end of the month) / 2

Monthly average equity investment = (book opening balance of equity investment at the beginning of the month + book ending balance of equity investment at the end of the month) / 2

Equity investment is the owner's equity on the balance sheet. When the owner's equity is less than the sum of paid-in capital (capital stock) and paid-up capital, equity investment equals the sum of paid-in capital (capital stock) and paid-up capital; when the sum of paid-in capital (capital stock) and paid-up capital is less than paid-in capital (capital stock), equity investment is equal to paid-in capital (capital stock).

Article 87 Interest expense as stipulated in Article 46 of the CIT Law includes the interest, guarantee fees, mortgage charges and other costs of an interest nature in relation to the direct or indirect related party debt investment.

Article 88 As stipulated in Article 46 of the CIT Law, the interest expense which cannot be deducted from the taxable income shall not be carried forward to the next taxable year. The allocation of the interest expense among related parties should be made in accordance with the proportion of actual interest paid to each related party in the total interest paid to related parties. For any of the non-deductible interest expense that can be allocated to a domestic related party with higher effective tax rate, a deduction will be allowed. Actual interest paid to overseas related parties directly or indirectly should be regarded as a dividend distribution, and enterprise income tax should be levied based on the difference between the income tax rates of dividend and interest. There shall be no tax refund if the withheld income tax exceeds the income tax calculated for deemed dividends.

Article 89 To apply for the deduction of interest expenses when the related party debt to equity ratio of the enterprise exceeds the standard ratio to be deducted from the taxable income, the enterprise should, in addition to what is required pursuant to the relevant provisions in Chapter 3 of the Measures, prepare, preserve, and, based on the requirements of the tax authorities, submit contemporaneous documentation. It should demonstrate that the debt investment amount, interest rate, term, financing conditions and debt to equity ratio are in line with the arm's-length principle by including the following contents:

(i) An analysis of the borrower's solvency and borrowing capacity;

(ii) An analysis of the borrowing capacity and the financing structure of the group;

(iii) An explanation of any changes in equity investment, such as the enterprise's registered capital;

(iv) The nature, purpose, and market situation of the related party debt investment;

(v) The currency, amount, interest rate, terms, and financing conditions of the related party debt investment;

(vi) The conditions and terms of the collateral provided by the enterprise;

(vii) The conditions of guarantor and terms of the guarantee;

(viii) The interest rate and financing conditions of loans of similar nature and terms;

(ix) The conversion condition of the convertible bonds;

(x) Other supporting documents that can prove compliance with the arm's-length principle.

Article 90 For an enterprise which has not prepared, maintained or provided contemporaneous documentation to prove that its investment amount, interest rate, term, financing conditions and debt to equity ratio of related party debt investment comply with the arm's-length principle, the interest expense for the debt that exceeds the standard ratio cannot be deducted from the taxable income.

Article 91 The "actual interest payment" refers to the interest booked as cost or expense on an accrual basis by enterprises. If there are transfer pricing issues regarding the interest actually paid to related parties, tax authorities should first conduct a transfer pricing investigation and make any necessary adjustments pursuant to Chapter 5 of the Measures.

Chapter 10 General Anti-avoidance Administration

Article 92 Pursuant to Article 47 of the CIT Law and Article 120 of its Implementation Rules, the tax authorities can launch a general anti-avoidance investigation on enterprises where the following tax avoidance arrangements are identified:

(i) Abusive use of tax preferences;

(ii) Abusive use of tax treaties;

(iii) Abusive use of the forms of enterprise organization;

(iv) Tax avoidance by means of tax havens;

(v) Other arrangements without reasonable business purposes.

Article 93 In order to identify whether an enterprise has a tax avoidance arrangement, the tax authorities should examine the following factors, following the principle of "substance over form":

(i) The form and the substance of an arrangement;

(ii) The time and effective period of an arrangement;

(iii) The implementation method of an arrangement;

(iv) The connection of each step or part of an arrangement;

(v) The changes in each party's financial situation involved in an arrangement;

(vi) The tax result of an arrangement.

Article 94 The tax authorities should redefine the tax avoidance arrangements in accordance with the enterprise's economic substance, and annul the tax benefit obtained by the enterprise from such tax avoidance arrangements. For enterprises without economic substance, especially those incorporated in tax havens and enabling tax avoidance by their related parties or non-related parties, the tax authorities are empowered to deny the existence of the enterprises from a tax collection perspective.

Article 95 The tax authorities should issue the "Tax Inspection Notice" to the enterprise in accordance with the relevant provisions in the Tax Collection Law and its Implementation Rules when launching a general anti-avoidance investigation. The enterprise shall present supporting evidence for justifying its reasonable business purposes within 60 days of receiving the Notice. If the enterprise fails to provide documentation within the period or the evidence provided fails to justify the reasonableness of its business purpose, the tax authorities can make an adjustment based on the information obtained and deliver a "Notice on Special Tax Investigation Adjustment."

Article 96 In conducting a general anti-tax avoidance investigation, the tax authorities may request the planners of the tax avoidance arrangement to provide relevant materials and supporting evidence in accordance with the provisions of Article 57 of the Tax Collection Law.

Article 97 Any general anti-avoidance investigation and corresponding tax adjustment shall be reported level by level upward to the State Administration of Taxation for approval.

Chapter 11 Corresponding Adjustments and International Negotiation

Article 98 If one party involved in the related-party transaction has had a transfer pricing adjustment imposed upon it, the other party should be allowed to make corresponding adjustments to avoid double taxation. If the corresponding adjustment involves related parties in a tax treaty country or region, upon an application from the enterprise, the State Administration of Taxation will undertake negotiations with the competent tax authorities of the other party of the tax treaty pursuant to the mutual agreement procedures provided in the tax treaty.

Article 99 In the case of the corresponding adjustment of the related party located in the tax treaty country (or location), the enterprise should submit in writing an "Application for Initiating Mutual Negotiation Procedure" to both the State Administration of Taxation and the competent tax authorities at the same time, with copies of the adjustment notice of the enterprise or its related parties and other relevant materials.

Article 100 The enterprise should apply for corresponding adjustments within three years of the day the enterprise or its related parties receives the transfer pricing adjustment notice. Any overdue applications will be inadmissible.

Article 101 Taxes paid relating to overseas related party interest, rent, and royalty payments involved in a transfer pricing adjustment will not be subject to a corresponding adjustment.

Article 102 Where the State Administration of Taxation accepts an application for a bilateral or multilateral APAs in accordance with Chapter 6 of the Measures, it should undertake negotiations with the competent tax authorities of the other party of the tax treaty pursuant to the mutual agreement procedures provided in the tax treaty.

Article 103 The corresponding adjustments or results of mutual agreement procedures are to be delivered by the State Administration of Taxation in written form through the governing tax authorities to the enterprise.

Article 104 Corresponding adjustment as provided by this chapter does not apply to the interest that is not deductible in calculating taxable income and the interest expenses deemed as dividend distribution as described in Chapter 9 of the Measures.

Chapter 12 Legal Responsibility

Article 105 Enterprises that fail to submit the annual reporting forms for the related-party transactions to the tax authorities or fail to preserve contemporaneous documentation or other related documents in accordance with the provisions in the Measures will be dealt with pursuant to Articles 60 and 62 of the Tax Collection Law.

Article 106 If an enterprise refuses to provide contemporaneous documentation and other information on related-party transactions to the tax authorities, or provides false or incomplete information that cannot truthfully reflect its actual related-party transactions, it will be dealt with pursuant to the provisions in Article 70 of the Tax Collection Law and Article 96 of its Implementation Rules as well as Article 44 of the CIT Law and Article 115 of its Implementation Rules.

Article 107 If the tax authorities make a special tax adjustment for the enterprise pursuant to the provisions in the CIT Law and its Implementation Rules, an additional interest payment should be charged for additional tax levied on transactions after 1 January 2008.

(i) The period for interest calculation is from 1 June of the year after the tax year applicable to the date of the tax payment (pre-payment).

(ii) The interest rate shall be calculated based upon the RMB loan benchmarking rate published by the People's Bank of China on 31 December of the tax year(s) to which the underpaid tax belongs for a loan of the same term as the period for which additional tax is payable ("base rate"), plus 5 percent. The benchmarking rate will be converted to a daily interest rate based on a 365-day year.

(iii) Where the enterprise can provide both the contemporaneous documentation and relevant materials, or the enterprise is exempted from preparing contemporaneous documentation in accordance with Article 15 of the Measures, yet it provides other relevant materials requested by the tax authorities, the interest rate can be calculated based on the benchmarking rate alone.

If the tax authorities levy an interest on the additional tax payment when an enterprise is exempt from preparing contemporaneous documentation in accordance with Paragraph 1 Article 15 in the Measures and where the enterprise's actual amount of related-party transactions reaches the threshold of preparing contemporaneous documentation, the provisions in Paragraph 2 of this Article should be applied.

(iv) The interest charges prescribed in this Article cannot be deducted when calculating taxable income.

Article 108 If an enterprise has prepaid tax before the tax authorities make a special tax adjustment, in case additional tax should be paid after receiving the tax payment notice, the tax year to which the prepaid tax belongs should be determined according to the order of the tax years to which the additional tax payment belongs. The interest should also be calculated up to the date of the prepaid tax.

Article 109 The enterprise should pay the additionally levied tax and interest within the time limit prescribed in the adjustment notice issued by the tax authorities. If the enterprise fails to pay the tax and interest due within the time limit due to special circumstances, an application for an extension of the tax and interest payment should be submitted in accordance with the provisions in Article 31 of the Tax Collection Law as well as Article 41 and Article 42 of its Implementation Rules. If the enterprise does not apply for an extension or pay the tax and interest due, the tax authorities shall deal with it pursuant to Article 32 of the Tax Collection Law and other relevant provisions.

Chapter 13 Supplementary Provisions

Article 110 Procedures for investigations and adjustments of the special tax adjustment issues other than the transfer pricing administration and APA administration can be found in Chapter 5 of the Measures.

Article 111 The state tax bureaus and local tax bureaus at all levels should strengthen their cooperation during the implementation of special tax investigation and adjustments. If needed, joint investigation teams can be formed to conduct such investigations.

Article 112 The tax authorities and the tax officials should preserve and use the information and documents provided by enterprises in accordance with the Circular of the State Administration of Taxation on the Provisional Measures for the Tax-related Confidential Information Management of Taxpayers (Circular Guoshuifa [2008] No. 93) and other relevant provisions on confidentiality.

Article 113 If the last day of the prescribed period in the Measures is a legal holiday, the next day after the holiday should be deemed as the last day of the prescribed period. If there are more than three continuous legal holidays in the period, the last day should be postponed for the length of the holidays.

Article 114 Figures given in this Regulation using the phrases: "above", "below", "within a certain number of days", "on the day of", "before", "less than", "lower than", and "more than" are inclusive of the figure provided.

Article 115 In principle, if the investigated enterprises apply to change business address or deregister its tax registration during the special tax investigation and adjustment period, the tax authorities will not approve such changes or deregistration

Supplemental Materials

until the conclusion of the investigation.

Article 116 The preparation of contemporaneous documentation regarding related party transactions during the 2008 tax year in accordance with Chapter 3 in the Measures can be extended to 31 December 2009.

Article 117 The Measures are subject to explanation and modification by the State Administration of Taxation.

Article 118 The Measures come into effect on 1 January 2008. Meanwhile, the "Administration of Tax on Business Transactions Between Affiliated Enterprises Rules" (Guoshuifa [1998] No. 59), "Administrative Regulations for Tax on Business Transactions Between Affiliated Enterprises Rules (Revised)" (Guoshuifa [2004] No. 143) and "Notice of the State Administration of Taxation on Distributing the (Trial) Implementing Rules for Negotiated Pricing for the Transactions Among Associated Enterprises" (Guoshuifa [2004] No. 118) will be annulled. If the previous provisions are different from the Measures, the Measures shall prevail.

This translation of the China Implementation Measures was provided for inclusion in this guide courtesy of KPMG China. The editors with to thank **Steven Tseng**, who serves as KPMG's Partner in charge for the China & Hong Kong SAR as well as Asia Pacific Leader of their Global Transfer Pricing Services for the translation. Mr. Tseng can be reached by phone at **+86 (21) 2212 2888 *ext 3408***, **+86 (21) 2212 3408** (direct), or **+86 1381 898 3223** (mobile). He can also be reached by fax at **+86 (21) 6288 1889** and by email at **steven.tseng@kpmg.com.cn**. The physical address of KPMG China (Advisory) Limited is 50th Floor, Plaza 66, 1266 Nanjing West Road, Shanghai 200040, China.

Supplemental Materials

China Implementation Measures Attached Forms

The China *Implementation Measures* include twenty-two attached forms, which are available translated into English to **Tax Director's Guide to International Transfer Pricing** purchasers and subscribers.

Space constraints prevent the inclusion of the forms and attachments in this volume, but they are available free of charge to subscribers who register their copy of the book (email us at info@gbisi.com or call +1 617 795-0519 to register your copy).

Here is a list of the Attached Forms:

Form 1	Function and Risk Analysis Form
Form 2	Financial Analysis Form for Related-party Transactions
Form 3	Comparability Analysis Form
Form 4	Form for Determination of Related-Party Relationships
Form 5	Form for Determination of Related-Party Transactions
Form 6	Form for Determination of Comparability Factors
Form 7	Notification of Special Tax Investigation Conclusion
Form 8	Negotiation Records
Form 9	Notice on Preliminary Adjustment Plan of Special Tax Investigation
Form 10	Notice on Special Tax Investigation Adjustment
Form 11	Meeting Minutes of Advance Pricing Arrangement
Form 12	Notice on Formal Negotiation of an Advance Pricing Arrangement
Form 13	Notice on Rejection of Advance Pricing Arrangement Application
Form 14	Formal Application for Advance Pricing Arrangement
Form 15	Application for Extension on Submission of Formal Application for APA
Form 16	Response to the Application for Extension on Submission of Formal Application of an Advance Pricing Arrangement
Form 17	Notice on Extension of Examination and Evaluation of an APA
Form 18	Advance Pricing Arrangement
Form 19	Bilateral (Multilateral) APA Implementation Agreement
Form 20	Application for Renewal of an Advance Pricing Arrangement
Form 21	Response to the Application for Renewal of APA
Form 22	Confirmation Notice of Chinese Resident Enterprise Shareholders of Controlled Foreign Corporation

Supplemental Materials

Commissioner's Directive on the Operation of Transfer Pricing
(Administrative Guidelines)
National Tax Agency of Japan

This document is a translation of the original Japanese-language Directive. The Japanese original is the official text.

Document ID: Large Enterprise Examination Division 7-1
International Operations Division 3-1
Office of Mutual Agreement Procedures 1-16
Corporation Taxation Division 6-7
Date: June 1, 2001 (latest amendment: Jun.25, 2007)
To: Regional Commissioners, Regional Taxation Bureaus
Regional Commissioner, Okinawa Regional Taxation Office
From: Commissioner, National Tax Agency

The following rules have been established in regard to the operation of transfer pricing and shall be followed from this date forward.
"Commissioner's Directive on Procedure for Confirmation of Transfer Pricing Methodologies to Determine the Arm's Length Price (Administrative Guidelines)" issued on October 25, 1999 [Document ID: Large Enterprise Examination Division 8-1] is hereby repealed.

(Purpose)
These procedures aim at the establishment of guidelines for operations related to Article 66-4 of the Act on Special Measures concerning Taxation "Special Taxation Measures of Transactions between Corporations and Foreign-related Persons" and the proper and smooth enforcement of transfer pricing taxation.

Chapter 1. Definitions and Basic Policies

(Definition of Terms)
1-1 In this Directive, the meaning of the terms listed below shall be as prescribed in the following respectively:
(1) CTA: The Corporation Tax Act.
(2) ASMT: Act on Special Measures concerning Taxation.

(3) CTA Directive: Commissioner's Directive on Interpretation of the CTA.
(4) ASMT Directive: Commissioner's Directive on Interpretation of the ASMT.
(5) Transfer pricing taxation: The provisions of Article 66-4 of the ASMT (except Paragraph 3).
(6) Consolidated corporation: A consolidated corporation prescribed in Item 12-7-4 of Article 2 of the CTA.
(7) Consolidated parent corporation: A consolidated parent corporation prescribed in Item 12-7-2 of Article 2 of the CTA.
(8) Final tax return: A final tax return prescribed in Item 31 of Article 2 of the CTA and attached documents.
(9) Taxable year: Taxable year prescribed in Article 13 of the CTA.
(10) Consolidated taxable year: Consolidated taxable year prescribed in Article 15-2 of the CTA.
(11) Foreign-related person: A foreign-related person prescribed in Article 66-4(1) and Article 68-88(1) of the ASMT.
(12) Foreign-related transaction: A foreign-related transaction prescribed in Article 66-4(1) and Article 68-88(1) of the ASMT.
(13) Arm's length price: Arm's length price prescribed in Article 66-4(1) of the ASMT.
(14) Method of calculation of arm's length price: The calculation method of arm's length price prescribed in Article 66-4(2) of the ASMT.
(15) Unrelated persons: Persons who have no "special relations", as prescribed in Article 66-4(1) of the ASMT, with the subject corporation.
(16) Comparable transactions: Comparable unrelated transactions prescribed in the ASMT Directive 66-4(2)-1.
(17) Profit split method: The profit split method listed in Item 1 of Article 39-12(8) of the Cabinet Order of the ASMT.
(18) Transactional net margin method: The transactional net margin method listed in Items 2, 3 and 4 of Article 39-12(8) of the Cabinet Order of the ASMT.
(19) Intangible properties: The intangible properties prescribed in ASMT Directive 66-4(2)-3-(8).
(20) Tax treaties: The tax treaties that Japan concludes for the avoidance of double taxation and/or the prevention of fiscal evasion with respect to taxes on income.
(21) Act on Special Provisions for the Enforcement of Income Tax Conventions: Act on Special Provisions of the Income Tax Act, Corporation Tax Act, and Local Tax Act for the Enforcement of Income Tax Conventions.
(22) Mutual agreement procedure: A negotiation procedure between the competent authority of Japan and the competent authority of a foreign country pursuant to the provisions of a tax treaty.
(23) APA: The confirmation made by a District Director of a Tax Office or a Regional Commissioner

of a Regional Taxation Bureau with regard to the methodologies of calculation of arm's length price and the specific details thereof (hereinafter referred to as "TPM") deemed to be the most reasonable to be adopted by a corporation.

(24) APA review: The review of an APA request conducted by the RTB division-in-charge.

(25) Pre-filing consultation: The consultation by the corporation intending to receive confirmation of the RTB division in charge (including, where necessary, the division in charge of the National Tax Agency and Office of Mutual Agreement Procedures) concerning the TPM for which an APA request is to be made (including anonymous consultations through an agent) prior to an APA request.

(26) RTB division in charge: The Corporation Taxation Division of the Second Taxation Department of the Regional Taxation Bureau (Taxation Department in the cases of the Kanazawa, Takamatsu, and Kumamoto Regional Tax Bureaus) and Corporation Taxation Division of the Okinawa Regional Taxation Office (hereinafter referred to as "RTB Corporation Taxation Divisions") or Advance Pricing Arrangement Division of the First Large Enterprise Examination Department of the Tokyo Regional Tax Bureau, Transfer Pricing Division of the First Large Enterprise Examination Department of the Osaka Regional Tax Bureau, International Examination of Large Enterprise Division of the Large Enterprise Examination Department of the Nagoya Regional Tax Bureau, International Examination of Large Enterprise Division of the Large Enterprise Examination and Criminal Investigation Department of the Kanto-Shin-Etsu Regional Tax Bureau, Management Division (Large Enterprise Examination) of the Large Enterprise Examination and Criminal Investigation Department of the Sapporo,

Sendai, Kanazawa, Hiroshima, Takamatsu, Fukuoka, and Kumamoto Regional Tax Bureaus, and the Large Enterprise Examination Division of the Okinawa Regional Taxation Office (hereinafter referred to as "RTB Large Enterprise Examination Divisions").

(27) NTA division in charge: The Corporation Taxation Division of the Taxation Department of the National Tax Agency, or the Large Enterprise Examination Division of the Large Enterprise Examination and Criminal Investigation Department of the NTA.

(28) NTA Office of Mutual Agreement Procedures: The Office of Mutual Agreement Procedures of the Commissioner's Secretariat of the National Tax Agency.

(29) Commissioner's Directive on OTPCC: Commissioner's Directive on the Operation of Transfer Pricing with regard to Consolidated Corporations (Issued on Apr. 28, 2005) [Document ID: Large Enterprise Examination Division 7-4, etc.].

(Basic Policies)
1-2 Operations of transfer pricing taxation need to be properly managed, taking into consideration the fact that this taxation system is based on the arm's length principles. For this reason, it shall be

operated in accordance with the basic policies stated below:
(1) It shall be closely examined whether the prices fixed for foreign-related transactions are equal to the prices normally fixed for uncontrolled transactions. In cases where any problem is found in the transactions, efforts shall be made to widely collect information regarding the market and the business for an appropriate examination as to the selection of the calculation method and comparable transaction, and adjustment for differences.
(2) To ensure the predictability of the corporation and to realize proper and smooth enforcement of transfer pricing taxation, the APA process shall be conducted in cases where an APA request regarding the TPM is submitted by the corporation, based on the contents of mutual agreement related to the APA request if there is any such agreement.
(3) To solve international double taxation caused by transfer pricing taxation, it is important for the tax authorities of each country to share an understanding of transfer pricing. Therefore, an examination or APA review shall be conducted in an appropriate manner by referring to the OECD Transfer Pricing Guidelines as necessary.

(Use of Reference Case Studies)
1-3 The "Reference Case Studies on Transfer Pricing Taxation" (supplement) describes the tax treatment of transfer pricing illustrated by examples based on certain preconditions. This shall be referred to in order to assist the proper administration of transfer pricing taxation while being mindful that there exist other cases as well as those described in the Case Studies that, though similar, may be treated differently for the purposes of transfer pricing due to being based on different preconditions.

Chapter 2. Examination

(Examination Policies)
2-1 When examining foreign-related transactions, the following points shall be taken into account, in order to correctly ascertain whether any problem exists in the transaction under transfer pricing taxation. In the examination process, each case shall be examined not perfunctorily but carefully, bearing in mind the circumstances of each transaction.
(1) Whether or not the gross profit margin or operating profit margin (hereinafter referred to as "profit margin and so on") arising from foreign-related transactions of the corporation is excessively low compared with other transactions, which are conducted by the corporation with unrelated persons in a similar market and which are similar in quantity, market level, and other respects.
(2) Whether or not the profit margin and so on arising from foreign-related transactions of the

corporation is excessively low compared with the profit margin and so on of other unrelated persons engaged in the same category of business similar in quantity, market level, and other respects with the corporation.
(3) Whether or not the corporation's profit arising from foreign-related transactions is relatively low compared with the foreign-related person's profit arising from the same transactions, in the light of the function performed or risks assumed by the corporation or the foreign-related person with respect to such foreign-related transactions.

(Points to Consider when Conducting Examinations)
2-2 Foreign-related transactions shall be examined on the basis of final tax returns and other materials or data collected through examinations. Prior to calculation of arm's length prices, examinations shall be conducted from various angles, including by the following methods, in order to determine whether there exist any problems regarding transfer pricing taxation and to ensure that the examinations are conducted effectively.
(1) Verification whether or not the profit margin of foreign-related transactions under the examination are within the range of the profit margin of uncontrolled transactions (hereinafter referred to as "transactions deemed comparable with the foreign-related transaction") in the same business category and substantially similar to the foreign-related transactions in terms of quantity, market level, and other respects.
(2) Use of the average value of the consideration or profit margin for foreign-related transactions or transactions deemed comparable with the foreign-related transactions during a reasonable length of time before and after such a taxable year or consolidated taxable year, if it is considered to be inappropriate to examine the price of inventory and so on of the foreign-related transactions based only on the information for each relevant taxable year or consolidated taxable year due to considerable changes in prices reflecting changes in public demand, product lifecycle, or other such factors.

(Examination of Attachment of Form 17-(3))
2-3 In cases where a corporation that conducts any foreign-related transaction fails to attach "Information on Foreign Related Persons" (Form 17-(3)) to its final tax return or to provide sufficient information in Form 17-(3), the corporation shall be urged to submit the Form or to revise the information provided, and endeavors to obtain more accurate information on the particulars of the transactions shall be made.

(Documents to Be Inspected at the Time of Examination)
2-4 In examinations, it shall be ascertained whether any problem under transfer pricing taxation

exists by obtaining information on the actual circumstances of the foreign-related transaction from documents, books and records, and other materials (hereinafter in 2-4 referred to as "documents"), such as:
(1) Documents that describe the capital relationship and details of business of the corporation and each foreign-related person:
   (a) Documents containing the capital and business relationship between the corporation and its affiliate(s);
   (b) Documents containing the history and any changes in major shareholders of the corporation and the foreign-related person;
   (c) Financial documents or financial statements and reports on the details of business with respect to the corporation, and corresponding reports for the foreign-related person;
   (d) Documents listing the major product lines of the corporation and the foreign-related person, and the transaction price, selling markets, and market size of each product;
   (e) Documents containing the results and characteristics of each business, the special circumstances of each taxable year, and other details of business of the corporation and the foreign-related person.
(2) Documents used by the corporation for the calculation of arm's length prices:
   (a) Documents containing the selection process of comparable transactions adopted by the corporation and the details of the comparable transactions;
   (b) In cases where the corporation calculates arm's length prices regarding more than one transaction as a single transaction, documents reporting the details of each original transaction on the basis of which the calculation is made;
   (c) Documents containing the reasons for adoption of the calculation method of the arm's length prices and any other document prepared by the corporation for calculating the arm's length prices;
   (d) Documents containing the adjustment method and reasons for adjustments, if differences are adjusted with respect to comparable transactions.
(3) Documents containing the details of foreign-related transactions:
   (a) Contracts or documents containing the content of contracts;
   (b) Pricing policy and documents containing the details of price negotiations between the corporation and the foreign-related person;
   (c) Documents containing the details of the business strategies of the corporation or the foreign-related person with regard to the foreign-related transactions;
   (d) Documents containing the statement of profits and losses of the corporation and the foreign-related person with regard to the foreign-related transactions;
   (e) Documents containing the functions performed or risks assumed by the corporation and the

foreign-related person with respect to the foreign-related transactions;
(f) Documents containing the details of the intangible properties used by the corporation or the foreign-related person for conducting the foreign-related transactions;
(g) Documents regarding the analysis of the market of the inventory and so on related to the foreign-related transactions;
(h) Documents containing the details of inventory and so on related to the foreign-related transactions;
(i) If there are any other transactions closely connected with the foreign-related transactions, documents containing the details of such transactions.
(4) Other documents
(a) Manuals and so on containing the details of the accounting standards of the corporation and the foreign-related person;
(b) Documents containing the details of the transfer pricing examinations or APA conducted with regard to the foreign-related person by foreign tax authorities;
(c) If the foreign-related person, under the system of a foreign country corresponding to transfer pricing taxation, has prepared any document pursuant to the rules that require the preparation of appropriate documents for supporting the effectiveness of the system (referred to as "Documentation Rules"), then the documents so prepared;
(d) Other documents as deemed necessary.

(Points to Note in Applying the Estimation Clause or the Rules of Inquiry and Inspection to Third Parties in the Same Trade)

2-5 In cases where a corporation is requested to present or submit documents, books, and records or copies (hereinafter referred to in 2-5 as "documents prescribed in Paragraph 7"), and the corporation fails to present such documents prescribed in Paragraph 7 without delay, the provisions of Paragraph 7 ("Estimation Clause") or Paragraph 9 ("Rules of Inquiry and Inspection to Third Parties in the Same Trade") of Article 66-4of the ASMT is applicable. In applying these rules, the following points shall be noted:
(1) When requesting the corporation to present or submit the documents prescribed in Paragraph 7, explanation shall be given to the corporation that if it fails to present or submit these documents without delay, Paragraph 7 or Paragraph 9 of Article 66-4 of the ASMT is applicable; also, the fact that the explanation has been given and how the documents are presented or submitted by the corporation after such explanation shall be recorded.
(2) Whether the corporation has presented or submitted the documents prescribed in Paragraph 7 without delay shall be judged in light of the period normally required for submission or presentation of such documents.

(3) In cases where any uncontrolled transaction (uncontrolled transaction prescribed in ASMT Directive 66-4(2)-1; hereinafter the same) recognized by applying the provisions of Article 66-4(9) of the ASMT is selected as a comparable transaction, explanation shall be given to the corporation about the conditions of such selection, the content of the comparable transaction, and the method of adjustment for difference. When the explanation is made, attention shall be paid to the provisions of Article 163 (Confidentiality of Staff) of the CTA and the fact that such an explanation has been given shall be recorded.

(Loans)
2-6 The following points shall be noted when examining loans:
(1) Loans to which the CTA Directive 9-4-2 (Regarding Loans Without Interest for Reconstructing a Subsidiary and so on) is applicable shall also be treated as legitimate transactions under transfer pricing taxation.
(2) In cases where the maturity date of a foreign-related transaction is unknown, the period of the loan shall be reasonably calculated in light of the purpose of the loan.

(Corporations Not in the Financial Business)
2-7 In conducting examinations on lending and borrowing activities between a corporation and a foreign-related person, in cases where neither party is engaged in lending or investment activities as a core business and also where the ASMT Directive 66-4(6)-4 is not applicable, the appropriateness of the interest rate applied to the lending or borrowing shall be examined by regarding the interest rate, calculated as follows, as the arm's length interest rate:
(1) The interest rate that would normally be applied to a loan, assuming that the lender involved in the foreign-related transaction made the loan from an unrelated bank under similar conditions in terms of currency, borrowing date, and borrowing period.
(2) The interest rate that would normally be earned on the funds involved in the foreign-related transaction, assuming that they were invested in government securities or the like under similar conditions in terms of currency, transaction date, and transaction period (exclusive of cases where the interest rate set forth in (1) is applicable).
(Note) In cases where the interest rate set forth in (1) is applicable, and the loan actually made from a bank and so on to the lender in the foreign-related transaction is a loan made under similar conditions as set forth in (1), whether the loan has a conditional relationship with the foreign-related transaction is of no relevance.

(Provision of Services)
2-8 The following points shall be noted when examining the provision of services:

(1) In some cases, the consideration for use of intangible properties is not included in the price for the provision of services, even though the intangible properties are used for rendering services. (Note) In the case where it is examined whether any intangible properties are used when services are rendered, it shall be noted that the provision of services and use of intangible properties are conceptually distinct. Consideration therefore needs to be given to such matters as whether the intangible properties used by the service provider when rendering services correspond to the intangible properties set forth in ASMT Directive 66-4(2)-3-(8), and what impact the provision of services has on the activities and functions of the service recipient.

(2) In some cases, the services are rendered in conjunction with the transfer and so on of tangible assets or intangible properties, and the value of the consideration related to the provision of services is included in the price of such transfers and so on of such properties.

(Provision of Services Incidental to the Original Business Activities)
2-9 In the case where the ASMT Directive 66-4(6)-5 is not applicable to the provision of services incidental to the original business activities conducted by the corporation with the foreign-related person, whether or not the consideration for rendering such services is appropriate shall be examined, assuming that the gross cost for rendering such services is an arm's length price.

In this case, the services incidental to the original business activities mean the services rendered incidentally or related to the original business activities of a corporation or a foreign-related person not mainly engaged in the provision of the services; e.g., a corporation that imports products from its foreign subsidiary provides technical guidance regarding the manufacturing facilities of the foreign subsidiary. The gross cost for the provision of services includes, as a rule, not only direct expenses related to the services but also indirect expenses, such as the general and administrative expenses of the department in charge or any assisting department, calculated in accordance with reasonable distribution standards.

(Note) As a rule, whether the provision of services is incidental to the original business is judged on the basis of the purpose of such rendering of services. Nevertheless, the gross cost incurred for the provision of services shall not be treated as an arm's length price if:

(a) The cost incurred for the provision of the services accounts for a considerable portion of the amount of costs or expenses of the corporation or the foreign-related person for the taxable year during which such services are rendered.

(b) It is deemed inappropriate to treat the gross cost for the provision of the services as a consideration of the service; this is because the intangible properties are used for the provision of such services, or for other similar reasons.

(Treatment of Intra-group Services)

2-10
(1) All transactions having commercial value between a corporation and its foreign-related persons fall under foreign-related transactions.

Thus, transfer pricing examinations shall be conducted bearing in mind that the following services have commercial value: services regarding management, finance, business, and administration (see list below), which are performed by the corporation for its foreign-related persons (or vice versa) and which are services that the foreign-related persons would need to acquire from unrelated persons by paying the consideration or would perform for themselves if they were not rendered by the corporation.

(a) Planning and/or coordination
(b) Budgeting and/or budgetary control
(c) Accounting, tax, and/or legal services
(d) Management of credit and/or factoring
(e) Operation, maintenance, and/or management of computer networks
(f) Supervision of cash flow and/or solvency
(g) Investing and/or raising of funds
(h) Management of interest and/or exchange rate risks
(i) Assistance in the fields of production, purchase, distribution, and/or marketing
(j) Recruitment and/or training of staff

In cases where the corporation continuously maintains staff and equipment that are ready to perform services for the foreign-related persons upon request at any time, maintaining this state of readiness is itself a service, thus transfer pricing examinations of these services shall be conducted depending on the respective conditions.

In cases where foreign-related persons acquire some services from unrelated persons or perform such services for themselves, services which the corporation duplicates for the foreign-related persons do not have commercial value and are not included in foreign-related transactions.

Exceptions are where the duplication of services is only temporary or where the duplication is undertaken to reduce the risk of a wrong business decision.

On the other hand, even if the activities performed by the corporation as the parent company for the foreign-related person are related to intra-group services, activities such as meetings of shareholders of the parent company or reporting requirements based on legislation, which the parent company performs in its capacity as a shareholder, do not have commercial value and are not included in foreign-related transactions; this is because they are not the type of activities that the foreign-related persons would acquire from unrelated persons by payment or would perform for themselves if they were not performed by the corporation. Whether these activities are included in activities which the parent company performs in its capacity as a shareholder, or monitoring and so on which are included in intra-group services, shall be determined based on whether the activities have commercial value or not.

(Intangible Properties to Consider in Examinations)
2-11 When determining, in examinations, how intangible properties contribute to the income of the corporation or foreign-related persons, properties such as the following that have material value and serve as a source of income shall be comprehensively considered:
  (a) Patents and trade secrets derived from technical innovation.
  (b) Know-how derived from experience by employees and other human resources through business activities such as management, front-office operations, production, research and development, and sales promotion.
  (c) Production process, negotiation procedures, and development, distribution, and financing networks.

When determining whether the intangible property of the corporation or foreign-related person serve as a source of income, in the case, for instance, where it is possible to identify a corporation without intangible properties serving as a source of income from among corporations engaging in the same category of business as the foreign-related transaction and having similar markets and scales of operation, it shall be noted that a comparison is made between the profit margin (or similar indices) of the foreign-related transaction of the corporation or foreign-related person and the profit margin of the corporation without such intangible properties, as well as analyzing the activities, functions, and so forth in relation to the creation of the intangible properties of the corporation or foreign-related person.
(Note) Regarding the relationship between the provision of services and intangible properties in cases where intangible properties are used when providing services, 2-8(1) Note shall be noted

(Contribution to the Formation, Maintenance or Development of Intangible Properties)
2-12 When examining licensing transactions of intangible properties, it shall be noted that not only the legal ownership of the intangible properties but also the degree of contribution of a corporation or a foreign-related person to the activities for the formation, maintenance or development of the intangible property (hereafter "the formation and so on") need to be taken into account.
In assessing the degree of the contribution to the said formation and so on, the functions that the corporation or the foreign-related person performed, such as decision making, rendering of services, bearing of costs, and risk management, shall be taken into account comprehensively. In this case, it is to be noted that the degree of contribution shall be assessed as low when the corporation or the

foreign-related person merely bears the cost of the formation and so on of the intangible properties that are expected to be the source of income.

(Transaction for the Licensing of Intangible Property)
2-13 In cases where either a corporation or a foreign-related person is using the intangible property owned by either of them without an agreement concerning its use, it is to be noted that the arm's length price of this transaction shall be calculated as a transaction for licensing, except when it is recognized as a transfer transaction.
The commencement date of the licensing shall be determined properly from among the dates when the intangible property concerned was provided, the use started or profit was recorded through the use, by considering examples of transactions between non-related persons.

(Cost Contribution Arrangement)
2-14 A Cost Contribution Arrangement (hereinafter referred to as "CCA") means a contract to share the cost required for the activities necessary for the achievement of a common purpose, such as development of a specific intangible property (hereinafter referred to as "Activities such as Research and Development,") between contracting parties (hereinafter referred to as "the Participant"), and to obtain the interest of the outcome yielded from Activities such as Research and Development in accordance with the proportion of the total amount of expected benefit (hereinafter referred to as
"the Expected Proportion of Benefit") of the earning that is expected to increase or the cost that is expected to decrease (hereinafter referred to as "the Expected Benefit") for each participant by the new outcome yielded from Activities such as Research and Development.
For instance, the following falls under a CCA: a contract to share the cost required for the development of the manufacturing technology between the corporation and foreign-related person, using the Expected Proportion of Benefit calculated on the basis of the Expected Benefit that would be enjoyed through the sale of new products to be manufactured by each of the corporation and foreign-related persons, and using the manufacturing technology concerned to obtain the interest of the new intangible property yielded from the development of the manufacturing technology in accordance with the cost to be shared by each of them.

(Treatment of CCA)
2-15 The cost contribution (including the adjustment of the amount of cost contribution) and acquisition of the interest based on a CCA concluded between the corporation and foreign-related person fall under foreign-related transactions, and in cases where the Expected Proportion of Benefit of a corporation in the CCA is recognized to be excessive compared with an appropriate proportion (the proportion calculated based on 2-16 and 2-18), it shall be noted that the amount for the part

corresponding to the proportion that became excessive out of the total cost borne by the corporation concerned may not be deducted from the taxable income as it exceeds the arm's length price.

(Note) The cost shared by a corporation shall be treated in accordance with prescriptions of the laws and regulations concerning corporation tax. Therefore, for instance, in cases where there are entertainment expenses and so forth in the cost required for Activities such as Research and Development which are provided in the provision of Articles 61-4(3) of the ASMT, the amount of entertainment expenses and so forth shared by the corporation based on a proper Expected Proportion of Benefit shall be treated in accordance with the provision of ASMT Directive 61-4(1)-23(1) ("Method of the Expenditure of Entertainment Expenses and So Forth"). Therefore, it is to be noted that entertainment expenses and so forth in the cost shall be subject to the calculation of non-deductible expenses under the provision of Paragraph 1 of the said Article.

(Points to Consider in Relation to CCA)
2-16 In cases where a corporation concluded a CAA with a foreign-related person, it shall be examined whether or not the amount of cost contribution of the corporation is appropriate, taking the following points into consideration.
- (a) Whether the range of the Activities such as Research and Development is clearly defined and the content is provided for concretely and in detail.
- (b) Whether all participants are expected to enjoy the benefit directly by using the outcome yielded from the Activities such as Research and Development for themselves.
- (c) Whether the amount of cost to be shared by each participant has been determined by allocating the total amount of cost required for the Activities such as Research and

Development, based on the Expected Proportion of Benefit which has been properly estimated.
- (d) In cases where it is difficult to estimate the Expected Benefit directly, whether the standard (sales amount, gross margin, operating profit, volume of production or sales and so forth) used for the calculation of the Expected Benefit is reasonable enough for assuming the degree of Benefit obtained from the outcome yielded from the Activities such as Research and Development.
- (e) Whether the Expected Proportion of Benefit is reviewed in accordance with the fluctuation of the standard used to calculate it.
- (f) Whether it has been examined if the estimation of each participant's Expected Benefit was appropriate when there was a remarkable difference between the Expected Proportion of Benefit and the realized proportion of benefit (which means the proportion of increased earning or decreased costs for each participant (hereinafter referred to as "the Realized Benefit") based on the outcome yielded from Activities such as Research and Development,

to the total of the Realized Benefit for each participant).

(g) In cases where there is a new entry in an active CCA or a withdrawal and there is intangible property and so forth, developed through Activities such as Research and Development, whether the intangible property and so forth are evaluated at the time of the new entry or a withdrawal, and whether the appropriate consideration of the intangible property and so forth is paid or received among the participants in proportion to the share of the intangible property and so forth.

(Use of Existing Intangible Property in CCA)
2-17 In cases where an existing intangible property owned by a participant (any properties other than intangible property acquired / developed through the CCA, hereafter the same) is used for Activities such as Research and Development in the CCA, it shall be noted that it is required to examine whether the participant who owns the existing intangible property has received the arm's length royalty or the cost shared has been calculated assuming that such an amount has been shared by the participant, except when such an intangible property is recognized to have been transferred to the other participants.
(Note) In cases where a corporation conducts development activities and so forth by itself in relation to Activities such as Research and Development, within the framework of the CCA, or the realized benefit of the foreign-related participant markedly exceeds its Expected Benefit, it is required to examine whether the existing intangible property owned by the corporation is used for Activities such as Research and Development concerned; in the case where it is recognized as being used, it is to be noted that the points in this main clause shall be taken into account in the examination.

(Documents to be Inspected at the Time of Examination on CCA)
2-18 While information on the actual circumstance of the foreign-related transaction is to be accurately obtained from the documents and other items listed in 2-4 above in examinations, when examining on CCA, it shall be determined whether or not there is any problem under transfer pricing taxation by requesting the submission of documents of CCA (including the attached documents describing the scope / content of the activities of research and development) and mainly the following documents, such as:
(1) Documents prepared at the time of concluding a CCA:
   (a) Documents describing the name, address, capital relations, description of business and other information of the participants,
   (b) Documents describing the details of negotiation / consultation leading to the conclusion of an agreement made by participants,
   (c) Documents describing the method of calculating the Expected Proportion of Benefit and the

reason to use such a method,
- (d) Documents describing the accounting standard used for calculating the amount of the cost shared and Expected Benefit,
- (e) Documents describing the details of adjusting the amount of cost shared in the case where there is the difference between the realized proportion of benefit and Expected Proportion of Benefit,
- (f) Documents describing the details of valuation of the intangible property and so on in cases where any new participation or withdrawal takes place,
- (g) Documents describing the details in relation to the modification of contractual terms and conditions, the revision, or termination of the CCA.

(2) Documents prepared after the conclusion of a CCA:
- (a) Documents describing the total amount of the cost and its breakdown required for Activities such as Research and Development, as well as the amount of the cost shared by each participant and the process of its calculation,
- (b) Documents describing the extent of the difference between the Expected and realized Proportions of Benefit in relation to Activities such as Research and Development,
- (c) Documents describing the change of the share of each participant in the intangible property and so forth, formed through Activities such as Research and Development (including the method of valuation of intangible property and so forth, formed through Activities such as Research and Development),
- (d) Documents describing the details of any new participation or withdrawal.

(3) Other documents:
- (a) Documents describing the content of the intangible property and details of calculating the royalty in cases where an existing intangible property concerned is used in Activities such as Research and Development,
- (b) Documents describing the name, address and other particulars of those who are scheduled to make use of the outcome yielded from Activities such as Research and Development, but who will not participate in the CCA

(Transfer of Money for Price Adjustment and So Forth)
2-19 In cases where a corporation transfers money back and forth with a foreign-related person nominally for the purpose of price adjustment, whether or not the transfer of money is made in fact for the adjustment of transaction prices shall be closely examined.

(Consideration Calculated by Foreign Tax Authority)
2-20 It shall be noted that since arm's length prices are calculated in accordance with the laws of

Japan, the consideration for a foreign-related transaction calculated for the purpose of taxation corresponding to transfer pricing taxation on a foreign-related person by a foreign tax authority is not necessarily an arm's length price (except for the cases where a mutual agreement has been reached).

(Relationship with Request for APA)
2-21

(1) It shall be noted that an examination is not interrupted by an APA request.
(2) Documents (except those as to facts) received from the corporation for the APA review (hereinafter referred to as the "applicant for APA") may not be used for the examination unless the corporation gives consent to the use of such materials.

(Transfer Pricing Taxation and Classification of Domestic/Foreign Source Income)
2-22 In cases where the provision of Article 69(1) (Foreign Tax Credit) of the CTA is applied together with transfer pricing taxation in examinations, it shall be noted that calculation of the creditable amount of foreign tax is made after the judgment of whether the increased income through the application of transfer pricing taxation is of domestic source or foreign source by applying the provisions of Article 138 (Domestic Source Income) to Article 140 (Details of the Scope of Domestic Source Income) of the CTA inclusive.

(Relationship with Thin Capitalization)
2-23 In cases where the provision of Article 66-5 (Special Rules of Interest on Indebtedness Pertaining to Foreign Control Stockholders) of the ASMT is applied together with transfer pricing taxation in examinations, it shall be noted that the portion of the "interest on borrowed funds" that exceeds the arm's length price may not be included when calculating the "interest on borrowed funds" prescribed in Paragraph 1 of the preceding article.

(Relationship with Withholding Tax)
2-24 In cases where, as a result of an examination, any difference is identified for the purpose of levying of the corporation tax between the amount of interest or royalty paid by the corporation to the foreign-related person and the arm's length price, it shall be noted that such difference does not affect the interest or the amount of royalty subject to withholding tax. Also it shall be noted that, under some tax treaties, the reduced tax rate is not applicable to such differences.

(Relationship with Consumption Tax)
2-25 Transfer pricing taxation covers the application of the CTA and other laws related to

Corporation Tax. Therefore, it shall be noted that the calculation of consumption tax is not affected by the application of such taxation in examinations.

Chapter 3. Points to Note in Calculating Arm's Length Prices

(Method for Adjusting Differences)
3-1 In adjusting the differences between a foreign-related transaction and a comparable transaction, the adjustment may be made by applying the method described below according to the circumstances of each case.
It shall be noted that an adjustment is made for differences if it is objectively clear that the differences would have an impact on the calculation of the consideration prescribed in Item 1(a) of Article 66-4(2) of the ASMT or the normal profit margin prescribed in Item 1(b) and (c) of preceding article, or on the calculation of the percentage prescribed in Item 2 and Item 3 of Article 39-12(8) of the Cabinet Order of the ASMT (by the same method as that given in Item 2(a) of Article 66-4(2) of the ASMT).

(1) In cases where the trade terms of one transaction is FOB (free on board)-based and the other transaction is CIF (cost, insurance & freight)-based, the amount equal to freight and insurance is added to or deducted from the consideration of the comparable transaction.
(2) In cases where there is a difference between the foreign-related transaction and a comparable transaction with respect to the period after sight of the bill, the amount equal to the interest that accrues during the period between the sight and settlement is added to or deducted from the consideration of the comparable transaction.
(3) In cases where any discount or rebate according to the quantity of the transaction is specified in the trade terms for the comparable transaction, the consideration resulting from application of the terms such as discount or rebate of the comparable transaction to the quantity of the foreign-related transaction is used.
(4) In cases where there is any difference as to function or risk, and the extent of such function or risk is considered measurable by the amount of expenses incurred by the parties with respect to the foreign-related transaction and the comparable transaction, such difference is adjusted using the percentage of the amount of the above-mentioned expenses to the total sales or sales cost related to such foreign-related transaction and the comparable transaction.

(Selection of Comparable Transactions for Foreign-Related Transactions with Use of Intangible Properties)
3-2 In cases where, when applying the provisions of ASMT Directive 66-4(2)-3, a corporation or foreign-related person engages in foreign-related transactions involving use of intangible properties,

it is to be noted that the similarity of intangible properties in terms of type, scope, mode of use, and so forth shall be considered when selecting comparable transactions.

(Calculating Arm's Length Prices for Some Comparable Transactions)
3-3 In calculating arm's length prices, where some comparable transactions are so similar to the foreign-related transaction in reference to factors which are prescribed in ASMT Directive 66-4(2)-3, it shall be noted that a mean of prices or margin profits arising from those comparable transactions may be used.

(Treatment of Common Expenses in the Profit Split Method)
3-4 When applying the profit split method, in cases where any cost of sales, and general, administrative and selling expenses incurred in connection both with the foreign-related transaction and other transactions (referred to in 3-4 as "Common Expenses") are included in such cost and expenses of the corporation or its foreign-related person, the profit to be split (as prescribed in ASMT Directive 66-4(4)-1: hereinafter the same) arising from the foreign-related transaction is calculated by dividing the cost and expenses in accordance with the proportion of reasonable factors. The reasonableness of these factors, such as sales, cost of sales, value of assets used for the transactions, number of employees involved in the transaction and so forth, shall be regarded in light of the content of both transactions and the nature of such expenses.
Also, it shall be noted that the common expenses are calculated based on the above method when calculating the factors to be used for attribution of profit to be split based on the amount of expenses.

(Treatment of Residual Profit Split Method)
3-5 When applying the residual profit split method prescribed in ASMT Directive 66 4(4)-5, "ordinarily gained profit out of the profit to be split that unrelated persons who do not possess material intangibles may obtain" shall be calculated based on profit indices, such as the ratio of operating profit to the value of business assets, or to the sales of a corporation (excluding a corporation that owns any material intangible asset) that is engaged in the same category of business as the foreign-related person and is similar in market size or scale of operation to the foreign-related person.

(Selling and General Administrative Expenses in Applying the Transactional Net Margin Method)
3-6 In calculating arm's length prices using the transactional net margin method, "selling and general administrative expenses for selling the inventory concerning the foreign-related transaction" shall contain the direct and/or indirect costs of selling. In cases where there are costs arising from both foreign-related transactions and other transactions, the costs shall be divided according to a rational

ratio of factors in light of the content of both transactions and the nature of such expenses, for example, sales, cost of sales, value of assets, and number of employees, according to the format of the individual transaction.

(Points to Note Concerning the Treatment of Taxation by Estimation)

(1) When applying the method set forth in Item 1 of Article 39-12(12) of the Cabinet Order of the ASMT, it shall be noted that the provisions of ASMT Directive 66-4(4)-1 to 66-4(4)-5 inclusive shall apply mutatis mutandis, and that the operating profit or corresponding sum (hereinafter referred to as "operating profit") arising from business involving foreign-related transactions according to the financial documents describing the consolidated assets and profit and loss situation of the business group to which the corporation and foreign-related persons belong, (hereinafter referred to as "consolidated financial statements") shall in principle be allocated to the corporation and foreign-related persons by splitting it according to the factors provided for in the said item.
(Note) In cases where the operating profit arising from business involving foreign-related transactions according to consolidated financial statements is not separated from operating profit arising from other business, the amount calculated by multiplying the operating profit arising from business including business involving foreign-related transactions by the proportion of (b) to (a) below may be allocated to the corporation.
   (a) Factors sufficient to estimate the degree of the contribution of the business group to the generation of operating profit from business including business involving foreign-related transactions.
   (b) Factors among those specified in (a) that are sufficient to estimate the degree of the contribution by the corporation through business involving foreign-related transactions.
(2) It shall be noted that when applying the method set forth in Item 4 of Article 39-12(12) of the Cabinet Order of the ASMT, ASMT Directive 66-4(5)-1 shall apply mutatis mutandis.

Chapter 4. Treatment of Foreign Transferred Income

(Treatment of Refund of Foreign Transferred Income)
4-1 In cases where a corporation that submitted the document prescribed in ASMT Directive 66-4(8)-2 has not received all or part of the refund stated in the document by the scheduled date, it shall be judged as to whether the application of the provision referred to above is appropriate after examining if there is any reasonable reason for there not having been a refund.
(Note) In the case where a corporation inquires about the form of the document prescribed in ASMT

Directive 66-4(8)-2, the corporation shall be informed that it may use "Application for Refund of Foreign Transferred Income" (appended Form 1).

(Treatment of Refund of Foreign Transferred Income with Corresponding Adjustment)
4-2 In cases where a foreign tax authority has imposed tax on a foreign-related person under a system corresponding to transfer pricing taxation, it shall be noted that if a corporation whose taxable income has been reduced by reason of a corresponding adjustment based on a mutual agreement has remitted the entire amount or part of the amount so reduced to the foreign-related person, the remitted amount may not be deducted from the taxable income.

(Treatment of Amounts Refunded to Foreign-Related Persons with Corresponding Adjustment)
4-3 In cases where taxable income has been reduced by reason of corresponding adjustment based on a mutual agreement, when the corporation shall remit the entire amount or part of the amount so reduced to the foreign-related person within a reasonable period, a request for correction to a tax return is made pursuant to the provisions of Article 7(1) of the Act on Special Provisions for the Enforcement of Income Tax Conventions ("Special Measures for Correction in the Case of Agreement Based on an Income Tax Convention Concerning the Amount of Compensation for Transactions") and the following particulars are reported in writing (using "Notification Regarding Refund of Foreign Transferred Income with Corresponding Adjustment" (appended Form 7)) to the District Director (Regional Commissioner in the cases of a corporation handled by the RTB Large Enterprise Examination Division), it shall be noted that the amount to be refunded is treated as an account payable to the foreign-related person.
   (a) Corporation name
   (b) Place of tax payment
   (c) Name of representative
   (d) Name and location of foreign-related person
   (e) Scheduled date of refund
   (f) Amount of refund (together with amount in foreign currency in the case of transactions in foreign currencies)
   (g) Method of refund

(Note) The amount reported as being refunded in respect of a transaction in a foreign currency shall be the yen equivalent calculated in accordance with the provisions of Corporation Tax Act Directive 13-2-1-2 ("Transactions in Foreign Currencies and Yen Conversions by the Accrual Calculation Method"). The difference between this amount and the yen equivalent converted by using the foreign exchange buying and selling rate on the day of the refund shall be included in gross revenue or loss in the taxable year in which the day of the refund falls.

Chapter 5. Advance Pricing Arrangements (APA)

(APA Policies)

5-1 In light of the fact that APA is intended to ensure the predictability of transfer pricing taxation for corporations and to assist proper and smooth enforcement of transfer pricing taxation, APA reviews shall be conducted in a balanced, accurate, and swift manner according to the complexity and importance of each case while paying full consideration to ensuring the taxation rights of Japan. Corporations shall also be eligible for appropriate pre-filing consultations in order to improve the convenience of and expedite the APA procedure.

(Filing Requests for APA)
5-2
  (1) Corporations are eligible to file requests for APA relating to some or all foreign-related transactions with the District Director (or the Regional Commissioner of the Regional Taxation Bureaus [hereinafter referred to as "RTB Commissioner"] in cases where the corporations are those under the jurisdiction of the RTB Large Enterprise Examination Division under the Ministry of Finance Ordinance No.49 of 1949; hereinafter the same) who has the responsibility for the corporation's returns.
  (2) Upon request for APA, an applicant shall file a "Request for APA of the TPM" (appended Form 2) (hereinafter referred to as "APA request") for each address in their country with the District Director of the precinct RTB. This will be done by the prescribed due date for the filing of final tax returns (the extended due date in cases where the due date is extended pursuant to the provisions of Article 75-2 (Special Rules for Extension of Due Date of Filing Final Returns) of the CTA pertaining to the first taxable year of the taxable years that the applicant is requesting to be confirmed (hereinafter referred to as "taxable years to be confirmed").
  (3) The APA request shall be filed in duplicate (in triplicate when mutual consultations are requested) in cases of a corporation handled by the RTB Large Enterprise Examination Division, or in triplicate (in quadruplicate when mutual consultations are requested) in cases of all other corporations (The same shall apply to the cases of 5-3, 5-8, and 5-9)

(Documents to Be Attached)
5-3 The District Director shall ask an applicant for APA to submit the following documents with the APA request:

  (a) Documents describing the outline of transactions to be confirmed and organizations conducting the transactions to be confirmed;
  (b) Documents describing the TPM to be confirmed and specific details thereof, and an explanation as to why it is the most reasonable;
  (c) Documents describing business and economic conditions essential to the APA and its continuation (hereinafter referred to as "critical assumptions");

(d) Documents providing a detailed explanation of transactions to be confirmed, including cash flow and currencies involved;
(e) Documents regarding direct or indirect capital relations or relations under substantial control between the foreign-related person pertaining to transactions to be confirmed (hereafter the "applicable foreign-related person") and the applicant for APA;
(f) Documents regarding the functions performed by the applicant for APA and the applicable foreign-related person in transactions to be confirmed;
(g) Operational and accounting information for the prior three (3) taxable years of the applicant for APA and the applicable foreign-related person (or alternate information, such as future business plans, business projections if the transactions to be confirmed relate to a new product or business and data for the prior three (3) taxable years is not available);
(h) Documents describing any transfer pricing examinations, appeals, lawsuits, and so forth pertaining to applicable foreign-related persons, and details of past taxation in their country;
(i) Documents required in order to explain concretely the TPM applied for by the applicant for APA, such as the results of application of the TPM for which the APA is requested to the three (3) taxable years prior to the taxable year to be confirmed;
(j) Other reference documents required for APA.

(Note) In addition to the documents set forth in (g) and (i), the RTB division in charge shall require the applicant for APA to submit documents for the two previous taxable years if it is deemed not possible to conduct a proper APA review using the documents for three (3) taxable years considering factors such as the lifecycle of the products involved in the transactions to be confirmed.

(Translation of Attached Documents)
5-4 Applicants for APA shall be requested to submit Japanese translations if any of the attached documents are written in foreign languages.

(Revision of APA Requests)
5-5 The Examination Group (Corporation) of the Tax Office (group in charge of corporation tax; hereinafter the same) or the RTB Large Enterprise Examination Division shall check the content of the APA request and documents as prescribed in 5-3. In the case where there are any misstatements or deficiencies, the applicant for APA shall be asked to revise the APA request.

(Forwarding of APA Requests and so on)
5-6 The Examination Group (Corporation) of the Tax Office shall promptly forward two (2) sets of the APA request received (or three (3) sets if the applicant for APA requests a mutual agreement procedure) to the RTB Corporation Taxation Division, and the RTB Corporation Taxation Division

shall promptly forward one (1) set of these (or two (2) sets if the applicant for APA requests a mutual agreement procedure) to the NTA Corporation Taxation Division. The RTB Large Enterprise Examination Division shall promptly forward one (1) set of the APA request received (or two (2) sets if the applicant for APA requests a mutual agreement procedure) to the Large Enterprise Examination Division of the Examination and Criminal Investigation Department of the NTA. If the applicant for APA requests a mutual agreement procedure, the NTA division in charge shall forward one (1) set of the APA request to the Office of Mutual Agreement Procedures of the NTA.

(Taxable Years to be Confirmed)
5-7 Taxable years to be confirmed are in principle from three (3) to five (5) taxable years.

(Amendments to APA Requests)
5-8 In cases where an applicant for APA submits documents pertaining to amendments to the filed request, the Examination Group (Corporation) of the Tax Office or the RTB Large Enterprise Examination Division shall process the request in accordance with the provisions of 5-5 and 5-6.

(Withdrawal of APA Requests)
5-9 In cases where an applicant for APA submits statements pertaining to the withdrawal of the APA request, the Examination Group (Corporation) of the Tax Office or the RTB Large Enterprise Examination Division shall process such statements in accordance with the provisions of 5-5 and 5-6.

(Pre-filing Consultations)
5-10
  (1) The RTB division in charge shall accede to requests from corporations for a pre-filing consultation. On receiving notice from the RTB division-in-charge, the NTA division-in-charge (including the Office of Mutual Agreement Procedures in the cases of consultations regarding an APA with mutual agreement; the same in (2)) shall in principle attend such consultations.
  (2) Mindful that pre-filing consultations are intended to help make APA procedures more convenient for corporations and to expedite APA procedures, the RTB division in charge (including the NTA division in charge involved in pre-filing consultations) shall pay attention to the following points when meeting with corporations for pre-filing
consultations in order to streamline the processing of APA requests by applicants for APA and to facilitate APA reviews after their request:
    (a) Matters necessary to APA procedures, including guidelines on the preparation of the

attached documents submitted with APA requests and deadlines for submission, shall be properly explained at the time of pre-filing consultations.
(b) Efforts shall be made to provide the information required in order to correctly ascertain the details of the foreign-related transactions that are the subject of the consultation, and to enable the corporation concerned to make an appropriate judgment as to whether to

apply for an APA and what kind of application to make.
(3) At pre-filing consultations, the RTB division in charge shall discuss issues and information that fall within the scope of the documents presented or submitted by the corporation requesting the consultation.

In the case where documents required due to the content of the pre-filing consultation are not presented or submitted, it shall be explained to the corporation why a proper pre-filing consultation cannot be held.
(4) In the case where an applicant for APA fails to attach the documents prescribed in 5-3 to an APA request, the applicant shall be informed that an APA request cannot be conformed pursuant to the provisions of 5-15(4) and 5-15(5), unless there are found to exist adequate grounds for being unable to submit some of the documents by the deadline for submission of the APA request at a pre-filing consultation that concerns the attachment of the documents prescribed in 5-3. In this instance, the RTB division in charge shall not be required to apply the provisions of 5-15(4) and 5-15(5) for a period deemed ordinarily necessary for the preparation of such documents (except where an extended period is required; hereinafter referred to as the "submission grace period").

In such a case, the RTB division in charge shall specify the submission grace period to the corporation requesting the pre-filing consultation, and explain that the APA review is in principle deferred for the duration of this period.

(Review of APA Requests)
5-11 The RTB division in charge shall evaluate the APA request in the following manner:
(1) The RTB division in charge shall commence the APA review promptly upon receipt of an APA request, and shall conduct the review in a balanced manner appropriate to the complexity and difficulty of the case while endeavoring to process the request correctly and swiftly. The NTA division in charge shall additionally be involved in APA review as necessary.

As the cooperation of the applicant for APA is essential to process an APA review swiftly, a better understanding of the applicant for APA on the importance of such cooperation shall be promoted.
(2) The RTB division in charge shall in principle perform APA reviews in accordance with the provisions of 2-1 and 2-2, and as otherwise prescribed in Chapter 2 and Chapter 3.

Supplemental Materials

It shall be noted that APA reviews do not constitute an examination or inspection of the taxpayer's books and records regarding Corporation Tax.

(3) In cases where documents other than those prescribed in 5-3 are found to be required for an APA review, the RTB division in charge shall explain this to the applicant for APA and request that the applicant for APA submit such documents.

In order to expedite the APA review process, the RTB division in charge shall set a deadline for the submission of such documents that is deemed reasonable in view of the circumstances of the applicant for APA in light of the period ordinarily required to prepare such documents.

(4) The RTB division in charge may request the applicant for APA to amend their requests in the case where the division concludes that the TPM requested is not the most reasonable.

(5) The NTA division in charge shall request the RTB division in charge to report on the status of the APA review process as necessary.

(Mutual Consultations Relating to APA)
5-12
(1) In cases where an applicant for APA has not filed a request for a mutual agreement procedure for the APA, the RTB division in charge shall provide information required by the applicant for APA to appropriately decide what kind of request to make; if it is confirmed that the applicant intends to request an APA with a mutual agreement procedure, it shall recommend that the applicant request for mutual consultation in order to avoid double taxation and ensure predictability.

(2) The RTB division in charge shall recommend the prompt requesting of a pre-filing consultation or filing of an APA request by a corporation in the case where it is identified that the corporation or foreign-related person held a pre-filing consultation or filed an APA request with a foreign tax authority.

(3) In cases where a mutual agreement procedure is requested, the RTB division in charge shall request the applicant for APA to file, in addition to APA requests, an Application for Mutual Consultation prescribed in the "Commissioner's Directive on Mutual Agreement Procedures (Administrative Guidelines)" issued on June 25, 2001 [Document ID: Office of Mutual Agreement Procedures 1-39].

(Coordination among the RTB division in charge and the NTA and the Office of Mutual Agreement Procedures)
5-13 In cases where an applicant for APA requests a mutual agreement procedure pertaining to the APA, the RTB division in charge, the NTA division in charge and the Office of Mutual Agreement Procedures shall consult with each other as necessary.
In this case, after completing its APA review, the RTB division in charge shall present its opinions on

the APA request to the Office of Mutual Agreement Procedures via the NTA division in charge. The Office of Mutual Agreement Procedures shall forward the contents of the mutual agreement to the RTB division in charge via the NTA division in charge.

(In the case where APA and Performance of APA Process Are Not Appropriate)
5-14 When conducting APA reviews, cases shall be appropriately handled as prescribed in (1) or (2) respectively in order to ensure the proper and smooth enforcement of transfer pricing taxation.
  (1) In cases such as the following where an APA is deemed inappropriate, the RTB division in charge shall, after consultation with the NTA division in charge (including the Office of Mutual Agreement Procedures in the cases of an APA with mutual agreement), request the applicant for APA to correct the APA request. In the case where the applicant fails to make such a correction, an explanation shall be given to the applicant that the APA is not possible.
  In the case where the content of a pre-filing consultation falls under (a) below, the following details shall be explained to the corporation requesting the pre-filing consultation.
    (a) In cases where it is found that the burden of tax in Japan would be reduced without reasonable economic grounds as a result of the transaction to be confirmed being of a form not ordinarily undertaken between unrelated parties.
    (b) In cases where the failure of the applicant for APA to submit information necessary for APA review or otherwise provide necessary cooperation would hinder an APA.
  (2) In cases such as the following where commencement or continuation of APA review is deemed inappropriate, the RTB division in charge shall, after consultation with the NTA division in charge (including the Office of Mutual Agreement Procedures in the cases of an APA with mutual agreement), explanation shall be given to the applicant for APA that the APA process will be deferred until such time that the commencement or recommencement of APA review is possible.
    (a) In cases where an applicant for APA files an APA request for transactions similar to those involving reassessment based on transfer pricing taxation, it is deemed necessary to conduct an APA review following adjudication on an appeal or finalization of a decision or judgment regarding such reassessment.
    (b) In cases where an applicant for APA files an APA request and a request for a mutual agreement procedure in respect of foreign-related transactions other than transactions to be confirmed, it is deemed necessary to conduct an APA review for such transactions to be confirmed following a mutual agreement.
    (c) In cases where it is deemed necessary to conduct an APA review after having obtained actual results of transactions to be confirmed due to it not being possible to ascertain the actual circumstances of business activities only from the documents, such as future business plans

and business projections, prescribed in the parenthesized clause to 5-3(g).

(Notification of Results of APA Review)
5-15
- (1) In cases where the RTB division in charge receives notification of a mutual agreement from the Office of Mutual Agreement Procedures via the NTA division in charge, the RTB division in charge shall promptly notify the District Director that the APA confirmation is made based on the results of agreement after the request has been suitably processed, including requesting the applicant for APA to correct the application according to the results of the agreement.
- (2) In cases where the RTB division in charge has received a notification that a mutual agreement had not been reached from the Office of Mutual Agreement Procedures via the NTA division in charge, the RTB division in charge shall ask the opinion of the applicant for APA regarding whether to withdraw its request for APA or to seek APA without a mutual agreement, and then promptly process the request in accordance with the provisions of 5-9, 5-15(3), or 5-15(4).
- (3) In cases where the RTB division in charge concludes after APA review that the TPM applied by the corporation is the most reasonable and no request has been filed for a mutual agreement procedure, the division shall promptly forward an APA notice to the District Director
- (4) In cases where the RTB division in charge concludes after APA review that the TPM applied by the corporation is not the most reasonable, the applicant for APA fails to submit the attaching documents prescribed in 5-3, the applicant does not submit the documents set forth in 5-11(3), or it is judged that an APA review can not be conducted in accordance with the provisions of 5-14(1), the division shall, after consultation with the NTA division in charge (including the Office of Mutual Agreement Procedures in the cases of an APA request with mutual agreement), promptly inform the District Director that the APA confirmation is not possible.
- (5) The District Director shall, upon receipt of the notice set forth in 5-15(1), 5-15(3), or 5-15(4) from the RTB division in charge, promptly send a notice for or against the APA using appended Form 3 ("Notification of Confirmation of Method of Calculation of Arm's Length Prices") or Form 4 ("Notification That Method of Calculation of Arm's Length Prices Cannot Be Confirmed"), as applicable, to the applicant for APA.

(Effect of the APA)
5-16 In cases where a corporation that has received a notice of APA confirmation set forth in 5-15(5) (hereinafter referred to as a "confirmed corporation") files tax returns complying with the content of the APA for the confirmed taxable years, the District Director shall treat the confirmed foreign-related transactions (hereinafter referred to as "confirmed transactions") as having been conducted at the arm's length price.

In cases where a taxable year to be confirmed has already elapsed at the time of confirmation, it shall be noted that an amended return submitted by the confirmed corporation to make the return filed for the taxable year to be confirmed comply with the content of the APA is not treated as corresponding to a "return filed foreknowing that corrections should be made" prescribed in Article 65(5) (Additional Tax for Deficient Returns) of the Act on General Rules for National Taxes.

(Submission of Reports)
5-17 Confirmed corporations shall be requested to submit reports with the following information no later than the prescribed due date for filing final tax returns concerning the confirmed transactions pertaining to each taxable year confirmed (hereinafter referred to as "confirmed taxable year") or within the period specified by the District Director. The report shall be filed in duplicate in the cases of corporations handled by the RTB Large Enterprise Examination Division, and in triplicate in the cases of all other corporations.
  (a) Statement that the confirmed corporation filed tax returns complying with the contents of the APA;
  (b) Profit or loss data of the confirmed corporation and the applicable foreign-related person relating to confirmed transactions (in the case where it is necessary, taking the content of APA into account);
  (c) Statement of fluctuations, if any, of material business and economic conditions based on which the APA was given;
  (d) Statement of adjustments made by the confirmed corporation provided in 5-19 in cases where the results of the confirmed transaction do not comply with the contents of the APA;
  (e) Financial and accounting data for the confirmed corporation and the applicable foreign-related person for the confirmed taxable years;
  (f) Other relevant information that helps the tax authorities determine whether the confirmed corporation filed tax returns complying with the contents of the APA.

(Treatment of Reports)
5-18
  (1) In cases where the report prescribed in 5-17 was filed by a confirmed corporation, the report shall be processed by the Examination Group (Corporation) of the Tax Office or the RTB Large Enterprise Examination Division in accordance with 5-5 or 5-6.
  (2) The RTB division in charge shall evaluate the report submitted and determine whether the confirmed corporation complies with the content of the APA. It shall be noted that report reviews correspond to examinations for corporation tax, and this shall be explained to the confirmed corporation by the RTB division in charge at the time of the report

review. In cases where it is found as a result of the report review that a return complying with the content of the APA has not been filed and the amount of income has been understated, the RTB division in charge shall explain to the confirmed corporation the result of review and that it is necessary to submit an amended return.

(Note) In cases where the confirmed corporation voluntarily files an amended return pursuant to the provisions of 5-19(2)(b) due to detection of such an understatement before it is deemed that the corporation knew of the report review by the RTB division in charge on account of visitation of the corporation by officials of the RTB division in charge for the purpose of report review or indication of such an understatement, the amended return is not treated as corresponding to a "return filed foreknowing that corrections should be made" prescribed in Article 65(5) (Additional Tax for Deficient Returns) of the Act on General Rules for National Taxes.

The judgment as to whether a return corresponds to a "return filed foreknowing that corrections should be made" is made on the basis of "Treatment of Additional Tax for Understatement and for Return After the Due Date (Administrative Guidelines)" issued on July 3, 2000 [Document ID: Corporation Taxation Division 2-9, etc.].

(3) The RTB division in charge shall report the results of report review to the NTA division in charge as required, and forward the results to the Office of Mutual Agreement Procedures via the NTA division in charge in cases where a mutual agreement was reached.

(Compensating adjustments)
5-19
(1) In cases where the confirmed corporation makes any adjustments required to comply with the contents of the APA in its financial statements, the District Director shall regard them as legitimate transactions for the purpose of transfer pricing.
(2) The RTB division in charge shall request the confirmed corporation to make compensating adjustments relating to the APA (hereinafter referred to as "compensating adjustments") as follows:
  (a) The confirmed corporation shall correct the taxable income on its final return in the case where it turns out that income is understated pertaining to the confirmed taxable years due to an inconsistency between the actual transaction and the results of applying the confirmed TPM before filing final tax returns.
  (b) The confirmed corporation shall promptly file amended tax returns in the case where it turns out that income was understated in the tax returns pertaining to the confirmed taxable years due to an inconsistency between the actual transaction and the results of applying the confirmed TPM after filing final tax returns.
  (c) In cases where a mutual agreement covers the APA (bilateral APA), the confirmed

corporation may correct the taxable income on the final returns based on the mutual agreement concerning compensating adjustments if it turns out that income in the financial statements pertaining to the confirmed taxable years is overstated due to a difference between the actual transaction and the results of applying the confirmed TPM after the closing date for financial statements and before filing final tax returns.
(d) In cases where a mutual agreement covers the APA (bilateral APA), the confirmed corporation may file a request for correction for the tax return as prescribed in Article 7(1) of the Act on Special Provisions for the Enforcement of Income Tax Conventions based on the mutual agreement concerning compensating adjustments if it turns out that income was overstated due to a difference between the actual transaction and the results of applying the confirmed TPM in the tax returns after filing final tax returns pertaining to the confirmed taxable years.

(Revisions to APA)
5-20 In cases where a request for revision is filed by the confirmed corporation because there arises a situation that causes material differences to business and economic conditions essential to the continuation of the APA in each of the confirmed taxable years, the District Director shall receive and process it in accordance with the relevant provisions of 5-1 to 5-19 inclusive.

(Cancellation of APA)
5-21
(1) In cases where the occurrence of any of the conditions below, the RTB division in charge shall forward a notice to the District Director that the APA, when conditions (a) through (c) below apply, relating to taxable years (consolidated taxable years in cases where they are applicable) subsequent to the year in which the applicable incident occurred, and when condition (d) applies, retroactively, is cancelled.
 (a) A confirmed corporation does not submit the request for revision prescribed in 5-20 even when material differences arise.
 (b) A confirmed corporation fails to comply with the contents of the APA in its tax returns.
 (c) A confirmed corporation fails to submit the report prescribed in 5-17, or the report contains material errors.
 (d) Any of the facts based on which the APA was given are revealed to be false, or the APA request contains material errors.
(2) Before forwarding a notice relating to cancellation under Subparagraph (1), the RTB division in charge shall consult with the NTA division in charge where necessary.
(3) In cases where Subparagraph (1) applies to an APA covered by a mutual agreement, the RTB

division in charge shall consult with the Office of Mutual Agreement Procedures via the NTA division in charge, and forward a notice to cancel the APA after receiving a notification of another mutual agreement which cancels the former mutual agreement.

(4) The District Director shall, upon receipt of a notice from the RTB division in charge, cancel the APA by sending the "Notification of Cancellation of Confirmation of Method of Calculation of Arm's Length Prices (appended Form 5)" to the confirmed corporation.

(Renewal of APAs)
5-22
In cases where a confirmed corporation files a request for renewal of its APA, the request shall be processed in accordance with the provisions of 5-1 to 5-21 inclusive, and the confirmed corporation shall file a request for renewal of its APA with the precinct District Director by the day before of the commencement of the taxable years to be confirmed, in principle.

(Applying the TPM to Tax Years Prior to the Confirmed Years)
5-23 In cases where an applicant for APA has the intention to apply the requesting TPM for years prior to the taxable years (consolidated taxable years if they are applicable; hereinafter the same in 5-23) to be confirmed, its APA request is accompanied by a request for a mutual agreement, and the confirmed TPM is regarded as the most reasonable even for years prior to the confirmed taxable years, the request shall be processed in accordance with the provisions of 5-15, 5-16, 5-19, and 5-21.

(Application to Transactions between the Head Office and Branches)
5-24 In cases where a foreign tax authority in the country where the head office of the corporation is located requests the commencement of a mutual agreement based on a request corresponding to the APA with respect to transactions between the head office or branch offices in foreign countries and the branch office in Japan that conducts businesses as set forth in Item 7 of Article 176(1) of the Cabinet Order of the CTA, and the branch office in Japan makes a request similar to a request for APA, necessary measures shall be taken in accordance with the provisions of 5-1 to 5-23 inclusive.

(Treatment of Corporation's Entry into Consolidated-Corporation Group)
5-25
(1) In cases where an applicant for APA becomes a member of a consolidated-corporation group and the concerned corporation files a request for APA, the precinct District Director shall request the consolidated parent corporation to promptly submit the "Application of Continuation of APA after Entry into Consolidated-Corporation Group (appended Form 6)".
The application shall be filed in duplicate (in triplicate if the consolidated parent corporation requests a mutual agreement) with the RTB Commissioner, or in triplicate (in quadruplicate if the

consolidated parent corporation requests a mutual agreement) with the District Director.

(2) In cases where the consolidated parent corporation as set forth in Subparagraph (1) submits Form 6 to the precinct District Director, the precinct District Director shall send a copy of the Form to the District Director who governs the district where the concerned corporation's head office or main office is located. The Examination Group (Corporation) of the Tax Office or the RTB Large Enterprise Examination Division shall handle the case in accordance with the provisions of 5-5 and 5-6. In cases where the concerned corporation requests a mutual agreement, the NTA divisions in charge shall send a copy of the Form to the Office of Mutual Agreement Procedures.

(3) In cases where the consolidated parent corporation submits Form 6, the Commissioner's Directive on OTPCC 5-1 to 5-25 inclusive shall apply to the APA concerning the concerned corporation, assuming that the request prescribed in Commissioner's Directive on OTPCC 5-2 has been made from the consolidated parent corporation to the precinct District Director.

Norway Regulations

Skatteetaten

Regulations relating to the Duty to Specify Controlled Transactions and Accounts Outstanding

Artikkel, 6. mars 2008

Uofisiell engelsk oversettelse/unofficial translation
Authority: Laid down by the Ministry of Finance on 7 December 2007 pursuant to Section 4-12, No. 6, of Act No. 24 of 13 June 1980 relating to Tax Administration (the Tax Administration Act).

I

Section 1. Exemptions from the duty to specify pursuant to Section 4-12, No. 1, of the Tax Administration Act
(1) The duty to specify pursuant to Section 4-12, No. 1, of the Tax Administration Act shall not apply to any company or entity that:

a. has, during the income year, controlled transactions with an aggregate fair value of less than 10 million kroner, and

b. has, as per the end of the income year, accounts outstanding with associated companies or entities in an amount of less than 25 million kroner, cf. Section 4-12, No. 4, of the Tax Administration Act.

(2) By controlled transactions are meant transactions and transfers between companies or entities that are classified as associated entities pursuant to Section 4-12, No. 4, of the Tax Administration Act, as well as dispositions between a permanent establishment and other parts of the enterprise.

(3) By accounts outstanding are meant all types of accounts receivable and accounts payable, as well as guarantees.

(4) By permanent establishment is meant a business activity that represents, or shall be deemed as, a permanent establishment pursuant to the provisions of tax treaties entered into by Norway. If the business activity of the enterprise does not fall within the scope of any tax treaty entered into by Norway, it shall, for the purposes of these Regulations, be deemed as a permanent establishment if the conditions stipulated in Article 5 of the OECD Model Tax Convention have been met.

II

These Regulations shall enter into force on 1 January 2008, and shall apply as from the 2007 income year.

Utskrift fra www.skatteetaten.no/Templates/Artikkel.aspx?id=73997&epslanguage=NO

Skatteetaten

Regulations relating to the Documentation of Price Determination for Controlled Transactions and Transfers

Artikkel, 6. mars 2008

Uofisiell engelsk oversettelse/unofficial translation
Laid down by the Ministry of Finance on 7 December 2007, pursuant to Section 4-12, No. 6, of Act No. 24 of 13 June 1980 relating to Tax Administration (the Tax Administration Act).

I

Section 1. Scope of the Regulations
These Regulations shall apply to enterprises that are obliged, pursuant to Section 4-12, No. 2, cf. Nos. 3 and 5, of the Tax Administration Act, to prepare and, at the request of the tax authorities, present written documentation as to how prices and terms are determined for controlled transactions.

The obligation to prepare and present documentation pursuant to Section 4-12, No. 2, cf. Nos. 3 and 5, of the Tax Administration Act, shall not apply to enterprises that:

a. during the tax year have controlled transactions with an aggregate fair value of less than 10 million kroner, and

b. have accounts outstanding with associated companies or entities in an amount of less than 25 million kroner as per the end of the tax year, cf. Section 4-12, No. 4, of the Tax Administration Act.

Section 2. Definitions

The following meanings shall for purposes of these Regulations be attributed to the expressions set out below:

Controlled transactions: Transactions and transfers between companies or entities that are classified as associated entities pursuant to Section 4-12, No. 4, of the Tax Administration Act, as well as dealings between a permanent establishment and other parts of the enterprise.

Arms' length principle: The principle that commercial and financial relations between associated enterprises shall take place on the same terms as if the transaction had taken place between independent enterprises under comparable conditions and circumstances, cf. Section 13-1 of the Tax Act and Article 9, No. 1, of the OECD Model Tax Convention.

Permanent establishment: A business activity that represents, or shall be deemed as, a permanent establishment pursuant to the provisions of tax treaties entered into by Norway. If the business activity of the enterprise does not fall within the scope of any tax treaty entered into by Norway, it shall, for the purpose of these Regulations, be deemed as a permanent establishment if the conditions stipulated in Article 5 of the OECD Model Tax Convention have been met.

OECD Model Tax Convention: The OECD Model Tax Convention on Income and on Capital, as updated on an ongoing basis and recommended used by the OECD Council.

OECD Guidelines: The Transfer Pricing Guidelines for Multinational Enterprises and Tax Administrations adopted by the Organisation for Economic Co-operation and Development (OECD) in 1995, with the subsequently adopted amendments, published in the report [C (95) 126/Final].

Internal comparable transactions: Comparable transactions that the enterprise has made with an independent enterprise, and that can be used as a benchmark when assessing whether the prices and terms applied to the controlled transactions of the enterprise are in conformity with the arms' length principle.

External comparable transactions: Comparable transactions made between independent enterprises, and that can be used as a benchmark when assessing whether the prices and terms applied to the controlled transactions of the enterprise are in conformity with the arms' length principle.
Section 3. General provisions

(1) The documentation prepared pursuant to Section 4-12, No. 2, of the Tax Administration Act shall provide a basis for evaluating whether the prices and terms of controlled transactions have been determined in conformity with the arms' length principle.

(2) The documentation shall contain the information, explanations and analyses outlined in Sections 4-13 below. The scope of such information, explanations and analyses shall be adapted to the financial magnitude and complexity of the controlled transaction, and to what is necessary to enable the tax authorities to evaluate whether the prices and terms of the transaction are in conformity with the arms' length principle.

(3) The documentation shall be organised in a readily understandable manner, but it is not a requirement that it adheres to the structure of Sections 4-13. The documentation shall, if it is extensive, contain a summary of its main features.

Section 4. Information concerning the enterprise, the group and the business activities

The documentation shall include a general description of the enterprise and the group to which it belongs, as well as the business activities operated thereby. It shall include:

a. A description of the legal ownership structure of the group and the geographical affiliation of the various entities.

b. A description of the operational structure of the group, hereunder the most important business areas of the various entities.

c. A brief historic description of the group, its business activities and any previously implemented reorganisations.

d. A description of the industry, hereunder important competition parameters.

e. A description of material changes to the enterprise or the group during the income year, hereunder an explanation of reorganisations and material changes to the functions performed by the enterprise, the property it uses in its business activities and the risks it assumes.

Section 5. Information concerning financial matters

(1) The documentation shall include information concerning the turnover and operating profits/losses for the last three years of the enterprise and other enterprises in the group with which the enterprise has had controlled transactions during the income year.

(2) An explanation shall be provided for any losses incurred by the enterprise during the last three income years.

Section 6. Information concerning the nature and scope of controlled transactions

(1) The documentation shall include a description of the controlled transactions that the enterprise has been involved in during the income year. The nature and scope of the transaction shall be specified in respect of each of the associated enterprises with which the enterprise has been involved in controlled transactions.

(2) Similar or closely related transactions may be described jointly (in aggregate). It shall be explained what transactions are described in aggregate.

(3) Furthermore, the transactions shall be described in relation to the five comparability factors stipulated in Chapter I of the OECD Guidelines. These are:

a. characteristics of the property or services;
b. a functional analysis, cf. Section 7;
c. contractual terms;
d. economic circumstances (market analysis); and
e. business strategies that may influence price setting.

(4) Any cost contribution arrangements in which the enterprise participates shall be explained, cf. Chapter VIII of the OECD Guidelines.

Section 7. Functional analysis

The functional analysis pursuant to Section 6, Sub-section 3, litra b, shall describe what functions each of the parties perform, what assets they use and what risks they assume, as well as the economic significance of the various functions, assets and risks in relation to the transaction.

Section 8. Special requirements pertaining to centralised services

In case a centralised service is provided within the group, hereunder services of an administrative, technical and financial nature, the enterprise receiving such services shall explain its expected benefits from the services. In case of cost-based allocation or price setting, the enterprise shall explain the cost base, the allocation ratio and any mark-up. If no mark-up is applied, this shall be explained separately by the enterprise providing the service.

Section 9. Special information concerning intangible property

A separate description shall be provided as to such intangible property of the group as is of relevance to the evaluation of the controlled transactions of the enterprise. The description shall include specification of the ownership, utilisation, development and maintenance of the intangible property.

Section 10. Information concerning the selection and application of the price setting method

The documentation shall include an explanation of the price setting method applied to a controlled transaction. It shall be explained why such method has been chosen, and why the price setting resulting from the use of such method is deemed to be in conformity with the arms' length principle. Furthermore, it shall be specified to what extent the price setting method is compatible with the methods described in Chapters II and III of the OECD Guidelines.

Section 11. Information concerning comparability analysis

(1) Unless otherwise set out below, the documentation shall include a comparability analysis that can, together with the information provided pursuant to Sections 4-10 and Section 12, form the basis for an evaluation as to whether the prices and terms of controlled transactions are in conformity with the arms' length principle.

(2) The comparability analysis entails the comparison of the prices and other terms of controlled transactions with the prices and other terms of transactions entered into between independent parties. The analyses shall be carried out on the basis of internal and external comparable transactions, taking into account the comparability factors described in Chapter I of the OECD Guidelines. Any adjustments made to improve comparability shall be explained. It shall also be explained what principles underpin the selection of comparable transactions.

(3) If there exist no internal comparable transactions, and it would be unreasonably difficult or costly to gather and process information concerning external comparable transactions, the obligation under Section 4-12, No. 2, of the Tax Administration Act shall be deemed to have been met without any comparability analysis as mentioned in Sub-section 2 being presented within the time limit stipulated therein. The enterprise shall in such case explain why no such analysis has been prepared, as well as explain what financial evaluations and analyses form the basis for the price setting that has actually taken place, and why this is deemed to be in conformity with the arms' length principle.

(4) The enterprise shall not be obliged to carry out database analysis, cf. nevertheless Section 15, Sub-section 2. If one or more database analysis has been carried out, these shall be enclosed with the documentation.

Section 12. Information concerning agreements, etc.

(1) The documentation shall include those agreements that are of relevance to the prices and other terms of controlled transactions.

(2) Agreements respecting the pricing of controlled transactions that the enterprise has entered into with the authorities in other countries shall be enclosed. The same shall apply to binding advance tax rulings or similar communications that the enterprise has obtained from foreign tax authorities and that relate to the pricing of the controlled transactions of the enterprise.

(3) Agreements respecting the pricing of controlled transactions that another enterprise has entered into with the authorities in other countries shall be enclosed if the enterprise invokes these as a basis for the pricing of controlled transactions. The same shall apply to binding advance tax rulings or similar communications that another enterprise has obtained from foreign tax authorities, if the enterprise invokes these communications as a basis for the pricing of its controlled transactions.

Section 13. Exemption pertaining to immaterial transactions

(1) The requirements stipulated in Sections 4-12 shall not apply to controlled transactions that are immaterial. As far as immaterial transactions are concerned, it shall only be specified what types of transactions the enterprise has engaged in that the enterprise itself deems to be immaterial.

(2) Transactions are deemed to be immaterial if they take place on a stand alone basis, are of limited economic significance and do not form part of the core business of the enterprise.

Section 14. Preparation and collocation of the documentation

Documentation in conformity with Sections 4-13 shall be gathered in respect of each income year. The enterprise shall have procedures that enable it to collocate and present documentation for each income year within 45 days after a request having been made by the tax authorities, cf. Section 4-12, No. 2, of the Tax Administration Act.

Section 15. Presentation at the request of the tax authorities

(1) The documentation shall, at the request of the tax authorities, be presented, submitted or sent within 45 days, cf. Section 4-12, No. 2, of the Tax Administration Act. The time limit stipulated in the preceding sentence shall be calculated by reference to, at the earliest, the expiry of the time limit for filing the tax return.

(2) If the documentation pursuant to Sub-section 1 does not include a comparability analysis, cf. Section 11, Sub-section 3, the tax authorities may request, following evaluation of the documentation received, the enterprise to present a comparability analysis. The tax authorities may, hereunder, request the enterprise to prepare a database analysis. The enterprise shall be granted a time limit of 60-90 days for complying with requests pursuant to the present Sub-section.

(3) The present Regulations entail no limitation as to the right of the tax authorities to request information pursuant to Section 4-8 and Section 4-10 of the Tax Administration Act, hereunder information expanding on descriptions and materials as mentioned in Sections 4-13.

Section 16. Concluding provisions

(1) The documentation shall be prepared in the Norwegian, Swedish, Danish or English language.

(2) The documentation shall be retained for a minimum of ten years after the end of the income year, cf. Section 4-12, No. 2, of the Tax Administration Act.

(3) The enterprise may opt to prepare the documentation in accordance with the Code of Conduct on Transfer Pricing Documentation for Associated Enterprises in the European Union (2006/C 176/01) of 28 July 2006. In such case the information required under Sections 4-13 shall be included either in the masterfile or in the country-specific documentation. The provisions of Section 3 and Section 12 to Section 16, Sub-section 2, inclusive, shall apply correspondingly.

II

These Regulations shall enter into force from 1 January 2008.

Utskrift fra www.skatteetaten.no/Templates/Artikkel.aspx?id=74000&epslanguage=NO

Act relating to Tax Administration (the Tax Administration Act)

Artikkel, 6. mars 2008

Uofisiell engelsk oversettelse/unofficial translation
Section 4-12. Duty to specify and document controlled transactions, etc.

1. Any company or entity with a duty to file a tax return pursuant to Section 4-2, No. 1, shall file a specification as to the nature and scope of transactions and accounts outstanding with associated companies or entities. This shall apply correspondingly to any company with a duty to file a company return pursuant to Section 4-9, No. 1.

2. Any company or entity mentioned in No. 1 shall prepare written documentation that provides a basis for evaluating whether the prices and terms of their transactions and accounts outstanding with associated companies and entities are in conformity with those that would have been adopted for transactions and accounts outstanding established between independent parties under comparable conditions and circumstances. The documentation shall be presented, submitted or sent within 45 days after a request having been made by the tax authorities, and shall be retained by the party obliged to prepare the documentation for a minimum of 10 years after the end of the income year.

3. Exempted from the duty to prepare and file documentation pursuant to No. 2 is any company or entity mentioned in No. 1 that has, in the relevant financial year and together with associated enterprises,

- fewer than 250 employees; and either
- sales income not exceeding 400 million kroner; or
- total assets not exceeding 350 million kroner.

Any company or entity mentioned in No. 1 that has transactions or accounts outstanding with an associated company or entity that is resident in a state from which Norway cannot demand information concerning the income and wealth of such other contracting party pursuant to an international law agreement, shall prepare written documentation in respect of such transactions and accounts outstanding irrespective or the limitations stipulated in the preceding sentence. Nor shall the said sentence apply to any company or entity liable to pay special tax pursuant to the Petroleum Taxation Act.

4. The following shall be deemed to be associated entities for purposes of Nos. 1, 2 and 3:

a. any company or entity that, directly or indirectly, is at least 50 percent owned or controlled by the entity obliged to specify or document;

b. any individual, company or entity that, directly or indirectly, has at least 50 percent ownership of, or control over, the entity obliged to specify or document;

c. any company or entity that, directly or indirectly, is at least 50 percent owned or controlled by any entity that is deemed to be an associated party pursuant to Item b; and

d. any parent, sibling, child, grandchild, spouse, cohabitant, parent of a spouse and parent of a cohabitant of any individual who is deemed to be an associated party pursuant to Item b, as well as any company or entity that, directly or indirectly, is at least 50 percent owned or controlled by such individuals.

5. The duty to specify and document as stipulated in Nos. 1-4 above shall apply correspondingly to any dealings effected between

a. any company or entity that is resident in Norway and its permanent establishments abroad.

b. any company or entity that is resident abroad and its permanent establishments in Norway.

6. The Ministry may lay down more detailed Regulations and Guidelines to supplement and implement the present provision, hereunder stipulate exemptions from the duty to specify and document.

Utskrift fra www.skatteetaten.no/Templates/Artikkel.aspx?id=73999&epslanguage=NO

Skatteetaten

Act relating to Tax on Wealth and Income (the Tax Act)

Artikkel, 6. mars 2008

Chapter 13. Discretionary assessment of wealth and income in case of community of interest
Uofisiell engelsk oversettelse/unofficial translation

Section 13-1. Community of interest

(1) Discretionary assessment may take place if the wealth or income of the taxpayer has been reduced as the result of a direct or indirect community of interest with another individual, company or entity.

(2) If the other individual, company or entity mentioned in Sub-section 1 is resident in a state outside the EEA, and there is reason to believe that the wealth or income has been reduced, such reduction shall be deemed to have resulted from a community of interest unless the taxpayer documents that such is not the case. The preceding sentence shall apply correspondingly if the other individual, company or entity is resident or domiciled in a state within the EEA, provided that Norway does not have the right to demand information concerning the wealth and income of such person pursuant to an international law agreement.

(3) Wealth or income shall be assessed discretionarily as if there had been no community of interest.

(4) If there is a community of interest between enterprises resident in Norway and abroad, and their commercial or financial relations are subject to arms' length terms laid down in a tax treaty between the respective states, the Transfer Pricing Guidelines for Multinational Enterprises and Tax Administrations adopted by the Organisation for Economic Co-operation and Development (OECD) shall be taken into consideration for purposes of determining whether wealth or income has been reduced as stipulated in Sub-section 1 and for purposes of the discretionary assessment of wealth or income pursuant to Sub-section 3. These Guidelines should, to the extent applicable, be correspondingly taken into consideration in other cases than those mentioned above. The above shall only apply to the extent that Norway has acceded to the Guidelines, and provided that the Ministry has not decided otherwise.

Utskrift fra www.skatteetaten.no/Templates/Artikkel.aspx?id=73998&epslanguage=NO

XII. Glossary

A Note About Transfer Pricing Terminology

The goal of this section is to offer a general sense of what some of the words and phrases that appear in this volume may indicate in a transfer pricing context. In no way should these entries be taken as definitive or technical in nature, especially since transfer pricing-related terms have different legal meanings in different jurisdictions.

In some cases, U.S. Transfer Pricing Regulations are quoted in these entries. While the hope is that these excerpts with prove useful in grasping the terms listed on a conceptual level, they may or may not be relevant to discussions of transfer pricing in other jurisdictions and even for U.S. transfer pricing, need to be considered in the context of other regulations, laws, rulings and court decisions.

Please consult with local tax counsel regarding the legal meaning of these terms in a given jurisdiction and fact pattern. If you have questions for the authors regarding what is meant by a given term, you may contact them directly using the phone numbers and email addresses provided.

Advance Pricing Agreements
Method By Which Related Parties May Value In Advance Goods To Be Transacted

Instead of waiting to see if your transfer pricing methodology is found to be acceptable by tax authorities, you may seek to enter into an Advance Pricing Agreement (APA) with the IRS. The IRS web site defines APAs as follows:

> The Advance Pricing Agreement (APA) Program is designed to resolve actual or potential transfer pricing disputes in a principled, cooperative manner, as an alternative to the traditional adversarial process. An APA is a binding contract between the IRS and a taxpayer by which the IRS agrees not to seek a transfer pricing adjustment under IRC § 482 for a covered transaction if the taxpayer files its tax return for a covered year consistent with the agreed transfer pricing method.

APAs are not available for all transactions and do have up-front costs. There is a fairly extensive process of fact-finding and negotiation that goes into the development of an APA. For the U.S. this process is described in IRS Revenue Procedure 2006-9, which was published on January 9, 2006. Details of the APA programs in other countries can be found in the Country Overview section.

Please note that in some countries, the term "Advance Pricing Arrangements" is used instead of "Advance Pricing Agreements," but is also abbreviated "APA."

Glossary

Arm's-Length Principle
What would a product cost if transacted by unrelated parties?

The "arm's-length principle" of transfer pricing states that the amount charged by one related party to another for a given product must be the same as if the parties were not related. An arm's-length price for a transaction is therefore what the price of that transaction would be on the open market. For commodities, determining the arm's-length price can sometimes be as simple a matter as looking up comparable pricing from non-related party transactions, but when dealing with proprietary goods and services or intangibles, arriving at an arm's length price can be a much more complicated matter. U.S. transfer pricing law requires that the best method rule be used to determine which transfer pricing methodology is most appropriate for determining the arm's-length price of a given transaction.

The official definition of the arm's length standard as it applies in the United States can be found in Section 482-1 (b) of the transfer pricing regulations:

> (b) Arm's length standard--(1) In general. In determining the true taxable income of a controlled taxpayer, the standard to be applied in every case is that of a taxpayer dealing at arm's length with an uncontrolled taxpayer. A controlled transaction meets the arm's length standard if the results of the transaction are consistent with the results that would have been realized if uncontrolled taxpayers had engaged in the same transaction under the same circumstances (arm's length result). However, because identical transactions can rarely be located, whether a transaction produces an arm's length result generally will be determined by reference to the results of comparable transactions under comparable circumstances. See Sec. 1.482-1(d)(2) (Standard of comparability). Evaluation of whether a controlled transaction produces an arm's length result is made pursuant to a method selected under the best method rule described in Sec. 1.482-1(c).
> (2) Arm's length methods--(i) Methods. Sections 1.482-2 through 1.482-6 provide specific methods to be used to evaluate whether transactions between or among members of the controlled group satisfy the arm's length standard, and if they do not, to determine the arm's length result.
> (ii) Selection of category of method applicable to transaction. The methods listed in Sec. 1.482-2 apply to different types of transactions, such as transfers of property, services, loans or advances, and rentals. Accordingly, the method or methods most appropriate to the calculation of arm's length results for controlled transactions must be selected, and different methods may be applied to interrelated transactions if such transactions are most reliably evaluated on a separate basis. For example, if services are provided in connection with the transfer of property, it may be appropriate to separately apply the methods

applicable to services and property in order to determine an arm's length result. But see Sec. 1.482-1(f)(2)(i) (Aggregation of transactions). In addition, other applicable provisions of the Code may affect the characterization of a transaction, and therefore affect the methods applicable under section 482. See for example section 467.

Best Method Rule
Which methodology should be appled to determine the arm's-length price?

The "best method rule" of transfer pricing requires that the methodology used to determine the transfer price be the one that offers the greatest precision in matching the price of an arm's-length transaction between unrelated parties. Some countries leave the decision as to which method is most appropriate for a given transaction up to the taxpayer, while others require that a particular methodology be employed. IRS regulations specify the best method for a given type of transaction. The official definition of the best method rule as it applies in the United States as well as a number of examples of its application can be found in Section 482-1 (c) of the transfer pricing regulations:

(c) Best method rule--(1) In general. The arm's length result of a controlled transaction must be determined under the method that, under the facts and circumstances, provides the most reliable measure of an arm's length result. Thus, there is no strict priority of methods, and no method will invariably be considered to be more reliable than others. An arm's length result may be determined under any method without establishing the inapplicability of another method, but if another method subsequently is shown to produce a more reliable measure of an arm's length result, such other method must be used. Similarly, if two or more applications of a single method provide inconsistent results, the arm's length result must be determined under the application that, under the facts and circumstances, provides the most reliable measure of an arm's length result. See Sec. 1.482-8 for examples of the application of the best method rule. See § 1.482–7 for the applicable method in the case of a qualified cost sharing arrangement.

Comparable Profits Method
How profitable are similar transactions among unrelated parties?

The Comparable Profits Method (CPM) attempts to measure how much profit a related party in a controlled transaction would have realized had that party been involved in an otherwise identical uncontrolled transaction. This method relies on identifying and evaluating comparable uncontrolled transactions. This method is available for both tangible and intangible property transactions in the United States, but is not available in many countries. The Transactional Net Margin Method (TNMN) is allowed in some jurisdictions that do not accept the CPM. The TNMN can be very similar to the CPM (some practitioners consider the terms to be virtually synonymous), but there are countries that specifically prohibit the use of the CPM and allow the TNMN, suggesting a perceived substantive difference by the tax authorities in those countries.

Here is the official definition from Section 1.482-5 of the U.S. regulations:

(a) In general

The comparable profits method evaluates whether the amount charged in a controlled transaction is arm's length based on objective measures of profitability (profit level indicators) derived from uncontrolled taxpayers that engage in similar business activities under similar circumstances.

(b) Determination of arm's length result

(1) In general

Under the comparable profits method, the determination of an arm's length result is based on the amount of operating profit that the tested party would have earned on related party transactions if its profit level indicator were equal to that of an uncontrolled comparable (comparable operating profit). Comparable operating profit is calculated by determining a profit level indicator for an uncontrolled comparable, and applying the profit level indicator to the financial data related to the tested party's most narrowly identifiable business activity for which data incorporating the controlled transaction is available (relevant business activity). To the extent possible, profit level indicators should be applied solely to the tested party's financial data that is related to controlled transactions. The tested party's reported operating profit is compared to the comparable operating profits derived from the profit level indicators of uncontrolled comparables to determine whether the reported operating profit represents an arm's length result.

(2) Tested party

(i) In general

For purposes of this section, the tested party will be the participant in the controlled transaction whose operating profit attributable to the controlled transactions can be verified using the most reliable data and requiring the fewest and most reliable adjustments, and for which reliable data regarding uncontrolled comparables can be located. Consequently, in most cases the tested party will be the least complex of the controlled taxpayers and will not own valuable intangible property or unique assets that distinguish it from potential uncontrolled comparables.

(ii) Adjustments for tested party

The tested party's operating profit must first be adjusted to reflect all other allocations under section 482, other than adjustments pursuant to this section.

(3) Arm's length range

See section 1.482-1(e)(2) for the determination of the arm's length range. For purposes of the comparable profits method, the arm's length range will be established using comparable operating profits derived from a single profit level indicator.

(4) Profit level indicators

Profit level indicators are ratios that measure relationships between profits and costs incurred or resources employed. A variety of profit level indicators can be calculated in any given case. Whether use of a particular profit level indicator is appropriate depends upon a number of factors, including the nature of the activities of the tested party, the reliability of the available data with respect to uncontrolled comparables, and the extent to which the profit level indicator is likely to produce a reliable measure of the income that the tested party would have earned had it dealt with controlled taxpayers at arm's length, taking into account all of the facts and circumstances. The profit level indicators should be derived from a sufficient number of years of data to reasonably measure returns that accrue to uncontrolled comparables. Generally, such a period should encompass at least the taxable year under review and the preceding two taxable years. This analysis must be applied in accordance with section 1.482-1(f)(2)(iii)(D). Profit level indicators that may provide a reliable basis for comparing operating profits of the tested party and uncontrolled comparables include the following--

(i) Rate of return on capital employed

The rate of return on capital employed is the ratio of operating profit to operating assets. The reliability of this profit level indicator increases as operating assets play a greater role in generating operating profits for both the tested party and the uncontrolled comparable. In addition, reliability under this profit level indicator depends on the extent to which the composition of the tested party's assets is similar to that of the uncontrolled comparable. Finally, difficulties in properly valuing operating assets will diminish the reliability of this profit level indicator.

(ii) Financial ratios

Financial ratios measure relationships between profit and costs or sales revenue. Since functional differences generally have a greater effect on the relationship between profit and costs or sales revenue than the relationship between profit and operating assets, financial ratios are more sensitive to functional differences than the rate of return on capital employed. Therefore, closer functional comparability normally is required under a financial ratio than under the rate of return on capital employed to achieve a similarly reliable measure of an arm's length result. Financial ratios that may be appropriate include the following--

(A) Ratio of operating profit to sales; and

(B) Ratio of gross profit to operating expenses. Reliability under this profit level indicator also depends on the extent to which the composition of the tested party's operating expenses is similar to that of the uncontrolled comparables.

(iii) Other profit level indicators

Other profit level indicators not described in this paragraph (b)(4) may be used if they provide reliable measures of the income that the tested party would have earned had it dealt with controlled taxpayers at arm's length. However, profit level indicators based solely on internal data may not be used under this paragraph (b)(4) because they are not objective measures of profitability derived from operations of uncontrolled taxpayers engaged in similar business activities under similar circumstances.

(c) Comparability and reliability considerations

(1) In general

Whether results derived from application of this method are the most reliable measure of the arm's length result must be determined using the factors described under the best method rule in section 1.482-1(c).

(2) Comparability

(i) In general

The degree of comparability between an uncontrolled taxpayer and the tested party is determined by applying the provisions of section 1.482-1(d)(2). The comparable profits method compares the profitability of the tested party, measured by a profit level indicator (generally based on operating profit), to the profitability of uncontrolled taxpayers in similar circumstances. As with all methods that rely on external market benchmarks, the greater the degree of comparability between the tested party and the uncontrolled taxpayer, the more reliable will be the results derived from the application of this method. The determination of the degree of comparability between the tested party and the uncontrolled taxpayer depends upon all the relevant facts and circumstances, including the relevant lines of business, the product or service markets involved, the asset composition employed (including the nature and quantity of tangible assets, intangible assets and working capital), the size and scope of operations, and the stage in a business or product cycle.

(ii) Functional, risk and resource comparability

An operating profit represents a return for the investment of resources and assumption of risks. Therefore, although all of the factors described in section 1.482-1(d)(3) must be considered, comparability under this method is particularly dependent on resources employed and risks assumed. Moreover, because resources and risks usually are directly related to functions performed, it is also important to consider functions performed in determining the degree of comparability between the tested party and an uncontrolled taxpayer. The degree of functional comparability required to obtain a reliable result under the comparable profits method, however, is generally less than that required under the resale price or cost plus methods. For example, because differences in functions performed often are reflected in operating expenses, taxpayers performing different functions may have very different gross profit margins but earn similar levels of operating profit.

(iii) Other comparability factors

Other factors listed in section 1.482-1(d)(3) also may be particularly relevant under the comparable profits method. Because operating profit usually is less sensitive than gross profit to product differences, reliability under the comparable profits method is not as dependent on product similarity as the resale price or cost plus method. However, the reliability of profitability measures based on operating profit may be adversely affected by factors that have less effect on results under the comparable uncontrolled price, resale price, and cost plus methods. For example, operating profit may be affected by varying cost structures (as reflected, for example, in the age of plant and equipment), differences in business experience (such as whether the business is in a start-up phase or is mature), or differences in management efficiency (as indicated, for example, by objective evidence such as expanding or contracting sales or executive compensation over time). Accordingly, if material differences in these factors are identified based on objective evidence, the reliability of the analysis may be affected.

(iv) Adjustments for the differences between the tested party and the uncontrolled taxpayers

If there are differences between the tested party and an uncontrolled comparable that would materially affect the profits determined under the relevant profit level indicator, adjustments should be made according to the comparability provisions of section 1.482-1(d)(2). In some cases, the assets of an uncontrolled comparable may need to be adjusted to achieve greater comparability between the tested party and the uncontrolled comparable. In such cases, the uncontrolled comparable's operating income attributable to those assets must also be adjusted before computing a profit level indicator in order to reflect the income and expense attributable to the adjusted assets. In certain cases it may also be appropriate to adjust the operating profit of the tested party and comparable parties. For example, where there are material differences in accounts payable among the comparable parties and the tested party, it will generally be appropriate to adjust the operating profit of each party by increasing it to reflect an imputed interest charge on each party's accounts payable.

(3) Data and assumptions

(i) In general

The reliability of the results derived from the comparable profits method is affected by the quality of the data and assumptions used to apply this method.

(ii) Consistency in accounting

The degree of consistency in accounting practices between the controlled transaction and the uncontrolled comparables that materially affect operating profit affects the reliability of the result. Thus, for example, if differences in inventory and other cost accounting practices would materially affect operating profit, the ability to make reliable adjustments for such differences would affect the reliability of the results.

(iii) Allocations between the relevant business activity and other activities

The reliability of the allocation of costs, income, and assets between the relevant business activity and other activities of the tested party or an uncontrolled comparable will affect the reliability of the determination of operating profit and profit level indicators. If it is not possible to allocate costs, income, and assets directly based on factual relationships, a reasonable allocation formula may be used. To the extent direct allocations are not made, the reliability of the results derived from the application of this method is reduced relative to the results of a method that requires fewer allocations of costs, income, and assets. Similarly, the reliability of the results derived from the application of this method is affected by the extent to which it is possible to apply the profit level indicator to the tested party's financial data that is related solely to the controlled transactions. For example, if the relevant business activity is the assembly of components purchased from both controlled and uncontrolled suppliers, it may not be possible to apply the profit level indicator solely to financial data related to the controlled transactions. In such a case, the reliability of the results derived from the application of this method will be reduced.

(d) Definitions

The definitions set forth in paragraphs (d)(1) through (6) of this section apply for purposes of this section.

(1) SALES REVENUE means the amount of the total receipts from sale of goods and provision of services, less returns and allowances. Accounting principles and conventions that are generally accepted in the trade or industry of the controlled taxpayer under review must be used.

(2) GROSS PROFIT means sales revenue less cost of goods sold.

(3) OPERATING EXPENSES includes all expenses not included in cost of goods sold except for interest expense, foreign income taxes (as defined in section 1.901-2(a)), domestic income taxes, and any other expenses not related to the operation of the relevant business activity. Operating expenses ordinarily include expenses associated with advertising, promotion, sales, marketing, warehousing and distribution, administration, and a reasonable allowance for depreciation and amortization.

(4) OPERATING PROFIT means gross profit less operating expenses. Operating profit includes all income derived from the business activity being evaluated by the comparable profits method, but does not include interest and dividends, income derived from activities not being tested by this method, or extraordinary gains and losses that do not relate to the continuing operations of the tested party.

(5) REPORTED OPERATING PROFIT means the operating profit of the tested party reflected on a timely filed U.S. income tax return. If the tested party files a U.S. income tax return, its operating profit is considered reflected on a U.S. income tax return if the calculation of taxable income on its return for the taxable year takes into account the income attributable to the controlled transaction under review. If the tested party does not file a U.S. income tax return, its operating profit is considered reflected on a U.S. income tax return in any taxable year for which income attributable to the controlled transaction under review affects the calculation of the U.S. taxable income of any other member of the same controlled group. If the comparable operating profit of the tested party

is determined from profit level indicators derived from financial statements or other accounting records and reports of comparable parties, adjustments may be made to the reported operating profit of the tested party in order to account for material differences between the tested party's operating profit reported for U.S. income tax purposes and the tested party's operating profit for financial statement purposes. In addition, in accordance with section 1.482-1(f)(2)(iii)(D), adjustments under section 482 that are finally determined may be taken into account in determining reported operating profit.

(6) OPERATING ASSETS. The term operating assets means the value of all assets used in the relevant business activity of the tested party, including fixed assets and current assets (such as cash, cash equivalents, accounts receivable, and inventories). The term does not include investments in subsidiaries, excess cash, and portfolio investments. Operating assets may be measured by their net book value or by their fair market value, provided that the same method is consistently applied to the tested party and the comparable parties, and consistently applied from year to year. In addition, it may be necessary to take into account recent acquisitions, leased assets, intangibles, currency fluctuations, and other items that may not be explicitly recorded in the financial statements of the tested party or uncontrolled comparable. Finally, operating assets must be measured by the average of the values for the beginning of the year and the end of the year, unless substantial fluctuations in the value of operating assets during the year make this an inaccurate measure of the average value over the year. In such a case, a more accurate measure of the average value of operating assets must be applied.

(e) Examples

The following examples illustrate the application of this section.

Example 1 -- Transfer of tangible property resulting in no adjustment.

(i) FP is a publicly traded foreign corporation with a U.S. subsidiary, USSub, that is under audit for its 1996 taxable year. FP manufactures a consumer product for worldwide distribution. USSub imports the assembled product and distributes it within the United States at the wholesale level under the FP name.

(ii) FP does not allow uncontrolled taxpayers to distribute the product. Similar products are produced by other companies but none of them is sold to uncontrolled taxpayers or to uncontrolled distributors.

(iii) Based on all the facts and circumstances, the district director determines that the comparable profits method will provide the most reliable measure of an arm's length result. USSub is selected as the tested party because it engages in activities that are less complex than those undertaken by FP. There is data from a number of independent operators of wholesale distribution businesses. These potential comparables are further narrowed to select companies in the same industry segment that perform similar functions and bear similar risks to USSub. An analysis of the information available on these taxpayers shows that the ratio of operating profit to sales is the most appropriate profit level indicator, and this ratio is relatively stable where at least three years are included in the average. For the taxable years 1994 through 1996, USSub shows the following results:

	1994	1995	1996	Average
Sales	500,000	560,000	500,000	520,000
Cost of Goods Sold	393,000	412,400	400,000	401,800
Operating Expenses	80,000	110,000	104,600	98,200
Operating Profit	27,000	37,600	(4,600)	20,000

(iv) After adjustments have been made to account for identified material differences between USSub and the uncontrolled distributors, the average ratio of operating profit to sales is calculated for each of the uncontrolled distributors. Applying each ratio to USSub would lead to the following comparable operating profit (COP) for USSub:

Uncontrolled Distributor	OP/S	US Sub COP
A	1.7%	$ 8,840
B	3.1%	16,120
C	3.8%	19,760
D	4.5%	23,400
E	4.7%	24,440
F	4.8%	24,960
G	4.9%	25,480
H	6.7%	34,840
I	9.9%	51,480
J	10.5%	54,600

(v) The data is not sufficiently complete to conclude that it is likely that all material differences between USSub and the uncontrolled distributors have been identified. Therefore, an arm's length range can be established only pursuant to section 1.482-1(e)(2)(iii)(B). The district director measures the arm's length range by the interquartile range of results, which consists of the results ranging from $19,760 to $34,840. Although USSub's operating income for 1996 shows a loss of $4,600, the district director determines that no allocation should be made, because USSub's average reported operating profit of $20,000 is within this range.

Example 2 -- Transfer of tangible property resulting in adjustment. (i) The facts are the same as in EXAMPLE 1 except that USSub reported the following income and expenses:

	1994	1995	1996	Average
Sales	500,000	560,000	500,000	520,000
Cost of Goods Sold	370,000	460,000	400,000	410,000
Operating Expenses	110,000	110,000	110,000	110,000
Operating Profit	20,000	(10,000)	(10,000)	0

(ii) The interquartile range of comparable operating profits remains the same as derived in EXAMPLE 1: $19,760 to $34,840. USSub's average operating profit for the years 1994 through 1996 ($0) falls outside this range. Therefore, the district director determines that an allocation may be appropriate.

(iii) To determine the amount, if any, of the allocation, the district director compares USSub's reported operating profit for 1996 to comparable operating profits derived from the uncontrolled distributors' results for 1996. The ratio of operating profit to sales in 1996 is calculated for each of the uncontrolled comparables and applied to USSub's 1996 sales to derive the following results:

Uncontrolled Distributor	OP/S	US Sub COP
C	0.5%	$ 2,500
D	1.5%	7,500
E	2.0%	10,000
A	1.6%	13,000
F	2.8%	14,000
B	2.9%	14,500
J	3.0%	15,000
I	4.4%	22,000
H	6.9%	34,500
G	7.4%	37,000

(iv) Based on these results, the median of the comparable operating profits for 1996 is $14,250. Therefore, USSub's income for 1996 is increased by $24,250, the difference between USSub's reported operating profit for 1996 and the median of the comparable operating profits for 1996.

Example 3 -- Multiple year analysis

(i) The facts are the same as in EXAMPLE 2. In addition, the district director examines the taxpayer's results for the 1997 taxable year. As in EXAMPLE 2, the district director increases USSub's income for the 1996 taxable year by $24,250. The results for the 1997 taxable year, together with the 1995 and 1996 taxable years, are as follows:

Glossary

	1995	1996	1997	Average
Sales	560,000	500,000	530,000	530,000
Cost of Goods Sold	460,000	400,000	430,000	430,000
Operating Expenses	110,000	110,000	110,000	110,000
Operating Profit	(10,000)	(10,000)	(10,000)	(10,000)

(ii) The interquartile range of comparable operating profits, based on average results from the uncontrolled comparables and average sales for USSub for the years 1995 through 1997, ranges from $15,500 to $30,000. In determining whether an allocation for the 1997 taxable year may be made, the district director compares USSub's average reported operating profit for the years 1995 through 1997 to the interquartile range of average comparable operating profits over this period. USSub's average reported operating profit is determined without regard to the adjustment made with respect to the 1996 taxable year. See section 1.482-1(f)(2)(iii)(D). Therefore, USSub's average reported operating profit for the years 1995 through 1997 is ($10,000). Because this amount of income falls outside the interquartile range, the district director determines that an allocation may be appropriate.

(iii) To determine the amount, if any, of the allocation for the 1997 taxable year, the district director compares USSub's reported operating profit for 1997 to the median of the comparable operating profits derived from the uncontrolled distributors' results for 1997. The median of the comparable operating profits derived from the uncontrolled comparables results for the 1997 taxable year is $12,000. Based on this comparison, the district director increases USSub's 1997 taxable income by $22,000, the difference between the median of the comparable operating profits for the 1997 taxable year and USSub's reported operating profit of ($10,000) for the 1997 taxable year.

Example 4 -- Transfer of intangible to offshore manufacturer

(i) DevCo is a U.S. developer, producer and marketer of widgets. DevCo develops a new "high tech widget" (htw) that is manufactured by its foreign subsidiary ManuCo located in Country H. ManuCo sells the htw to MarkCo (a U.S. subsidiary of DevCo) for distribution and marketing in the United States. The taxable year 1996 is under audit, and the district director examines whether the royalty rate of 5 percent paid by ManuCo to DevCo is an arm's length consideration for the htw technology.

(ii) Based on all the facts and circumstances, the district director determines that the comparable profits method will provide the most reliable measure of an arm's length result. ManuCo is selected as the tested party because it engages in relatively routine manufacturing activities, while DevCo engages in a variety of complex activities using unique and valuable intangibles. Finally, because ManuCo engages in manufacturing activities, it is determined that the ratio of operating profit to operating assets is an appropriate profit level indicator.

(iii) Uncontrolled taxpayers performing similar functions cannot be found in country H. It is determined that data available in countries M and N provides the best match of companies in a similar market performing similar functions and bearing similar risks. Such data is sufficiently complete to identify many of the material differences between ManuCo and the uncontrolled comparables, and to make adjustments to account for such differences. However, data is not sufficiently complete so that it is likely that no material differences remain. In particular, the differences in geographic markets might have materially affected the results of the various companies.

(iv) In a separate analysis, it is determined that the price that ManuCo charged to MarkCo for the htw's is an arm's length price under section 1.482-3(b). Therefore, ManuCo's financial data derived from its sales to MarkCo are reliable. ManuCo's financial data from 1994-1996 is as follows:

	1994	1995	1996	Average
Assets	$24,000	$25,000	$26,000	$25,000
Sales to MarkCo.	25,000	30,000	35,000	30,000
Cost of Goods Sold	6,250	7,500	8,750	7,500
Royalty to DevCo	1,250	1,500	1,750	1,500
Other	5,000	6,000	7,000	6,000
Operating Expenses	1,000	1,000	1,000	1,000
Operating Profit	17,750	21,500	25,250	21,500

(v) Applying the ratios of average operating profit to operating assets for the 1994 through 1996 taxable years derived from a group of similar uncontrolled comparables located in country M and N to ManuCo's average operating assets for the same period provides a set of comparable operating profits. The interquartile range for these average comparable operating profits is $3,000 to $4,500. ManuCo's average reported operating profit for the years 1994 through 1996 ($21,500) falls outside this range. Therefore, the district director determines that an allocation may be appropriate for the 1996 taxable year.

(vi) To determine the amount, if any, of the allocation for the 1996 taxable year, the district director compares ManuCo's reported operating profit for 1996 to the median of the comparable operating profits derived from the uncontrolled distributors' results for 1996. The median result for the uncontrolled comparables for 1996 is $3,750. Based on this comparison, the district director increases royalties that ManuCo paid by $21,500 (the difference between $25,250 and the median of the comparable operating profits, $3,750).

Example 5 -- Adjusting operating assets and operating profit for differences in accounts receivable.

(i) USM is a U.S. company that manufactures parts for industrial equipment and sells them to its foreign parent corporation. For purposes of applying the comparable profits method, 15 uncontrolled manufacturers that are similar to USM have been identified.

(ii) USM has a significantly lower level of accounts receivable than the uncontrolled manufacturers. Since the rate of return on capital employed is to be used as the profit level indicator, both operating assets and operating profits must be adjusted to account for this difference. Each uncontrolled comparable's operating assets is reduced by the amount (relative to sales) by which they exceed USM's accounts receivable. Each uncontrolled comparable's operating profit is adjusted by deducting imputed interest income on the excess accounts receivable. This imputed interest income is calculated by multiplying the uncontrolled comparable's excess accounts receivable by an interest rate appropriate for short-term debt.

Example 6 -- Adjusting operating profit for differences in accounts payable.

(i) USD is the U.S. subsidiary of a foreign corporation. USD purchases goods from its foreign parent and sells them in the U.S. market. For purposes of applying the comparable profits method, 10 uncontrolled distributors that are similar to USD have been identified.

(ii) There are significant differences in the level of accounts payable among the uncontrolled distributors and USD. To adjust for these differences, the district director increases the operating profit of the uncontrolled distributors and USD to reflect interest expense imputed to the accounts payable. The imputed interest expense for each company is calculated by multiplying the company's accounts payable by an interest rate appropriate for its short-term debt.

Comparable Uncontrolled Price Method

Simple Method for Transfer Pricing of Tangible Goods Where Unrelated Party Transactions Are Available for Comparison

The comparable uncontrolled price method is perhaps the simplest way of determining the arm's-length price for the sale of tangible goods between related parties, but it requires that there be similar transactions between unrelated parties to use for comparison. The method simply requires that the goods in question be standard enough to be sold on an open market. For this reason, patented products, or those containing trade secrets or other unique characteristics are not well-suited to this method, which is described in 26CFR 1.482-3(b) of the U.S. transfer pricing regulations:

(b) Comparable uncontrolled price method
(1) In general
The comparable uncontrolled price method evaluates whether the amount charged in a controlled transaction is arm's length by reference to the amount charged in a comparable uncontrolled transaction.
(2) Comparability and reliability considerations
(i) In general
Whether results derived from applications of this method are the most reliable measure of the arm's length result must be determined using the factors described under the best method rule in section 1.482-1(c). The application of these factors under the comparable uncontrolled price method is discussed in paragraph (b)(2)(ii) and (iii) of this section.
(ii) Comparability
(A) In general
The degree of comparability between controlled and uncontrolled transactions is determined by applying the provisions of section 1.482-1(d). Although all of the factors described in section 1.482-1(d)(3) must be considered, similarity of products generally will have the greatest effect on comparability under this method. In addition, because even minor differences in contractual terms or economic conditions could materially affect the amount charged in an uncontrolled transaction, comparability under this method depends on close similarity with respect to these factors, or adjustments to account for any differences. The results derived from applying the comparable uncontrolled price method generally will be the most direct and reliable measure of an arm's length price for the controlled transaction if an uncontrolled transaction has no differences with the controlled transaction that would affect the price, or if there are only minor differences that have a definite and reasonably ascertainable effect on price and for which appropriate adjustments are made. If such adjustments cannot be made, or if there are more than minor differences between the controlled and uncontrolled transactions, the comparable uncontrolled price method may be used, but the reliability of the results as a measure of the arm's length price will be reduced. Further, if there are material product differences for which reliable adjustments

cannot be made, this method ordinarily will not provide a reliable measure of an arm's length result.

(B) Adjustments for differences between controlled and uncontrolled transactions

If there are differences between the controlled and uncontrolled transactions that would affect price, adjustments should be made to the price of the uncontrolled transaction according to the comparability provisions of section 1.482-1(d)(2). Specific examples of the factors that may be particularly relevant to this method include--

(1) Quality of the product;
(2) Contractual terms, (e.g., scope and terms of warranties provided, sales or purchase volume, credit terms, transport terms);
(3) Level of the market (i.e., wholesale, retail, etc.);
(4) Geographic market in which the transaction takes place;
(5) Date of the transaction;
(6) Intangible property associated with the sale;
(7) Foreign currency risks; and
(8) Alternatives realistically available to the buyer and seller.

(iii) Data and assumptions

The reliability of the results derived from the comparable uncontrolled price method is affected by the completeness and accuracy of the data used and the reliability of the assumptions made to apply the method. See section 1.482-1(c) (Best method rule).

(3) Arm's length range

See section 1.482-1(e)(2) for the determination of an arm's length range.

(4) Examples

The principles of this paragraph (b) are illustrated by the following examples.

Example 1 -- Comparable sales of same product

USM, a U.S. manufacturer, sells the same product to both controlled and uncontrolled distributors. The circumstances surrounding the controlled and uncontrolled transactions are substantially the same, except that the controlled sales price is a delivered price and the uncontrolled sales are made f.o.b. USM's factory. Differences in the contractual terms of transportation and insurance generally have a definite and reasonably ascertainable effect on price, and adjustments are made to the results of the uncontrolled transaction to account for such differences. No other material difference has been identified between the controlled and uncontrolled transactions. Because USM sells in both the controlled and uncontrolled transactions, it is likely that all material differences between the two transactions have been identified. In addition, because the comparable uncontrolled price method is applied to an uncontrolled comparable with no product differences, and there are only minor contractual differences that have a definite and reasonably ascertainable effect on price, the results of this application of the comparable uncontrolled price method will provide the most direct and reliable measure of an arm's length result. See section 1.482-3(b)(2)(ii)(A).

Example 2 -- Effect of trademark

The facts are the same as in Example 1, except that USM affixes its valuable trademark to the property sold in the controlled transactions, but does not affix its trademark to the property sold in the uncontrolled transactions. Under the facts of this case, the effect on price of the trademark is material and cannot be reliably estimated. Because there are material product differences for which reliable adjustments cannot be made, the comparable uncontrolled price method is unlikely to provide a reliable measure of the arm's length result. See section 1.482-3(b)(2)(ii)(A).

Example 3 -- Minor product differences

The facts are the same as in Example 1, except that USM, which manufactures business machines, makes minor modifications to the physical properties of the machines to satisfy specific requirements of a customer in controlled sales, but does not make these modifications in uncontrolled sales. If the minor physical differences in the product have a material affect on prices, adjustments to account for these differences must be made to the results of the uncontrolled transactions according to the provisions of section 1.482-1(d)(2), and such adjusted results maybe used as a measure of the arm's length result.

Example 4 -- Effect of geographic differences

FM, a foreign specialty radio manufacturer, sells its radios to a controlled U.S. distributor, AM, that serves the West Coast of the United States. FM sells its radios to uncontrolled distributors to serve other regions in the United States. The product in the controlled and uncontrolled transactions is the same, and all other circumstances surrounding the controlled and uncontrolled transactions are substantially the same, other than the geographic differences. If the geographic differences are unlikely to have a material effect on price, or they have definite and reasonably ascertainable effects for which adjustments are made, then the adjusted results of the uncontrolled sales may be used under the comparable uncontrolled price method to establish an arm's length range pursuant to section 1.482-1(e)(2)(iii)(A). If the effects of the geographic differences would be material but cannot be reliably ascertained, then the reliability of the results will be diminished. However, the comparable uncontrolled price method may still provide the most reliable measure of an arm's length result, pursuant to the best method rule of section 1.482-1(c), and, if so, an arm's length range may be established pursuant to section 1.482-1(e)(2)(iii)(B).

(5) Indirect evidence of comparable uncontrolled transactions

(i) In general

A comparable uncontrolled price may be derived from data from public exchanges or quotation media, but only if the following requirements are met--

(A) The data is widely and routinely used in the ordinary course of business in the industry to negotiate prices for uncontrolled sales;

(B) The data derived from public exchanges or quotation media is used to set prices in the controlled transaction in the same way it is used by uncontrolled taxpayers in the industry; and

(C) The amount charged in the controlled transaction is adjusted to reflect differences in product quality and quantity, contractual terms, transportation costs, market conditions, risks borne, and other factors that affect the price that would be agreed to by uncontrolled taxpayers.

(ii) Limitation

Use of data from public exchanges or quotation media may not be appropriate under extraordinary market conditions.

(iii) Examples

The following examples illustrate this paragraph (b)(5).

Example 1 -- Use of quotation medium

(i) On June 1, USOil, a United States corporation, enters into a contract to purchase crude oil from its foreign subsidiary, FS, in Country z. USOil and FS agree to base their sales price on the average of the prices published for that crude in a quotation medium in the five days before August 1, the date set for delivery. USOil and FS agree to adjust the price for the particular circumstances of their transactions, including the quantity of the crude sold, contractual terms, transportation costs, risks borne, and other factors that affect the price.

(ii) The quotation medium used by USOil and FS is widely and routinely used in the ordinary course of business in the industry to establish prices for uncontrolled sales. Because USOil and FS use the data to set their sales price in the same way that unrelated parties use the data from the quotation medium to set their sales prices, and appropriate adjustments were made to account for differences, the price derived from the quotation medium used by USOil and FS to set their transfer prices will be considered evidence of a comparable uncontrolled price.

Example 2 -- Extraordinary market conditions

The facts are the same as in Example 1, except that before USOil and FS enter into their contract, war breaks out in Countries X and Y, major oil producing countries, causing significant instability in world petroleum markets. As a result, given the significant instability in the price of oil, the prices listed on the quotation medium may not reflect a reliable measure of an arm's length result. See section 1.482-3(b)(5)(ii).

Cost Plus Method
Generally used in cases of the manufacture, assembly, or other production of goods

The Cost Plus Method measures the comparable uncontrolled cost of manufacturing a product plus an "appropriate" profit margin. It is described in 26CFR 1.482-3(d) of the U.S. transfer pricing regulations:

(d) Cost plus method
(1) In general
The cost plus method evaluates whether the amount charged in a controlled transaction is arm's length by reference to the gross profit markup realized in comparable uncontrolled transactions. The cost plus method is ordinarily used in cases involving the manufacture, assembly, or other production of goods that are sold to related parties.
(2) Determination of arm's length price
(i) In general
The cost plus method measures an arm's length price by adding the appropriate gross profit to the controlled taxpayer's costs of producing the property involved in the controlled transaction.
(ii) Appropriate gross profit
The appropriate gross profit is computed by multiplying the controlled taxpayer's cost of producing the transferred property by the gross profit markup, expressed as a percentage of cost, earned in comparable uncontrolled transactions.
(iii) Arm's length range
See section 1.482-1(e)(2) for determination of an arm's length range.
(3) Comparability and reliability considerations--
(i) In general
Whether results derived from the application of this method are the most reliable measure of the arm's length result must be determined using the factors described under the best method rule in section 1.482-1(c).
(ii) Comparability
(A) Functional comparability
The degree of comparability between controlled and uncontrolled transactions is determined by applying the comparability provisions of section 1.482-1(d). A producer's gross profit provides compensation for the performance of the production functions related to the product or products under review, including an operating profit for the producer's investment of capital and assumption of risks. Therefore, although all of the factors described in section 1.482-1(d)(3) must be considered, comparability under this method is particularly dependent on similarity of functions performed, risks borne, and contractual terms, or adjustments to account for the effects of any such differences. If possible, the appropriate gross profit markup should be derived from comparable uncontrolled transactions of the taxpayer involved in the controlled sale, because similar

Glossary

characteristics are more likely to be found among sales of property by the same producer than among sales by other producers. In the absence of such sales, an appropriate gross profit markup may be derived from comparable uncontrolled sales of other producers whether or not such producers are members of the same controlled group.

(B) Other comparability factors

Comparability under this method is less dependent on close physical similarity between the products transferred than under the comparable uncontrolled price method. Substantial differences in the products may, however, indicate significant functional differences between the controlled and uncontrolled taxpayers. Thus, it ordinarily would be expected that the controlled and uncontrolled transactions involve the production of goods within the same product categories. Furthermore, significant differences in the value of the products due, for example, to the value of a trademark, may also affect the reliability of the comparison. Finally, the reliability of profit measures based on gross profit may be adversely affected by factors that have less effect on prices. For example, gross profit may be affected by a variety of other factors, including cost structures (as reflected, for example, in the age of plant and equipment), business experience (such as whether the business is in a start-up phase or is mature), or management efficiency (as indicated, for example, by expanding or contracting sales or executive compensation over time). Accordingly, if material differences in these factors are identified based on objective evidence, the reliability of the analysis may be affected.

(C) Adjustments for differences between controlled and uncontrolled transactions.

If there are material differences between the controlled and uncontrolled transactions that would affect the gross profit markup, adjustments should be made to the gross profit markup earned in the comparable uncontrolled transaction according to the provisions of section 1.482-1(d)(2). For this purpose, consideration of the operating expenses associated with the functions performed and risks assumed may be necessary, because differences in functions performed are often reflected in operating expenses. If there are differences in functions performed, however, the effect on gross profit of such differences is not necessarily equal to the differences in the amount of related operating expenses. Specific examples of the factors that may be particularly relevant to this method include--

(1) The complexity of manufacturing or assembly;
(2) Manufacturing, production, and process engineering;
(3) Procurement, purchasing, and inventory control activities;
(4) Testing functions;
(5) Selling, general, and administrative expenses;
(6) Foreign currency risks; and
(7) Contractual terms (e.g., scope and terms of warranties provided, sales or purchase volume, credit terms, transport terms).

(D) Purchasing agent

If a controlled taxpayer is comparable to a purchasing agent that does not take title to property or otherwise assume risks with respect to ownership of such goods, the commission earned by such purchasing agent, expressed as a percentage of the purchase price of the goods, may be used as the appropriate gross profit markup.

(iii) Data and assumptions

(A) In general

The reliability of the results derived from the cost plus method is affected by the completeness and accuracy of the data used and the reliability of the assumptions made to apply this method. See section 1.482-1(c) (Best method rule).

(B) Consistency in accounting

The degree of consistency in accounting practices between the controlled transaction and the uncontrolled comparables that materially affect the gross profit markup affects the reliability of the result. Thus, for example, if differences in inventory and other cost accounting practices would materially affect the gross profit markup, the ability to make reliable adjustments for such differences would affect the reliability of the results. Further, the controlled transaction and the comparable uncontrolled transaction should be consistent in the reporting of costs between cost of goods sold and operating expenses. The term COST OF PRODUCING includes the cost of acquiring property that is held for resale.

(4) Examples

The following examples illustrate the principles of this paragraph (d).

Example 1. (i) USP, a domestic manufacturer of computer components, sells its products to FS, its foreign distributor. UT1, UT2, and UT3 are domestic computer component manufacturers that sell to uncontrolled foreign purchasers.

(ii) Relatively complete data is available regarding the functions performed and risks borne by UT1, UT2, and UT3, and the contractual terms in the uncontrolled transactions. In addition, data is available to ensure accounting consistency between all of the uncontrolled manufacturers and USP. Because the available data is sufficiently complete to conclude that it is likely that all material differences between the controlled and uncontrolled transactions have been identified, the effect of the differences are definite and reasonably ascertainable, and reliable adjustments are made to account for the differences, an arm's length range can be established pursuant to section 1.482-1(e)(2)(iii)(A).

Example 2. The facts are the same as in EXAMPLE 1, except that USP accounts for supervisory, general, and administrative costs as operating expenses, which are not allocated to its sales to FS. The gross profit markups of UT1, UT2, and UT3, however, reflect supervisory, general, and administrative expenses because they are accounted for as costs of goods sold. Accordingly, the gross profit markups of UT1, UT2, and UT3 must be adjusted as provided in paragraph (d)(3)(iii)(B) of this section to provide accounting consistency. If data is not sufficient to determine whether such accounting differences exist between the controlled and uncontrolled transactions, the reliability of the results will be decreased.

Example 3. The facts are the same as in EXAMPLE 1, except that under its contract with FS, USP uses materials consigned by FS. UT1, UT2, and UT3, on the other hand, purchase their own materials, and their gross profit markups are determined by including the costs of materials. The fact that USP does not carry an inventory risk by purchasing its own materials while the uncontrolled producers carry inventory is a significant difference that may require an adjustment if the difference has a material effect on the gross profit markups of the uncontrolled producers. Inability to reasonably ascertain the effect of the difference on the gross profit markups will affect the reliability of the results of UT1, UT2, and UT3.

Example 4. (i) FS, a foreign corporation, produces apparel for USP, its U.S. parent corporation. FS purchases its materials from unrelated suppliers and produces the apparel according to designs provided by USP. The district director identifies 10 uncontrolled foreign apparel producers that operate in the same geographic market and are similar in many respect to FS.

(ii) Relatively complete data is available regarding the functions performed and risks borne by the uncontrolled producers. In addition, data is sufficiently detailed to permit adjustments for differences in accounting practices. However, sufficient data is not available to determine whether it is likely that all material differences in contractual terms have been identified. For example, it is not possible to determine which parties in the uncontrolled transactions bear currency risks. Because differences in these contractual terms could materially affect price or profits, the inability to determine whether differences exist between the controlled and uncontrolled transactions will diminish the reliability of these results. Therefore, the reliability of the results of the uncontrolled transactions must be enhanced by the application of a statistical method in establishing an arm's length range pursuant to section 1.482-1(e)(2)(iii)(B).

Cost of Services Plus Method

When the same services are being offered to related and to unrelated parties, the value of those services is the price paid by unrelated parties.

The Cost of Services Plus Method, introduced in the August 1, 2006, is useful when one entity provides essentially the same services to unrelated parties as it does to related ones. In such cases, the price charged to unrelated parties for those services can be used to value the same services when they are provided to related parties. It is defined in the "Final and TemporaryRegulations on Intercompany Services" issued by the Internal Revenue Service on August 1, 2006.

Here is the official definition from Section 1.482-9T(e) of the U.S. regulations:

(e) Cost of services plus method--(1) In general. The cost of services plus method evaluates whether the amount charged in a controlled services transaction is arm's length by reference to the gross services profit markup realized in comparable uncontrolled transactions. The cost of services plus method is ordinarily used in cases where the controlled service renderer provides the same or similar services to both controlled and uncontrolled parties. This method is ordinarily not used in cases where the controlled services transaction involves a contingent-payment arrangement, as described in paragraph (i)(2) of this section.

(2) Determination of arm's length price--(i) In general. The cost of services plus method measures an arm's length price by adding the appropriate gross services profit to the controlled taxpayer's comparable transactional costs.

(ii) Appropriate gross services profit. The appropriate gross services profit is computed by multiplying the controlled taxpayer's comparable transactional costs by the gross services profit markup, expressed as a percentage of the comparable transactional costs earned in comparable uncontrolled transactions.

(iii) Comparable transactional costs. Comparable transactional costs consist of the costs of providing the services under review that are taken into account as the basis for determining the gross services profit markup in comparable uncontrolled transactions. Depending on the facts and circumstances, such costs typically include all compensation attributable to employees directly involved in the performance of such services, materials and supplies consumed or made available in rendering such services, and may include as well other costs of rendering the services. Comparable transactional costs must be determined on a basis that will facilitate comparison with the comparable uncontrolled transactions. For that reason, comparable transactional costs may not necessarily equal total services costs, as defined in paragraph (j) of this section, and in appropriate cases may be a subset of total services costs. Generally accepted accounting principles or Federal income tax accounting rules (where Federal income tax data for comparable transactions or business activities are available) may provide useful guidance but will not conclusively establish the appropriate comparable transactional costs for purposes of this method.

(iv) Arm's length range. See §1.482-(e)(2) for determination of an arm's length range.

Cost-Sharing Arrangements
Method By Which Related Parties May Cooperate to Develop Intangible Property and Attribute Cost Proportionately To Anticipated Benefits

Entities seeking to develop intangible property may enter into cost-sharing arrangements, which allow the parties to the agreement to attribute proportional shares of costs relating to the development of intangible property based on their anticipated share of the benefits to be derived from that property. Cost-sharing arrangements have been particularly popular among U.S. software developers with affiliated entities abroad. In some countries, as well as in the OECD guidelines, cost-sharing arrangements are referred to as cost-contribution arrangements. The IRS issued new proposed cost-sharing regulations in 2005, which have drawn sharp criticism from many business groups. Until those proposed regulations are finalized, the current regulations, described in 26CFR 1.482-7, remain in effect:

(a) In general--(1) Scope and application of the rules in this section. A cost sharing arrangement is an agreement under which the parties agree to share the costs of development of one or more
intangibles in proportion to their shares of reasonably anticipated benefits from their individual exploitation of the interests in the intangibles assigned to them under the arrangement. A taxpayer may claim that a cost sharing arrangement is a qualified cost sharing arrangement only if the agreement meets the requirements of paragraph (b) of this section. Consistent with the rules of Sec. 1.482-1(d)(3)(ii)(B) (Identifying contractual terms), the district director may apply the rules of this section to any arrangement that in substance constitutes a cost sharing arrangement, notwithstanding a failure to comply with any requirement of this section. A qualified cost sharing arrangement, or an arrangement to which the district director applies the rules of this section, will not be treated as a partnership to which the rules of subchapter K apply. See Sec. 301.7701-3(e) of this chapter. Furthermore, a participant that is a foreign corporation or nonresident alien individual will not be treated as engaged in trade or business within the United States solely by reason of its participation in such an arrangement. See generally Sec. 1.864-2(a).

Gross Services Margin
New method for pricing services is similar to the resale price method for tangible property

The "gross services margin" method is one of the six methods for determining the value of service transactions under the final and temporary regulations issued on August 1, 2006. This method takes the same approach to valuing services as the resale price method takes to valuing tangible property. This method values services provided among related parties by reference to profit margins of comparable services being provided among unrelated parties. The method is ordinarily used in transactions involving three or more parties where two parties that are not related conduct a main transaction, but a third party that is related to one of them provides some of the services associated with the transaction, either on a contract or supplemental basis to the main transaction.

The official definition of gross services margin as it applies under United States transfer pricing rules can be found in propose Section 482-9T(d) of the U.S. transfer pricing regulations:

> (d) Gross services margin method--(1) In general. The gross services margin method evaluates whether the amount charged in a controlled services transaction is arm's length by reference to the gross profit margin realized in comparable uncontrolled transactions. This method ordinarily is used in cases where a controlled taxpayer performs services or functions in connection with an uncontrolled transaction between a member of the controlled group and an uncontrolled taxpayer. This method may be used where a controlled taxpayer renders services (agent services) to another member of the controlled group in connection with a transaction between that other member and an uncontrolled taxpayer. This method also may be used in cases where a controlled taxpayer contracts to provide services to an uncontrolled taxpayer (intermediary function) and another member of the controlled group actually performs a portion of the services provided.

On August 21, 2006 the IRS issued a release (IRB 2006-34) discussing the new regulations. Here's what they had to say about the Gross Services Margin provisions:

> The 2003 proposed regulations provided for a gross services margin method, which evaluated the amount charged in a controlled services transaction by reference to the gross services profit margin in uncontrolled transactions that involve similar services. The method was analogous to the resale price method for transfers of tangible property in existing §1.482-3(c).
>
> Under the 2003 proposed regulations, this method would ordinarily be used where a controlled taxpayer performs activities in connection with a "related uncontrolled transaction" between a member of the controlled group and an uncontrolled taxpayer. For example, the method may be used where a controlled taxpayer renders services to another member of the controlled group in connection

with a transaction between that other member and an uncontrolled party (agent services), or where a controlled taxpayer contracts to provide services to an uncontrolled taxpayer and another member of the controlled group actually performs the services (intermediary function).

The 2003 proposed regulations defined the terms "related uncontrolled transaction," "applicable uncontrolled price," and "appropriate gross services profit". A "related uncontrolled transaction" is a transaction between a member of the controlled group and an uncontrolled taxpayer for which a controlled taxpayer performs either agent services or an intermediary function. The "applicable uncontrolled price" is the sales price paid by the uncontrolled party in the related uncontrolled transaction. The "appropriate gross services profit" is the product of the applicable uncontrolled price and the gross services profit margin in comparable uncontrolled services transactions. The gross services profit margin takes into account all functions performed by other members of the controlled group and any other relevant factors.

One commentator mistakenly interpreted the term "related uncontrolled transaction" to suggest that the comparable transaction under this method is one that takes place between controlled parties. While this was not intended, the Treasury Department and the IRS agree that the nomenclature is potentially confusing, and as a result, these regulations substitute the term "relevant uncontrolled transaction" in lieu of "related uncontrolled transaction" wherever that appeared. In other respects, the gross services margin provisions in these temporary regulations are substantially similar to the provisions in the 2003 proposed regulations.

Indirect Costs

To what extent should costs relating to operations, brand recognition, and R&D be included in transfer pricing calculations?

One of the most difficult and controversial calculations in a transfer pricing analysis can be the attribution of "indirect costs" to a transaction. To the extent that a U.S. parent company has conducted research and development on a product or has invested in advertising to build the product's acceptance and recognition, those costs may be applicable to a transfer pricing analysis. These considerations are particularly relevant to the transfer pricing of intangible property, which is often developed in cooperation between related parties across national borders.

The official definition of indirect costs as it applies in the United States can be found in Section 482-2 of the transfer pricing regulations:

(iii) Indirect costs or deductions are those which are not specifically identified with a particular activity or service but which relate to the direct costs referred to in paragraph (b)(4)(ii) of this section. Indirect costs or deductions generally include costs or deductions with respect to utilities, occupancy, supervisory and clerical compensation, and other overhead burden of the department incurring the direct costs or deductions referred to in paragraph (b)(4)(ii) of this section. Indirect costs or deductions also generally include an appropriate share of the costs or deductions relating to supporting departments and other applicable general and administrative expenses to the extent reasonably allocable to a particular service or activity. Thus, for example, if a domestic corporation's advertising department performs services for the direct benefit of a foreign subsidiary, in addition to direct costs of such department, such as salaries of employees and fees paid to advertising agencies or consultants, which are attributable to such foreign advertising, indirect costs must be taken into account on some reasonable basis in determining the amount of costs or deductions with respect to which the arm's length charge to the foreign subsidiary is to be determined. These generally include depreciation, rent, property taxes, other costs of occupancy, and other overhead costs of the advertising department itself, and allocations of costs from other departments which service the advertising department, such as the personnel, accounting, payroll, and maintenance departments, and other applicable general and administrative expenses including compensation of top management.

Intangible Property

Before valuing intangible assets, it is necessary to identify them.

Section Sec. 1.482-4(b) of the U.S. Internal Revenue regulations defines intangible property as:

(b) Definition of intangible. For purposes of section 482, an intangible is an asset that comprises any of the following items and has substantial value independent of the services of any individual--
(1) Patents, inventions, formulae, processes, designs, patterns, or know-how;
(2) Copyrights and literary, musical, or artistic compositions;
(3) Trademarks, trade names, or brand names;
(4) Franchises, licenses, or contracts;
(5) Methods, programs, systems, procedures, campaigns, surveys, studies, forecasts, estimates, customer lists, or technical data; and
(6) Other similar items. For purposes of section 482, an item is considered similar to those listed in paragraph (b)(1) through (5) of this section if it derives its value not from its physical attributes but from its intellectual content or other intangible properties.

Profit Split Method
Comparable Profit Split and Residual Profit Split Approaches to Valuing Related-Party Transactions

While the IRS Regulations refers to the "profit split method," they might have referenced "profit split methods," since there are two distinct approaches authorized under that heading. Both variations rely on the contribution of the parties to a transaction to the combined operating profit or loss associated with the business activity in question. The first variation, the comparable profit split method — described in 26CFR 1.146-6(c)(2) — evaluates the profitability of the transaction in reference to a comparable uncontrolled transaction. In cases where there are no comparable uncontrolled transactions whose profitability can be examined, the residual profit split method is used, as described in 26CFR 1.146-6(c)(3). The residual profit split method attempts to allocate income and expenses associated with the business activity between the parties in the transaction using a structured methodology described in this section. The level of detail required to conduct a residual profit split analysis can be significant, particularly in complex business activities involving multiple vendors and shared expenses. These methods are available for transactions involving both tangible and intangible property. The official definition of this method can be found in 26CFR 1.482-6 of the transfer pricing regulations:

§ 1.482–6 Profit split method

(a) In general. The profit split method evaluates whether the allocation of the combined operating profit or loss attributable to one or more controlled transactions is arm's length by reference to the relative value of each controlled taxpayer's contribution to that combined operating profit or loss. The combined operating profit or loss must be derived from the most narrowly identifiable business activity of the controlled taxpayers for which data is available that includes the controlled transactions (relevant business activity).

(b) Appropriate share of profits and losses. The relative value of each controlled taxpayer's contribution to the success of the relevant business activity must be determined in a manner that reflects the functions performed, risks assumed, and resources employed by each participant in the relevant business activity, consistent with the comparability provisions of § 1.482– 1(d)(3). Such an allocation is intended to correspond to the division of profit or loss that would result from an arrangement between uncontrolled taxpayers, each performing functions similar to those of the various controlled taxpayers engaged in the relevant business activity. The profit allocated to any particular member of a controlled group is not necessarily limited to the total operating profit of the group from the relevant business activity. For example, in a given year, one member of the group may earn a profit while another member incurs a loss. In addition, it may not be assumed that the combined operating profit or loss from the relevant business activity should be shared equally, or in any other arbitrary proportion. The specific method of allocation must be determined under paragraph (c) of this section.

(c) Application—(1) In general. The allocation of profit or loss under the profit split method must be made in accordance with one of the following allocation methods—(i) The comparable profit split, described in paragraph (c)(2) of this section; or (ii) The residual profit split, described in paragraph (c)(3) of this section.

Glossary

Related-Party Transaction
To which types of transactions do transfer pricing rules apply?

Since transfer pricing law applies exclusively to "related-party transactions," it makes sense to examine the legal definition of this class of transaction. While it would be simple to say that a related-party transaction is any transaction that is not at arm's-length, that begs the question, since a transaction that may or may not be between related parties would similarly be unclear as to whether it was arm's-length. For example, is a joint venture between two companies that do not share common ownership a related-party transaction? To find a statutory definition, we can turn to Section 6038A of the U.S. regulations, which offers the following:

(2) Related party
The term "related party" means -
(A) any 25-percent foreign shareholder of the reporting corporation,
(B) any person who is related (within the meaning of section 267(b) or 707(b)(1)) to the reporting corporation or to a 25-percent foreign shareholder of the reporting corporation, and
(C) any other person who is related (within the meaning of section 482) to the reporting corporation.

While (A) is further defined within Section 6038A, (B) and (C) refer to three other sections. Section 267(b) offers the following set of definitions:

(b) Relationships
The persons referred to in subsection (a) are:
(1) Members of a family, as defined in subsection (c)(4);
(2) An individual and a corporation more than 50 percent in value of the outstanding stock of which is owned, directly or indirectly, by or for such individual;
(3) Two corporations which are members of the same controlled group (as defined in subsection (f));
(4) A grantor and a fiduciary of any trust;
(5) A fiduciary of a trust and a fiduciary of another trust, if the same person is a grantor of both trusts;
(6) A fiduciary of a trust and a beneficiary of such trust;
(7) A fiduciary of a trust and a beneficiary of another trust, if the same person is a grantor of both trusts;
(8) A fiduciary of a trust and a corporation more than 50 percent in value of the outstanding stock of which is owned, directly or indirectly, by or for the trust or by or for a person who is a grantor of the trust;
(9) A person and an organization to which section 501 (relating

to certain educational and charitable organizations which are exempt from tax) applies and which is controlled directly or indirectly by such person or (if such person is an individual) by members of the family of such individual;
(10) A corporation and a partnership if the same persons own -
(A) more than 50 percent in value of the outstanding stock of the corporation, and
(B) more than 50 percent of the capital interest, or the profits interest, in the partnership;
(11) An S corporation and another S corporation if the same persons own more than 50 percent in value of the outstanding stock of each corporation;
(12) An S corporation and a C corporation, if the same persons own more than 50 percent in value of the outstanding stock of each corporation; or
(13) Except in the case of a sale or exchange in satisfaction of a pecuniary bequest, an executor of an estate and a beneficiary of such estate.

Section 707(b)(1) adds:

(b) Certain sales or exchanges of property with respect to controlled partnerships
(1) Losses disallowed
No deduction shall be allowed in respect of losses from sales or exchanges of property (other than an interest in the partnership), directly or indirectly, between -
(A) a partnership and a person owning, directly or indirectly, more than 50 percent of the capital interest, or the profits interest, in such partnership, or
(B) two partnerships in which the same persons own, directly or indirectly, more than 50 percent of the capital interests or profits interests.
In the case of a subsequent sale or exchange by a transferee described in this paragraph, section 267(d) shall be applicable as if the loss were disallowed under section 267(a)(1). For purposes of section 267(a)(2), partnerships described in subparagraph (B) of this paragraph shall be treated as persons specified in section 267(b).

That leaves us to look for a definition of "related" in Section 482. While it does not provide a specific definition, it does offer the phrase, ". . owned or controlled directly or indirectly by the same interests. . ." This broad language is subject to IRS and judicial interpretation. The IRS has taken the position that when parties that lack common ownership cooperate to shift income and deductions, they become related parties for purposes of transfer pricing law. (See Technical Advice Memorandum 200230001.)

Glossary

So what about that joint venture? Does it constitute a related-party transaction? The answer in some countries is clear. For example, Italy specifically includes joint ventures in their definition of relationships controlled by transfer pricing law. However, since the Unites States uses a functional analysis, whether a given joint venture is subject to transfer pricing constraints may depend on the facts of the case in question.

Resale Price Method
Method uses comparable profits in unrelated-party sale of tangible goods to determine profit ratios

The resale price method compares the gross profit realized when an entity resells goods to a related party to the gross profits realized by comparable entities in uncontrolled transactions. Comparable profitability is determined by calculating the ratio of the initial purchase price of comparable tangible goods to their resale price to an unrelated party. This ratio (expressed as a percentage) is then used to calculate the value of the goods in a related-party transaction. The official definition of this method can be found in 26CFR 1.482-3(c) of the U.S. transfer pricing regulations:

(c) Resale price method—(1) In general

The resale price method evaluates whether the amount charged in a controlled transaction is arm's length by reference to the gross profit margin realized in comparable uncontrolled transactions. The resale price method measures the value of functions performed, and is ordinarily used in cases involving the purchase and resale of tangible property in which the reseller has not added substantial value to the tangible goods by physically altering the goods before resale. For this purpose, packaging, repackaging, labelling, or minor assembly do not ordinarily constitute physical alteration

Further the resale price method is not ordinarily used in cases where the controlled taxpayer uses its intangible property to add substantial value to the tangible goods

(2) Determination of arm's length price—(i) In general. The resale price method measures an arm's length price by subtracting the appropriate gross profit from the applicable resale price for the property involved in the controlled transaction under review

(ii) Applicable resale price. The applicable resale price is equal to either the resale price of the particular item of property involved or the price at which contemporaneous resales of the same property are made. If the property purchased in the controlled sale is resold to one or more related parties in a series of controlled sales before being resold in an uncontrolled sale, the applicable resale price is the price at which the property is resold to an uncontrolled party, or the price at which contemporaneous resales of the same property are made. In such case, the determination of the appropriate gross profit will take into account the functions of all members of the group participating in the series of controlled sales and final uncontrolled resales, as well as any other relevant factors described in § 1.482–1(d)(3)

(iii) Appropriate gross profit. The appropriate gross profit is computed by multiplying the applicable resale price by the gross profit margin (expressed as a percentage of total revenue derived from sales) earned in comparable uncontrolled transactions.

Services Cost Method
New regulations eliminate "Simplified-Cost Based Method" and replace it with "Services Cost Method."

On August 1, 2006 the IRS issued final and temporary transfer pricing services regulations. These new regulations make significant changes to the proposed regulations issued in 2003, including the elimination of the heavily criticized Simplified-Cost Based Method, which has been replaced in the new regulations by the Services Cost Method. According to the Treasury Department, the Services Cost Method is intended to reduce complexity for valuing low-margin services. The Services Cost Method includes a safe-harbor rule for reducing services transaction valuations by amounts paid for support services that was not available in the Simplified-Cost Based Method, which was roundly criticized as being too complicated by tax practitioners.

Other changes from the 2003 proposed regulations include the narrowing of the "shareholder stewardship activities" definition, the inclusion of stock-based compensation in the calculation of costs charged to affiliates, and the addition of a section on "Shared Services Arrangements" between related parties.

A complete copy of the new regulations can be found on USTransferPricing.com.

XIII. Directory of Contributors

Directory of Contributors

Brian Andreoli
Partner, DLA Piper

1251 Avenue of the Americas
New York, New York 10020-1104
+1 212 335-4553 phone
+1 212 884-8453 fax
brian.andreoli@dlapiper.com

Brian E. Andreoli focuses his practice on transfer pricing, international tax matters, and state tax matters. Mr. Andreoli has been a tax professional for more than 30 years, with experience in public, accounting, corporate (both foreign and domestic) law and litigation. He was Corporate Tax Leader at a major pharmaceutical company for 16 years. He has tried cases and administrative hearings in the states of New York, Connecticut, Ohio, California, Virginia, North Carolina, South Carolina, Pennsylvania and Washington. These cases have concerned corporate income tax, sales and use tax, franchise tax and property tax. He also practices in voluntary disclosures for both corporations and individuals, concerning both civil and criminal penalties.

Mr. Andreoli is admitted before the bars in Connecticut, New York, Massachusetts, and the District of Columbia, and is a Certified Public Accountant. He is licensed to practice in the United States Tax Court, Second Circuit Court of Appeals, the United States Supreme Court, and the Federal District Courts of the District of Columbia, Connecticut, Massachusetts, and New York (Southern and Eastern).

He is also known as a frequent speaker on international tax issues and transfer pricing matters in the United States, the United Kingdom, and Canada and has spoken on state tax issues in the United States. He recently spoke on two radio programs about the GlaxoSmithKline IRS dispute, cases involving cross border corporate tax structures, and advice for businesses going international with their products. The archived radio programs may be accessed through the following links:

- The first program was with Sky Radio Network's FORTUNE Magazine Radio Channel, which can be heard on American and Northwest Airlines. It is a short discussion of how to avoid the tangle of international tax laws: http://www.skyradionet.com/player.cfm?ID=4129
- He also appeared on the LawBusiness Insider program where he spoke in greater detail about these issues: http://www.lbishow.com/talkshow_2006_09_23.html

Directory of Contributors

Svein G. Andresen
Tax Partner/Attorney-At-Law, KPMG

+47 40 63 90 22 phone
+47 21 09 29 45 fax
svein.andresen@kpmg.no

Sven G. Andresen has been with KPMG for 13 years and has extensive experience within the banking, insurance, shipping, oil service and processing industry. Before joining KPMG, Svein worked four years as a tax consultant at the Norwegian Directorate of Taxes and as a legal advisor at the Central Taxation Office of large sized entities.

Svein is the tax partner in charge of Global Transfer Pricing Services (GTPS) and Global Tax Outsourcing (GTO) in KPMG Norway. Professional experience includes international taxation (especially cross-border tax planning and reorganisation), and transfer pricing. His clients are mainly listed Norwegian companies and large foreign multinationals with operations in Norway. Svein frequently is a speaker at seminars on International Corporate Tax and Transfer Pricing issues, and he has published several articles.

Svein has been listed as a leading transfer pricing adviser in Norway in Euromoney Legal Media Group for the last six years. In addition, he has been mentioned twice as one of the leading tax advisors in Norway in International Tax Review.

Svein holds his degree as a candidate in jurisprudence from the University of Oslo, which he completed in 1990.

Directory of Contributors

Robert D. Baldassarre
Managing Director, KPMG LLP

99 High Street
Boston, MA 02110
+1 617 988-1813 phone
+1 617 904-1638 fax
rbaldassarre@kpmg.com

Robert Baldassarre is a managing director in KPMG's Global Transfer Pricing Services practice in the United States; he is based in Boston. Baldassarre focuses on providing economic analysis, valuation analysis, and transfer-pricing planning and compliance studies for clients. His industry base includes software development, financial services, e-Commerce, consumer electronics, industrial equipment, and pharmaceuticals.

Mr. Baldassarre has 14 years of professional experience in economic analysis and tax consulting. Prior to joining KPMG, he served as an internal management consultant in logistics and operations research at Compaq Computer Corporation. He has also held positions in the private sector as an economist and forecast manager at Standard & Poor's/DRI and in the public sector as a development economist for the Massachusetts Executive Office of Economic Affairs under Governor Weld. He began his career as a budget policy analyst for the Massachusetts legislature.

Mr. Baldassarre received a B.A. in international relations and economics and an M.B.A in finance and economics from Boston University and studied European law and economics at the University of Padova in Italy.

Directory of Contributors

Anthony J. Barbera
Vice President, The Ballentine Barbera Group, a CRA International Company

1201 F Street, NW
Suite 700
Washington DC 20004
+1-202-662-7830 phone
tbarbera@crai.com

Anthony J. Barbera is a former principal of The Ballentine Barbera Group, LLC, and has more than 20 years of experience providing consulting services on a wide range of economic issues in both the government and private sectors. Since 1989, Dr. Barbera's primary practice has been in the economics of intercompany pricing. His specializations include detailed market analyses, cost-sharing agreements, intellectual property valuation, and product price analyses for numerous industries. Dr. Barbera has developed innovative transfer pricing ideas concerning trademarks and marketing intangibles that have proven useful and workable in a tax-planning context and he has assisted several large U.S. companies implement these ideas.

Anthony Barbera holds a Ph.D., Economics from the University of Maryland and a B.S. in Mathematics from Loyola College.

Directory of Contributors

Marius Basteviken
Transfer Pricing Economist /Attorney-at-Law, KPMG

+47 40 63 90 32 phone
+47 21 09 29 45 fax
marius.basteviken@kpmg.no

Marius Basteviken assists several multinational companies with their transfer pricing compliance work in Norway. He has experience in preparing management accounts as a lecturer at the Norwegian School of Economics and Business Administration.

Marius has held several presentations in both Norwegian and English. In addition, he has been the co-author of numerous articles relating to transfer pricing published in both domestic and international journals.

Marius holds the 'siviløkonom' degree (business economist) from the Norwegian School of Economics and Business Administration (NHH), Bergen, a Postgraduate Diploma in Legal Practice from the College of Law, London, and a Graduate Diploma in Law from Kingston University, London.

Directory of Contributors

Anjali D. Bhasin
Vice President, The Ballentine Barbera Group, a CRA International Company

1201 F Street, NW
Suite 700
Washington DC 20004
+1 703 201-8869
abhasin@crai.com

Anjali Bhasin is a member of CRA's Competition practice. Dr. Bhasin has over thirteen years of experience in conducting economic analyses of intercompany pricing of services and tangible and intangible property. Her engagements have included APAs, global tax planning, transfer pricing documentation studies, and audit defense in transfer pricing-related tax controversies. Dr. Bhasin has been involved in a wide variety of projects including intellectual property migration, calculation of buy-in payments, royalty rates, business enterprise valuations, cost sharing arrangements, cost allocation models, management service fees, and centralization of entrepreneurial functions and risks with limited risk distributors, contract manufacturers, and service providers. Her industry experience spans telecommunications, software, satellites, pharmaceutical, broadcasting, entertainment, financial services, IT consulting services, and medical equipment. Prior to joining CRA, Dr. Bhasin was a director in PricewaterhouseCoopers' transfer pricing practice.

Anjali Bhasin holds a Ph.D. in Economics from Indiana University, an M.A. in Economics from Indiana University, an M.A. in Economics from Christ Church College, Kanpur University, and a B.A. in Commerce from Christ Church College, Kanpur University.

Directory of Contributors

Patrick Breslin
Founder, PTB Consulting, LLC

1741 Kenyon St. NW
Washington, DC 20010
+1 202 518-0471 phone
+1 202 518-0472 fax
+1 202 468-9347 mobile
pbreslin@ptbconsultingllc.com

Patrick Breslin has extensive experience conducting economic analysis of intercompany transactions with a focus on intangible property valuation. He has been involved in planning, business restructuring, cost sharing arrangements, APA applications, and audits, including IRS settlement negotiations yielding a 75 percent reduction in a multi-hundred million dollar income adjustment. Mr. Breslin's transaction experience includes Internet commerce platforms, electronic payment systems, software, biotechnology, trademarks, and other intangible property. Client engagements have also involved consumer, pharmaceutical and medical products, agricultural products, oil and gas, and various industrial products and services.

Prior to forming PTB Consulting, Mr. Breslin was a principal at the Ballentine Barbera Group. Prior to that, he was a director with PricewaterhouseCoopers and managed major engagements in the economic consulting practices of Baker & McKenzie and KPMG. Mr. Breslin was also founder and CEO of Relatable, a software company providing copyright monitoring and royalty allocation solutions for the electronic distribution of music and media. He has also consulted on international trade and environmental policy issues.

Mr. Breslin holds a M.A. in International Economics and Finance from Brandeis University and a B.A. in Political Science, *cum laude*, from Boston College.

Directory of Contributors

George Carlson
Director, Deloitte Tax LLP

555 Twelfth St. NW
Suite 500
Washington, D.C. 20004
+1 202 378-5241 phone
+1 202 661-1978 fax
gcarlson@deloitte.com
www.deloitte.com.

George N. Carlson is a Director in Deloitte Tax LLP's National Tax Office in Washington D. C. His areas of specialization are transfer pricing, international tax planning, and state and local taxation.

Dr. Carlson has prepared transfer pricing studies for clients in the apparel, automobile, computer software, distilled spirits, electronics, investment banking, medical products, pharmaceutical, sporting goods, and telecommunications industries. The economic analyses prepared by Dr. Carlson have been used in obtaining advance pricing agreements; developing cost sharing and intangible property migration structures; audit defense at both the examination and appeals levels; litigation support; and contemporaneous documentation studies.

Before joining the private sector, Dr. Carlson served for 14 years in the U.S. Treasury Department's Office of Tax Policy, including Director of the Office of Tax Analysis and Director of the International Tax Staff. In that capacity, Dr. Carlson participated in developing policy positions on domestic and international tax issues. Treasury Secretary James A. Baker III awarded Dr. Carlson the Treasury's Exceptional Service Award in 1986. Earlier in his Treasury tenure, Dr. Carlson served as a U.S. representative to the Organization for Economic Cooperation and Development (OECD) Group on transfer pricing that wrote the report Transfer Pricing and Multinational Enterprises, 1979.

Dr. Carlson received a Ph.D. from the University of Illinois, and an undergraduate degree from the University of Washington, both in Economics. He has published numerous articles in books and professional journals on transfer pricing and tax policy issues, and is a frequent speaker at national and international tax conferences.

Directory of Contributors

Philip W. Carmichael
Director of Economics, Baker & McKenzie Consulting, LLC

1114 Avenue of the Americas
New York New York 10036
+1 212 626-4291 phone
Philip.Carmichael@bakermckenzie.com
http://www.bakermckenzie.com/PhilipCarmichael/

Philip W. Carmichael is the Director of the Economics Group and Baker & McKenzie in New York. Mr. Carmichael specializes in transfer pricing, where he has led a wide range of engagements for his clients, including restructuring intercompany arrangements for tax planning, preparing U.S. and foreign documentation; valuing intangible assets; and audit defense.

During his seventeen years of transfer pricing practice, Mr. Carmichael has served as the global transfer pricing adviser for several key client accounts. In this role, he was intimately familiar with the intercompany transactions and tax strategies of the client; coordinated and directed resolution of transfer pricing matters inside and outside the United States; advised on opportunities for tax planning; and led the preparation of global documentation.

A particular focus of Mr. Carmichael's practice has been the structuring and valuation of intercompany transactions of intellectual property in the context of global business restructurings. He has led numerous important engagements for clients in which licensing, cost-sharing and/or intellectual property migration have been a central strategy. His work has spanned a number of industries, including business products; industrial products; software; and technology.

Mr. Carmichael has assisted clients in addressing transfer pricing documentation requirements around the world, responding to needs in the United States, Canada, Europe, Latin America, Asia, and the Pacific. In addition, he has assisted U.S.- and foreign-based multinationals in transfer pricing audits.

Previously, Mr. Carmichael was a managing director in the Economic and Valuation Services practice of KPMG LLP.

Mr. Carmichael has led a number of large tax planning/restructuring engagements for major clients, covering multiple product lines and multiple tax jurisdictions. These engagements have involved converting entities to contract and toll manufacturers; converting sales offices to commission agents and commissionaires; creating new HQ operations; restructuring service entities; migrating intangible property; and establishing cost sharing arrangements.

Mr. Carmichael received his B.A. from the University of Notre Dame in 1984. He received his M.B.A. from Georgetown University in 1989.

Directory of Contributors

Jose Casas Chavelas
Partner, KPMG

Bosque de Duraznos 55
Col Bosques de las Lomas
Mexico City 11700
MEXICO
+52 55 5246 8364 phone
+52 55 5246 8359 fax
jcasas@kpmg.com

Jose Casas Chavelas is the Partner in charge of KPMG Mexico's Global Transfer Pricing Services Practice. He has more than ten years of experience in the analysis of intercompany transactions for multinational groups.

His role includes the development of transfer pricing documentation for Mexican companies that belong to multinational groups as well as obtaining Advanced Transfer Pricing Agreements, assisting companies to restructure their transactions based on transfer pricing, and assisting companies during a transfer pricing audit performed by the tax authorities.

Mr. Casas has experience in several industries including pharmaceutical, maquila, wholesale, retail, chemical, automotive, manufacturing and service companies, as well as financial entities, among others.

Prior to joining KPMG, Mr. Casas was chief of department of transfer pricing audits, as well as of the audit department of foreign residents, of the Ministry of Finance.

Mr. Casas holds a Masters Degree in Public Accountanting from the Escuela Bancaria y Comercial where he specialized in international taxation. He also studied the tax specialization at the Escuela Bancaria y Comercial. He teaches accounting at the Instituto Tecnológico de Estudios Superiores Monterrey (Campus Estado de México).

Mr. Casas is a member of the College of Public Accountants of Mexico, in which role he also has been an instructor in their transfer pricing degree program. Currently he is the president of the transfer pricing commission of the Mexican Institute of Public Accountants.

Mr. Casas has been a speaker at several transfer pricing and international taxation forums in Mexico and abroad. He has also written articles on transfer pricing, in several publications.

Mr. Casas has been considered by the International Tax Review journal as one of the transfer pricing experts in Mexico.

Directory of Contributors

Patrick Cauwenbergh
Tax Partner, Deloitte Touche Tomatsu

Berkenlaan 8A
Diegem B-1831
BELGIUM
+322-600-6927 phone
+322-600-6703 fax
pcauwenbergh@deloitte.com

Patrick Cauwenbergh is a tax partner in the Brussels office of Deloitte Touche Tohmatsu's Belgium affiliate. He joined Deloitte in 1999 and is now the partner in charge of Deloitte's Brussels transfer-pricing practice.

Mr. Cauwenbergh has specialized in transfer pricing and international tax planning since 1992, as both practitioner and academic. He is a member of the Institute of Accountancy and Tax Advisers (IAB).

Mr. Cauwenbergh participates in and conducts transfer pricing and international tax-planning assignments for Europe-based companies (including many of the largest Belgian controlled groups) regarding their relations with other EU member states, eastern European countries, Japan and the U.S.. His team at Deloitte consists of fully dedicated transfer pricing and international tax planning specialists (tax lawyers and economists) who are active in such areas as fiscal reengineering, European transfer-pricing documentation (including comparables searches), competent authority (including arbitration) procedures, advance pricing agreements, and defence audits. Industry studies include chemicals, automotive, consumer goods, telecommunications, paper and pulp industry, financial services, electronics, general trading, and pharmaceuticals.

Mr. Cauwenbergh is the only Belgian lawyer with a PhD on the Belgian and foreign tax aspects of international transfer pricing. He has been a professor at the University of Antwerp in international tax law since 1997. He also lectures on transfer-pricing topics at the University of Leuven (European Tax College) and at the University of Ghent.

Mr. Cauwenbergh participates in many seminars on transfer pricing and international tax planning, and is the author of two monographs and a large number of articles in national and international professional journals.

Directory of Contributors

Tanmoy Chakrabarti
Senior Transfer Pricing Consultant, Ernst and Young

AXA Building
41 Shortland Street
Auckland 1010
NEW ZEALAND
164 274899867 phone
tanmoy.chakrabarti@nz.ey.com
http://www.ey.com/NZ

Tanmoy Chakrabarti is a Senior Transfer Pricing Consultant with Ernst and Young, New Zealand. Previously, Tanmoy has worked with PricewaterhouseCoopers and BMR Advisors, India in their respective transfer pricing practices. Tanmoy specializes in tax effective supply chain planning involving cross-border transactions and have been advising various multinational clients across various industries like Financial Services, Information technology and Distribution. He has worked on Indian Regulations, OECD, Australian as well as New Zealand IRD Guidelines. Other than transfer pricing regulations Tanmoy has also worked on WTO issues, Corporate Governance and Sarbanes-Oxley Law. Tanmoy holds a master degree in Economics with specialization in International Trade and Finance from Jawaharlal Nehru University, New Delhi, India.

Directory of Contributors

Pamela T. Church
Partner, Baker & McKenzie LLP

1114 Avenue of the Americas
New York NY 10036
USA
+1 212 626 4976 phone
Pamela.T.Church@bakernet.com

Pamela Church is a member of both the Firm's Global Corporate & Mergers and Acquisitions Practice Group and the North American Intellectual Property Practice Group. She is the head of the New York Intellectual Property Practice. Her practice in the New York office includes general corporate counseling with a concentration in international transactions, mergers and acquisitions, venture capital, business reorganizations, leveraged buy-outs, start-ups and joint ventures, particularly in the media, technology and luxury goods fields. Ms. Church also concentrates on intellectual property matters involving licensing, technology transfer, research and development collaboration, print and electronic publishing, e-commerce, television, and motion pictures transactions.

Ms. Church has counseled major publishing, cosmetics, entertainment, and high fashion companies, as well as pharmaceutical and biotechnology companies, in the establishment and implementation of comprehensive trademark and copyright registration, licensing, merchandising, enforcement, and anti-piracy programs for world-famous trademarks. Ms. Church also represents publishers and advertisers in preparing sponsorship and endorsement contracts, reviewing and clearing advertising for use in on-line and off-line media, drafting advertising agency, product placement and media production agreements and advising clients in respect of compliance with federal and state regulations governing contests and sweepstakes. Ms. Church came to Baker & McKenzie from Coudert Brothers LLP, where she served on the Firm's Executive Board.

A native English speaker, Ms. Church is also fluent in French and German and conversant in Greek. She holds a J.D. from New York University School of Law and a B.A. (*cum laude*) from Yale University.

Directory of Contributors

Jeffrey Cole
Partner, TPA Global

2111 Wilson Blvd., Suite 700
Arlington, VA 22201
USA
+1 703 351-5009 phone
j.cole@tpa-global.com
www.tpa-global.com

Jeffrey Cole has extensive experience in the valuation of intangible assets in support of IRS audits, documentation studies, and business reorganizations. His specializations include financial statement analysis and asset pricing, including the valuation of intangible assets. He is currently focusing on serving a small number of large clients where he typically provides broad and ongoing economic support related to valuation issues surrounding transfer pricing audits, documentation efforts, and planning strategies.

Mr. Cole also advises clients on the value of intangible assets consistent with arm's length expectations during periods of significant restructuring of their global operations. In this role, he has helped develop innovative strategies for valuing the rights, risks, and intangibles assets that often get transferred during these periods of transition. Examples range from estimating appropriate statutory royalties due to newly created intangible holding companies to valuing the economic risks that get allocated to newly created licensees of a company's trademarks.

Directory of Contributors

Xavier Daluzeau
Senior Associate, CMS Bureau Francis Lefebvre

1/3 Villa Emile-Bergerat
92522 Neuilly-sur-Seine
Paris
FRANCE
+33 1 47 38 42 25 phone
+33 1 47 38 86 75 fax
xavier.daluzeau@cms-bfl.com

Xavier Daluzeau joined the International Taxation Department of CMS Bureau Francis Lefebvre in 1997. He holds a postgraduate degree of HEC (1997) and University of Paris XI (1997) in corporate law. He was two years in secondment in CMS Bureau Francis Lefebvre Berlin.

He specialises in international taxation and his main practice areas are transfer pricing, transactional operations, reorganisations and acquisitions.

He is fluent in English and German.

He is the co-author of the chapter on rulings of a book on French tax procedures published in 2005. He regularly publishes articles on international tax matters in French and international publications.

Directory of Contributors

Christopher Desmond
Managing Director, CETERIS

55 West Monroe, Suite 2900
Chicago, IL 60603
USA
+1 312-253-0920 phone
+1 773-426-1212 mobile
+1 312-253-0968 fax
christopher.desmond@ceterisgroup.com

Christopher Desmond is a Managing Director based at Ceteris' Chicago headquarters with over ten years of experience advising clients on a variety of transfer pricing matters. Christopher has served on multiple transfer pricing teams involving expert witness testimony for cases in the U.S. Federal Tax Courts. Prior to joining Ceteris, Christopher was a transfer pricing economist with both PricewaterhouseCoopers LLP and Ernst & Young LLP. Christopher has experience working with clients in the agricultural, alcohol & tobacco, consumer products, commodity trading, automotive, medical devices, healthcare, pharmaceutical, hotel, retail, food & beverages, logistics, publishing, tobacco, technology, media, consumer goods, industrial and specialty chemicals.

Throughout his career, he has also led initiatives related to global transfer pricing policies and how transfer pricing impacts the U.S. states. Recently, he has assisted companies with implementing the new Service Regulations, FIN 48 and Sarbanes Oxley 404 as it relates to transfer pricing. Christopher obtained his MBA with a concentration in International Business and a Bachelors of Science in Management from Eastern Illinois University. An award-winning speaker, he has spoken at numerous conferences and seminars throughout the nation as well as authored articles and chapters regarding transfer pricing for international publications.

Directory of Contributors

Hareesh Dhawale
Managing Director, KPMG LLP

355 South Grand Avenue
Los Angeles, CA 90071-1568
USA
+1 213 593-6769 phone
+1 202-403-3863 fax
hdhawale@kpmg.com

Hareesh Dhawale is a managing director in KPMG LLP's Washington National Tax practice, specializing in transfer pricing. Dr. Dhawale has conducted numerous transfer pricing studies for clients in industries and sectors as diverse as pharmaceuticals, telecommunications, internet services, computer software, semiconductors, express transportation services, oil & gas exploration and drilling, and automotive parts. The transfer pricing studies have been used to assist clients obtain bilateral advance pricing agreements (APAs) and to develop, document, and defend their transfer pricing and cost sharing policies. Within the pharmaceutical sector, Dr. Dhawale has prepared numerous planning, documentation and cost sharing studies. These studies have employed econometric and statistical tools to value intangible property as well as detailing and promotional activities.

Dr. Dhawale has prepared economic analysis in the following areas:
- APAs: Automotive parts, express transportation services, recreational vehicles;
- Documentation: Automotive parts, consumer goods, express transportation services, oil and gas exploration and drilling, internet services and pharmaceuticals;
- Cost Sharing: Pharmaceuticals;
- Planning Studies: Pharmaceuticals and telecommunication sectors; and
- Examination Issues: Software and pharmaceuticals.

Prior to joining KPMG, Dr. Dhawale worked in the transfer pricing practice of another big public accounting firm. Dr. Dhawale has also served as a faculty member in the Economic Department of the U.S. Naval Academy, where his teaching and research interests were in the areas of macroeconomics, monetary economics, and econometrics. As a law clerk with Silverstein and Mullens, Dr. Dhawale provided research and editorial assistance in the preparation of BNA's Transfer Pricing Portfolio Series.

Dr. Dhawale received his Ph.D. in economics from the University of Maryland at College Park and his J.D. from The George Washington University National Law Center. He is a member of the District of Columbia and the Virginia bars.

Directory of Contributors

Horacio Dinice
Tax Partner, Deloitte Argentina

Peron 646, 2nd Floor
Buenos Aires C1038AAN
ARGENTINA
+54 11 4321 3002 phone
+54 11 4320 4066 fax
hdinice@deloitte.com

Horacio Dinice is a tax partner with Deloitte Argentina, where he leads the transfer-pricing practice. He has engaged mainly in international tax consulting and transfer-pricing matters. His experience encompasses advising multinational corporations on the tax implications of cross-border acquisitions/transactions, the establishment of foreign operations in Latin American countries (Argentina, Bolivia, Paraguay, and Uruguay) and leads various regional transfer-pricing projects throughout the region. His experience covers a wide range of industries.

Mr. Dinice graduated from the University of Buenos Aires, with a certified public accounting degree, in 1986. He was a professor of tax law at the State University, and has written tax articles for international publications.

Mr. Dinice is member of the IFA branch in Buenos Aires, and participated in training courses organized by Deloitte for professional personnel. He participated in technical meetings of improvement and professional development in other countries.

He is a frequent speaker at conferences focusing on international tax and transfer-pricing issues.

Directory of Contributors

Pierre-Jean Douvier
Partner, CMS Bureau Francis Lefebvre

1/3 Villa Emile-Bergerat
92522 Neuilly-sur-Seine
Paris
FRANCE
+33 1 47 38 56 76 phone
+33 1 47 45 86 75 fax
pierre-jean.douvier@cms-bfl.com

Pierre-Jean Douvier is Partner within CMS Bureau Francis Lefebvre, in charge of the international department. He joined CMS Bureau Francis Lefebvre in 1986. Mr. Douvier specialises in international law (transfer pricing, crossborder transactions – including M&A, financing, refinancing, hybrid financing and restructuring, financial leasing, international taxation, energy law, trusts). His recent experience in the life sciences industry sector includes:
- Acquisition of a worldwide OTC department.
- Restructuring of Pharmaceutical activities contracts within Europe
- Re engineering of functions within companies taking into account regulatory aspects
- Set up in Eastern countries.

Mr. Douvier had been with Coopers & Lybrand (1981-1984) and Ernst & Whinney (1984-1986). He graduated from Paris II Assas and Business School. His professional memberships include the Institute for Tax Advisors (IACF), International Fiscal Association (IFA), International Bar Association and is the honorary vice-president of the Trusts Committee (IBA).

Mr. Douvier's publications & conference presentations include: *International taxation : 20 case studies* (LITEC), *Tax law in international relationships* (PEDONE), *The regime of permanent establishment* (IBFD Amsterdam 2005), *Treasury management* (Ed. F. Lefebvre) and *The regime of partnerships* (IBFD Amsterdam 2006).

Pierre-Jean Douvier is a lecturer in international taxation at University of Paris II Assas and also in conferences with topic such as: transfer of domicile, trusts, assets reorganisation. His native language is French and he also speaks English, German, and Italian.

He holds a master degree in Business Law from the University of Paris II Assas (1981) and is a graduate of the E.S.L.S.C.A Business School (1979).

Directory of Contributors

Sean F. Foley
Principal, KPMG LLP

2001 M. Street, NW
Washington, DC 20036
+1 202 533 5588 phone
+1 202 315 3087 fax
sffoley@kpmg.com

Sean Foley is the principal in charge of KPMG's Global Transfer Pricing Services practice in the United States; he is based in Washington, D.C. Foley focuses on Advance Pricing Agreements (APA) and Competent Authority matters, transfer pricing risk management, and other related matters. Prior to joining KPMG, Foley was the Director of the Internal Revenue Service APA program.

Mr. Foley has an LL.M. in Taxation (with distinction) and a J.D. (summa cum laude) from the Georgetown University Law Center. He clerked for Justice Ruth Bader Ginsburg when she served on the U.S. Court of Appeals and served as legislative director to Congressman Sander Levin, a member of the House Ways and Means Committee.

From 2005 to 2007, Sean Foley was an adjunct law professor at the Georgetown University Law Center. He writes a monthly column for the International Tax Review on U.S. international tax developments and is the current chair of the American Bar Association's transfer pricing subcommittee on services.

Directory of Contributors

L. David Fox
Fasken Martineau DuMoulin LLP

Toronto Dominion Bank Tower
P.O. Box 20, Suite 4200
66 Wellington Street West
Toronto-Dominion Centre
Toronto Ontario M5K 1N6
CANADA
+1 416 865 4480 phone
+1 416 364 7813 fax
dfox@fasken.com
www.fasken.com

David Fox practices in the areas of corporate tax, personal tax planning and wealth management in the Toronto office of Fasken Martineau DuMoulin LLP. A large portion of David's practice is devoted to advising corporate clients on domestic and international tax matters, including transfer pricing. He also regularly advises clients in respect of federal and provincial tax audits, objections and appeals and, in this context, has represented clients in Canada's tax courts. David's practice also involves working with companies to address employee payroll and non-resident withholding tax issues. In addition, David assists clients in addressing the tax aspects of trust and estate matters. David is a licensed Certified Public Accountant (U.S.) and, prior to joining Faskens, worked as an auditor and tax accountant at an international public accounting firm.

David obtained a Bachelor of Science in Business Administration, majoring in accounting, from Nichols College in Massachusetts and earned his Bachelor of Laws degree from the University of Western Ontario.

Directory of Contributors

Sheila Geraghty
Of Counsel, DLA Piper US LLP

1251 Avenue of the Americas
New York, New York 10020-1104
+1 212 335-4599
Sheila.Geraghty@dlapiper.com

Sheila Geraghty focuses her practice on transfer pricing and international tax matters. Ms. Geraghty has been a tax professional for more than 20 years, with experience in both public accounting and Fortune 500 corporate tax practices. She is currently "Of Counsel" with DLA Piper US LLP and is licensed to practice law in Ohio, Connecticut and Colorado.

Directory of Contributors

Tamara Berner Gracon
Managing Director, KPMG LLP

500 E Middlefield Rd
Mountain View CA 94043
+1 650 404-4705 phone
+1 650 897-9984 fax
tgracon@kpmg.com

Tamara Berner Gracon is a managing director in KPMG's Global Transfer Pricing Services practice in the United States; she is based in Mountain View, Calif. She focuses on economic and financial analyses to companies interested in establishing or reorganizing operations in other tax jurisdictions.

Ms. Gracon's experience includes transfer pricing, intangible property valuation, as well as financial and profitability analysis. She has assisted multinational clients of all sizes in tax structuring, pricing, and documenting intercompany transactions to comply with U.S. and OECD regulations. In addition, she has worked with a wide variety of software and hardware companies and is familiar with transfer pricing issues relevant to the high-tech sector.

Ms. Gracon earned a master's degree in business administration with an emphasis in finance at Georgetown University's McDonough School of Business. She also holds a B.A. in both economics and political science from the University of Colorado at Boulder.

Directory of Contributors

Michael E. Granfield
Senior Managing Partner, FTI Consulting

2001 Ross Avenue, Suite 400
Dallas TX 75201
USA
+1 214 397-1610 phone
+1 214 397-1785 fax
michael.granfield@fticonsulting.com

Dr. Michael Granfield is a senior managing partner with FTI Consulting's national transfer pricing group specializing in large clients in retailing, global sourcing, motor vehicles and high technology.

He has been a leading academic and professional transfer pricing economist for over 25 years, starting with comprehensive transfer pricing, planning and execution strategies for such firms as Westinghouse, FCIC, Schlumberger, Hyundai, Wal-Mart, Alcatel, Pier 1, Nissan, Conner Peripherals, Seagate, Pioneer, and Tyson Foods. In the early and mid-eighties, he was the IRS's leading external economist in the first big global in-bound transfer pricing cases involving the Japanese automobile companies. Subsequently, he also provided extensive transfer pricing training to the Australian Tax Office and worked on a series of big transfer pricing projects for the ATO including advance pricing agreements and their documentation regulations. More recently, Michael's work has concentrated on the crucial area of the transfer of intellectual property involving trademarks, trade names, business strategies, software and related services.

In terms of related efforts in the area of public policy, Dr. Granfield was a senior economist with the Council on International Economic Policy in the Ford White House from 1975 to 1977. Before this assignment, he was the chief minority economist for the U.S. Senate antitrust and monopoly subcommittee. Michael was also the only economist invited to testify and make recommendations to the U.S. House of Representatives Ways and Means oversight committee (the so-called pickle hearings), which was assessing the effectiveness of U.S. transfer pricing administration by the IRS and Treasury.

Dr. Granfield was also a professor of managerial economics at UCLA's Anderson Graduate School of Management. While at UCLA, Michael was an academic administrator, as well, serving as vice-chancellor for planning and budgeting (CFO), associate vice-chancellor for academic policy, and associate dean for academic affairs. Michael's last position with the University of California was as dean of the Graduate School of Business Administration at the University of California, Riverside.

Directory of Contributors

Thijs Heijenrath
International Tax Partner, Deloitte Belastingadviseurs BV

Oostmaaslaan 71,
3063 AN Rotterdam,
THE NETHERLANDS
+31 10 880 1059 phone
+31 10 880 1880 fax
theijenrath@deloitte.nl
www.deloitte.nl

Thijs Heijenrath is an international tax partner with Deloitte Belastingadviseurs BV, the Netherlands affiliate of Deloitte Touche Tohmatsu, based in Rotterdam. He leads Deloitte's Transfer Pricing / Tax-Aligned Supply Chain group in the Netherlands. He is an active member of the Global Transfer Pricing Strategy board of Deloitte. In his capacity as Dutch service line leader, he is responsible for all Transfer-Pricing / Tax Aligned Supply Chain engagements of the Dutch firm.

Mr. Heijenrath and his team serve major Dutch and foreign-based multinational companies operating in a wide range of industries and a variety of transfer pricing topics. His team is most frequently involved in:
- transfer pricing planning and business reengineering projects, including tax-aligned supply-chain projects;
- negotiating and obtaining advance pricing arrangements;
- transfer pricing controversy/audit defence;
- advising multinational companies in competent authority and arbitration procedures; and
- global and pan-European transfer pricing risk management projects, including transfer pricing documentation projects.

Mr. Heijenrath has broad experience in international taxation and transfer pricing, and has served clients from a wide range of industries. He started his professional career in 1988 with the Dutch tax authorities. Prior to joining Deloitte in 1995, he was a tax inspector of the rulings team - the predecessor of the current APA team. He has extensive experience in designing and negotiating APAs, both from the government's and the taxpayer's perspectives.

Mr. Heijenrath is a regular speaker at seminars, and is the author of numerous articles on transfer pricing issues. He is a lecturer in the LL.M. program of the European Tax College of the Universities of Tilburg and Leuven, and the international master's program of the International School of Economics in Rotterdam.

Directory of Contributors

Tobin Hopkins
Principal, Ernst & Young LLP

233 South Wacker Drive
Chicago, IL 60606
USA
+1 312 879-3137 phone
tobin.hopkins@ey.com

Tobin Hopkins is a Principal in Ernst & Young's National Transfer Pricing Practice in the U.S. and focuses on assisting multinational corporations on transfer pricing and implementation issues within the context of Tax Effective Supply Chain Management (TESCM).

Consulting exclusively on transfer pricing for over thirteen years, Tobin has been involved in the economic and financial analysis of intercompany transactions related to TESCM and other prospective planning issues, audit defense, documentation, and advanced pricing agreements. Additionally, Tobin completed a three-year rotation at the U.S. Transfer Pricing Desk in Amsterdam where he focused on assisting U.S. and European multinational in driving tax efficient structures built around business change.

Tobin has an M.B.A. from the University of Chicago and B.S. in Economics from Vanderbilt University.

Directory of Contributors

Lyndon James
Leader, Transfer Pricing Team, PricewaterhouseCoopers

Darling Park, Tower 2
201 Sussex Street
Sydney NSW 2000
AUSTRALIA
+61 2 8266 3278 phone
+61 2 8286 3278 fax
+31 6 1098 0117 mobile
lyndon.james@au.pwc.com
www.pwc.com/au

Lyndon James is the leader of PwC's transfer pricing team in Australia.

Lyndon has specialised in transfer pricing since 1996 and in that time has conducted a wide variety of complex transfer pricing assignments for some of the world's leading multinational companies across all industries in Australia and Asia. Lyndon specialises in transfer pricing controversy and dispute resolution matters. He has been recognised by the International Tax Review as one of Australia's leading transfer pricing advisors.

Lyndon has an honours degree in economics from the University of Wales, UK and is a member of the Institute of Chartered Accountants in Australia and the Taxation Institute of Australia.

Erik Jan van Sten
Manager Transfer Pricing, Deloitte

Rotterdam, Netherlands
+31 10 880 1051 phone
+31 10 880 1880 fax
+31 6 1098 0117 mobile
evansten@deloitte.nl

Erik Jan van Sten is a manager in the Deloitte Transfer Pricing Group in the Netherlands, based in the Rotterdam office. Erik Jan has experience in various industries.

Erik Jan has over 8 years of experience in international transfer pricing. Before joining Deloitte in June 2005, he started his career at the transfer pricing team of another Big-4 firm.

As manager in the Dutch firm, Erik Jan is responsible for project coordination and managing teams of transfer pricing specialists on a wide range of engagements, from transfer pricing documentation to supply chain management.

Erik Jan is frequently involved in a wide variety of projects:
- Designing transfer pricing policies with respect to intercompany transactions of tangible goods, services, intellectual property and financial services;
- Performing pan-European and local documentation studies and benchmark analyses;
- Performing tax valuations of group companies and intellectual property;
- Performing conversion analyses regarding intercompany reorganizations or the implementation of new transfer pricing policies;
- Performing risk assessment analyses of a company's transfer pricing systems and related issues including permanent establishments;
- Assisting clients in unilateral and multilateral Advance Pricing Agreement procedures;
- Assisting clients under transfer pricing audit by the Dutch tax authorities.

Erik Jan is experienced in a number of industries, including pharmaceutical and health care, consumer electronics, industrial electronics, fashion apparel, and financial markets. He holds a Masters Degree in Economics from the Erasmus University in Rotterdam.

Satoko Kawamura
Economist, Baker & McKenzie GJBJ

Tokyo Aoyama Aoki Koma Law Office
(Gaikokuho Joint Enterprise)
The Prudential Tower
13-10, Nagatacho 2-chome
Chiyoda-ku, Tokyo 100-0014 Japan
+813 5157 4304
+813 5157 4300
satoko.kawamura@bakernet.com
www.taalo-bakernet.com
www.bakernet.com

Satoko Kawamura is an Economist specializing in transfer pricing and international tax planning. She advises on a broad range of transfer pricing issues, such as designing global transfer pricing policy, and transfer pricing documentation. Satoko has been involved in many APA (advanced pricing arrangement) cases covering Japan, the US, China, Korea, Australia and so on, and assisted many multinational companies in resolving transfer pricing disputes at bilateral competent authority proceedings. She also works as a part of the team providing economic analysis and valuation for an array of transfer pricing and international tax matters.

Directory of Contributors

Yukiko Komori
Economist, Baker & McKenzie GJBJ

Tokyo Aoyama Aoki Koma Law Office
(Gaikokuho Joint Enterprise)
The Prudential Tower
13-10, Nagatacho 2-chome
Chiyoda-ku, Tokyo 100-0014 Japan
+813 5157 2789
+813 5157 4300
yukiko.komori@bakernet.com
www.taalo-bakernet.com
www.bakernet.com

Yukiko Komori is an Economist specializing in transfer pricing and international tax practice. She advises on a broad range of transfer pricing issues, and has participated in a vast array of governmental research projects. Her various articles on transfer pricing issues have been widely published in Japan and several other countries.

Directory of Contributors

Ted Keen
Vice President, Ballentine Barbera Group International (A CRA International Company)

1 Undershaft
London EC3A 8EE
UNITED KINGDOM
+44 (0) 20 7664 3671 phone
+44 (0) 20 7664 3998 fax
tkeen@crai.com

Dr. Ted Keen has 16 years of experience consulting on a wide range of economic issues in the United States and in Europe. For the past twelve years he has specialized in developing innovative applications of economic theory to transfer pricing and valuation matters. Based in London since 1997, Dr. Keen has advised multinational clients on transfer pricing planning, compliance, audit defence and alternative dispute resolution in numerous jurisdictions in Europe, Asia Pacific, and North America.

His particular areas of expertise include global transfer pricing system design, planning and compliance; post-merger integration of transfer pricing systems; valuation, cost-sharing and royalty arrangements for transfers and migration of intellectual property; transfer pricing in human capital-intensive service businesses; and establishing and defending principal-agent arrangements, including contract and toll manufacturing, commissionaires, contract research and development, contract marketing, and purchasing and procurement companies.

Dr. Keen has spoken at numerous seminars and conferences on transfer pricing and intangible property valuation. He has advised the Russian Ministry of Taxation on the application of the OECD transfer pricing guidelines. He has also addressed and led working groups of tax ministers at the invitation for the EU's Fiscalis project, which seeks to develop transfer pricing expertise in the tax ministries of new EU and candidate member states.

Prior to joining CRA and BBG, Dr. Keen was a Partner with KPMG in London, where he was responsible for the training, development, and professional practices for KPMG's Global Transfer Pricing practice. Before joining KPMG, Dr. Keen was an economist for an economic consulting firm in Los Angeles, where he specialized in research and preparation of expert witness testimony in the areas of antitrust litigation, economic policy analysis, and the calculation of economic damages from breach of contract, infringement, and fraud. While completing his dissertation, Dr. Keen held teaching positions at Pomona College, Claremont McKenna College, Scripps College, Pitzer College, Claremont Graduate University, and Laverne University.

Directory of Contributors

Elizabeth King
Founder, Beecher Consulting

9 Beecher Road
Brookline MA 02445
USA
+1 617 730-8138
+1 208 988-1013
eking@latte.harvard.edu

Elizabeth King, Ph.D. is the founder of Beecher Consulting LLC, an independent firm specializing in transfer pricing and valuation issues. She has worked in these fields for over 20 years, first as an industry economist with the Internal Revenue Service, then as a senior manager with Price Waterhouse, and now as a principal with Beecher Consulting. Dr. King has been qualified and has testified as an expert in the U.S. federal courts, and has consulted to several of the big U.S. accounting firms on commodities trading and other specialized issues.

Dr. King has published extensively on transfer pricing issues and the valuation of tangible and intangible assets. Her publications include: "Transfer Pricing and Valuation in Corporate Taxation" (The Netherlands: Kluwer Academic Publishers 1994); "The Role of Economic Analysis in Transfer Pricing" in Lowell, Cym H et al, International Transfer Pricing (New York: Warren Gorham & Lamont 1994, 1997); and "The Valuation of an Assembled Workforce Intangible" in The Valuation of Intangible Assets in Global Operations (Westport CT and London: Quorum Books 2001). Dr. King is currently working on a forthcoming book on transfer pricing, to be published by Springer Verlag in 2008.

Dr. King held a post-doctoral position at the Harvard Business School, received her Ph.D. in economics from New York University, and earned her BA from Sarah Lawrence College. She has worked on a wide variety of cases in a broad range of industries, among them: The trading of crude oil, petrochemicals, natural gas, metals and other physical commodities; financial products and services; the provision of telecommunications services; the rendering of research, design, engineering, strategic consulting, procurement, quality assessment and other services; the provision of manufacturing, selling and packaging services; the manufacture and sale of medical equipment; the manufacture and distribution of pulp and paper, firearms, industrial purging compounds and graphic arts equipment and consumables; the development, importation and distribution of kitchen appliances, consumer electronics, fine jewelry, personal care products and apparel; the fabrication and distribution of window coverings; the manufacture of magnetic disks; the online distribution of rich media content; the operation of online loyalty programs; and many other Internet-based and traditional businesses.

Directory of Contributors

Andreas Köster-Böckenförde
Partner, Jones Day

Grüneburgweg 102
60323 Frankfurt am Main
60323 Frankfurt am Main 60323
Federal Republic of Germany
+49 69 9726 3968 phone
+49 69 9726 3993 fax
akboeckenfoerde@jonesday.com
http://www.jonesday.com/akboeckenfoerde

Andreas Köster-Böckenförde has substantial experience in M&A transactions, both in corporate and tax law. He focuses primarily on multinational transactions such as M&A and corporate reorganizations in preparation of a disposition or as part of a post-acquisition integration. He also advises on optimized VAT structures of multinational clients, on cross-border issues, and on the development, amendment, and implication of stock option plans and real property transactions as well as assists clients in tax audits.

Prior to joining Jones Day, Andreas was a senior tax manager in the Frankfurt tax practice of PricewaterhouseCoopers (PwC), where his primary focus was mergers and acquisitions. He has reorganized tax structures for several international and domestic clients to optimize their tax position and also has been involved in IPOs. In 1994, Andreas led a multinational team in an enterprise screening project for the East European Development Bank in St. Petersburg.

Andreas is a member of the Frankfurt Bar Association (Anwaltskammer) and the Frankfurt Tax Advisors Bar (Steuerberaterkammer). He has published numerous articles in publications such as Practical European Tax Strategies and Tax Planning International European Union Focus. He is fluent in German and in English.

Joanna Lam Luk Yu
Transfer Pricing Senior Manager, Deloitte Touche Tohmatsu

35/F One Pacific Place
88 Queensway, Hong Kong
CHINA
+852 2852 6373 phone
+852 2805 1579 fax
joalam@deloitte.com.hk
www.deloitte.com

Joanna Lam is a senior manager in the Transfer Pricing Group in Deloitte Touche Tohmatsu's Hong Kong office. Prior to her re-joining to the Hong Kong office, Joanna was the Transfer Pricing Manager stationed in Deloitte Shenzhen office for more than 3 years. She was our Senior Consultant under the Corporate and China Tax Group in Deloitte Hong Kong for years 2001 to 2004.

Joanna's area of specialization extend across a wide range, including Hong Kong taxation, cross-border transactions between Hong Kong and China, transfer pricing management, regional tax planning and group reorganization. Joanna has also established a close connection with China Tax Bureaus in major cities of the Guangdong Province.

Joanna has comprehensive skills and competence in serving MNCs that have various forms of investment in Asia Pacific regions and advising them on transfer pricing planning, supply chain optimization, service/R&D cost sharing arrangements, and tax- efficient structuring for cross-border transactions. Joanna has advised clients in a wide range of industries, including the apparel, electronics, freight forwarding and manufacturing sections.

Joanna is a member of The Association of Chartered Certified Accountants.

Directory of Contributors

Ryan Lange
Associate, Ceteris, Inc.

55 West Monroe, Suite 2900
Chicago, IL 60603
+1 312 253-0914 phone
+1 312-404-4543 mobile
+1 312 253-0968 fax
Ryan.Lange@ceterisgroup.com

Ryan Lange (Chicago) – As an associate with Ceteris, Inc., Ryan performs various transfer pricing analyses for multinational companies for both tangible, intangible property, and services transactions. In addition, he has experience with business valuations for tax purposes. Prior to joining Ceteris, Ryan worked as a credit analyst in Merrill Lynch's Business Financial Services Division. While there, he received formal credit training and was responsible for the financial analysis, evaluation and subsequent underwriting of commercial loans covering a variety of transactions (working capital, equipment, real estate, etc.) and spanning numerous industries (retail, agriculture, industrial, etc). Ryan obtained a Bachelor of Business and Administration in Finance, Investment and Banking and a Bachelor of Business and Administration in Real Estate and Urban Economics from the University of Wisconsin-Madison.

Directory of Contributors

Ben Lannan
Partner – Transfer Pricing, PricewaterhouseCoopers

Riverside Centre
Level 15, 123 Eagle Street
Brisbane, QLD 4000
AUSTRALIA
+61 7 3257 8404 office
+61 414 618 948 mobile
ben.lannan@au.pwc.com
http://www.pwc.com/au

Ben Lannan is a Partner in the PricewaterhouseCoopers Transfer Pricing Team based in Brisbane. He has over twelve years full time experience in transfer pricing, assisting a range of clients to develop and implement defendable transfer pricing strategies. Ben's focus has concentrated on Value Chain Transformation initiatives which provide multi national corporations with innovative business and tax structures to facilitate their international commercial operations.

Ben has successfully managed a range of complex projects to develop and implement tax advantaged business models, with responsibility for co-ordinating resources throughout the Asia Pacific region to secure effective outcomes across a range of diverse business issues. This includes advising on the feasibility, design and implementation of regional and global business structures involving the establishment of principal arrangements, commissionaire arrangements, limited risk distributors and contract/toll manufacturing models.

Ben has a B.Ec (Honours) and is an Associate Member of the ICAA.

Directory of Contributors

Marc M. Levey
Partner, Baker & McKenzie LLP

1114 Avenue of the Americas
New York NY 10036
USA
marc.m.levey@bakernet.com
+1 212 891-3944 phone
+1 212-310-1644 fax
marc.m.levey@bakernet.com

Marc Levey is a partner in the New York office of Baker & McKenzie. He has over 30 years of experience in international taxation and is a nationally recognized expert in his field, particularly in structuring and defending transfer pricing strategies. He has frequently been acknowledged by Euromoney as one of the "World's Leading Tax Advisors," included in its "Best of the Best" global tax experts.

Mr. Levey's practice focuses on transfer pricing and cross-border transactions; tax controversies and litigation; general corporate, international and partnership taxation, and restructuring multinational company's global operations. He has worked in various industries such as pharma/life sciences, financial institutions, energy, automotive, chemicals, electronics, consumer goods, gaming, fashion and luxury products. Mr. Levey serves as the Chair of the firm's Global Transfer Pricing Steering Committee and Co-Chair of the Firm's Fashion and Luxury Goods Practice Group.

Mr. Levey previously served as Tax Attorney with the International Tax Ruling Group of the National Office of the IRS from 1975 to 1977. He acted as Senior Trial Attorney with the Tax Division of the U.S. Department of Justice from 1977 to 1981. He was the Special Attorney to the Attorney General of the U.S. Department of Justice in 1982. Mr. Levey was formerly a partner in a Big Five firm, where he headed the transfer pricing practice for the greater metropolitan New York area and was member of the firm's international task force. In addition, Mr. Levey was a tax partner at a prominent New York-based law firm.

Mr. Levey represents a wide range of clients in proceedings before the IRS and Federal courts and has substantial experience in handling tax controversies. He has been, and currently is, tax counsel to numerous high profile Tax Court cases including Club Med Sales, Inc. v. Commissioner; Astra USA Inc. v. Commissioner; Saint Gobain Corporation et al. v. Commissioner; Frette SA v. Commissioner; Andres Courrage Inc. v. Commissioner; Framatome Connectors USA v. Commissioner; and El Paso Maquila Sales Inc. v. Commissioner. He has also successfully negotiated conclusions to numerous IRS tax audits.

Directory of Contributors

Fernando Pereira de Matos
Partner, Deloitte Touche Tohmatsu

Rua Alexandre Dumas 1981
Chácara Santo Antonio
São Paulo SP
BRAZIL
+55 11 5186 1179 phone
fmatos@deloitte.com

Fernando Pereira de Matos is a tax consulting partner with Deloitte Touche Tohmatsu's Brazilian member firm. He has experience in production costing and management, integrated with accounting for managerial and tax purposes, tax management, transfer-pricing management and control, and tax and corporate planning.

Mr. Matos has been with Deloitte since 1982, and has experience in the tax area, with active participation in the application of Brazilian transfer-pricing legislation focused on the determination of comparable prices, identification of import and export prices charged between related companies, price management, analysis of tax and financial impacts of this legislation, assessment of alternatives to avoid double taxation, and experience in tax planning and corporate reorganization through mergers, spin-offs and incorporation of companies, having structured and implemented sophisticated projects in these areas for a number of companies.

Mr. Matos has assembled an expert team of professionals serving in the transfer-pricing practice, with over 50 specialized professionals fully dedicated to services of this nature throughout Brazil. He leads the Deloitte team that was recognized as "Brazil Transfer Pricing Firm of the Year" by the readers of International Tax Review magazine in 2007.

Mr. Matos authored the book *Transfer Pricing in Brazil*. With his team and under his coordination, he has achieved major progress in the development of creative solutions for clients, and to this end, developed pioneer software in Brazil for complying with transfer-pricing legislation and in the process of controlling and administrating transfer pricing with related parties, as well as their tax and financial effects.

Mr. Matos has made presentations at numerous seminars regarding Brazilian transfer pricing legislation.

Mr. Matos holds a bachelor's degree in accounting.

Directory of Contributors

Niels Melius
Senior Economic Consultant, Deloitte Tax LLP

50 Fremont St # 31
San Francisco, CA 94105
+1 415 783-6741 phone
+1 415 592-1085 fax
nmelius@deloitte.com

Niels Melius is a senior economic consultant in Deloitte Tax LLP's San Francisco transfer pricing group. He joined the firm in 2005 after graduating from Georgetown University, where he obtained a Bachelor of Science in International Political Economy. Niels assists clients on advance pricing agreements (APAs), cost sharing arrangements, local and global documentation studies, business restructuring, and planning studies. He has assisted taxpayers in the automotive, technology, pharmaceutical, food, consumer goods, retail, apparel, medical equipment and financial services industries.

Niels Melius has prepared economic analyses for the following industry clients:
- APAs: apparel and automotive industries
- Documentation: automotive, pharmaceutical, food, consumer goods, retail, apparel, medical equipment and financial services industries;
- Cost sharing: retail industry;
- Planning studies: food, retail and apparel industries; and
- Business restructuring: pharmaceutical industry.

Mr. Melius earned his BSFS in International Political Economy from Georgetown University in 2005.

Directory of Contributors

Robert Miall
Director, Ernst & Young

Becket House
1 Lambeth Palace Rd
London, SE1 7EU
United Kingdom
+44 2 07 951 1411 phone
rmiall@uk.ey.com

Robert Miall is a Director in Ernst & Young's UK Transfer Pricing Practice with over twenty year's experience of applying economics to business. He has specialized in transfer pricing for more than 10 years.

In his current position, he is a member of a team with global responsibility for coordinating transfer pricing services to Ernst & Young's priority accounts.

Mr. Miall previously led a pan-European practice based in Amsterdam. Robert has worked on a wide range of assignments, analyzing complex markets and business structures and evaluating and designing and defending transfer pricing policies. He has spoken at a number of conferences on the application of economic analysis to transfer pricing.

Robert Miall has played a leading role in developing transfer pricing methodologies and project management frameworks for application throughout Ernst & Young's Global Transfer Pricing Service Line. He holds Bachelors and Masters degrees in economics from the London School of Economics.

Directory of Contributors

D. Clarke Norton
Principal Economist, Co-Head, Transfer Pricing Practice, DLA Piper LLP

1251 Avenue of the Americas
New York NY 10020-1104
USA
+1 212-335-4817 phone
+1 917-778-8817 fax
clarke.norton@dlapiper.com

D. Clarke Norton is a principal economist in DLA Piper's Tax group and co-head of the Transfer Pricing practice. With nearly 20 years of experience, she is recognized as a leading authority on transfer pricing, dispute resolution and avoidance.

Ms. Norton comes to DLA Piper from Duff & Phelps, where she was co-leader of the Transfer Pricing practice. She and her team currently advise Fortune 500 companies on all aspects of transfer pricing, including APA and Competent Authority matters. As the foremost expert in transfer pricing for the apparel and footwear industries, Ms. Norton focuses her practice on consumer products and retail operations and has extensive experience in supply chain and procurement transfer pricing for multinational corporations.

Ms. Norton has served as an expert economist to the US Attorney's Office and is a frequent speaker and author on transfer pricing, business planning and intellectual property. International Tax Review has named her one of the World's Leading Transfer Pricing Advisors.

Prior to working at Duff & Phelps in 2006, Ms. Norton founded and led the transfer pricing practice at FTI Consulting. Before that, she was a partner at KPMG and a senior economist at NCR Corporation. She also served as the chief economist of the IRS Associate Chief Counsel's Advance Pricing Agreement Program, helping to negotiate hundreds of bilateral tax agreements with governments around the world.

Ms. Norton holds an M.P.I.A. in international management and finance and a B.A. in economics from the University of California at San Diego.

She is the co-author of "Transfer Pricing for Global Sourcing – in a Recession," Supply Chain Brain, September 14, 2009 and the author of "Transfer Pricing in a Recession," Transfer Pricing Week, August 19, 2009.

Directory of Contributors

Alexander R. T. Odle
Principal, Baker & McKenzie Amsterdam N.V.

Claude Debussylaan 54
1082 MD Amsterdam
NETHERLANDS
+31 (20) 551-7157 phone
alexander.odle@bakernet.com

Alexander Odle heads the Intellectual Property practice of the Amsterdam office. He specializes in all aspects of intellectual property law, mass-media law and advertising law. In addition to providing advice on various intellectual property laws and mass-media law, he regularly represents clients in legal proceedings in connection with infringement of intellectual property rights, wrongful statements and comparative advertising.

He also has a great deal of experience in drafting and negotiating licensing agreements, R&D agreements and transfer of technology agreements.

Alexander Odle has successfully represented numerous clients in connection with trademark infringement, use of confusing trade names and infringement of copyrights and model rights on the design of product packaging. He has represented numerous clients with respect to mass-media law issues in legal proceedings involving wrongful statements and misleading and comparative advertising.

Alexander Odle has also advised clients in drafting and negotiating exhibition agreements under which Dutch art has been loaned to foreign museums.

Mr. Odle's publications, presentations and articles include:

- *Privacy en de Vrijheid van Meningsuiting* – Industrieele Groote Club, Amsterdam, March 2005
- *Building and Enforcing IP Value* – IP Value 2004, An international guide for the boardroom, Globe White Page, January 2004
- *Data Protection at National and International Level* – Nationaal Rapport voor AIPPI (voorzitter van de Nederlandse werkgroep), October 2003
- *Mogelijke gevolgen van de implementatie van de Modellenrichtlijn en de inwerkingtreding van de Modellenverordening* – BMM bulletin 02/3, 2002
- *Protecting Website Content: The Netherlands* – joint publication, PLC Practice Manual, October 2001 and Global Counsel, December 2000/January 2001
- Teacher, post-doctoral course Internationale Intellectual Property Law at Asser College Europe from 1995 through 2000
- *Parallel Import: een ware uitputtingsslag* – Dossier Ondernemingszaken Nr. 23, March 1996

Directory of Contributors

Ken Okawara
Head of Transfer Pricing and Economic Analysis, Baker & McKenzie GJBJ

Tokyo Aoyama Aoki Koma Law Office
(Gaikokuho Joint Enterprise)
The Prudential Tower 13-10, Nagatacho 2-chome
Chiyoda-ku, Tokyo 100-0014 Japan
+813 5157 2965 phone
+813 5157 2904 fax
ken.okawara@bakernet.com
www.taalo-bakernet.com
www.bakernet.com

Ken Okawara, Ph.D, is the Head of Transfer Pricing and Economic Analysis at Baker & McKenzie in Tokyo. Ken is a Licensed Tax Attorney (Zeirishi) and a recognized expert in transfer pricing matters and economics. He has assisted many multinational companies in negotiations with tax authorities in Japan and several other countries. He has helped clients to resolve transfer pricing disputes at bilateral and multilateral competent authority proceedings. He has been involved in more than 60 APA/CA cases covering Japan, the US, Canada, the UK, Switzerland, Germany, Australia, Singapore, Malaysia, Korea and China. Ken also has significant experience in designing global transfer pricing policy for a variety of companies. He has published numerous articles and books on international tax and transfer pricing issues.

Directory of Contributors

Danny Oosterhoff
Partner, Ernst & Young

Antonio Vivaldistraat 150
1083 HP Amsterdam
The Netherlands
+31 88 40 71007 phone
+31 20 546 6007 office
+31 88 40 70 968 fax
danny.oosterhoff@nl.ey.com
www.ey.nl

Danny Oosterhoff is responsible for Ernst & Young's transfer pricing group in Amsterdam. Danny has specialized in transfer pricing services since 1996 and joined Ernst & Young's economic consulting practice in Chicago for one year in 1998 as a member of the European transfer pricing desk.

He has worked with many multinational enterprises in the field of transfer pricing planning, risk management and dispute resolution. His experience covers a wide range of industries, including the chemicals, pharmaceutical, high-tech and technology, consumer products, media and telecommunications sectors. He has negotiated a significant number of Advance Pricing Agreements with the Dutch authorities, on both unilateral and multilateral levels. He has also effectively used APAs and roll-back mechanisms to resolve transfer pricing disputes. Within this field he developed specific approaches for the organizational design of such centralized supply chain and trading companies that specifically account for the increased tax authority focus on economic reality.

Danny is a frequent contributor to Dutch and international professional journals on a variety of transfer pricing matters. He is listed as one of the leading Transfer Pricing Experts in both the 2004 and 2005 "Guide to the Word's Leading Transfer Pricing Advisers."

Danny holds a degree in tax law from the University of Tilburg.

Directory of Contributors

Kari Pahlman
Partner, Global Transfer Pricing Services, KPMG

8th Floor
Prince's Building
10 Chater Road
Hong Kong
CHINA
+852 2143 8777 phone
+852 2845 2588 fax
kari.pahlman@kpmg.com.hk

Kari Pahlman has nine years of experience in tax and financial advisory in relation to international taxation, transfer pricing and valuations. Prior to joining KPMG China to start the Hong Kong transfer pricing function, he worked for KPMG in Europe, responsible for transfer pricing advisory, tax effective supply chain planning, IP valuations, purchase price allocation and asset impairment studies. He specialises in various economic advisory assignments in relation to transfer pricing, tax effective supply chain management and asset valuations and has served as an engagement leader for numerous regional and global projects in these areas.

Kari's industry experience in transfer pricing work spans across industrial and consumer markets, financial services as well as information and communications industries. His recent engagements in Asia include regional transfer pricing and supply chain management work, both from compliance and planning perspectives, for global consumer product manufacturers, industrial product suppliers, banking and insurance institutions, asset management corporations as well as IT and media companies.

Kari holds an MBA from the Helsinki School of Economics and an LL.M. from the University of Amsterdam. He is an accredited member of American Society of Appraisers.

Directory of Contributors

Michael Plodek
International Tax Counsel, Lockheed Martin

Michael Plodek is the International Tax Counsel at Lockheed Martin. He earned his JD in 2002 from Boston University and an LLM in Taxation from New York University in 2003. Mr. Plodek was previously an associate with Jones Day in Washington, D.C.

Directory of Contributors

Nathan Richards
Director, Global Transfer Pricing Services, KPMG

8th Floor
Prince's Building
10 Chater Road
Hong Kong
CHINA
+852 2685 7645 phone
nathan.richards@kpmg.com.hk

Nathan Richards is a director in KPMG's Global Transfer Pricing Services (GTPS) group in Hong Kong. Nathan has over nine years of expertise in Tax and Transfer Pricing advisory in relation to international taxation and tax effective supply chain management. His Tax and transfer pricing experience includes four years in the US and four years in Switzerland prior to joining KPMG in China/Hong Kong SAR. He specializes in various economic advisory services including transfer pricing planning and tax effective supply chain management, with a particular focus upon business tax restructurings, conversion analyses, branding and technology IP management strategies and asset valuation. Nathan has experience completing transfer pricing analyses according to IRS Sections 482 and 6662, OECD Transfer Pricing Guidelines, as well as various local country specific regulations. He has extensive experience as an engagement leader for large global and regional tax restructurings as well as Master File transfer pricing compliance projects. Nathan has provided Tax and Transfer Pricing advisory services to a wide range of industries including the automotive, aviation, consumer goods, financial services, industrial products, medical, mining, pharmaceutical, and power generation industries.

He holds a Bachelor of Arts in International Political Economy from The Colorado College (USA) and a Master of Arts in International Economics and Finance from Brandeis University International Business School (USA).

Silvia B. Rodriguez
Tax Manager, Deloitte & Co. S.R.L.

Peron 646, 2nd Floor
Buenos Aires C1038AAN
ARGENTINA
+54 11 4320 2700 ext. 4714
+54 11 4320 4021
silviarodriguez@deloitte.com

Silvia Rodriguez is Tax Manager with Deloitte in Argentina, with experience in transfer pricing since its creation. Mrs. Rodriguez graduated from University of Lomas de Zamora with a degree in Certified Public Accounting in 1998 and she earned a Master's degree in business administration from University of CEMA in 2002.

Mrs. Rodriguez has led several integrating transfer pricing planning projects with worldwide tax strategies and provided assistance in transfer pricing audits.

She has served as a lecturer at various international taxation conferences as well as instructor at Asociación Argentina de Estudios Fiscales (AAEF) (Argentine tax studies association) and at Consejo Profesional de Ciencias Económicas de la Ciudad Autónoma de Bs As. (Professional council in Economics of Buenos Aires City). She is a member of AAEF's Transfer Pricing Committee.

J. Linwood Smith
**Senior Manager, Tax Services & Transfer Pricing,
Deloitte Touche Tohmatsu**

35/F One Pacific Place
88 Queensway, Hong Kong
CHINA
+852 2852 1953 phone
+852 2815 8006 fax
+852 9572 3748 mobile
linwsmith@deloitte.com.hk
www.deloitte.com/cn

Linwood Smith is a Senior Manager of Tax Services and Transfer Pricing at Deloitte in Hong Kong. He previously served as the Director of EdgarStat LLC, a consulting firm that provides transfer pricing services to tax agencies and private corporations. Linwood also oversees the day-to-day operations of the EdgarStat database, subscription-based Internet service that provides corporate financial information to transfer pricing professionals.

Linwood has more than a decade of experience as a transfer pricing consultant. For the past five years, the majority of his engagements have involved assisting tax authorities in litigating transfer pricing controversies. He has also performed numerous transfer pricing engagements for clients ranging from small corporations to Fortune 500 multinationals. He has extensive experience in preparing transfer pricing planning studies, § 6662 documentation reports, Advance Pricing Agreements, and cost sharing arrangements. His engagements have involved diverse industries, including pharmaceuticals, software, financial products, oil & gas, chemicals, engineering and professional services, commodities, and consumer goods.

He has also worked as a corporate law associate at a large D.C. law firm and as an International Tax Manager at a Big 4 accounting firm.

Linwood Smith holds a B.S. in Finance from Florida State University and a J.D. from George Mason University School of Law.

Directory of Contributors

Geoffrey K. Soh
Executive Director, Transfer Pricing, KPMG Singapore

16 Raffles Quay #22-00
Hong Leong Building
Singapore 048581
+65 6213 3035 phone
+65 6225 0984 fax
geoffreysoh@kpmg.com.sg
http://www.kpmg.com/sg

Geoffrey Soh is Head of Transfer Pricing in KPMG Singapore. He has 20 years of professional experience, including 12 years in providing transfer pricing advisory to clients. Prior to joining KPMG Singapore, Geoff worked for over five years in KPMG Vancouver's transfer pricing practice. He transferred to Singapore in 2003, to develop KPMG's transfer pricing practices in the region.

Geoff has managed over 500 international transfer pricing engagements, including those for clients in the hospitality and gaming industry, consumer markets, information, communication, and entertainment (ICE) sector, and the financial services industry, among others. His projects have encompassed the compliance, tax planning, audit defense, and Advance Pricing Arrangements/dispute resolution aspects of transfer pricing. He has also led the transfer pricing work in a number of tax efficient supply chain restructuring projects. He was also the lead economist for a bilateral advance pricing agreement involving a U.S. Fortune 100 company.

Geoff has presented at a number of regional transfer pricing conferences and has published articles on Singapore and Canadian transfer pricing developments. He has been cited by the International Tax Review's World Tax Guide for transfer pricing in Singapore.

Geoff holds a Bachelor of Arts in Economics (Honours) degree from the University of Calgary, Canada and a Master of Arts in Economics degree from the University of Alberta, Canada.

Directory of Contributors

Monique van Herksen
Principal, Baker & McKenzie Amsterdam N.V.

P.O. Box 2720
1000 CS Amsterdam
The Netherlands
+31 (20) 551 7137 phone
+31 20 626 7949 fax
monique.vanherksen@bakernet.com
www.bakernet.com/amsterdam

Monique van Herksen heads the European Transfer Pricing Team of Baker & McKenzie. She specializes in international and corporate tax law with an emphasis on transfer pricing, exchange of information, treaties, competent authority issues and litigation. She has been involved in a great variety of transfer pricing issues and Advance Pricing Agreements, including the printing industry, pharmaceutical products and medical devices, chemical products, the apparel and sporting goods industry, the luxury goods industry, secured transportation and other courier services, the automotive industry, financial products, the semiconductor industry, the telecommunication industry, the software industry, pulp/paper/cardboard products, the coal mining industry, the oil and gas industry, and more recently, the planning/implementing of a CDM structure under the Kyoto Protocol.

Monique van Herksen has taught transfer pricing to foreign government officials of the United States, The Netherlands, India, Vietnam, Brazil and Denmark and teaches a transfer pricing course at the Leiden University International Tax LL.M. program since its inception in 1998. She has taught in the Postgraduate International Tax Law Program of Vienna University and the European Tax College LLM program in Louvain, Belgium, and has presented papers and issues in her field of expertise to governmental organizations such as the OECD and EU, including the 2005 and 2006 Fiscalis Programme that serves to provide internal training to the tax authorities of EU member countries on economic analyses and benchmarking for transfer pricing and transfer pricing and intangibles, and to private interest groups such as the Tax Executives Institute, the American Tax Institute, the International Fiscal Association, the International Bureau for Fiscal Documentation, the Dutch Association of Tax Lawyers and the Dutch Organization of Tax Advisers.

She was assigned the responsibility of reporting for the Netherlands for the International Fiscal Association 2007 Conference on transfer pricing and intangibles.

Directory of Contributors

Kimberley Webb
Manager, KPMG in China

8th Floor, Prince's Building
10 Chater Road Central, Hong Kong
CHINA
+852 2685 7645 phone
+852 2845 2588 fax
kimberley.a.webb@kpmg.com.hk

Kimberley Webb has over five years experience in transfer pricing and corporate income tax. She has assisted clients across a broad range of industries with developing and implementing transfer pricing policies and the preparation of the necessary supporting documentation. Her client based includes global multinationals in the financial services sector and the fast moving and durable consumer goods markets. Kimberley has experience in the integration of transfer pricing policies with other taxes, including customs duty and excise.

Kimberley has is a full member of the New Zealand Institute of Chartered Accountants and holds an honour's degree in accounting and a BA in economics/statistics from the University of Auckland (New Zealand).

Jens Wittendorff
Tax Partner, Deloitte

Weidekampsgade 6
Copenhagen S 2300
DENMARK
+45 36 10 34 11 phone
+45 36 10 20 40 fax
jwittendorff@deloitte.dk

Jens Wittendorff has seventeen years of professional experience as an international tax adviser. He is working in the Deloitte Copenhagen office and has previously worked in the London office of Deloitte. He is trained as a Master of Science in International Business Administration and Commercial Law. Jens serves large national and international MNCs, mainly on tax planning issues involving transfer pricing, mergers & acquisitions, reorganizations, and other cross-border transactions. He is a member of the Deloitte Global Transfer Pricing Team.

Jens speaks frequently to professional groups on international tax issues and transfer pricing and is the author of numerous articles and books on international tax law. He is the author of the Danish National Report on Transfer Pricing and Intangibles for the 2007 IFA Congress as well as the co-author of the Danish National Report on Financial Derivatives for the 1995 IFA Congress.

Looking for Comparables?

There is only one transfer pricing database designed *by transfer pricing professionals, for transfer pricing professionals*. By special arrangement with EdgarStat LLC, we are pleased to offer our readers the opportunity to try this powerful transfer pricing tool:

EdgarStat Interactive Transfer Pricing Database

Whether preparing transfer pricing documentation or negotiating an Advance Pricing Agreement (APA), if you use a profit-based transfer pricing method, you need financial information derived from comparable companies. In the past, getting these data required either laborious research, data extraction, conversion, compilation, and analysis, or large fees for generic company data that may or may not meet your transfer pricing needs. The other option was to pay a consultant to assemble the data for you. EdgarStat offers a better option: exactly the data you need at a reasonable price.

Ease-of-Use With Advanced Functionality

With a simple user interface, EdgarStat makes it easy for a novice user to search for comparables and analyze financial data. Behind this simple interface is a wealth of functionality and data, including:
- Business descriptions and direct access to 10-K annual reports for virtually all non-banking public companies in the United States since 1999
- Automatic computation of operating margin, gross margin, operating markup, and other commonly used profit level indicators;
- Built-in statistical functions to analyze data, including interquartile range; and
- Technical support provided by experienced transfer pricing professionals

Why EdgarStat?

- Developed by transfer pricing professionals
- Easy-to-use interface requires little or no training
- Streamlined format for quick searches and determinations of comparability
- Data at every stage of the analysis may be downloaded into Excel for use in written reports or off-line anlysis
- Fraction of the price of competing databases

Breakthrough Pricing

- An annual subscription to EdgarStat costs $2,500.
- Competing databases that lack EdgarStat's transfer pricing functions cost $14,000 to $25,000 or more per year.

Try EdgarStat Risk-Free

For more information or to sign up for a free demo of EdgarStat today, please visit **USTransferPricing.com** or call **(617) 795-0519**.